a

Henry Guze

PSYCHOPATHOLOGY OF SCHIZOPHRENIA

Officers of the

AMERICAN PSYCHOPATHOLOGICAL ASSOCIATION

for 1964

PSYCHOPATHOLOGY OF SCHIZOPHRENIA

Edited by **PAUL H. HOCH, M. D.**
Department of Mental Hygiene, State of New York; College of Physicians and Surgeons, Columbia University, New York City.

and **JOSEPH ZUBIN, Ph. D.**
Department of Mental Hygiene, State of New York; Department of Psychology, Columbia University, New York City.

THE PROCEEDINGS OF THE FIFTY-FOURTH ANNUAL MEETING OF THE AMERICAN PYSCHOPATHOLOGICAL ASSOCIATION, HELD IN NEW YORK CITY, FEBRUARY 1964.

GRUNE & STRATTON

NEW YORK • LONDON • 1966

SAMUEL W. HAMILTON AWARDS

NAME		SYMPOSIUM
Clarence P. Oberndorf, M.D.	1952	*Depression*
John C. Whitehorn, M.D.	1953	*Psychiatry and the Law*
David M. Levy, M.D.	1954	*Psychopathology of Childhood*
Stanley Cobb, M.D.	1955	*Experimental Psychopathology*
Sandor Rado, M.D.	1956	*Psychopathology of Communication*
Karl M. Bowman, M.D.	1957	*Problems of Addiction and Habituation*
Bernard Glueck, Sr., M.D.	1958	*Trends in Psychoanalysis*
Sir Aubrey Lewis, M.D.	1959	*Comparative Epidemiology in the Mental Disorders*
Franz J. Kallmann, M.D.	1960	*Psychopathology of Aging*
Nolan D. C. Lewis, M.D.	1961	*Future of Psychiatry*
Franz Alexander, M.D.	1962	*Evaluation of Therapy*
Heinrich Klüver, Ph.D.	1963	*Psychopathology of Perception*
Paul H. Hoch, M.D.	1964	*Psychopathology of Schizophrenia*

HENRY M. AND LILLIAN STRATTON AWARDS

Name		*Symposium*
James Birren, Ph.D.	1960	*Psychopathology of Aging*
Benjamin Pasamanick, M.D.	1961	*Future of Psychiatry*
Heinz E. Lehmann, M.D.	1962	*Evaluation of Therapy*
Charles W. Eriksen, Ph.D.	1963	*Psychopathology of Perception*
Ronald Melzack, Ph.D.	1963	*Psychopathology of Perception*
Robert W. Payne, Ph.D.	1964	*Psychopathology of Schizophrenia*
Kurt Salzinger, Ph.D.	1964	*Psychopathology of Schizophrenia*

Library of Congress Catalog Card No. 65-26740

Grune & Stratton, Inc.
381 Park Avenue South
New York, N.Y. 10016

Printed in U.S.A. (K-B)

CONTENTS

Preface ix

Paul H. Hoch: Samuel W. Hamilton Memorial Lecturer, 1964, *Jerome D. Frank* xi

Part I: Phenomenology and Clinical Aspects

1. History of the Nosology and the Evolution of the Concepts of Schizophrenia, *Nolan D. C. Lewis* 1
2. A Psychodynamic View of Pseudoneurotic Schizophrenia, *James P. Cattell* 19
3. Schizophrenic Cognition, *Silvano Arieti* 37
4. Formal Qualities of Hallucinations: A Comparative Study of the Visual Hallucinations in Patients with Schizophrenic, Organic, and Affective Psychoses, *David A. Frieske and William P. Wilson* 49
5. Understanding the Adaptive Struggles of Schizophrenic Patients, *Sandor Rado* 63

Discussion, *Sidney Malitz, Recorder* 71

Part II: Psychology

6. The Measurement and Significance of Overinclusive Thinking and Retardation in Schizophrenic Patients, *R. W. Payne* 77
7. Verbal Behavior in Schizophrenics and Some Comments Toward a Theory of Schizophrenia, *Kurt Salzinger, Stephanie Portnoy, and Richard S. Feldman* 98
8. The Prediction of Performance in Schizophrenia, *Norman Garmezy* 129
9. Behavior Patterns of Chronic Schizophrenics, *Eugene I. Burdock and Anne S. Hardesty* 182
10. Presidential Address: Contributions of Behavioral Scientists Toward a World without War, *Jerome D. Frank* 205

Discussion, *Lissy Jarvik, Recorder* 219

Part III: Neurochemistry and Genetics

11. Current Biochemical Research in Schizophrenia, *Seymour S. Kety* 225
12. Biologic Maladaptation in Schizophrenia, *Jacques S. Gottlieb, Charles E. Frohman, and Peter G. S. Beckett* 233
13. Long-Term Follow-Up (10-15 Years) of Schizophrenic Patients with Funkenstein (Adrenalin-Mecholyl) Tests, *George E. Vaillant and Daniel H. Funkenstein* 244
14. Current Reproductive Trends in Schizophrenia, *L. Erlenmeyer-Kimling, John D. Rainer, and Franz J. Kallmann* 252
15. A Neurotropic Compound Identified in Urine of Schizophrenic Patients, *Arnold J. Friedhoff and Elnora Van Winkle* 277
16. Schizophrenia, *Paul H. Hoch* 283

Discussion, *Jonathan Cole, Recorder* 302

Part IV: Clinical Research in Schizophrenia

17. Evaluation of Outcome in Schizophrenia (The Long-Term Prognostic Test Index), *Zygmunt A. Piotrowski and Herman Y. Efron* 312
18. The Prediction of Schizophrenia in Infancy: II. A Ten-Year Follow-Up Report of Predictions Made at One Month of Age, *Barbara Fish, Renée Wile, Theodore Shapiro, and Florence Halpern* 335
19. The Concept of Plasticity in Childhood Schizophrenia, *Lauretta Bender* 354
20. Office Treatment of the Chronic Schizophrenic Patient, *Alexandra Adler* 366
21. Schizophrenia among Adolescent Street Gang Leaders, *Howard Davidman and Edward Preble* 372

Discussion, *Bernard Holland, Recorder* 384

Part V: Therapy

22. Pharmacotherapy of Schizophrenia, *H. E. Lehmann* 388

23. The Effect of Somatic Treatments on Clinical Course, Psychopathological and Pathophysiological Research in Schizophrenia, *Lothar B. Kalinowsky* 412

24. Effect of Diet on Schizophrenic Behavior, *H. H. Berlet, C. Bull, H. E. Himwich, H. Kohl, K. Matsumoto, G. R. Pscheidt, J. Spaide, T. T. Tourlentes, and J. M. Valverde* 425

25. Inhibitory Conditional Responses in Schizophrenic Patients, *Joseph H. Stephens, Soon Mo Choi, and John E. Peters* 453

Discussion, *William Goldfarb, Recorder* 464

Part VI: Diagnosis, Classification, and Prognosis

26. Social Competence, the Process-Reactive Distinction, and the Nature of Mental Disorder, *Leslie Phillips* 471

27. A Cross-Cultural Approach to Classification in Schizophrenia and Other Mental Disorders, *Joseph Zubin and Mitchell L. Kietzman* 482

28. Two Years of a Home Care Study for Schizophrenics, *Benjamin Pasamanick, Joseph L. Albini, Frank R. Scarpitti, Mark Lefton, and Simon Dinitz* 515

29. Release and Community Stay Criteria in Evaluating Psychiatric Treatment, *Lee Gurel* 527

Discussion, *Morton Kramer, Recorder* 553

Appendix

Membership of the American Psychopathological Association 561

Past and Present Officers of the American Psychopathological Association 570

Index 572

PREFACE

SCHIZOPHRENIA in one form or another has bedeviled mankind long before Bleuler renamed Kraepelin's "dementia praecox." In a sense, the history of schizophrenia is the history of psychopathology itself, for as early as 3300 years ago its characteristics were already noted and differentiated from other types of mental deviation. Despite its long history, it is as baffling to us today as it was to the ancient Hindus when the *Ayura Veda* was written. General paresis, pellagra with psychosis, PKU, and mongolism—to name but a few—have yielded the secret of their origins, but schizophrenia still defies us. It is a most debilitating disease, sapping the strength of nearly one per cent of the population and accounting for two-thirds of the patients in our mental hospitals. The estimated direct cost for maintenance and indirect loss of income attributable to this illness total approximately $.66 billion annually.

Because it has defied all attempts at discovering its cause, it now ranks as the greatest challenge in the field of mental disorders. The current symposium has attempted to indicate the wide front on which this disease is now being attacked.

The reader is cautioned that only a small portion of the current research in this field is contained in this volume, but it is hoped that it is a representative sample.

THE EDITORS

Paul H. Hoch

PAUL H. HOCH, M.D.

Hamilton Memorial Award Lecturer, 1964

DR. PAUL H. HOCH needs no introduction to members of the American Psychopathological Association. As Chairman of our Program Committee for over 15 years, he has borne the major responsibility for organizing programs on practically every significant psychiatric topic and has seen to it that they have received permanence as published volumes. But this is among the least of his achievements. As a summary of his career reveals, he has made important contributions to virtually every aspect of American psychiatry.

Born in Budapest, he received his medical training at the University of Göttingen and his psychiatric training in Zurich. Before coming to the United States in 1933, he was Assistant Professor of Psychiatry and Neurology at the University of Göttingen and Director of the Outpatient Department and of the Brain Research Division of the Neuropsychiatric Clinic.

He began his career in the United States at the Manhattan State Hospital, where he headed the newly created shock treatment unit, and in 1942 became Chief Medical Officer of the Hospital for War Neuroses at Gladstone, New Jersey. The following year he joined the staff of the New York State Psychiatric Institute and became Director of the Department of Experimental Psychiatry in 1948 and Professor of Clinical Psychiatry in 1956. The Institute has been the locus of his major teaching, research, and clinical activities.

Since 1955 he has been Commissioner of Mental Hygiene of the State of New York. Under his forward-looking, energetic, and wise leadership, the New York State program for hospital and community treatment of the mentally ill has become a pace-setter for the nation.

Dr. Hoch has held many consultantships, and the national and international associations in which he has been a member or an officer are far too numerous to recount. He has been president of five, including this one. Among the many honors he has received are the Adolf Meyer Memorial Award for Psychiatric Research and the Nolan D. C. Lewis Award for outstanding contributions to the field of neuropsychiatry.

A most productive researcher, he has published over 150 articles in psychiatric and professional journals and has written or edited 20 books on psychiatric subjects. He has also maintained a private practice and is widely respected as an astute diagnostician and skillful therapist.

Having had the pleasure of working with him on two committees, I have never ceased to marvel at his quick and penetrating grasp of issues, his practical common sense, the breadth of his information, and his imperturbability. Despite his immense responsibilities and multifarious activities, he never seems harassed and never loses his good humor.

He is a man of prodigious industry, encyclopedic knowledge, excellent judgment, and outstanding leadership ability. As a teacher, researcher, administrator, and clinician, his impact on contemporary American psychiatry cannot be overestimated. A phrase used to characterize Benjamin Franklin fits him well: Paul Hoch is a harmonious human multitude.

High among Dr. Hoch's professional interests is schizophrenia. It is therefore especially fitting that a meeting devoted to his perennially fascinating and challenging subject be the occasion for conferring upon him the Samuel W. Hamilton Award.

JEROME D. FRANK, M.D.

Part I: Phenomenology and Clinical Aspects

1

HISTORY OF THE NOSOLOGY AND THE EVOLUTION OF THE CONCEPTS OF SCHIZOPHRENIA

by NOLAN D. C. LEWIS, M.D.*

THE CONDITION KNOWN CURRENTLY as "schizophrenia" has probably always existed among civilized peoples. Ancient records, non-medical as well as medical, mention and sometimes give descriptions of human behavior which in many ways are similar to those applied in modern psychopathology to schizophrenic states. Man as an observer has always been impressed by such manifestations among his own kind (peculiar mannerisms and speech, hallucinations, catatonic rigidity, unusual attitudinizing, and stupors—all of which belong in the schizophrenic categories), although in the early days of psychiatry these states were not clearly differentiated from mental deficiency and some other conditions.

I have elected the task of attempting to trace the historical pathway of the concepts that seem to have a bearing on the topic under consideration today. To start as far in the past as possible and still rely on relatively safe sources of information, one could begin by pointing out that the early Hindu Vedas or "Works of Wisdom," while not particularly rich in accounts having a direct psychiatric bearing, do contain suggestive phrases. Fragments from the Ayur-Veda (1400 B.C.), an ancient system of medicine of India, reveal a first classification of deranged mental functions which were ascribed to the malevolent activities of various devils. However, such descriptive phrases as "one who is gluttonous, filthy, walks naked, has lost his memory and moves about in an uneasy manner" are highly suggestive of schizophrenic disorders, particularly as they are differentiated in

*Professor Emeritus of Psychiatry, Columbia University, New York, N.Y.

that same text from toxic confusions from ingestion of poisons, from alcoholics, and from types that resemble the elated phases of the manic-depressive reaction.

The Greek physician Hippocrates (circa 460-377 B.C.) described a situation in which the patient moved about thinking and seeing something else than reality and expressing himself in terms of strange visions. This probably has a schizophrenic meaning since he differentiated it from alcoholic mental disturbances, acute febrile reactions, depressions, and epilepsy. Plato saw a variety of mental trouble as "stuporous and demented." There is good reason to believe that mental disease was just as prevalent in relation to the size of the population as it is today. Moreover, any review of the ancient literature suggests that most of the different reaction types now known to us were present in antiquity.

In 50 to 25 B.C. Aurelius Cornelius Celsus, who was not a physician but a scholar and astute observer, enters the history of psychiatry. He was a recorder of medical thought in the times of the Roman rulers Tiberius, Caesar, and Caligula, and his writings are of encyclopedic dimensions. He described difficult mental types of disturbances such as acute fevers or phrenitis and melancholia. From his description of "a third kind of insanity," one is inclined to believe he referred to cases of schizophrenia and paranoia. This third type was liable to be prolonged, not dangerous to life, and was characterized in some cases by false images but in others by impaired judgment. Aretaeus (30-90 A.D.), in his comments and decriptions of mental disorders, mentioned cases called "secondary dementia."

We may well be on somewhat shaky ground in interpreting the meaning of symptoms mentioned by ancient writers, but when the patients are described as having hallucinations and delusions as prominent features, although such are also found in nonschizophrenic disorders where "splitting" is present, we are probably justified in assuming that there were schizophrenics among them, particularly when the writer at the same time outlined other groups with toxic deliria, brain injuries, and what resembled manic attacks, as well as hysterical phenomena (Asclepiades, Celsus, and Galen).

The history of schizophrenia is really that of psychiatry as a whole, but in the attempt to segregate the topic as clearly as possible our main attention should be given to the last two centuries, which are the most important of all. The most tenaciously held impressions in psychiatry have always been the contrasting pictures of excitement and depression, acuteness and chronicity, and also of "dementia" or deterioration. Deterioration of the type dealt with today was described by Willis,[1] the famous British anatomist, in 1674 in terms of "stupidity" and "morosity" in certain young individuals. Two years earlier (1672) he had recorded that a great number of young persons underwent deterioration even though they had been lively minded and even brilliant in their childhood. This passing into "deterioration" during adolescence apparently was not always necessarily permanent or continuous, for he states: "On the other hand, others formerly dull may brighten up through the evaporation of fluid." The notion that termination in deterioration indicated a specific disease is not to be found (as far as I can determine) in any literature previous to that of Willis.

Many such patients undergoing deteriorating processes must have been schizophrenics, as were similar ones described by Sydenham (1672) under "stupidity." Moreover, since during the course of the disorder many cases show swings of excitement, elations, and depressions, such older terms as "acute and chronic mania" and "acute and chronic melancholia" must have included a host of schizophrenic syndromes, just as later and even today some of the cases complicated by affective swings of mood are wrongly diagnosed and classified with the manic-depressive reaction group. Only a relatively few years ago a symptom complex seen frequently in schizophrenia—namely, catalepsy—was described and classified as a separate distinct disorder.

In the 1800's we find that Pinel (1809), his distinguished pupil Esquirol (1814), Spurzheim, and others of the earlier days described unquestionable cases of dementia praecox under different names, although the term *dementia praecox* was first used by Morel in 1856. However, our present concepts have developed chiefly from the contributions of Kahlbaum (1863) and from the more widely known writings and teachings of Kraepelin (1895), Bleuler (1911), Adolf Meyer (from 1903), Kretschmer (1925), Bumke (1924), and deJong and Baruk (1930).

We shall now consider in more detail the concepts developed by these pioneers. Starting with the early French "school," Philippe Pinel (1745-1826) in the last part of the 18th century and first part of the 19th was writing philosophical evaluations of medicine and nosology in an attempt to integrate the philosophy and psychology of John Locke with that of the French and with his own experience as a physician. He described patients with symptoms similar to those reported earlier by Willis. Among these was a case obviously of the catatonic type with deterioration, which in Pinel's list of terms for mental disorder (mania, melancholia, monomania or "limited insanity," dementia) did not fit well enough, but did in his opinion come under "idiotism," a term then used for abolition of intellectual and affective faculties. Therefore, these deteriorating patients were labeled as "idiotism."[2]

Esquirol (1772-1840) in his *Des Maladies Mentales*[3] used the term "accidental or acquired idiocy" for this same developmental defect which appeared during the adolescent years. He considered that it represented a failure to reach maturity of mind regardless of a favorable start and also that the condition passed on into idiocy, having been provoked by excessive bleeding during the acute phases of the psychosis, by suppression of menses, by masturbation, or by trauma to the head.

It was an important step when the term "idiocy" was reserved to the actually congenital or genuine early defects and "dementia" found an application to the acquired defects, but the term was applied also at times to temporary or transitory reversible conditions. After some limitation of the term "dementia" to the organic types, including senile states, the other psychoses were divided into total and partial insanities by the French psychiatrists. In addition to the fundamental forms of mania and melancholia, there were concepts of confusion and also of *délires* or delusional states which in Germany had been called "paranoia," a term used by Vogel in 1764 in a more general way and by Heinroth in 1818 for *Verruckung* and by Zeller and Ellinger in 1815.[4]

In the 1850's Morel applied the first use of the term "démente précoce" to a type of *stupidité*. Morel (1809-1873) was physician-in-chief to the Asylum for the Insane, Saint-yon. In his book[5] dealing with mental disorders he describes a boy, 13-14 years of age, about whom he was consulted. This boy was bright in his studies but underdeveloped physically, a condition about which he felt humiliated when among others. Gradually he changed from active interests into a "gloomy, taciturn" person inclined to seek seclusion. This state became worse, and he developed a hatred for his father whom he thought of killing. He was taken to the institution for treatment and he improved physically, but the mental condition became worse and eventually hopeless. Morel considered it a case of "hereditary insanity"—one of *une démence précoce*. Thus it was "constitutional" and not just accidental in origin (the patient's mother was "insane" and his grandmother eccentric enough perhaps to qualify also).

Therefore, Morel taught that the disorder was inherited by later generations and that it bore an unfavorable prognosis as it moved in the direction of what he termed "degeneracy." He apparently originated the concept of "degeneration" in a psychiatric sense, and constructed a theory that pathological changes could be brought about by the environment—including disrupting family influences, malnutrition, toxins, and disease—and that such changes could induce a high percentage of "moral depravities," neurotics, criminals, and paupers. In the third generation the taint could appear in severe physical defects, sterility, and a gradual dying out of the family line. What Morel taught, with his concept of degeneracy, could fill a lengthy chapter in the history of psychiatry. For some time the idea of degeneracy was prominent among the French psychiatrists, which did not always mean that the patient drifted into a dementia.

> The French worked more problematically with the degenerate and the nondegenerate with circular insanity as opposed to vesania (i.e., total insanity) and primary and secondary, or acute and chronic confusion, and the "délires" or delusional states, among which Mangan singled out as definitely "nondegenerative" his "délires chronique a évolution systématique"—our present-day paranoid dementia praecox (schizophrenia) and paraphrenia. Austrian and German psychiatrists evolved the amentias and Wahsinns, thereby keeping clear the manias and melancholias as largely recoverable affective psychoses and paving the way for Kraepelinian conceptions.[6]

Morel always sought for unity for a syndrome of cause, course, and outcome, and in 1863 Kahlbaum (1828-1899) with new concepts made the attempt to utilize Morel's ideas of the whole disease as a unit to include etiology, course, all the physical and mental data, and the prognosis. He strove for a true nosology of definite clinical entities. "His vesania or 'insaneness' concept covers the cases of 'general insanity' (or paraphrenia), with melancholia, mania, confusion, and dementia forming successive stages. In its comprehensiveness it represents actually our modern dementia praecox".[6]

The various concepts that have influenced the formulation of the disorder and its subgroupings into the hebephrenic, catatonic, paranoid, and simple forms have an interesting history. Kahlbaum,[7] out of his paraphrenia or "general insanity," selected a certain reaction pattern with motor tension symptoms which he named "Katatonia" and described in 1868 and again in a monograph in 1874 ("Spannungsirresein" or vesania catatonica). In 1870 his assistant Hecker[8] had described hebephrenia as a disorder related to puberty and adolescence and leading to deterioration. Both disorders were presented as distinct disease entities.

In 1884 heboidophrenia was described and again in 1890, based on the fact that not all of the early age-bound disorders were as serious as hebephrenia in their outcome. These nosological ideas of Morel and Kahlbaum were largely buried, temporarily, by the growth of the conception of paranoia in the field of psychiatry. Ellinger (1845) and Snell (1865) developed a concept of primary paranoia which was accepted by Griesinger in 1868, by Westphal in 1876, Krafft-Ebing and Schüle (1880-1905), Meynert (1863-1892) and Cramer, and Ziehen (1894)—all of whom contributed actively to the "exploitation of a formal psychological paranoia concept." However, Spitzka (1852-1914) and Kiernan in America accepted catatonia as an entity at a time when most others were reluctant. Spitzka, in his textbook *Manual of Insanity* (1887) defines "Katatonia" as "a form of insanity characterized by a pathetical emotional state, and verbigeration combined with a state of motor tension."[9] He goes on to say that "this well marked, though not generally recognized mental disorder, was first demarcated by Kahlbaum and Görlitz about eight years ago. In the course of the writer's study of the pauper insane at Ward's Island he became impressed with the genuineness of the grounds on which Kahlbaum based this classification, and the subsequently published, and more recently reprinted, paper of Kiernan based on a study of the same patients was the first confirmation of the important and practical proposition of the Prussian alienist."

Then follows a description of the condition, including initial depressed phases, excited turmoil, confusions and cataleptic states, the stereotypies, the grimaces, the hallucinations, and other descriptive terms still today in use for different symptoms of catatonic schizophrenia—thus showing an excellent grasp of the clinical picture before Kraepelinian psychiatry came into it. In his book Spitzka also seems to be the first to devote a separate chapter under the caption "Paranoia." He says in the Preface: "The alternative designation of Paranoia has been adopted in this volume as a preferable term (i.e., to monomania) for reasons similar to those which actuated Mendel in his recent proposition to substitute it for the German vernacular term *Verrücktheit*."

Emil Kraepelin (1856-1926), professor of psychiatry successively at Dorpat, Heidelberg, and Munich, is considered by many to be the greatest of all descriptive psychiatrists whose concepts increased and enriched the knowledge of this discipline. Without doubt, he was the foremost systematizer in the present psychiatric era, reminding one in some ways of Asclepiades of Bithynia and of others who, following periods of active analysis, have attempted a great synthesis of more or less scattered facts and ideas.

In the third edition (1887) of his textbook[10] he devoted a chapter to Kahlbaum's contributions under the heading "Degenerative Psychoses," pointing out in 1893 that he considered dementia praecox as synonymous with hebephrenia and presenting catatonia and "dementia paranoides" as separate independent types of disorders on the same standing as dementia praecox. But in 1894 when Ziehen published his textbook filled with descriptions of "acute paranoias," Kraepelin seriously objected to this "paranoification of psychiatry" (Meyer's characterization). In his concept of deterioration processes Kraepelin combined all of the so-called "primary" and "secondary" dementias into one dementing disorder. At the historic Heidelberg meeting of 1898 he formally presented dementia praecox as a specific entity. There was considerable opposition, especially without more convincing etiological and pathological information, to calling it a metabolic disorder such as myxedema and paresis; these diseases were used, of course, only as analogies.

Kraepelin made his studies after the fashion of those who work in natural history in that he followed the course of mental disorders in the individual cases from the earliest expressions on through to the termination, and he had a large amount of clinical and laboratory material with which to work. He rejected the concept of secondary dementia as taught by his predecessors. He was after the cause, the course, the outcome of mental diseases with reference to any possible pathological lesions. He was after a definite nosology. He had a keen clinical sense for the acute disorders and divided them into recoverable forms and those leading to deterioration, making this distinction an important principle of classification. His method of analyzing cases from the viewpoint of course and outcome rather than from the stream of consciousness made the sequence of events the main issue, as in an experiment. While the discovery of a pathological lesion was his goal, he always admitted that the cause was unknown, that the course was variable, and the outcome uncertain. He recognized that many cases did not terminate in apathetic deterioration.

Before Kraepelin's innovation, Clouston (1840-1915), a Scotch psychiatrist, had described these cases as "adolescent insanity." Kraepelin in 1896 in the fifth edition of his *Lehrbuch* had dementia praecox, catatonia, and dementia paranoides arranged as disorders of metabolism associated with damage to the brain cortex. Later, with great thoroughness and attention to method he worked over his material and realized that the original assumption (that the products of disordered organ metabolism circulating in the body fluids had damaged the cortex) was not supported by the laboratory findings. Thus the idea of "deterioration" on the basis of toxicity and of the type seen in organic conditions was abandoned. Kraepelin defined dementia praecox as a "series of disease pictures, the common feature of which is the termination in a special kind of state of mental weakness," but he also emphasized that the end result might not always be unfavorable and that whatever damage may have occurred in the cortex was partially recoverable in certain cases. He pointed out the great variability of the temporary aspects of the disorders encountered in the course of the disease, but he held that certain fundamental features, although often disguised, were practically always present and observable, particularly in the terminal stages. This latter fact led to one of his most radical steps—namely, the placement of the type of outcome in the position of a classification criterion.

In addition to the termination in deterioration processes, Kraepelin considered as fundamental the clinical combination of hallucinations, delusions, odd distorted emotional expressions, disorders of attention, negativism, stereotypies of motion and attitudes, lessened capacities for work, disorders of judgment, and the dilapidation and shattering of the thought processes, associated with relatively intact perception capacities, clear sensorium, and memory retention. He qualified all of these symptoms in various ways, emphasizing their numerous settings. He traced the life histories of his patients with meticulous care and finally grouped them from the standpoint of symptoms and prognosis into hebephrenic, catatonic, and paranoid forms.

Numerous and multiform attempts have been made to investigate selected clinical aspects or syndromes occurring in, or characteristic of, some of the forms of dementia praecox, among which catatonia was studied physiologically, biochemically, and clinically, resulting clinically in little else than renaming of some of the special features—e.g., the "etonnement" of Heshard, "akinetic fixity" of Stern, and the "bradyphrenia" or dullness and slowness of thought of Naville. Almost from the beginning the term "dementia praecox" was the focus of a great deal of critical discussion, since on the one hand there were cases in the experience of every psychiatrist where partial or complete social recoveries occurred after so-called "deterioration" had set in, to say nothing of the recoveries of milder cases, and on the other hand many cases were noted where the first overt symptoms characteristic of the disorder appeared during the adult years even after 30 or 40 years of age and very occasionally as late as the end of the fifth decade.

Those psychiatrists who accepted deterioration as a definite criterion for classification in the dementia praecox group rather consistently changed the diagnosis to manic-depressive psychosis on any schizophrenic who recovered and did not progress into deterioration, regardless of the mental content. This attitude remained for quite some time as any survey of the old records of mental hospitals (including those in New York State) will show. To many psychiatrists, including those of today, Kraepelin's designation favored a fatalistic attitude toward this whole group of cases.

The next phase was an attempt to formulate dynamic genetic conceptions of processes tending toward deterioration. From 1896 on through 1906 a constitutional-psychogenic scheme was developed by Adolf Meyer, August Hoch, Smith Ely Jelliffe, and others. For quite a time this influenced and represented much of the work in this area in America.

In 1903 the eminent psychologist G. Stanley Hall gave an address, "Arrest of Development in Adolescence," before the National Educational Association. Adolf Meyer in his discussion of the paper described what he called "adolescent deterioration," which he thought was largely due to "disharmonies" of thinking, of habits, and of interests which cause shunting in one direction or another. He said that "physicians do not have the opportunity to see the candidates for deterioration early." Others, such as friends who have been present early, describe[10] . . . "dilapidation of interest, erratic attention, and social indifference. Most prominently lacking is the sense of actuality. They become self-conscious, suspicious, and solitary . . . which fail to be corrected by healthy social or other normal activities. The touch with actuality is lost more and more. . . . the unreal and half understood things are eagerly elaborated into delusions and offered for explanation of peculiar sensations."[11]

It is obvious that this is a clear-cut Kraepelinian description of dementia praecox, although the term did not appear in this account, thus indicating that it had not come into a common use here by 1903 or that Meyer had a reluctance which was not the case a year or so later in his review of psychiatric literature.[12] Although Adolf Meyer is usually thought of as dealing with schizophrenia in terms of psychological origin engendered by "pathological habit twists" in the thought processes, one should note what he said about toxins. In a paper entitled "The Nature and Conception of Dementia Praecox" read at the 1910 Meeting of the American Neurological Association in Washington, D.C., Dr. Meyer said: "I am not a priori opposed to the favorite explanation of all and every lesion of the nervous system on ground of the action of special toxins. Considering the liberal interpretation of the concept "toxin," and the inclusion under it of all disorders of enzymes and hormones, it may become possible to demonstrate some specific short circuits or chemical principles besides mere oxidation (Koch) in such processes as are grouped under dementia praecox. The point is that today the simple formula is not available and therefore a mere postulate."[13]

In contrast to the rigid descriptive and nosological attitudes and presumptions which held the field for so many years in America, the trend gradually changed toward the acceptance of psychobiological integrative concepts in line with Adolf Meyer's lead, who from the early 1900's evolved and elaborated the idea of genetic-dynamic factors in force in all types of human behavior.[14] His early formulation of the "reaction types" in psychiatry in general, and specifically in connection with what he called "essential schizophrenia," was seen by him to be the result of "progressive maladjustment with poor adaptation and uneven personality growth." Some years later this was followed by his "parergasias," including a parergastic-paranoid reaction type, all "based on a frankly pleuralistic psychological integration concept," which included the opportunity to study and evaluate the numerous elements entering the picture from all levels of integration and which opened the way for therapeutic modification of those factors susceptible to change, but which excluded the tendency to fixed or rigid prognostic trends. He coined the term "parergasia" for use in preference to "dementia praecox" or "schizophrenia." By it he meant those disturbances developing in particular constitutional types and expressed in vague autistic fantasies, projections, paranoid systematizations, incongruity of affect, motility disturbances, etc., in order to avoid a one-sided bias or emphasis and to escape from nosological nomenclature. His general pathergiastic terminology did not find acceptance with many psychiatrists.

Contemporary in this general era was what may be called the Jung-

Bleuler development with a strong emphasis on psychodynamic factors and mechanisms. Jung was earlier more interested in schizophrenia than was Freud, judging from what each said and published about it. In 1907 he emphasized complex-determined mechanisms, but with a possible toxin involved in the process. Later he developed the idea of introversions and special types, one of which had been anticipated by August Hoch in what he called the "shut-in" personality. Jung was an extremely profound student. His contributions—which include an extension of the knowledge of schizophrenia, the elaboration of important associative tests, a differentiation of introverted and extroverted types, an outstanding advancement of the knowledge of symbolism, and an enrichment of the whole field of folklore and racial psychology —deserve a more thorough consideration in relation to schizophrenia than can be given here. His *Psychology of Dementia Praecox*[15] is a classic in schizophrenic phenomenology and interpretation.

Eugen Bleuler (1857-1939), the eminent Burgholzi professor, in addition to his own original investigations in mental disorders became interested, from as early as 1900 on, in the works of Freud and those of Karl Abraham. Among Bleuler's numerous original contributions that have vitalized psychiatry for many years is the psychology of "schizophrenia," a term he introduced to indicate the alterations in the thinking processes and disharmony of affect, including the phenomena of ambivalence and autistic thinking. His major work, *Dementia Precox oder die Gruppe der Schizophrenien,*[16] was published in 1911. Later he delineated the "schizoid" and "syntonic" personality types.[17]

He saw in schizophrenia a fundamental disease, a "splitting" of the personality which at first he conceived as due to a toxin causing cortical gliosis, which in turn produced serious basic associative disorders with secondary symptoms composing the overt clinical picture. Thus he saw it as an organic disease. The term "schizophrenia" is now in use everywhere, but with the development of the concept, which greatly elucidated disorders of the thought processes, the classification became even more confused since for a time the terms "schizophrenia" and "dementia praecox" were used interchangeably in many psychiatric hospitals. Professor Bleuler's analysis and grouping of the symptoms made some 50 years ago have not been used in a practical way in this country to the extent they deserve. He divided the manifestations into primary and secondary, each with a number of characteristics which may be listed briefly as follows:

I. Primary Symptoms in Thought Processes in Schizophrenia:
   1. Logically unrelated ideas, related in the patient's mind.
   2. Combinations of ideas in a condensation process.
   3. Symbols used when a normal consciousness would have suppressed them and utilized a real object.
   4. General vague notions utilized when concrete statements would be easier understood.
   5. Alliteration.

II. Secondary Symptoms in Schizophrenia:
   1. Autism
   2. Delusions
   3. Illusions of Memory
   4. Hallucinations
   5. Negativism
   6. Stereotyphy
   7. Most of the catatonic symptoms

Since these "secondary" symptoms occur, at least, in part, in a variety of mental conditions and settings, and since many cases classed as simple schizophrenia may have few if any of the active ones, some workers have thought that this so-called simple type should be excluded from the schizophrenic group and perhaps the term "dementia praecox" retained for it. Bleuler considered these "secondary" symptoms, which constituted the main part of the formal picture of Kraepelin, as secondary elaborations of the primary disturbance of the associations and affectivity. Bleuler's ideas and theoretical constructions were the result of systematization of observations on a truly enormous amount of empiric material. His findings strongly supported the fact that schizophrenic subjects do not necessarily deteriorate, but he did utilize some of the external characteristics of Kraepelin's system and did not follow very deeply into the rapidly developing "Freudian system" of his later years, although he was influenced to some extent by Freud's early contributions, particularly those on infantile sexuality and on the unconscious nature of psychologic conflicts.

With Bleuler's concepts of autism and ambivalence and Freud's narcissism doctrine and a little later his analysis of ego tendencies, interests in nosology became subordinated to psychodynamic ones to make for rapid progress in psychopathology. Griesinger (1817-1868) as early as 1845 in his book *Pathologie und Therapie des psychischen Krankheiten*[18] made many statements indicating that he was aware of several of the psychological phenomena which were later fully developed and elaborated into a system by Freud. He gave a rather comprehensive definition of the dynamic unconscious and its role in mental life; he spoke of repression of the instincts, of hunger and love as motivations of conduct; he discussed dreams as wish fulfillment; he indicated the importance of a strong, well-integrated ego and pointed out that anxiety and depression result from conflicts. He even used the term "complex," which was later particularized by Jung. These and numerous streaks of brilliant insight by other pre-Freudian authors, often pointed out by modern writers as antedating Freud, certainly in no way deduct from his originality and genius, since the detailed, patient, tedious, working through of these mechanisms is something quite different from a mere flash of an idea or one that is briefly treated.

Freud published an article, "Defense Neuro-psychoses" (Weitere Bermerkungen über die Abwehr-neuropsychosen)[19] in 1896, the same year as Kraepelin's 1896 edition of the textbook. This was largely a descriptive-explanatory account of a hallucinatory paranoid state in which he pointed out the various psychological mechanisms observed. In 1900 his *Interpretation of Dreams* appeared, and in 1901 *Psychopathology of Everyday Life.* In 1912 came his outspoken dynamic study of the famous Schreber case.[20] These and other important supportive studies uncovered a new field of empiric psychological data which gradually led to a deeper understanding of psychodynamics.

To the historian discovery is seldom a unitary event attributable to some particular man, time, or place, but it seems fair to say that Kraepelin furthered astute clinical psychiatric observation, that Bleuler presented the pictures of ideational and affective content, and that Freud illuminated and interpreted this content. The work of these three men developed contemporaneously and the contribution of each was not in opposition to the others.

Kretschmer in 1918[21] singled out and described a syndrome of sensitivity, the *sensitive Beziehungswahn* indicating the delusions of self-reference of the sensitive individual, thus deviating from the original Kraepelinian pattern, and in 1925 the French brought into more active use the terms *schizomania* and *schizothymia* to better designate those cases of schizophrenia showing active or overt affective components. Through the years many names have been proposed for different syndromes within the schizophrenic framework or related thereto.

To pursue the mainstream of developments, the anthropological constitutional studies should be mentioned next. Peculiarities of body build have been discussed for many years in terms of predispositions to various diseases. More recently in psychiatry, the contributions of Kretschmer,[22] Sheldon,[23] Parnell,[24] and others are well known. Kretschmer[25] in 1925 with his concept of constitution, which stimulated a liberal number of workers along the same lines, occupies a special place in the history of schizophrenia in particular and the story of psychiatric research in general.

In the search for causes of disease, the end of the great era (initiated by Pasteur, Koch, and others) of the identification of the bacterial and other micro-organismal exciting agents seems to be in sight. There are a number of disorders—including neoplastic diseases, some bodily organ degenerations, and the majority of psychiatric disorders—that have not been elucidated, as far as etiology is concerned, by external factors. Therefore, recent trends are rapidly on the increase in the direction of constitutional studies in which genetics is in a central position. We are apparently on the threshold of another phase of medical history where it may be possible to show eventually that genetics and associated biochemical factors determine the onset and mold the course of many unsolved problems.

Genetics in psychiatry has made outstanding progress since the early studies of Rudin's group pointed toward the assumption of a hereditary disposition to schizophrenia. From 1938 Kallmann[26] has been the foremost contributor to the knowledge of inheritance in mental disorders in general and in schizophrenia in particular. He and his associates are actively continuing and enlarging the investigations. Other workers in various countries are also actively engaged in genetic studies in psychiatry, notably Slater[27] in England.

Biochemical studies are now widespread and may eventually lead to an understanding based on etiology and therefore a new terminology. In recent years in psychiatric and allied literature reports illustrate how various groups of investigators have pursued independent lines of biochemical research in an effort to find a correlation with personality, with moods, and with changes in the mental state of man. These studies include chemical factors in carbohydrate metabolism, toxicity of body fluids, indole bases and acids, neuramic acid, and tryptophane metabolism. Drugs producing model psychoses are apparently linked to enzyme systems in the brain, but as yet the results are scattered. However, there are certain trends running through these results, showing similarities sufficient to suggest that a biochemical factor (or factors) is involved in schizophrenia. Accumulating the rest of the evidence and synthesizing it is a challenge for future search and research. Psychogenic approaches apparently deal largely with superstructures in psychic life. Freud in his *Outline of Psychoanalysis* said: "The future may teach us how to exercise a direct influence by means of particular chemical substances, upon the amounts of energy and their distribution in the apparatus of the mind. It may be that there are other undreamed of possibilities of therapy."

The student interested in the schizophrenic type of psychosis discovers that he is dealing with an extremely large group of individuals. From the presenting symptoms it does not appear to be a homogenous group, and he cannot be sure that the patients are suffering from a unitary disorder. He has no specific criterion such as the Wasserman, colloidal gold test, or the Widal, for example, such as he has for syphilis and some other conditions with multiform analogies. Despite all such handicaps one finds it useful to talk about a "schizophrenic group," albeit one cannot but be impressed with the number and variety of etiological factors, hypothetical and speculative, that have appeared in print during the past 25 years. Some of these proposed courses are the result of assumptions constructed on skimpy evidence, while others are based on careful but inconclusive experimental work. Attempts are still active to explain the unknown by another unknown. However, such are not without value if presented in the form of a working hypothesis to be tested by experiment and experience. Faith is not enough, nor soothing words, regarding apparent therapeutic successes adequate to gain the needed facts. We should be willing to recognize and admit the defeats in research and therapy since they serve to reduce the areas and eliminate inadequate methods, thus leaving what is still to be investigated.

The current concepts of etiology can be arranged readily into two principal categories: (1) that it is a distorted reaction pattern originating from certain experiences and situations in early life, and (2) that the disorder is predetermined by hereditary and other constitutional conditions of unknown origin and of obscure pathology which predispose the individual to a breakdown when confronted with the various stresses inherent in life and living and which have to be met by all.

Since nosology based on etiology is not yet possible, we follow one based on "telesmatics" (Southard's term) or the art of effects; therefore all classifications of mental disorders, including the present one in use (1963), statistically rest on a set of multiple events and are based on precipitating stress, brain and other bodily diseases, exogenic factors, age levels, and on constellations of clinical symptoms. Proof of the causes of these symptoms is not yet available, and thus much remains in the realm of belief and speculation.

The schizophrenias have been grouped in many different ways, both for statistical recording and for purposes of study in attempts to segregate the reaction types for comparison and special evaluation. Although no classification has been entirely satisfactory for research purposes, the following four categories are recognized by most clinicians and could serve fairly well for study group purposes.

1. The "nuclear" or central group with progressive and finally severe deterioration—the so-called "process" schizophrenia.
2. The acute turmoil state (Campbell).
3. Simple deterioration type.
4. The atypical schizophrenias: (a) Schizoaffective, (b) Pseudoneurotic[28] (Hoch and Polatin), (c) Pseudopsychopathic[29] (Hoch).

Since all classifications of schizophrenias are based on shifting clinical pictures, there are naturally numerous differences of opinion regarding labels, depending on what 'clusters" of symptoms are emphasized. There would be less diagnostic blunders and much might be corrected and further elucidated by carefully organized studies of the outcome. Although a few such studies have been made, it seems that the most needed follow-up investigations are less popular than those in other areas of the problem and also less attractive to financial aid.

In summary, our information about schizophrenic mechanisms has been considerably enlarged by such individual contributions as those of Jung with his ideas of "complexes" and special types, by Bleuler's fundamental conception of association disorders, by Kleist's elaboration of motility phenomena (following Wernicke), by the outstanding dynamic contributions of Freud, and again by Bleuler's concept of autism and ambivalence, and by Schilder's explanations of the ego tendencies. New foci of interest arose with Kretschmer's description of constitutional bodily types, by several endocrine studies, by the investigations into hereditary factors by Rudin and especially by Kallmann, and finally by what has been accomplished in recent years and currently in biochemical areas.

These productions seem quite remarkable when we consider the distance covered during the last 160 years, since it was about then that Immanuel Kant insisted that the subject of mental diseases belonged to philosophy and not to the physician, nor was psychology considered to be a sufficiently respectable subject until about 140 years ago when August Comte reserved a special place for it in his classification of the sciences.

A statement made by Nicolaus Steno (1638-1686) in a lecture on "Anatomy of the Brain" in 1669 apparently still applies. He said, "Beautiful are the things we see, more beautiful is what we know, but far the greatest are the things we do not know."

REFERENCES

1. Willis, T.: De Anima Britorum. Amsterdam, 1674, p. 497.
2. Pinel, P.: Traité Médico-Philosophique sur l'Aliénation Mentale. Paris, Richard Caille and Ravier, 1801.
   ——: A Treatise on Insanity (trans. D. D. Davis). London, Codell and Davies, 1806.
3. Esquirol, J. E. D.: Des Maladies Mentales. Paris, J. B. Ballière, 1838.
4. Zeller: Allg. Ztschr. f. Psychiat. Berlin, 1844, Vol. I.
5. Morel, B. A.: Traité des Maladies Mentales. 1960.
   ——: Traité des Dégénérescences Physiques Intellectuelles et Morales. Paris, J. Bailliere, 1857.
6. Meyer, A.: The Evolution of the Dementia Precox Concept (Vol. V of Schizophrenia, 1925: Proc. Assn. for Research in Nerv. & Ment. Dis.). New York, Paul B. Hoeber, 1928.
7. Kahlbaum, K.: Der Katatonic oder das Spannungsirresein. 1874.
8. Hecker, E.: Arch. f. path. amat. Berlin, 50:11, 1870.
9. Spitzka, E. C.: Insanity: Its Classification, Diagnosis and Treatment (2nd ed.). New York, E. B. Treat, 1887.
10. Kraepelin, E.: Psychiatrie; ein Lehrbuch für Studierende und Ärtzte (8th ed.). Leipzig, Barth, 1913 (3rd ed., 1887).
11. Taken from private stenogram made on the occasion.
12. Meyer, A.: A review of recent problems in psychiatry. *In* Nervous and Mental Diseases (4th ed.). Church and Peterson, 1904, pp. 650-668.
13. ——: The Nature and Conception of Dementia Precox. J. Abnorm. Psychol. 5:274-285, 1910-11.
14. ——: Arch. Neurol. Psychiat. 8:121.

15a. Jung, C. G.: The Psychology of Dementia Precox (trans. A. A. Brill). *In* Nervous and Mental Diseases, Monograph #3. New York, Nerv. and Ment. Dis. Publishing Co., 1907.

15b. ——: On the Psychogenesis of Schizophrenia. J. Ment. Sci. 85:999, 1939.

15c. ——: Die Schizophrenie. Schweiz. Arch. Neurol. Psychiat. 81:163, 1958.

16a. Bleuler, E.: Dementia Praecox oder die Gruppe der Schizophrenien (trans. J. Zinkin). Leipzig, Deuticke, 1911, New York, International University Press, 1950.

16b. ——: Textbook of Psychiatry (trans. A. A. Brill). New York, Macmillan, 1930.

17. ——: Die Problem der Schizoide und der Syntonie. Berlin and Leipzig, Ztschr. f.d.ges. Neurol. Psychiat. 78:373.

18. GRIESINGER, W.: Die Pathologie und Therapie der Psychischen Krankheiten für Ärtzte und Studierende. Stuttgart, Adolph Krabbe Verlag, 1845.
19. FREUD, S.: Weitere Bemerkungen über die Abwehr-Neuropsychosen. Leipzig, Neurol. Centralblatt, 15:434, 1896.
20. ——: The Standard Edition of the Complete Psychological Works. Vol. XII (1911-13) London: Hogarth Press, 1958.
21. KRETSCHMER, E.: Die Sensitive Beziehungswahn. Berlin, Springer (1st ed., 1918; 3rd ed., 1950).
22. ——: A Textbook of Medical Psychology (trans. E. B. Straus). London, Hogarth Press, 1952.
23. SHELDON, W. H.: The Varieties of Temperament. New York, Harper, 1942.
24. PARNELL, R. W.: Behavior and Physique. London, Arnold, 1958.
25. KRETSCHMER, E.: Physique and Character (trans. W. J. H. Sprott). London, Kegan Paul, French and Trubner, 1925.
26a. KALLMANN, F. J.: The Genetics of Schizophrenia. New York, J. J. Augustin, 1938.
26b. ——: The genetic theory of schizophrenia: An analysis of 691 schizophrenic twin index families. Amer. J. Psychiat. 103:309, 1946.
26c. ——: Heredity in Health and Mental Disorder. New York, Norton, 1953.
26d. —— AND ROTH, B.: Genetic aspects of preadolescent schizophrenia. Amer. J. Psychiat. 112:599, 1956.
27a. SLATER, E.: Psychotic and Neurotic Illnesses in Twins: Special Report of Medical Research Council. London, H.M.S.O., 1953, p. 278.
27b. ——: Psychiatry. *In* Clinical Genetics (ed. A. Sorsby). London, Butterworth, 1953.
27c. ——: The monogenic theory of schizophrenia. Basel, Acta Genet. 8:50, 1958.
28a. HOCH, P. H., AND POLATIN, P.: Pseudoneurotic forms of schizophrenia. Psychiat. Quart. 23:248, 1949.
28b. —— and CATTELL, J. P.: The diagnosis of pseudoneurotic schizophrenia. Psychiat. Quart. 33:1, 1959.
29. DUNAIF, S. L., AND HOCH, P. H.: Pseudopsychopathic schizophrenia. *In Psychiatry and the law* (eds. P. H. Hoch and J. Zubin). New York, Grune & Stratton, 1955.
30. KRAEPELIN, E.: One Hundred Years of Psychiatry. New York, Philosophical Library, 1962.
31. TERRY, G. C., AND RENNIE, T. A. C.: Analysis of Parergasia, Monograph #64. New York, Nerv. and Ment. Dis Pub. Co., 1938.

2

A PSYCHODYNAMIC VIEW OF PSEUDONEUROTIC SCHIZOPHRENIA

by JAMES P. CATTELL, M.D.*

THE CRITERIA FOR THE DIAGNOSIS of pseudoneurotic schizophrenia are well established[1,2] and have come to be increasingly recognized and accepted in psychiatric facilities. One report of the investigation of the course and outcome of over 100 patients with this syndrome has been published.[3] The literature contains a number of papers on the diagnosis, psychodynamics, and treatment of similar or related symptom constellations. These include publications on the borderline case, patient or state;[5-9] latent schizophrenia;[10,11] and ambulatory schizophrenia.[12,13] In May 1961 at the Annual Meeting of the American Psychiatric Association in Chicago, Dr. Paul H. Hoch chaired a panel discussion on the psychodynamics and treatment of pseudoneurotic schizophrenia. The other participants were Drs. G. Bychowski, S. Rado, M. O. Strahl, and the author.

In an earlier presentation[2] we delineated the primary clinical symptoms of pseudoneurotic schizophrenia: disorders of thinking and associations—form and content; disorders of emotional regulation—form and content and disorders of sensorimotor and autonomic functioning. The secondary clinical symptoms of the syndrome were enunciated as pan-anxiety, pan-neurosis and pan-sexuality (chaotic sexuality). (See tables 1-4.)

We noted in that paper that the role of anxiety in the formation of the primary and secondary symptoms is not clear. Anxiety, its vicissitudes, and the defenses against it are prominent in every psychodynamic frame of reference. We noted that symptoms may be regarded as a means of coping with anxiety—a restitutive function—or as they become more dominating and disabling, they may have a disintegrative effect.

At a given time in a patient's life and illness, either trend may be

*Assistant Clinical Professor of Psychiatry, Columbia University, New York, N.Y.

TABLE 1.—The Diagnosis of Pseudoneurotic Schizophrenia

The Primary Clinical Symptoms:
1. Disorders of thinking and associations: Process; content.
2. Disorders of emotional regulation: Form; content.
3. Disorders of sensorimotor and automatic functioning.

The Secondary Clinical Symptoms:
1. Pan-anxiety.
2. Pan-neurosis: Neurotic symptomatology, acting-out behavior and character-disorder symptoms.
3. Pan-sexuality.

TABLE 2.—Primary Clinical Symptoms of Pseudoneurotic Schizophrenia

Disorders of Thinking and Associations—Process:
1. Evidence of characteristics of primary process thinking.
2. Disturbances in thought continuity and goal-directed thought.
3. Disturbances of thought flow.
4. Disturbances of awareness, attention, anticipation, and concentration.
5. Impairment in the process of concept-formation.

Disorders of Thinking and Associations—Content:
1. Content dominated by stereotyped, anachronistic concepts and attitudes.
2. Distorted concepts of self, body image, the world, and the interrelationships of these.
3. Rigid and distorted concepts of the meaning and utilization of intellect, emotion and behavior.
4. Chaotic concepts of sexuality.

more in evidence. One can postulate that the qualitative and quantitative aspects of such trends are influenced by constitutional factors and by environmental factors and their interaction. For convenience, we can define the constitutional factors as those associated with deficiencies in basic endowment and those related to the vicissitudes of gestation and delivery. Following parturition, the child can be subjected to any portion of a broad spectrum of physical, emotional, social, and other experiences in his environment. This environment can be basically deficient in a variety of ways. It is the interaction of the strengths and weaknesses of the constitutional factors and the environmental opportunities that determines the outcome of the individual's relative health or lack of it.

Environmental opportunities necessarily include not only the early nurturing experiences, but the later experiences in living. Psychotherapy, psychoanalysis, and other types of medical assistance are part of these later experiences.

We recognize that the designation of prepartum factors as constitutional and postpartum experiences as environmental is arbitrary and that there are a number of other ways in which one might view these factors. Our approach is one way to define an area of discussion, and such definition is our goal as a preface to this presentation.

The title of this paper, "A Psychodynamic View of Pseudoneurotic

TABLE 3.—Primary Clinical Symptoms of Pseudoneurotic Schizophrenia (*Continued*)

Disorders of Emotional Regulation—Form:

1. Evidence of some of the characteristics of primary process functioning.
2. Low threshold to anxiety.
3. Heterogeneity of emotional response. Emotional volatility with dysregulation of emotional depth.
4. Inertia in initiating, sustaining, and terminating emotional response.
5. Impairment of ability to select and regulate aggression and assertion.
6. Complex-bound emotional reactions.
7. Latent period between perceiving stimulus and conscious recognition of associated emotional reaction.
8. Somatization of emotional reactions.

Disorders of Emotional Regulation—Content:

1. Intolerance of tension, and diffuse anxiety.
2. Impairment of feeling tone, and anhedonia.
3. Impairment of empathy. Sensitiveness with low threshold to withdrawal reaction.
4. Exploitation of others in effort to experience emotion.
5. Emotional feelings repudiated. Intellectualization of emotion.
6. Craving for stimulation; craving for protection and dependency.
7. Striving for quick, magical gratification of needs.

TABLE 4.—Primary Clinical Symptoms of Pseudoneurotic Schizophrenia (*Concluded*)

Disorders of Sensorimotor and Autonomic Functioning:

1. Impairment of integration of sensory perceptions.
2. Impairment of ability to select and maintain motor responses.
3. Somatization of emotional reactions. Autonomic dysfunction.
4. Impairment of sensorimotor-autonomic integration in psychosexual functioning.
5. Energy dysregulation. Intolerance of sustained activity toward a future goal.
6. Pursuit of sensory and motor patterns as substitutes for stimulus-appropriate thought, feeling or action.

Schizophrenia," was selected to emphasize one aspect of this kind of illness. The major portion of this presentation is devoted to Henry, a disguised name with a disguised history. He is a prime representative of the well-endowed individual who was subjected to numerous environmental vicissitudes. However, his distorted, stereotyped, and anachronistic attitudes, concepts, and patterns of behavior proved to be malleable in a series of dynamic and growth-promoting opportunities.

This psychodynamic view of Henry presents his problems at the time of entering treatment, his history and certain aspects of his behavior and growth during the course of treatment. The latter, in turn, reflect many aspects of his earlier inhibition, symptoms, and anxiety. Maturation is the most accurate mirror of the extent of earlier failure to achieve it.

Identification

Henry is a 34-year-old married man who owns and operates a thriving import-export firm. Personable in appearance, his clothes reflect his European background and cosmopolitan life. He is somewhat taller than average, has a good build inclined toward stockiness, and with his thinning hair and black-rimmed glasses he is an impressive looking person. He speaks with quiet assurance and there is scarcely a trace of foreign accent, though he is equally at home with several languages. A nonsmoker, he sometimes busies his hands with glasses, keys, or a coin. He is an animated conversationalist and has a wide variety of interests. We wish to review the emergence of this picture of Henry from that which he presented 10 years earlier.

Presenting Complaints

Henry sought private treatment, through the suggestion of a medical friend, just before his twenty-fourth birthday. He was miserable, frightened, and helpless; he was disabled in almost every sphere of daily functioning and found no satisfaction or pleasure in living. Depression, anxiety, a variety of obsessive-compulsive-phobic complaints, facial tics, indecisiveness, work inhibition, and a peptic ulcer were the leading symptoms. Despondency and tension plagued him most of the time and there were apparently inexplicable episodes of severe depression from time to time. There were brief periods of feeling "high" but these were characterized more by agitation than elation. He lived with his parents and continued to view his father as a threatening ogre, against whom he had passively rebelled in early youth.

Mother was the most important person in his life. She showered him with solicitude and he enjoyed his frequent bouts of "flu," for she nursed him as if he were a boy of six. Feelings of irritation and defiance about this infantilization were mostly unexpressed, in part because the foundation of his identity was in her being, of which he saw himself as an extension.

There was some social life, which he described as compulsive, but he was in constant fear of being revealed as a frightened, guilty child in social relationships. He classified most people according to a few stereotyped categories and inevitably felt threatened. Employed as a copywriter in a small advertising agency, he paternalized his boss, produced little because he felt blocked, and earned $25 a week, a paltry wage at that time.

There was a renewed fear of being drafted by the Army, a problem that had arisen initially five years before when he was in college. At that time he had developed a peptic ulcer and was rejected for military service, but he had recently been notified that he was to be reexamined. There had been an attendant exacerbation of ulcer symptoms and he was under the care of an internist. He protested that he had no fear of combat but dreaded the regimentation, loss of freedom, and the arbitrary power that crude superiors would have over him in the Army. The primitive aspects of barracks living and the anticipated coarseness and horseplay of soldiers were repugnant to him. His fear of bodily damage in this context was particularly prominent and he regarded himself as defenseless and vulnerable to physical, including sexual, assault. This was linked with his fascination and fear that he might be homosexual. In addition, he feared air flights, having fantasies of crashing, and he had several phobias in association with driving his car. There was frequent concern that he would "black out" while negotiating slopes or curves in the road. He felt panicky driving through the tunnel he traversed daily and developed unreality feelings on at least one such occasion. Henry's appearance was a subject of obsessive rumination and he was greatly concerned about thinning hair and receding hairline, which he saw as a defect jeopardizing his body integrity and making him less manly. This was linked to his fascination with pubic hair, which figured prominently in his masturbatory fantasies, and with his anxiety about obesity. Guilty fear pervaded these activities and interests. These, in turn, were related to compulsive eating, particularly chocolate foods, which occurred when he felt anxious and lonely. He found some tension release in this and in masturbation but it was often negated by reverberations of guilt and fears of damage.

Concepts and attitudes about sexuality were confused and poorly integrated. Heterosexual experience, at the time of entering treatment, had been confined to petting to orgasm. On kissing a girl, he often felt a tight knot in his abdomen which disappeared when it became clear that there was no opportunity for intercourse. When sexually aroused with one girl he felt "certain sado-masochistic impulses in my sexual parts and a wish to be hurt slightly to indicate a certain violence of passion." A feeling of constriction in the penis was experienced when he worried about being fat, but disappeared when he exercised. A comparable sensation occurred when he thought about growing older and accomplishing nothing in life. He spoke of his fears of the Army as fears a child has about castration and referred to entering the Army as amputation without anesthesia. The avoidance of intercourse he explained as fear of involvement with women, being trapped into marriage and responsibility, and a conviction that he would not perform satisfactorily in intercourse.

Fascination with pubic hair was evidenced in dream, fantasy, and action. To avoid obsessive preoccupation with being drafted, he daydreamed about a harem and shaving the girls' pubic hair. "It hides something that would be more attractive than what girls have before puberty. Without it, the appearance is similar to prepuberty, but different and more sexual." At this time his experience was limited to stimulating the genital area of partially clothed women, but he imagined the shaved area would appear "redder than lips." However, the vagina would be more attractive if painted with iodine, though it seemed more important to so paint the nipples. He had cut and shaved his own pubic hair at times, found this activity sexually stimulating and was pleased with "the removal of this ugliness." There were fantasies of sewing up a girl's vagina or of cutting off the clitoris in a sexual context, as well as of cutting off his penis when disgusted with himself for masturbating or being indecisive. There were manifest dreams and fantasies of incest, castration, of being a woman, of women with male equipment, as well as dreams with sado-masochistic and voyeur-exhibitionistic content. He was very sensitive to odors, preoccupied with anal and genital odors, and evinced confusion about a woman's anal and genital anatomy and functioning.

Henry spoke of his college group as a "social smorgasbord" and of having lived in a house full of homosexuals. Instances of several real or imagined "passes" by men were recounted and he expressed fearful interest in this kind of activity.

Other areas of concern included bowel consciousness, some anxiety about toilet contamination; self-consciousness about chronic nail-biting; a wish to take up riding, neutralized by a fear of horses; a wish to do free-lance writing, impaired by a writing block; concern about facial tics and facial acne, and fearful confusion about aggressiveness. He was almost convinced that if ever provoked to rage, he would lose control, become demoniacal, and kill his adversary. There were fantasties of his boss supine on the floor, the patient sitting on him and bashing his head against the floor, with attendant fear of retaliation.

This fairly comprehensive survey of Henry's symptoms and functioning at the time he began treatment gives an indication of the ubiquitousness of his anxiety and ambivalence, the range of his defensive maneuvering, and the paucity of pleasure in his day-to-day living. We might note, parenthetically, that if one "considers the uses of sexuality," one finds that he pursued sexual activity for almost every conceivable purpose except for simple gratification of his sexual need. In this, as in the other areas of his thinking and functioning, we see illustrations of the primary and secondary clinical symptomatology of pseudoneurotic schizophrenia.

Past History and Onset of Illness

Henry was born into an upper middle class, cultured home in a western European country. His father, a brilliant professional man of orthodox Jewish faith, was of central European origin and had established himself initially in his native land. Political circumstances had necessitated his abrupt migration to the country of Henry's birth, where he again achieved prominence in his chosen work. The later immigration to the United States was also politically determined and again he built a reputation in a short time. A man of determination, austere habits, and definite opinions, he apparently expended his tolerance, patience, and flexibility in devoted pursuit of his work, leaving little available for his family. Henry's mother, a native of another western European country, was a member of a family traditionally engaged in one phase of the import-export business, which the patient subsequently decided to make his career. During Henry's youth she had been a glamorous and subtly flirtatious beauty and a musician and painter of some talent. She later opened her own firm in the family tradition. One gains the impression of a blithe spirit, a personality quite in contrast to that of her husband, sensitive, moderately hedonistic, and somewhat anxious, with a penchant for dramatizing in a somewhat irresponsible way and having a facade of calm self-assurance.

Henry's infancy was marked by acute ear infections requiring three serious surgical operations before he learned to talk. He reported that he had been a "sickly child" until he was 15 years old, though one could say that this characterization continued to apply through the time he began treatment, in view of the peptic ulcer and frequent, disabling respiratory infections. His poor health may have expedited a number of developments, particularly the closeness and reciprocal dependency with his mother, her infantilizing solicitude, and the father's relative isolation from both of them. In addition, there had initially been a wet nurse and subsequently a child's nurse, who cared for him until age 7, freeing the mother to come and go as she pleased. Feelings of fear and hate were prominent in his recollections of his father, a stranger in the house from whom he was protected by the mother. Henry recounted vivid memories of sitting in the bathroom talking with his mother, at her request, while she bathed; of seeing her naked body and being fascinated by the breasts floating in the water. This phase of his education went on at least from ages 5 to 7, the father's objections going unattended until he had finally insisted that Henry was "too old" for this sort of thing. However, Henry does not recall ever having seen his father's body and adult maleness remained a mystery to him.

His reaction at 8 or 9 to his father kissing his mother was: "What right does he have to do that?" On two occasions his father slapped his face, once for not having prayed and once for failing to have a sufficiently good report card. Henry learned to avoid his father's wrath by telling him what he wanted to hear, feeling that the truth was unimportant. His resentment was further underlined by his father's requiring him to have Hebrew lessons, adding another frightening school situation in which he felt cowed by father-surrogates and intimidated by classmates. These lessons also accentuated his awareness of the father's Jewish, central-European origin, and thus his own, which he wished to repudiate in favor of identifying himself with the western-European country of his birth.

During the course of treatment, a number of vivid experiences of childhood and adolescence appeared in association with current activities and dreams. He recalled his sister, two years his junior, showing him her clitoris when he was 11 years old. Later, he was amazed to discover that the clitoris of his current girl friend was so small, recalling that his sister's was much larger. There were many recollections about interest in his mother's breasts. At 11 or 12, the father commented on her new brassiere on an occasion when she was wearing a wool-knit dress. Henry put his hand on one of her breasts, a gesture which she seemed to encourage, and then he felt guilty and somewhat frightened. He first masturbated, using suntan lotion as a lubricant, at an unrecalled age. When he mentioned this to friends, he was shocked and hurt by their disapproval. Between the age of 11 and 14, he masturbated before a mirror wearing one of his mother's girdles or brassieres. There were associated fantasies of her forcing him into these garments or beating him, as well as manifestly incestuous daydreams. All this was the subject of much guilt, with attendant fear of discovery by father and subsequent anxiety that such practices would somehow be revealed to the world at large. Around this time he learned about circumcision, which his mother helpfully explained as "taking the front part of the penis off." He was angrily aware that this had been done at his father's insistence, on religious grounds, but he held his mother responsible also for not having interfered.

In view of his frail health, his mother took him to summer resorts throughout his childhood, the father remaining at home. There, she would often go out in the evening with one or another escort, and he has indelible and awe-provoking memories of this statuesque princess, delicately perfumed and moving in an aura of mystery. This picture was to influence his later attitude toward women of this type, for whom he felt a compelling fascination, regarding them as the unattainable ideal. In contrast, girls lacking any of the characteristics of this idealized woman, in terms of physical configuration, culture and poise, were regarded as second best, no matter how attractive they were. They seemed more easily available, for he could approach them with less fear, but they were not the prized objects of his desire. This stereotyped view of women was to be dramatized in 70 to 80 relationships before it was finally resolved.

The relationship between Henry and his sister, apparently a healthy girl who married in her early twenties, was good throughout childhood and adult life. She was favored by the father and apparently no rival to the patient for the mother's affection. The family moved to the

United States when Henry was 15 and he attended camp the first two summers he was here. He hated camp, felt that he was a misfit, and experienced some of the fears he later expressed about barracks life, when he was in danger of being drafted into the Army. Certain aspects of his college life were alluded to above and he was graduated from a coeducational school at the age of 19 with a bachelor of arts degree. A few months later, he began working as a copywriter in the promotion department of a large firm but had no interest in the technical nature of the material. After a year or so, he left this job and moved to the advertising agency where he was still employed at the time he began treatment at age 24.

Developments during Treatment

Henry's subsequent history is a study in anxiety, dependence, and ambivalence with a gradual and episodic emergence of his more recent, relatively stable and successful way of life. During the decade of the present study, he was in and out of treatment, the earlier interruptions representing a dramatization of his ambivalence about the therapy. He came for treatment sessions about once a week during the first two years. His $25 a week salary precluded his coming more frequently. He adamantly refused to seek financial assistance from his parents, wanting to keep the whole thing a secret from them. After two years of weekly visits with increasingly frequent interruptions, he was suddenly fired, for personality reasons, from a good job he had held for 14 months. He agreed to begin psychoanalysis, which continued for 3 years with three or four sessions each week. At the end of this 3-year period he went abroad for 6 months in order to improve his occupational status and initiate his own business. During the second 5 years of the decade, he would return for a few visits to work out some specific problem or emotional reaction.

Throughout the period under consideration, he held several full-time and part-time jobs and indecisively considered a dozen other job opportunities. These positions were involved with some sort of journalistic and promotional activities, but the situation was often marred by his difficulties in getting along with associates and his inclination to paternalize his superiors. With the passage of time, he became increasingly proficient in promotional work, progressively better able to handle interpersonal relationships, and was offered more and more remunerative opportunities. Meanwhile, he constantly debated entering the import-export business in the family tradition. There was much talk of writing magazine articles in this field and, after much procrastination, he occasionally produced a few. In addition, he lectured before various organizations on topics in this field. As he began to pursue the import-export business on a part-time basis while holding a part-time promotional job, he began to receive offers to join established firms of the former type and to enter into partnerships. Each of these offers appealed to him as providing safe, parental protection but each was ultimately vetoed on the basis of being restrictive and away from his special interests in the field. Gradually he came to devote full time to his own firm and used his promotional abilities in a subtle and conservative manner to facilitate the growth of his business. Such an approach, unique in this field of endeavor, proved to be quite successful, and he gradually achieved increasing stature and expanded his firm.

There were growth and development in other areas of behavior more or less concurrent with those in the occupational sphere. Fairly early in treatment, there were beginnings of emancipation from parents and home, the initial move being his setting up his own apartment and finally occupying it amid much doubting and fear of the consequences. Would his parents object? Would he be able to take care of himself in it? Would he not be awfully lonely and realize the full impact of having no friends and being helpless? Would not such private facilities make it possible, or obligatory, to be intimate with girls and lead to dangerous sexual situations or emotional involvements? Henry ruminated on these and other issues and many of them were analyzed in treatment with slow realization that such a bold step on his part would not be catastrophic. At times, he longed to be at home again and have the protection of the parental umbrella. For a while, he would return home for maternal care during bouts of "flu," though this inclination faded as he became more confident and as he had fewer such illnesses with progressively less disability. The view of his father as a formidable, frightening tyrant and his mother as a possessive but understanding angel became modified much more gradually.

Emotional emancipation from parents and parent figures was a slower process than the physical emancipation. However, he became more adventurous socially and joined a group of contemporaries in renting a summer house at a nearby resort. This was quite a departure for one who had always spent summer weekends and vacations with parents. He was amazed and pleased that he enjoyed himself and that he was liked and respected by the others in the group. Having some interest and a little experience in sailing with friends, he bought a small sailboat but was filled with fear that he would be incapable of handling it, only to be surprised at his own facility. This represented a further departure from family interests and a challenging of his fear of physical activities and concern about bodily integrity. As he tested his abilities and gained more experience in import-export merchandise, he became more able to rely on his own taste and judgment, even when they clashed with his mother's aesthetic ideas or his father's conservative business concepts. Social mobility increased and he was progressively less intimidated by wealthy clients, aggressive dowagers, and social-register families. A view of this development at the half-way point, as it were, can be seen in his first trip abroad, away from the protective shelter of home-town, parents, and analyst.

At the end of 3 years of psychoanalysis, which had followed 2 years of psychotherapy, he went to Europe for 6 months with a view to expediting his business interests. While there, he visited many cities and was amazed at his freedom in social situations, business transactions, and in relationships with attractive women. However, all was not wonderful. Anxiety and depression plagued him from time to time. There was much indecisiveness about accepting various promotional jobs in Paris, either for temporary support while he established his own business or as a decisive step in a career in promotional work. Much of the discomfort was anticipatory and he was repeatedly surprised that he functioned so well in action, handling people and situations in a successful manner which had not been possible before.

He wrote some long letters during his absence and some of his remarks illustrate these points: "On my arrival in Paris, the chief emotional impulse was 'No,' with a feeling of banishment from home to a cold, wintry place, away from all familiar surroundings and friends. These things seemed most important during the first few days, though not at all now (a month later). New objects and surroundings become friendly and familiar so quickly and the essence of friends is the art of making them, which I also discovered I command." Referring to a dominating woman relative with whom he spent some time: "She is amazingly possessive towards me, almost jealous, urging me to see this or that girl she introduced me to and then jealous of the time I spend with them. . . . She resents it when I follow my own inclinations socially. But all this has proved to be no real problem, and something I could cope with to my satisfaction and I think hers."

During his fourth month abroad he wrote: "One of the strongest emotional things in Europe, revisiting ———, the setting of so much of my childhood. Spent the first few days wandering around ——— (the capital), the sections I knew best, visiting the schools I'd been to, looking up a couple of old teachers who were still around and remembered me vividly, visiting our old housekeeper. The city quite unchanged, but how changed I am! What a long way I've come: not just because I've lived elsewhere, but because I've grown up. Particularly the last few years. Never felt the impact of analysis as much as in that city." He resolved the job issue by agreeing to work as editorial and promotional consultant for a magazine for 6 weeks, insuring some income for living expenses but avoiding a 6 months' commitment which his employers had requested. On this situation, he noted: "I'm facing new business and social problems which are new only in terms of the actors, not really in terms of the problems themselves—problems and situations which not very long ago would have thrown me into sleeping fits and probably into being fired. I think I have learned a great deal the last 3-4 months in Europe . . . or learned and discovered them probably in your office. But worked them out in practice, put them to work on actual problems, and without half trying as the saying goes. And particularly the past few weeks: deciding things, working, traveling, meeting girls. Of course, problems. But on the whole, I've never felt so happy in my life. Done so much. Felt so confident, without feeling that some house of cards would collapse tomorrow because of my very confidence. . . ." As for deciding about following journalism and advertising or his own import-export business: ". . . Then as for my own business, the only way to tell is to try it. I'd known that before but kept worrying. Now I find that the percent of worrying has declined to a very low and infrequently occurring amount. . . . I had been trying to create a life out of an imaginary and not too realistic catalog of futures; that's one way of describing my pattern. I now find that I have grown out of this largely."

Henry's emergence as a person in his own right in occupational and social areas of behavior proceeded apace in the second half of the decade under consideration. Taking a slight lag into account, the same may be said of his development to adult sexuality. He came to be able to perform easily and well, to the satisfaction of the woman concerned and himself. The most problematical area was that involving close emotional relationships with women, which, of course, is intimately related to certain aspects of his developmental history. His episodic returns for brief series of treatment sessions during the second half of the decade were motivated by various difficulties in developing such close emotional relationships. This important aspect of his life, which involved 70 to 80 women over a 10-year period, warrants presentation in some detail.

The utter chaos of his concept of male and female anatomy and physiology and his confused attitudes about sexuality, emotional closeness, family relationships, assertiveness, and relationships to authority have been noted in the section on presenting complaints. During the early months of treatment, the range of his sexual fantasies was encyclopedic, some of the content of which was mentioned. Social activity with women was limited to one or two and sexual activity was restricted to occasional petting to orgasm, though compulsive, guilt-laden masturbation was rampant. Not infrequently, he escorted his sister to parties, including those over weekends in nearby cities. On some weekends the family would go to a resort, and on these occasions patient and sister would usually occupy the same room. In the ninth month of treatment, and after he had been chiding himself for not having had intercourse, the patient met a new girl. In the thirty-eighth session, he reported that he had had intercourse four times with her on their fourth date together. He had apparently performed satisfactorily but stated that it had not been pleasurable and that he had experienced many anxious reverberations, including fears that he would be expected to repeat the performance. Subsequently he had intercourse with her on several occasions, with some pleasure at times but always with anticipatory and retrospective anxiety. He was relieved when she left for Europe a few weeks later.

Henry's stereotyped concept of the ideal woman was based on his view of his mother during his earlier years. As was noted in the section on that era of his life, she had been an awesome, statuesque princess, who had moved in an aura of mystery at times. She had been a warm, need-fulfilling, maternal protectress at other times and had encouraged his interest in her ample bosom. As Henry became somewhat freer and socially more mobile, he engaged in an ambivalent pursuit of these two sets of characteristics. As might be expected, he found elements of both sets of characteristics in a wide variety of combinations.

He was usually awed by the glamorous type of woman, became stiff and shy as he worshipped her from afar, and thus invited the rebuff he had expected. More time was devoted to youthfully maternal and protective women, who in a sense wooed him socially and sexually, only to become increasingly possessive and demanding. He functioned quite well sexually with these girls and enjoyed their initial dedication to his welfare but became frightened as he felt increasingly trapped and carried toward marriage.

Another influential factor in his reaction to women was his idea about parental expectations of a proper marriage for him and his own concept that it would be expeditious to marry a wealthy woman, whose means would nourish the development of his business. He had variably intimate social relationships with a number of minor heiresses but found each one unacceptable. Gradually he was able to recognize that the parental and financial standards he had set were defensive maneuvers against long-term involvement with any woman.

However, this development was slow. During the 6 months in Europe, he had felt much more spontaneous with women, had met many traveling about, and had availed himself of some of the sexual opportunities that occurred. There, he had none of the fear of being trapped, partly because he was moving around a lot and partly because he was free of the restraining parental influence he had felt in his home city. During the months after he returned, he found himself increasingly in demand at social gatherings as an eligible bachelor but felt increasingly bored by casual relationships, social or sexual or both. He wished to meet someone with whom he could share more interests and to whom he could become attached. However, many of the eligible young women impressed him as rather provincial products of fashionable Eastern schools, in contrast to his more cosmopolitan experience.

His infrequent visits to treatment during the second 5 years were motivated primarily by problems and indecisiveness about a more permanent relationship with a woman. He suddenly reported that he was taking an attractive divorcee with him on one of his periodic trips to Central and South America. There was some trepidation since he had never done this before nor had he ever spent so much time continuously with one woman. He thoroughly enjoyed the experience, was quite enthusiastic about the girl, and no longer had as many fears about protracted and intimate association with a woman. However, it developed that the girl was deeply involved with a "mad artist," inextricably embroiled in a sado-masochistic relationship. The trip with Henry, though perhaps designed to be a final break, turned out to be only a leave of absence from this man. Though Henry understood that the girl was involved in her own problems and that he was probably fortunate in avoiding entanglement in a "sticky triangle," he regarded the situation as a severe rejection and felt lost and depressed. He welcomed every opportunity to talk with the girl, as she continued to dramatize her own ambivalence. There was anger, petulance, despondency, and the "human bondage" reaction. These gradually faded after the girl went to her home in another part of the country, but Henry kept wondering whether he would ever find a woman about whom he could feel as he had with her on their trip.

At about this time, he hired an assistant in his firm, a bright, "bouncy," young woman, who very quickly became a superb Girl-Friday. She was warm, sympathetic, seemed to be able to anticipate his needs and wishes, and to cheer him out of his despondent mourning of the loss of the other girl. Soon she was attending business-social functions with Henry, since it was simpler for him to be accompanied by a presentable girl and she was available. He felt paralyzed about renewing relationships with other girls he had known and about initiating new ones. Though he was aware of his vulnerability and his need to invite the maternal ministrations of this girl, he proceeded to do just that. Soon he was spending social evenings and recreational nights and weekends with her, as well as working days. Then he became perplexed and irritated that she was increasingly possessive and demanding. He felt fond of her, valued her talents in the business, and found her to be a convenient social and sexual partner. However, he did not love her and he resented her petulance and fits of despondency in response to his increasing interest in doing things without her. Henry engaged in long debates with himself about the girl and his relationship to her and increasingly contrasted her and compared her with another woman, much more his peer, in whom he had a growing interest. Girl-Friday was characterized as safe and predictable, devoted to him and to the business but not as inspiring to him emotionally, intellectually, or physically as he wished. The other girl was viewed as being much more of a person in her own right with definite resources in writing and teaching, which she was already exploiting. In a word, he saw in her an interesting and stimulating partner, adaptable but undemanding, in contrast to a business partner. Henry went alone on a business and vacation trip to Central America, though Girl-Friday had expressed a wish to go with him. A few months later he went to Europe and was soon joined by the other girl. There, they became better acquainted, developed increasing fondness for each other, and they were married shortly after returning to this country.

The marriage occurred at about the time of the follow-up study several years ago. At the time of the follow-up interview, his business was thriving, he was becoming increasingly prominent in his field, and was recognized as an authority in many countries in this hemisphere and in some abroad. He was showing great interest in writing in his field but the writing came easily and was not disturbed by procrastination and blocking.

Discussion

This relatively extensive account of certain segments of Henry's life contains, we hope, some psychodynamic illumination of the anxious, inhibited, and symptom-ridden person who came for treatment initially. Issues of family migration; the personality structure of the father, mother, and sister; the patient's many illnesses and his reactions to various family members; his dramatized ambivalence in every area of behavior: social, sexual, emotional, intellectual, occupational—all of these illustrate and document the development of the Henry who began treatment.

The course of his illness and increasing health during the course of ten years of observation and treatment provide further enlightenment about his concepts, attitudes, and patterns of behavior. His growth and change are a commentary on his basically sound endowment and his flexibility and his ability to undertake new concepts and patterns of living.

This report is focused on psychodynamic considerations and alludes to the treatment only parenthetically. We are commenting on some of the factors that may have influenced the development of this man at the time he began treatment and we are recounting some of the changes that occurred during the period he was under observation and treatment. The extent to which he was influenced by psychoanalysis and psychotherapy, the nature and reverberations of transference phenomena, and other considerations in this realm are beyond the scope of this presentation. These data will be considered at another time.

It is important to note that at the time of the follow-up interview Henry could not be regarded as completely free of anxiety, inhibition, or symptom. He had not yet really confronted all of the experiences implicit in married living: the commitments and responsibilities of a spouse; the possible collisions between his work and his wife's career in another field; the household changes and the joys and demands of his own children; the curtailment of the freedom to travel freely at home and abroad of his bachelor days, and the final fulfillment of his adolescent fantasies.

In one of his later papers, Freud commented that analysis is never finished. It stops at some point and hopefully the growth process continues in the individual.[14] Hopefully, that will be true for Henry.

REFERENCES

1. Hoch, P. H., and Polatin, P.: Pseudoneurotic forms of schizophrenia. Psychiat. Quart. 23:248, 1949.
2. ——and Cattell, J. P.: The diagnosis of pseudoneurotic schizophrenia. Psychiat. Quart. 33:17, 1959.
3. ——, Cattell, J. P., Strahl, M. O., and Pennes, H. H.: The course and outcome of pseudoneurotic schizophrenia. Amer. J. Psychiat. 119:106, 1962.
4. Cattell, J. P.: Psychodynamic and clinical observations in a group of unmarried mothers. Amer. J. Psychiat. 111:337, 1954.
5. Knight, R. P.: Borderline states. Bull. Menninger Clin. 17:1, 1953.
6. Stern, A.: Psychoanalytic investigation of and therapy in the borderline group of neuroses. Psychoanal. Quart. 7:467, 1938.
7. Wolberg, L.: The borderline patient. Amer. J. Psychother. 6:694, 1952.
8. Rangell, I.: The borderline case. Report of a panel meeting. J. Amer. Psychoanal. Ass. 3:285, 1955.
9. Robbins, L. L.: The borderline case. Report of a panel meeting. J. Amer. Psychoanal. Ass. 4:550, 1956.
10. Bychowski, G.: The problem of latent psychosis. J. Amer. Psychoanal. Ass. 1:484, 1953.
11. ——: Psychic structure and therapy of latent schizophrenia. *In* Schizophrenia in Psychoanalytic Office Practice (ed. A. N. Rifkin). New York, Grune & Stratton, 1957.
12. Zilboorg, G.: Ambulatory schizophrenias. Psychiatry 4:149, 1941.
13. ——: Further observations on ambulatory schizophrenias. Amer. J. Orthopsychiat. 27:677, 1957.
14. Freud, S.: Analysis terminable and interminable. *In* Collected Papers. London, Hogarth Press, 1953, 5:316.

3

SCHIZOPHRENIC COGNITION

by SILVANO ARIETI, M.D.*

THERE IS A TREND TODAY among some students of schizophrenia to see the disorder exclusively or predominantly as a result of abnormal family psychodynamics. Even the cognitive alterations of the schizophrenic patient have been interpreted as the result of abnormal communication (Bateson et al.[12]) or as direct transmission of irrationality from the parents (Wynne et al.[33]) There is no doubt that interpersonal relations play a very important role in the engendering of the disorder, inasmuch as they elicit the anxiety which may lead to the psychosis or inasmuch as they deprive the patient of antischizophrenic defenses (Lidz et al.[22]). There is no doubt that these interpersonal factors must be intensively studied in the psychotherapeutic process: first, because they are the variables which are the most affected by this type of therapy; second, because probably they are the variables necessary to actualize at a clinical level vaster psychopathological potentialities.

Nevertheless, the writer feels that this important approach remains a partial one in the understanding of the multifarious schizophrenic process and especially of schizophrenic cognition. For instance, if we study the family background of a patient suffering from the paranoid type of schizophrenia, we may find that the mother of the patient had an attitude toward the world characterized by suspiciousness and hostility. According to her, "People are dangerous because they are after you, ready to cheat you or hurt you." Now we may easily see a relation between the mother's attitude and the patient's paranoid delusions. We may even say that the patient's delusions have a great deal to do with what he introjected from his mother. However, to think that the "irrationality" has been "transmitted" with such a simple and direct mechanism is, in my opinion, a fallacious point of view. Although the attitude of the mother is pathological, it may still be viewed as a wrong philosophy of life or, as Sullivan would say, as a para-

*Department of Psychiatry, New York Medical College, New York, N.Y.

taxic distortion. However, when her son believes that people plot to kidnap him, call him a spy, and had put poison in his food, this irrationality cannot be considered any longer expression of a philosophy of life or of a parataxic distortion. What may have started as an interpsychic parataxic distortion has become an intrapsychic autistic conception for whose development a transformation of the cognitive faculty was necessary.

Particular clusters of psychodynamic factors may occur more frequently in the life or family of preschizophrenics than of other people, but these factors do not necessarily lead to schizophrenia. They lead to schizophrenia when they become translated into those specific psychological *forms* which are the schizophrenic symptoms.

An alteration in cognition—that is, the adoption of new cognitive mechanisms—is a constant feature in all schizophrenic syndromes; I mean of those cases which are no longer prepsychotic, latent, or borderline. Some researchers may disagree on this point, because usual psychological tests may reveal no thinking disorders in some initial or not clear- cut cases. In these instances our tests seem less sensitive than our clinical evaluation, which "senses" the alteration, and less reliable than the observations of friends, teachers, parents, and other members of the family who have noticed not only a change in the behavior of the patient but also a decline from previous cognitive performances. Other authors deny the presence of cognitive alterations because the latter are not constantly found, even when the patient has other obvious schizophrenic symptoms. To this criticism we must answer that although these alterations consist of intrapsychic mechanisms, they are dynamically determined. They tend to occur when the complexes of the patient or the anxiety connected with deductions reached with normal thinking make the patient escape from normal or higher levels of cognition. Later in the illness, however, these alterations tend to extend to larger and larger areas of the psyche.

The Concept of Progressive Teleologic Regression

From a formal point of view the cognitive alterations of the schizophrenic can be seen as expressions of a *progressive teleologic regression actualized by various forms of concretization.*[4, 6] These terms require some clarification.

Fundamentally, schizophrenia assumes the form of a regression. Regression, as the term is used here, is not limited to the Freudian concept of return to earlier levels of adaptation, but includes the Jacksonian concept of return to lower levels of functionality. Whereas the *content* of symptoms may reproduce, in either identical or symbolic fashion, earlier ontogenetic experiences and their derivatives, the *forms* that the symptoms assume may be the ones generally used in lower forms of cognition or even those which once appeared at earlier phylogenetic levels. In the schizophrenic's psychological structure an attempt is made *to fit a higher content into a lower form.*

For instance, the abstract, almost indefinite, imperceptible and unverbalizable feeling-idea that the world is hostile, threatening, and unsafe—which the patient had prior to the onset of the psychosis—may be transformed into the feeling that *someone in particular* is against the patient. The vague, huge menace becomes a concretized fear, a definite persecutor. In another instance, a patient who prior to the onset of the psychosis had the feeling that he had "a rotten personality" now has an olfactory hallucination: he smells a bad odor emanating from his body. The rotten personality has become the rotten body which smells.

The second term, teleologic, implies that the regression is purposeful, or at least tends to be purposeful, in the sense that it aims (although it is not very successful) to remove excessive anxiety and reestablish some kind of psychic equilibrium. This concept is not necessarily vitalistic or animistic; it is an additional application of concepts developed in general medicine by Claude Bernard and in psychiatry by Sigmund Freud. It is not a denial that psychological and psychopathological phenomena follow physical determinism (according to which causes have effects), but it is an additional affirmation that the living organism, in health or disease, seems to be subject to both mechanical and teleologic causalities.

An example from physical medicine may clarify the matter. An infective disease produces an invasion of foreign proteins in an organism, and foreign proteins bring about a temperature rise—that is, fever. All this follows mechanical causality. We know, however, that fever has a purpose: to combat the invasion of the foreign proteins. Here the organism seems to follow teleologic causality. Obviously in the course of evolution only those organisms survived which had such inherited biochemical properties that enabled them to respond with fever to bacterial invasion. To us, who are interested in survival, the mechanism seems teleological. It is teleological at our level of human values. In the same way we may admit that in the evolution of the nervous system, even at high psychological levels, only those species survived which had the capacity of readjusting at least at some psychopathological levels. A defense, as a mechanism described in psychoanalysis, is a pathological readjustment—teleologic, although determined by previous causes. Incidentally, the new science of cybernetics aims at finding a reconciliation between a deterministic and a teleologic interpretation of biological phenomena.

Schizophrenic regression, contrary to other types, is progressive because even though it is to some extent purposeful, with few exceptions it fails of its purpose and tends to repeat itself. A human being who is deprived of the highest levels of integration can in a very rough way be compared to an animal experimentally deprived of the neopallic cortex. This animal will not be in a physiological condition comparable to that of an organism of a low species which does not possess that cortex. Rather, it remains in an abnormal condition, because its whole organism is attuned to the neopallic cortex, or integrated with the functions of the cerebral cortex.

In a similar way the schizophrenic patient will *regress to,* but not *integrate at,* a lower level; he will remain disorganized. The organism then defends itself from the disorganization with further regression to an even lower level. The process repeats itself in a vicious circle that can lead to complete dilapidation. The situation is thus different from that occurring in other psychopathologic conditions. For instance, the phobic patient also undergoes a regression. His phobia is a regressive form under which his higher-level problems are expressed. However, the phobic patient as a rule remains arrested at a phobic level, without progression toward lower mechanisms. His illness may become worse, because the phobias may become more intense or more numerous, but they will still be phobias.

The Process of Active Concretization

According to Kurt Goldstein the schizophrenic process is an expression of what he called "the concrete attitude." Goldstein believes that the schizophrenic abandons the realm of the abstract and withdraws into the concrete.[14, 15]

There is no doubt that Goldstein has opened a path of fruitful inquiry. Nevertheless, we must recognize that his formulations are incomplete and at times even somewhat inaccurate, suffering from the fact that originally Goldstein worked only with organic patients. Life, experienced only or predominantly at a concrete level, is a reduced life, but not necessarily a psychotic one. A brain-injured patient may not be able to solve problems of higher mathematics, but may remain in the realm of a limited reality. Goldstein himself states that the concrete attitude may be a realistic attitude. A subhuman animal, which does not possess the ability to conceive categories or platonic universals, lives in a limited but nevertheless realistic world.

Goldstein too realizes that the concreteness of the schizophrenic is not the same as that of the organic patient, but he interprets the difference simply as the result of different levels of concreteness.

This explanation is not satisfactory. We find different degrees of concreteness in various organic defects and also in mental deficiencies, but these conditions are not necessarily accompanied by psychosis. As a matter of fact, an organic defect may even eliminate a psychosis, as it does at times in psychosurgery and, possibly in a reversible form, even in shock therapy. To this author schizophrenic cognition seems to result not from a reduction to a concrete level but from a *process of active concretization.* It is not a question here of just different semantics. The process is viewed differently.

By active concretization is meant that the psyche is still to a certain degree capable of conceiving the abstract, but not able to sustain it, because it is too anxiety-provoking or too disintegrating. It has to transform it immediately into a concrete representation. For instance, the previously mentioned patient who has a pervading feeling that the whole world is menacing, hostile, and rejecting transforms such concepts into the idea that "someone" or "they" are against him. The patient who has the feeling that he has a "rotten personality" translates this concept into a concrete olfactory hallucination: his body emanates a bad odor. In this aspect the schizophrenic is similar to the dreamer, the fine artist and the poet who transform abstract concepts into perceptual images. The higher level impinges itself upon a lower form. Contrary to what happens in artistic production, however, in schizophrenic cognition the abstract level disappears within the concrete form and the patient is no longer aware of it.

In the following sections important forms of schizophrenic concretizations will be taken into consideration: adualism, paleologic thought, and awholism.

Adualism

One of the most perplexing problems connected with schizophrenic cognition is the finding of an explanation for the fact that concrete delusional concepts are accepted as real by the patient in spite of lack of corroborating evidence. The explanation is in a certain way a circular one: the patient is deprived of the abstract faculty which would permit him to correct his errors. For instance, in a very acute or advanced stage of the disorder we have the following phenomenon: a patient visualizes the scene in which some people who played an important role in his childhood and who are now dead come to visit him in the hospital. As soon as he has these thoughts, he sees those dead people in the hospital, already there in the act of visiting him. As a matter of fact, some fellow inmates are misidentified as these dead people. *Emotionally loaded thoughts become reality, actual things, or events.* Odier[23] also studied this phenomenon and applied it to Baldwin's[11] concept of adualism and Piaget's[24] concept of realism. For Baldwin, adualism is lack of dualism, the inability (often found in young children) to distinguish between the world of the mind and the external world—that is, between acts of consciousness and objects. For Piaget realism is the capacity to attribute one's own psychic qualities to external objects and persons and to accept the attributed qualities as real.

Baldwin's and Piaget's formulations are correct, but they can hardly be called interpretations; they reinstate the phenomenon with more adequate descriptive terms. It seems to me that the phenomenon of adualism can be seen as a special form of the general process of active concretization.

The mind which has regressed to an advanced stage of concretization cannot conceive the possible, but only the actual. An occurring thought cannot be conceived as a possibility—a possibility being an abstraction. Such qualities as being fictitious, metaphorical, potential, assumed, and presumed are not always possible for schizophrenic ideation.

The delusions and the hallucinations, which for us are either fictitious or symbolic, are neither fictitious nor symbolic for the patient, but as real as they are experienced. Contrary to the severely injured organic patient and the severe mental defective, the schizophrenic is able to conceive potentialities and assumptions; but if they are too anxiety-provoking or if they have something to do with his complexes, he is not able to sustain them and he immediately translates them into real facts. If we ask these severely ill schizophrenics to explain why they believe their strange ideas in spite of lack of evidence, they do not attempt any demonstration of the validity of them. Each patient almost invariably gives this simple answer: "I know," meaning "I know that it is so." The belief of the patient is more than a strong conviction; it is a certitude, because for him "something which is known" is equivalent to "something which exists." What for us are truth and error share for the patient equal right to existence, inasmuch as they are both acts of consciousness. Moreover, the patient quite often feels urged to act in accordance with his new and unparalleled certainty, and this course of action puts him almost immediately into trouble with his fellow men.

Biologically or neurophysiologically it is very difficult to explain the phenomenon of concretization in general and of adualism in particular. Obviously a complete explanation would require a knowledge of molecular changes occurring in the central nervous system. From a general point of view we may consider it, as we have already done in a previous section of this paper, as a return to a lower level of integration in a Jacksonian sense. This return, however, would not be necessarily determined by physical causes, but by psychodynamic mechanisms operating in presence of biological predispositions.

Paleologic Thought

At times the process of active concretization is arrested at a level at which explanations are still attempted by the patient. At this level the patient does not say simply "I know" to corroborate what seems to us absurd beliefs. In other words, he does not do what the patient suffering from adualism does, but he tries to give himself or others a logical explanation by resorting to a logic *sui generis* which has been called paleologic[2-7, 9] (from the Greek *pallo*-old, archaic). Paleologic thought—also referred to in different terminologies or theoretical frameworks as dereistic, autistic, archaic, primitive, prelogic, or paralogic primary process thinking—has been studied from many angles.

A didactical presentation that the present author has found useful is to consider this type of thinking as subject to that type of organization which has been described by Von Domarus.[29] Von Domarus' principle states that whereas the normal person accepts identity only upon the basis of identical subjects, the schizophrenic may accept identity based upon identical predicates. For instance, if the following information is given to a normal man: "All men are mortal; Socrates is a man," this normal person will be able to conclude that "Socrates is mortal." As traditional Aristotelian logic teaches us, this conclusion is valid because the subject of the major premise (all men) contains the subject of the minor premise (Socrates). If, on the other hand, a schizophrenic happens to think, "The Virgin Mary was a Virgin; I am a virgin," she may conclude, "I am the Virgin Mary." This delusional conclusion is reached because the identity of the predicate of the two premises (being virgin) makes the schizophrenic accept the identity of the two subjects (the Virgin Mary and the patient).

We can easily conclude that in this type of thinking the predicate is a very important part. The predicate, furthermore, may refer not only to a quality inherent in the objects which are identified, but also to spatial and temporal contiguity. For instance, two objects or facts may be identified just because they happen to be in the same place or to have occurred at the same time.

Even the most bizarre delusions of schizophrenic patients can be interpreted in the light of Von Domarus' principle.[2-5, 29] The application of Von Domarus' principle, however, extends far beyond schizophrenia. The whole phenomenon of Freudian symbolism may be linked to this type of cognitive organization. Freud has demonstrated that a person or object *A*, having a certain characteristic of *B* (that is, a common predicate with *B*), may appear in dreams as being *B* or a composite of *A* and *B*. The wife of a dreamer may appear in a dream as having the physical appearance of the dreamer's boss. The two persons are identified in the dream because the dreamer is preoccupied with a common predicate of them (their domineering attitude). Any similarity may lead to an identification. The symbol is not only something which stands for something else but it is also something which has at least a common characteristic (predicate) with the thing it symbolizes.

This type of thinking is also found in normal young children, especially from 1 to 3½ years of age.[4] In children the occurrence of this type of thinking is a transient phenomenon, manifesting itself with great variations. In many normal children only minimal traces of it are detected, whereas in children manifesting various degrees of pathology this type of thinking may become very pronounced (Kanner[19, 20]).

This way of thinking or of cognitive organization, which Arieti has called paleologic,[2, 4] can be interpreted with formulations which apparently differ from Von Domarus' principle, but actually refer to the same phenomena. We may, for instance, state that the cognitive faculty organizes classes or categories which differ from those of normal thinking. For normal persons a class is a collection of objects to which a concept applies. For instance, Washington, Jefferson, Lincoln, Roosevelt, Truman, etc., form a class of objects to which the concept "'President of the United States" applies. In paleologic thinking (or thinking which follows the primary process) a class is a collection of objects which have a predicate or part in common (for instance, the state of being virgin), and which, by virtue of having such predicate or part in common, become identified or equivalent. Whereas the members of a secondary (or normal) class are recognized as being similar (and it is actually on their similarity that their classification is based), the members of a primary class are freely interchanged (for instance, the patient becomes the Virgin Mary).

It is easy to understand why it is so. In primary classification it is only the common element which counts; all the rest is not important or not noticed or reacted to by the organism. The common element is the part (or, in some cases, what we, using logical language, call a predicate) to which the organism reacts.

This form of thinking may be linked to the biological fact that part-perception precedes phylogenetically whole-perception.[7, 8, 10] Studies from various sources (Von Senden's on the congenital blind, who later underwent cataract operations and acquired eyesight;[30] Hebb's theoretical work on perception;[17] Riesen's studies on chimpanzees raised in darkness;[26] Pritchard, Heron, and Hebb's experimental works on the stabilized image on the retina[25]) confirm this point. Some findings of Tinbergen on animal instincts can also be interpreted in a similar way.[28] Neurological studies, especially on visual agnosias (Adler,[1] Goldstein,[16] Jossman,[18] Wilbrand and Sanger,[31] Wolpert[33]) reaffirm the occurrence of part-perception. An organism which reacts to a "part" with a particular response tends to respond in the same way to different objects which have that part in common. To respond in the same way is for a primitive cognitive organization to identify. Part-perception and the formation of part-objects have also been described by Melanie Klein in infants.[21]

In some psychopathologic conditions this obsolete form of cognitive organization reappears in various degrees or mixtures.

The difficulty to form secondary categories (that is, concepts which refer to wholes) affects also the language of the schizophrenic. Words may lose their connotation power. What instead acquires prominence is the verbalization—that is, the word becomes predominantly a phonetic entity, not a carrier of meaning.[2, 4] These findings have been confirmed experimentally by Goldman.[13]

Awholism

There are several cognitive mechanisms which are less organized than paleologic thinking. One of them is what I have designated as *awholism.*[7, 10] In my experience this phenomenon occurs frequently in the most severe or acute forms of schizophrenia, but to a milder degree appears also in chronic cases. The very regressed or very acutely ill patient is unable to perceive or conceive what to the normal person appear wholes or segregated units. At first the patient must divide big or complex wholes into small units. For instance, a patient looking at the nurse could not see or focus on her as a person, but perceived only her left or right eye or her hand or her nose, etc. Another patient, who while she was in a state of dangerous excitement was put into a seclusion cell, remembered that she could not look at the whole door of the cell. She could see only the knob or the keyhole or some corner of the door. At first the whole or the bigger unity is divided into the smaller unities of which it is composed, but later, if the excitement increases, even the smaller unities are divided into smaller fragments. Thus a return to a pre-gestalt level occurs. Pronounced fragmentation of wholes takes place in states of acute confusion, of which the patient retains only a vague memory, also in some toxic-infective deliria, and in very bizarre, almost entirely forgotten dreams. One of the reasons why the phenomenon has not been described in the literature in reference to schizophrenia is the difficulty that patients have in remembering it. These amnesias are probably determined by the fact that disintegrated wholes have no names or cannot be classified according to schemata of previous experiences, similarly perhaps to what according to Schachtel occurs in childhood amnesias.[27] At times during the very acute episode the patient is aware that he is losing the perception of wholes or the capacity to see the world as divided into unities, and he makes conscious efforts to reconstruct these wholes but the attempts are only partially successful. The wholes turn out to be different from the original ones and distortions result.

Phenomena similar to what I have called awholism have also been described by Kanner[19, 20] in children affected by what he called early infantile autism. It is obvious that in the phenomenon of awholism a part assumes a supremacy over the whole. Only a part of what is normally a whole perception or conception is responded to by the patient. But whereas at the level of paleologic thinking there was an attempt to identify or to associate parts in order to identify different wholes which had that part in common, such identification does not occur at the level of awholism. At times, however, a part may stand for the whole to which it belongs or for any other part of the whole. In many cases the part remains a part, with little or no further organization. Thus the phenomena of perceptual and apperceptual fragmentation and word-salad may ensue.

REFERENCES

1. Adler, A.: Disintegration and restoration of optic recognition in visual agnosia. Arch. Neurol. Psychiat. 51:243, 1944.
2. Arieti, S.: Special logic of schizophrenic and other types of autistic thought. Psychiatry 11:325, 1948.
3. ——: Autistic thought: its normal mechanisms and its relationships to schizophrenia. J. Nerv. Ment. Dis. 111:288, 1950.
4. ——: Interpretation of Schizophrenia. New York, Brunner, 1955.
5. ——: Schizophrenic thought. Amer. J. Psychother. 13:537, 1959.
6. ——: Schizophrenia: the manifest symptomatology, the psychodynamic and formal mechanisms. *In* American Handbook of Psychiatry (ed. S. Arieti). New York, Basic Books, 1959, Vol. 1, p. 455.
7. ——: The Loss of Reality. Psychoanalysis 48:3, 1961.
8. ——: The microgeny of thought and perception. Arch Gen. Psychiat. 6:454, 1962.
9. ——: Studies of thought processes in contemporary psychiatry. Amer. J. Psychiat. 120:58, 1963.
10. ——: In preparation.
11. Baldwin, J. M.: Quoted by Piaget, J., in La Représentation du Monde chez l'enfant. Paris, Alcan, 1932.
12. Bateson, G., Jackson, D. D., Halex, J., and Weakland, J.: Toward a theory of schizophrenia. Behavioral Sci. 1:251, 1956.
13. Goldman, A. E.: Symbolic representation in schizophrenia. Vol. 28, 3:293-316, 1960.
14. Goldstein, K. The Organism. New York, American Book, 1939.
15. ——: The significance of psychological research in schizophrenia. J. Nerv. Ment. Dis. 97:261, 1943.
16. ——: Some remarks on Russel Brain's articles concerning visual object agnosia. J. Nerv. Ment. Dis. 98:148, 1943.
17. Hebb, S. O.: The Organization of Behavior. New York, Wiley, 1949.
18. Jossman, P.: Zur Psychopathologie der Optigchagnostischen Storungen. Mschr. Psychiat Neurol. 72:81, 1929.
19. Kanner, L.: Early infantile autism. J. Pediat. 25: 211, 1944.
20. ——: Irrelevant and metaphorical language in early infantile autism. Amer. J. Psychiat. 103:242, 1946.

21. Klein, M.: Contributions to Psychoanalysis. London, Hogarth Press, 1948.
22. Lidz, T., Cornelison, A. R., Fleck, S., and Terry, S.: The intrafamilial environment of schizophrenic patients: II. Marital schism and Marital skew. Amer. J. Psychiat. 114, 241, 1957.
23. Odier, C.: Anxiety and Magic Thinking. New York, International Universities Press, 1956.
24. Piaget, J.: La Representation Du Monde Chez L'Enfant. Paris, Alcan, 1932.
25. Pritchard, R. M. Heron, W., and Hebb, S. O.: Visual perception approached by the method of stabilized images. Canad. J. Psychol. 14:67, 1960.
26. Riesen, A. H.: The development of visual perception in man and chimpanzee. Science 106:107, 1947.
27. Schachtel, E. G.: Metamorphosis. New York, Basic Books, 1959.
28. Tinbergen, N.: The Study of Instinct. Oxford, Oxford University Press, 1951.
29. Von Domarus, E.: The specific laws of logic in schizophrenia. *In* Language and Thought in Schizophrenia: Collected Papers (ed. J. S. Kasanin). Berkeley, Univ. of California Press, 1944.
30. Von Senden, M.: Space and Light: The Perception of Space and Shape in Congenitally Blind Patients before and after Operation. London, Mcthuen & Co., Ltd., 1960.
31. Wilbrand, H., and Sanger, A.: Die Neurologie des Auges. Wiesbaden, J. F. Bergmann, 1917, Vol. 7.
32. Wolpert, C.: Die Simultanagnosie—Stözung der Gesamtauffassung. Ztschi. Ges. Neurol. Psychiat. 93:397, 1924.
33. Wynne, L. C., Ryckoff, I. M., Day, J., and Hirsch, S. I.: Pseudo-mutuality in the family relations of schizophrenics. Psychiatry, 21:205, 1958.

4

FORMAL QUALITIES OF HALLUCINATIONS: A COMPARATIVE STUDY OF THE VISUAL HALLUCINATIONS IN PATIENTS WITH SCHIZOPHRENIC, ORGANIC, AND AFFECTIVE PSYCHOSES

by DAVID A. FRIESKE, M.D., and WILLIAM P. WILSON, M.D.*

VISUAL HALLUCINATIONS ARE a relatively neglected facet of psychopathology. Both patients and psychiatrists have usually been most interested in the content and meaning of these false perceptions. Investigations have, for the most part, focused on the relation of content to personality factors and mental mechanisms of defense. Bleuler[1] studied psychotic hallucinations extensively and applied analytic techniques to their understanding. He believed that their contents were related to mental dynamics and the premorbid personality of the patient. Jung[2] argued that hallucinations are the outward projection of psychic elements. He felt that they are much like dreams in that they present symbolically distorted fragments of "complexes." Rorschach[3] related the sensory modality of the hallucinatory experience to the personality type. More recently, Brosin[4] has indicated that hallucinations, like dreams, are defensive efforts of a severely stressed individual. Havens[5] studied the hallucinations of schizophrenics with regard to their placement in space. He related the position of the vision or voice to the severity and chronicity of the psychosis.

In addition to his study of the meaning and content of hallucinations, Bleuler[2] was concerned with the more formal characteristics such as duration, intensity, distinctness, reality, and projection. However, he gave only qualitative descriptions of these properties. Further studies have been fragmentary. In spite of the lack of data, Jaspers[6] has argued that while some knowledge of content is necessary in order to understand hallucinations, particularly in relation to personality

*Duke University Medical Center, Durham, N.C.

and mental mechanisms, it is equally important to investigate the formal qualities of these productions. As Arieti has repeatedly emphasized, the study of form offers an escape from the limitless diversity of content which may obscure the actual nature of psychiatric phenomena. For Jaspers all psychic events may be divided into form and content. For example, the content of hypochondriasis may present in a number of ways: as bodily delusion, as a voice, or as a compulsive idea. He directs psychopathology toward the goal of "clear understanding" of the "real phenomenological gulfs that exist" and also to the transitions between them. Content has a much more "accidental" character than form. Certainly, Weinstein's[7] studies of delusional and hallucinatory phenomena in Virgin Islanders substantiate this position.

In view of the dearth of descriptive and comparative studies of the form of hallucinations, we have made it the purpose of the investigation to ascertain whether any "real phenomenological gulfs" exist between schizophrenic, organic, and affective visual hallucinations. Our approach is that of careful scrutiny of the individual's immediate, subjective experience. We feel that our findings may be useful in achieving a "clear understanding" of these phenomena. In addition, we hope that the knowledge acquired will be useful in interpreting the results of past and future experimental studies relating to hallucinosis. Certainly, a reliable phenomenological framework will be needed for eventual synthesis with accumulating neurophysiologic data into a more comprehensive understanding of these remarkable psychic events.

Method

Qualities of visual hallucinations were investigated by means of structured interviews with patients selected from the population of the Duke Medical Center and the Veterans Administration Hospital, Durham, N.C., and John Umstead State Hospital at Butner, N.C. Three patient groups were selected: one schizophrenic, one organic, and one affective. Only patients with reasonably certain diagnoses were utilized. Each diagnosis was corroborated using the criteria listed in the Diagnostic and Statistical Manual of the American Psychiatric Association. Briefly, schizophrenia was diagnosed on the basis of autism, manifest ambivalence, unequivocal disturbances in associations, and minimal or inappropriate affect. Manic-depressive psychosis was diagnosed when a pervasive disturbance of affect was apparent associated with appropriate biological concomitants, such as disturbances of sleep, appetite, sex, and psychomotor activity. In both categories, a clear sensorium was required. Physiological or anatomic brain disease was diagnosed when disturbances of orientation, memory, retention, recall, and calculation could be documented by examination. Only patients who would freely discuss their false perceptions were used. They were asked specific questions relative to their hallucinations. Cross-checking was performed throughout the interview to ascertain the reliability of their answers. Patients giving unreliable answers were probed further until some idea of what they meant was reached. If this could not be done, their responses were not used.

The qualities investigated may be divided into several groups. *First,* they were asked questions concerning the temporal relations of their sensations: whether they occurred during the day, at night, or both. They were also asked to estimate how long they had been having the sensations. *Second,* they were asked questions concerning the complexity of the sensations: whether they were accompanied by other sensory modalities; whether the various sensations occurred in meaningful combinations similar to the "feelies" described by Huxley in *Brave New World.*[8] *Third,* questions concerning the *reality* of the objects were asked. These were whether they seemed complete or incomplete, real or dream-like; whether they could be produced or stopped at will; and whether they led to any overt action, such as running away. *Fourth,* the patients' reactions to the experiences were ascertained: whether they had a special reference to him or whether they were completely impersonal, accidentally seen objects; whether they were pleasant or frightening or viewed with indifference. *Fifth,* the projections of objects were determined: whether they were perceived as coming from outside or inside the person. If they were seen as coming from outside, it was further determined whether they were nearby or far away (at least outside the room); whether they were perceived with eyes open or closed or in both ways. *Finally,* questions relative to the actual nature of the perceptions were asked. These included the color of the objects (whether in black and white or technicolor); the intensity of the lighting of objects (dull or bright); and the size of objects (normal or life-sized as opposed to smaller or larger than normal). Also, we determined whether changes in the size, shape, or numbers of objects occurred; whether the objects were seen as three dimensional as opposed to flat or two dimensional; whether they were seen clearly and distinctly as opposed to vaguely or poorly defined; and whether the objects moved in any way or were completely still.

The data were tabulated in a form suitable for analysis by an IBM 7090 computer. Counts and Chi-square tests of statistical significance were performed by the computer.

Results

Some general characteristics of the groups studied will be considered first (table 1). There were a total of 95 patients, 50 schizophrenics, 30 deliria, and 15 affective disorders. No attempt was made to sub-divide the schizophrenic groups into subtypes. The deliria were predominantly acute psychoses due to withdrawal from alcohol, narcotics, barbiturates, other drugs, and one case of lead encephalopathy. In the affective group, there were 4 manics and 11 depressives. The age of the patients ranged from 16 to 70 years; the nonschizophrenics were slightly older. There were 56 males and 39 females. The increased proportion of males in the schizophrenic group was related to the selection of many of them from the population of the Veterans Administration Hospital. The racial distribution approximated that in our area. Educational achievement was consistent for the three groups.

The only significant difference, other than diagnosis, was length of illness. The schizophrenics were a group of chronically ill patients with an average length of illness approximating 10 years. Conversely, the comparison group was composed of patients with acute psychotic episodes. The organic group, especially, consisted of rather brief psychoses (mean duration less than one month).

Table 1.—General Characteristics

	Total	Schizophrenic	Organic	Affective
Numbers	95	50	30	15
Length of Illness (Mean No. Years)	5.8	10.3	<0.1	0.8
Mean Age (Years)	40.6	38.4	43.0	39.6
Sex: Male	56	36	14	6
Female	39	14	16	9
Race: White	76	36	26	14
Negro	19	14	4	1
Education (Mean No. Years)	9.4	8.6	10.3	10.3

Temporal Aspects (*Table 2*)

The schizophrenic had usually been hallucinated for many years. The mean duration of his hallucinosis was 8 years and 1 month. The nonschizophrenics, as was expected, had much shorter periods of visual hallucinosis. The affective group had a mean duration of about 3 months, the organics less than 10 days. During a 24-hour period, the schizophrenics had their hallucinations a greater percentage of the time. Thus, 74 per cent of this group had visual sensations both during the day and at night. Frequently, their visions would cease only when they slept. Affective and organic groups had a much higher proportion occurring only at night (37 per cent organics vs. 20 per cent affectives vs. 10 per cent schizophrenic). This difference between the schizophrenics and the other groups was statistically significant for the organic group ($X^2 = 8.4$, $p = 0.05$), but not for the affective group.

Complexity (*Table 3*)

The schizophrenic invariably had hallucinations in more than one sensory modality; that is, visual sensations were always combined with another type of sensory phenomena. Very often, there were combinations of three or more modalities. The most frequently occurring combinations were with auditory sensations (voices, music, or noise, 96 per cent). Other sensory experience was represented less often, but with surprising frequency. Tactile phenomena such as pain, touch, kinesthesia, heat or cold, and electrical sensations, or combinations of these, were combined with visual hallucinations in 64 per cent of the cases. Olfactory false perceptions were reported by 48 per cent, and unusual tastes were experienced by 22 per cent of this group of visually hallucinating schizophrenics. There were no cases in which only visual hallucinations occurred.

TABLE 2.—Temporal Aspects

	Total Length of Hallucinations (Mean No. Years)	Hallucination During Day and Night	Day Only	Night Only
Schizophrenics	8.1	37 (74%)	8 (16%)	5 (10%)
Organic	0.03	15 (50%)	4 (13%)	11 (37%)*
Affective	0.28	11 (73%)	1 (7%)	3 (20%)

*Statistically significant: $X^2 = 8.4$, $p = 0.05$.

TABLE 3.—Complexity

	Schizophrenics (N = 50)	Organic (N = 30)	Affective (N = 15)
Visual + Auditory	48 (96%)	16 (53%)[1]	14 (93%)
Visual + Tactile	32 (64%)	7 (23%)[2]	6 (40%)[5]
Visual + Olfactory	24 (48%)	2 (11%)[3]	1 (7%)[6]
Visual + Gustatory	11 (22%)	0 (0%)[4]	0 (0%)[7]
Visual Alone	0	10 (33%)	1 (7%)
Connected Sequences Occurred	22 (44%)	9 (30%)	8 (53%)

Statistically significant: [1]$X^2 = 21.3$, $p = 0.001$
[2]$X^2 = 13.1$, $p = 0.001$
[3]$X^2 = 15.0$, $p = 0.001$
[4]$X^2 = 7.8$, $p = 0.01$
[5]$X^2 = 3.1$, $p = 0.05$
[6]$X^2 = 8.6$, $p = 0.01$
[7]$X^2 = 4.0$, $p = 0.05$

The comparison (i.e., nonschizophrenic) groups had much less complex experiences. The patients with affective psychosis had very frequent combinations with auditory sensations, but this was significantly less true in the organic group which had concurrent auditory phenomena in only 53 per cent of cases ($X^2 = 21.1$, $p = 0.001$). With all other modalities, the control group experienced simultaneous sensations much less often. Thus, there is a statistically significant difference in the frequency of tactile phenomena experienced by the control group when compared to the schizophrenic group ($X^2 = 13.1$, $p = 0.001$; and $X^2 = 3.1$, $p = 0.05$). Similarly, olfactory hallucinations were quite rare in both affectives and organics ($X^2 = 15.0$, $p = 0.001$ for organics; $X^2 = 8.6$, $p = 0.01$ for affectives). No gustatory hallucinations occurred in the comparison groups. Only the comparison group had isolated visual hallucinations without other sensations. This happened in the organic group in 33 per cent of cases, and also in one affective disorder.

Another measure of complexity is the frequency with which the visual hallucinations are linked in coordinated sequences with the phenomena of other modalities. If patients with complex hallucinations are compared, it is noted that this type of "motion picture" activity occurred with about the same frequency in all groups: 44 per cent

TABLE 4.—Reality

	Schizophrenics (N = 50)	Organic (N = 30)	Affective (N = 15)
Completely Real	36 (72%)	25 (83%)	11 (73%)
Passive Experience	47 (94%)	26 (87%)	13 (87%)
Action Causing	27 (54%)	20 (67%)	10 (67%)

of the schizophrenics, 53 per cent of the affectives, and 30 per cent of the organics.

Reality (*Table 4*)

The great majority (72 per cent) of schizophrenics indicated that their visual sensations were complete and real as opposed to being in any way dream-like and incomplete. Ninety-four per cent indicated that they could not elicit the experience by will or imagination, nor could they cause them to stop. In other words, they experienced them passively, as one does everyday events. A slight majority were so impressed that they undertook some activity directly related to the visions, such as telling others about them, hitting at the objects, or running away. The nonschizophrenic groups had much the same kind of evaluation of their visual sensations. There were no statistically significant differences in any of these variables.

Reaction (*Table 5*)

The schizophrenics tended to believe that their sensations had some very personal implication (88 per cent of cases). In a majority of instances, they were frightened by them. The affective group reacted in much the same way, but the organic group was quite different. Although they most often were frightened by their visions, only half

TABLE 5.—Reaction

	Schizophrenics (N = 50)	Organic (N = 30)	Affective (N = 15)
Personal	44 (88%)	17 (57%)*	15 (100%)
Frightening	31 (62%)	19 (63%)	11 (73%)
Pleasant or Indifferent	19 (38%)	11 (37%)	4 (27%)

*Statistically significant: $X^2 = 10.2$, $p = 0.01$.

TABLE 6.—Projection

	Schizophrenics (N = 50)	Organic (N = 30)	Affective (N = 15)
Projection:			
External	44 (88%)	29 (97%)	13 (87%)
Internal	6 (12%)	1 (3%)	2 (13%)
Eyes:			
Open Only	44 (88%)	24 (80%)	14 (93%)
Closed Only	0	1 (3%)	0
Both	6 (12%)	5 (17%)	1 (7%)

of the patients responding attributed some personal special significance to the phenomena. They otherwise frequently believed that they were witnessing some frightening event which, however, had no relation to them—e.g., a train wreck. This difference was statistically significant ($X^2 = 10.2$, $p = 0.01$).

Projection (Table 6)

The sensations perceived by the schizophrenic were projected into the external world in 88 per cent; only 12 per cent "imagined" or saw them in their "mind's eye." Of the subjects who saw objects in the environment, most of them indicated that they were "nearby," usually within four feet or at least within the room. The others said that their false perceptions were either very far away or at least outside the room (table 7). Most subjects saw these visions only when their eyes were open. The nonschizophrenic group projected their objects in almost exactly the same way. However, organics occasionally saw their visions only with eyes closed; this did not occur in the schizophrenics or affectives.

TABLE 7.—Distance

	Schizophrenic (N = 44)	Organic (N = 29)	Affective (N = 13)
External: Nearby	31 (72%)	21 (72%)	10 (77%)
External: Far Away or Outside Room	13 (28%)	8 (28%)	3 (23%)

Perceptual Qualities (Table 8)

The false perceptions of the schizophrenic group tended to have the properties of actual, life-like perceptions. The objects were seen as three dimensional—i.e., with depth—in 96 per cent of the cases. They were seen in technicolor, usually with many vivid colors (84 per cent). The objects were clearly defined and precisely visualized (82 per cent). The objects changed frequently in size, shape, and/or number as opposed to remaining the same (88 per cent), but they were usually viewed as "life size" or normal size, not elephantine or lilliputian (68 per cent). Seventy per cent of the objects moved. A majority of visions (62 per cent) were brightly lighted, many with shining or glowing objects; the remainder were dull or drab.

In the nonschizophrenic group, all of the perceptual variables were quite similarly described. There were no statistically significant differences between any of the variables with the exception of movement.

In summary, the visual hallucinosis of schizophrenia may be described as follows. The patient hallucinates throughout his illness, and 75 per cent have continuous hallucinations broken only by sleep. Experiences in other sensory modalities always accompany the visual sensations. Frequently, complex combinations of three or four other types of sensory perception are reported. Sounds occur most frequently followed by touch, smell, and taste in descending frequency. The various senses tend to remain isolated from each other, without connected sequences. Three-fourths of the false perceptions seem completely real. Almost all are reported as passive experiences which

TABLE 8.—Perceptual Qualities

	Schizophrenics (N = 50)	Organic (N = 30)	Affective (N = 15)
Color (Technicolor)	42 (84%)	27 (90%)	11 (73%)
Intensity (Bright)	31 (62%)	18 (60%)	8 (53%)
Size (Normal Only)	34 (68%)	19 (63%)	12 (80%)
Changes in Objects	44 (88%)	24 (80%)	10 (67%)
Movements of Objects	35 (70%)	27 (90%)*	12 (80%)
Three Dimensional	48 (96%)	26 (87%)	14 (93%)
Clarity: Clear	41 (82%)	25 (87%)	9 (60%)

*Statistically significant: $X^2 = 4.3$, $p = 0.05$.

cannot be altered by the will. A slight majority cause some type of activity. The patients usually feel that their hallucinations have some personal significance which frightens them.

Objects are usually placed outside the observer, most often inside the room or nearby. They are seen only with the eyes open. The objects seem life-sized, three dimensional, vividly colored, and bright. They are seen in fine detail. Frequently the objects change in size, shape, or number. They may move about in the visual field.

Visual hallucinosis in patients with organic or affective diseases differs significantly from the schizophrenics' in (1) duration of hallucinosis, (2) time of occurrence, (3) self-reference, (4) frequency of combination with other sensory modalities, and (5) movement. Differences are more marked in the organic group, but there is an impressive formal similarity in the visual hallucinations of all diagnostic categories. There are no statistically significant differences in the incidence of the following categories: (1) connected sequences, (2) reality, (3) causation, (4) activity, (5) affective response, (6) color, (7) intensity, (8) size, (9) changes in objects, (10) dimension, (11) clarity, (12) projection, and (13) placement.

Discussion

The composite picture of visual hallucinations given above documents the essential similarity between various types of visual experience suspected by previous authors. Thus, Bleuler's[2] classification of hallucinations as secondary symptoms of schizophrenia implies that there is a universal predisposition to sensory deception. Schizophrenics do not discard the false images because of their autism. Jung[2] agreed with Bleuler that "hallucinations are ubiquitous," that schizophrenia simply sets dream mechanisms loose in the waking state. Jaspers[6] compared visual hallucinations to a number of normal phenomena such as after-images, sense-memory, fantastic visual phenomena, subjective eidetic imagery, and pseudo-hallucinations. He placed all types of visual sensations on a spectrum extending from hallucinations to imagery. Hallucinations seem real, objective, constant, complete, clearly detailed, and vividly colored. They are perceived externally and cannot be controlled. Imagery has all the opposite qualities, and must be actively produced. Earlier experimental and clinical studies supported this viewpoint. Thus, Mitchell[9] experienced vivid, realistic, detailed scenes and figures while intoxicated with mescaline. Horrax[10] collected 12 patients with temporal lobe gliomas who had striking visual hallucinations. These tumors produced mobile, vividly colored, realistic and changing false perceptions.

More recently, Oswald[11] has theorized that dreams, imagery, pseudo-hallucinations, hypnagogic phenomena, and visual hallucinations all amount to the same thing neurophysiologically. He views dreams, for example, as "hallucinations at the time they were experienced." Snyder[12] relates visual hallucinations, highway hypnosis, night terrors, daydreaming, dreaming, and sensory deprivation phenomena to the same "biomechanism." Several studies list visual sensation as the dominant sensory modality in dreams.[13, 14] Objects in dreams are described as clearly delineated, "cinema-like," and externally placed.[14] Penfield and Jasper[15] describe "psychical hallucinations" where objects are seen "as they exist in reality." Moreover, they indicate that these hallucinatory auras resemble dreams or visual hallucinations, not altered perceptions or illusions. Both dream-like experiences and complex visual sensations can be produced by electrical stimulation of the diseased temporal lobes. They differ from the crude, less complex "sensory seizures" of the anterior parietal cortex. Experimental and accidental sensory deprivation produce remarkable visual sensations in nonpsychotic subjects. Prolonged sensory isolation[16] results in some type of hallucination in the great majority of subjects. Usually, visual sensations are outstanding; objects seem vivid, real, externally located, mobile, and uncontrollable by the will. Some subjects visualize complex, full-blown scenes. Similar visual sensations were observed in eight nonpsychotic respirator patients.[17] Even brief periods of perceptual isolation have been reported to be associated with hallucinations.[18] Finally, further evidence for a unity of form in visual hallucinosis comes from experiments with psychotomimetic drugs. The induced visual hallucinosis is quite similar to schizophrenia even though the total clinical picture resembles a toxic state.[19, 20] Conversely, Lewis[21] describes lilliputian hallucinations in functional psychoses which are quite similar to those generally regarded as characteristic of toxic and organic states.

If the accumulated evidence for a unity of form is utilized to begin a synthesis of phenomenology and neurophysiological data, we find that our knowledge in the latter area is limited. Fink[22] has postulated an involvement of the reticular activating system in hallucinosis. However, certain evidence indicates that this system is only secondarily involved, if at all, in the production of hallucinations. The evidence against such a concept is as follows: (1) The lack of sensorial aberration in patients with schizophrenia and affective disorders indicates minimal or no involvement of this system which is so important in maintaining consciousness; (2) drugs which produce depression of the reticular system tend to reduce the incidence of hallucinations rather than cause them; (3) increases in the level of activity of the reticular system[23] may be associated with hallucinosis—e.g., amphetamine intoxication. However, many other hallucinogenic drugs decrease the level of reticular activity.[24] Thus, there are no consistent findings to document Fink's postulated primary involvement of the reticular system.

The involvement of temporal lobe mechanisms in hallucinosis does, however, have much consistent supporting evidence. (1) Hallucinations of classical form arise with irritative lesions of this system.[10, 15] (2) Hallucinogenic drugs such as LSD, mescaline, psilocin, psilocybin, atropine, and JB-329 all consistently alter the electrical activity of the hippocampus.[25, 26] (3) Drug alterations of hippocampal activity are not dependent on the integrity of the reticular system.[26]

Finally, our knowledge tends to indicate that specific afferent systems are not primarily involved in hallucinosis. Hallucinogenic drugs do not produce alterations of activity in the specific afferent pathways.[27,28] Moreover, the ability of the schizophrenic and depressed patient to perceive and interpret normally is well known.

In conclusion, it is apparent that a satisfactory explanation of the neurophysiologic origin of hallucinations is not available. Further investigations may add more to our understanding of these processes. The work reported here will, we hope, afford a better understanding of the process per se, since it documents the hypotheses of others and provides a surer foundation for extending our neurophysiologic investigations into unstudied systems.

Summary

The formal qualities of visual hallucinations were studied in 50 schizophrenic patients. They were compared to similar phenomena in 30 organic and 15 affective patients. The results indicate an impressive similarity in perceptual qualities among all three groups, although there were some differences in duration, interpretation, and reaction. The possible implications for neurophysiologic research in hallucinosis were considered.

Acknowledgments

The authors wish to acknowledge the invaluable assistance of Dr. J. L. Cathell, Superintendent, and Dr. Pedro Irigaray of the John Umstead Hospital, Butner, N.C.

REFERENCES

1. Bleuler, E.: Dementia Praecox or the Group of the Schizophrenias. New York, International Universities Press, 1955.
2. Jung, C. G.: Psychology of dementia praecox. *In* Psychogenesis of Mental Disease. New York, Pantheon, 1960, pp. 3-151.
3. Rorschach, H.: Psychodiagnostics (5th ed). New York, Grune & Stratton, 1951.
4. Brosin, H. W.: Contributions of psychoanalysis to the study of the psychoses. *In* Dynamic Psychiatry (eds. F. Alexander, and H. Ross). Chicago, University of Chicago Press, 1952, pp. 287-289.
5. Havens, L. L.: The placement and movement of hallucinations in space, phenomenology and theory. Int. J. Psychoanal. 43:426-35, 1962.
6. Jaspers, K.: General Psychopathology. Chicago, University of Chicago Press, 1963.
7. Weinstein, E. A.: Cultural Aspects of Delusion. New York, Free Press, 1962.
8. Huxley, A.: Brave New World. New York, Harper, 1932.
9. Mitchell, S. W.: Remarks on the effects of Anhelonium lewinii (the mescal button). Brit. Med. J. 2:1625-1629, 1896.
10. Horrax, G.: Visual hallucinations as cerebral localizing phenomenon. Arch. Neurol. Psychiat. 10:532-547, 1923.
11. Oswald, I.: Sleeping and Waking, Physiology and Psychology. New York, American Elsevier Publishing Co., 1962.
12. Snyder, F.: The new biology of dreaming. Arch. Gen. Psychiat. 8:381-391, 1963.
13. Kleitman, N.: Sleep and Wakefulness. Chicago, University of Chicago Press, 1963.
14. Pegge, C. D.: The mode of the dream. J. Ment. Sci. 108:26-36, 1962.
15. Penfield, W., and Jasper, H.: Epilepsy and the Functional Anatomy of the Human Brain. Boston, Little, Brown & Co., 1954.
16. Heron, W.: Cognitive and physiological effects of perceptual isolation. *In* Sensory Deprivation (eds. P. Solomon et al.). Cambridge, Harvard University Press, 1961, pp. 6-34.
17. Mendelson, J., Solomon, P., and Lindemann, E.: Hallucinations of poliomyelitis patients during treatment in a respirator. J. Nerv. Ment. Dis. 126:421-428, 1958.
18. Murphy, D. B., and Myers, T. I.: Occurrence, measurement and experimental manipulation of visual "hallucinations." Percep. Motor Skills 15:47-54, 1962.
19. Heath, R. G.: Psychotomimetic compounds. *In* Psychosomatic Medicine (the first Hahnemann Symposium) (eds. H. H. Nodine and J. H. Moyer). Philadelphia, Lea & Febiger, 1962, pp. 337-354.
20. Hoch, P. H.: Pharmacologically induced psychoses. *In* American Handbook of Psychiatry (ed. S. Arieti). New York, Basic Books, 1959, Vol. 2, pp. 1697-1708.

21. Lewis, O. J.: Lilliputian hallucinations in the functional psychosis. Canad. Psychiat. Ass. J. 6:177-185, 1961.
22. Fink, M.: Effect of anticholinergic compounds on post convulsive electroencephalogram and behavior of psychiatric patients. Electroenceph. Clin. Neurophysiol. 12:359-369, 1960.
23. Morrell, L., and Morrell, F.: Non-random oscillation in the response-duration curve of electrographic activation. Electroenceph. Clin. Neurophysiol. 14:724-730, 1962.
24. Spradlin, W., Hughes, J., and Wilson, W. P.: Unpublished data.
25. Adey, W. R., Bell, F. R., and Dennis, B. J.: Effects of LSD-25, psilocybin and psilocin on temporal lobe EEG patterns and learned behavior in the cat. Neurology 12:591-602, 1962.
26. Wilson, W. P., and Sternberg, W.: Unpublished data.
27. Rovetta, P.: Effect of mescaline and L.S.D. on evoked responses, especially of the optic system of the cat. Electroenceph. Clin. Neurophysiol. 8:15-24, 1956.
28. Killam, K. F., and Killam, E. K.: The action of LSD on central afferent and limbic pathways in the cat. J. Pharmacol. Exp. Ther. 116:35-36, 1956.

5

UNDERSTANDING THE ADAPTIVE STRUGGLES OF SCHIZOPHRENIC PATIENTS

by SANDOR RADO, M.D., D.POL.SC.*

> We must bear in mind that all our psychological ideas are, as it were, provisional (*psychologische Vorlaufigkeiten*) and will have, therefore, at some future time to be based on an organic foundation.
>
> *Freud, 1914*

METHODOLOGY

THE DIVERSE RESEARCH PROJECTS and findings in the psychiatric exploration of schizotypal disorders lack coordination. As a first step toward improving this situation, I have attempted to work out a general *methodological scheme*, which consists of *the three interdependent elements of the total investigative procedure—observation, formation of theory, and validation*—and of the outline in table 1.

The prevailing tendency of investigators to avoid dealing with theories is most unfortunate. In methodological fact, theories are *coding systems* that make the existence, the organization and, by their creative impact, the growth of science possible. Investigation moves from working theory to established theory. That theories need not be true but must be *fruitful* is by now a methodological commonplace.

The chief investigative function of clinical science is the clear description of the clinical pictures.

Introspectional sciences use three investigative methods: (1) communicated surface introspection (as used in daily life), (2) communicated *deep* introspection (the psychoanalytic method), and (3) introspectional interpretation and understanding of inspectional observations.

Introspectional findings can be stated only in the language of introspection (also called psychological language). They are not

*President and Dean, New York School of Psychiatry, New York, N.Y.

TABLE 1.—Survey of Resources and Integration of Findings

1. Clinical Science
2. Basic Sciences, operationally classified as
   (a) introspectional
   (b) inspectional
3. Continuous Integration of Findings
   (a) obtained by introspectional operations
   (b) obtained by inspectional operations
   (c) transoperational (psychophysiological) correlations, leading to
   (d) *a comprehensive behavioral theory (correlated pathodynamics) of schizotypal disorders*

accessible to quantitative measurement. The understanding of introspectional language, and with it of the individual concerned, depends upon and is mediated by the investigator's emotional resonance, emotional self-experience, and emotional self-understanding. This fact confirms in full the unique value of Socrates' teaching: "Know thyself."

Inspectional findings are stated in the language of inspection (also called physical language). They culminate in quantitative measurement.

Introspectional science makes emotional as well as intellectual understanding of the patient's behavior possible. It provides a biologically grounded conceptual scheme of psychoanalytic thought which I have termed "adaptational psychodynamics." It defines the part played in the organization of behavior by both the organismic and societal mechanisms of motivation and control. Working toward psychophysiological correlation, it seeks to evolve appropriate descriptive terms and formulate well-defined concepts.

As complementary resources, adaptational psychodynamics uses information derived from psychodynamic sociology, anthropology, and history, as well as from descriptive and experimental psychology.

In the inspectional domain, the needed contributions come from the group of disciplines dealing with the structural and functional organization of the brain. This group includes the physiological and pathological branches of what is now called behavioral science. A resource of rapidly increasing importance is behavioral genetics, the physiology and pathology of inheritance and variation.

The supreme investigative task is, of course, to integrate our introspectional and inspectional findings—the view from within and the view from without—into one organized theory.* "Mind" is produced by the living brain, and culture in turn by the inventive mind. The crucial question is how. To find the answer, we must go on cross-interpreting our two classes of findings. By ever increasing their correspondence we should eventually arrive at a correlated dynamics of behavior. We may hope that such a psychophysiological theory will create the foundation upon which to build scientific therapy.

At present, our knowledge of integration is at a less than elementary stage. When the newcomer turns to reading the literature, he cannot help but feel that the diverse schools and approaches compete with one another in the pursuit of self-sufficiency rather than seeking consensus and uniting in the pursuit of integration. The techniques of cross-interpretation and correlation are still to be discovered. To my knowledge, no systematic treatise on this subject exists.

A peculiar difficulty complicates the relationship between adaptational psychodynamics and the underlying physiology in every area of behavioral inquiry, including the one here concerned. Since the diagnosis of schizophrenia and the evaluation of spontaneous or therapeutic changes is based primarily on psychodynamic findings, the first step in the basic science investigation should be the construction of a working theory of the psychodynamics of schizotypal disorders that will pose the essential problems calling for physiological study. Otherwise, the physiological investigator gropes in the dark. But our chances of validating psychodynamic propositions by means of psychodynamics itself are rather limited. For obvious reasons, psychodynamics cannot be expected to develop methods of validation equalling those of the physical sciences. As I have stated elsewhere, behavioral science has a unique composition: without psychodynamics it has no worthwhile problems, and without physiology, no binding solutions. Definitive validation of psychodynamic formulations can be achieved only through correlation with the underlying brain physiology. The hard fact is that the organism is dominated by the "psyche," which is produced by the brain. Operationally, the psyche is introspectional and the brain is inspectional. Only inspectional evidence can be put on public display.

---

*Let me emphasize that the existence of two views—one from within and one from without—is a fact of neurology, not a theory of Descartes, and that a third "neutral and superordinated" view does not exist today, nor can it be invented tomorrow. Descartes' dualistic theory reflects the spirit of his time; the hope for a neutralistic theory reflects the cybernetic spirit of our time.

A Working Theory of the Schizotype

Since the late 1940's, clinical observation of patients suffering from schizophrenia and, in particular, pseudo-neurotic schizophrenia, made the need for a deeper psychodynamic study of this disorder imperative. The working theory emerging from this study was first presented in the broader framework of my "Academic Lecture" at the American Psychiatric Association in May, 1953. The results of continued studies were reported in subsequent publications, of which the most recent one was a contribution to a symposium on "The Outpatient Treatment of Schizophrenia," held in Minnesota in 1959 and sponsored by the U.S. Public Health Service.

Looking forward to a future correlated pathodynamics that would embrace the relevant genetic and physiological findings, from the beginning I took my clue from Franz J. Kallmann's "Genetic Theory of Schizophrenia," which gave evidence for the existence of schizophrenic genotypes. Accordingly, schizophrenic patients are called in the language of genetics "schizophrenic phenotypes"; for psychiatric purposes I abbreviated the term into *schizotypes.* No established findings existed then (or exist today) concerning the physiology of the schizotype. I have therefore attempted to abstract from clinical observation those traits that may constitute the psychodynamic expression of the mutated genes and have formed from them a working adaptational theory which I have called schizotypal organization and behavior.

Like a number of observers before me, I traced the clinical manifestations concerned to shortcomings of central integration. The psychodynamic "integrative apparatus" appeared to be affected by two basic damages of genetic origin. One was termed "integrative pleasure deficiency," and the other, temporarily, was termed "proprioceptive diathesis." Pleasure deficiency damages structure and function of the entire integrative apparatus. At the basic level of "hedonic self-regulation" pleasure and pain are the organism's fundamental instruments for its navigation on the sea of life. This makes the consequences of pleasure deficiency obvious. At the next higher levels of preverbal emotion and emotional thought, the welfare emotions, built on the experiencing of pleasure (affection, love, joy, pride, etc.), are contracted. Because of the absence of the buffering effect of the welfare emotions, the emergency emotions, built on the anticipation of pain, are expanded. Thus, fear and rage may rise to exorbitant strengths. In consequence of these damages of the integrative apparatus, the pleasure deficiency will produce more or less serious disordering effects in every phase of life in every area of behavior. So-called "anhedonia" is not, as older psychiatrists thought, merely one of the symptoms, but a fundamental defect of the whole individual's psychodynamic organization. The organism's inherited capacity for pleasure may be further diminished—first by inadequate maternal care in early life, and subsequently through the inhibitions associated with psychiatric disorders.

The manifold proprioceptive disturbances appearing in the clinical picture of schizotypal disorders distort the patient's awareness of his bodily self, thus impairing his relationship to himself—his "action self"—as well as to his environment. Therefore, their significance is not symptomatic but organizational.

Thanks to its powers of self-regulation, the innately damaged schizotypal organism does promising repair work by evolving a system of compensatory adaptation: (1) the schizotype remains extremely overdependent throughout his life; (2) he shifts the tasks ordinarily solved by warm (i.e., pleasurable) feelings to the level of unemotional thought; (3) he uses a scarcity economy of pleasure. Success with these mechanisms depends largely upon the total balance between the organism's liabilities and its resources. From patient to patient, the grade of inherited damage varies from low to high; intelligence, from subnormal to genius; creative talent, from nil to unique; socioeconomic status and opportunity, from one extreme of the scale to the other. If the balance becomes unfavorable, the patient's excessive fears and rages precipitate emergency dyscontrol, signalling that the system of compensatory adaptation is breaking down.

In addition to the three compensatory mechanisms just described, the organism develops a fourth one which, however, is *maladaptive* from the outset. The patient's infantile craving for magic is vastly increased, eventuating in wishful delusions in which he relies on magic.

This theory enables us to interpret the clinical forms of schizophrenia as developmental stages of schizotypal behavior: compensated, decompensated, disintegrated, and deteriorated.

(1) Compensated schizotypal behavior is seen in the so-called schizoid patients who may go through life without a breakdown. (2) Decompensated schizotypal behavior appears in the clinical pictures designated by Paul Hoch and Philip Polatin as the "pseudoneurotic form of schizophrenia." (3) Disintegrated schizotypal

behavior is clinically known as overt schizophrenic psychosis. (4) Deteriorated schizotypal behavior may be due to lack of proper care. It is marked by a progressive cessation of function, a nearly complete withdrawal from the adaptive task.

In this scanty outline, I had to omit the solid mass of clinical observations and psychodynamic mechanisms presented in my previous publications. Nor was it possible to discuss the chances of psychotherapeutic intervention, in particular at the stage of decompensated schizotypal behavior (pseudoneurotic schizophrenia). But the point I had intended to make is, nevertheless, clear: understanding the patient's adaptive struggle leads to much more dependable clinical diagnosis and points up problems of the utmost importance that the investigators in the inspectional basic sciences could not otherwise detect. And the theory is formulated in a technical language that will make correlation with brain physiology possible.

Clinical scrutiny of the theory of schizotypal organization and behavior has been—and still is—going on continuously for more than a decade. I have used the theory with my own patients and observed its use by generations of residents who have been introduced to it through my lecture courses, clinical conferences, and their treatment of patients at the outpatient clinic.

As an example, let me quote here one observation of a twenty-year-old single girl treated in our outpatient clinic. Her "presenting problems" are recorded in her case history in her own words:

> 1. I can't function socially, I can't relate to people, no matter how hard I try. I feel I am being ridiculous, that I am not going to make an impression, that I am not an individual. At times I contradict them and I even contradict myself, and I am aware that I am spoiling the relationship but I still can't help it. I am so preoccupied with analyzing them or thinking about myself that I don't get involved in the situation. If I am enjoying being with somebody for a little while (and it occurs very rarely), I feel I am using him or that I am being used. I can say very nasty things or be cruel in the most subtle ways. I am conscious of it but I can't help it and it's very frustrating. They say that I am calm, composed, that I have good control, but I laugh in myself because I am very tense and I can cover it up. They even consider me the most independent of a group because I can leave them in the middle of a party or not pay any attention to the conversation, but actually I am withdrawn, thinking in myself about myself. I am very introverted and I am aware of it, but there's nothing I can do about it. I feel bored and I know that my boredom is merely a defense and that I am very inadequate. I've stopped going out. I've restricted my social life.
>
> 2. I've stopped dating boys because I didn't know what to tell them. I felt

bored. I can't reciprocate emotionally or physically; I am never sure of my emotions if I have any. If I had the guts, if I had the least respect and consideration for me and for them, I would at least talk to them honestly, freely. I would tell them that I am not sure of my feelings, but keep avoiding discussing the question and act ridiculous, like a five-year-old child. I fear responsibilities. I don't let boys have intercourse with me because after I begin, it would be too easy for me and I would do it with everybody. I can't because I can't trust anybody. Besides, when a friend makes love to me, I get tense, I can't relax. I get frozen. I enjoy it but not like I should. What kind of a mother would I be? I can't give affection; I can't control my anger; my child would be deprived like me. It's terrible.

3. I can't function in school. I wonder how I could make passing grades. I had high marks in grammar school and high school, mostly "A's" and "B's" but now I go to finals unprepared. I put off my mark and go to make-up exams. The only subject I am still good at is history, where one does not have to think, because I can no longer think clearly and logically. I can't put my thoughts together. I am mixed up, disorganized. I always had difficulty writing, but now it's worse. What is clear is what my classmates explain to me. I may have terrific insights but it does not last and I doubt. I torture myself. My teachers know that I've some difficulty but they don't know it's so serious.

4. I've always felt nervous but it's worse now, and I feel tired. I have no energy. I drag myself and I force myself to work. I don't sleep well either. And I hate myself because I overeat. I am almost addicted to food. I am nervous or afraid. I have to eat and eat and eat. . . .

5. Recently I've had anxiety attacks. I felt very shaky, nervous within myself, afraid, incapable of concentrating. I just can't explain it well, put it into words. It frightened me. It happened three or four times and could last from fifteen minutes to a few hours. The first time, I was reading an autobiography because I have to do the critique of it for my term paper, and I guess I was identifying too much with the author. He was hated by his family. . . . The second time, I was thinking that I had to take supper with my parents and I started shaking like a leaf; how will I ever be able to pass the examination?

6. I've always been depressed but it has been worse during the last two years; it's just a combination of the previous years. My past is too painful. I pity my mother, I hate my father; they never gave me any affection, they beat me up, they insulted me, they hated me, my sister hated me. Now I feel very inferior, inadequate. I feel sad, depressed. I don't find life worth living. Before I moved out of their house, I thought of killing myself in the bathroom; they would have been embarrassed at finding my body . . . but it alleviated my depression pretty much when I started living in my own apartment.

7. I feel very disintegrated, disunified. I can feel as if my body and my mind were two different entities, apart. My body sensations are not my body sensations like they used to be. I feel I am a part of a group or in contact with another person sometimes when I am alone. These experiences happen very often; it can be continual. I am completely removed, I have no desire. I am aware of it and it does not make any difference.

When the patient introduced herself with these complaints, she had no idea of her diagnosis or of the psychiatric literature on the subject.

From the outset we have abandoned the collection of symptoms listed in the various textbooks. Instead, we have learned to see and understand our patients as diseased human beings who struggle and rarely succeed in achieving a tolerable existence. The phrase, "understanding our patients as human beings," does not refer to a romantic approach of some sort, but to sharply delineated psychodynamic mechanisms. The theory has also served as an indispensable guide in our experiments with psychotherapeutic intervention, the focal point of which is the patient's relationship to himself. We help him to learn to adjust himself to the schizotypal nature of his individuality. Experience has shown that by achieving self-adaptation, the patient may develop a degree of realistic foresight which enables him to avoid many of the troubles he used to have.

I am looking forward to critical analyses and clinical experiences of observers other than my pupils.

REFERENCES

List of author's previous publications: (1) on the schizotype; (2) on some of the underlying psychodynamic principles.

1. Chapter on "Schizotypal Disorders in Dynamics and Classification of Disordered Behavior." Now in the author's Collected Papers, Vol. I (pp. 274-283). New York, Grune & Stratton, 1956.

Schizotypal Organization: Preliminary Report on a Clinical Study on Schizophrenia (with B. Buchenholz, H. Dunton, S. H. Karlen, and R. Senescu). Now in Collected Papers, Vol. II (pp. 1-10). New York, Grune & Stratton, 1962.

Discussion of Dr. Whitehorn's paper on schizophrenia. Now in Collected Papers, Vol. II (pp. 49-51).

Chapter on "Differential Diagnosis in Obsessive Behavior." Now in Collected Papers, Vol. I (pp. 75-78).

"Theory and Therapy: The Theory of Schizotypal Organization and its Application to the Treatment of Decompensated Schizotypal Behavior." Now in Collected Papers, Vol. II (pp. 127-140).

2. "From the Metapsychological Ego to the Bio-Cultural Action-Self." Now in Collected Papers, Vol. II (pp. 42-48).

Hedonic self-regulation of the organism. *In* The Role of Pleasure in Behavior (ed., R. G. Heath). New York, Hoeber Medical Division, Harper & Row, 1964, pp. 257-264.

Discussion

Recorder: SIDNEY MALITZ, M.D.

COMMENTS ON DR. CATTELL'S PRESENTATION

DR. JEROME D. FRANK: Dr. Cattell's paper brings up the problems of retrospective distortions in the narrative account, although it also demonstrates the skill and selectivity of the writer. Papers describing new syndromes follow the law of diminishing returns after the first few papers on the subject are published. Most readers, if not convinced by the first few papers on the subject are unlikely to be convinced by subsequent ones. I would be interested in learning what Dr. Cattell was attempting to accomplish in writing this paper.

DR. RÜMKE: I am allergic to the word "anxiety." There are so many forms of anxiety. The schizophrenic has a specific way of being anxious. The concept of pan-sexuality also distresses me. The schizophrenic seems to work out his sexuality in a specific way.

DR. LEON MOSES: Could Dr. Cattell give some figures on the incidence of major psychosomatic disorders associated with pseudoneurotic schizophrenia? I question the basic validity of the concept of pseudoneurotic schizophrenia. Pseudoneurotic schizophrenia symptoms are uncommon in psychosomatic patients in my experience except in ulcerative colitis and obesity patients. Few of the latter have become acutely psychotic.

DR. CATTELL: In response to Dr. Frank's comments, we have presented this paper because there are so few case studies of pseudoneurotic schizophrenia in the literature and we feel it is an important clinical entity. In reply to Dr. Moses, at least 60 per cent of our pseudoneurotic schizophrenia patients have psychosomatic disorders. Patients with pseudoneurotic schizophrenia rarely go on to become overtly psychotic.

COMMENTS ON DR. ARIETI'S PRESENTATION

DR. PIOTROWSKI: I would like to clarify Von Demaros' principal as being compatible with Kurt Goldstein's ideas.

DR. DAVID WECHSLER: I would like to differentiate between our understanding the patient and what he does. I have seen nonvirgins who thought they were virgins.

DR. J. ZUBIN: Alfred North Whitehead differentiates two types of abstracting: abstraction from possibility and abstracting from actuality. Both mathematicians and paranoid schizophrenics are adept at the former. Recent sociological studies of middle and lower class Negro children have indicated that the latter cannot abstract as well, because they have not been exposed as frequently to abstractions in speech. There is a great need for controls here. Before we can say schizophrenics demonstrate concrete thinking we will have to compare schizophrenics with different social and cultural backgrounds.

DR. RÜMKE: Is concrete thinking always a regression? Schizophrenics might be thought of as progressing in the area of irrational thinking. We seem to take for granted that irrationality is a low level of thinking. There is irrationality in poetry but it is on a very high level. I admire some schizophrenics and I think this would be impossible if they were only regressing.

Concretization is not always a sign of regression either. The neologisms of the schizophrenic may be the best words he has to describe his feelings. I should like to describe the progression of irrationality rather than its regression.

RESPONSE BY DR. ARIETI: The schizophrenic shows a tendency to translate the abstract into the concrete because he cannot maintain the abstract at that level. I have never compared the schizophrenic's concreteness to that of the organic patient with a parietal lobe tumor. There is a dynamic meaning to the schizophrenic's concretization which is most prominent when their complexes are involved.

In regard to Dr. Wechsler's remarks, the nonvirgins also identifying with the Virgin Mary affirms my point about using the same predicates. There is no great disagreement between Professor Rümke and myself. Freud also spoke of the restitutive as well as the regressive aspects of symptoms. I am aware of beautiful expressions sometimes used by schizophrenics which are reminiscent of expressions used in the creative process, since the latter also uses primitive forms of thinking.

COMMENTS ON DR. FRIESKE AND DR. WILSON'S PRESENTATION

DR. HAROLD ESECOVER: Drs. Frieske and Wilson are to be thanked for having focused our attention on a neglected aspect of visual hallucinatory experience—that is, their formal qualities. They have thoughtfully explored such varied and important aspects as temporal relationship, complexity, reality, color, size, movement, dimensionality, clarity, and projection of object.

The method they have used is that of the structured interview. The major difficulty with all phenomenological research on hallucinations rests with the methodology. Here I see two main problems: the possible bias introduced by suggestion due to the researcher's using leading questions; and a sampling bias introduced by virtue of the fact that only patients who talk readily about these experiences are ever included in such studies. With this in mind, I would appreciate it if the authors furnish us with some details about the following:

1. What was the percentage of hallucinating patients who were not willing to talk about their experiences and thus were excluded from the study?
2. Could the authors provide us with some of the actual questions used in the interviews?

Modell has provided us in his study of schizophrenic hallucinations with a model of an intensive exploratory approach, with at times 30 to 40 interviews of one patient being done. This approach supplies a good deal of data on small samples. Drs. Frieske and Wilson's approach yields less intensive data on a larger sample. Although Modell selected from the onset patients who talked readily of their hallucinations, his approach through the establishment of a relationship between researcher and patient over a period of time seems to have the potential of elucidating data from the less communicative patient. Both approaches are valid and important and perhaps an integration of the two would be fruitful in future research.

The authors, in their attempt to find a unity of form in visual hallucinations, generalize their findings to include the effects of psychotomimetic drugs and sensory deprivation studies. It is here that I believe they run into difficulty. In our experience (Malitz, Wilkens, and myself) and that of other workers (such as Feinberg, Bliss and Clark, and Zucker), there appears to be some striking differences between schizophrenic visual hallucinations and those induced by psychotomimetic drugs. Firstly, visual hallucinations in schizophrenia appear abruptly without prodromata, whereas those induced by psychotomimetic agents are preceded by unformed visual sensations and then by the so-called "form constants" initially described by Kluver with mescaline (latticework, geometrical shapes, cobwebs). All of these are absent in schizophrenic hallucinations. The hallucinations of psychotomimetic agents involve considerable distortions of the subject's entire visual perceptual world with marked illusionary experience. The visual hallucinations of the schizophrenic are superimposed on a visual environment that is usually normal. Drug-induced visual hallucinations appear with eyes closed or in a darkened surrounding as opposed to eyes open in the schizophrenic. Lastly, hallucinations of psychotomimetic drugs are almost exclusively visual. In our study of 100 subjects there was a 97 per cent incidence of visual hallucination with only 3 per cent of other kinds of hallucinations.

The visual hallucinations induced by sensory deprivation are described by Heron as follows:

"The hallucinations seemed to show a great many characteristics of drug-induced hallucinations as well as those produced by Grey Walter by means of flickering light. Typically, the hallucinations progress from simple to complex. Firstly, lightening of the visual field; then dots or lines or lights, geometrical figures, and patterns, followed by isolated objects against a homogenous visual field."

Thus, the visual hallucinations of psychotomimetic drugs and of sensory deprivation seem close to one another and seem to show some striking differences from those of schizophrenia.

The authors in their discussion of the neurophysiology of hallucinations emphasize the involvement of temporal lobe mechanisms and question the role of the reticular activating system. There is certainly a large literature of supporting evidence that visual hallucinations can be produced at the cortical level, particularly of the temporal lobe. Penfield's temporal lobe stimulation studies add to this evidence. Yet, Lhermitte and Van Bogaert have demonstrated hallucinations with lesions of the mesencephalic tegmentum. It would seem that almost all levels of organization of the CNS can produce these phenomena with the right pathological, physiological or biochemical changes.

The work of Evarts, Marazzi, and Fink suggest a model of inhibition of symaptic transmission and hallucinatory behavior which can then be fitted into a theory of perceptual release (Jackson and West) that seems useful. Certainly there are great gaps in our knowledge, and one must really conclude by agreeing with the authors that a "satisfactory explanation of the neurophysiological origin of hallucinations is not available."

DR. MARTIN ROTH: I should like to point out that schizophrenic hallucinations occur in clear consciousness and that the schizophrenic lacks insight into the character of his hallucinatory experiences. In this paper, the way that the hallucinations and delusions are intertwined in schizophrenia was not sufficiently emphasized. Any psychiatric research requires adequate numbers before valid conclusions can be drawn. Two borderland areas requiring more research are alcoholic hallucinosis and amphetamine psychosis. In the former, auditory hallucinations predominate but visual hallucinations sometimes occur. The syndrome seems quite close to schizophrenia in many respects. The hallucinations occur in clear consciousness in both. In amphetamine psychosis the hallucinations are also predominantly auditory and it resembles paranoid schizophrenia very closely also.

DR. VAILLANT: Nerve gas poisons produce increased dreaming but not an increase in hallucinations. Scopalamine, on the other hand, increases hallucinations but produces dreamless sleep and inhibits the rhombocephalic phase of sleep. Physostigmine increases the rhombocephalic phase of sleep and is analogous in its effect to the nerve gasses.

RESPONSE BY DR. FRIESKE: In answer to Dr. Esecover's questions, 20 to 25 per cent of the subjects wouldn't talk even though we spent an average of one and a half hours with them. We asked specific questions and filled out a special form. It was sometimes hard to pin down ambivalent schizophrenics, but we tried to push them until they gave a consistent answer more than 2 or 3 times in a row. It was our impression that certain formal qualities of all visual hallucinations were similar, and perhaps there exists some unifying substrate like the temporal lobe.

COMMENTS ON DR. RADO'S PRESENTATION

DR. GLUECK: I should like to take issue with the transoperational pessimism of Dr. Rado. We have recently learned of the existence of "adaptive enzymes" in mammals which sounds quite exciting.

DR. KETY: Dr. Rado and I are both students of Bacon. We need theories in clinical medicine that explain the whole problem at once because we are faced with the treatment of the entire problem at once. In neurophysiology and chemistry we don't need an answer by 5 P.M., so we can dispense with theories that attempt to explain the entire problem and can focus on details.

Thudicum was a biochemist who advanced the theory that many forms of insanity are due to toxic substances. Then he promptly ignored his theory and spent the rest of his life on the minute aspects of the chemistry of the brain. By working in the darkness without theory, he illuminated it. Would he have accomplished as much if he had tied himself down to a premature theory of biochemical action? I do not recommend that scientists in other fields take up this theory which attempts to answer too much.

DR. HOCH: Dr. Rado emphasizes the adaptational frame of reference which, until we know more about the specific etiology of schizophrenia, remains extremely important. We tend to treat schizophrenics as all one type. This is incorrect. There are smart schizophrenics and stupid ones. There are also schizophrenic genuises. The impact of schizophrenia on intelligence and whether it enhances or detracts would make an interesting study.

I do not agree with Dr. Rado that the anhedonia and proprioceptive disturbances in schizophrenics are primary. I feel that they are already secondary to some other fundamental disturbance, probably biochemical.

RESPONSE BY DR. RADO: You were all very kind to me. I did not mean that the physiologist should wait for the psychodynamic psychologist to tell him what to do, but rather that the latter ask the former, "Would you please look into this?" How the physiologist does this is his privilege. This is a free country. It is my feeling that the anhedonia and proprioceptive disturbance in the schizophrenic is related to a mutated gene.

Part II: Psychology

6

THE MEASUREMENT AND SIGNIFICANCE OF OVERINCLUSIVE THINKING AND RETARDATION IN SCHIZOPHRENIC PATIENTS

by R. W. PAYNE, PH.D.*

THE PRESENT PAPER WILL SUMMARIZE a series of investigations, which have been carried out over the past few years, into the nature of thought disorder in schizophrenic patients.

KRETSCHMER'S THEORY OF SPALTUNGSFÄHIGKEIT

When Bleuler coined the term "schizophrenia," it was partly to draw attention to the particular type of thought disorder which he thought characterized this condition. He believed that many schizophrenic symptoms could be attributed to a fragmentation of intellectual functioning which resulted in the relative isolation and lack of interaction between one set of thought proceses and another. Kretschmer was very influenced by this idea, and he used the term "Spaltungsfähigkeit" (dissociation) to refer to this disorder. Kretschmer thought that Spaltungsfähigkeit was only one of a number of physical and psychological characteristics associated with the more fundamental constitutional factor "schizothymia-cyclothymia." He believed that Spaltungsfähigkeit was continuously distributed throughout the normal and the abnormal population, an extreme degree of dissociation producing schizophrenic thought disorder, but an extreme degree of its opposite (integration) contributing towards manic-depressive symptoms. Kretschmer and his followers developed a number of objective tests of Spaltungsfähigkeit, which they administered to both normal and psychotic groups, in order

*Department of Behavioral Sciences, Temple University Medical School, Philadelphia, Pennsylvania.

This paper is one of two granted the Henry M. and Lillian Stratton Award for 1964.

to show that normal pyknic and leptosomatic individuals showed similar but smaller differences to those found between schizophrenics and manic depressives.

Neither Kretschmer nor his followers carried out the crucial test of this theory to discover whether or not these tests measured anything in common. In the first study to be described,[17] Kretschmer's tests of Spaltungsfähigkeit, along with a number of new measures of this disorder derived from the same theory, were administered to an unselected but heterogeneous group of 100 normal subjects. Only chance intercorrelations were obtained, although it was demonstrated that many of the measures were highly reliable. This unexpected result suggests that a number of different measures of the tendency to keep various psychological processes independent of one another have nothing in common. In other words, the tendency or ability to divide one's attention successfully is purely a function of the particular tasks involved.

This finding was followed up by an extensive review of the German literature[5] and as a result of this, it was concluded that there is no evidence that these tests in fact discriminate between schizophrenics and manic depressives, or between normal pyknics and leptosomes in any consistent way. Accordingly, one must conclude that the theory about the nature of schizophrenic thought disorder which led Bleuler to coin the term "schizophrenia" has not been supported by the experiments which have been carried out. It has frequently been contended that schizophrenics are not a homogeneous group, and it is of interest that a specific type of schizophrenic thought disorder of the sort postulated by Bleuler evidently cannot provide a common characteristic with which to define this disorder.

A Pilot Study of the "Overinclusion" Hypothesis

A somewhat different explanation of schizophrenic thought disorder was that put forward by Norman Cameron.[7-10] As a result of early studies using sorting tests, Cameron concluded that schizophrenic thought disorder was unlike that which characterized organic patients, and was also not similar to the normal thought processes of children, as suggested by the "regression" hypothesis. Cameron hypothesized that a central feature of schizophrenic thought was "overinclusive thinking." This is characterized by an inability to preserve conceptual boundaries, so that ideas which are only distantly related, or even irrelevant to a concept become incorporated into it, and are regarded as a necessary part of it. Because of this, thinking becomes more abstract and less precise.

Payne, Matussek, and George[25] suggested that this theory was of considerable importance because of the number of predictions that could be made from it. They speculated that overinclusion could be regarded as being the result of an abnormal amount of stimulus generalization, to use a learning theory concept. Put in terms of a rather different approach to cognitive theory, and using a concept which Broadbent[6] has found experimentally useful, they suggested that overinclusive thinking might be regarded as due to a defect in some hypothetical central "filter" mechanism, the function of which is to screen out irrelevant data, both internal (in the form of irrelevant thoughts and associations) and external (in the form of irrelevant stimuli), to allow for the most efficient processing of incoming information. In a pilot study, a number of predictions were tested about the differences which should be found between an acute schizophrenic group and a group of hospitalized neurotic patients matched for age, previous intellectual level as assessed by a vocabulary test, and other relevant variables. Some of the predictions which were verified were as follows:

1. In a specially constructed "object classification test"[19, 22] it was predicted that, because of their overinclusiveness, schizophrenics should consider many more data as relevant to the task, and should accordingly be able to discover more methods of sorting the material. These would include a not significantly smaller number of normal categories (e.g., shape, weight, hue, etc., of the objects), but would also include categories based on data ignored by nonschizophrenic patients (shadows cast by the objects, unintentional scratches on the objects, personal associations to the objects, etc.). Both expectations were confirmed.

2. In the Goldstein "object sorting test," which consists of a set of everyday objects, during the "handing over" experiment the subject is invited to select all those objects which belong together with a given "point of departure." It was predicted that schizophrenics should select significantly more objects because of the "overinclusive" category they establish. This was also confirmed.

3. If the Benjamin Proverbs test was given with no time limit, and if the examiner did not give the next proverb until he received a positive indication from the patient that he had finished, it was predicted

that schizophrenics would use significantly more words per answer. It was agreed that for schizophrenic patients, proverbs illustrate a more complex, overinclusive concept which should take longer to explain. This prediction was confirmed,[24] but only when answers were recorded on tape, probably because psychologists tend to paraphrase and condense answers when taking them down in longhand, despite their best intentions.

4. It was argued that "Einstellung" rigidity is a special case of the development of a set which in this particular case is a disadvantage. It was predicted that schizophrenics should be less susceptible to the development of Einstellung rigidity. Using a modified version of Luchin's[15] "water-jar" test in which the "set" was made stronger, this was shown to be the case.[24] In this particular case, overinclusive thinking was thus an advantage.

A Pilot Study of Babcock's "Slowness" Hypothesis

An entirely different explanation of schizophrenic thought disorder was put forward by Harriet Babcock.[1, 2] She suggested in essence that a main cause of schizophrenic thought disorder is an extreme degree of generalized motor and mental retardation. Schizophrenics take so long to work out the answer to even a simple question that, in response to the social pressure of normal conversation to answer, they produce a response before they have had time to formulate an appropriate reply. Babcock in several large scale studies showed that schizophrenics as a group are indeed very slow at a wide range of tasks. Payne[16] in an experimental study of a single schizophrenic patient showed that, at least in this case, thought disorder could be manipulated strikingly by manipulating the social pressure and the response time allowed.

A Study of Overinclusive Thinking, Retardation and "Concreteness" in Several Diagnostic Groups

The fourth major explanation of schizophrenic thought disorder has been that it is similar to that found in brain damaged patients, and is due to "concreteness." In the studies which have sought to find evidence for this hypothesis, "concreteness" was usually defined operationally as an inability to produce adequately explained abstract sortings on the Goldstein or other sorting tests. However, an inspection of the criteria for an "abstract performance" used for these tests in conjunction with Goldstein and Scheerer's[14] 8-point definition of the abstract attitude, suggested that it might not be possible operationally to distinguish this from "general intelligence." In order to test this and other hypotheses, Payne and Hewlett[24] administered five tests of concreteness, and four tests of general intelligence to a group of 20 normals, 20 neurotics, 20 depressives, and 20 schizophrenics. The groups were matched for age, sex, education, occupational level, and preillness intelligence as assessed by a vocabulary scale. The tests of concreteness did not differentiate significantly between the groups. Further, as expected, these tests correlated as highly with the other tests of intelligence as the latter correlated among themselves. When the battery of tests was factor-analyzed, tests of concreteness and tests of intelligence were equally good measures of a factor which was labelled intelligence, factor scores of which similarly failed to differentiate the groups. It was concluded that concreteness, at least as measured by these tests, did not appear to characterize any of these three abnormal groups.

In the same study, 13 different measures of overinclusive thinking, including the tests referred to above and others, were given to the subjects. On each of these 13 tests, the schizophrenic group produced the most extreme (overinclusive) mean score, although only six of these differences attained statistical significance. The entire test battery was factor-analyzed, and the first three centroid factors extracted by Thurstone's procedure were determined. That discriminant function of these three centroid factors which discriminated best between the schizophrenics and the depressives was calculated. By premultiplying the three resulting discriminant function weights into the three columns of centroid factor loadings, a single set of factor saturations was obtained which defined that single rotated factor which would best discriminate the schizophrenics from the other groups. It was predicted that this would be a factor of "overinclusive thinking," and, as expected, the eight highest factor loadings on this factor were all obtained by tests of overinclusive thinking. This factor differentiated the schizophrenics from the other groups better than any individual test. It was concluded that evidence had been produced that these tests were measuring something in common which differentiated the groups as predicted from the theory of overinclusion. It was concluded that overinclusive thinking appeared to characterize only schizophrenic patients. However, from an inspection of the histograms of the individual test scores and the factor score, it was clear that only about half the schizophrenic group was abnormal in this respect. The remainder were within the normal range, the bottom range of the distributions of all the groups coinciding.

Payne and Hewlett also administered a group of 24 measures of speed of performance to the four groups, ranging from very simple tests of motor speed taken from Babcock and Levy's[3] battery, to Furneaux's[13] tests of the speed of inductive reasoning. A group of 17 measures of Eysenck's[11] factor of "psychoticism" was also included, many of which were also speed tests. This was done to test the hypothesis that tests of "psychoticism" differentiated psychotics from non-psychotics insofar as they were measures of speed of functioning. The mean differences between the groups substantiated this hypothesis. All the test of speed, regardless of their complexity, differentiated the psychotics from the other two groups. The other measures of "psychoticism" did not yield significant differences. By a procedure identical with that described above, that rotated factor was obtained which maximized the difference between the psychotics as a group and the remaining subjects. As expected, the resultant factor was defined almost exclusively by speed tests, 25 of the 31 loadings greater than .30 on this factor being obtained by measures of speed. However, the factor was perfectly general, simple motor tests, and complex reasoning speed tests tending to have equally high loadings. It was concluded that there does seem to be a general factor of retardation which characterizes psychotics as a whole, and that Eysenck's factor of "psychoticism" could well be relabelled "retardation." It was found that this factor was relatively independent of overinclusive thinking, there being a correlation of only .377 between them. Both factors were independent of the factor of general intelligence.

One further finding was that, while the depressives all tended to be homogeneously retarded but not overinclusive, the schizophrenics were extremely heterogeneous with respect to retardation, both on the factor score and on individual test scores. Approximately half the group was sufficiently fast to be within normal limits. However, the other half of the group was more retarded than even the depressives. There was also a significant tendency for those schizophrenics who were overinclusive not to be retarded, and for those who were retarded not to be overinclusive. The two types of thought disorder tended not to coexist in the same schizophrenic patient.

This descriptive study suggested that there may be two different types of thought disorder in schizophrenics, and that this might provide another basis for subdividing this rather heterogeneous group of patients. Further studies were designed to throw further light on the specific implications and correlates of each type of thought disorder, its response to treatment, and its possible cause. These studies are still continuing, but some of the more striking results will be discussed briefly.

The Effect of Remission of Psychiatric Symptoms on Thought Disorder

The investigations described above do not demonstrate that either overinclusive thinking or retardation is a feature of the illness of these patients. It is possible that they are a relatively permanent constitutional characteristic of certain people which might predispose them to breakdowns, but which could not explain symptoms peculiar to the illness itself. In order to investigate this possibility, Payne, Ancevich, and Laverty[20] administered tests of overinclusive thinking and retardation to 16 deluded schizophrenics, 17 schizophrenics without delusions, and 21 nonschizophrenic mental patients matched for age and vocabulary level after these patients had all been treated and were judged to be free of symptoms. The groups were not significantly different from each other either on measures of overinclusion or retardation, and all were within the normal range as defined by other studies. These patients were also compared with exactly similar groups of 15 deluded schizophrenics, 15 schizophrenics without delusions, and 15 nonschizophrenic patients tested at the same hospital immediately after admission, and prior to the onset of treatment by Payne, Caird, and Laverty.[21] As expected, and as shown in previous studies, the schizophrenic patients who were tested while ill suffered from both types of thought disorder.

This study suggests that both overinclusive thinking and retardation appear to be a feature of the illness of schizophrenic patients, and that they are not a permanent constitutional characteristic. This suggests that tests of both these types of thought disorder might be used to help assess the recovery of such patients.

The Relationship of Overinclusive Thinking to Delusions

It was though possible that overinclusive thinking might be one important factor in the formation of delusions in schizophrenic patients[18] for several reasons. The classical explanation of paranoid delusions is that they are due to unconscious homosexual urges. The individual "denies" his love and successfully represses this by consciously feeling the opposite emotion, "hate." However, in order to justify expressing this hatred, the individual first "projects" it, attributing it to the person to whom he is unconsciously attracted sexually. This explanation emphasizes emotional rather than intellectual factors. While emotional factors are undoubtedly important, this hypothesis does not explain adequately how it is that delusions often become so general, involving a whole group of people such as the F.B.I. (is the patient really attracted sexually to *all* its members?), or how it is that they are frequently associated with thought disorder as judged clinically.

It seems probable that there are several factors which can cause delusions. Some patients may experience hallucinations which are so compelling that they can only explain them in a way which necessarily appears delusional to somebody not sharing these experiences, but which is not completely illogical given these experiences. It is possible that the traditional account of delusions also applies to some cases. However, it also seems likely that overinclusive thinking can produce delusions. Delusions nearly always involve logical contradictions. That is to say the deluded patient can entertain two incompatible ideas at the same time. Overinclusive thinking could produce an extension of the boundaries of concepts in such a way that two normally mutually exclusive categories or concepts could overlap, containing elements in common. Thus, for the normal person, while the only possibilities are "either—or," the overinclusive person can also conclude "both."

In one sense, both overinclusive thinking and delusions are by definition unwarranted generalizations from the data. Thus, for example, a patient may correctly believe that a certain individual dislikes him. However, his overinclusive "concept" of this may extend to other similar people (e.g., all foreigners, all dark men, all policemen, etc.), so that he may develop the same negative reactions to this entire category of people, being incapable of the necessary discrimination. His negative reactions to this group may itself occasionally produce retaliation which would further reinforce the delusional belief. Thus the development of an extensive paranoid reaction could well be partly a function of overinclusive thinking. This theory is consistent with one other clinical observation to which attention is seldom drawn. Many paranoid patients appear to perceive an unusually wide range of stimuli. Thus, for example, a patient may note that one of the two men across the street in shabby raincoats has a folded copy of the *Times* in his pocket, and that he periodically touches this in an unusual way. This the patient may interpret as a signal with some special significance. The delusion is, of course, abnormal, but what may also be abnormal is the amount of detailed perception on which the delusion is based. In normal people the range of perceptions around whatever engages the attention is very limited; such details go unnoticed and could therefore not form the basis of delusions.

In order to test this hypothesis, Payne, Caird, and Laverty[21] gave a test of overinclusive thinking (the Proverbs test as described above) and several tests of retardation to matched groups of 15 deluded schizophrenics, 15 schizophrenics with no apparent delusions, and 15 non-deluded nonschizophrenic mental patients. The patients were tested before treatment had commenced. As predicted, the nonschizophrenics were nearly all within the normal range on the test of overinclusive thinking. This group obtained the lowest mean score. The deluded schizophrenics were significantly more overinclusive as expected. The nondeluded schizophrenics fell in between, and this was thought not to be surprising, because it is often difficult to be sure that a psychotic patient is not deluded, since many are defensive about their beliefs, and a number in this group may in fact have secretly harbored delusions. These results were thought to be consistent with the hypothesis. The tests of retardation, on the other hand, did not differentiate significantly between the three groups. Thus there is no evidence that retardation is specifically related to this symptom.

Thought Disorder in Chronic Schizophrenics

All the studies so far described, and apparently nearly all the studies of overinclusive thinking reported in the literature, were carried out on acute schizophrenics. There seem to be no data on the status of chronic schizophrenic patients.

If it is the case that overinclusive thinking is the main factor in the progressive intellectual deterioration shown by some schizophrenics, it should be the case that chronic schizophrenics should be more overinclusive on tests than acute patients. A pilot study to test this hypothesis was carried out at Oakwood Hospital in Maidstone, Kent, by A. R. Dabbs.[19] Thirty-seven chronic schizophrenic patients were given the Object Classification test. Unexpectedly, they did not differ from normals in the number of their unusual responses, although they gave fewer total responses, a result which suggested that they were not abnormally overinclusive. Presumably therefore, their clinical status was the result of some other type of thought disorder. This pilot study was not well controlled, since the influence of such factors as age, drugs, and education was not established.

This study was followed up by a more elaborate investigation carried out at the Ontario Hospital in Kingston.[23] Forty long-stay chronic schizophrenics were given a test of overinclusive thinking (the Proverbs test) and tests of retardation. They were found not to be significantly more overinclusive than normal people, although they were extremely retarded on the measures of speed used. This initial finding was ambiguous, however, as nearly all the patients were being given maintenance doses of phenothiazine drugs, and this could have alleviated their overinclusive thought disorder. To test this hypothesis, they were taken off all drugs for a six-weeks period. Unfortunately, the staff concerned were aware of this (probably placebo medication should have been substituted with no one's knowledge). Before the end of the six-weeks period, 11 patients were thought to have become sufficiently disturbed that they were put back on drugs, and were lost to the experiment. At the end of the six-weeks period the remaining patients were retested on the tests they had received before, and were also given another test of overinclusive thinking (the Object Sorting Test), which they had not seen before. Although they were now slightly more overinclusive than they had been prior to the withdrawal from drugs, this difference was not significant. As a group, they were still not significantly overinclusive by comparison with normal people. These patients were then divided into two matched groups. In a double-blind experiment, one group received placebo for a further six weeks, while one group was given "Proketazine," a high-potency phenothiazine. After six weeks the groups were retested on the Object Sorting Test, and were given a test of overinclusive thinking which they had not seen before (the Object Classification Test). The groups were not significantly different, nor did either group show any significant treatment effect. There was still no evidence for a significant amount of overinclusive thinking in either group. Independent clinical ratings before and after treatment also suggested that their ward behavior had not changed significantly with the phenothiazine drug, although this fact was not so surprising, because presumably their resistance to phenothiazine treatment was a major factor in their still being in hospital.

It was concluded that overinclusive thinking does not seem to characterize chronic schizophrenics as a group, but an extreme degree of retardation does. One possible implication is that the presence of overinclusive thinking in an acute patient is a relatively good prognostic sign, while an extreme degree of retardation is a bad prognostic sign. This hypothesis is currently being tested by a long-term follow-up study.

The Response of Overinclusive Thinking to Phenothiazine Treatment in Acute Schizophrenic Patients

In view of the above findings, it was thought possible that it is overinclusive thinking which responds well to phenothiazine treatment in acute schizophrenic patients, as contrasted with severe retardation which does not. To test this hypothesis, 43 new admissions to the Ontario Hospital, Kingston, were tested within a few days of their arrival, with tests of overinclusive thinking and retardation. These patients were selected as being typically psychotic, and such patients do not represent a very high proportion of the intake of this particular hospital. As in previous studies, there was a statistically significant tendency for the overinclusive subjects to be diagnosed as "schizophrenic," whereas the retarded subjects were diagnosed as both "depressive" and "schizophrenic."

The patients were divided into two matched groups. One group was given phenothiazine treatment, and the other group received other forms of treatment. It was planned to retest the patients six weeks later. For various unforeseen reasons, only 21 of these original patients were available for reassessment after this period, 11 of whom had been receiving phenothiazine drugs. The groups were no longer very well matched, as the reduced phenothiazine group was now younger and more intelligent. The retests showed that both groups were slightly but not significantly improved, both on the tests of overinclusion and on the tests of retardation. However there were no significant differences between the groups, nor were there even any consistent tendencies.

The experiment therefore was unable to demonstrate a specific response of overinclusive thinking to phenothiazine treatment. While no firm conclusions can be drawn from this pilot study, the hypothesis must now be entertained that the recovery of overinclusive thinking which is known to accompany the disappearance of psychotic symptoms in schizophrenics may be due to factors other than the phenothiazine treatment which most schizophrenic patients receive.

There is similarly no evidence that retardation responds to phenothiazine treatment in acutely ill schizophrenic patients, but this is consistent with the hypothesis already advanced that severe retardation in such patients has a poor prognosis, and that very retarded patients tend to remain retarded, and remain in hospital.

The Relationship Between Thought Disorder and Reaction Time

One of the earliest and most reliably reported findings in schizophrenics has been the observation that, in a reaction time task, they tend to be extremely slow and variable. It was argued that because the factor of "retardation" described earlier seemed general, patients who were slow on the tests of retardation should also be slow in their reaction time. The earlier studies, of course, throw no light on the nature or cause of this retardation. However, there seemed no reason why retarded patients should be especially variable in their reaction time performance.

It was also argued, however, that overinclusive thinking could be associated with both a slow and a variable reaction time. If it is the case that overinclusive thinking results from some defective "filter" mechanism, the function of which is to screen out irrelevant stimuli, then this same defect should make overinclusive patients very distractible in a reaction-time situation. Indeed, a simple reaction-time task for such patients should often become a discrimination reaction-time task, because irrelevant stimuli, instead of being "screened out" when they occurred, would be attended to and "processed" along with the relevant stimulus. Errors would not necessarily occur, but reaction time would be delayed. Similarly, in a multiple choice reaction-time task, overinclusive subjects should behave as if they were processing more information than that conveyed by the stimulus array, since irrelevant stimuli would not be screened out but would be processed along with the relevant stimuli. Again, errors need not occur, although reaction times should be slower. They should also be more variable, since the number of unintentional distractions present should be variable.

In order to discover how important each of these factors might be in determining reaction times in psychotic patients, Payne and Caird in a study as yet unpublished administered a series of reaction-time tests to the 15 deluded schizophrenics, the 15 nondeluded, and the 15 nonschizophrenic patients referred to above. The subjects were required to respond by depressing a morse key to a tone, or one of a group of tones presented at random. These tones all came from the same source, one of a pair of earphones lying on the table. In addition, a series of distracting tones coming from another source, a loudspeaker in the corner of the room, provided distractions, which were varied from none at all to several. In one further condition, "meaningful" distraction was used, consisting of a tape recording of speech and laughter made at a party, played at a volume a little too low to make out exactly what was being said. Again this came from the loudspeaker in the corner of the room.

Table 1 shows the correlations which were obtained between the reaction time, the overinclusion score derived from the Proverbs test, and a retardation score derived from the three of Babcock's simple psychomotor speed tests used by Payne and Hewlett.[24]

TABLE 1.—Correlation between Reaction time, and Overinclusive Thinking and Retardation in a Mixed Psychotic Group

	Simple R.T.		Choice R.T.	
Conditions	*Correlation with Overinclusion*	*Correlation with Retardation*	*Correlation with Overinclusion*	*Correlation with Retardation*
No distraction	.299	.520	.331	.364
Mild distraction	.737	.110	—	—
Moderate distraction	.697	.149	.748	.185
Seveve distraction	.675	.184	—	—
Meaningful distraction	.738	.170	.738	.441

It can be seen that, as expected, both types of thought disorder are significantly associated with a slow reaction time. As one might expect, retardation is the most important determinant of reaction time only when simple reaction time is measured under conditions of no distraction. When distraction is added, overinclusive thinking becomes the more important determinant of slow reaction time.

An attempt was made in this study to minimize all distraction by giving the subjects a reaction-time test in which the stimuli were administered through padded earphones, and all other sounds were thus excluded. Visual stimuli were also excluded by a blindfold. It was though that under these conditions overinclusive patients might speed up. This prediction was not confirmed. The patients became even slower under these conditions. However, many of the patients found this situation very distressing, especially some of the patients who were deluded, and it is possible that these attempts to exclude all external distractions were themselves more distracting than those which were eliminated, because of the worries and fears which were aroused by the experimental conditions. This result was thus thought to be ambiguous.

One unexpected finding was that while overinclusive subjects were clearly very slow in reaction time, they did not get slower as more distractions were added in this experiment. The data suggested that the "mild" distraction consisting of a single, easily distinguished irrelevant tone from another source produced a maximum amount of slowness in the overinclusive patients, so that any further increase in the number of distractors had no further effect. In short, it appeared as if there were a certain "asymptote" of slowness beyond which the patients did not go. This observation has led to the formulation of the following hypothesis which is currently being tested.

It is postulated that the number of different stimuli to which an individual can react correctly in a choice reaction-time experiment involving different responses is limited. The limiting factor is the capacity of the subject's "span of apprehension" or "immediate memory span." This is because he must keep constantly in his memory span the different specific alternative responses to be made. When the data are so numerous that the possible responses exceed the capacity of his memory span, performance is impaired, but not by a further reduction in speed. Instead, information which cannot be held in the memory span is "lost," and incomplete data are processed. This would produce a limit on the amount of slowness which would occur. However, beyond this point, errors would be introduced, and these would increase as the amount of data increased. It is thought that in the experiment described above, overinclusive patients may have been working at this slowness asymptote under the conditions of "mild distraction." The added distractors merely produced more errors. Unfortunately, errors were not recorded in this experiment, and a further experiment will shortly be conducted to test the details of this hypothesis.

One other implication of this hypothesis is that normal people are in fact able to "screen out" stimuli to which they are told not to attend in a reaction time experiment, even if the task itself involves attending to and discriminating between a number of relevant stimuli, and even when the "distractors" are very similar to these "relevant" stimuli. In a complementary study with university summer school students it was demonstrated that this was the case. A group of nine normal subjects found no difficulty in "screening out" irrelevant stimuli, even when they were close to the threshold of their powers of discrimination. The presence and number of such distractions, at least in this pilot study, had no significant effect on reaction time, which was, however, a function of the number of *relevant* stimuli which had to be discriminated. This suggests that in normal people "filtering" can be amazingly effective. Even when the discrimination between that which is to be attended to and that which is to be filtered is very difficult, performance is not impaired.

It was concluded from these experiments that it is still a tenable hypothesis that overinclusive thinking is the cause of the slow and variable reaction times of some schizophrenic patients.

It was the aim of a different study to compare the different effects of distraction in "overinclusive" and "retarded" psychotic patients. In a very small-scale pilot study it was shown that over-inclusive patients were made significantly slower by distraction, as predicted by the theory. They were also variable as expected. Retarded patients, on the other hand, were very slow, but their slowness was not significantly affected by the distractions used. In this respect they were like the normal subjects tested. On the other hand, they showed a distinct and significant tendency to become slower as the experiment progressed, unlike the normals or the overinclusive subjects. It is conceivable that retarded patients are unusually susceptible to the development of some fatigue-like process, and that this may even be a factor in their initial retardation. This hypothesis will be tested further in subsequent experiments with a larger number of cases.

In the experiments planned in this area, it is intended to apply an "information theory" analysis to these reaction-time experiments in order to obtain a quantification of the complexity of the task as it relates to reaction time, and in order to attempt to measure exactly how much irrelevant information is processed by overinclusive subjects, and under what conditions.

The Relationship between Thought Disorder and Perception

The relative inability to screen out "irrelevant" perceptual data could easily result in perceptual symptoms in patients with this disorder. In normal people, perception is in part a process whereby stimulus patterns presented by the environment are simplified, and "irrelevant" details are excluded. Presumably, this results from many years of discrimination learning which has taught us that, in general, only certain common elements of stimulus compounds go together, so that we learn to ignore the sensory data which don't "fit in." If, however, the "filter" which is responsible for this exclusion becomes ineffective, additional sensations would presumably be allowed into consciousness. This must make the world seem unusual or altered in some way, and it is conceivable that the particular perceptual symptom (Wahnstimmung) thought by some authorities to precede the development of delusions in schizophrenic patients, in which the patient feels that his environment has changed in a way which he cannot specify but which is in some way more "meaningful," may represent the patient's awareness of such a percentual change.

It was thought that if such a perceptual change existed, it might best be detected at the threshold of recognition. The apparatus used in the study to be described was a replica of that used by Brengelmann[4] in his picture-recognition test. The subjects are asked to look into an illuminated box through an aperture which is covered by a self-operated tachistoscopic shutter. They are allowed a standard series of exposures starting at 1/200 seconds and increasing in length. The task is merely to say what the picture in the box is. The test consists of a number of pictures exposed in this way. As soon as a subject recognizes a picture correctly, the next card is given. Brengelmann used the test to measure the threshold of recognition. However, it is the case that at shorter speeds than that needed for correct identification of the pictures, normal people sometimes make incorrect guesses. It was predicted that overinclusive subjects would find the pictures much more meaningful than normal people do, when they were presented at speeds too short to allow correct identification. Thus the score taken was merely the total number of incorrect guesses made in a series of pictures presented tachistoscopically, prior to the correct identification of the picture. (The normal response tends to be "I couldn't say.") A mixed group of 43 psychotic patients was tested immediately after admission to hospital prior to the onset of treatment. They received the test already described, and thy were also given the object classification test as a measure of overinclusive thinking. There was found to be a correlation coefficient of .90 between the "incorrect" guesses score and the overinclusive score, a value higher than any found in previous experiments between different tests of overinclusive thinking. This correlation is probably as high as the reliabilities of these particular test scores would allow. This result appeared to support the hypothesis. It would also appear that a simple perceptual test of this sort, which is easy to give to even disturbed patients, may be the most reliable way of measuring this type of thought disorder.

A study is now being conducted to determine whether or not the drug L.S.D. can produce similar results in normal subjects, in both a tachistoscopic perceptual experiment, and on other measures of overinclusive thinking. Some preliminary results suggest that L.S.D. does indeed produce this effect in normal subjects, but precise figures are not yet available.

Overinclusive Thinking and Generalization in Learning

A number of studies which have been reviewed by Payne[18] suggest that when schizophrenics are told to sort objects (e.g.) pictures or words presented on cards) into specific categories, they tend to make errors of overinclusion; that is, they incorrectly include those irrelevant objects which are most similar to the relevant object. It is also known that this tendency can be demonstrated when they are asked to underline all those words (out of a presented group) which they believe to represent an essential part of a concept denoted by a stimulus word. In such experiments it is fairly clear that at the time those concepts (e.g., these words) were initially learned, the patients probably did *not* acquire an overinclusive definition. This overinclusive extension of the boundaries of the concept probably developed much later, along with other symptoms. Earlier studies have not investigated the acquisition of *new* concepts in overinclusive subjects. If overinclusive thinking can be regarded as an unusual amount of stimulus generalization, this should affect the acquisition of new concepts.

To test this hypothesis, the 43 newly admitted psychotic patients described above who had been given a standard test of overinclusive thinking also took part in a concept-learning experiment. The material consisted of two decks of special cards. They were told only that they were to sort the cards into two piles. However, each time they made an error, they were corrected. No two cards contained identical figures, so that the subjects had gradually to *learn* the concept which identified each pile by having a characteristic common to each group of figures consistently reinforced. One set of cards depicted meaningless line diagrams of different shapes and sizes, some shaded and some not. The other set contained pictures of objects. In the latter set, subjects had to learn to sort all the pictures of fruit into the right-hand pile and all the other pictures into the left-hand pile. It was expected that the overinclusive subjects would learn as quickly as normals to discriminate the dissimilar objects (the nonedible objects) but would persist in misclassifying the vegetables with the fruits. The "meaningless" set of cards was similar in that some figures were intentionally made very similar to the "correct" object, while some were easily distinguished. However, in this set of material no single word (previously learned concept) was adequate to describe the category which was being reinforced.

The results of this experiment were clearly contrary to prediction. In this learning situation, there was no significant tendency on either set of cards for overinclusive subjects to make the predicted type of errors. Indeed, no type of error proved to be significantly associated either with overinclusive thinking as measured by the other tests (the Object Classification test, the tachistoscopic test), or with retardation as assessed by simple motor-speed tests.

This surprising finding suggests that perhaps it is a mistake to regard overinclusive thinking as being associated with a *learning* defect. It may be the case that it only develops slowly, and that it only applies to concepts which have been learned for some time. Put another way, it may be that overinclusion does not develop until a very much later stage in the learning process, and that it is some failure of the *maintenance* of the inhibition, which circumscribes and defines concepts, rather than some failure in the initial development of this inhibition.

Studies are now being planned to assess more exactly the relationship between overinclusive thinking and stimulus generalization in both classical conditioning and in learning experiments.

Summary and Conclusions

It is difficult to provide a succinct summary of the experimental results which have been described, since they have already been presented in outline form, omitting the details of the experimental conditions and the numerical data yielded by each particular experiment. It is perhaps more useful to restate the hypotheses which have been suggested by these experiments in very speculative and rather imprecise terms, but in a way which perhaps makes the present ideas slightly clearer.

Overinclusive thinking is basically not a thinking disturbance at all. It is an impairment of some central filtering process whose function it is actively to inhibit external sensations, and internal thoughts which are not relevant to whatever is the focus of attention at a given time. This filter is of crucial importance, because it reduces the number of incoming data to the point at which they can be manipulated within the span of apprehension without losing crucial components. It is only this which makes rational thinking possible. Overinclusion is a relatively rare disorder which is found in at most 50 per cent of a typical sample of acutely ill mental patients who are diagnosed as schizophrenic. It can also be produced in normal people by the use of so-called hallucinogenic drugs such as lycergic acid, L.S.D., and mescaline. It is usually a relatively short-lived condition, which is conceivably the result of some toxic agent. It does not appear to respond to any known drug, but in most cases it clears up with the passage of time in a month or two, so that relatively few patients with this disorder are chronically ill, although relapses may occur. It may first be experienced as a feeling, difficult to verbalize, that things look different, that sensations are more intense than normal, and that things have changed in some way. This may be interpreted by the patient as having some special significance which cannot be specified. Gradually, delusions may develop as a result of complex interactions between the resulting attention defect and the errors of thought which tend to produce unjustified generalizations. These delusions may cause the patient to behave in such a way that the environment itself reacts (becomes hostile, for example), thus reinforcing the belief. Delusions also receive a quite different kind of reinforcement from doctors who by their "ums" and "ahs" may well encourage a patient not only to talk about his false beliefs, but to continue to hold them. In this way it is possible that in some patients the delusions become functionally autonomous and persist long after the overinclusion which gave rise to them has disappeared. Thus a proportion of patients who are initially hospitalized because of overinclusive phenomena remain long after the primary illness has passed. In such patients, an active program of reeducation would seem to be called for.

Retardation, on the other hand, is a much less well understood phenomenon. It characterizes most depressed patients, and at least half those who are labeled schizophrenic. It may not be a unitary phenomenon, perhaps having several quite different causes. However, it appears to be the basis of what has been called "psychoticism" by Eysenck.[11] In schizophrenic patients it may be a relatively bad prognostic sign. It does not seem to respond dramatically to any drugs and seems to characterize most chronic mental patients. Eysenck[12] has hypothesized that it is perhaps the result of an abnormal tendency to develop reactive inhibition, which dissipates extremely slowly, and the studies suggest that the retardation shown by at least some patients might be associated with an unusual build-up of some neurological fatigue process.

REFERENCES

1. Babcock, H.: Time and the Mind. Cambridge, Mass., Sci-Art Publishers, 1941.
2. ——: Dementia Praecox, a Psychological Study. New York, Science Press, 1933.
3. —— and Levy, L.: Manual of Directions for the Revised Examination of the Measurement of Efficiency of Mental Functioning. Chicago, Stoelting, 1940.
4. Brengelmann, J. C.: Validierung des Bilderkennungstestes im Gruppenversuch. Z.f.Diag.Psychol. u.Persönlichkeitsforschung. Vol. 6, No. 1, 1958.
5. ——: Spaltungsfähigkeit als Personlichkeitsmerkmal (Kritischer Literaturbericht). Z.f.d.exp.u.angew.Psychol. 2:455, 1954.
6. Broadbent, D. E.: Perception and Communication. London, Pergamon, 1958.
7. Cameron, N.: Reasoning, regression and communication in schizophrenics. Psychol. Monogr. 50:1-30, 1938.
8. ——: A study of thinking in senile deterioration and schizophrenic disorganization. Amer J. Psychol. 51:650-664, 1938.
9. ——: Deterioration and regression in schizophrenic thinking. J. Abnorm. Soc. Psychol. 34:265-270, 1939.
10. ——: Schizophrenic thinking in a problem-solving situation. J. Ment. Sci. 85:1012-1035, 1939.
11. Eysenck, H. J.: The Scientific Study of Personality. London: Routledge & Kegan Paul, 1952.
12. ——: Reminiscence, drive and personality theory—revision and extension of a theory. Brit. J. Soc. Clin. Psychol. 1:127-140, 1962.
13. Furneaux, W. D.: Manual of Nufferno Speed Tests. London, Nat. Foundation of Educational Research, 1956.
14. Goldstein, K., and Scheerer, M.: Abstract and concrete behaviour. An experimental study with special tests. Psychol. Monogr. 53, No. 2, 1941.
15. Luchins, A. S.: Mechanization in problem solving: the effect of Einstellung. Psychol. Monogr. 54, No. 6, 1942.

16. PAYNE, R. W.: The role of the clinical psychologist at the Institute of Psychiatry. Revue de Psychologie Appliquée, 3:150-160, 1953.
17. ——: Experimentelle Untersuchung zum Spaltungsbegriff von Kretschmer. Z.f.d.exp.u.angew.Psychol. 3:65-97, 1955.
18. ——: Cognitive abnormalities. *In* Handbook of Abnormal Psychology (ed. H. J. Eysenck). New York, Basic Books, 1961.
19. ——: An object classification test as a measure of overinclusive thinking in schizophrenic patients. Brit. J. Soc. Clin. Psychol. 1:213-221, 1962.
20. ——: ANCEVICH, S. S., AND LAVERTY, S. G.: Overinclusive thinking in symptom-free schizophrenics. Canad. Psychiat. Ass. J. 8:225-234, 1963.
21. ——, CAIRD, W. K., AND LAVERTY, S. G.: Overinclusive thinking and delusions in schizophrenic patients. J. Abnorm. Soc. Psychol. 68:562-566, 1944.
22. ——, AND FRIEDLANDER, D.: A short battery of simple tests for measuring overinclusive thinking. J. Ment. Sci. 108:362-367, 1962.
23. ——, FRIEDLANDER, D., LAVERTY, S. G., AND HADEN, P.: Overinclusive thought disorder in hospitalized chronic schizophrenic patients and its response to "Proketazine." Brit J. Psychiat. 109:523-530, 1963.
24. —— AND HEWLETT, J. H. G.: Thought disorder in psychotic patients. *In* Experiments in Personality (ed. H. J. Eysenck). London: Routledge & Kegan Paul, 1960, Vol. II.
25. ——, MATUSSEK, P., AND GEORGE, E. I.: An experimental study of schizophrenic thought disorder. J. Ment. Sci. 105:627-652, 1959.

7

VERBAL BEHAVIOR IN SCHIZOPHRENICS AND SOME COMMENTS TOWARD A THEORY OF SCHIZOPHRENIA*

by KURT SALZINGER, Ph.D.,† STEPHANIE PORTNOY, M.A.,‡ and RICHARD S. FELDMAN, M.A.‡

IF IT IS FAIR TO DESCRIBE the verbal behavior of the schizophrenic patient as following the law of least effort, then we can perhaps best describe the research concerning schizophrenic language as following the laws of least data and most theory.

Over its recognized course of existence, schizophrenia has changed in many respects. It has changed its symptomatology; it has accepted new types of treatment; it has even taken on a new name. Through it all, clinicians have retained the interview as a means for diagnosis, prognosis, determination of type of treatment, and assessment of outcome of treatment.

---

*This study was supported in part by Research Grant MH 07477 from the National Institutes of Health. The speech samples were originally collected in previous studies[33,34,38] supported by Research Grants M 586, M 1541, MY 2785, and M 4842 from the National Institutes of Health. We are indebted to the following people for making groups of subjects available to us: F. Hardesty and G. DeLeon of the City College of New York; A. Niyekawa of Brooklyn College; D. W. Chapman, S. Novak, J. Church, M. Franklin, H. Smith, and L. J. Stone of Vassar College. The hospitalized schizophrenic sample was made available by N. Beckenstein, Director of the Brooklyn State Hospital, A. Glenn, L. Olinger, and M. Portnoy. The hospitalized normal sample was made available by L. C. Kolb, R. Senescu, B. Schoenberg, and J. Oppenheim. We wish to thank C. Osterhout, who gathered and tabulated the data on the reconstruction technique, and G. Smith, B. Rabin, and J. Tanur, who did much of the analysis of the data from all the techniques reported on. Finally, special thanks are due to J. Zubin for his constant interest and assistance in this research.

†Biometrics Research, N.Y. State Department of Mental Hygiene, and Polyclinic Institute of Brooklyn, N.Y.

‡Biometrics Research, N.Y. State Department of Mental Hygiene, and Columbia University, New York, N.Y.

This paper is one of two granted the Henry M. and Lillian Stratton Award for 1964.

Yet, despite the central importance accorded to the verbal behavior of the schizophrenic patient, very little has been done to study that behavior in an objective, quantitative manner in a situation free of contaminating and interacting variables. Our earlier work[32, 34, 36, 38] concentrated on showing that the interviewer influences the verbal output of the schizophrenic patient and does so in a lawful way—that is, in a way to be predicted from our knowledge of behavior theory. We were able to show furthermore that the speed with which the interviewer influence wears off (extinction) is greater for a schizophrenic than for a normal individual.[33] Finally, the rate of conditioning of schizophrenic patients (that is, the degree to which the patient becomes influenced by the interviewer) appears to be a prognostic indicator, with a significantly larger number of high conditioners than low conditioners out of the hospital at the end of a 180-day follow-up period.[36]

Having investigated some of the important parameters of the situation in which the verbal behavior of the schizophrenic patient is typically emitted, we turned our attention to the nature of that behavior itself. The literature describing the language of schizophrenia is large but contains little more than labels, such as paralogical, paleological, concrete, pseudoconcrete, abstract, overinclusive, and egocentric. Quantitative study and objective examination have both constituted the nonpreferred methods of study. To this date the method of choice is that of citing dramatic examples with "interesting" interpretations. Most recently, perhaps, Maria Lorenz[19] suggested "criticism, a technique more familiar in the arts than in the sciences," for the study of schizophrenic speech. Much earlier, we have von Domarus' principle[7] concerning paralogical thinking, and more recently Arieti's[1] idea of paleological thinking, but there has been no attempt to identify the frequency of occurrence of such thinking, whether it refers to incidence within a given patient or incidence in a group of patients. In addition, review of schizophrenic speech samples provides rather little evidence for the universality of such reasoning among schizophrenic patients.

While we have no time to review the literature on schizophrenic language thoroughly, it seems not unfair to summarize it by saying that schizophrenic speech can best be characterized as noncommunicative or hard to understand. In a paper describing one of the few attempts to analyze schizophrenic language by quantitative techniques,[47] this point is made: namely, that the schizophrenic patient has a tendency to maximize his own convenience by minimizing the effort expended to make himself understood. Perhaps the most extreme example of a failure in communication appeared in a recently cited case of "opposite speech,"[18] where the patient regularly exchanged "yes" for "no," "right" for "wrong" and "do" for "don't" in his speech. Ferreira recently called attention to the fact that the schizophrenic patient uses a private language and that he "does so *not to communicate* his thoughts for, in fact, he much fears to be understood"[10] (p. 134). Other evidence for a defect in communication on the part of the schizophrenic patient comes from the area of sorting tests.[28] Although the classical interpretation has been that schizophrenic failure to sort correctly is due to concrete thinking, a more detailed analysis of a sorting task[21] has shown that it is primarily the privacy of the criteria for sorting which results in normal-schizophrenic differences, and thus there is no deficit in abstract ability but rather a loss in social communication.

It is these considerations which give rise to our idea that it would be useful to assess the degree to which a schizophrenic patient communicates with other individuals. It is certainly no accident that the clinician relies on the patient's verbal behavior to learn something about him. Verbal behavior is what most of us engage in most of the time, and thus it is often verbal behavior which brings to the attention of relatives, friends, or legal authorities the fact that the schizophrenic is actually disturbed. Since the impact of the patient's verbal behavior can be assumed at least to contribute to his hospitalization, it seemed to us to be most important to assess the effect of the speech of schizophrenic patients on other people. The effect we decided to study was the degree of communicability.

The idea of assessing looseness of association, or, put even more simply, whether the patient "makes sense" when he talks, is, of course, used by the clinician. In a recent paper[22] an attempt was made to deal directly with the problem of looseness of association. Using the speech samples obtained from schizophrenic patients, the investigators first divided the material into "units of thought" and then observed the number of times an "abnormal shift" appeared between any two units of thought. They defined abnormal shift "as a break in the stream of associations which the scorer judged would not occur in nonpsychotic subjects" (p. 31). We will use indirect techniques for the measurement of breaks in the stream of associations. Rather than ask our scorers whether they can detect abnormal shifts in association—i.e., to make subjective judgments—we have required the scorers to respond to aspects of the speech in such a way that the structure of the speech itself must determine the response, and the complex response of judging degree of disorganization is not necessary.

It might be in order here to say a few words about the relative advantages of using speech to understand better the disease of schizophrenia. Perhaps the most persistent problem faced by the investigator of schizophrenia is that which has gone under the various names of attitude, motivation, cooperation, or involvement in the task set for him, and which can perhaps best be described experimentally as the amount of stimulus control required by the task. Shakow[41] recently reported how apparent differences between schizophrenics and normals were reduced or even completely eliminated when cooperation level was taken into account. It is obvious, for example, that a subject instructed to report the presence or absence of a light stimulus must at the very least be looking in the direction of the light—that is, at a fixation point—in order for the experimenter to make a valid statement about the subject's dark-adaptation curve. Thus, if the subject views the fixation point part of the time only, then the resulting "dark adaptation" curve will be some complex function of the extent to which the subject "cooperates" in viewing the fixation point and the state of the photochemical receptors in the eye. The fact is that many of the differences found between schizophrenics and normals can be ascribed to differences in stimulus control rather than to differences in psychophysical thresholds, learning ability, thought disorder, shallowness of affect, or whatever the investigator is interested in. As a result, many investigators have chosen to train both patients and normals until their behavior has stabilized. Yet what these investigators have overlooked has been the fact that the adult schizophrenic is an individual who has been reinforced for talking for decades and that therefore his verbal behavior has reached a stability unlike that of any new behavior which the experimenter typically has time to introduce by his training methods. Furthermore, a long training procedure may interfere with ongoing projected therapeutic programs or may be interfered with by the patient's changing accessibility to training. Thus we are going to suggest in this paper that the relative stability of verbal behavior makes it ideal for use in studying schizophrenia. It might be noted, by the way, that it is this great stability which has been so useful for shedding light on cases of disputed authorship as early as 1887[25] and as recently as 1963.[4]

In giving these arguments for the use of verbal behavior to provide information on schizophrenia, it is important to point out that these arguments hold only for the case where language is studied as behavior rather than as a report on what the subject "feels" or does. It is to be noted that the experimental psychologist, as well as the clinician, has contributed to the false notion that language must be accepted as information about something else rather than as raw data subject itself to the usual objective techniques of analysis. The psychopathologist interested in the study of complex behavior which he takes great pains to teach his patient (by way of a sorting test, for example) would do much better to study the already present complex behavior called language. By studying it as behavior rather than as report, he also gets around any problem of simulation, where the patient's response is controlled by variables extraneous to the experimental situation and likely to obscure relationships of his pathology.

Another advantage which can be ascribed to the study of verbal behavior in schizophrenic patients stems from the fact that the entire area of verbal behavior has recently undergone great improvement in techniques of study.[40] Perhaps the best evidence for the potential usefulness of our present understanding of verbal behavior in general for gaining insights into pathological processes lies in a recent report of a conference[26] which applied the many different techniques for the study of verbal behavior to the problem of aphasia.

Finally, it is worthwhile to discuss the relative merits of examining production versus perception of speech in schizophrenics. While there have been some interesting studies of perception of speech, it seemed to us again that it would require less cooperation from our patients simply to have them speak than to have them respond in a way that would signify the extent to which they understood a message.

It is for the reasons listed above that we decided to make use of speech samples obtained under conditions requiring only that the subject talk. In one study[15] we compared the rate of repetition of words in schizophrenic and normal speech samples and found that schizophrenic patients tended to use the same words more frequently than normals for passages 900 words in length. This finding can, of course, be viewed as evidence for lower communicability if we follow Whitehorn and Zipf's interpretation.[47] In another study[39] we used the cloze procedure to compare schizophrenic and normal speech samples in ability to communicate and found that normals communicate better than schizophrenics. The cloze procedure is based on the assumption that language is redundant—that is, that successive elements in a sentence contain overlapping bits of information. Thus a person listening to another individual over the telephone can generally understand him even if there are interruptions or disturbances over the line; in other words, he can fill in gaps of information. The cloze procedure, which originated as a measure of readability,[44, 45] involves the following: A given passage of verbal material is mutilated by deleting words systematically and is then given to a group of subjects who are asked to guess these deleted words. Each passage can then be described in terms of the number of words guessed correctly. Taylor[44, 45] suggested this technique to determine which passages are more readable, assuming that those passages whose gaps can be most easily filled are more readable. Since then this technique has been used to investigate statistical approximations to English,[37] the effect of drugs on speech,[16, 35] differences between suicide notes and control letters,[27] the effect of psychotherapeutic interaction on predicting the speech of patients,[8] and finally the nature of aphasic speech.[11]

Two studies so far have employed the cloze technique to test pathology in perception of speech. Honigfeld[17] compared the relative ability of schizophrenic patients to understand normal, psychotic, and pseudo-psychotic speech (i.e., speech under the influence of psilocybin), and Taylor[46] is developing a cloze procedure variant to determine the speed with which schizophrenic patients can fill in the missing words in very simple short sentences.

We added two other techniques for assessing the communicability of schizophrenic speech in an effort to evaluate contingencies between longer units of speech (see ref. 31 for an extended discussion of the problem of unit size) than the cloze procedure is sensitive to. The first of these is what we have called the method of reconstruction and was suggested to us by a study by Becker, Bavelas, and Braden,[3] in which the investigators used subjects' ability to agree on reconstructing a series of sentences presented in random order as a criterion for validating an index of sentence contingency. In view of the fact that our material is oral rather than written, and since there are a number of different ways to divide it into sentences, in some cases only with the help of unusual punctuation, we decided to break the material up into equally long speech segments without any punctuation. As for reconstructability, we have measured both the amount of agreement among subjects reconstructing the passages (as done in the original study) and their agreement with the original order of the passages, since it is conceivable that subjects may agree highly among themselves on an order which is quite different from the original sequence in the speech sample.

The second additional procedure which we employed in this study is what we have called the method of unitization. It stemmed in part from the fact that transcription of speech into written prose is by no means simple. Among the problems which occur in the punctuation of speech is that the many idiosyncratic, incomplete, or ambiguous structures make it very difficult to apply the usual rules reliably. It was our thought that asking groups of subjects to divide unpunctuated speech samples into grammatical sentences and to cross out any words which could not be fitted into such sentences would provide us with additional measures of the communicability of schizophrenic speech. One can hypothesize, for example, that to the extent that schizophrenic speech is less coherent than normal speech, one would have to cross out more words.

Thus, in this study we will explore further the utility of the cloze procedure, particularly by relating it to outcome of illness. We will test out the other two techniques, which are sensitive to structural and semantic coherence and therefore potentially useful for measuring the communicability of schizophrenic speech and its relationship to outcome of illness. The relationship of the reconstruction technique and outcome will be specifically examined. Finally, we shall apply our findings and those of others toward a theory of schizophrenia.

Procedure

Speech Samples and Subjects

The speech samples used in this study were the beginnings of either extended samples of continuous speech obtained by the monologue procedure, which was devised to make interviewer questions unnecessary,[38] or uninterrupted portions of our standardized interviews.[33]

The monologue procedure consists of instructing the patient to begin speaking about the reason for his being hospitalized and to continue talking about any topic he wishes, such as his friends and his hobbies, until told to stop. The interview procedure begins in much the same way, except that general questions are asked whenever the patient is silent for more than two seconds, and unlike the monologue procedure, where the patient and interviewer are separated from each other by a screen, the interview is carried out under face-to-face conditions.

The method of reconstruction was applied to the speech samples of 13 schizophrenic patients (11 acute and 2 chronic) at the Brooklyn State Hospital and 12 nonpsychiatric patients at Presbyterian Hospital, both in New York City. These patients were selected so as to provide 13 schizophrenic-normal pairs (one normal patient was paired with two different schizophrenics) matched for sex, age, formal education, and, where possible, for ethnic group. Background data are summarized in part A of table 1.

The method of unitization utilized speech samples of 10 of the above pairs. Three male acute schizophrenic patients and their matches of

TABLE 1.—Background Information

		Schizophrenic-Normal Comparisons					
		A. Reconstruction			B. Unitization		
		Schizophrenics	*Normals*	*Diff.**	*Schizophrenics*	*Normals*	*Diff.**
N		13 (2 chronic, 11 acute)	12†	—	10 (2 chronic, 8 acute)	9†	—
Sex		2F, 11M	2F, 10M	—	2F, 8M	2F, 7M	—
Age in Yrs.	Range	19-44	18-46	0-16	20-44	18-41	1-8
	Median	33	32	3	32	35	2.5
Yrs. of Formal Educ.	Range	8-16	6-16	0-4	8-16	6-16	0-4
	Median	12	12	0	12	12	0
First Admissions		7	—	—	6	—	—

		Prognosis	
		C. Reconstruction Sample	D. Cloze Procedure Sample
N		*10 Acute Schizophrenics*	*23 Acute Schizophrenics*
Sex		2F, 8M	9F, 14M
Age in Yrs.	Range	20-44	19-44
	Median	37	36.3
Yrs. of Formal Educ.	Range	8-12	8-16
	Median	12	12
First Admissions		4	10

*The ranges are taken over the differences for each pair, and the medians taken for the resulting distributions of differences.

†One male normal was matched with two different schizophrenics.

the above group were not included. Background data are summarized in part B of table 1.

The evaluation of the cloze procedure as a prognostic index was based partly on speech samples of 10 of the 13 schizophrenic patients comprising the method of reconstruction group and described above; the cloze procedure data for these 10 subjects had been collected in a previous study.[39]

Two of the patients (the chronic schizophrenics) were excluded from the prognostic study because they were interviewed 463 and 1365 days after coming to the hospital, while the remaining patients in the sample were interviewed within 14 days of their arrival at the hospital, during which time they had received no drugs or somatotherapy. One acute schizophrenic male patient was transferred to another hospital and his record was not available for follow-up.

In addition to the remaining 10 patients described above, the speech samples of another group of 13 schizophrenic patients were selected. The resultant group of 23 acute schizophrenic patients is described in part D of table 1.

Outcome of illness was determined by counting the number of days that the patient spent in the hospital within the 180-day period immediately following the current admission; if the patient left and returned within this period, days of hospitalization were cumulated. The number of days in the hospital ranged from 22 to 180, with a median of 101 days.

Description of Methods of Evaluation of Communicability

Method of Reconstruction. The first 200 words of each speech sample, preceding any reinforcement periods or interviewer utterances except, of course, the initial instructions, were divided into 10 successive 20-word segments and typed on 2 by 6 inch white cards in two lines of 10 words each (whenever space permitted) without any punctuation. All subjects in this experiment were college students and native speakers of English and were paid for their time. Each was tested individually and was given the following instructions:

> I am going to place before you a series of cards. On each card there is a segment of speech selected from tape-recorded samples of the continuous speech of one person. The segments are now in scrambled order. You are to read them carefully and rearrange them into the order in which they were originally spoken. Put the first card with the typed material facing up beside the number 1, the next beside the number 2 and so on. When in their correct

> order, the segments will form a continuous, uninterrupted excerpt from the speech of one person.
>
> You will have up to three minutes to sort these cards. Although I am not primarily interested in the time it takes you, I will record the time. Do you have any questions?

After the subject had ordered the speech segments of one person, he was given another set and told to perform the same task. Twenty subjects ordered the speech segments of seven schizophrenic patients and their normal matches and another group of 20 subjects ordered the speech segments of the six other schizophrenic patients and their matches. None of the subjects was told that any of the speech samples came from schizophrenic patients. Both the order of segments within a speech sample and the order of the speech samples themselves were randomized.

Cloze Procedure. The initial section of each speech sample, preceding any reinforcement periods or interviewer utterances except, of course, the initial instructions, was mimeographed on a separate page, without any punctuation and with every 5th word deleted (except numbers and proper nouns) and a blank substituted, for a total of 40 blanks per passage. Wherever the fifth word was a number or proper noun, the next word was deleted. The corresponding number of words was added to the passage so that there were always forty blanks with 4 words following the last blank. This resulted in the actual passage lengths for the normals ranging from 204 to 212 words, with a median of 206. For the schizophrenics the range was 204 to 213 words, with a median of 205. The passages were then distributed to groups of college students, all native speakers of English, who were told that they were being given samples of continuous speech and that they were to fill in each blank with whatever single word they thought belonged there.

Ten speech samples were presented to the subjects in groups of four passages containing two schizophrenic-normal pairs. There were 17 completed cloze forms for one patient, 16 for four patients, 15 for four patients, and 30 for one patient. Thirteen of the speech samples were given to the subjects in groups of four patients. Of these, there were 14 completed cloze forms for two patients, 16 for six patients, 17 for two patients, and 18 for three patients.

Unitization Procedure. The passages on which the cloze procedure was based were mimeographed and distributed to college students, all native speakers of English, who were tested in groups. They were given the following instructions:

> On the following pages you will find the verbatim typescripts of tape-recorded speech samples. Each page is taken from the speech of a different person. We know that most people do not always speak in perfect, grammatical sentences, but instead speak with some repetitions, incomplete sentences, corrections of words spoken just previously, etc. Some speech has very little of this; some has quite a bit.
>
> Your task is to divide the following speech samples into complete grammatical sentences in the best way you can. The only change you may make is to *cross out* words. You may not add or change words or rearrange the words already present. Indicate the sentences by enclosing them in parentheses. Indicate the words to be eliminated by drawing a line through them.

Seven pairs of speech samples were presented in sets of 2—i.e., one patient and his normal match. There were five pairs of passages unitized by 17 subjects, one pair unitized by 18, and one pair unitized by 19. Three pairs of speech samples were administered in sets of 4—i.e., two patients and their normal matches. Fifteen subjects unitized one pair and 16 the two remaining pairs of passages.

Results and Discussion

Schizophrenic—Normal Comparisons

Method of Reconstruction. These data were analyzed in terms of five different measures:

1. Kendall's coefficient of concordance, W,[42] was used to measure the amount of agreement among the subjects' orderings of the 10 speech segments, thus giving us a measure of general contextual constraint.

2. Spearman's rank order correlation coefficient, rho,[42] was employed to measure the amount of agreement between the subjects' orderings and the order in which the segments were actually emitted by the speaker, thus providing us with a measure of the communicability of the different speech samples.

3. A sequence error score was constructed to measure the extent to which each subject ordered successive pairs of speech segments the way the speaker emitted them, thus giving us another measure of communicability. The score itself consists of the number of pairs placed in an order different from the spoken one and thus can vary from 0 to 9 for each subject.

Two additional error scores were obtained separately for the first half and the last half of each speech sample by counting the number of incorrectly ordered pairs for cards 2-5 and cards 6-9. The first and last cards were omitted from this analysis, so that all cards of each set had surrounding context in the original speech.

4. A sequence error agreement score was devised in order to measure the extent to which subjects agreed on the same incorrect sequences. Presumably, if subjects agree on an order which is at variance with the spoken order, then these results would indicate not only that there is a general fault in communicability, but that the structure is consistently misleading to the hearer. The score is based on the ratio of the number of different incorrect segments placed immediately preceding a given segment to the total number of such incorrect pairings. The resulting ratios, except those where either one or no error was made, were averaged across cards to yield the final ratio for that speech sample.

5. Mean log time to complete the reconstruction task was taken as a measure of the degree of difficulty in ordering the speech segments, and we assume that such difficulty is another aspect of communicability. It was measured from the time the subject was first exposed to the segments to the time he indicated that he was finished with them.

The first point that can be made about the coefficients of concordance in fig. 1 is that all but one of them are statistically significant at the .05 level (two-tail) or better (X^2 test for significance[42]; the only exception is one schizophrenic patient's speech sample which just misses reaching significance. The result is, of course, evidence for the fact that any English language sample, even a schizophrenic sample, exerts enough contextual constraint to produce a great deal of agreement among a group of English speaking subjects. Furthermore, the rank order correlations (fig. 1) are all quite high, showing again that the structure of English is such that speech can withstand a good deal of mutilation (in this case segmentation) and still be restorable to the order in which it was emitted.

Fig. 1 also allows us to compare performance on the normal and schizophrenic speech samples. Nine of the 13 pairs of speech samples show a greater amount of agreement for the normal than for the schizophrenic (there is no statistical test for the significance of the difference between two W's). It is noteworthy that both female speech samples go in a direction opposite to the majority of the group. The small size of the sample prohibits our making any conclusions about sex differences, however. As far as restoring the original order is con-

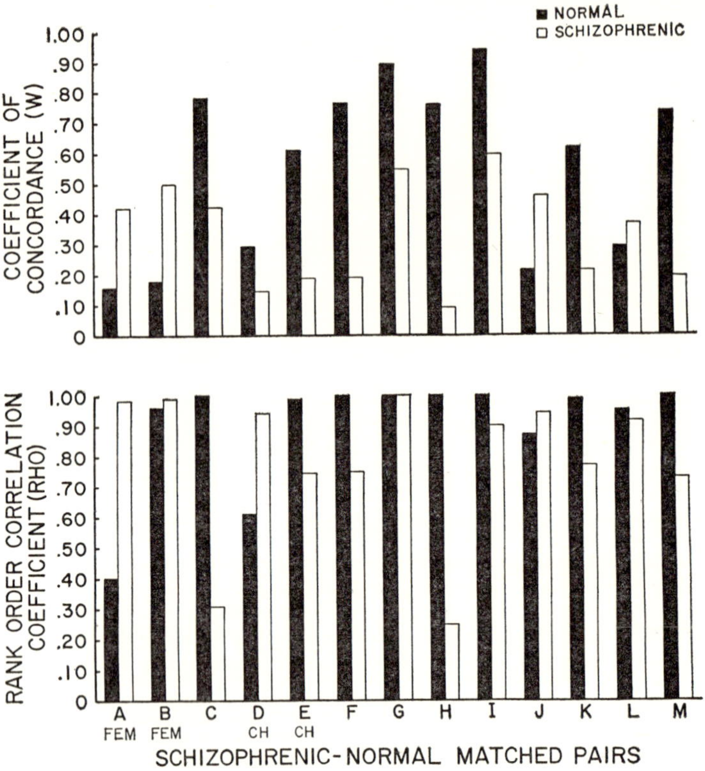

FIG. 1.—Reconstruction technique. *Top:* Kendall's coefficient of concordance for agreement among subjects' orderings of normal and schizophrenic speech segments. *Bottom:* Rank order correlation coefficients between subjects' orderings of normal and schizophrenic speech segments and the order of the segments in the original speech. Results on each measure are shown separately for each schizophrenic-normal matched pair. Pairs A and B are females; pairs D and E each include a chronic schizophrenic.

cerned, the rank order correlation coefficients show that subjects have greater ability to restore the original order of the normal than of the schizophrenic speech samples in eight of the matched pairs, that they are equally able to restore the order in one pair, and that they show greater ability to restore the schizophrenic speech sample in four pairs. Again, both female pairs go in a direction opposite to the majority of the group. It is to be noted that the rank order correlation coefficient as used here was based on the ordering given by the subjects as a group, thus allowing for the cancellation of idiosyncratic errors in ordering and resulting in the relatively high positive relationship between subject and speaker order.

Although there is no statistical test for the significance of the difference between two Spearman rank order correlation coefficients, we used the parametric equivalent to give us some notion of significance. Of the eight pairs for which R_s is higher for the normal speech, seven are significant at the .002 level or better and one is above .05; of the four pairs for which R_s is higher for the schizophrenic speech, two are significant at the .02 level or better and two are above .05 (all one-tail tests). We made use of the sequence error score in order to take into account each individual's deviation from the speaker's order.

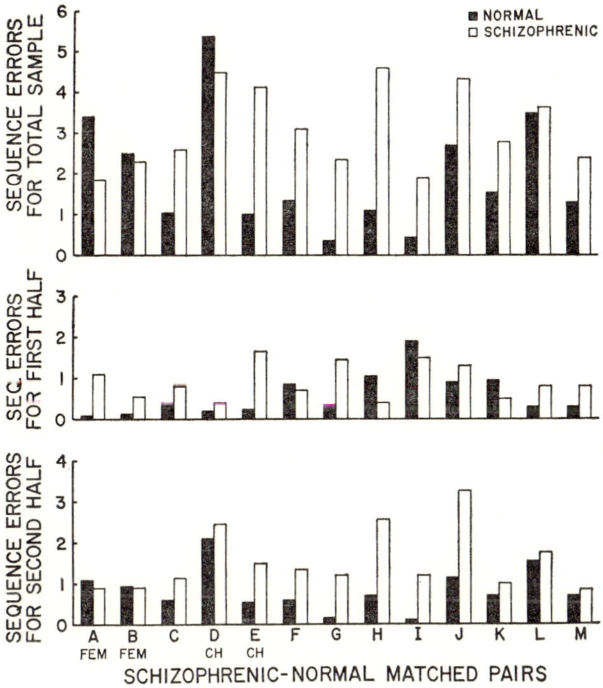

FIG. 2.—Reconstruction technique. Sequence errors in subjects' orderings of segments of normal and schizophrenic speech for the total sample (top), the first half of each sample only (middle), and the second half of each sample only (bottom). Results on each measure are shown separately for each schizophrenic-normal matched pair. Pairs A and B are females; pairs D and E each include a chronic schizophrenic.

Inspection of fig. 2 shows 10 of the 13 pairs to have more errors on the schizophrenic than the normal speech samples, and again both female pairs are opposite in direction to the majority of the group. (Nine of the 10 show a significant difference by the matched pairs signed ranks test at .04 and better; the other one has a $p = .46$. Of the three others, only one is significant at .001; the others have p's

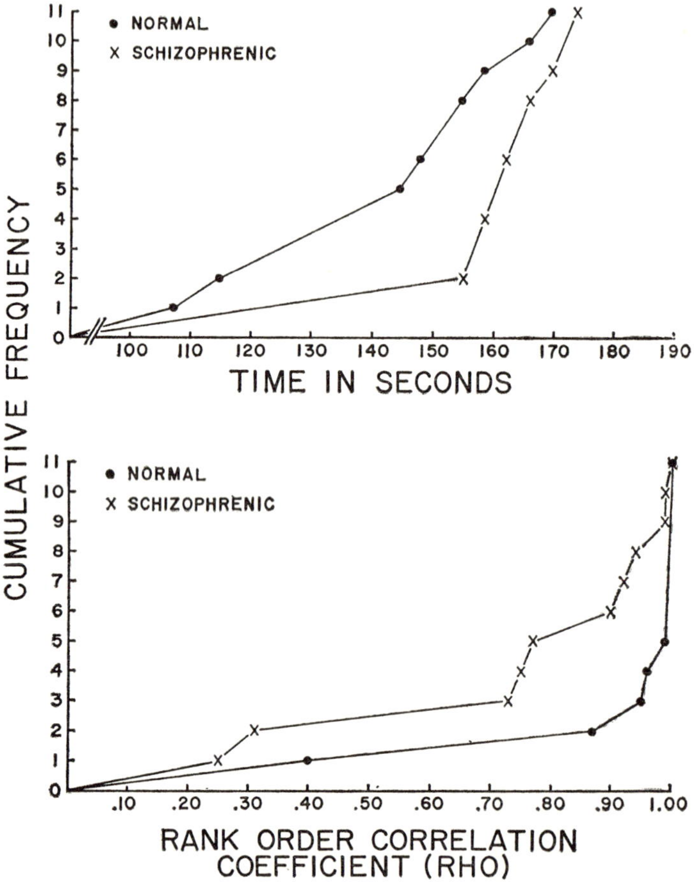

FIG. 3A.—Reconstruction technique. *Top:* Cumulative frequency distributions of time taken by subjects to complete the reconstruction of samples of normal and schizophrenic speech. Each point is a geometric mean of the subjects' reconstruction times for a given speech sample. *Bottom:* Cumulative frequency distributions of rank order correlation coefficients between subjects' orderings of normal and schizophrenic speech segments and the orders of the segments in the original speech.

of .17 and .25; all are one-tail tests.) Thus, this score yields a stronger indication of difficulty in communicability of schizophrenic speech than the scores dealt with above. The sequence error score has another advantage: it can be broken down into scores for first and second halves of each speech sample. A previous study[39] on the cloze procedure indicated not only a difference between the communicability of schizophrenic and normal speech samples, but also that the second half of the speech samples differentiated the groups better than the first. Inspection of fig. 2 shows a similar finding for the reconstruction technique. Cards 2-5 of the speech sample show that nine schizo-

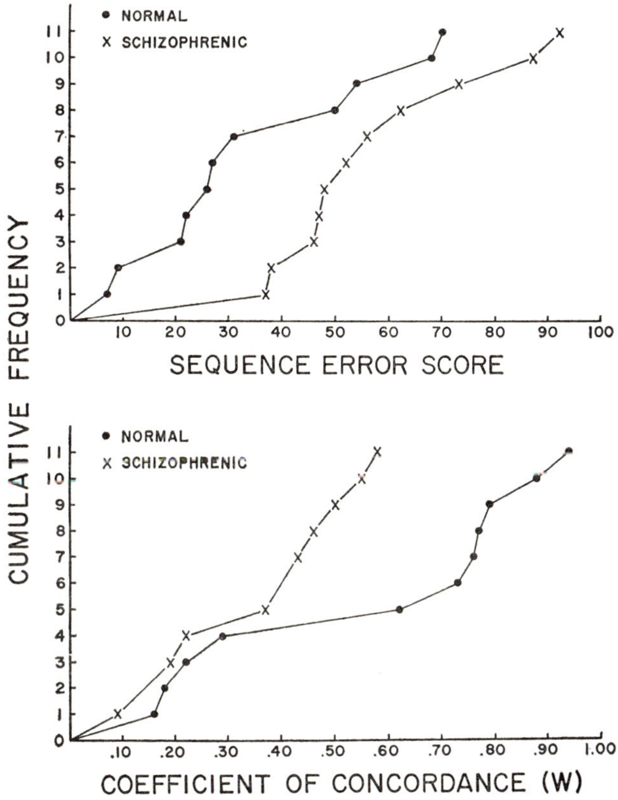

FIG. 3B.—Reconstruction technique. *Top:* Cumulative frequency distributions of sequence error scores for subjects' orderings of normal and schizophrenic speech segments. *Bottom:* Cumulative frequency distributions of Kendall's coefficient of concordance for agreement among subjects' orderings of normal and schizophrenic speech segments.

phrenic members have more sequence errors than the normals, while cards 6-9 indicate that 11 schizophrenic members have more sequence errors than the normals; and this time, only the two female pairs yield results opposing the rest of the group. Thus we have more evidence for the notion that the schizophrenic patients' speech communicates less as their responses come to depend more and more on their own previous responses and are guided less and less by external stimuli, such as instructions or the interviewer's questions.

Despite our matching procedure, we thought it might be worthwhile to examine the data for the group as a whole. In view of the fact that we were dealing with a comparison of groups, we omitted from consideration the two chronic patients (and their matches) who were interviewed as indicated above after having spent a long time in the hospital, rather than a few days after admission as was true for the other patients. The cumulative frequency distribution of the coefficients of concordance (fig. 3B) shows a rather interesting result. From a W score of 0 to about .30 there is an equal likelihood that a given individual will be a normal or a schizophrenic. Between .30 and .60 the probability appears to be 0 that such an individual will be normal and 1.00 that he is a schizophrenic patient. Finally, should an individual's speech sample result in W scores above .60, then the probability appears to be 1.00 that he is normal and 0 that he is schizophrenic. The small size of the sample, however, prevents us from recommending it as a diagnostic aid. Nevertheless, these findings do suggest that schizophrenic speech leads to a medium amount of agreement in the reconstruction task—i.e., that on the whole communicability of schizophrenic speech is poorer than that of most normal speech but in the majority of cases better than the poorest normal speech.

The cumulative frequency distribution of the rank order correlation coefficients (fig. 3A) shows, as did the comparison in pairs, that most speech samples, whether normal or schizophrenic, result in rather high correlations between group ordering and the order in which the segments were originally emitted. Nevertheless, one can see that six normal speech samples give rise to correlations of 1.00 and only one schizophrenic speech sample does as well; furthermore, five schizophrenic speech samples produce correlations of .80 or less, while only one normal speech sample does as poorly. Again the score suggests itself as a possible diagnostic index.

Finally, inspection of the cumulative distribution of the sequence errors (fig. 3B) shows that seven normals have scores below 32 while no schizophrenics do.

The sequence error agreement score showed, for nine of the 13 pairs, that when the subjects placed normal speech segments in the incorrect order, they were more apt to agree on this order than when they placed schizophrenic speech segments in the incorrect order, thus suggesting that normal speech samples exert greater contextual constraint than schizophrenic speech samples, even when the constraint produces an order differing from that of the speaker. Since only eight of the 13 pairs yielded this result, and since this score cannot, unlike the other scores above, be evaluated statistically (each patient-normal pair giving rise to only one score), these results must be viewed with caution.

The time it takes the subjects to order the speech segments constitutes the last measure on the reconstruction task. All but one of the patient-normal pairs showed that it took longer to reconstruct the schizophrenic speech sample than the normal speech sample (see fig. 4). The one exception is again one of the female pairs. Matched pairs signed ranks tests (performed on log seconds) were used to assess the significance of the difference for each pair. The one exception to the general trend was not significant ($p = .13$). The 12 pairs which went in the predicted direction had the following

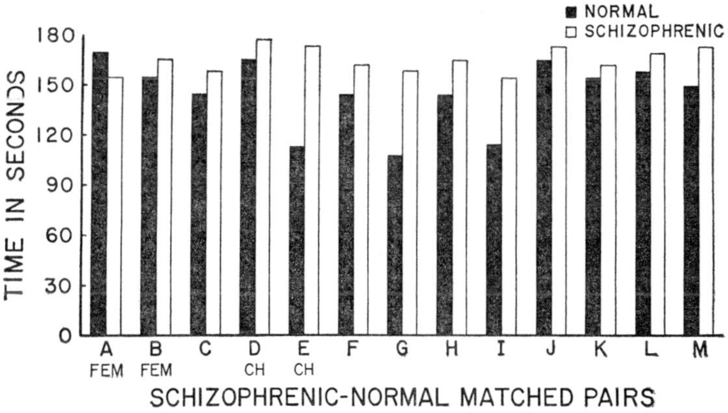

FIG. 4—Reconstruction technique. Time (geometric mean of subjects' reconstruction times for a given speech sample) taken by subjects to complete the reconstruction of samples of normal and schizophrenic speech. Results are shown separately for each schizophrenic-normal matched pair. Pairs A and B are females; pairs D and E each include a chronic schizophrenic.

one-tail p levels: four matches, p = .001; two matches, p = .004; and one each of .005, .02, .06, .07, .09, and .13. Thus again, and perhaps most clearly, we have an indication of a deficit in communicability of schizophrenic speech.

In summary, one can conclude on the basis of the method of

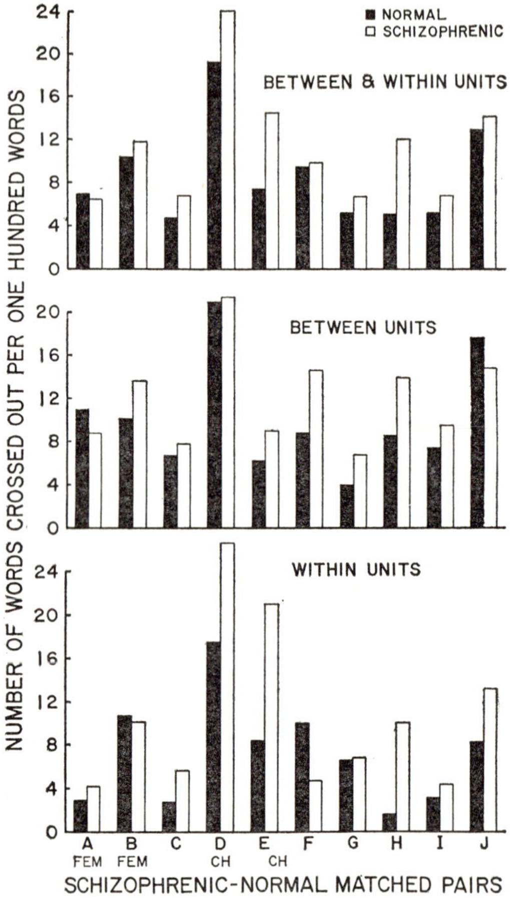

FIG. 5.— Unitization technique. *Top:* Total number of words (between and within units) which subjects crossed out per 100 words of the speech sample. *Middle:* Number of words crossed out between units only, per 100 words of the speech sample. *Bottom:* Number of words crossed out within units only, per 100 words of the speech sample. Results on each measure are shown separately for each schizophrenic-normal matched pair. Pairs A and B are females; pairs D and E each include a chronic schizophrenic.

reconstruction that there is less ability to communicate in schizophrenic than in normal speech, whether one considers short units as in the cloze procedure[39] or long units as in the reconstruction technique. Differences in the kinds of information yielded by the two techniques will be considered later.

Method of Unitization. These data were analyzed in terms of the following measures:

1. Number of units (sentences) per 100 words of text
2. Number of words per unit
3. Number of words crossed out per 100 words of text:
   a—between units
   b—within units
   c—total

The first two measures—namely, number of units and length of unit—do not differentiate normals from schizophrenics, p levels being considerably larger than .05 on the basis of matched pairs signed ranks tests applied to the 10 matched pairs. On the other hand, the number of words crossed out because they cannot be fitted into units does differentiate between the schizophrenic and normal subjects (see fig. 5) with one-tail p levels of .05, .03, and .005 for the difference in number of words crossed out respectively between units, within units, and between plus within units. Furthermore, comparisons made separately between members of each pair show for the most part highly significant p levels. These results also indicate that most words to be crossed out occur between units but that the total number of words crossed out discriminates best.

In summary, schizophrenic speech is characterized by having a larger number of intrusions (as measured by number of words crossed out) than normal speech; this result suggests that the greater difficulty in filling in the cloze procedure blanks of schizophrenic speech samples stems at least in part from words which cannot be related to the surrounding speech even when they are actually supplied to the "listener" and which therefore would certainly be very difficult to predict. Such a finding is consistent with the study by Sommer, Dewar and Osmond,[43] who found that schizophrenics emit less common associates in a word association test than normals do, but goes beyond their finding to suggest that schizophrenic speech contains more words not related at all to their context.

Speech Rate. The length of time the original speakers took to emit the speech samples used for the method of reconstruction above was measured.

A matched pairs signed ranks test applied to the above 13 pairs (and including one normal twice who was matched to a chronic and to an acute schizophrenic patient) showed the patients to speak significantly more slowly ($p < .001$, two-tail). This significant difference remained ($p < .02$, two-tail) when the two chronic patients and their matches were eliminated (in which case each normal is included only once). Goldman-Eisler[12] has already demonstrated that most of the variation in speed of talking can be accounted for in terms of pauses between words rather than in terms of time spent in vocalization, and she also showed[13] that an increase in pause length before a word

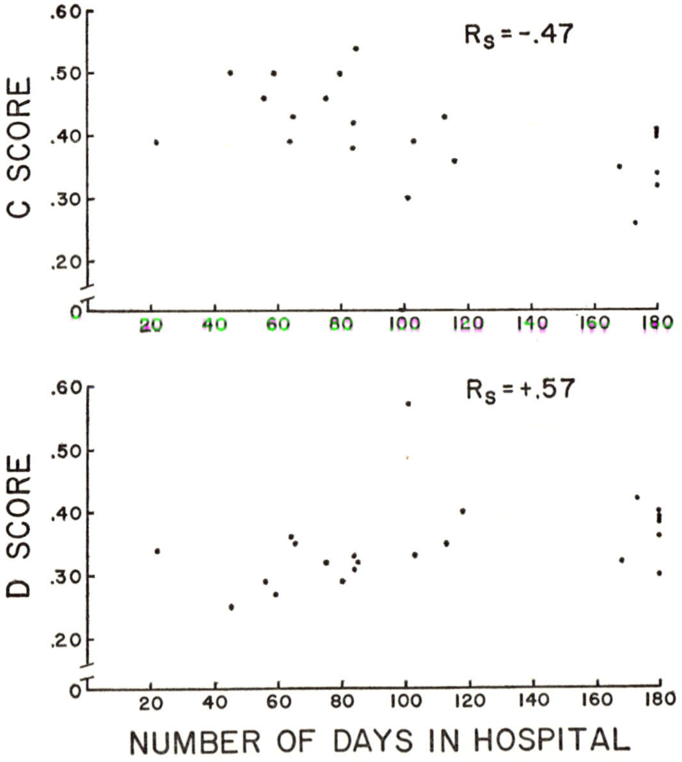

FIG. 6.—Rank order correlation scatter diagrams relating cloze procedure scores to outcome of illness (as measured by number of days in hospital during 180-day follow-up period) for 23 acute schizophrenic patients. The correlation is —.47 with C score (top) and +.57 with D score (bottom).

indicates an increase in information. Translated into the terms of our cloze procedure it means a smaller number of correct guesses of a deleted word after a long pause, and it therefore constitutes still more evidence for difficulty in schizophrenic communication. This led us to compute a rank order correlation between length of time to emit 200 words for the 23 schizophrenics for whom we have cloze procedure data and their cloze procedure scores. The correlation was —.42 ($.01<p<.05$, one-tail), thus verifying our hypothesis that slower speech will produce difficulty in communicability. In another study in our laboratory we examined the effect of chlorpromazine on speech rate as well as on the predictability of speech,[35] and we found a reduction in both speech rate and in cloze score—i.e., in communicability as a function of increasing dosage. Finally, Feldstein and Jaffe[9] found a larger number of filled pauses in schizophrenic than in normal speech as well as a positive relationship between irrelevant elements in speech and the proportion of filled pauses.

Communicability and Outcome of Illness

Another way of testing the utility of our measures of speech disorganization is to relate them to outcome of illness with an eye to employing them as prognostic indexes.

Cloze Procedure. Two cloze procedure scores were used and are more fully described by Salzinger, Portnoy and Feldman.[39]

1. The C score consisted of the proportion of correct guesses out of total guesses made. A correct guess was one which matched the deleted word exactly.

2. The D score consisted of the proportion of all incorrect guessed words which were different from each other.

The rank order correlation of the C score and outcome (see procedure section) was —.47 ($.01<p<.05$, one-tail); the data are plotted in fig. 6. Thus the better a patient communicates, the shorter his stay in the hospital. When relating outcome to the C score based on the first 100 words only, however, the rank order correlation was —.29 ($p>.05$, one-tail); for the second 100 words it was —.48 ($.01<p<.05$, one-tail). Thus, as in our previous study[30] on the cloze procedure and schizophrenic-normal differences, when the patient is further removed from the external stimuli and has to rely more and more on what he himself produces as stimuli for further speech, more of his pathology appears (there are larger differences between normals and schizophrenics and therefore his speech becomes better related to outcome of illness.

The rank order correlation between the D score and outcome is +.57 ($p<.01$, one-tail) and the data are plotted in fig. 6. Thus we find that the greater the D score (the less the contextual constraint as measured by agreement on the incorrect responses), the longer the stay in the hospital and, one may assume, the more seriously ill the patient. The correlation of the D score for the first 100 words with outcome is +.41 ($.01<p<.05$, one-tail), and like that for the C score is higher for the second than for the first 100 words (+.53, $p<.01$, one-tail). It is interesting to note that while the D score does not differentiate normals from schizophrenics, it does seem to differentiate degrees of psychopathology. The interesting question presents itself as to whether the D scores on the normals might serve as predictors of psychopathology in normal individuals.

Method of Reconstruction. Correlations between outcome of illness and the following variables were all quite low and nonsignificant ($p>.05$, one-tail): time to complete the reconstruction task, W, and the rank order correlations between the subjects' ordering and the original speaker's ordering. However, the sequence error score yielded a rho of +.66 ($.01<p<.05$, one-tail), indicating that the more difficult the subjects found it to order the speech segments, the longer those patients stayed in the hospital (see fig. 7). In addition, we find again that the relationship is much clearer for the second than for the first 100 words; the correlation is +.21 ($p>.05$, one-tail) for the first half of the speech sample, but +.88 ($p<.01$, one-tail) for the second half.

The sequence error agreement score (see fig. 7) correlated —.74 ($p = .01$, one-tail) with number of days spent in the hospital, indicating that the less the agreement on reconstructing incorrect orders of the speech segments (the greater the sequence error agreement score), the shorter the stay in the hospital. This seems at first to contradict the results on the D score in the cloze procedure, which showed a high positive correlation with number of days spent in the hospital. The explanation must lie in the different lengths of the units involved in the two techniques and the effects of different kinds of errors in producing important changes in the passages. Since the method of reconstruction deals with larger units, with each incorrectly placed speech segment involving 20 words or 10 per cent of the sample and each cloze procedure error involving only about

.5 per cent of the sample, agreement on its errors reveals in addition to high contextual constraint significant misunderstanding of the speech sample. Even though relatively high agreement on errors in the cloze procedure is associated with a short stay in the hospital because it shows integrity of the speech sample, such agreement in the method of reconstruction is associated with a long period of hospitalization because it shows gross misunderstanding of schizophrenic speech. In view of this explanation it is not surprising that the W score correlated +.02 with stay in the hospital, since it incorporates in one score the contextual constraint which leads to correct

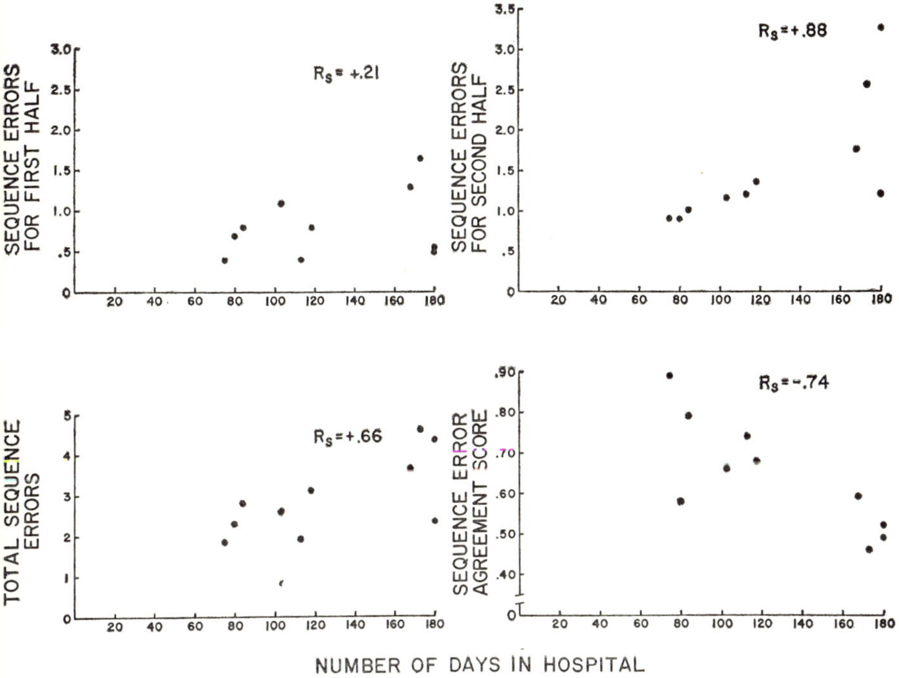

Fig. 7.—Rank order correlation scatter diagrams relating reconstruction technique scores to outcome of illness (as measured by number of days in hospital during 180-day follow-up period) for 10 acute schizophrenic patients. The correlation is +.21 with sequence errors in reconstructing the first half of each speech sample (top left), +.88 with sequence errors for the second half (top right), +.66 for sequence errors in reconstructing the total sample (bottom left) and —.74 for the sequence error agreement score among subjects reconstructing the total sample (bottom right).

as well as to incorrect responses, the two types of constraints being opposite in effect as far as communicability is concerned.

Since we could follow up only eight schizophrenic patients on the unitization technique, we decided to await a larger sample before testing the relationship of its measures to outcome.

Interrelationship of the Three Measures of Aspects of Communicability

Final conclusions on the interrelationship of the three techniques will have to await empirical correlations. Some comments on the theoretical relationships are, however, in order. The cloze procedure appears to us to be the most comprehensive way of measuring communicability since both the semantic and the syntactic properties of the speech sample would seem to determine the cloze score; it appears to be the most direct way of measuring communicability since the respondent must supply the correct word in order to demonstrate his understanding of the speech sample. The other two techniques appear to concentrate more on ways of describing the structure of the speech samples and appealed to us primarily as determinants of communicability rather than as overall measures of communicability. Thus one can conceive of a passage which might be almost completely incomprehensible semantically and yet one which, because of good syntactic structure, could be reconstructed easily.

Only the intrusions—that is, the words which subjects cross out in the unitization technique—seem close to a direct measure of communicability, but even these need not reduce communicability drastically as in the case of words repeated immediately. It appears that both the nature of the speech samples as measured by the techniques of unitization and reconstruction, and their communicability as measured by the cloze procedure, relate to psychopathology. The actual degree of independence of these techniques will be investigated in a later paper.

Some Comments Toward a Theory of Schizophrenia

Our findings probably do not serve as a source of embarrassment to any of the leading theories of schizophrenia presently extant. Mednick,[23, 24] for example, has suggested in his theory of schizophrenia that the greater anxiety, or what he now terms the greater arousal level, to be found at least in the beginning of schizophrenia is associated with greater stimulus generalization and a tendency to make responses which avoid further anxiety, with the result that the schizophrenic patient will "experience atypical thought sequences and tangential intrusions into his stream of ideation"[24] (p. 172). He goes on to suggest that remote associations are more likely to be positively reinforced than are close associations because they result in a drop in anxiety and so are drive-reducing. Our data are certainly not in conflict with the predictions of such a theory, although we may not agree with the usefulness of a concept like drive reduction. The theory of the "double-bind"[2] suggests that the only way in which the schizophrenic patient can extricate himself from the double-bind is to make what we like to call avoidance responses. These investigators have pointed out that the patient makes utterances which are rich in metaphor, that the patient is unaware of speaking in metaphors, and that this is one of the methods which he has learned in order to escape from and respond to the double-bind situation. The schizophrenogenic mother sets up a conflict in which she punishes him for his behavior (no matter what it is) but does not allow him to react to her as a source of punishment. Furthermore, our results appear to agree, at least in general outline, with the idea of some language difficulty as suggested by Arieti,[1] or Goldstein.[14] These theories do not, however, explain some other findings in the literature about differences between normals and schizophrenics. Among these are differences in psychophysical tasks. An experiment by Lovinger,[20] to take but one example, has shown that schizophrenic patients in poor contact show less object constancy than do normals. The schizophrenic patients react to the immediate stimuli which impinge upon them. In this particular experiment the subjects seem to react to the visual angle on the retina, rather than to their experience which should have made the distance factor and the visual angle influence their judgment. Object constancy is, after all, an important aspect of a person's experience. An individual who stands on top of the Empire State Building and who is asked to judge the height of a person down below, even though the visual angle would be very tiny indeed, would not judge the height of a human being as one inch but would instead judge this individual to be approximately five feet. In other words, a normal individual reacts not only to the immediate stimuli that impinge upon him but reacts to the immediate stimuli plus the history surrounding these particular stimuli. That the schizophrenic patient has a tendency to be ahistorical is a finding which has been in the literature for a while. In one of our own experiments, for example,[33] we found that schizophrenic patients extinguish faster than do normals. This finding has been confirmed in experiments by

Rickard, Dignam, and Horner,[29] who found rapid extinction during minimal reinforcement periods, and by Dinoff, Horner, Kurpiewski, and Timmons,[6] who found rapid extinction when reinforcement was withheld. In other words, the schizophrenic patient reacts immediately to the cessation of reinforcement. The schizophrenic patient acts as if there had been no previous conditioning or relatively little conditioning before extinction had set in, while the normal individual accounts for his history in his subsequent behavior. In still another experiment done in our laboratory,[30] it was demonstrated that the schizophrenic patient, in a task of absolute judgment, had a tendency to react to the immediate effect of an anchor rather than to the instruction which preceded the anchor and which told him to take the effect of the anchor weight into account. The normal individuals, on the other hand, were able to so adjust their judgments of the weights that they compensated for the effect of the anchor. Again, we have evidence here that the schizophrenic patient reacts to the immediately effective stimuli rather than to past stimuli.

For a long time now investigators of schizophrenia have pointed out that schizophrenics have a tendency to react to such extraneous stimuli as the amount of dirt on cards used for sorting tasks, rather than to the design to which they were instructed to react. It was Chapman[5] who showed by means of an experiment that schizophrenic patients have a greater tendency to react to distracting stimuli on cards on a sorting task than do normal individuals. Again our interpretation is that schizophrenic patients react to those stimuli which are immediately present. In fact, they react to them in a way which is not selective. It is for this reason that Chapman found that schizophrenic patients' performances became worse as the number of distracting stimuli increased. This was not true for the normal control group used in Chapman's experiment.

The question might be asked, "How does all this relate to language?" One of the most important aspects of language is the fact that a speaker in emitting his words must react not only to the word he has just uttered but to the last two words, the last three words, and usually to many words he has uttered previously. One would then expect that an individual who is unable to react to stimuli remote either in time or in space would have difficulty in making himself understood. This is, in fact, what we have found. We might also remind the reader of another study done in our laboratory,[15] where we found that schizophrenic patients tended to repeat their words as well as sequences of words over shorter intervals than did normal individuals. Interestingly enough, a study by Yavuz[48] has demonstrated a tendency of schizophrenics to repeat bigrams, in a letter-listing task, more frequently than normals. Again this seems to give evidence for the notion that schizophrenic patients have difficulty in reacting to stimuli which are not immediate. Thus we are suggesting that what looks like thought disorder might more generally be viewed as a prepotency of immediate stimuli over remote stimuli.

The schizophrenic patient's hallucinatory behavior can perhaps also be explained in terms of the effect of immediate stimuli. In the absence of any external stimulation powerful enough to capture his attention, his thoughts become the "voices" which control his behavior.

If one accepts the notion that a schizophrenic patient reacts prepotently to immediate stimuli, then this has a number of implications about treatment. One clear implication, for example, is that one has to use stimuli which are powerful and which are immediate, if one is interested in controlling the behavior of a schizophrenic patient. This is really not a surprising remark for any person who has ever worked with schizophrenics. All but the most disturbed patients can be gotten to pay attention as long as one tries hard enough with sufficiently powerful stimuli. Thus, if one wants to control the behavior of a schizophrenic patient, one would probably have to use such immediate stimuli all of the time in order to be able to restrain the patient from his psychopathological behavior and allow normal behavior to occur. Presumably, if the reinforcing stimuli could also be very powerful after the normal or more nearly normal behavior is emitted, this would then be a potential technique for modifying the behavior of the schizophrenic patient so that eventually he may not have to depend upon powerful immediate external stimulation. In regard to this, we might consider the possibility that tranquillizers may work against this approach by lowering the patient's reactivity to any external stimulation. Salzinger, Pisoni, Feldman, and Bacon[35] have already collected data supporting the hypothesis that chlorpromazine reduces the amount of control exerted by reinforcement.

Finally, one ought to consider the possibility that the reason the schizophrenic patient is quite so difficult to treat successfully is that he is basically ahistorical, and that if this be true, then schizophrenic patients must be people who should be exposed to such powerful immediate external stimulation all of the time, in order to keep them going along as normal individuals.

Summary

In this chapter we presented three objective techniques for the assessment of communicability of schizophrenic speech, examined their ability to distinguish normal from schizophrenic language (as possible diagnostic measures), and related them to degree of psychopathology within the schizophrenic group (as a possible prognostic index). The first assessment technique, the method of reconstruction, consists of having normal subjects put randomized speech segments into the order in which they think the speaker uttered them. The second technique, the method of unitization, consists of having normal subjects divide unpunctuated speech samples into complete sentences, deleting any words which could not be fitted into these sentences. The third technique, the cloze procedure, consists of having normal subjects guess words which have been systematically deleted from the speech samples. All three techniques were found to yield useful measures.

The results of this study, together with data from other experiments, led us to propose the notion that the basic deficit in the schizophrenic patient's behavior consists of his being controlled primarily by stimuli immediate in space or in time. It is for this reason, we contended, that he has difficulty in sorting tests, that at least in the more deteriorated stage he shows less object constancy, that he extinguishes faster after conditioning (to give but a few examples from areas outside language), and that in language he shows "loose association" and poor ability to communicate because language requires that the speaker react to long-range stimuli.

REFERENCES

1. Arieti, S.: Interpretation of Schizophrenia. New York, Robert Brunner, 1955.
2. Bateson, G., Jackson, D. D., Haley, J., and Weakland, J.: Toward a theory of schizophrenia. Behav. Sci. 1:251-264, 1956.
3. Becker, S. W., Bavelas, A., and Braden, M.: An index to measure contingency of English sentences. Lang. Speech 4:138-145, 1961.
4. Brinegar, C. S.: Mark Twain and the Quintus Curtius Snodgrass letters: a statistical test of authorship. J. Amer. Stat. Ass. 58:85-96, 1963.
5. Chapman, L. J.: Distractability in the conceptual performance of schizophrenics. J. Abnorm. Soc. Psychol. 53:286-291, 1956.
6. Dinoff, M., Horner, R. E., Kurpiewski, B. S., and Timmons, E. O.: Conditioning verbal behavior of schizophrenics in a group therapy-like situation. J. Clin. Psychol. 16:367-370, 1960.
7. von Domarus, E.: The specific laws of logic in schizophrenia. *In* Language

and Thought in Schizophrenia (ed. J. S. Kasanin). Berkeley, University of California Press, 1944.
8. Feldstein, S., and Jaffe, J.: Language predictability as a function of psychotherapeutic interaction. J. Consult. Psychol. 27:123-126, 1963.
9. ——: Schizophrenic speech fluency: a partial replication and an hypothesis Psychol. Rep. 13:775-780, 1963.
10. Ferreira, A. J.: The semantics and the context of the schizophrenic's language. Arch. Gen. Psychiat. 3:128-138, 1960.
11. Fillenbaum, S., and Jones, L. V.: An application of "cloze" technique to the study of aphasic speech. J. Abnorm. Soc. Psychol. 65:183-189, 1962.
12. Goldman-Eisler, F.: The determinants of the rate of speech output and their mutual relations. J. Psychosom. Res. 1:137-143, 1956.
13. ——: Speech production and the predictability of words in context. Quart. J. Exper. Psychol. 10:96-106, 1958.
14. Goldstein, K.: Methodological approach to the study of schizophrenic thought disorder. *In* Language and Thought in Schizophrenia (ed. J. S. Kasanin). Berkeley, University of California Press, 1944.
15. Hammer, M., and Salzinger, K.: Some formal characteristics of schizophrenic speech as a measure of social deviance. Ann. N.Y. Acad. Sci. 105:861-889, 1964.
16. Honigfeld, G.: The effect of an hallucinogenic agent on verbal behavior. Psychol. Rep. 13:383-385, 1963.
17. ——: The ability of schizophrenics to understand normal, psychotic, and pseudo-psychotic speech. Dis. Nerv. Syst. 24:692-694, 1963.
18. Laffal, J., Lenkoski, L. D., and Ameen, L.: "Opposite speech" in a schizophrenic patient. J. Abnorm. Soc. Psychol. 52:409-413, 1956.
19. Lorenz, M.: Criticism as approach to schizophrenic language. Arch. Gen. Psychiat. 9:235-245, 1963.
20. Lovinger, E.: Perceptual contact with reality in schizophrenia. J. Abnorm. Soc. Psychol. 52:87-91, 1956.
21. McGaughran, L. S., and Moran, L. J.: "Conceptual level" versus "conceptual area" analysis of object-sorting behavior of schizophrenic and nonpsychiatric groups. J. Abnorm. Soc. Psychol. 52:43-50, 1956.
22. Meadow, A., Greenblatt, M., and Solomon, H. C.: "Looseness of association" and impairment in abstraction in schizophrenia. J. Nerv. Ment. Dis. 118:27-35, 1953.
23. Mednick, S. A.: A learning theory approach to research in schizophrenia. Psychol. Bull. 55:316-327, 1958.
24. ——: Schizophrenia: A Learned Thought Disorder. Proc. 14th Internat. Congr. of Applied Psychol., Copenhagen, 1961.
25. Mendenhall, T. C.: The characteristic curves of composition. Science, 9:237-246, 1887.
26. Osgood, C. E., and Miron, M. S.: Approaches to the Study of Aphasia. Urbana: Univ. of Illinois Press, 1963.
27. Osgood, C. E., and Walker, E. G.: Motivation and language behavior: a content analysis of suicide notes. J. Abnorm. Soc. Psychol. 59:58-67, 1959.
28. Payne, R. W.: Cognitive abnormalities. *In* Handbook of Abnormal Psychology (ed. H. J. Eysenck). New York, Basic Books, 1961.

29. Rickard, H. C., Dignam, P. S., and Horner, R. F.: Verbal manipulation in a psychotherapeutic relationship. J. Clin. Psychol. 16:363-367, 1960.
30. Salzinger, K.: Shift in judgment of weights as a function of anchoring stimuli and instructions in early schizophrenics and normals. J. Abnorm Soc. Psychol. 55:43-49, 1957.
31. ——: Some problems of response measurement in verbal behavior: the response unit and intraresponse relations. Paper read at Conference on Methods of Measurement of Change in Human Behavior, Montreal, Canada, 1962.
32. Salzinger, K., and Pisoni, S.: Reinforcement of affect responses of schizophrenics during the clinical interview. J. Abnorm. Soc. Psychol. 57:84-90, 1958.
33. ——: Reinforcement of verbal affect responses of normal subjects during the interview. J. Abnorm. Soc. Psychol. 60:127-130, 1960.
34. ——: Some parameters of the conditioning of verbal affect responses in schizophrenic subjects. J. Abnorm. Soc. Psychol. 63:511-516, 1961.
35. Salzinger, K., Pisoni, S., Feldman, R. S., and Bacon, P. M.: The effect of drugs on verbal behavior. Paper presented at symposium, Control of Verbal Behavior. Amer. Ass. Adv. Sci., Denver, Colorado, 1961.
36. Salzinger, K., and Portnoy, S.: Verbal conditioning in interviews: application to chronic schizophrenics and relationship to prognosis for acute schizophrenics. J. Psychiat. Res. 2:1-9, 1964.
37. Salzinger, K., Portnoy, S., and Feldman, R. S.: The effect of order of approximation to the statistical structure of English on the emission of verbal responses. J. Exper. Psychol. 64:52-57, 1962.
38. ——: The experimental manipulation of continuous speech in schizophrenic patients. J. Abnorm. Soc. Psychol. 68:508-516, 1964.
39. ——: Verbal behavior of schizophrenic and normal subjects. Ann. N.Y. Acad. Sci. 105:845-860, 1964.
40. Saporta, S. (Ed.): Psycholinguistics. New York, Holt, Rinehart and Winston, 1961.
41. Shakow, D.: Psychological deficit in schizophrenia. Behav. Sci. 8:275-305, 1963.
42. Siegel, S.: Nonparametric Statistics for the Behavioral Sciences. New York, McGraw-Hill, 1956.
43. Sommer, R., Dewar, R., and Osmond, H.: Is there a schizophrenic language? Arch. Gen. Psychiat. 3:665-673, 1960.
44. Taylor, W. L.: Cloze procedure: a new tool for measuring readability. Journalism Quart. 30:415-433, 1953.
45. ——: Recent developments in the use of cloze procedure. Journalism Quart. 33:42-48, 1956.
46. ——: Application of cloze procedure to the verbal behavior of mental patients. Paper read at Study Section on Verbal Behavior, American College of Neuropsychopharmacology, Washington, D.C., 1963.
47. Whitehorn, J. C., and Zipf, G. K.: Schizophrenic language. Arch. Neurol. Psychiat. 49:831-851, 1943.
48. Yavuz, H. S.: The production of random letters sequences in schizophrenics. J. Psychol. 56:171-173, 1963.

8

THE PREDICTION OF PERFORMANCE IN SCHIZOPHRENIA*

by NORMAN GARMEZY, PH.D.†

THIS CHAPTER FOCUSES on an apparent paradox related to the performance of schizophrenic patients—namely, the discrepant effects produced by rewards and punishments on their behavior in contrast to the influence exerted by these same classes of reinforcers on more normally functioning individuals.

The paradox is one not wholly unique to psychopathology. Since 1913, when Thorndike[101] first presented his view that punishment and reward had obvious and unvarying consequences (to weaken or to strengthen stimulus-response connections), the role played by punishment has become a source of ambiguity and contradiction, whereas Thorndike's original position regarding reward has remained essentially unchanged.

Five decades after Thorndike's original formulation, Church,[24] in summarizing the varied effects of punishment on behavior, noted:

> Considerable uncertainty remains today regarding the effect of punishment, and there does not appear to be any single reliable effect. Much experimental evidence indicates that punishment decreases the probability of occurrence of a response or increases the latency, but there is also much conflicting evidence. In some experiments punishment has only a temporary suppressing effect on a response, or none at all, and in other experiments punishment actually has the paradoxical effect of increasing the strength of the response it follows. (p. 369)

Church then goes on to observe that there has been a "continuing search" to unravel these "paradoxical effects of punishment."

The atypicality of the schizophrenic's response to learned punishments and rewards may be expressed in the following manner: (1) A normal individual, following punishment, will frequently produce

---

*The preparation of this chapter was facilitated by USPHS grants MH-(K6)-14, 914-02 and MH-06170-02, and a grant awarded by the Graduate School of the University of Minnesota.

†Department of Psychology, University of Minnesota, Minneapolis, Minnesota.

more variable behavior simply because he remains unaware of which response among an array of potentially appropriate alternatives is the correct one; by contrast, the schizophrenic's response to punishment characteristically tends to become more stereotyped, more inflexible, and less solution-oriented. (2) Learned rewards for normal subjects generally produce rather stable effects in maintaining activity and in providing information as to the adequacy of past responses and the direction of subsequent ones. If punishment increases behavior variability, rewards induce response stability and hence usually lead to improved performance in most learning situations. But here, too, schizophrenics are different. The outcome of a regimen of positive reinforcements for the schizophrenic patient's performance is, at best, equivocal. In many studies, the patient remains oblivious to the presumed power of a reward and gives little indication that it possesses motivated properties for him.

In the sections that follow, I shall present some data that bear on the relative effectiveness of punishments and rewards in modifying the behavior of schizophrenic patients.

The Role of Punishment

More than a decade ago, Eliot Rodnick and I, with the assistance of many of our student colleagues, initiated a research program that focused on the effects of social censure on schizophrenic performance.[42, 85] In the course of a series of experiments, our research group was seemingly able to demonstrate the existence of a functional relationship between censure and deficit behavior in such diverse tasks as auditory and visual discrimination, concept formation, verbal learning and retention, and size estimation. On the basis of this evidence, we initially expressed our view of the relationship in this way:

> We shall try to demonstrate that schizophrenic patients can and do respond adaptively in tasks of considerable complexity and difficulty provided that these tasks have been made sufficiently interesting to insure the cooperation of the patient. This adaptability, however, is a tenuous one which can be disturbed by the introduction of minimal censure into an experiment. Under these conditions the deficit behaviors which have been described as characteristic of the schizophrenic patient appear. (p. 116)

It is now clear that the above summary, although applicable to the data of the Duke studies, is a generalization that cannot be supported by the results obtained by other investigators. For example, a number of studies employing shock or white noise as aversive stimuli indicate that such "punishments" produce behavior facilitation in schizophrenic patients.[20, 26, 60, 79, 86]

In many of these studies, employing physically noxious stimuli, the aversive stimulus appeared with the onset of a signal and was terminated only after an appropriate response had been made. Thus, the basic experimental paradigm utilized in these investigations was one of *instrumental escape training,* the subject's instrumental response, in effect, resulting in cessation of the noxious stimulus. Under such training conditions, the frequency of punished responses produced by schizophrenic patients underwent a marked reduction, since escape from painful stimulation was possible only when the subject responded correctly.

Although the results of these studies are somewhat consistent, theoretical explanations of the relationship that obtains are rather disparate. Cohen,[27] in an unpublished paper, has suggested three theoretical positions that could account for these results: (1) a characteristically low general motivational state in schizophrenic patients that can, in part, be compensated for by the energizing effects of any strong noxious stimulus; (2) a deficiency in responsiveness to acquired social reinforcers in schizophrenic patients—one that is not present when primary (biological) reinforcers are used to motivate behavior; (3) a heightened sensitivity on the part of patients to negative or aversive reinforcement as opposed to a relative insensitivity to positive reinforcement.

With regard to the first position, other evidence appears to contradict the hypothesis that schizophrenics are characterized by a generalized low level of drive that can be made more optimal by noxious stimulation. Such a concept of a drive deficit is contraindicated by some excellent data provided by Malmo, Shagass, and Smith,[69] who employed a variety of stressors (including pain stimulation) with chronic schizophrenic patients and secured concomitant physiological and behaviorial measures in response to such stress stimuli. On the basis of behavioral measures, the patients, relative to controls, not only showed markedly lowered responsiveness (including a reduction in the frequency with which they physically withdrew from pain-stimulation), but they even failed to signal overtly their response to pain. However, in terms of physiological indexes of responsiveness, the schizophrenic patients showed heightened muscular tension, heart rate, and diastolic blood pressure in comparison with the control subjects. Malmo and his colleagues concluded:

> In order to understand this finding we must distinguish between those aspects of responsiveness which involve background physiological activities (such as heart rate, blood pressure, and level of muscular tension), and those aspects which involve "purposive" acts (such as pressing the button to indicate pain, performing size discriminations, and mirror drawings). The first class of activities are diffuse in character, largely involuntary, and frequently associated with emotional arousal. "Purposive" acts are selective rather than diffuse in character, largely voluntary, and less regularly associated with emotional arousal. . . .
>
> Our data thus indicate that in schizophrenia those aspects of responsiveness which are associated with emotional arousal may remain intact, while the mechanisms underlying overt, "purposive" acts may be defective or inoperative. This conclusion is counter to the traditional view that "affect is flat" in chronic schizophrenia. Typically, the run-of-the-mine *chronic* schizophrenic *appears* emotionally unresponsive to the observer (e.g., in a psychiatric interview).
>
> But this observation may be due more to lack of "purposive" response to the questions of the examiner than to any general decrease in affectivity. Our chronic schizophrenic group, it should be emphasized, would similarly have been judged as unresponsive, had only measures of response to the specific painful stimuli been available. However, measures reflecting general level of activity suggested the opposite—that the chronic schizophrenic was quite "responsive." (pp. 371-372)

(It is this deficit in purposive functioning that may well explain the behavioral inadequacy of the schizophrenic patient in many experimental tasks despite the motivational increment presumably provided by painful stimulation.)

These results have been confirmed by a recent experiment conducted by Ray,[82] who measured GSR activity in response to a sequence of stressful stimuli using chronic schizophrenics (hospitalized for a minimum of eight years) and normal controls. His stressors included word associations to affective and neutral words, verbal threat of pain, sham pain, and actual pain stimulation. Ray found differences between the patient and normal groups primarily in GSR amplitudes during a period of initial perception of the verbal stimuli and "in shifts of conductance levels while establishing sets to respond and . . . while giving overt verbal responses." However, with reference to the wide variety of stimuli used in the study, Ray concludes:

> The data showing near equivalence between chronic schizophrenics and normals in levels of autonomic activation and reactivity to a wide variety of stimuli casts serious doubt on the validity of some common terms in the parlance of mental hospitals such as the "burned-out chronic" or even the notion of "vegetative existence" insofar as these terms imply an inferior level of autonomic functioning.
>
> The results also fail to support the hypothesis that chronic schizophrenic

subjects are autonomically less reactive than normal control subjects to threats of pain, sham-pain, and pain stimuli. . . .

For those inclined to consider psychopathology primarily in perception terms it may be of interest to note that since autonomic reactions occurred to conceptually presented threat of pain and sham-pain even before pain was introduced, it is assumed that both perception and intellectual discrimination occurred. Under the threat-pain conditions, then, it would seem that the perceptual process is intact, that the intervening intellectual analysis or understanding of the meaning of stimuli is intact, and that the affective (autonomic) processes are intact. (pp. 21-22)

Thus, Ray finds it necessary to conclude with Malmo that the deficit in schizophrenia lies not in faulty levels of activation, but in differences in readiness to produce overt-voluntary responses. Consistent with these findings are the observations of Venables and Wing[104] that there is a high positive correlation between arousal and withdrawal in long-stay schizophrenic men.

Cohen's second hypothesis that primary reinforcers may be more effective than secondary reinforcers in modifying the behavior of schizophrenic patients retains its status as an interesting speculation, but only that. Unfortunately, there has been no systematic group of studies conducted under near-identical experimental conditions with the same (or comparable groups) of subjects to test the behavioral effects of such classes of reinforcers. Such a program of research is clearly needed. Data garnered in this manner may enable us to evaluate the relative power of a predictive model for schizophrenic behavior based on the energizing aspects of drive as advocated by Broen and Storms[15] in contradistinction to one based upon the associative aspects of drive in which the emphasis is placed upon avoidance responses that are cued off by specific types of anxiety-evoking stimuli.[85] This issue has had its counterpart in some of the controversy that has been generated by studies of the effects of anxiety on learning.[34, 97, 100] In this area, too, explanations of decremental behavior evinced in learning tasks by anxiety-prone individuals have centered on both the energizing role of anxiety and the specific kinds of habits that such persons are more likely to exhibit under stress.[22]

Although the issue does not involve a simple "either-or" choice, this differentiation between the associative (or steering) as opposed to the nonassociative (or energizing) properties of motives would appear relevant in studying the effect of punishment variables on schizophrenic performance. The studies that have been cited previously in which shock and white noise constituted the stressors were primarily concerned with the energizing aspects of schizophrenic behavior. Such physical stressors, when used in escape situations of relative simplicity such as reaction time, can act to heighten schizophrenic performance, particularly in patients who, as Lang noted, are already reasonably "motivated" to perform well. Thus, if we examine the studies cited earlier, we find that Cavanaugh's[20] subjects are described as meeting the criteria of "contact and cooperativeness"; Pascal and Swensen's[79] patients prove to be first-admission cases who were apparently well motivated, since they constituted part of an available pool of patients that could be used in the study; Rosenbaum[86] and his associates excluded from their study long-term chronic patients by eliminating those who had been hospitalized for a period exceeding three years. It is interesting that among these several studies it was Lang,[60] employing a more chronic group, who secured such minimal improvement under aversive stimulation that he was led to question the hypothesis of a basic motivational deficit in schizophrenia that could be modified by aversive stimulation.

The fact that schizophrenic patients in all of these studies still failed to approach the performance level of normal control subjects would suggest that even for the simplest tasks, a complex of internal competing responses may be present to interfere with efficient performance. Certainly it seems reasonable to postulate that the schizophrenic patient brings to all situations strong habit predispositions oriented toward withdrawal, preoccupation and rumination, excessive autism, uncooperativeness, etc. Although noxious stimulation may partially rectify the imbalance in the habit strengths of these responses relative to those of more task-oriented behaviors, it cannot completely overcome the power of the task-irrelevant patterns. In part, the reduction in variability of the patient groups observed in a number of these studies may be due to just such modifications in the relative strengths of habits of fairly homogeneous samples of patients whose cooperativeness is an initial requisite for participation in the experiment (i.e., the habit strength of competing preoccupations in such subjects is not unduly high and hence potentially capable of displacement in the patient's response hierarchy).

An evaluation of specific response patterns of schizophrenic patients may, in the long run, prove of greater theoretical significance than vague allusions to a basic deficit of "biological" motivation in schizophrenia. Can we possibly hope to substantiate the existence of a distorted biological substrate through observation of the gross molar behaviors of the schizophrenic patient? Is it not more reasonable to expect that the ultimate resolution of the issue of the contribution of biological components to schizophrenia is more likely to reside in the results of investigations conducted by physiologists, biochemists, and others of comparable training and persuasion?

Nor can our knowledge of the schizophrenic process be clarified by designating the patient as a "social motive" defective. The critical questions for research into motivational processes in schizophrenia are more likely to be these: What types of stimuli create differential states of arousal in patients? How do such stimuli come to possess significant cue value for the schizophrenic patient? Are there predictable classes of responses in patients that are associated with these stimuli? Can such classes of responses assist in our prediction of the performance of patients in various laboratory tasks? Questions such as these are related to Cohen's third hypothesis that the schizophrenic patient may be selectively reactive to negative as opposed to positive reinforcement.

It is obvious that these questions reflect a bias heavily weighted toward consideration of the associative properties of specific drive states in the schizophrenic patient as a basis for predicting his behavior. Earlier, I suggested that the schizophrenic patient brings to experimental situations strong predispositions toward withdrawal. It is interesting to note that Child and Waterhouse,[23] in their significant theoretical paper on the effects of frustration on performance, consider habits of persistence vs. withdrawal as classes of responses that are particularly relevant for predicting adequacy or inadequacy of behavior under frustration stress. The differential habit strengths of such responses are presumably a function of their prior association with anxiety-reduction. In the case of the schizophrenic patient, withdrawal responses have been extensively used to escape from potentially frustrating situations.

It may be instructive to illustrate the pervasiveness of this mechanism by quoting from Goldstein,[43] who has contributed so greatly to the study of the impairment of abstraction in schizophrenia.

> This impairment of abstraction might suggest that schizophrenia is an organic disease. But such an assumption did not seem appropriate. Looking for another explanation of the symptoms, I did a careful study of the phenomena in the concrete behavior of schizophrenics and compared these with the phenomena in the behavior of organic patients. The results were illuminating: the comparison showed essential differences between the two groups. . . . The pattern which

> the organic patient shows in his concrete behavior can be understood as being due more or less to disintegration of sensory, motor, or mental processes. . . . The schizophrenic, on the other hand, develops characteristic individual patterns in his concrete procedure which reveal influences from the patient's ideas, feelings, etc. . . . This origin would be found in consideration of this defect in its relation to the totality of the schizophrenic picture. . . . It may be sufficient to point to the disturbance of abstraction in relation to one symptom of schizophrenia which is generally considered outstanding—the withdrawal of the patient from the world—and to consider why the schizophrenic withdraws. Could the impairment of abstraction be considered a means to guarantee this withdrawal? . . . Is the concreteness of the schizophrenic a means of avoiding dangers which arise for him out of our world, dangers based on conflicts between him and our world which may lead him to catastrophe and anxiety? . . . Persons who later became schizophrenic often show symptoms of this tendency—shyness, suspicion, anxiety, withdrawal—at an early age, before the disease, under the pressure of special conflicts, breaks out.
>
> From this point of view, the abnormal concreteness appears as a secondary phenomenon, a protective mechanism against unbearable danger and anxiety. . . . The assumption that the danger arises from the world of personal relations, and that the patient tries to withdraw because of the anxiety stimulated by it, makes a number of peculiarities in the patient's behavior understandable. In this respect I must mention that, if lack of abstraction is a protective mechanism, the withdrawal will be utilized only, or particularly, in situations which are dangerous for the patient; it will be less evident when there is no danger. (pp. 1341-1342)

As for the origins of withdrawal, there seems to be some consensus among clinicians[2, 51, 56] that early parent-child relationships constitute one learning context for the acquisition of these maladaptive response patterns. Jenkins sees schizoid withdrawal as a defensive pattern produced by "a parent overpowering to a child, a parent with whom it would be more than usually difficult for the child to establish his individuality, his selfhood, without doing so through negativism or schizoid withdrawal" (p. 739). Arieti relates the ubiquitous nature of schizophrenic withdrawal to the patient's constant expectancy of disapproval in childhood—an expectancy that ultimately produces an extreme sensitivity "to the slightest sign of the oncoming reproach."

In the light of these clinical hypotheses, it seems reasonable to conclude that the use of censure in laboratory tasks should heighten the evocation of withdrawal behavior in schizophrenic patients. Thus, responses elicited in experimental tasks that are followed by some signal suggesting criticism or disparagement should undergo a marked reduction in response strength. Although we can predict a modification of responsiveness on the basis of censure, we cannot predict the adequacy of the patient's performance on a task without knowledge of the response alternatives that are available to him. Alternative choices may be one or many, structured or unstructured.

In terms of available alternatives, we can define those situations that are most and least evocative of performance deficits.

1. The likelihood of behavior decrements will be heightened if the experimental procedures provide simply for a general devaluation of the patient's performance at some point in the experimental sequence; such decrements will be accentuated if the task permits a multiplicity of response alternatives. Since the criticism is nonspecific with regard to the inappropriateness of the subject's previous responses, the schizophrenic patient can be expected to become either less responsive or more grossly inappropriate in his behavior as the experiment proceeds. Compounding the effect of punishment will be the oft-noted difficulty of the patient in maintaining a mental set[91] and his propensity for discontinuing task-oriented activity.[83]

The role played by an unstructured failure-threat in accentuating deviant responding in schizophrenia is readily seen in a study conducted by Wilensky[106] on the effects of failure on task performance for schizophrenic and normal subjects. Typically, all subjects were given tasks requiring auditory and visual memory as well as auditory and visual perception. If the subject responded incorrectly, he was so informed without the nature of his error being specified. Wilensky reports that an analysis of the patient's qualitative responses following frustration revealed an increment in bizarre responding, perseverative errors and refusals to respond. Although both groups of subjects were similar in *how* they responded prior to frustration, during the post-frustration period the schizophrenic patients were more prone to abandon the tasks. Wilensky also reports that a small number of the patients even sustained hallucinatory and irrelevant fantasy experiences following mild frustration. Apparently the patient's predisposition toward schizoid withdrawal was accentuated by the use of verbal punishment in a situation that failed both to provide adequate information as to the nature of error and no clearly specified alternative response.

These results are not too dissimilar to those obtained by Webb,[105] who administered successively two comparable forms of a similarities test and mildly criticized the performance of one group of patients following the administration of the first form of the test, whereas a control group of patients was not censured at all. Although the control group showed marked improvement in conceptualization on the second form of the test, the censured group failed to improve, showed a decline in higher level abstractions with a concomitant increase in *very poor quality* responses as well as some trend toward greater verbal imprecision and tangentiality. Furthermore, following frustration, it proved necessary to "prod" the experimental subjects to respond more frequently (but with substantially less probability of eliciting a scorable response)—a pattern that did not obtain for the control subjects.

A study by Brooker[16] provides a comparison of the effects of an irrelevant devaluation and a response-relevant devaluation on task performance in schizophrenia.* In the first of two experiments, Brooker utilized a task-irrelevant censure threat and secured marked conceptual deficits from schizophrenic patients. Schizophrenic and normal subjects were required to learn to sort the Wisconsin cards using color as the sorting base. All subjects were told "Right" following a correct response and were provided with no information after an incorrect sort. After every five card sorts, all subjects were required to judge two weights. Half of the schizophrenic and normal groups were told "Right" following their judgments, while the other half were told that they had been "Wrong" on the interpolated task. Under this irrelevant punishment procedure, the performance of the schizophrenic group was seriously disrupted, a pattern not observed under the reward condition. By contrast, the performance of normal subjects remained inviolate in the face of either interpolated reinforcement condition.

A second experiment conducted by Brooker provides an interesting contrast to the first study. In this experiment, identical to the first in most respects, the punishment was made task-relevant through the use of the verbal statement "Wrong" following incorrect sorts for one group, in contrast to a rewarded group that continued to receive "Right" for each (appropriate) correct response. Under this regimen, punished schizophrenic subjects, relative to their counterparts who received reward, showed equivalent conceptual improvement throughout the experiment. The reason for this latter result may become more apparent in the discussion that follows.

2. In many studies, the experimental procedures that have been employed have involved a punishing signal that is administered immediately following an experimenter-designated, incorrect response. As

*I am grateful to Professor Alexander Buchwald, who served as Dr. Brooker's advisor, for bringing this study to my attention.

we have seen, such a signal, in some studies, takes the form of a noxious (pain) stimulus that is terminated only when *S* makes the appropriate response. This probably constitutes the *optimal* condition for behavior improvement since the stimulus literally *forces* the patient to respond correctly—a situation that doesn't readily permit irrelevant response sets to be retained.

However, in other studies censure (rather than a physically noxious stimulus) has been used in the form of a "Wrong" signal following an error in responding; but the termination of such a psychologically noxious event is *not made dependent* upon the subject's choice of the correct alternative. As we shall see shortly, in such paradigms the effectiveness of the censure is best revealed on the trial that *follows* the one on which the patient's response has been punished. Given the simplest situation in which there are two highly structured response alternatives (such as those requiring simple motor movements), one of which is followed by a punishing signal, we can predict that the schizophrenic patient will show more frequent responding with the alternative response that avoids the censure.

If this is a highly probable consequence, the prediction of deficit or incremental behavior in schizophrenia becomes a rather straightforward one: *If the response alternative that permits avoidance of the censuring signal is a task-congruent response, behavior facilitation should follow: if the response alternative is non-congruent, performance deficits should ensue.**

An analysis of several studies tends to support this hypothesis. The first is provided by some unpublished data collected by Bleke[10] in a

*This formulation modifies an earlier statement that censure and deficit are invariant.[85] The author published it as part of a Presidential Address to the North Carolina Psychological Association (May 1960) unaware that Cohen had independently presented a comparable formulation the previous spring at the Midwestern Psychological Association meetings. In addition, the essential statements were also contained in a series of studies[20, 21, 60, 66] conducted by a number of investigators under the direction of Dr. Walter Cohen, whose astute conceptual analysis initially clarified the overgeneralized nature of the censure-deficit hypothesis[42, 85] but who, unfortunately, propounded in turn a generalization that appears equally questionable—namely, that tasks using an escape paradigm produce facilitation of the schizophrenic's performance, whereas those using avoidance designs tend to produce decremental behavior.[21] Recently, Silverman[93] published a substantial review of these and other studies of the effects of punishment on psychological deficit in schizophrenia, using a comparable context for his analysis. Since this chapter cites only a selected number of studies, the interested reader should review Silverman's excellent article.

study of verbal learning by schizophrenic and normal subjects. Bleke had his groups learn a pattern of push and pull movements of a switch lever to 14 neutrally toned nouns which were projected successively on a screen. Half the subjects learned under a "punishment" condition in which a lever movement resulted in the screen lighting up briefly to read *Wrong;* for correct movements under this condition, the screen merely lighted. The remaining subjects were tested under a "reward" condition in which *Right* flashed on the screen following correct lever movements, whereas incorrect responses were indicated by lighting the screen. In this experiment, Bleke demonstrated that one subset of schizophrenic patients—those characterized by chronically inadequate patterns of social and sexual behaviors prior to their illness ("poor premorbids")—under punishment showed tendencies toward greater interferences in learning as measured by greater frequency of errors and number of trials required to learn to criterion.

The clues for understanding this decrement are contained in two factors: (1) the pattern of reversal movements followed a *Wrong* signal (i.e., an alternation of response from the previous one); and (2) the structure of the list that the subjects had to learn. Reasoning that a subject's effort to avoid punishment would be revealed by his reversal of that lever movement that had immediately preceded the *Wrong* signal, a tabulation was made of the patient's proportion of reversal movements in early trials following each *Right, Wrong,* and light signal. These results are presented in table 1.

Table 1 reveals that all groups more typically used a pattern of reversals rather than nonreversals following correct responses. Normals

TABLE 1.—Mean Per Cent of Reversal Movements Following Correct and Incorrect Responses by Poor and Good Premorbid Schizophrenic and Normal Groups under Reward and Punishment Conditions

Per Cent Reversal Following							
Incorrect Responses				Correct Responses			
Condition	*Poors*	*Goods*	*Normals*	*Condition*	*Poors*	*Goods*	*Normals*
Punishment (*Wrong* if incorrect)	50.2	48.4	32.3	Punishment (Light if correct)	56.8	58.3	54.0
Reward (Light if incorrect)	36.3	39.4	38.3	Reward (*Right* if correct)	51.8	59.8	60.8

tended not to reverse, however, following errors, whereas the schizophrenic groups showed tendencies toward increased reversals. Statistical tests indicated that schizophrenics (both those who had made good and poor premorbid social and sexual adjustments) showed significantly more reversals than normals following *Wrong* signals, a finding that did not obtain when merely a light signal was used to indicate error.*

Some conjecture regarding these different strategies employed by the two groups seems warranted. The normal pattern reveals a negative recency effect similar to that observed by Goodnow and Pettigrew[45] in subjects receiving short-run 50-50 probability sequences. The choice patterns of such groups show a marked tendency to persist with an unsuccessful response. In Bleke's experiment it seems reasonable to assume that most subjects perceived that the sequence of left-right choices was designed to provide for essentially a 50-50 probability model. Hence, the adoption of a strategy that an unsuccessful choice was best maintained on the following trial. It is interesting to note that schizophrenic patients too maintain such a pattern when a light signal provides the more neutral information cue regarding error. Following a *Wrong* signal, however, the schizophrenic subjects abandon this strategy and reveal a greater propensity for random responding, with reversals hovering near the 50 per cent mark. This variation in response to a more salient as opposed to a less salient failure signal suggests that formulations of alternation behavior stressing the subject's efforts to make optimum the amount of stimulus variability or complexity[30] available to him are not applicable in this instance.

For the schizophrenic patient the pattern of alternations following *Wrong* suggests a more extreme response to error—a tendency that varies markedly among individuals. As Goodnow[44] has noted: "Differences among individuals in their fear of erring may, in fact, be a fairly general trait and be extremely helpful in explaining differences in behavior where judgments are to be made and action taken." Certainly the clinical literature would lend credence to this intense fear of erring by schizophrenic patients.

That these different response strategies would have a demonstrable effect upon task performance is best seen by examining the correct

*Unlike the poor premorbid schizophrenic patients, the good premorbids, after showing marked reversals on the very first trial, shifted subsequently to a more adaptive nonreversal strategy similar to the one used by normals; poor premorbids, however, failed to modify their aversive pattern over trials.

response sequences for Bleke's two lists of words. These are reproducd in table 2.

TABLE 2.—Pattern of Correct Lever Movements Used in Bleke's Experiment

List I	List II
1. Pull	1. Push
2. Push^{R}	2. Pull^{R}
3. Pull^{R}	3. Push^{R}
4. Push^{R}	4. Push^{NR}
5. Push^{NR}	5. Pull^{R}
6. Push^{NR}	6. Push^{R}
7. Pull^{R}	7. Pull^{R}
8. Push^{R}	8. Pull^{NR}
9. Pull^{R}	9. Pull^{NR}
10. Pull^{NR}	10. Push^{R}
11. Push^{R}	11. Pull^{R}
12. Pull^{R}	12. Push^{R}
13. Push^{R}	13. Push^{NR}
14. Pull^{R}	14. Pull^{R}

R = reversal; NR = nonreversal

Examination of the lists for successive correct responses reveals that 10 of 13 possibilities for List I, and 9 of 13 possibilities for List II, provide for an alternation or reversal sequence. It is, therefore, apparent that the likelihood of obtaining a correct response following an incorrect lever movement would be heightened by a nonreversal strategy and decreased by a reversal set. The schizophrenic patients, bringing into Bleke's experiment strong predispositions toward avoidance of censure, find themselves inadvertently confronted with an experimental environment that can only exacerbate the likelihood of heightened maladaptive and decremental behavior.

Bleke's results are supported by a subsequent study conducted by Zahn,[111] who had schizophrenic and normal subjects respond to an unsolvable discrimination task in which two identical pictures were projected successively on a screen at a very rapid exposure rate. Each subject was required to *pull* a lever if he perceived the two pictures to be identical and to *push* the lever if they appeared to be different. Then, arbitrarily, on 13 of 15 trials, *E* flashed a *Wrong* signal to indicate an incorrect judgment. Zahn's reversal data for good and poor premorbid schizophrenic patients and normal controls, as seen in table 3, essentially confirm Bleke's findings.

TABLE 3.—Mean Number of Reversals* by Schizophrenic and Normal Subjects on Unsolvable Discrimination Task (from Zahn)

Group		*Mean*
Poor Premorbid Schizophrenic	(N = 11)	6.27
Good Premorbid Schizophrenic	(N = 13)	4.77
Normal Controls	(N = 20)	3.55

*Based upon 12 possible reversals.

The poor premorbid schizophrenic group showed a significantly greater number of reversals compared to normals ($p < .01$); the good premorbid patients who fell intermediate between these two groups did not differ reliably from either. As in the case of Bleke's data, random responsiveness on the part of the *poors* under censure is suggested. However, when Zahn eliminated one subject who had responded to all presentations of the discrimination problem as if all stimulus pairs were identical, the mean reversal value of the poor premorbid group rose to 6.9, which proved to be significantly above ($p < .025$) the expected chance level of six reversals, suggesting the operation of a process other than random responding.

Zahn made a further analysis of five trials in which the punished stimulus pair was followed by its identical reproduction. Using as cut-off points two or fewer reversals vs. three or more, Zahn found that the distribution of subjects in his schizophrenic and control groups confirmed his previous analysis. These data, which are presented in table 4, produced an X^2 of 10.30, which for 2 df is significant below the .01 level.

The applicability of the formulation that has been suggested can also be seen in studies conducted by investigators in other laboratories.

TABLE 4.—Number of Schizophrenic and Normal Subjects Showing High and Low Reversal Scores Involving Successive, Identical Discriminations (from Zahn)

	Number of Reversals (Based on Five Trials)		
	0-2	3-5	Total
Goods	9	4	13
Poors	2	9	11
Normals	15	5	20

$X^2 = 10.30$
$p = <.01$

Cavanaugh, Cohen, and Lang[21] tested schizophrenic patients in a disjunctive reaction time procedure under several conditions: One group was presented with a neutral tone whenever the subject's response was "too slow"; another group was verbally censured for responding slowly. This was accomplished by the transmission of a tape-recorded message delivered via earphones to the subject ("That was too bad—too slow") whenever responses fell below the median RT on a previous block of seven trials. A control group received no information following their performance. In a subsequent experiment, a reward group ("That was good—very fast" for rapid responses) was also employed. Of all the experimental conditions, censure appears to be most significant for improving speed of performance in the schizophrenic groups. In seeking to reconcile discrepancies between their own research findings and those of the Duke studies, Cavanaugh et al. suggested that if censure provides additional information cues or knowledge of results to the psychotic subject, which can then help him to focus on the task, modify his set, and eliminate distractions, then improvements in performance are likely to occur.*

Why is there improvement in reaction time under conditions in which the subject's performance is obviously disparaged? Two facts related to reaction time help to frame the experimental findings of the Cavanaugh, Cohen, and Lang[21] experiment: (1) "RT is long when the stimulus is very weak and becomes shorter as the stimulus increases to medium and high intensities" (p. 19)[109]; (2) RT is quickened by extra motivation.

The verbal censuring message has great stimulus intensity for the schizophrenic subjects; its arousal properties are immediate and acute. The more rapidly the patient reacts, the greater the likelihood that he can avoid the punishing signal and damp down the anxiety that has been aroused. In this instance, the avoidance response facilitates RT

*These authors also suggest an "alternative" explanation for the decrements observed in the Duke studies—namely, that these are a consequence of the schizophrenic's learning responses that lead to the avoidance of punishment. The "alternative" nature of this interpretation is somewhat puzzling, since it is similar to an earlier explanation advanced by the Duke group.[39, 85] Furthermore, an explanation to interpret behavioral improvement based on the additional information cues provided by punishment is not without its problems. Garmezy, in a study of stimulus generalization,[40] demonstrated that patients provided with the additional information of a *Wrong* signal not only failed to benefit (unlike normals) with this cue, but showed a flattened gradient that was a function of efforts by patients to avoid the response alternative that could produce a *Wrong* signal.

and leads to a behavioral improvement. Furthermore, in this study, as in Bleke's, the experimental procedure may also lend itself to behavior facilitation. In a personal communication, Dr. Cavanaugh provided me with the order of presentation used in his disjunctive RT procedure. Subjects had received 21 preinformation trials conducted under the usual RT conditions followed by 21 information trials during which the various reinforcement conditions were employed as described earlier. This sequence was, in turn, followed by 21 postinformation trials which were comparable to the preinformation sequence. Inspection of Dr. Cavanaugh's order of trials indicates that for both the 21 pretest and the 21 information trials there were 13 reversals (i.e., left to right, right to left) and seven nonreversals. For the posttest sequence, the reversal:nonreversal ratio was 12.8. This reversal emphasis in the trials sequence could facilitate reaction time if the schizophrenic subject following a censure message is more readily oriented (on the subsequent trial) to the alternative response key.

To return to Bleke's experiment once again, is it not reasonable to postulate that it may be possible to reconstruct Bleke's list to make a reversal strategy following a *Wrong* signal facilitating? This could be accomplished by insuring a greater frequency of nonalternating runs within the list than those that would follow an alternating sequence. If the schizophrenic patient is predisposed toward a reversal strategy when in error, the list will, in effect, take over responsibility to prevent a chained sequence of errors from occurring. In this instance, the patient would encounter a more "sympathetic environment"—one far less prone to disadvantage him for his learned habits to punishing events than the experimental environment Bleke had inadvertently created.

It appears that, given knowledge of the habit structures of the schizophrenic patient in response to specific motivational conditions, a careful examination of the nature of the task and its response requirements can help to predict increments or decrements in the patient's performance. Avoidance versus escape paradigms is not the central issue. The primary information that is needed is (1) knowledge of the cues that have relevance for the schizophrenic patients, (2) the responses that have been learned to these cues, and (3) the congruence or noncongruence of these responses to the task-response.

A study by Leventhal[61] employing a verbal reinforcement procedure with schizophrenic, neurotic, and normal patients provides the most striking illustration of these points. All subjects were required to construct sentences containing both a verb (as indicated on a card) and one of four pronouns: *I, We, He, They*. Four groups of schizophrenics were used in the experiment. (The data for comparable groups of neurotics and normals will be ignored.)

Group R, a partial reward group, was told "good" following each *I* or *We* sentence; *E* did not respond to *He* and *They* sentences.

Group P, a partial punishment group was told "not so good" immediately following a *He* or *They* sentence; *E* did not respond to *I* or *We* sentences.

Group R-P, a continuously rewarded and punished group was told "good" immediately following *I* and *We* sentences, and "not so good" for *He* and *They* sentences.

Group C, a control group, received no response from *E* irrespective of the type of pronoun used.

The results of the experiment (as seen in figure 1) were quite conclusive. Schizophrenic Groups P and R-P showed marked acquisition of *I* and *We* responses, whereas the reward and control groups gave little evidence of learning. It is the R-P condition, evaluated against the performance of the individual R and P Groups, that provides an understanding of the apparent adequacy of learning revealed by patients in the P and R-P Groups. Apparently, for schizophrenic subjects reward is an inadequate reinforcer and punishment is not. First, we note that the response that is being measured is the frequency of *I* and *We* sentences. Under the P and R-P conditions, *E's* criticism is directed toward the patient whenever he utters a *He* or *They* sentence. With his powerful prepotent habits of withdrawal developed to censure or threat, the schizophrenic subject tends to avoid those responses (*He/They*) that are followed by punishment, and to produce only those alternatives (*I/We*) that are available to him in the experiment. The fact that these are congruent with the experimenter's dependent variable produces the appearance of behavioral adequacy revealed by the P and R-P subjects. It is clear from data provided by the R condition that it is not the approach tendency to *I* and *We*, but rather avoidance of *He* and *They*, that produces the appearance of facilitated learning under censure in the schizophrenic group. It is true, as Leventhal has indicated, that schizophrenic patients learned under punishment, but their learning was primarily a function of prepotent habits of avoidance developed to censure which in this experiment produced behavior that was quite consonant with the experimenter's arbitrary designation of his dependent variable.*

---

*In a somewhat different experimental context, Atkinson and Robinson[3] examined paired associate learning under conditions of personal and impersonal

Although the effects of punishment appear to be dissimilar to those obtained by Bleke, the two studies are completely congruent once one perceives the nature of the habit structures that are associated with particular drive stimuli in the schizophrenic patient and their consonance or incompatibility with the response requirements of the experimental tasks.

Symbolic Stimuli and Avoidance Behavior

We have considered two types of studies involving punishment: (1) those providing for a general devaluation of performance, and (2) those in which a punishing signal is applied to specific experimenter-designated responses. For each category of studies there is evidence that punishment evokes powerful aversive habits in schizophrenics, although the consequences of such aversiveness may differ in each instance.

There is a third category of studies that is more difficult to classify since it represents something of a grab-bag of miscellaneous methods and experimental procedures. In general, however, this category is best described as one in which investigators make use of stimuli that *symbolize* threat or punishment. Here, too, a careful analysis of the schizophrenic patient's responses to such contents reveals the operation of aversive habits. The range and diversity of studies that fall under this rubric are best revealed by several brief examples.

Feffer,[35] in a study of conceptual behavior in schizophrenia, devised a figure-ground task that provided for the placement of affective and

---

reward and punishment and were able to demonstrate that when incorrect responses and failures to respond were reproved, schizophrenics learned more rapidly under this type of regimen than under one utilizing mild reward or nonreinforcement. In a more recent study, McCarthy[72] has illustrated the pervasiveness of this censure-avoidance phenomenon by presenting schizophrenic patients with pairs of self-reference statements reflecting needs for dependence vs. independence. Subjects initially ascribed one of the two paired statements to themselves. Subsequently, they were tested under conditions in which they were asked to respond in a way that would indicate how "they could someday be." A censured group received a *Wrong* signal for statements of dependency; a praised group was given a *Right* indicator for selecting statements descriptive of independent behavior. Patients exposed to censure learned the appropriate responses of independence more rapidly than those who were praised for this same class of responses. However, retests to evaluate the magnitude of change to subsequent endorsements of independence-dependence statements proved similar for both groups. Furthermore, there was little evidence that either group generalized these verbal behaviors to other test situations.

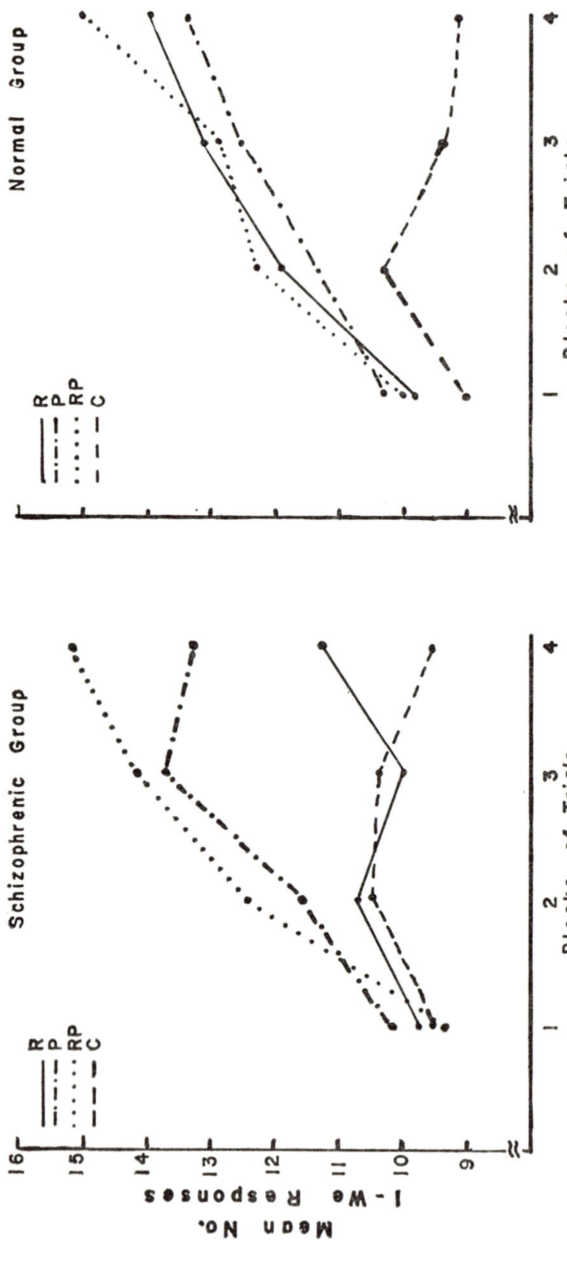

FIG. 1.—Mean number of *I* plus *We* responses for the normal and schizophrenic groups over four blocks of trials (20 per block). (From Leventhal.)

neutral words (as determined by the Luria technique) in either the central or peripheral areas of the stimulus field. Feffer found that when the affective contents constituted the figure, the patients focused on the more peripheral aspects of the field and produced intrusion responses that reflected the more neutral background contents. When the affectively toned stimuli were a component of the ground, patients focused on the figure contents, thus clearly revealing their aversiveness to anxiety-arousing stimuli. Feffer suggests that his data are consistent with the general hypothesis that "pathologically concrete thinking in schizophrenia represents an avoidant reaction to affective stimuli," a conclusion that is consonant with Goldstein's position.

Baxter and Becker[7] used reports of differentiated patterns of deviant family relationships for good and poor premorbid schizophrenic patients to infer the affect-arousing contents of specific TAT cards devoted to mother-son (6 BM) and father-son (7 BM) relationships. A rating scale was devised that would permit measures of avoidance and anxiety ratings to be derived from the test protocols. Avoidance was determined by four factors: "the amount of displacement of person, place, and/or time evident in the theme; the predominant direction of movement implied—i.e., toward or away from an affectively meaningful, spatially proximal relationship; the amount of verbal productivity in thought units; and the degree to which objectively presented figures were ignored in the themes produced" (p. 433). Baxter and Becker report that the *poor* premorbid group significantly exceeded their good premorbid counterparts in the magnitude of manifest avoidance content to both cards; *goods,* however, showed a trend toward avoidance behavior on the father-son card.

Silverman,[92] in an unpublished study, presented schizophrenic and normal subjects with counterbalanced lists of words (negative, positive, and neutral in import) that were projected on a screen at an extremely rapid speed of exposure. The subject sat before a lever that could be moved in one of two directions—either toward or away from himself. The subject's task was to indicate his judgment of the nature of the stimulus word by pushing the lever away if he perceived the word to be a negative one and to pull the lever toward him if he judged it to be either positive or neutral. By pushing or pulling the lever, the screen on which the stimulus word appeared could be simultaneously moved either away from or toward the subject. Silverman hypothesized that the patient's hypersensitivity to threat of punishment would result in more accurate discrimination and reduced latencies in responding to the noxious stimuli relative to neutral items. Data from the experiment indicate that the hypothesis of hypersensitivity was supported. But it is also evident from the data that schizophrenic subjects have a response bias in the direction of pushing both lever and screen away from themselves, even during the presentation of 20 blank stimuli that were introduced both prior to and following the judgment task. The response measure introduced by Silverman is somewhat unusual, and one may speculate whether inadvertently (as in other experiments that have been cited) the selection of this specific measure of hypersensitivity may not provide congruence between the index of the patient's aversive behavior (frequency of "movement away" of lever and screen) and the experimenter-designated appropriate response.

In many instances of spatial conflict, movement toward is often associated with approach behavior, movement away with avoidance.[74] Forewarned of the presence of "unpleasant" stimuli, a predisposition toward warding off such contents could have heightened the patient's selection of a push response. Since such a response is associated with noxious stimulus identification, high push-responding would readily lend itself toward an interpretation of hypersensitivity. To reject the notion of highly generalized avoidance response tendencies would require a more detailed analysis of the push-pull responses to the various stimulus word (including blank) categories used in the experiment. Furthermore, it would be best to mount another study that reversed the response measures that Silverman employed to identify his noxious and nonnoxious contents.

Finally, an unpublished study by Alvarez,[1] drawn from the Duke investigations, provides the most unequivocal evidence of how a neutral stimulus, simply by virtue of its contiguous pairing with a censure signal, can become a symbolic cue for withdrawal behavior.

In this experiment, poor and good premorbid schizophrenic patients, together with normal controls, initially rated their preferences for pictures of men and women selected because these evoked a wholly neutral response in a pilot investigation. Two sets of pictures, with equivalent preference ranks as determined by each subject's rating, were then used in a judgment task. For this task, the subject was required to predict, on the basis of physiognomic cues alone, certain presumed actions and preference choices of the individuals pictured. Prior to rendering a judgment about the individual, the photograph was placed in an apparatus set before the subject. This apparatus also contained two box inserts, the fronts of which were covered with opaque ground glass. When the boxes were illuminated, one lighted to read *Right*, the other *Wrong*. The subject was told that the lighting of one of the boxes would signify whether he had correctly or incorrectly predicted that photographed person's response to a given question. The experimenter then arbitrarily paired one set of pictures with the reward signal (nine of ten trials for one picture and eight of ten for the other), while a comparable set was paired in identical fashion with the punishment signal. Following this, all subjects again rated their preferences for the photographs.

The results of the experiment are presented in figure 2. Poor premorbid schizophrenic subjects showed a significant decline in their preference for pictures that had been contiguously paired with the *Wrong* signal, whereas the good premorbid schizophrenic and normal groups remain uninfluenced by the experimental manipulation. Reward effects were negligible for all groups—a finding more readily understandable for *goods* and *normals* whose preference choices, unlike that of the *poor* premorbid group, remained extremely stable. Consistent with Silverman's interpretation of his own findings, Alvarez' study, which may be viewed as a conditioning paradigm, offers striking evidence of the hypersensitivity of the schizophrenic to minimal

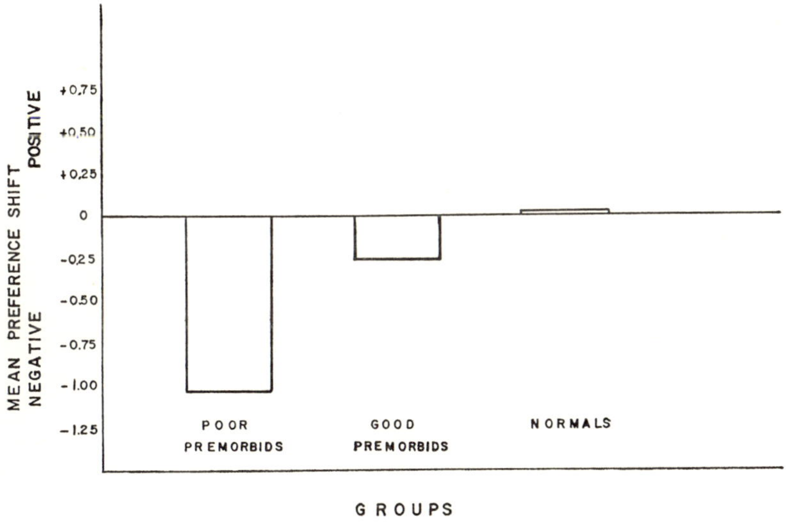

FIG. 2.—Mean shift in preference scores for censured pictures by schizophrenic and normal subjects. (From Alvarez.)

signs of censure. Such cues can provide an affective coloration to previously neutral components in the patient's environment, which, in turn, can come to serve as stimuli capable of evoking avoidance behavior.* If any study is needed to set at rest the concept of the schizophrenic as one who is generally deficient in acquired social motivation, the Alvarez study should suffice. Quite the contrary, the schizophrenic patient is extraordinarily sensitive to a specific class of psychologically noxious reinforcers—a sensitivity that is inferred from the types of habits that he uses to remove himself as rapidly as possible from the many anxiety-arousing situations that assail him.

Factors Influencing Predictions of Schizophrenics' Behavior under Censure

Premorbid Adjustment

Some cautions must be introduced in citing the effectiveness of censure in modifying the behavior of schizophrenic patients. Results of the Duke studies consistently revealed that withdrawal under censure was characteristic largely of a subset of patients who had exhibited chronic social and sexual maladjustment prior to the onset of psychosis. Such patients, as measured by the Phillips Scale,[81] are defined primarily in terms of their manifest avoidance of interpersonal interactions with others. By contrast, those schizophrenic patients whose case histories reveal adequate social and sexual adaptation tended to behave more nearly like normal persons in response to both learned punishments and rewards.† *Good* premorbid patients appear to possess a more flexible set of responses under stress—an observation that is

*Neiditch[77] has demonstrated a similar effect with a group of functional psychotics, many of whom were undoubtedly schizophrenic (since a criterion for inclusion in the study was an 18-35 age requirement). His subjects initially rated their preference for nine paper and pencil tests. A test intermediate in preference value was then contiguously paired with the frustration imposed by efforts to complete an unsolvable task. Subsequent preference ratings revealed that the psychotic group significantly downgraded the neutral test that had been associated temporally with the failure experience. By contrast, the judgments of normal control subjects remained uninfluenced by the interpolated frustration.

†A high positive relationship ($r = +.84$) has been shown recently to exist between scores on the Phillips Scale of Premorbid Adjustment in Schizophrenia and Becker's revision of the Elgin Scale.[8] Therefore, it seems appropriate to view the good premorbid-poor premorbid dimension derived from the Phillips Scale as one that is equivalent to the process-reactive continuum as defined by the Becker-Elgin Scale .[112]

supported by the results of studies conducted by Bleke, Zahn, and Alvarez. Cavanaugh, in a personal communication, has indicated that his schizophrenic group was composed of chronically ill patients who "for the most part would be characterized as poor premorbids on the Phillips Scale." Leventhal does not describe his subjects in terms of their status as either process-reactive or poor premorbid-good premorbid patients. In his study, he used only first admissions who had been hospitalized for less than four months, suggesting a preponderance of more acutely ill cases within his sample. This factor alone, however, does not allow one to make a judgment of premorbid adequacy. All poor premorbid cases were at one time "acute" patients in terms of first admission status and brief period of hospitalization. The determination of premorbid adaptation is irrelevant to the criteria used by Leventhal in selecting the subjects for his experiment. Since an additional criterion for admission to his study required participants to be in the age range 20-49, we can assume (on the basis of age-specific incidence data) that the experimental psychotic group was an admixture of schizophrenic patients varying markedly in quality of premorbid adaptation. Data on marital status would help to clarify this important distinction. However, given a sample of schizophrenics "drawn from six hospitals in Iowa," one can assume a substantial representation of poor premorbid cases since the ratio of *poors* to *goods* in most state hospitals runs substantially in favor of the former.

Since evidence in favor of strong aversive tendencies following threat of censure is more uniquely the habitual response of poor premorbid patients, the results of a study performed by Losen[66] involving censure and a sample of good premorbid schizophrenic patients should occasion no surprise. Although Losen's use of censure involved a somewhat nonspecific and general devaluation of the patients' performance, they still appeared to profit from his criticism. We have seen how such a diffuse form of reproof inevitably produces withdrawal in poor premorbid patients. Losen's findings that *goods* can profit even under this trying regimen attests to their adaptive efforts at active problem-solving under failure-threat in contradistinction to the more characteristic use of flight and withdrawal by *poors*.

The evidence derived from these and other experiments unequivocally supports the necessity for investigators who are interested in evaluating the effects of learned punishments on schizophrenic behavior to design their experiments to provide for adequate control of the variable of premorbid social competence.

Effects of Tranquilizing Medication

In an article that raises some provocative issues of the relevance of drug studies with animals to psychopathological processes in man, Evarts[32] has indicated a strategy for determining the specific role played by the tranquilizing drugs in modifying the behavior of schizophrenic patients. The first step, he suggests, is to set up an analogue of schizophrenic processes by imposing upon experimental animal subjects a disorganizing regimen designed so as to avoid producing either a gross neurological defect or severe disturbances of sensory processes or motor skills. The impairment to be induced by the drug, Evarts urges, should be a selective one (as opposed to a diffuse and pervasive one) that can be equated functionally with those primary psychological defects characteristically schizophrenic. The reversal of an impairment resulting from disorganizing stimulus events by specific chemical agents can then be used to predict the therapeutic potential of the agent in psychopathology.

In commenting on Evarts' suggestion, it is somewhat gratuitous for me to note that the growing usefulness of tranquilizing agents in modifying emotional processes such as fear, anxiety, and severe tension states in psychiatric patients[53, 102] has been accompanied (and in some instances preceded) by a number of systematic studies of the effectiveness of such drugs in ameliorating experimentally induced conditioned emotional reactions in rats, cats, and other species.[13, 14, 48, 50, 75] In general, these experiments lend support to the hypothesis that ataractic drugs reduce emotional responsivity to stimuli that have been contiguously associated with pain or fear-arousing stimuli. A number of these studies indicate that the drugs are effective in depressing conditioned avoidance reactions of the barrier-crossing or lever-pressing type.

Although concepts such as "fear" and "anxiety" have been used to describe such conditioned emotional responses, these behaviors remain questionable analogues of psychiatric states[54] and most unsatisfactory when applied to Evarts' demand for behaviors that are equivalent to the primary psychological defects of schizophrenia. Nevertheless, there is a uniquely challenging parallel to be seen in the effect of such drugs on the extinction of aversive reactions to conditioned stimuli following noxious experiences in animals and a comparable diminution in avoidance responding under censure in schizophrenia. Studies of the latter sort are few; worse yet, they lack the rigorous research design and methodological controls (e.g., double-blind, variation in dosage level, placebo usage, repeated testing of drug effects on same subjects) that are prerequisites for theorizing about drug action.[88] Despite these limitations, a brief review of some relevant data may be instructive. In each of the studies conducted by Zahn and Alvarez, independent groups of drug (primarily chlorpromazine) and drug-free poor premorbid and good premorbid schizophrenic patients were used, in addition to a drug-free normal control group. In table 5 data drawn from Zahn's experiment offer tentative evidence that chlorpromazine may modify the reversal pattern of *poors* following a *wrong* signal.

TABLE 5.—Reversals on Punished Pictures Following *Wrong* by Drug and Nondrug Patients (from Zahn)

	Drug Group (Chlorpromazine)		*Nondrug Group*	
	Mean	σ	Mean	σ
Goods	4.00	1.53	4.77	2.10
Poors	3.75	1.48	6.27	2.16
Normals	—	—	3.55	2.54

The means for both schizophrenic groups under drugs approximate the mean of the normal group, with the most striking reduction in reversal behavior apparent for the poor premorbid group.

Data derived from Alvarez' experiment supports Zahn. It will be recalled that in this study of shifts in preference choice for photographs that had been contiguously paired with either a *Right* or a *Wrong* signal, poor premorbid subjects showed a heightened aversiveness to "punished" pictures. When Alvarez' schizophrenic subjects were separated on the basis of their drug status, it became evident that these effects were the contribution largely of a selected subset of nondrug *poors*. These data are presented in table 6.

TABLE 6.—Mean Negative Preference Shifts for Censured Pictures by Drug and Nondrug Patients (from Alzarez)

Subgroup	*N*	*Mean*	σ
Nondrug Goods	7	—0.36	1.22
Drug Goods	13	—0.23	0.99
Nondrug Poors	13	—1.38	1.13
Drug Poors	7	—0.21	0.89
Normals	20	—0.07	1.38

Statistical analysis revealed that the two good premorbid subgroups differed neither from each other nor from the normal controls; nondrug *poors,* however, showed a significantly greater aversive response to the censured pictures than all other subject groups, including their drug counterparts. To complete the picture, the stability in preference choice of the drug *poors* was virtually identical to the nonshift behavior exhibited by both the normal group and the two subgroups of *goods.*

Two facts provided by Alvarez offer a cautionary note. First, table 6 reveals that twice the number of *goods* were receiving drugs in comparison with *poors.* Second, within each group the drug apparently had been prescribed for the more acute as opposed to the more chronic cases. Thus, a decision as to whether or not a psychiatrist prescribes drugs appears to be a joint function of both premorbid status and an acuteness-chronicity factor. Alvarez notes that among *goods* the acute patient is very likely to receive the drug, whereas the probability of this occurrence with a chronic case is not different from chance. On the other hand, a chronic *poor* is not a likely candidate for drug therapy, whereas in terms of acuteness *poors* divide evenly among the drug and nondrug groups.

Although his N's are very small, Alvarez concludes:

> Thus, the psychiatrist appears to maintain an implicit premorbid scale of his own, using variables which are quite similar in some ways to the Phillips Scale. . . . The basic assumptions here too seem to involve the belief that the more recently hospitalized patient can best benefit from the drug, particularly if the patient previously had made a good premorbid adjustment. The chronic patient, on the other hand, may not be deemed sufficiently promising to warrant drug therapy, especially if he has always had a marginal social-sexual premorbid adjustment. (p. 104)

Since a greater number of acutely ill patients were receiving chlorpromazine, the presumed reduction in avoidance responding under censure may merely reflect, in these subjects, the significantly lower habit strength associated with such aversive tendencies.

One further bit of evidence may be helpful in considering the effect of the ataractic drugs on avoidance behavior. Dr. Leventhal, whose study of verbal conditioning of schizophrenic subjects provided dramatic evidence of the power of censure in reducing the frequency of responses associated with such negative reinforcement, has reported in a personal communication that only four of the schizophrenic subjects used in his study were receiving tranquilizing medication at the time of testing. This fact, in part, may account for the consistency between Leventhal's data and the Duke studies.

Before leaving the drug area, however, a final point warrants discussion. I have concentrated thus far solely on the likelihood that a consequence of the physiological action of the tranquilizers is to lessen the severity of the distressing affects that accompany a threat-arousing stimulus; by raising the threshold for such stimuli, the intensity of the patient's defensive avoidance reactions may be reduced. An alternative hypothesis to account for this change in the schizophrenic's behavior (and one that would be far less adaptive in the long run) would be a perceptual one. The drugs may reduce the efficiency with which the patient can perceive and differentiate aversive situations from more neutral events. Experimental evidence to support this alternative formulation is sparse. Himwich[52] has suggested that chlorpromazine acts to block the reticular formation and to inhibit the alerting response. However, he indicates that an awareness of the painful stimulus is maintained by other cortical mechanisms but that "the severity of the associated distressing emotional accompaniment of the stimulus is greatly mitigated."

In a completed but as yet unpublished study, Bradford[12] had drug and nondrug good and poor premorbid schizophrenic patients evaluate two experimentally contrived mothers who discussed their techniques of child-rearing in the course of a tape-recorded pseudo-interview. The attitudes and practices of one mother were overpoweringly "schizophrenogenic," the other warmly democratic. Bradford found the responses of all nondrug patient groups and normals to these mothers, as measured by a modified Semantic Differential, to be comparable and appropriately discriminative. However, schizophrenic patients under drug therapy (and particularly the poor premorbid group) tended to equate the two mothers, failing to discriminate the specific stimulus attributes that had been assigned to each. Unfortunately, Bradford's study failed to provide a test of these alternative hypotheses, since patients were not required to manifest either approach or avoidance responses toward the two maternal figures.

On the other hand, Clarke,[25] who developed Bradford's procedure in an earlier study of conformity behavior to the two types of mothers, found that groups of drug and nondrug *poors* could not only discriminate between the two figures, but that the nondrug group showed marked conformity in response to the dictates of the powerful maternal figure. Clarke makes the following association between his study and other studies of aversive responding to punishment by schizophrenics.

> In the present study, the negative mother may be viewed as functionally comparable to the 'wrong' signal, and it can be thus hypothesized that she is viewed by the patient as a potent source of punishment for behavior that deviates from her own behavior or from her expectations. Under these circumstances, the patients were expected to choose the response that had the highest probability of avoiding the threatened punishment, in this case, conformity. (p. 50)

The drug poor premorbid group, however, revealed (as did all other groups in the experiment) accurate perception of the mothers, but far less intense conformity behavior. This finding would suggest that accurate perception of the threatening and nonthreatening stimuli was intact, but that the intensity of reaction to a negative stimulus was markedly reduced. These findings suggesting that perceptual acuity is not at issue are somewhat congruent with those by Sampson et al.,[80] who found that schizophrenic patients receiving fairly large doses of chlorpromazine (800 mg. daily) in comparison with a placebo group were able more readily both to identify photographs of patients housed on their wards and to name them more accurately.

Nevertheless, one can only conclude at this point that the issue of modification of responsiveness vs. perceptual accuracy remains unsettled because of the lack of strongly supportive data. Only through a series of carefully controlled investigations—a forlorn hope in this period of haphazard and indiscriminate drug usage—will it be possible to specify the action of ataractic medication on specific response systems in schizophrenic patients.

Reinforcing Effects of Learned Rewards

Although punishment appears to produce inflexibly maladaptive behavior in the schizophrenic patient, in some ways his response to rewards may be more unusual when matched against the normative behavior of others. All individuals, psychotic or otherwise, are motivated to avoid punishment. The differences between schizophrenic and normal subjects appear to reside more in the former's sacrifice of a problem-solving set in the interest of avoiding threat. With reference, however, to the effectiveness of learned rewards such as approval, prestige, and praise in modifying behavior, it is quite clear that reinforcers such as these play a major role in directing the learning activities of most children and adults.[59] For most individuals, such acquired or secondary rewards typically serve to strengthen old behaviors and to facilitate the acquisition of new ones. Atkinson and Robinson[3] report that a survey of studies of the comparative effectiveness of rewards and punishments in normal individuals revealed only one study in which punishment effects outweighed the positive aspects of reward. By contrast, a review of a large number of comparable studies of schizophrenic patients suggests that the likelihood of modifying their behavior through the mechanisms of praise and approval is, at best, equivocal. Hunt and Cofer[55] noted this in their early review of studies of psychological deficit in schizophrenia when they suggested that the slowness of patients on reaction time tasks, and their failure to maintain experimentally established sets to react reflected a partial extinction of responses to social stimuli. The latter were those derived from social interaction with the experimenter, an implicit desire to please him, and in turn to receive his commendation, approval, and support. More recent investigations have tended to confirm their earlier observations of Hunt and Cofer. Although several studies indicate an enhancement of the schizophrenic's performance following positive evaluation, such improvements are usually not very striking.[29, 78, 96, 99] By contrast, a larger number of investigators report failure to alter schizophrenics' behavior in the service of achieving rewards.[3, 21, 28, 46, 61] Finally, there are a number of studies in which the experimenter's intermingling of positive and negative reinforcers makes it difficult to evaluate the individual contributions provided by each,[1, 9, 40, 57] although the evidence appears to run in favor of a heavier commitment by the schizophrenic patient toward the avoidance of punishment than toward the achievement of reward.

The relative power of these two classes of reinforcers for schizophrenic and normal subjects can be seen in Leventhal's data as presented in figure 1. It is apparent that his schizophrenic group remained unresponsive to the presumably rewarding effects of the experimenter's verbal message "good" for specific pronoun usage. *E's* verbal admonition, "not so good," produced pronounced avoidance of the punished response class. Normal subjects, by contrast, found both the positive and negative reinforcement conditions facilitating.

Alvarez' experiment provides even more striking evidence of the ineffectiveness of reward. Measures of preference shift for rewarded pictures revealed no differences between *normals, goods* and *poors.* But this apparent similarity among the groups in response to reward is rather deceptive. *Normals* and *goods* remained uninfluenced by the interpolated procedure in which they were rewarded or punished for their predictions of the behaviors of the photographed persons. This was indicated by the subsequent stability of their preference choices for rewarded, punished, and control photographs. On the other hand, *poors,* as I have indicated, did show a substantial downward shift on the punished set of pictures. Hence, a compensatory increment in preference for other pictures in the series was indicated. Although the set of rewarded photographs had the twin advantages of greater familiarity and positive reinforcement—factors that ordinarily conduce to preferential evaluations—there was no evidence that the interpolated rewards had any effect on the choice behavior of the poor premorbid group. Indeed, whatever positive shifts were necessary to compensate for the negative trend away from punished stimuli were indiscriminately divided between the neutral and rewarded sets of stimulus pictures.

Although the trend is clearly toward the nonreinforcing effects of reward, the reconciliation of other studies that suggest enhancement of performance is not easily achieved. Some speculations, however, may be fruitful:

1. D'Alesio and Spence[29] have suggested that the level of task difficulty and the type of response required of the subject may be significant factors. In those studies reporting performance increments, the tasks that have been used, such as digit-symbol substitution and finger dexterity, have been relatively simple and thus have minimized response competition. It is of interest to note that in the only study in which task complexity was varied, the facilitating effects of reward were relegated largely to the simpler tasks.[99] Perhaps of even greater importance has been the nonverbal nature of the response demanded of the subject. It is interesting to observe that Bleke,[10] using a complex paired-associate learning task, required his subjects to use a motoric (lever) response and found some evidence for behavior facilitation under conditions of reward reinforcement. On the other hand, Atkinson and Robinson[3] employed a comparable type of task and failed to secure improvement under conditions in which the subject had to say the response associates aloud. (Other procedural variations, however, including the method of dispensing rewards and the difficulty of the material to be learned, could also account for the obtained differences.) Other learning studies that required verbal responses and revealed failures to learn under reward were those conducted by Leventhal[59] and Cohen and Cohen.[28] The very act of verbal

interaction with another may be sufficiently anxiety-arousing for the schizophrenic patient to insure interference with efficient learning. However, other studies do not support this conjecture.[96]

2. Rewards also appear to have a negligible effect on the behavior of schizophrenic patients when used in studies in which these are paired simultaneously with social punishments.[1, 40, 103] Thus, for schizophrenic subjects, the generalization effects produced by punishment may far outweigh those of reward. (At least, this would be reasonable to assume for poor premorbid patients. Unfortunately, the experimental literature with regard to level of premorbid adaptation and the effectiveness of social rewards on performance is rather meager.)

A reanalysis of the data of one of the author's previous papers may illumine this point.[40] Schizophrenic (largely poor premorbid) and normal subjects were tested in an auditory discrimination task under two conditions. For the first condition, *Reward Only,* subjects learned to *pull* a lever to a (training) tone and subsequently were tested on both the training stimulus and other stimuli that varied along the dimension of pitch. For each correct response (pull) to the training tone, a box lighted to read *Right;* there were no other signals provided if the subject responded to the other stimuli either with an appropriate (push) or an inappropriate (pull) response. In a second condition, *Reward-Punishment,* subjects again were rewarded with a *Right* signal for pulling to the training tone but were punished by the lighting of a *Wrong* signal if they pulled the lever upon hearing the most distant and hence the most dissimilar tonal stimulus.

Here then we have a procedure in which the schizophrenic patient is confronted with an array of stimuli varying along a defined dimension; a response to one stimulus in the array is associated with punishment, whereas that same response when made to another stimulus elsewhere in the continuum is followed by reward. If schizophrenics are more readily influenced by the rewarding as opposed to the punishing consequences of their behavior, one would predict maximum responding at the point of reward with the frequency of responding to other stimuli in the dimension determined largely by their similarity to the rewarded stimulus. If, however, punishment is more effective than reward for motivating schizophrenic behavior, there should be a decline in the frequency of a given response if it can eventuate in either punishment or reward. Furthermore, the frequency of responding to the generalized stimuli in the array should be a function of the dissimilarity of these stimuli to the one that has been associated with punishment. Stated in a somewhat different fashion, the gradient of generalization of avoidance of a punished stimulus should be flatter than the generalization gradient of approach to a rewarded one.

The results of the study tend to support this hypothesis. Under the *Reward Only* condition, schizophrenic and normal subjects produced generalization gradients of equivalent steepness. However, with the introduction of punishment for incorrect responses to the most ex-

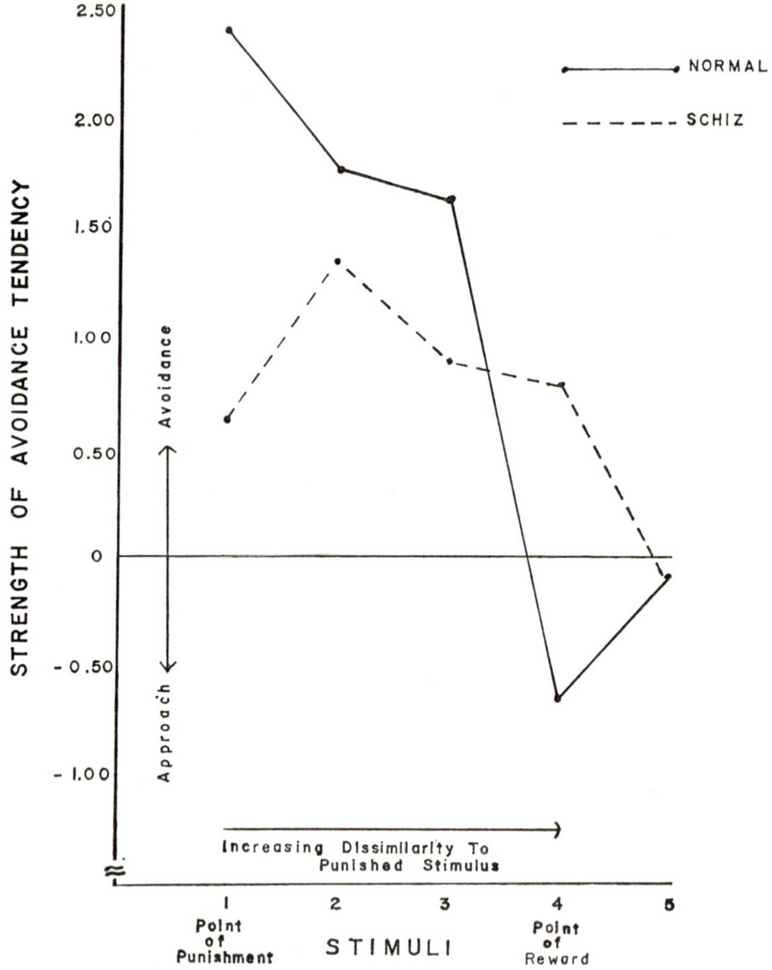

FIG. 3.—Hypothetical gradients of avoidance for schizophrenic and normal subjects. (From Garmezy.)

treme tone in the pitch dimension, normals benefited by the additional information cue with the result that their improved discrimination resulted in a correspondingly steeper response gradient. Schizophrenic patients, however, failed to profit from such cues and instead revealed a lessened ability to discriminate, as suggested by their markedly flatter response gradient. The factor of heightened avoidance under punishment in the schizophrenic group was seen further in a reduction in the frequency of appropriate (pull) responses to the training stimulus. Although such a maneuver by the patients lessened the likelihood of acquiring punishments, it also reduced the probability that they would receive social rewards. Comparison of the first 20 and last 20 trials in the experiment indicated that schizophrenic subjects did, indeed, make fewer pull responses to every stimulus with the greatest relative decline manifested at the training stimulus where such a response was wholly inappropriate.

Suppose we assume that the empirical gradients obtained under both experimental conditions represent an algebraic summation of both approach (to pull) and avoidance (of pulling) tendencies that are present at each stimulus point.[17] Since comparable rewards operate under both conditions, it seems reasonable to suggest that the strength of approach tendencies in each instance is equivalent. With the introduction of censure, however, under the *Reward-Punishment* condition it seems equally appropriate to assume that the strength of the avoidance tendency is now increased relative to *Reward Only*. Thus, by positing a simple subtractive relationship between the approach and avoidance tendencies at each stimulus point, it is possible to derive the hypothetical gradient of avoidance to which reference was made earlier.* These

*This hypothetical avoidance gradient can be secured by computing the difference between the frequency of pull responses at each point under the Reward Only and Reward-Punishment conditions. If we let AP represent the strength of approach under Reward Only and AV the strength of avoidance under Reward-Punishment with av to signify the reduced strength of the avoidance tendency for the Reward Only condition, then the operations above may be symbolized by the following notation:

Condition	*Hypothetical Approach Tendency*	*Hypothetical Avoidance Tendency*
Reward-Punishment	AP	AV
—Reward Only	—AP	—av
Residual hypothetical gradient of avoidance		$= \text{av}_{\text{residual}}$

hypothetical avoidance gradients are presented graphically in figure 3. It can be seen that patients, relative to normal subjects, reveal a low and flattened avoidance gradient from the point of punishment to the most distant stimulus along the pitch dimension. Although normal subjects show more marked avoidance to the punished tone, approach behavior increases as the training stimulus is neared, suggesting that their gradient is a function of heightened discrimination rather than indiscriminate avoidance. On the other hand, approach behavior for the schizophrenic patients seems to be determined primarily by the distance of a stimulus point from the locus of punishment. For the schizophrenic subjects, heightened generalization under punishment appears to be a function of the patient's efforts to escape censure by relinquishing those responses which, if made in error, can produce a *Wrong* signal. Since these same responses, however, can serve to produce a *Right,* it seems reasonable to assume that the patient is motivated more toward withdrawal and avoidance of punishment than he is toward the acquisition of social rewards.

Alternative explanations, however, have been provided by others for the failure of schizophrenic patients to profit from social rewards. First, the complexity of unraveling the informational as opposed to the reinforcing aspects of various verbal reinforcement combinations (e.g., *Right* vs. *Nothing, Wrong* vs. *Nothing, Right* vs. *Wrong*), independent of the additional problems superimposed by using psychopathological groups, has been discussed by Spence[95] and Buchwald.[18] The presence of schizophrenia undoubtedly adds to the complexities of interpretation. Spence, in personal correspondence with the author, has indicated that in several of the studies that she and her colleagues have conducted, poor premorbid (or nonremitted) patients exhibit marked differences in two-alternative studies in which *Right* is paired with no signal (*Right-Nothing*) as compared with a *Wrong-Nothing* combination. Such patients, Spence asserts, "couldn't utilize *Nothing* as effectively as an overt response in either combination but were especially poor in translating *Nothing* into *Wrong.* Thus, she suggests, behavioral deficits in poor premorbid patients may be related more to deficient cue utilization in specific verbal reinforcement combinations than to their motivational or emotional reactions to praise and censure.

Buchwald has also suggested in personal correspondence that alternative explanations of the results of studies of reward on performance in schizophrenia should also give attention to the nature of the reinforcement combinations that have been employed. In the interest of precision, I should prefer to quote at some length from Professor Buchwald's letter:

> . . . interpreting the lack of learning with positive verbal reinforcement in schizophrenics as due to the lack of effectiveness of approval is only one possible interpretation. I would like to suggest the following alternative.
>
> 1. In any learning experiment, in particular in multiple-choice or selective learning, at least two different outcomes or consequences are used. Typically, one of these (the "reinforcement") follows some particular response while the other, no environmental change or "nothing" for short, occurs after all other behaviors.
>
> 2. For systematic (learned) changes in behavior to occur, one of the consequences must be a stronger (positive) reinforcer than the other. For example, in a lever "push-pull" experiment, if *S* were told *Right* whenever he either pushed or pulled, the mean number of pushes would not increase over trials.
>
> 3. From #2 it follows that if schizophrenics, or poor premorbids, do not learn as well as normals under verbal approval, it indicates that the difference between the reinforcement value of *Right* and that of *nothing* is less in the slower learning group. We usually think of this as being due to the value of *Right* being greater in one group than the other. We are equally justified in attributing it to a disparity in the values of *nothing* in the two groups.
>
> 4. Consider that the (poor premorbid) schizophrenic has a very strong aversion to social censure. Lack of social censure—i.e., *nothing*—can conceivably then be very positively reinforcing. More generally, assuming that *nothing* is strongly positively reinforcing to schizophrenics fits with the description of the schizophrenic as withdrawing from others. Lack of another's response to him is preferred to the other's response (which might be censure). *Nothing*, in the verbal outcome situation, is a lack of response on the part of the other individual.

The observations advanced by Drs. Buchwald and Spence have cogency. Their comments add importance to those studies in which the pairing of *Right-Wrong* in contrast to *Right-Nothing*[40, 61] and *Wrong-Nothing*[61] suggest that punishment, when paired with reward, may be more effective in modifying the behavior of schizophrenic patients. However, an analysis, such as the one that I have advanced, can at this point only be viewed as suggestive.

To determine the effects of rewards uncontaminated by the patient's perception of implicit or explicit punishments is not an easy task. Nevertheless, the fact that so few studies fail to reveal even nominal acceleration of performance stamps the schizophrenic patient's response to social rewards as an aberrant one. However, discrepancies do exist in the literature, and our current difficulties in attempting to resolve these incongruencies have been well summarized by D'Alesio and Spence:[29]

> Lumping together all types of schizophrenics, all types of laboratory tasks, and the total class of manipulations characterized as social incentives and motivations, has not produced a simple empirical generalization about the effect that social incentives have on the performance of schizophrenics, let alone a generalization about the differences in reaction to social incentives between schizophrenics and normals. If the seeming contradictions among empirical findings are to be resolved, more refined analyses of the relevant experimental variables and their interaction with schizophrenic characteristics appear to be demanded. (p. 393)

Speculations Regarding the Origins of Avoidance Behavior in Schizophrenia

Two facets of schizophrenic reactivity have been described: (1) inflexible and persistent withdrawal from psychologically noxious events, and (2) a lessened responsiveness to social rewards. How does an organism prone to behaviors so contradictory to ordinary expectations develop? In this final section, I shall attempt to speculate on the early origins of such response systems solely from the standpoint of social learning considerations. I am not suggesting that alternative considerations utilizing physiological, biochemical, or genetic variables are not equally tenable. Obviously, a definitive theory of schizophrenia will require attention to all of these factors. But for the moment, I wish to speculate exclusively on the learned aspects of the schizophrenic patient's response to social punishments and social rewards.

Are tendencies toward social withdrawal, avoidance of others, extreme shyness, excessive sensitivity, and interpersonal aversiveness inherited? Some investigators are unequivocal in asserting that the general dimension of introversion-extraversion is strongly influenced by genetic factors.[33, 47] However, many investigators oriented toward genetic causation in schizophrenia perceive problems in explanations based exclusively upon the transmission of genetically determined trait structures. Rosenthal,[87] confronted with the prospect of integrating a diverse array of scientific findings collected on a set of quadruplet schizophrenic women, reviewed the evidence in favor of the possible inheritance of premorbid personality patterns and concluded:

> . . . no literature exists on the possible inheritance of certain day-to-day behavioral patterns during schizophrenic illness when the behaviors are not

considered as specific features of clinical subtypes or amount of deterioration. (p. 530)

The premorbid personality patterns that interested Rosenthal were those usually subsumed under the rubric of the "shut-in" personality[11, 38, 108]—pervasive introversiveness, alienation from others, excessive sensitivity, proneness to fantasy rather than problem-solving behavior. These attributes, although they appear to antedate the disorder, are said to provide the habit continuity for the schizophrenic's subsequent withdrawal from social interactions with others. However, as Rosenthal indicates, such continuities may not reflect antecedents to the disorder at all but rather the earliest consequents of a disease process. Their role then as precursors to schizophrenia and as genetic indicators of fundamental temperament attributes may be somewhat less determinate than the genetically minded propose. Furthermore, such behaviors may be explicated on the basis of social learning components as well as genetic predispositions. Whether introverted, excessively timid, and hypersensitive normal individuals respond to positive and negative reinforcers in a manner congruent with those of schizophrenic patients requires a study that has not yet been done. I fear that we are more concerned at the moment with such control variables as age, education, and (occasionally) social class when matching psychotic and normal groups of subjects. Were we to direct our experimental inquiries toward persons possessing trait manifestations not unlike those characteristic of the early schizophrenic or preschizophrenic individual, we would, perhaps, be more effective in our search for the types of social learning experiences that predispose some individuals (and not others) to more malignant forms of social maladaptation.

In the vacuum created by a lack of data, interesting speculations abound. Recently, Meehl[73] has argued for a fundamental genetic defect in the appetitive and aversive systems in the brain of the schizophrenic. He perceives the anhedonia (a defect in pleasure capacity) and interpersonal aversiveness so characteristically schizophrenic as derivatives of an imbalance produced by a malfunctioning reward center of the limbic system in relation to a normally functioning aversive center. To this genetically faulty neurological base, Meehl, fully cognizant of the clinician's reports of familial role interactions, would add the disordered social learning environment that is provided by a "schizophrenogenic" mother. Indeed, Meehl sees the maternal figure as a potentiator of the disorder, thus providing, in Rosenthal's words, that "unhappy collusion of nature and nurture" that may be uniquely schizophrenic.

But is it necessary to invoke a genetic substrate in searching for the roots of the schizophrenic patient's response to positive and negative social reinforcements? A flourishing child-development literature provides many exclusively behavioral formulations of the origins of specific forms of children's behavior that also allow for extension into more aberrant interpersonal processes.[4, 31, 36, 49, 58, 62, 90]

Elsewhere[41] I have suggested that pervasive withdrawal may have its roots in the unhealthy symbiosis that is presumed to characterize the relationship that exists between mother and preschizophrenic child. These reports of a pathological family milieu have not been the exclusive province of any one group of clinical observers. Lidz' studies of the intrafamilial environment of the schizophrenic,[64, 65] Stierlin's symbiosis[98] with its emphasis on the child's adaptation to the reality of the stronger maternal figure, Wynne's concept of pseudo-mutuality,[110] Bateson and Jackson's views of the "double bind"[5] —all stress the distorted patterns of interaction between family members and the preschizophrenic child. It is this pattern that has led Bateson[6] to state:

> . . . the schizophrenic communicates *as if* he expected to be punished every time he indicates he is right . . . and repeated experience of punishment . . . will lead the individual to behave habitually as if he expected such punishment. (p. 97)

It may be helpful to summarize Otto Will's[107] perception of the pathogenic aspects of the family milieu of the preschizophrenic child, since Will's formulation shares many components with those advocated by Bateson and his colleagues. Will emphasizes the mother's ability to generate acute and persistent conflict in her child by providing him with discrepant but repetitive messages in which speech and action belie one another. As a result, the child is confronted recurrently with contradictory commands that provide him with a never-ending unclarity between words and actions. Adding to the stress of such discrimination conflicts are continuing threats by mother of a disruption of her relationship with her child—a threat that (in the light of the child's vulnerability) is best overcome through dissociation. But this separation of cognition and affect has its own pathological consequences in hindering subsequent learning, inhibiting perceptual clarity, and warping the child's developing sense of reality. Will describes other disturbing influences arising from the family's distorted views of the culture. Excessive fears, proneness to denials of reality, and a failure to expose its members to external social experiences that would, in time, insure the development of valid and culturally appropriate discriminations—all serve to produce the counterfeit social currency that the child must subsequently use in interpersonal exchanges. For both Will and Bateson, a key attribute of the family environment of the preschizophrenic child is the presence of contradictory messages that continually pass from mother to offspring. In considering the consequences that may be expected to ensue from repetitive and ubiquitous sequences of subtly discrepant communications, I ask you to reflect for a moment on the behaviors produced by prolonged discrimination conflicts in Pavlov's dogs,[80] Masserman's cats,[71] or Liddell's sheep.[63] Liddell noted:

> In the course of months or years of training in the conditioned reflex laboratory a progressive change in the animal's behavior is observed and in our experience this behavior moves toward the pathological terminus which we call the experimental neurosis. . . . Another fundamental characteristic of the method is the intimacy which develops during training between animal and experimenter. In the course of months or years this intimate relationship alters infallibly, first in the direction of dependence and solicitation, but later toward avoidance or hostility. (p. 392)

Although the analogy is rather fetching, I would not be inclined to view multiple discrimination conflicts per se as a significant antecedent for the development of prepotent withdrawal responses in the preschizophrenic child. Rather, I believe that the more crucial element resides in the child's anticipation of consequences that would ensue for unacceptable responses to the many discrimination problems that are presented to him. This is the component that Will refers to as "repeated threats to the continuance of the relationship of the infant with those who care for him." It has been suggested more explicitly by Bateson et al.,[5] who view the learning context for the preschizophrenic child as one characterized by the extensive use of negative reinforcers. Referring to the use of such negative injunctions, Bateson writes:

> This may have either of two forms:
>
> (a) "Do not do so and so, or I will punish you;" or
>
> (b) "If you do not do so and so, I will punish you." Here we select a context of learning based on avoidance of punishment rather than a context of reward seeking. There is perhaps no formal reason for this selection. We assume that the punishment may be either the withdrawal of love or the expression of hate or anger—or most devastating—the kind of abandonment that results from the parent's expression of extreme helplessness. (p. 253)

I find this passage a very insightful one, made all the more comprehensive by the inclusion of a component in which efforts to escape the conflict are "made impossible by certain devices which are not purely negative—e.g., capricious promises of love, and the like."

Two clinical vignettes—the first a ward observation that illustrates the "double bind," the second a brief moment in a therapeutic interaction—offer a useful vehicle for reflecting on the social learning antecedents of schizophrenic behavior.

> A young man who had fairly well recovered from an acute schizophrenic episode was visited in the hospital by his mother. He was glad to see her and impulsively put his arm around her shoulders, whereupon she stiffened. He withdrew his arm and she asked, "Don't you love me any more?" He then blushed, and she said, "Dear, you must not be so easily embarrassed and afraid of your feelings." The patient was able to stay with her only a few minutes more and following her departure he assaulted an aide and was put in tubs.[5] (p. 259)

The second incident was provided by Dr. Alan Clarke, a former research associate, who reported the following exchange in the course of a therapeutic session with an adolescent schizophrenic boy:

PATIENT: You know what my mother's like?

THERAPIST: No, Bill—tell me.

PATIENT: She's like a destroyer. She sits in the middle of the ocean and there's a whole bunch of little fishing boats around her.

THERAPIST: Uh . . . fishing boats?

PATIENT: Yeah, like me, my Dad, brother and sister. . . .

THERAPIST: Oh.

PATIENT: And none of 'em know what to do. They don't know whether to sit still or sail away. But they know that if they move, she will train her guns on 'em and blast 'em out of the water.

Both incidents are helpful in formulating a social learning explanation of patients' habitual responses to rewards and punishments. In preparing this paper, I asked a number of my departmental colleagues with a cathexis for learning theory to suggest the early training regimen of an adult who on the one hand is hypersensitive to censure and pervasively committed to flight from it and who, on the other hand, is at best minimally responsive to signs of social approval. There seems to be some agreement that two types of reinforcement schedules could account for these effects. The first would require an environment in which the ratio of rewards to punishments was so heavily weighted in favor of the latter that there would be little likelihood that approval or praise would develop strong secondary reinforcing properties. In this type of pervasively punishing environment, highly generalized aversive responses possessing great habit strength would develop as the dominant response to frustration. A meager admixture of rewards would be insufficient to prevent the extinction of more approach-oriented or problem-solving behaviors under frustration. This hypothetical schedule of reinforcement, however, when suggested as modal for the schizophrenic patient's early years, leaves me quite dissatisfied. Lu's[67] description of the preschizophrenic child as one who was "good," obedient, dependent, and submissive, seeking to live up to (and often meeting) parental expectations and aspirations, makes it unlikely that such a child would have long foregone positive reinforcements from his parents or other significant parental surrogates in his environment.

The second learning paradigm for producing aversive behaviors that are strongly resistant to extinction may be a more adequate representation of the preschizophrenic sequence. This is one in which rewards and punishments have been consistently associated with the same goal response during learning.[70] Were the punishments to outweigh the rewards, the training situation would be even more favorable for the development of generalized avoidance. I believe that this paradigm comes closer to the evidence cited by clinicians for family pathology in schizophrenia. Bateson's observation of the ward interaction of patient and mother gives us a glimpse into the reward/punishment inconsistencies to which I make reference. The patient's initial and spontaneous gesture of affection toward his mother suggests the expectation of a counter-rewarding response from her. His momentary approach behavior identifies the response as one that has had some association with a prior amount of reward reinforcement. The contradictory aspect of the exchange resides in the mother's unresponsiveness. By withholding an anticipated reward, she exacts an unexpected "punishment"[76] for the patient's approach efforts.

If the "double-bind" has meaning at all, it is this sequence that I believe is the crucial one for the development of schizophrenic pathology: (1) The preschizophrenic child is confronted with numerous difficult and repetitive discriminations that involve cues so subtle that he is incapable of utilizing them for efficient problem-solving. (2) Initial efforts to respond adaptively to these (essentially) unsolvable discriminations encounter an apparently arbitrary schedule of both rewarding and punishing consequences. (3) As more problem-oriented behavior meets with continued negative reinforcement, less adaptive, highly stereotyped and fixated habits (primarily avoidant in direction) begin to develop.

Studies that have followed the paradigm of rewarding and punishing the same goal response have been restricted largely to subhuman species, but they are nonetheless instructive in detailing the rigid and perseverative behaviors that subsequently develop. One is reminded both of Masserman's[71] "counter-phobic" cats immobilized after having been shocked at the food box which previous to shock had only been associated with food reward, and Rigby's[84] report of rats who when faced with a comparable form of (temporal) conflict either crouched in fear or made vigorous efforts to leave the field. But, of the small number of investigations applicable to our problem, none are more revealing than the extensive studies of frustration and fixation behavior conducted by Maier.[68] Initially, Maier trained his rats to jump from a stand to one of two cards in a discrimination apparatus. One card, made readily discriminable by a design on the face, gave way if the rat leaped against it, thus providing the animal with a food reward that had been placed behind the card; the other card (different in design) was locked in place so that all the animal received for its efforts if it leaped against it was a punishing strike on its nose and a fall into a net placed below the discrimination apparatus. Maier noted that if each card was consistently designated as *either rewarding or punishing*, the animals could learn the discrimination and would consistently jump toward the rewarded card. If, however, the cards were then latched in an irregular order so that neither a particular card nor a particular position was consistently rewarded or punished, a new response pattern appeared. The animal, after an initial stage of variable choice behavior, soon refused to jump. This resistance could be overcome by directing an air blast at the animal as it stood on the jumping platform. Subsequently, however, the animal developed a "position habit" so rigid and stereotyped that it has been termed an "abnormal fixation." Such habits prove remarkably resistant to extinction, even to the extent of being maintained on trials in which food is exposed in the alternate position. Why then does the habit persist? Mowrer[76] has pointed out that the position habit is simpler than any alternate choice and probably provides the rat with no more punishment than it would experience if it sought for a more adequate solution to the problem. But more significant for our search for an analogue to schizophrenic processes is Mowrer's suggestion that "hope," which had earlier become conditioned to the positive card during training, is extinguished once frustration is initiated. The positive card then becomes as "equally punishing" as the negative one had been. With the extinction of hope, the strength of responding adaptively to the positive cue in the environment is destroyed, and a simpler pattern of behavior thenceforth prevails. As Bull and Strongin[19] have noted, the initial reaction to a frustration of deprivation or threat is anger, but a later consequence (if the responses generated by anger prove unsuccessful in reducing frustration) is discouragement and despair.

Although its tone may sound metaphorical, Mowrer's explanation of Maier's data seems pertinent as an analogue to the stylized passivity exhibited so often by the preschizophrenic child in response to a persistently frustrating familial environment. Parental air blasts designed to move the child off his jumping stand can produce responses that represent compromise solutions to demanded approach and preferred avoidance; fantasy, language distortions that conceal one's ambivalences, and paralogical thinking can all come to represent cognitive symbolizations of aversiveness. Gradually, behavior can grow more ritualistic, singularly more stereotyped and more camouflaged, until its only functional intent is to provide escape from those who have been perceived as the creators of a persistently noxious environment.

In terms of the effects of the joint imposition of rewards and punishments for the same behavior, a study by Fisher,[37] described in detail by Martin,[70] has some relevance to our analysis since it examines the consequences of such training on social interaction. The subjects of the experiment consisted of two groups of puppies who for a period of 15 weeks were either rewarded (petted and fondled) for approach behavior to the experimenter (indulged group), or both rewarded and punished (swatted, handled roughly, or shocked) for similar behavior (punished-indulged). A series of dependency tests based upon the amount of time each puppy spent near a human was run during the early and late course of training, as well as several days after the 15-week period had ended. Results indicated both greater dependency upon and greater fearfulness (as measured by a timidity test) toward humans.

This study underscores Hartup's[49] summary of the results of many experimental studies of dependency behavior in humans. Specifically, Hartup indicates that "frustration and inconsistency" on the part of adults toward children elicit greater dependency interactions than "consistent attention and approval."

It is such characteristics, which if present with great consistency in the early home environments of schizophrenic patients, could contribute to the emergence of a pattern of behavior characterized by compliance, heightened sensitivity, estrangement from others, avoidance of new situations, and rigidly inflexible rather than solution-oriented behavior toward new learning experiences. Behaviors such as these are indeed alien to many of us, but their seeming uniqueness needn't represent a genetic anomaly but could reflect consistent, albeit disguised, social learning histories quite distinguishable from those most of us have experienced.

In conclusion, I would merely offer a caution that sensitizes me to the entire problem of accounting for the effects of contemporaneous punishments in terms of events that have long preceded the current scene. Recent articles by Church[24] and Solomon[94] have pointed to the many complexities inherent in predicting behavioral effects produced by punishment. Solomon expresses the problem in this manner:

> . . . to predict in even the grossest way the action of punishment on a response, one has to know *how* that particular response was originally inserted in the subject's response repertoire. Is the response an instrumental one which was strengthened by reward? Is it instead a consummatory response? Is it an innate sequential response pattern? Is it a discrete reflex? Was it originally established by means of punishment? *Where,* temporally, in a behavior sequence, was the punishment used? How *intense* was it? These are but a few of the relevant, critical questions, the answers to which are necessary in order for us to make reasonable predictions about the effects of punishment. Thus, to conclude, as some psychologists have, that the punishment procedure is typically either effective or ineffective, typically either a temporary suppressor or a permanent one, is to oversimplify irresponsibly a complex area of scientific knowledge, one still containing a myriad of intriguing problems for experimental attack.
>
> Yet, the complexities involved in ascertaining the effects of punishment on behavior *need not* be a bar to useful speculation ultimately leading to experimentation of a fruitful sort.

From the standpoint of trying to understand the behavior of psychotics under punishment, one must add to Solomon's impressive list of difficulties the complexities that inhere in the schizophrenic process itself: the problems posed by efforts to recreate the past through retrospective accounts posed by highly prejudiced informants and recorded by theoretically biased observers; our current, insurmountable problem of trying to partial out the contributions of innate aspects of temperament as opposed to more socially acquired behaviors; and, finally, the fact that many individuals with comparable trait manifestations and disturbed family backgrounds never approximate schizophrenia. These manifold difficulties require that all speculations—genetic, biological, or behavioral—as to the origins of schizophrenic behavior be offered with a formal caveat that suggests that an idea has been offered supported with something less than a full-fledged warranty.

REFERENCES

1. Alvarez, R. R.: A comparison of the preferences of schizophrenic and normal subjects for rewarded and punished stimuli. Unpublished Ph.D. Dissertation, Duke University, 1957.
2. Arieti, S.: Interpretation of Schizophrenia. New York, Robert Brunner, 1955.
3. Atkinson, Rita L., and Robinson, Nancy M.: Paired associate learning by schizophrenic and normal subjects under conditions of personal and impersonal reward and punishment. J. Abnorm. Soc. Psychol. 62:322-326, 1961.
4. Bandura A., and Walters, R. H.: Social Learning and Personality Development. New York, Holt, Rinehart & Winston, 1963.
5. Bateson, G., Jackson, D. D., Haley, J., and Weakland, J.: Toward a theory of schizophrenia. Behav. Sci. 1:251-264, 1956.
6. Bateson, G.: The group dynamics of schizophrenia. *In* Chronic Schizophrenia (eds. L. Appleby et al.). Glencoe, Ill., Free Press, 1960, pp. 90-105.
7. Baxter, J. C., and Becker, J.: Anxiety and avoidance behavior in schizophrenics in response to parental figures. J. Abnorm. Soc. Psychol. 64:432-437, 1962.
8. Becker, W. C.: A genetic approach to the interpretation and evaluation of the process-reactive distinction in schizophrenia. J. Abnorm. Soc. Psychol. 47:489-496, 1956.
9. Benton, A. L., Jentsch, R. C., and Wahler, H. J.: Effects of motivating instructions on reaction time in schizophrenia. J. Nerv. Ment. Dis. 130:26-29, 1960.
10. Bleke, R. R.: Reward and punishment as determiners of reminiscence effects in schizophrenic and normal subjects. Ph.D. Dissertation, Duke University, 1953.
11. Bower, E. M., Shellhower, T. A., and Daily, J. M.: School characteristics of male adolescents who later became schizophrenic. Amer. J. Orthopsychiat. 30:712-729, 1960.
12. Bradford, N.: Comparative perceptions of mother and maternal roles by schizophrenic patients and their normal siblings. Ph.D. Dissertation, University of Minnesota, 1965.
13. Brady, J. V.: Assessment of drug effects on emotional behavior. Science 123: 1033-1034, 1956.
14. ——: Comparative psychopharmacology: animal experimental studies on

the effects of drugs on behavior. *In* Psychopharmacology: Problems of Evaluation (eds. J. O. Cole and T. W. Girard). Washington, D. C., National Academy of Sciences, National Research Publication 583:46-63, 1959.

15. Broen, W. E., Jr., and Storms, L. H.: A reaction potential ceiling and response decrements in complex situations. Psychol. Rev. 68:405-415, 1961.
16. Brooker, H.: The effects of differential verbal reinforcement on schizophrenic and non-schizophrenic hospital patients. Unpublished Ph.D. Dissertation, Indiana University, 1962.
17. Brown, J. S.: Principles of intrapersonal conflict. Conflict Resolution 1:135-154, 1957.
18. Buchwald, A. M.: Variations in the apparent effects of "Right" and "Wrong" on subsequent behavior. J. Verbal Learn. Verbal Behav. 1:71-78, 1962.
19. Bull, N., and Strongin, E.: The complex of frustration: a new interpretation. J. Nerv. Ment. Dis. 123:531-535, 1956.
20. Cavanaugh, D. K.: Improvement in the performance of schizophrenics on concept formation tasks as a function of motivational change. J. Abnorm. Soc. Psychol. 57:8-12, 1958.
21. ——, Cohen, W., and Lang, P. J.: The effect of "social censure" and "social approval" on the psychomotor performance of schizophrenics. J. Abnorm. Soc. Psychol. 60:213-218, 1960.
22. Child, I. L.: Personality. Ann. Rev. Psychol. 5:149-171, 1954.
23. Child, I. L., and Waterhouse, J. K.: Frustration and the quality of performance. II. A theoretical statement. Psychol. Rev. 60:127-139, 1953.
24. Church, R. M.: The varied effects of punishment on behavior. Psychol. Rev. 70:369-402, 1963.
25. Clarke, A. R.: Conformity behavior of schizophrenic subjects with maternal figures. J. Abnorm. Soc. Psychol. 68:45-53, 1964.
26. Cohen, B. D.: Motivation and performance in schizophrenia. J. Abnorm. Soc. Psychol. 52:186-190, 1956.
27. ——: Verbal reinforcement, punishment and motivational level in schizophrenia. Unpublished paper delivered at the Midwestern Psychological Association, Chicago, 1959.
28. Cohen, E., and Cohen, B. D.: Verbal reinforcement in schizophrenia. J. Abnorm. Soc. Psychol. 60:443-446, 1960.
29. D'Alesio, G. R., and Spence, Janet T.: Schizophrenic deficit and its relation to social motivation. J. Abnorm. Soc. Psychol. 66:390-393, 1963.
30. Dember, W. N.: Alternation behavior. *In* Functions of Varied Experience (eds. D. W. Fiske and S. R. Maddi). Homewood, Ill., Dorsey Press, 1961, pp. 227-252.
31. Donnelly, Ellen M.: The quantitative analysis of parent behavior toward psychotic children and their siblings. Genet. Psychol. Monogr. 62:331-376, 1960.
32. Evarts, E. V.: A discussion of the relevance of effects of drugs on animal behavior to the possible effects of drugs on psychopathological processes in man. *In* Psychopharmacology: Problems in Evaluation (eds. J. O. Cole

and T. W. Girard). Washington, D.C., National Academy of Sciences, National Research Council, 1959.

33. Eysenck, H. J.: The inheritance of extroversion-introversion. Acta. Psychol. Amsterdam, 12:95-110, 1956.
34. Farber, I. E.: The role of motivation in verbal learning and performance. Psychol. Bull. 52:311-327, 1955.
35. Feffer, M. H.: The influence of affective factors on conceptualization in schizophrenia. J. Abnorm. Soc. Psychol. 63:588-596, 1961.
36. Finney, J. C.: Some maternal influences on children's personality and character. Genet. Psychol. Monogr. 63:199-278, 1961.
37. Fisher, A. E.: The effects of differential early treatment on the social exploratory behavior of puppies. Unpublished Ph.D. Dissertation, Pennsylvania State University, 1955.
38. Frazee, Helen E.: Children who later became schizophrenic. Smith Coll. Stud. Soc. Work 23: 125-149, 1953.
39. Garmezy, N.: Approach and avoidance behavior of schizophrenic and normal subjects as a function of reward and punishment. Amer. Psychol. 7:334, 1952 (abstract).
40. ——: Stimulus differentiation of schizophrenic and normal subjects under conditions of reward and punishment. J. Pers. 20:253-276, 1952.
41. ——: Adaptive mechanisms in schizophrenia. Paper presented at the Menninger School of Psychiatry, 1963.
42. Garmezy, N., and Rodnick, E. H.: Premorbid adjustment and performance in schizophrenia; implications for interpreting heterogeneity in schizophrenia. J. Nerv. Ment. Dis. 129:450-465, 1959.
43. Goldstein, K.: The organismic approach. *In* American Handbook of Psychiatry (ed. S. Arieti). New York, Basic Books, Inc., 1959, Vol. II.
44. Goodnow, Jacqueline J.: How people deal with probable events. *In* Trends in Psychology (eds. K. R. Walker, W. M. O'Neal, and J. S. Clark). Melbourne, Australia, A.C.E.R., Press, 1957.
45. Goodnow, Jacqueline J., and Pettigrew, T. F.: Effect of prior patterns of experience upon strategies and learning sets. J. Exper. Psychol. 49:381-389, 1955.
46. Goodstein, L. D., Guertin, W. H., and Blackburn, H. L.: Effects of social motivational variables on choice reaction time of schizophrenics. J. Abnorm. Soc. Psychol. 62:24-27, 1961.
47. Gottesman, I. I.: Heritability of personality: a demonstration. Psychol. Monogr. 77:7 (Whole No. 572), 1963.
48. Grossman, S. P.: Effects of chlorpromazine and perphenazine on bar-pressing performance in an approach-avoidance conflict. J. Comp. Physiol. Psychol. 54:517-521, 1961.
49. Hartup, W. H.: Dependence and independence. *In* Child Psychology. The Sixty-Second Yearbook of the National Society for the Study of Education (ed. H. W. Stevenson). Chicago, University of Chicago Press, 1963.
50. Heistad, G. T.: Effects of chlorpromazine and electroconvulsive shock on a conditioned emotional response. J. Comp. Physiol. Psychol. 51:209-212, 1958.

51. Hill, L. B.: Psychotherapeutic Intervention in Schizophrenia. Chicago, University of Chicago Press, 1955.
52. Himwich, H. E.: Biochemical and neurophysiological action of psychoactive drugs. *In* Drugs and Behavior (eds. L. Uhr and J. G. Miller). New York, John Wiley & Sons, 1960, pp. 41-89.
53. Hoch, P. H.: The effect of chlorpromazine on moderate and mild mental and emotional disturbances. *In* Chlorpromazine and Mental Health. Philadelphia, Lea & Febiger, 1955, pp. 99-111.
54. Hunt, H. F.: Some applications of conditioned "fear." *In* Drugs and Behavior (eds. L. Uhr and J. G. Miller). New York, John Wiley & Sons, 1960, pp. 227-231.
55. Hunt, J. McV., and Cofer, C. H.: Psychological deficit. *In* Personality and the Behavior Disorders. (ed. J. McV. Hunt). New York, Ronald Press, 1944, Vol. II, pp. 971-1032.
56. Jenkins, R. L.: The schizophrenic sequence: withdrawal, disorganization, psychotic reorganization. Amer. J. Orthopsychiat. 22:738-748, 1952.
57. Johannsen, W. J.: Responsiveness of chronic schizophrenics and normals to social and non-social feedback. J. Abnorm. Soc. Psychol. 62:106-113, 1961.
58. Kagan, J., and Moss, H. A.: Personality and social development: family and peer influences. Review of Educational Research 31:463-474, 1961.
59. Kimble, G. A.: Conditioning and Learning (2nd ed.). New York, Appleton-Century-Crofts, 1961.
60. Lang, P. J.: The effect of aversive stimuli on reaction time in schizophrenia. J. Abnorm. Soc. Psychol. 59:263-268, 1959.
61. Leventhal, A. M.: The effects of diagnostic category and reinforcer on learning and awareness. J. Abnorm Soc. Psychol. 59:162-166, 1959.
62. Levy, D. M.: Maternal Overprotection. New York, Columbia University Press, 1943.
63. Liddell, H. S.: Conditioned reflex method and experimental neurosis. *In* Personality and the Behavior Disorders (ed. J. McV. Hunt). New York, Ronald Press, 1944, Vol. I, pp. 389-412.
64. Lidz, Ruth, W., and Lidz, T.: The family environment of schizophrenic patients. Amer J. Psychiat. 106:332-345, 1949.
65. Lidz, T., Cornelison, A., Fleck, S., and Terry, D.: The intrafamilial environment of the schizophrenic patient. VI. The transmission of irrationality. A.M.A. Arch. Neurol. Psychiat. 79:305-316, 1958.
66. Losen, S. M.: The differential effects of censure on the problem-solving behavior of schizophrenic and normal subjects. J. Personality 29:258-272, 1961.
67. Lu, Yi-chuang.: Mother-child role relations in schizophrenia. Psychiatry 24:133-142, 1961.
68. Maier, N. R. F.: Frustration: the Study of Behavior without a Goal. New York, McGraw Hill, 1949.
69. Malmo, R. B., Shagass, C., and Smith, A. A.: Responsiveness in chronic schizophrenia. J. Personality 19:359-375, 1951.
70. Martin, B.: Reward and punishment associated with the same goal response. Psychol. Bull. 60:441-451, 1963.
71. Masserman, J. H.: Behavior and Neurosis: an Experimental Psycho-

analytic Approach to Psychobiologic Principles. Chicago, University of Chicago Press, 1943.

72. McCarthy, J. F.: The differential effects of praise and censure upon the verbal responses of schizophrenics. Amer Psychol. 19:459, 1964 (abstract).

73. Meehl, P. E.: Schizotaxia, schizotypy, schizophrenia. Amer. Psychol. 17:827-838, 1962.

74. Miller, N. E.: Liberalization of basic S-R concepts: extensions to conflict behavior, motivation and social learning. *In* Psychology: a Study of a Science (ed. S. Koch). New York, McGraw-Hill, 1959, Vol. II, pp. 196-292.

75. Miller, R. E., Murphy, J. V., and Mirsky, I. A.: The effects of chlorpromazine on fear-motivated behavior in rats. J. Pharmacol. Exp. Ther. 120:379-387, 1957.

76. Mowrer, O. H.: Learning Theory and Personality Dynamics. New York, Ronald Press, 1950.

77. Neiditch, S. J.: Differential response to failure in hospital and non-hospital groups. J. Abnorm. Soc. Psychol. 66:449-453, 1963.

78. Olson, G. W.: Failure and the subsequent performance of schizophrenics. J. Abnorm. Soc. Psychol. 57:310-313, 1958.

79. Pascal, G. R., and Swensen, C.: Learning in mentally ill patients under conditions of unusual motivation. J. Personality 21:2, 240-249, 1952.

80. Pavlov, I. P.: Conditioned Reflexes (trans. G. V. Anrep). London, Oxford University Press, 1927.

81. Phillips, L.: Case history data and prognosis in schizophrenia. J. Nerv. Ment. Dis. 117:515-525, 1953.

82. Ray, T. S.: Electrodermal indications of levels of psychological disturbance in chronic schizophrenics. Unpublished paper. Presented at American Psychological Association meetings, Philadelphia, 1963.

83. Rickers-Ovsiankina, M.: Studies in the personality structure of schizophrenic individuals. II. Reaction to interrupted tasks. J. Gen. Psychol. 16:179-196, 1937.

84. Rigby, W. K.: Approach and avoidance gradients and conflict behavior in a predominantly temporal situation. J. Comp. Physiol. Psychol. 47:83-89, 1954.

85. Rodnick, E. H., and Garmezy, N.: An experimental approach to the study of motivation in schizophrenia. *In* Nebraska Symposium on Motivation (ed. M. R. Jones). Lincoln, University of Nebraska Press, 1957, pp. 109-184.

86. Rosenbaum, G., MacKavey, W. R., and Grisell, J. L.: Effects of biological and social motivation on schizophrenic reaction time. J. Abnorm. Soc. Psychol. 54:364-368, 1957.

87. Rosenthal, D. (ed.): The Genain Quadruplets. New York, Basic Books, Inc., 1963.

88. Russell, R. W.: Psychopharmacology. *In* Annual Review of Psychology (eds. P. R. Farnsworth, Olga McNemar, and Q. McNemar). Palo Alto, Calif., Annual Reviews, Inc. 15:87-114, 1964.

89. Sampson, Patsy N., Ray, T. S.., Pugh, L. A., and Clark, M. L.: Picture

recognition as an index of social sensitivity in chronic schizophrenics. J. Consult. Psychol. 26:510-514, 1962.

90. Sears, R. R., Whiting, J. W. M., Nowlis, V., and Sears, Pauline S.: Some child-rearing antecedents of aggression and dependency in young children. Genet. Psychol. Monogrs. 47:135-234, 1953.

91. Shakow, D.: Psychological deficit in schizophrenia. Behav. Sci. 8:275-305, 1963.

92. Silverman, J.: Noxious cue sensitivity in schizophrenia. Unpublished Ph.D. Dissertation, University of Michigan, 1962.

93. ——: Psychological deficit reduction in schizophrenia through response-contingent noxious reinforcement. Psychol. Rep. Monogr. Suppl. 2, 13:187-210, 1963.

94. Solomon, R. L.: Punishment. Amer. Psychol. 19:239-253, 1964.

95. Spence, Janet T.: Verbal discrimination performance under different verbal reinforcement combinations. J. Exp. Psychol. 67:195-197, 1964.

96. Spence, Janet T., Lair, C. V., and Goodstein, L. D.: Effects of different feedback conditions on verbal discrimination learning in schizophrenic and non-psychiatric subjects. J. Verbal Learn. Verbal Behav., 2:339-345, 1963.

97. Spence, K. W.: A theory of emotionally based drive (D) and its relation to performance in simple learning situations. Amer. Psychol. 13:131-141, 1958.

98. Stierlin, H.: The adaptation to the "stronger" person's reality: some aspects of the symbiotic relationship of the schizophrenic. Psychiatry 22:143-152, 1959.

99. Stotsky, B. A.: Motivation and task complexity as factors in the psychomotor responses of schizophrenics. J. Personality 25:327-343, 1957.

100. Taylor, Janet A.: Drive theory and manifest anxiety. Psychol. Bull. 53:303-320, 1956.

101. Thorndike, E. L.: Educational Psychology. Vol. I. The Psychology of Learning. New York, Teachers College, Columbia University, 1913.

102. Uhr, L., and Miller, J. G. (eds.): Drugs and Behavior. New York, John Wiley & Son, 1960.

103. Ullman, L. P., and Forsyth, R. P.: Responses by normal and schizophrenic subjects under positive and negative examiner reinforcement in a probability learning situation. Amer. Psychol. 14:407-408, 1959.

104. Venables, P. H., and Wing, J. K.: Level of arousal and the subclassification of schizophrenia. Arch. Gen. Psychiat. 7:114-119, 1962.

105. Webb, W. W.: Conceptual ability of schizophrenics as a function of threat failure. J. Abnorm. Soc. Psychol. 50:221-224, 1955.

106. Wilensky, H.: The performance of schizophrenic and normal individuals following frustration. Psychol. Monogr. 66:12 (Whole No. 344), 1952.

107. Will, O. A., Jr.: Human relatedness and the schizophrenic reaction. Psychiatry 22:205-223, 1959.

108. Wittman, Mary P., and Steinberg, D. L.: A study of prodromal factors in mental illness, with special reference to schizophrenia. Amer. J. Psychiat. 100:811-816, 1944.

109. Woodworth, R. S., and Schlosberg, H.: Experimental Psychology. New York, Henry Holt & Co., 1954.

110. Wynne, L. C., Ryckoff, I. M., Day, Juliana, and Hirsch, S. I.: I. Pseudo-mutuality in the family relationships of schizophrenics. Psychiatry 21:205-220, 1958.

111. Zahn, T. P.: Acquired and symbolic affective value as determinants of size estimation in schizophrenic and normal subjects. Ph.D. Dissertation, Duke University, 1956.

112. Zlotowski, M., and Solomon, L. F.: The relationship between the Becker and Phillips scales of premorbid adjustment. J. Nerv. Ment. Dis. 1964 (in press).

9

BEHAVIOR PATTERNS OF CHRONIC SCHIZOPHRENICS*

by EUGENE I. BURDOCK, PH.D., and ANNE S. HARDESTY, M.S.†

THIS CHAPTER DESCRIBES BEHAVIORAL PATTERNS of hospitalized mental patients elicited by means of a psychological interview. The patterns of two groups of resident patients and one sample of recent admissions have been analyzed according to sex, age, and length of illness.

The interviews were conducted in accordance with a specially designed protocol, the *Structured Clinical Interview* (hereafter the SCI), which consists of an interview schedule and an accompanying inventory of maladaptive behaviors indicated by the patient's responses. The interview is intended to provide a uniform stimulus context for the expected behavior. In this respect it resembles an individual clinical test such as the WAIS or the Stanford-Binet. The inventory in turn requires the examiner to indicate the presence or absence of preselected items of evoked behavior. The patient's verbal responses, physical appearance, and comportment are recorded on the inventory during the progress of the interview. The dichotomous items cover a wide range of psychopathological indicators and yield a quantitative assessment of degree of psychopathology.

The interview is constructed so as to direct the patient's attention toward significant areas of adaptation. However, the stimulus material is essentially neutral, making only an oblique approach to areas of potential pathology. The interview thus resembles a projective technique in that the interviewer's statements or questions serve as ambiguous stimuli which the patient, to some extent, invests with

---

*The authors wish to express their appreciation to Mrs. Marylin Wechselblatt who faithfully and uncomplainingly supervised the collection of data and verified the computations.

†Biometrics Research, Columbia University Department of Psychiatry and N.Y. State Department of Mental Hygiene, New York, N.Y.

his own meanings. But the responses are standardized by being recorded on the inventory in units of behavior. Typical questions are:

> "Tell me, what's troubling you now?"
> "What kind of an imagination do you have?"
> "What has your social life been like?"
> "How has your family been getting along?"
> "Tell me something that interests you in the news."

These questions are always presented in precisely these forms, but if the answer is ambiguous, the interviewer may ask: "Can you tell me more about it?" or he may repeat the question.

Answers to "What kind of an imagination do you have?" vary from a noncommittal "All right" to frank report of delusional or hallucinatory experiences. An "all right" may be belied by obvious indication of hallucination.

The aim of the instrument is to increase objectivity by penetrating beneath the level of generalization, which characterizes most global evaluations and in which disagreement is rife, to the underlying observable behaviors.

The inventory is so constructed that each molecule of maladaptive behavior is given a positive weight. Thus the greater the pathology, the more molecules of maladaptive behavior will be observed. A total score is determined by simply summing the observed items of maladaptive behavior. Total scores appear to reflect general severity of illness and have been found useful in comparing patients with each other and in evaluating changes within a single patient after treatment. Justification for use of total score as a measure of level of pathology is derived from studies of the internal consistency of the SCI, a preliminary form of which was reported on at the Eastern Psychological Association in 1962.[3] Point biserial correlations were computed between items and total score for several different samples, and 95 per cent confidence limits constructed so as to exclude a zero correlation. In this way it was found that the bulk of the items contributed significantly to total score. Certain critical behaviors of infrequent occurrence have been retained in spite of insignificant correlations with total score because of their intrinsic significance for psychopathology.

The SCI is composed of ten separate subtests which describe behaviors in the following areas: (1) Anger-Hostility, (2) Conceptual Dysfunctioning, (3) Fear and Worry, (4) Incongruous Behavior, (5) Incongruous Ideation, (6) Lethargy-Dejection, (7) Perceptual

Dysfunctioning, (8) Physical Complaints, (9) Self-Depreciation, and (10) Sexual Deviance. Because the frequency distributions of scores for both total and subtests appear to follow an exponential decay curve, an appropriate transformation has been applied to the raw scores in order to stabilize the variance. Table 1 shows the frequency

TABLE 1.—Frequency Distributions of Scores on Subtests and Total of the *Structured Clinical Interview* for a Sample of 48 Normals

	Subtest										
Raw Score	*1*	*2*	*3*	*4*	*5*	*6*	*7*	*8*	*9*	*10*	*Total*
0	37	29	42	35	47	28	48	44	35	42	12
1	9	14	4	10	1	15		3	6	4	10
2	1	5	1	3		4		1	2	1	7
3			1						3	1	7
4	1					1			1		2
5									1		3
6											2
7											1
8											1
9											1
10											
11											
12											
13											
14											1
15											
16											1

distributions of raw scores for a sample of normal subjects whose scores provided a baseline against which to compare the profiles of the mental patients. The ten subtests contain different numbers of items. Therefore, the transformed scores have been converted to scaled scores with mean of 50 and standard deviation of 10, respectively, so as to facilitate profiling of a subject's scores on the different subtests and to allow for comparisons among individuals and groups.

Four criteria were used for assigning items to subtests: (1) Initially, items were assigned to subtest areas *a priori* on the basis of clinical and theoretical criteria. (2) Point biserial correlations were then computed between items and subtests. (3) Frequency of occurrence of each item was balanced against magnitude of correlation in order not to exclude rare but critical items. (4) Stability of correlation was

TABLE 2.—Composition and Reliability of Subtests of the *Structured Clinical Interview* on a Sample of 410 Hospitalized Mental Patients

Subtest 1 (Anger-Hostility)				Subtest 2 (Conceptual Dysfunctioning)				Subtest 3 (Fear and Worry)				Subtest 4 (Incongruous Behavior)				Subtest 5 (Incongruous Ideation)			
Item No.	*Freq.*	rpb_1	rpb_T	*Item No.*	*Freq.*	rpb_2	rpb_T	*Item No.*	*Freq.*	rpb_3	rpb_T	*Item No.*	*Freq.*	rpb_4	rpb_T	*Item No.*	*Freq.*	rpb_5	rpb_T
14	15	.17	.15	1	2	.06	.16	21	38	.39	.17	2	7	.10	.12	17	93	.12	.04
16	4	.07	—.01	8	43	.22	.12	22	24	.35	.14	3	40	.09	.02	18	1	.08	.04
26	5	.12	.02	9	13	.29	.15	23	29	.28	.20	4	77	.24	.12	29	5	.38	.12
80	17	.21	.11	10	15	.35	.21	24	28	.28	.19	5	66	.24	.20	34	6	.27	.20
81	18	.22	.17	11	2	.15	.06	25	4	.16	—.04	6	33	.29	.19	46	2	.02	.02
82	23	.23	.21	12	53	.27	.14	27	49	.31	.11	7	0	0	0	48	10	.15	.11
83	24	.06	.04	13	268	.17	.03	35	78	.38	.10	15	12	.14	.09	49	0	0	0
84	2	.10	.12	42	59	.30	.27	61	81	.44	.36	132	11	.15	.20	54	4	.11	.12
85	23	.26	.18	43	11	—.03	.02	63	42	.14	.29	147	83	.27	.18	62	71	.50	.48
88	108	.10	.18	53	153	.22	.10	68	58	.23	.27	151	21	.05	.05	65	19	.38	.31
92	13	.14	.18	109	4	.15	.12	156	21	.08	.16	152	17	.30	.30	70	0	0	0
93	0	0	0	116	112	.48	.42					153	6	.19	.09	76	2	.14	.13
94	50	.24	.24	117	15	.32	.28					154	12	.19	.23	86	16	.27	.22
95	7	.12	.11	118	71	.47	.41					157	9	.25	.13	87	21	.35	.23
99	18	.41	.24	119	119	.24	.29					158	9	.12	.19	96	38	.41	.42
110	8	.38	.31	120	36	.22	.17					159	34	.27	.18	97	29	.37	.30
111	2	.22	.10	126	16	.39	.30					160	83	.43	.34	98	3	.06	.13
113	13	.38	.20	127	11	.29	.29					166	35	.30	.29	100	17	.40	.21
133	42	.12	.12	128	33	.31	.33					167	5	.17	.12	101	14	.48	.24
134	4	.22	.15	129	27	.22	.15					169	41	.20	.26	102	14	.34	.26
140	0	0	0	130	13	.32	.29					171	0	0	0	108	13	.31	.18
141	1	.17	.06	135	140	.17	.12					172	1	.10	.07	122	7	.42	.24
143	1	.10	.05	161	75	.27	.24					178	4	.07	.08	123	10	.37	.23
148	1	.17	.05	163	26	.28	.16					180	17	.07	.08	124	17	.42	.34
149	0	0	0	164	13	.12	.13									174	19	.03	0
168	29	.30	.18	175	7	.26	.29												
179	4	.26	.16	177	4	.04	.07												
				182	13	.33	.22												

TABLE 2. (*Continued*)—Composition and Reliability of Subtests of the *Structured Clinical Interview* on a Sample of 410 Hospitalized Mental Patients

Subtest 6 (Lethargy-Dejection)			
Item No.	*Freq.*	rpb_6	rpb_T
50	52	.15	.17
103	25	.35	.14
104	38	.40	.22
106	163	.24	.32
115	135	.35	0
121	69	.32	.19
137	20	—.07	.10
138	41	.09	—.04
139	99	.45	.29
150	38	.25	.19
162	60	.39	.26
165	169	.38	.11
170	72	.41	.23
176	49	.10	.14
181	11	.13	.15
183	2	.02	—.06

Subtest 7 (Perceptual Dysfunctioning)			
Item No.	*Freq.*	rpb_7	rpb_T
32	1	.16	.04
36	1	—.01	—.01
39	14	.35	.09
40	8	.20	.21
51	3	.09	.11
66	0	0	0

Subtest 8 (Physical Complaints)			
Item No.	*Freq.*	rpb_8	rpb_T
37	16	.14	—.03
44	35	.18	.10
45	18	.10	.09
47	35	.25	.12
52	32	.23	.06
55	11	.20	.17
69	42	.18	.08

Subtest 9 (Self-Depreciation)			
Item No.	*Freq.*	rpb_9	rpb_T
20	5	.18	.06
28	3	.05	.02
30	34	.10	.31
31	18	.18	.06
33	6	.12	.08
38	24	.30	.08
56	29	.09	.05
57	21	.33	.13
58	6	.32	.19
59	27	.35	.18
60	47	.14	.09
64	59	.27	.14
71	113	.15	.20
79	41	.21	.14
89	8	.28	.13
90	35	.29	.22
91	26	.30	.24
105	71	.36	.19
107	43	.31	.28
125	30	.19	.08

Subtest 10 (Sexual Deviance)			
Item No.	*Freq.*	rpb_{10}	rpb_T
72	70	.43	.27
73	22	.36	.22
74	9	.17	.17
75	1	.03	.05
77	39	.36	.32
78	56	.34	.18
144	2	.08	.13
145	2	.12	.15
155	1	.08	.08

determined by replication of the point biserial correlations in samples of chronic resident patients, new admissions, and normals.

The authors examined each item in the light of the four criteria and reassigned items on the basis of discussion and agreement. After several reshufflings of items and recomputations of the point biserials, when no further improvement could be obtained, the final assignments of items to subtests were cross-validated on a fresh sample and intercorrelations among the subtests were determined. Table 2 displays the point biseral correlations of each item with its subtest and with the total, together with its frequency of occurrence, for a sample of 410 hospitalized mental patients from among whom the 361 subjects for this study were selected. In Table 3 the intercorrelations among the subtests and the total are shown for the sample of normal subjects who provided the baseline for standardization of scores.

The interviews were conducted by psychologists from the staff of *Biometrics Research.* The reliability of the interviewers' observations was tested on samples of interviews for which two or more interviewers took turns interviewing and making concomitant observations. Interobserver agreement was then assessed by two-way analysis of variance.[1] On total scores one pair of observers, recording the behavior of 26 patients, had an intraclass correlation of .87; for another pair on 83 patients, the intraclass R was .83; for a group of three observers, an intraclass R of .89 was obtained across 25 patients. Intraclass correlations have also been determined for the subtests

TABLE 3.—Intercorrelations among Ten Subtests and Total of the Structured Clinical Interview

(Normals: N = 48)

Subtests	*1*	*2*	*3*	*4*	*5*	*6*	*7*	*8*	*9*	*10*	*Total*
1		.19	.42	.20	—.06	.27	0	.03	.56	.22	.65
2			.08	.21	—.11	.28	0	.12	.29	.14	.49
3				.12	—.05	.27	0	.21	.78	.54	.74
4					.41	.09	0	.03	.23	.06	.41
5						.08	0	—.04	.05	—.05	.09
6							0	—.13	.22	.36	.54
7								0	0	0	0
8									.44	.01	.30
9										.53	.88
10											.61

TABLE 4.—Reliability of Subtests of the *Structured Clinical Interview* (Intraclass Correlations between two Observers on 26 Patients)

Subtest	R
1	.66
2	.73
3	.75
4	.48
5	.81
6	.71
7	—.04
8	.79
9	.89
10	.73
Total	.87

on the first sample of 26 patients observed by the above pair of observers (table 4.) The correlation of —.04 of subtest 7 is based on only two items (on which the two observers disagreed). This subtest, which deals with Perceptual Dysfunctioning, contains items of very infrequent occurrence. A more representative estimate of its reliability will have to await analysis of a larger sample.

In addition to the interview inventories, *Ward Behavior Inventories*[4] were obtained on a subsample of patients. Total scores on the SCI and WBI, despite the different character of the two observational situations, showed a correlation of .41.

The patients for the study were drawn from chronic intensive treatment programs in two New York State mental hospitals and from new admissions to a research hospital. The patients ranged in age from 18 through 50 years, the two sexes being about equally represented. The 272 chronics had schizophrenic diagnoses and histories of one or more hospitalizations dating back at least two years before the beginning of the study. In selecting patients for inclusion in the two intensive treatment programs, the psychiatrists in charge had screened out very aggressive or extremely deteriorated patients.

While the range of pathology in the chronic sample was somewhat attenuated by the method of selection, the sample of 82 schizophrenics from the research hospital were successive admissions interviewed within one week of admission. Though some of these patients had had previous hospitalizations, all were interviewed during an acute phase of their illness on admission to the hospital. The composition of the sample is detailed in table 5.

TABLE 5.—Composition of Sample of Hospitalized Mental Patients by Age, Sex, and Admission Status

	MALES		FEMALES		TOTAL
Age Group	Chronic Resident Schizophrenics				
	Continuously Hospitalized	*Intermittently Hospitalized*	*Continuously Hospitalized*	*Intermittently Hospitalized*	
18-34	48	35	21	44	148
35-50	42	12	22	48	124
Total	90	47	43	92	272
	NEWLY ADMITTED PATIENTS				
	Schizophrenics				
	First Admission	*Previous Admission*	*First Admission*	*Previous Admission*	
18-34	4	22	11	28	65
35-50	4	5	4	4	17
Total	8	27	15	32	82
	Psychoneurotics				
18-34	1	1	2	—	4
35-50	1	—	2	—	3
Total	2	1	4	—	7
Grand Total					361

PATTERN ANALYSES

Figure 1 compares the SCI patterns of the two samples of chronic schizophrenics. In this and the following figures, the higher the score, the greater the indicated pathology. The patterns of the two institutions are quite similar, but the patients at Institution B show a slightly higher level of pathology than those in Institution A. The most marked deviation from normality occurs in the area of Conceptual Dysfunctioning, where the patients are approximately two standard deviations above the normals. The second highest score is on the subtest for Lethargy-Dejection.

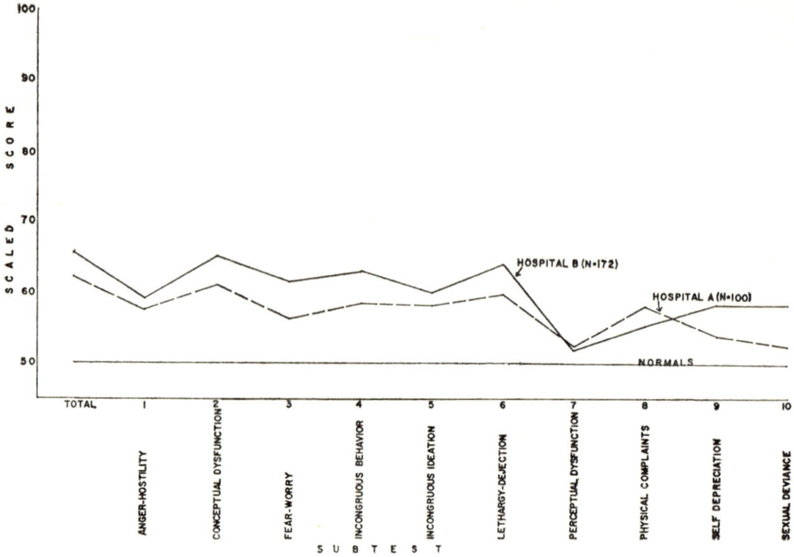

Fig. 1.—Mean SCI scores of two groups of chronic resident schizophrenics.

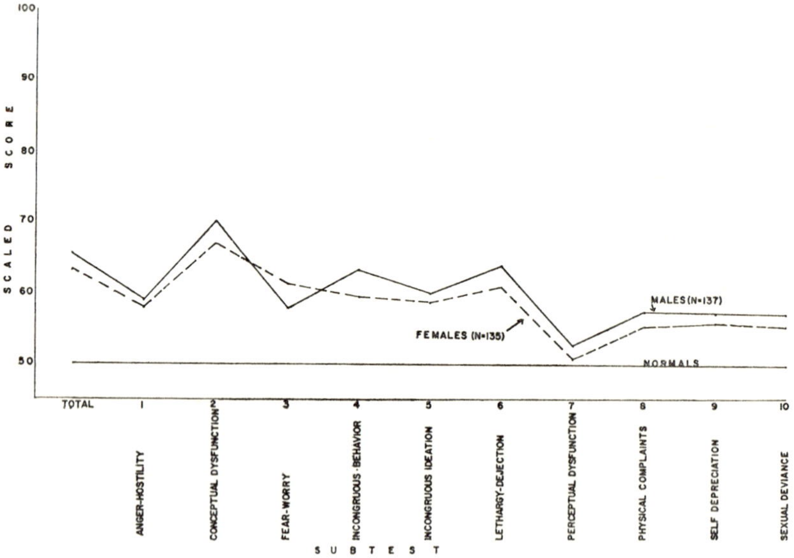

Fig. 2.—Comparison of mean SCI scores of male and female chronic resident schizophrenics.

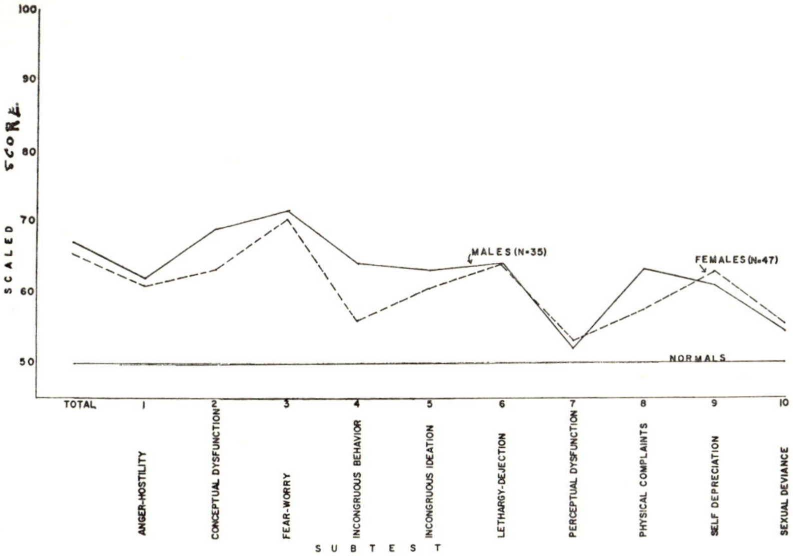

FIG. 3.—Comparison of mean SCI scores of male and female schizophrenics in an admission sample.

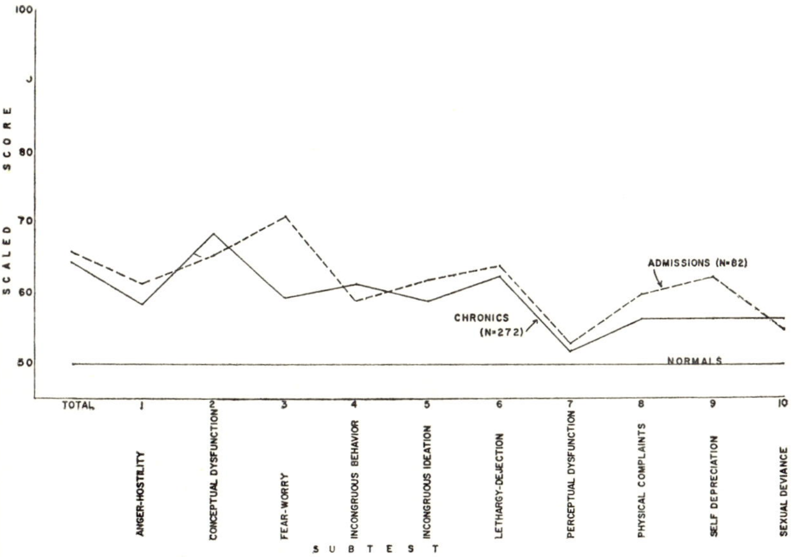

FIG. 4.—Mean SCI scores of new admissions and chronic residents with diagnosis of schizophrenia.

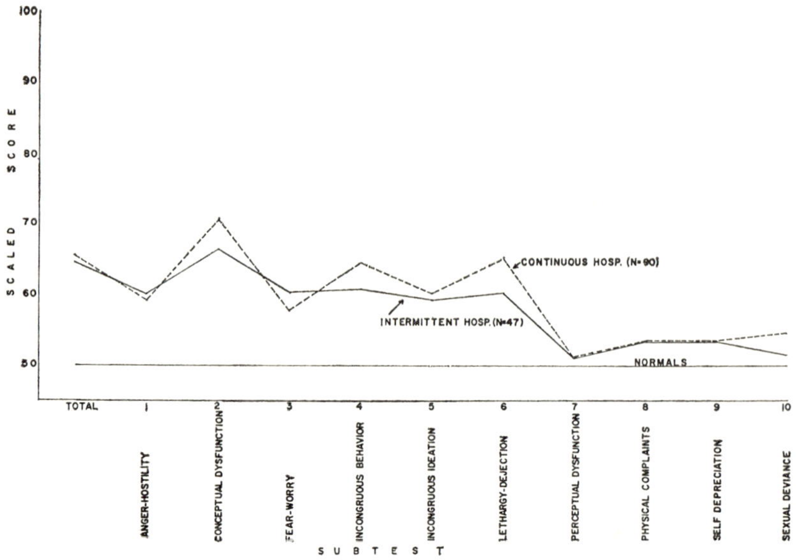

FIG. 5.—Mean SCI scores of male chronic schizophrenics compared for intermittent versus continuous hospitalization.

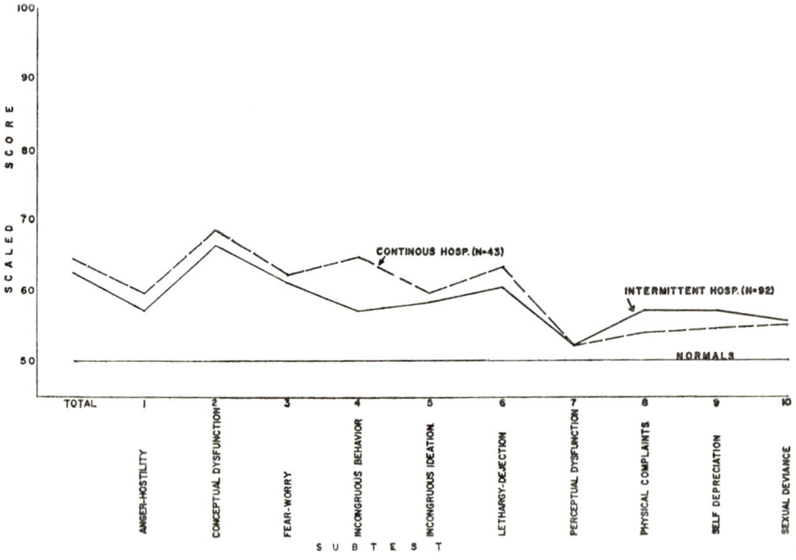

FIG. 6.—Mean SCI scores of female chronic schizophrenics compared for intermittent versus continuous hospitalization.

Figure 2 shows the profiles of the males and females across both institutions. Male chronics show consistently higher pathology on all but one of the ten subtests, Fear and Worry, where the females take over the lead.

Figure 3 shows the SCI patterns of males and females in the admission sample. Here too, as with the chronics, males exceed females in observed pathology. The males display greater pathology in the areas of Conceptual Dysfunctioning, Incongruous Behavior, and Physical Complaints.

Figure 4 contrasts the mean scores of the total admission sample with the corresponding scores of the total chronic sample. The new admissions show greater pathology in the areas of Fear and Worry, Physical Complaints, and Self-Depreciation.

In Figure 5 the male chronic schizophrenics are divided into two groups: a group of 90 who had been continuous residents for the two years preceding interview, and a group of 47 whose stays had been interrupted by at least one release during the preceding two years. The group of continuous residents show generally more pathological behavior than the intermittent residents. Their scores are higher on Conceptual Dysfunctioning, Lethargy-Dejection, and Sexual Deviance, but the intermittent residents exceed the continuous residents in Fear and Worry.

Figure 6 presents mean subtest patterns of the corresponding two groups of female patients. The female chronics with continuous hospitalization during the preceding two years, like the males, show more pathology than the chronic group with intermittent hospitalization. Unlike the males, the continuously resident female chronics show as much Fear and Worry as the intermittent residents. The two groups of females do not differ on Sexual Deviance. For both sexes, the continuous residents show peaks on Conceptual Dysfunctioning, Incongruous Behavior, and Lethargy-Dejection. Some of the discrepancies between the two sexes may be due to the reversal of the ratios of continuous to intermittent residents. Among the females there are twice as many with intermittent hospitalization as there are with continuous hospitalization; exactly the reverse is the case with the males, although the totals for the two sexes are equal.

The newly admitted schizophrenics were divided into those for whom this was the first admission and those with previous admissions. These patients were all interviewed within one week of admission. Figure 7 shows the profiles of the two groups of males among the new admissions. The two profiles are quite different. The first admissions show peaks of pathology on Fear and Worry, Lethargy-Dejection, Physical Complaints, and Self-Depreciation. Those with previous admissions show, in addition to elevated Fear and Worry, evidence of Conceptual Dysfunctioning, Incongruous Behavior, Incongruous Ideation, and somewhat greater Anger and Hostility.

In Figure 8 are seen the corresponding profiles for the newly admitted females. As with the males, both groups of females show elevations on Fear and Worry, with first admissions having the higher scores. The first admission females also show elevated Self-Depreciation. But female patients with previous admission show more Lethargy-Dejection.

In order to examine the effect of age on scores, the sample was divided into younger (ages 18 to 34) and older (ages 35 to 50) subgroups. Figures 9 and 10 draw the contrasts between the two age groups for the chronic males and females. As can be easily seen in the graphs, there is relatively little difference in the two pairs of profiles. Among the admissions, on the other hand, there is some divergence between the two age groups for both sexes. Figure 11 presents the profiles for the two age groups of newly admitted male schizophrenics. The younger age group shows somewhat higher scores except for Physical Complaints, where the older group is higher. There is another sharp divergence between the two age groups on Incongruous Ideation, where the younger age group shows an excess in contrast to the older admissions. Similarly, on Sexual Deviance the younger group shows some elevation, whereas the older group is below average. Figure 12 shows the profiles of the two age groups of newly admitted female schizophrenics. The younger group exceeds the older group in Fear and Worry and Self-Depreciation, but shows less Anger-Hostility and less Incongruous Behavior.

The largest diagnostic subgroup across the two samples is the paranoid schizophrenics. The mean subtest scores for patients with this diagnosis are shown in figure 13 for the chronics and in figure 14 for the admissions. In each figure the paranoids are shown in comparison with the catatonics, of whom there are an equal number among the chronics. In the chronic group there is relatively little separation between these two diagnoses, a somewhat surprising finding that is not paralleled among the admissions. The admission sample is, of course, much smaller in size, a fact which may be related to the heightened contrast it displays between the paranoids

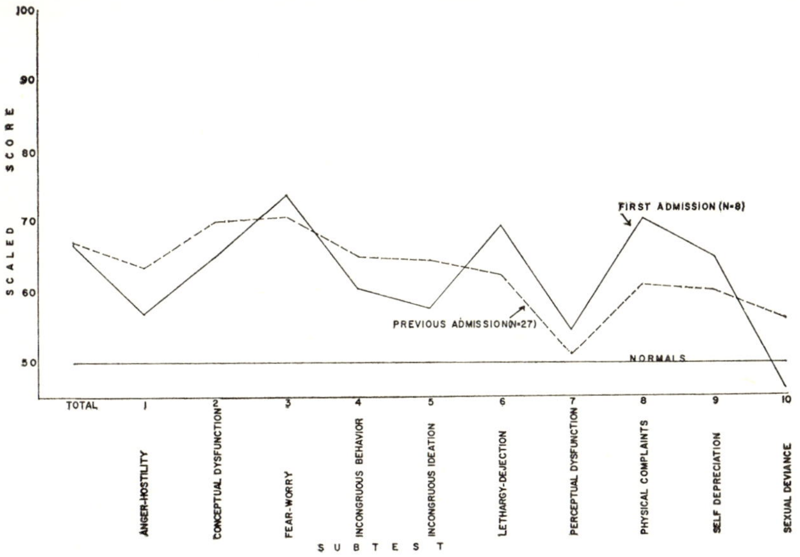

FIG. 7.—Mean subtest scores of two groups of male schizophrenics interviewed within one week of admission to hospital.

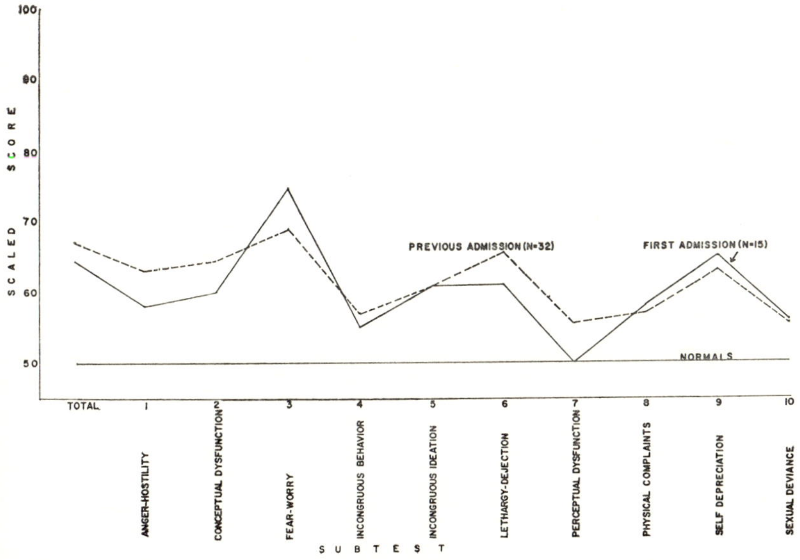

FIG. 8.—Mean subtest scores of two groups of female schizophrenics interviewed within one week of admission to hospital.

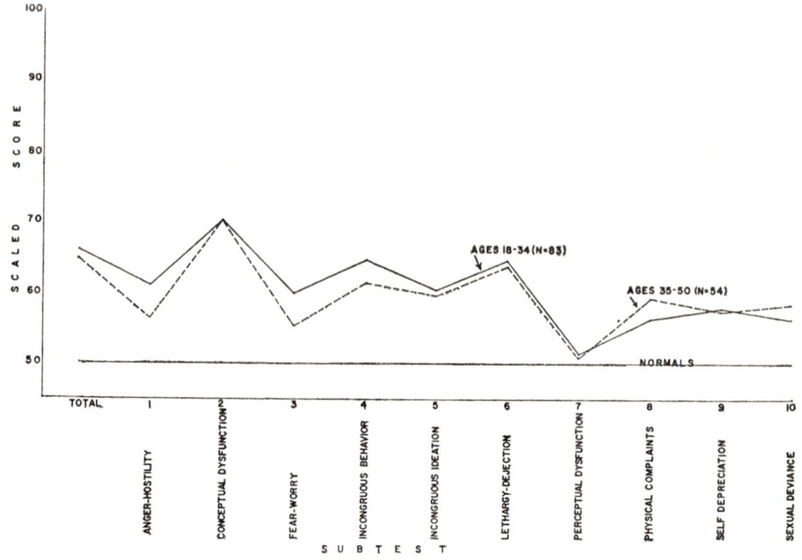

FIG. 9.—Mean SCI scores of two age groups of male chronic schizophrenics.

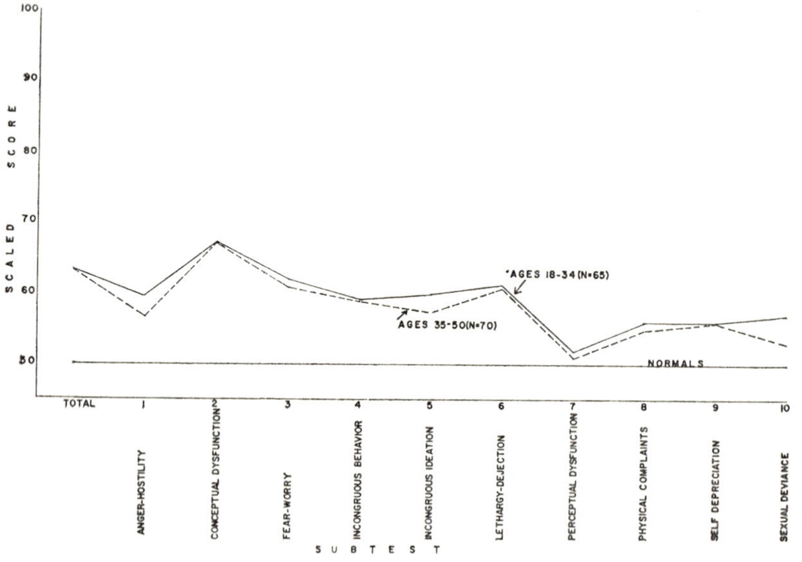

FIG. 10.—Mean SCI scores of two age groups of female chronic schizophrenics.

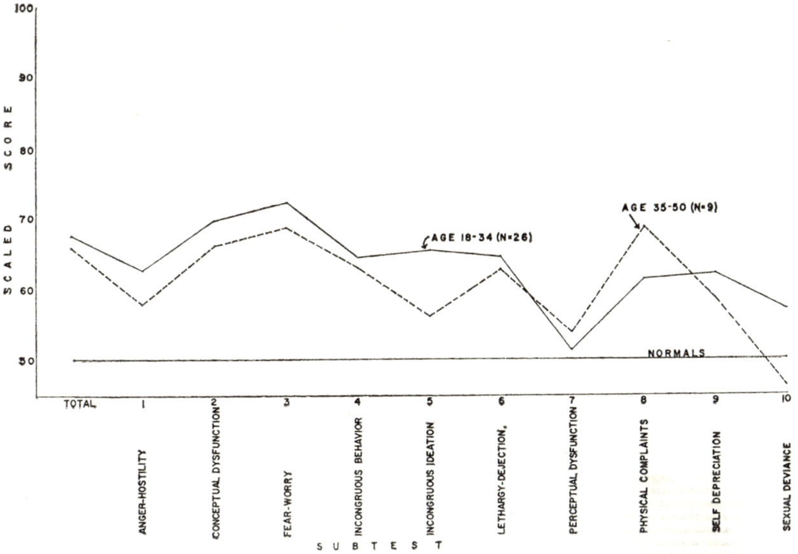

FIG. 11.—Mean SCI scores of two age groups of newly admitted male schizophrenics.

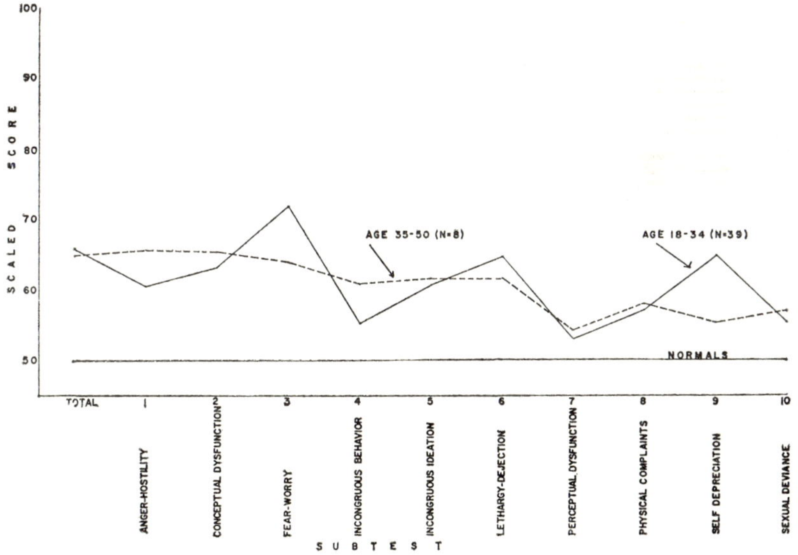

FIG. 12.—Mean SCI scores of two age groups of newly admitted female schizophrenics.

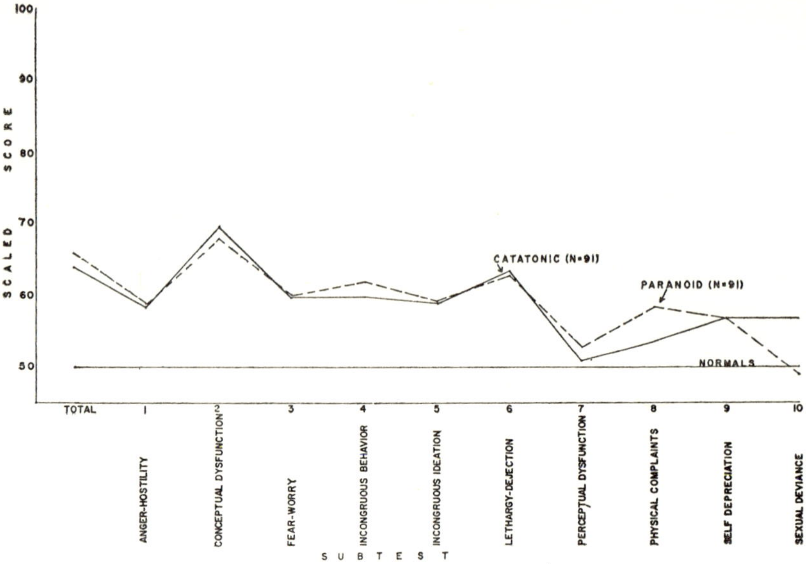

FIG. 13.—Mean SCI scores of two diagnostic subgroups of chronic schizophrenics.

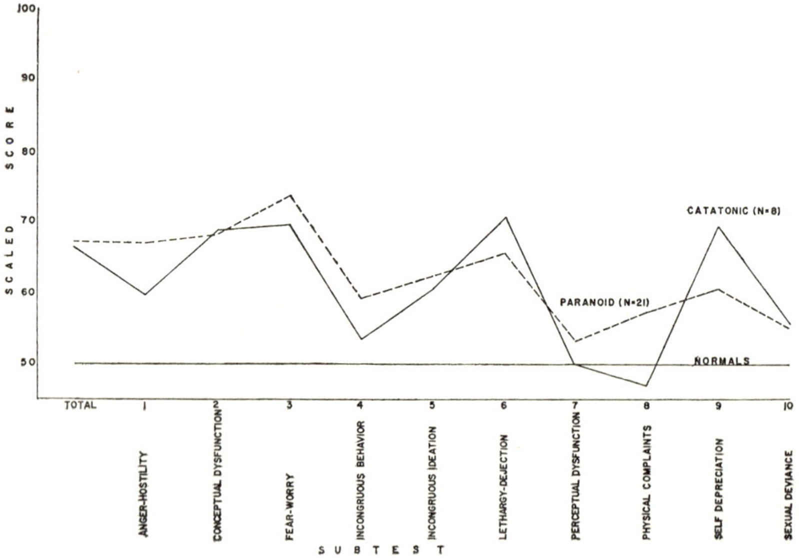

FIG. 14—Mean SCI scores of two diagnostic subgroups of newly admitted schizophrenics.

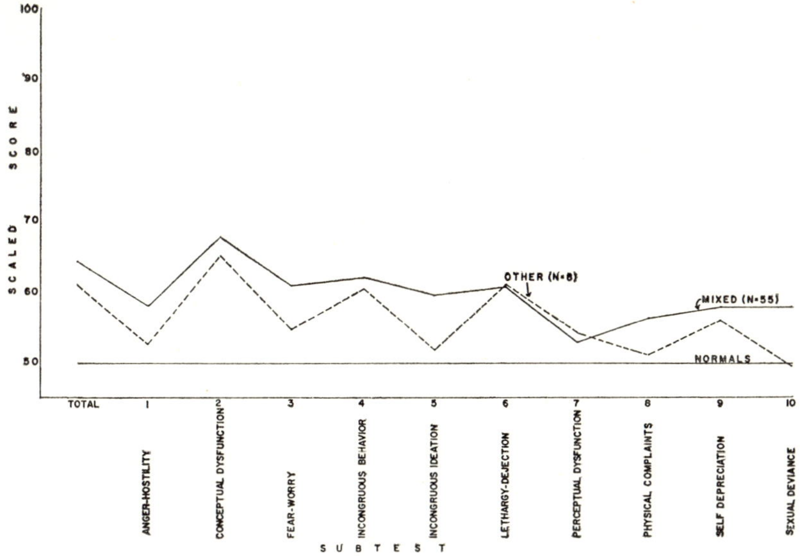

FIG. 15.—Mean SCI scores of two diagnostic subgroups of chronic schizophrenics.

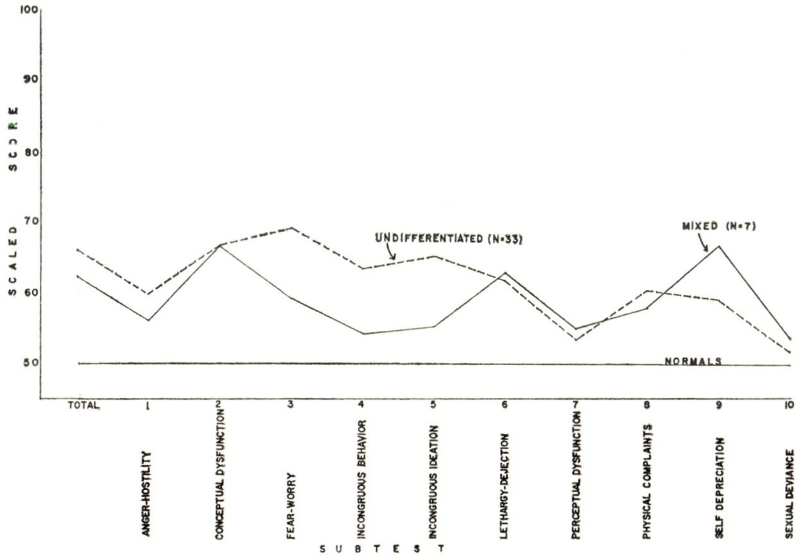

FIG. 16—Comparison of interview profiles of two groups of newly admitted schizophrenics.

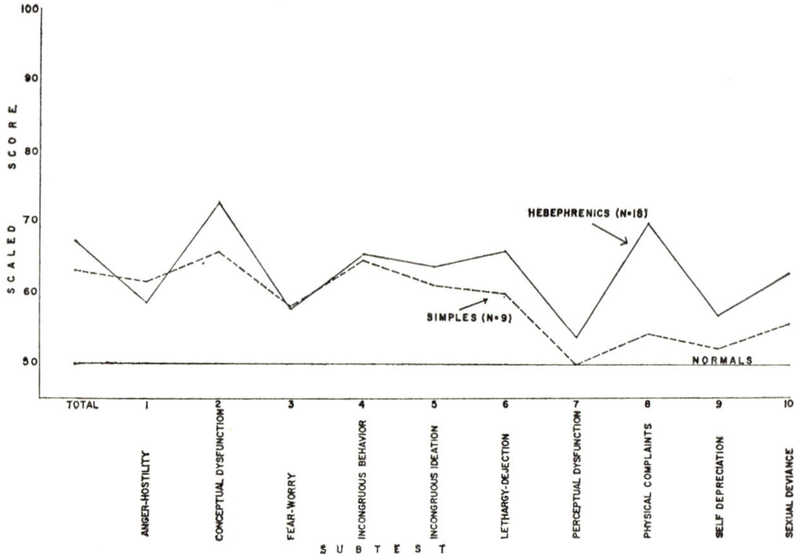

FIG. 17.—Interview profiles of chronic hebephrenics and of chronics with simple schizophrenia.

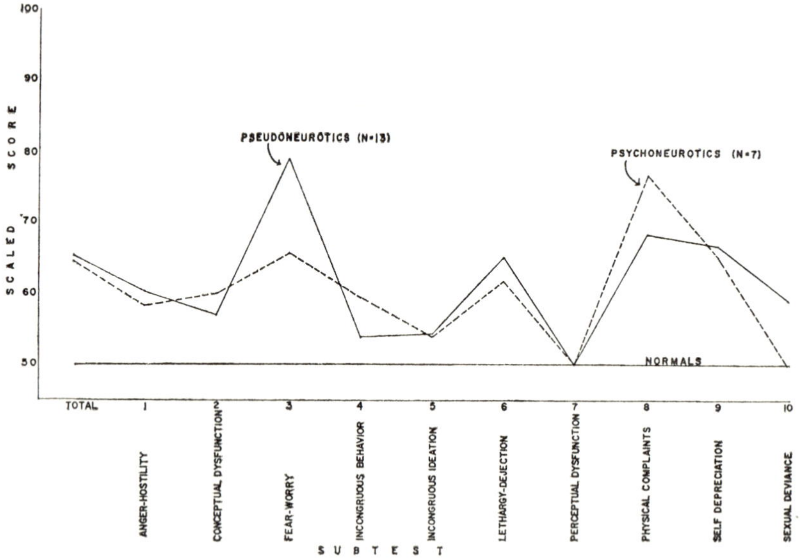

FIG. 18.—Interview profiles of pseudoneurotic schizophrenics and of psychoneurotics in an admission sample.

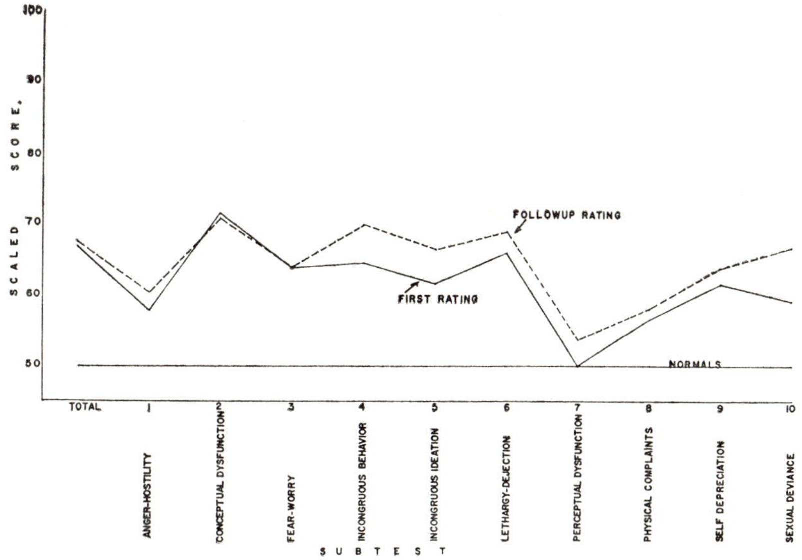

FIG. 19.—Test-retest profiles of a group of nine continuously hospitalized chronic schizophrenics reinterviewed on a six-months follow-up.

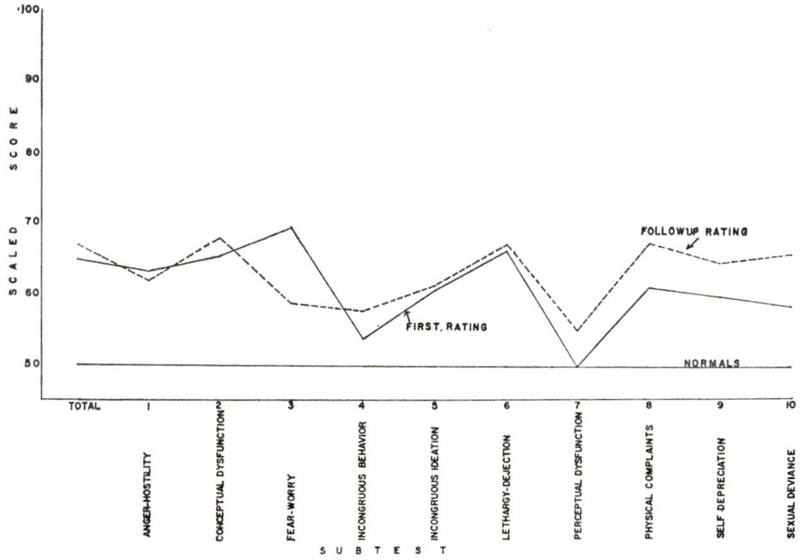

FIG. 20.—Test-retest profiles of a group of seven chronic schizophrenics with histories of intermittent hospitalization reinterviewed after six months with no intervening release.

and the catatonics. In the sample of admissions, as figure 14 makes clear, the catatonics exceed the paranoids in Lethargy-Dejection and Self-Depreciation, whereas the paranoids show more Fear and Worry, Anger-Hostility, Physical Complaints, and Incongruous Behavior.

Figure 15 is a comparison of the diagnoses, mixed and other, for the chronic sample. The mixed group, which is much larger, shows a generally higher degree of pathology, rising most sharply above the "other" group in Incongruous Ideation. In figure 16 an analogous comparison is drawn between the mixed and undifferentiated in the admission sample. The undifferentiated are by far the larger category among the admissions. They exceed the mixed group in Fear and Worry, Incongruous Behavior, and Incongruous Ideation, but the mixed group show more Self-Depreciation.

Figure 17 contrasts a group of chronic hebephrenics with a group of chronics diagnosed as simple schizophrenics. The hebephrenics are much higher than the simple schizophrenics in Conceptual Dysfunctioning and Physical Complaints, and also exceed in Lethargy-Dejection, Self-Depreciation, and Sexual Deviance.

In Figure 18 a group diagnosed as pseudoneurotic schizophrenics is compared with a group of psychoneurotics. For the most part, the two profiles are fairly similar, but the pseudoneurotics show marked elevation on Fear and Worry while the psychoneurotics are much higher on Physical Complaints.

A small subsample of chronics who had remained in hospital and had been returned to the regular continued treatment services from the special intensive treatment unit were reinterviewed some six months after the first evaluation. Figures 19 and 20 show the before and after profiles. Figure 19 deals with those who had a history of at least two years of continuous hospitalization; figure 20 contains those chronics whose hospitalization had been intermittent during the preceding two years. But neither group had had a release between the two interviews. The continuously hospitalized group show relatively little change. Their two profiles are parallel, but the subsequent one shows some increases in Incongruous Behavior, Incongruous Ideation, and Sexual Deviance. The intermittent group shows more variability. Although the total score remains at about the same level, there is a marked decline in Fear and Worry, balanced by some increase in Physical Complaints, Self-Depreciation, and Sexual Deviance.

Summary

As can be seen in table 4, there are three groups of patients in the sample: (1) the major component consisting of 272 chronic resident schizophrenics, (2) a group of 82 newly admitted schizophrenics, and (3) a small supplementary group of 7 psychoneurotics brought in to contrast with the pseudoneurotic schizophrenics. Analyses of the behavioral patterns of the patients were based on a reference sample of 48 normals. Since the 272 chronic resident schizophrenics came from two different hospitals, patterns of the two institutions were first compared to identify any significant differences between the two institutions. Only a slight difference in overall level of pathology was found between the two hospitals. The chronics were then pooled for subsequent comparisons. The admission sample, when compared with the sample of chronic residents, showed greater Fear and Worry, more Physical Complaints, and greater Self-Depreciation. Within each of the major samples, chronics and admissions, the two sexes were compared with one another. In both samples male schizophrenics showed greater pathology than females, but there was a more consistent elevation among the chronics. Comparisons were then made within the chronic sample between continuous and intermittent residents, separately for each sex. An analogous set of comparisons was also drawn among the admissions between the first admissions and those with previous admissions. These comparisons were followed by a series of comparisons in which the old and young patients in each subsample were compared with each other, separately by sex. The next set of comparisons draws attention to differences between diagnostic subgroups. Two unexpected findings among these comparisons are the relatively little differentiation between the chronic paranoids and chronic catatonics, and the striking difference between the pseudoneurotic schizophrenics and the psychoneurotics. A final comparison is of two small subsamples of the chronic schizophrenics who were reinterviewed. One of these latter, a continuously hospitalized group, show less variation on reinterview than the other group who had histories of intermittent hospitalization.

REFERENCES

1. Burdock, E. I., Fleiss, J. L., and Hardesty, Anne S.: A new view of interobserver agreement. Personnel Psychol. 16:373-384, 1963.

2. Burdock, E. I., and Hardesty, Anne S.: Observational inventories for the

assessment of mental patients. Psychopharmacol. Serv. Cent. Bull. 2:14-16, 1962.

3. Burdock, E. I., and Hardesty, Anne S.: Structured clinical interview and inventory. Paper presented at Eastern Psychological Association, Atlantic City, N.J., May 1962.

4. Burdock, E. I., Hakerem, G., Hardesty, Anne S., and Zubin, J.: A. Ward Behavior Rating Scale for mental hospital patients. J. Clin. Psychol. 16:246-247, 1960.

10

PRESIDENTIAL ADDRESS: CONTRIBUTIONS OF BEHAVIORAL SCIENTISTS TOWARD A WORLD WITHOUT WAR*

by JEROME D. FRANK, M.D.†

WE ARE LIVING IN A TIME of the most rapid and drastic changes in the conditions of human life that mankind has ever known. These changes, brought about by science and technology, are creating new hopes and new dangers. For the first time we can realistically envisage a world without poverty, hunger, ignorance, or chronic disease, closely knit by communication and transportation, in which the brotherhood of man could become a reality. At the same time, humanity has at last achieved the power to exterminate itself. The challenge to our generation is to change ingrained patterns of perception and behavior swiftly and drastically enough to overcome the dangers and realize the hopes. As Kenneth Boulding has said: "If the human race is to survive it will have to change its ways of thinking more in the next 25 years than it has done in the last 25,000."[1]

As so often seems to be the case in human affairs, the threatened evil is imminent, the hoped-for benefit problematical. The world of human brotherhood and enduring peace lies in the distant future; the suicide of mankind can occur any day.

President Kennedy put it metaphorically: "Every man, woman, and child lives under a nuclear sword of Damocles, hanging by the slenderest of threads, capable of being cut at any moment by accident, miscalculation, or madness."[2] In more prosaic terms it has been estimated that the United States and the Soviet Union have in deliverable form about one-eighth of the amount of fissionable material required to wipe out life on earth, and all signs point to further increase as other nations begin to make their own nuclear weapons.

---

*This chapter originally appeared in Comprehensive Psychiatry 5:283-293, 1964.

†Professor of Psychiatry, Henry Phipps Psychiatric Clinic, Johns Hopkins Hospital, Baltimore, Md.

Political and military leaders and scientists agree that the unlimited destructive power of modern weaponry has made the eventual elimination of war necessary for human survival. Since war is woven into all aspects of modern society and has afforded a way of satisfying all sorts of human drives, both aggressive and altruistic, eliminating it will require an immense effort. Not only must we forestall its outbreak, but for the long pull we must find other means of satisfying human needs that war has met in the past and develop new methods of resolving international conflicts that are suited for the nuclear age. This task can be accomplished only by massive, concerted, and persistent efforts of experts in human behavior, along with those in many other fields. The purpose of this presentation is to offer concrete illustrations of contributions psychiatrists, psychologists, and other students of human nature are actually making toward the goal of a world without war.

To be sure, determinants of war and peace lie primarily in the realms of politics, economics, and military science, as do hopes of finding substitutes for war and creating an enduring peace. However, national leaders, not nations, interact, and weapons do not fire themselves, unless men finally decide to abdicate this function to computers. Considerations of national policy, military and economic strength, and the like determine the behavior of leaders to a large extent, but psychological factors may also powerfully influence their decisions.

There can be little doubt that mental illness of national leaders occasionally changed the course of history. Woodrow Wilson's cerebral arteriosclerosis, which enhanced the rigidity of his personality, probably kept the United States out of the League of Nations. Hitler's pathological bitterness and hatreds shaped the catastrophic course of Nazism. These examples are, of course, exceptional, and there is probably nothing psychiatrists could have done about them in any case. They can, however, make relevant information about mental illness available to national leaders and diplomats to help them evaluate the persons with whom they deal. A psychiatrist, Mottram Torre, and a political scientist, William Glaser, have done just this by collaborating on a richly documented monograph describing the major types of mental illness or aberrant behavior that diplomats may display and by suggesting how best to deal with them.*

That psychological reactions of normal healthy leaders may play

*Parts of the monograph have been published.[3]

an important role in determining the fate of nations is being brilliantly demonstrated by a political scientist, R. C. North, and his colleagues at Stanford. They have been studying the "conflict spiral" leading up to World War I by quantitative content analysis of official and unofficial state papers, newspapers, and the like in the six weeks following the assassination at Sarajevo.[4, 5] They found that decision makers of each of the five major powers saw themselves as agents of friendship, but three (Austria-Hungary, Germany, and France) also saw themselves as targets of hostility. They felt themselves to be victims of injury, and the feelings were most intense when they were making the most crucial policy decisions—that is, when calm was most needed. North's analyses confirm the clinical observation that strong emotions distort perception and reduce flexibility of behavior. As tensions rose, decision-makers tended increasingly to select from incoming information those data that supported their preconceived views. Intelligence gatherers in the field reinforced this trend by overemphasizing information which they thought the central leadership wanted to receive. This lead to mounting mutual misperceptions and a progressive narrowing of perceived alternatives for resolving the conflict, culminating in the outbreak of war. Furthermore, "soft" indexes of psychological tension traced a pattern over time almost identical with "hard" economic indexes such as gold flow, securities prices, and commodity futures, and levels of hostility were significantly correlated with levels of mobilization of European armies.

These findings open the exciting possibility of developing quantitative measures of national suspiciousness, hostility, and the like. Just as Dow-Jones averages and freight car loadings help policy makers to foresee and forestall economic depressions, so periodic determinations of national psychological states might help national leaders to avoid war. As North puts it: ". . . such research can enrich wisdom gained through experience, clarify the ambiguities of common sense, and provide more precise tools through which to assess the incredible complexities of international relations."[4] This increases the decision maker's freedom of action and helps to reduce the likelihood of catastrophic misjudgments.

It is somewhat ironic that this convincing demonstration of the importance of psychological factors in international affairs should be made by a political scientist. Perhaps his example will stimulate behavioral scientists to become more active in this field.

Space does not permit review of certain interesting armchair attempts to apply psychological principles and knowledge to the full range of phenomena of the arms race and international relations.[6-8] Instead, a few of the efforts to gather facts about specific problem areas, or proposals for dealing with them, that can be empirically explored will be briefly presented. These can be grouped into five categories, arranged roughly in order of closeness to the problem of war prevention: forestalling the outbreak of war, developing better methods of guarding against cheating on disarmament agreements, making negotiations more effective, overcoming hostile and suspicious national attitudes, and developing nonlethal methods of conducting group conflict.

Today, main reliance for preventing the outbreak of a hot war is placed on deterrence—the mutual threat to inflict so much damage on a potential nuclear aggressor that he will not launch an attack. A prominent missile expert, Dr. Lester Van Atta, has observed that since a massive exchange of nuclear weapons would be an incalculable disaster for both sides, one must assume that neither intends to use them—that is, that their sole function is to deter. He continues: "But deterrence is a psychological effect, not a physical effect. We have made the untested assumption that the more numerous and sophisticated our weapons, the greater their deterrent effect. On their side, the Soviets apparently have assumed that the more megatons per weapon, the greater their deterrent power. I leave to you, as psychologists, the question as to whether either of these assumptions is supportable."[9]

One psychologist, Thomas Milburn,[10] has accepted the challenge. His Project Michelson is undertaking studies of deterrence which are realistic enough to be sponsored by the Navy. Milburn's point of departure is the recognition that threat of punishment, though it may inhibit undesired behavior, leaves the underlying motivations unchanged and stimulates resentment toward the threatener. Therefore the inhibited behavior may reemerge even more strongly after the threat is withdrawn. On the other hand, reward reinforces the desired behavior and also creates a more favorable attitude toward the rewarding agent. Milburn, therefore, suggests that deterrence should be viewed as having positive as well as negative forms. It should be used not only to prevent or inhibit behavior of the adversary we do not wish, but to reward behavior that we approve. The sale of wheat to Russia is an example of a positive deterrent, since it rewards the Russians for diverting resources from armaments to food.

Project Michelson supports over 30 related studies in 15 universities and independent research organizations.[11] The researches are based mainly on computer analyses of speeches of decisionmakers today, historical documents such as those used by North, and literature on various aspects of military strategy. Some findings are tested by giving the data in disguised form to subjects in simulated international conflict situations and observing how closely the march of events in the artificial situation resembles that of the real one. So far, only preliminary results have been reported, but they are highly promising. Those with the most immediate applicability concern the distorting effects of the "information filters" of our adversaries and allies, a phenomenon also noted by North, and that we shall meet again in studies of international person-exchange programs and negotiations.

A psychological pitfall involved in trying to prevent an adversary from attacking by outarming him is illustrated by a public opinion study of attitudes of builders of private fallout shelters. As contrasted with a carefully matched sample of nonshelter builders, shelter builders were found to rely more on military strength as a major deterrent of war, were more inclined to believe that the military position of the United States had become stronger during the preceding year, and believed shelters would reduce the chance of war. At the same time they were more certain war would occur. This apparently paradoxical finding can be explained by the hypothesis that having built a shelter as protection in the event of war, to justify the effort the builder is impelled to believe that the outbreak of war is more, rather than less, likely.[12]

This example of the universal need for self-justification suggests one reason why arms races are so difficult to halt. The more resources a nation invests in weaponry to deter an attack, the more it is tempted to find evidence that its enemy plans to attack to justify its investment. This, in turn, stimulates it to build still more weapons.

The prevention of a hot war is at best only a holding operation until complete disarmament under adequate safeguards can be achieved and other effective ways of resolving international conflicts are created. A major psychological obstacle to reaching disarmament agreements is each side's fear of secret violations by the other; and each side would be strongly tempted to cheat because of its conviction that the other is doing the same. Because caches of weapons can be so easily concealed, and even secretly manufactured, physical inspection will probably never be enough. Hidden weapons are useless, however, unless leaders know where they are and an organization exists that is able to launch an attack with them. This suggests that inspection of people might be more effective than inspection of weapons. Behavioral scientists are exploring two promising approaches to knowledge inspection. Both assume that since disarmament is the official goal of all nations and to the advantage of all, each would intend to keep a disarmament agreement. Each would want to convince the others that it is doing so, and the main danger of violations would be by clandestine groups. One proposal for exposing them has been termed "inspection by the people."[13] This would require laws within each country encouraging the populace to reveal to an international inspectorate any cheating that they know of. It has been worked out in considerable detail, including methods of protecting informers and making sure that the inspectorate can communicate freely with the citizens of the countries involved. Leo Szilard had an opportunity to present this proposal personally to Premier Khrushchev and reports that he "got the point, got it fully and his answer was very gratifying."[14] Since then it has been under serious discussion by Soviet and American scientists.

Public opinion polls in the United States, Western Europe, India, and Japan have shown that 70 to 90 per cent of the respondents would approve such an inspection organization and that they themselves would report any such attempts at manufacturing forbidden weapons to this worldwide inspection agency. Whether people would actually behave as they say they would is, of course, uncertain; but the polls at least suggest that the possibility of inspection by the people is not as fantastic as might appear at first glance.

The second approach to knowledge inspection is through direct interrogation of people who might know of violations. Ralph Gerard, a leading neurophysiologist, believes that lie detection techniques using physiological indexes, including new ones such as changes in brain-wave patterns, could be raised to a level of over 90 per cent certainty and that these hold out substantial hope for checking whether an official's public statements or statements to an adversary in negotiations really are true.[15]

Improved methods of inspection would probably help achieve disarmament agreements, but at best such agreements can be only one step along the road to a warless world. In fact, many would claim that focus on disarmament puts the cart before the horse—that disarmament will become possible only after nations relinquish or reconcile mutually threatening national goals, and after other forms of resolving international conflicts, in which nations have confidence, have been evolved.

International negotiations have been the chief means for approaching these goals. Behavioral scientists cannot do much about the conflicts of national purpose which negotiations attempt to resolve, but they can clarify formal properties of the negotiating process and cultural differences in habitual approaches to problems that may complicate and confuse substantive issues.

A psychologist, Robert Blake, has been illuminating certain characteristics of the negotiating process that hamper negotiations through his studies of union-management bargaining.[16] A typical example is his analysis of "hero-traitor dynamics." A "traitor" is a negotiator who seems to capitulate to the adversary and lose for his group. The "hero" wins for his group by devastating the adversary. Unfortunately, heroic behavior in this sense is usually contrary to what the resolution of the issue requires, and the negotiator who shows appropriate problem-solving behavior is in danger of being labeled a traitor by his group. Blake suggests an ingenious solution to this dilemma—"the crisscross panel." Each group puts up a set of nominees from which both contending groups select the panel. Now both groups are obliged to accept the panel's decisions. Since its members represent both groups, they can more readily escape from the hero-traitor dynamic and are more inclined to examine issues from the points of view of both groups than from that of their own group alone. Obviously, the crisscross panel is not usable for most international conferences, but it does warrant exploration in conjunction with, for example, international negotiations on scientific matters in which some participating scientists have the confidence of all nations.

The most direct behavioral science contribution to smoothing the negotiators' path may lie in analysis of the obstacles arising from differences in national value systems and attitudes of the negotiating countries. A good example is psychiatrist Bryant Wedge's description of stumbling blocks in the United States-Soviet university student exchange program, created by differences in national preconceptions concerning the relation of the individual to the state.[17] The Soviet government approached student exchange as a matter between governments, which decide and speak for their citizens and institutions; the American government saw itself simply as the agency of individuals and institutions. The Soviet Ministry of Education selected students, presented their names and degrees to the American committee, and expected them to be automatically accepted. When the American committee requested more data to determine where the students could best be placed and finally rejected eight of them, the Soviets regarded this both as a reflection on the value of Soviet academic degrees and a capricious rejection of official government judgments.

On the other hand, Americans, raised in the tradition of free scholarship, were very frustrated when they found that they were expected to accept programs given them by the Soviet educational authorities. Thus, despite the sincere desire of each side to make the program work and to be maximally accommodating to the other, each believed the other was being unreasonably obstructionistic in the service of motives related to the cold war.

Dr. Wedge has continued his studies of Russian-American negotiations by an analysis of verbatim records of the first 116 sessions of the eighteen-nation committee on disarmament conducted in 1962 and 1963.[18] He clearly shows how differences in Russian and American negotiation mores impede the negotiation process, and makes constructive suggestions for the behavior of Americans at the negotiating table that have received official attention.

An inescapable effect of the shrinkage of the world and the unlimited destructive power of weaponry is the obsolescence of the sovereign national state. Human survival depends on the eventual replacement of international anarchy by supranational institutions for conflict resolution operating under world law and with power to enforce their decisions. For this to come about, mutual hostility and mistrust between nations must be overcome, and people of all countries must become much more aware than they are today that they are members of an increasingly interdependent world community. Psychologists and psychiatrists are making two types of contribution toward this goal. They are helping to improve the effectiveness of foreign aid and exchange of person programs, and are experimentally investigating nonviolent methods of resolving group conflicts.

A major pitfall of international exchange programs is the fact that members of all national groups tend to distort information about other groups to fit their own preconceptions. As a result, personal contacts between citizens of different nations may increase mutual tensions rather than resolve them. Social scientists are clarifying these national stereotypes and learning how to counteract them by visiting other lands and by studying reactions of foreign visitors to this country.

An impressive example of the contributions a trained observer in another country can make is afforded by a Russian-speaking social psychologist, Urie Bronfenbrenner, who has spent most of the last two years in Russia studying its educational system and its effects on character formation.[19] On the basis of systematic interviews with members of various segments of Soviet society, he has shown that in many respects the Russian image of the United States is the mirror image of our picture of them. They believe that we are the aggressors, that our government misleads and deludes the people, that our government leaders are not to be trusted, and so on. He analyzes factors tending to support such mutual distortions. One is the "strain toward consistency"—the tendency, once one has decided whether the other country is good or bad, to make every bit of information fit that assumption. This may reach such a pitch that even if one side or the other makes a genuine concession, the adversary first views it as an effort to gain a hidden advantage. Another perpetuator of mutual distortion is the so-called Asch phenomenon—the tremendous pressure a group consensus exerts on an individual with a deviant view.[20] A third is the self-confirming nature of the mirror image, in that it impels each nation to act in a manner which confirms and enhances the fears of the other. Awareness of these sources of mutual mistrust may lead to greater success in overcoming them.

Because of the availability of opportunity, most of the studies of international communication at the personal level have been made on visitors to the United States. These investigations are so numerous that no attempt will be made even to list them. Groups studied range from children in Children's International Summer Villages[21] and students[22] to leaders of other nations who are guests of the United States Department of State.[23]

All these studies confirm the same points. To establish tension-reducing communications with members of other lands, one must be alert not only to their cultural biases but to their particular forms of social intercourse, so as to avoid unintended insults, such as seeming to be talking down to the visitor.

A more subtle difficulty arises when symbolic terms used by the members of one culture to define their positive and negative values have incompatible meanings in the other. For example, to many Latin Americans the term "Capitalism" evokes images of exploitation, and "Socialism" represents social justice and welfare. To many Americans the terms obviously have quite different value connotations.

On the positive side, a visitor gains a favorable impression of the host country if he is treated as a person in his own right, rather than as a member of a category. A very effective way of doing this is to involve him in an on-going enterprise—that is, to treat him as a regular member of the organization whose participation is wanted and needed. In short, visitors are most likely to form favorable attitudes if the exchange experience provides new information about the host country in the context of a positive interaction with some of its people.[24]

The same rule applies in efforts of Americans abroad to create a favorable image of the United States. Foreign aid projects that ignore it may create more ill will than good. The offer of aid in itself implies an inferior status of the recipient, which damages his self-esteem. He will, therefore, be motivated to deny the donor's good intentions and to be particularly attentive to any weaknesses or flaws in the program or to ulterior motives behind it. The challenge is to find ways of giving aid that will enhance the recipient's status rather than implicitly lower it. This can be done through defining the aid project as a collaborative effort toward self-help in which the visitor uses the special knowledge and skills of his host and trains him to take over as soon as possible. To the same end, it is important that the program personnel live in the same style as the local population and in direct informal contact with them. The Peace Corps has put these principles into practice. Its success is due in no small measure to the insights of psychologists, psychiatrists, and other social scientists who have played a major role in formulating its general policies, screening and training applicants, and in planning, conducting, and evaluating its programs. These are tailored to meet the specific psychological as well as technological requirements of the different host countries.

Studies of exchange and foreign aid programs and the Peace Corps represent naturalistic, empirical approaches to the reduction of international mistrust and hostility. Many behavioral scientists are also approaching this problem by systematically manipulating the variables of experimental bargaining and competitive situations. Most of these studies derive from game theory and are too esoteric and remote from real-life conflicts to warrant reporting here, but one, conducted by the Sherifs at a boy's camp some years ago, has proved uncannily relevant to the international scene.[25] Eleven-year-old, middle-class American, Protestant, well-adjusted boys, all strangers to each other, were brought to an experimental camp and divided into two groups.

During the first six days the groups were isolated from each other until each became a cohesive organization with definite leadership structure, local customs and a name—the Eagles and the Rattlers. In the following week the two groups were subjected to a series of competitive activities in which victory for one side inevitably meant defeat for the other. This produced a high level of mutual hostility, analogous to that displayed by nations at war. The children attributed self-glorifying qualities to their own groups and assigned traits to the other which justified treating it as an enemy. They improvised and hoarded weapons, raided each other's property, and indulged in other shows of power. Efforts were then made to restore peace. It was found that simply bringing the boys together in social events did no good. The boys used the occasions to indulge in mutual recriminations and accusations. The hostility was, however, successfully resolved through a series of planned crises that could only be overcome by collaborative efforts of both groups. One was the surreptitious interruption of the camp water supply. In another the food-carrying truck on a camping trip ran into a ditch and stalled. The efforts of all the campers were required to tow it out. The cumulative effect of these interactions rapidly reduced the hostility to the point that the boys in each group were again choosing friends from the other.

One cannot, of course, generalize very far from an experiment involving a handful of well-adjusted eleven-year-old boys. What makes the experiment exciting is the apparent analogies at the international level. The areas in which Russia and the United States have made progress in mutual trust are precisely those that involve superordinate goals that both want but neither can attain alone. These include the International Geophysical Year and the International Weather Watch, and now the limited nuclear test ban, in which, as President Kennedy said, "all humanity is the gainer." Probably the most fruitful area for promoting this type of trust-creating activity will prove to be exploration of outer space.

Even in that far-off day when all nations fully understand and appreciate each other, intense conflicts will probably arise that will strongly tempt the antagonists to seek violent solutions. For the long range, therefore, new forms of power not based on violence and new nonlethal methods of waging conflict must be developed. The nonviolent civil disobedience campaigns of recent years offer a rewarding field of exploration toward these ends. It is obvious that these campaigns are largely irrelevant to international conflict today. Their interest lies in the fact that they have highlighted certain aspects of human nature and conduct that in the long run may be crucial to the creation of a world without war. On the basis of extensive interviews with participants in freedom rides and sit-in campaigns, for example, two psychiatrists, Jacob Fishman and Frederic Solomon, have shown that this mode of waging conflict can afford a socially useful outlet for aggressive trends.[26] The sit-ins, as it were, tempt the whites to act out their own aggressive impulses. At the same time, through refusing to use violence, the sit-ins gain a sense of moral superiority to their opponents and a heightened sense of manliness. These campaigns, as did Gandhi's before them, demonstrate that it is possible to create group standards strong enough to reverse the deeply ingrained equation of courage with willingness to threaten and use violence. Much of the psychological impetus for resort to violence to settle disputes seems to lie in each side's fear of appearing afraid to itself or to the adversary. Nations, like individuals, respond to threats by threats and to violence by violence, at least partly to convince themselves and their opponents that they cannot be intimidated. The demonstration that it is possible to break the link between violence and courage suggests that one of the main psychological obstacles to the elimination of war may be circumventable. This should encourage the search for new forms of resolving international conflict that are compatible with survival in the nuclear age.

In summary, the overriding psychological threat today to the continuance of human existence is the force of habit. When faced with new problems and threats, we inevitably resort to methods of resolving them that worked in the past, even though they are obviously no longer appropriate. National leaders have no choice; they cannot abandon tried and true methods of preserving national security and promoting national goals in favor of methods that exist only in the imagination. They are well aware of this predicament. One high Defense Department official, for example, has stated that "we have tens or hundreds of times more missiles than we would drop even in an all-out war," and Secretary McNamara, after admitting that the main function of our huge nuclear armaments is to be able to destroy the enemy after they have hit us, adds plaintively: "It exceeds the extent of my imagination to conceive of how these forces might be used and of what benefit they would be to our nation."[27]

Behavioral scientists, through realistic, down-to-earth analyses of existing modes of international relations and sober explorations of new alternatives, are contributing to the creation of new institutions for conflict resolution that must eventually replace war if human existence is to continue. Few of their studies are spectacular, and many have simply demonstrated what should be apparent to common sense but unfortunately often is not. But their cumulative effect is considerable, and policy makers are lending an increasingly sympathetic ear to them. Students of human nature can make major contributions toward the achievement of safeguarded disarmament, effective nonlethal substitutes for war, and a world order in which mankind, freed from the threat of self-destruction, can apply the enormous resources of knowledge now available to the realization of its full potential.

REFERENCES

1. Boulding, K.: After civilization, what? Bull. of the Atomic Scientists 18:2-6, 1962, p. 6.
2. Kennedy, J. F.: Speech at United Nations, Sept. 25, 1961. Quoted in SANE World, Jan. 1, 1964.
3. Torre, M.: How does physical and mental illness influence negotiations between diplomats? Circulated to participants in the First International Congress of Social Psychiatry, August 1964.
4. North, R. C., et al.: Crisis and crises. Stanford Today. Series 1, No. 4, March 1963, p. 14.
5. Holsti, O. R., Brody, R. A., and North, R. C.: Violence and hostility: the path to world war. Paper, Studies in International Conflict and Integration, Stanford University, Feb. 1964.
6. Frank, J. D.: Breaking the thought barrier: psychological challenges of the nuclear age. Psychiatry 23:245-266, 1960.
7. Psychiatric Aspects of the Prevention of Nuclear War. Report No. 57. New York, Group for the Advancement of Psychiatry, 1964.
8. Osgood, C. E.: An Alternative to War or Surrender. Urbana, Ill., University of Illinois Press, 1962.
9. Van Atta, L. C.: Arms control: human control. Amer. Psychologist 18:37-46, 1963, p. 39.
10. Milburn, T. W.: The concept of deterrence: some logical and psychological considerations. J. Soc. Issues 17:3-11, 1961.
11. Higgs, L. D., and Weinland, R. G.: Project Michelson, Preliminary Report, February 1, 1963, Technical Progress Report 309. China Lake, California, U. S. Naval Ordnance Test Station, March 1963.
12. Berrien, F. K.: Shelter owners, dissonance and the arms race. Soc. Problems 11:87-91, 1963.
13. Melman, S.: Inspection by the people. *In* Preventing World War III: Some Proposals (eds. Q. Wright, W. M. Evan, and M. Deutsch). New York, Simon and Schuster, 1962.

14. SZILARD, L.: "Minimal deterrent" vs. saturation parity. Bull. of the Atomic Scientists 20:6-12, 1964, p. 10.
15. GERARD, R. W.: Truth detection. *In* Preventing World War III: Some Proposals (eds. Q. Wright, W. M. Evan, and M. Deutsch). New York: Simon and Schuster, 1962.
16. BLAKE, R. R.: Psychology and the crisis of statesmanship. Amer. Psychologist 14:87-94, 1959.
17. WEDGE, B. M.: A note on Soviet-American negotiation. *In* Proceedings of the Emergency Conference on Hostility, Aggression and War (ed. M. Miller). Washington, American Association for Social Psychiatry, 1961.
18. WEDGE, B., AND MUROMCEW, C.: Psychological factors in Soviet disarmament negotiation. J. Conflict Resolution 9:18-36, 1965.
19. BRONFENBRENNER, U.: The mirror image in Soviet-American relations: A social psychologist's report. J. Soc. Issues 17:45-56, 1961.
20. ASCH, S. E.: Social Psychology. New York, Prentice-Hall, 1952.
21. BJERSTEDT, A.: Informational and noninformational determinants of nationality stereotypes. J. Soc. Issucs 18:24-29, 1962.
22. WATSON, J., AND LIPPITT, R.: Crosscultural experience as a source of attitude change. J. Conflict Resolution 2:61-66, 1958.
23. WEDGE, B. M.: Visitors to the United States and How They See Us. Princeton, D. Van Nostrand Co., 1965.
24. KELMAN, H. C.: Changing attitudes through international activities. J. Soc. Issues 18:68-87, 1962.
25. SHERIF, M., ET AL: Intergroup Conflict and Cooperation: The Robbers Cave Experiment. Norman, Oklahoma, University of Oklahoma Press, 1961.
26. FISHMAN, J. R., AND SOLOMON, F.: Psychological observations on the student sit-in movement. *In* Proceedings of the Third World Congress of Psychiatry. Toronto, University of Toronto Press, 1962.
27. MCNAMARA, R. S.: Testimony before House Armed Services Committee, 1963. Quoted by Senator G. McGovern, August 2, 1963, Congressional Record.

Discussion

Recorder: LISSY JARVIK, M.D., PH.D.

COMMENTS ON DR. PAYNE'S PRESENTATION

DR. WELCH: Dr. Welch asked for clarification on the difference between retardation and preoccupation as well as for a discussion on the effects of tranquilizers.

DR. ZUBIN: Dr. Zubin commented that "thought-disorder" was not mentioned by Dr. Payne, and he expressed his agreement with this: "It is true that schizophrenics think differently from normals, but so does the genius. Is overinclusiveness a schizophrenic characteristic? Perhaps the lack of precision characteristic of overinclusiveness has its roots in the family situation, in cultural differences, where there is often a lack of necessity to be very definite." Dr. Zubin further pointed out that schizophrenics who tend to be conceptually confused, but are perceptually and psychomotorically intact, have a good prognosis, and vice-versa if they have a poor prognosis. In other words, patients who have been found to be perceptually confused or show psychomotor impairment have a poor prognosis despite conceptual intactness.

DR. BURDOCK: Dr. Burdock elaborated on Dr. Zubin's comments and discussed some of the data gathered by the Biometrics Research group which agree with those reported by Dr. Payne.

DR. WECHSLER: Dr. Wechsler inquired whether the patient was "pushed to go further." By way of illustration, he cited some of his own work with the Vigotsky test: First, the test was conducted in the standard manner and then the subjects were asked to sort again and again and again, using their own principles. After four or five sortings, normal subjects produced typically schizophrenic responses.

DR. PAYNE: With respect to Dr. Wechsler's question, Dr. Payne reported that, indeed, they had tried to push the subjects and found exactly what one would expect from Dr. Wechsler's comments. Subjects began to sort according to such strange principles as the shadows cast by the objects. However, the overinclusive patients did not show this change; they had already failed to differentiate between the normal and the bizarre under original conditions. With respect to Dr. Zubin's comments on "thought-disorder," Dr. Payne agreed that there was probably not a disorder in thought *processes,* but rather a disorder in thought *content.* Since administration of lysergic acid diethylamide (LSD) led to overinclusive thinking, the disturbance probably involves more than social or cultural differences. Regarding the differentiation of preoccupation and retardation, Dr. Payne commented that preoccupation is expected to be more of a handicap in complex than in simple tasks, while retardation appears to offer the same handicap regardless of the complexity of the task.

Comments on Dr. Salzinger's Presentation

Dr. Rümke: Dr. Rümke brought up the problem of differentiating the aphasic from the schizophrenic patient and inquired about differential test results in the two groups. He pointed out further that chronic schizophrenics will switch from normal to abnormal speech and back again, and that often they exhibit paraphasia.

Dr. Lehmann: "Is the method clinically applicable? Do several writers agree on the reconstruction? Do the writers possess the same cultural idioms as the patients?"

Dr. Hunt: Dr. Hunt stressed the importance of the context in which speech is emitted, giving as examples different motivations produced by stress, avoidance, defense, or desire.

Dr. Zubin: Dr. Zubin pointed out that Dr. Salzinger's studies involved a medium (language) which has commonly been used in subjective and clinical evaluations. As a matter of fact, it has been the major component of clinical evaluation (speech), which has now been transformed into a quantitative index. Using this measure, it has been demonstrated that schizophrenics lack certain measurable qualities. The differences, however, are small and when examining graphs of normals and schizophrenics, they do not loom large.

Dr. Fieve: "How well were the educational backgrounds matched?"

Dr. Hunt: "Does the schizophrenic begin to shape his verbal behavior in order to get out of the hospital?"

Dr. Mendelssohn: Dr. Mendelssohn inquired about the effect of LSD on language and related his own experiences following the ingestion of LSD. He concluded that subsequent to his LSD experience, he has been able to understand his schizophrenic patients much better than he did before the experience.

DR. CHEEK: Dr. Cheek reported that administration of LSD-25 to ten alcoholic patients produced significant differences (at the 1 per cent level of confidence) in the cloze procedure.

DR. BRUCH: "Were any patients in active psychotherapy at the time of the study?"

DR. SALZINGER: The differentiation of aphasics, schizophrenics, and normals presents no problems with the techniques employed which will pick up small consistent differences.

The groups *were* matched for education, sex, etc. It is planned to study the speech community of the respondent as well as the speaker.

The techniques presented today are still in the category of research tools rather than clinically practicable methods.

According to a study by Dr. Honigfeld, it becomes difficult to predict speech following the administration of LSD-25. Even a single low dose (75-125 mg.) leads to increased difficulty in understanding the subject's speech.

As to psychotherapy, the therapist's understanding of the patient's language does not appear to increase with an increasing number of sessions.

COMMENTS ON DR. GARMEZY'S PRESENTATION

DR. SALZINGER: Schizophrenics persistently withdraw in response to stimuli. Although they are not ahistorical, they are *not* affected by conditioned aversive stimuli. Yet, positive reinforcement *does* work with schizophrenics.

DR. LINDSLEY: Dr. Lindsley expressed his concern that people look for "the" schizophrenic—an abstraction. From daily observation during the past ten years (some 2,000 hours on a single patient) it is clear that no two reactions to punishment or reward are alike. Although it is possible to give a summary for 22 patients, in terms of their most likely reaction, it is *not* possible to characterize any single patient. As a matter of fact, there has been no correlation between any recorded data and the official American Psychiatric Association diagnoses; for this reason subclassification may be more valuable than single comprehensive diagnostic categories.

DR. FISH: Dr. Fish stressed that organisms are not biologically homogeneous; she stated that many studies have ignored the biological differences in experiments designed to assess the effects of punishment and reward. One of the major problems concerns the question: Why are certain experiences not rewarding, or not punishing, to the potentially schizophrenic child when they do have such effects on normal children? Differences in reaction time, proprioception, and vestibular mechanisms are among those which cannot be ignored, and in judging responses adjustment has to be made in the tempo of the input to conform to the child's reaction time.

DR. ZUBIN: Dr. Zubin commented on Garmezy's notion of "the burnt child" and asked how this can be conceptualized without a hereditary basis. "Is not the notion of vulnerability essential to our understanding of schizophrenia?"

DR. GARMEZY: With respect to the issue of vulnerability—hereditary predisposition—Dr. Garmezy stated that "it would be so much easier to resort to vulnerability than to blame the mother." Yet, Dr. Garmezy strongly believes that a specific kind of sequence of reinforcing events is far more important than any vulnerability which may exist. Dr. Garmezy felt it unnecessary to give first place to biological facts in examining the development of schizophrenia, since the "shut-in type characteristic of schizophrenia" is not characteristic of all schizophrenics. "If you can show me the neurological defect, we will be glad to incorporate it into our experiments. At the moment, such complex longitudinal studies would be needed that the present base rate of schizophrenia makes them almost prohibitive." He cited the histories of the Genain quadruplets, as reported by Dr. Rosenthal, and concluded that their social learning history was so bad that "you don't need any biological facts" to understand the development of schizophrenia in them. With respect to individual differences in responses, Dr. Garmezy stressed that "all people can become averse to punishment, but none are insensitive to reward; therefore, more studies on reward are needed."

COMMENTS ON DR. BURDOCK'S PRESENTATION

DR. LORR: Dr. Lorr commented upon the construction of experimental scales in the absence of unifying concepts. He requested information on the reliability of profiles, the reliability of elements, and the independence of various elements making up the scales. He suggested further that there was no evidence of congruence of the two approaches except for a correlation of .41 for the total score.

Dr. Roth: Dr. Roth emphasized the importance of distinguishing between two groups of schizophrenics, the acute and the chronic. Because of their vastly different prognosis, it would be a tremendous advance if any test could detect the acute florid group. As to the relationship between early therapy and prognosis, there is suggested evidence that early therapy leads to better prognosis, but further research in this area is clearly needed. He stated that in his own research on schizophrenia of the aged, two stages were found—the first showing insidious onset up to a given level, and the second characterized by the sudden onset of hallucinations. The outcome of therapy was better if patients were seen during the first stage.

Dr. Zubin: Dr. Zubin pointed out that the difference in prognosis between acute and chronic schizophrenia may well be analogous to the difference in prognosis between those accident patients seen immediately and those seen after ten days: "Spontaneous recoveries don't occur after ten days." He emphasized the value of controlled interviews for research purposes and stressed the fact that there need be no correlation between the amount of pathology and the outcome of the disease.

Dr. Rümke: Dr. Rümke commented that the acute group may well include cases that are not schizophrenic and have a better prognosis than the schizophrenics. Inquiring whether Dr. Burdock's group had tried "a little schizophrenic language in the interview," he reported his own experiences in eliciting various kinds of responses when speaking schizophrenic language to his patients.

Dr. Roth: "Does the acute case of schizophrenia have an inherently better prognosis?" The salient features of acute schizophrenia have been described and should be subjected to statistical analysis. The question of learning versus inheritance has bearing on this discussion. "In everything there is something learned—even in Huntington's Chorea." When considering schizophrenia, we must keep in mind that childhood schizophrenia does not have a better prognosis than adult schizophrenia, "even though childhood schizophrenics are seen at an age when learning takes place most readily."

DR. BURDOCK: The statistical approach suggested by Dr. Roth is exactly what we are trying to do here. The questions raised by Dr. Lorr are as yet unanswered. Looking for these answers is precisely what we are programming now.

We have not classified the schizophrenics as acute and chronic because the patients represent two types: The new patients are a mixture of all types, an admission cohort, while the chronic patients represent the residue of such cohorts.

Part III: Neurochemistry and Genetics

11

CURRENT BIOCHEMICAL RESEARCH IN SCHIZOPHRENIA

by SEYMOUR S. KETY, M.D.*

BIOCHEMICAL RESEARCH IN SCHIZOPHRENIC ILLNESS, which the author had occasion to review in 1959,[1] has yielded new information over the past five years which it may be of interest to examine and summarize. Some of these studies have been directed at abnormalities in plasma proteins, while others may relate to the process of biological transmethylation. These two lines of effort will be the basis of this review.

Interest in the possible presence of an abnormal protein constituent of the blood in schizophrenia was stimulated by a report by Heath and his associates at Tulane in 1957:[2] that a serum fraction obtained from schizophrenic patients was capable of causing some of the symptoms of that disorder when injected into nonschizophrenic volunteers. The substance, which was given the name "taraxein," appeared to have some relationship to ceruloplasmin, a copper-containing globulin found in normal plasma.[3]

One attempt to replicate the production of psychotic symptoms in volunteers by injections of material similarly prepared was not successful,[4] and to date the original findings have not been confirmed in a significant and well-controlled series. Following this report, however, a number of groups have independently obtained evidence which is compatible with the thesis that an abnormal protein is present to a greater extent in the blood of some schizophrenics than in normals, and that this substance is capable of producing certain behavioral,

*Chief, Laboratory of Clinical Science, National Institute of Mental Health, National Institutes of Health, Bethesda, Maryland.

metabolic, or cellular changes in lower animals. Haddad,[5] by an ingenious and careful series of studies replicating and extending an earlier report by Malis,[6] found evidence for an antigenic abnormality in the pooled serum of chronically ill schizophrenic patients. This was done by sensitizing animals with serum from schizophrenics, desensitizing with serum from nonpatients, and challenging with the sensitizing pool. Bishop[7] found evidence for the effect of plasma from schizophrenic patients upon learning and retention of learning in the rat. Other investigators, Winters and Flataker,[8] and more recently, Bergen and his associates,[9] found a slowing of rope climbing activity in rats injected with certain fractions of the serum of psychotic patients as compared with normal plasma fractions. German[10] reported an effect of serum of schizophrenics on cortical-evoked responses of animals which separates them clearly from normals and other psychotics. In what appear to be the best controlled studies to this time of the effects of plasma from psychotic patients on behavior, Ferguson and Fisher[11] recently reported studies using a precision timing task in cebus monkeys in which a highly significant delay in responsiveness was produced by the injection of plasma from some newly admitted catatonic patients. It is of interest that in their studies plasma from normal individuals under preoperative stress produced similar but not as marked slowing of response.

Frohman, Gottlieb, and their associates[12] reported increases in the ratio of lactate to pyruvate in the medium after chicken erythrocytes were incubated in plasma or plasma fractions of some schizophrenic patients as compared to normal controls. Mangoni and associates[13] have been unable to confirm this, while Buhler and Ihler[14] were unable to demonstrate an effect of such plasma on the oxidation of labeled glucose, which had previously been claimed.[15] In a more recent paper, Frohman and associates[16] have been able to demonstrate this difference in the lactate:pyruvate ratio only when the subjects have engaged in moderate exercise before the blood samples are drawn, no appreciable difference being found when the subjects are at complete rest, in normal activity, or exercising vigorously. This—plus the fact that the degree of exercise to which the subjects were exposed affects the lactate:pyruvate ratio in the incubation mixture more than does the presence or absence of schizophrenia—suggests the need for more evidence that this property of the plasma is characteristic for schizophrenia rather than a concomitant of reduced exercise tolerance or other features of chronic hospitalization.*

Attempts are being made by some of these groups to fractionate plasma proteins of schizophrenic patients and to purify and characterize the source of the abnormal biological activities. These studies have not to date been successful in producing a purified, reasonably stable material or in characterizing it beyond its presumed presence in the alpha-2 globulin fraction.

The evidence in this area is far from conclusive at the present time. Further confirmation in a rigorously controlled situation is required of the report, now eight years old, that a substance in the blood of schizophrenic patients is capable of causing some of the symptoms of schizophrenia in nonschizophrenic volunteers.

Fessel and coworkers[18] have reported qualitative and quantitative abnormalities in various serum proteins in a considerable proportion of schizophrenic patients and the ability to differentiate schizophrenic from manic depressive patients on the basis of an abnormally high macroglobulin level in the former. Certain of these findings have been confirmed by two independent groups.[19, 20]

Further work is necessary and some of it is in progress to determine to what extent the abnormalities in serum, demonstrated by physical chemical analysis or by the various bioassays, are characteristic of schizophrenia or a reflection of the stress, exposure to chronic endemic infections, dietary or other adventitious factors which accompany the disorder. In this connection it is of interest to read some comments by Dunn and Pearce[21] in their review of the plasma proteins in a wide variety of diseases:

> The common findings of . . . mild to severe elevation of the alpha-2 globulins and variable alterations in the other fractions [constitutes] a nonspecific response to such varied stimuli as infection, malignancy, hypertension, disorders of metabolism, or trauma. This constellation of findings is similar to that recently labelled the stress pattern. Many investigators have regarded such patterns as specific when considering an isolated disease or group of diseases.

*Recently, Durell and Ryan[17] succeeded in demonstrating an increase in anaerobic glycolysis of chicken erythrocytes with increased lactate production in association with most human plasmas. They found, further, that this phenomenon is clearly associated with hemolysis and that the plasma of certain individuals shows ability to hemolyze such erythrocytes through the action of a heterogenetic antibody. Their findings in a blind study of hospitalized schizophrenics, nonschizophrenic psychotics and nonhospitalized normal controls do not support the thesis that this property is confined to or characteristic of schizophrenic individuals.

Mueller[22] has demonstrated an abnormality in the response of plasma free fatty acids to insulin in six of twelve schizophrenic patients. Seeman and O'Brien[23] have reported a highly significant increase in the sodium-potassium-activated ATP-ase in erythrocytes of schizophrenic patients. The presence of abnormal lymphocytes in blood smears from schizophrenic patients has permitted Fessel and Hirata-Hibi[24] to identify such smears with remarkable accuracy. These findings await further extension and independent confirmation.

In 1952 Osmond and Smythies pointed out some similarities between mescaline psychosis and schizophrenia, and between that drug and adrenaline.[25] They included a biochemical note by Harley-Mason which stated, in part:

> It is extremely probable that the final stage in the biogenesis of adrenaline is a transmethylation of noradrenaline, the methyl group arising from methionine or choline. It is just possible that a pathological disordering of its transmethylation mechanism might lead to methylation of one or both of its phenolic hydroxyl groups instead of its amino group. . . . Methylation of phenolic hydroxyl groups in the animal body is of rare occurrence but a significant case has been reported recently. . . . It is particularly interesting to note that out of a series of phenylethylamine derivations tested by Noteboom, 3,4-dimethoxyphenylethylamine was the most potent producing catatonia in animals.

Since that time the transmethylation of noradrenaline to adrenaline has been established,[26] and Axelrod[27] has demonstrated the O-methylation of both catecholamines as an important step in their normal metabolism.

The suggestion that pathological transmethylation might occur in schizophrenia was further strengthened by the recognition that a number of psychotomimetic agents, in addition to mescaline, were methylated congeners of normal body metabolites. On this basis, Hoffer and associates[28] used niacin and niacinamide, methyl accepters, in an effort to inhibit competitively the possible abnormal process. Their report of beneficial results in schizophrenia has not been extensively confirmed. In 1961, Pollin, Cardon, and Kety[29] tested this hypothesis by administering large doses of L-methionine to chronic schizophrenic patients. This substance is an essential precursor of S-adenosylmethionine, the active substance which transfers its methyl group to acceptor compounds in the process of transmethylation.[30] In some of the patients during the administration of the L-methionine there was a temporary exacerbation of psychotic symptoms. This finding has since been confirmed by three other groups,[31-33] and, in addition, Brune and Himwich[34] found that betaine, another CH_3 donor, was equally effective in accentuating psychotic symptoms in schizophrenics. Further work by investigators in our laboratory have contributed to other aspects of this problem. Baldessarini and Kopin[35] found that feeding L-methionine to rats produced a significant increase in S-adenosylmethionine concentration in the liver and brain. Axelrod[36] demonstrated the presence in normal mammalian tissue of an enzyme capable of methylating normal metabolites—i.e., tryptamine and serotonin—to their dimethyl derivatives for which Szara[37] and others[38] had reported psychotomimetic properties under certain experimental conditions.

In the past two years, Friedhoff[39] at New York University has demonstrated the frequent occurrence in the urine of schizophrenic patients of the substance (3,4-dimethoxyphenylethylamine), which Harley-Mason had emphasized as a possible abnormally methylated metabolite. This compound is a dimethylated derivative of dopamine and closely related to mescaline, which represents a trimethylated congener of this biogenic amine. He has also reported the ability of liver cells to produce this substance from dopamine.[40]

These findings are clearly compatible with the hypothesis that the process of biological transmethylation is somehow disturbed in schizophrenia, with the production of excessive amounts of methylated derivatives of normal metabolites capable of inducing some of the symptoms of schizophrenia. The hypothesis, however, is far from having been validated. Although methionine is the only one of a large number of amino acids which were capable of intensifying the psychotic state in some patients, and although similar effects are produced by betaine, it has not been established that the clinical changes resulted from any specific methylated derivatives, and the possibility that this was a nonspecific toxic psychosis or a peculiarly schizophrenic response to nonspecific toxic changes has not been ruled out. Although we treated five nonpsychotic volunteers with methionine and saw no remarkable mental effects, neither we nor any other group have clearly demonstrated that schizophrenics are especially sensitive to methionine. Although Kopin and Baldessarini have demonstrated the ability of methionine to elevate brain and liver levels of S-adenosylmethionine, it is difficult on purely biochemical grounds to defend the thesis that a vital biological process like transmethylation should become so readily the victim of dietary changes in methionine. By means of C^{14}-methionine we are attempting to find evidence of the methylated compounds in the schizophrenics treated with methionine, but have been unsuccessful thus far. Although Friedhoff was unable to find the dimethoxyphenylethylamine in normal urine, other workers[41] have found it in normal populations, albeit not as frequently as in schizophrenia. There is only preliminary evidence that this substance is produced endogenously in the body rather than being a dietary component, and no direct evidence that it is responsible for any of the symptoms of schizophrenia.

Recently, Kuehl[42] and Bourdillon[43] reported studies essentially confirming the findings of Friedhoff, in that a substance which had the characteristics of 3,4-dimethoxyphenylethylamine was present in the urine of a high percentage of schizophrenics, but was rare in the urine of nonschizophrenic psychotic patients or normal volunteers. Although many alternative explanations have not been ruled out, the hypothesis that an alteration in biological transmethylation plays a significant role in some forms of schizophrenia remains a plausible and parsimonious explanation of a fairly diverse range of observations; such an explanation merits further evaluation.

REFERENCES

1. Kety, S. S.: Biochemical theories of schizophrenia. A two-part critical review of current theories and of the evidence used to support them. Science 129:1528-1532, 1590-1596, 1959.
2. Heath, R. G., Martens, S., Leach, B. E., Cohen, M., and Feigley, C. A.: Behavioral changes in nonpsychotic volunteers following the administration of taraxein, the substance obtained from serum of schizophrenic patients. Amer. J. Psychia. 114:917-920, 1958.
3. Leach, B. E., Cohen, M., Heath, R. G., and Martens, S.: Studies of the role of ceruloplasmin and albumin in adrenaline metabolism. A.M.A. Arch. Neurol. Psychiat. 76:635-642, 1956.
4. Robins, E., Smith, K., and Lowe, I. P.: *In Neuropharmacology.* Transactions of the Fourth Conference (ed. H. A. Abramson). New York, Josiah Macy Jr. Foundation, 1957, pp. 123-136.
5. Haddad, R. K., and Rabe, A.: An antigenic abnormality in the serum of chronically ill schizophrenic patients. *In* Serological Fractions in Schizophrenia (ed. R. G. Heath). New York, Harper & Row, 1963, pp. 151-157.
6. Malis, C. Y.: K Etiologii Schizofrenii. Medgiz, Moscow, 1959.
7. Bishop, M. P.: Effects of plasma from schizophrenic subjects upon learning and retention in the rat. *In* Serological Fractions in Schizophrenia (ed. R. G. Heath). New York, Harper & Row, 1963, pp. 77-91.
8. Winter, C. A., and Flataker, L.: Effect of blood plasma from psychotic patients upon performance of trained rats. A.M.A. Arch. Neurol. Psychiat. 80:441-449, 1958.
9. Bergen, J. R., Pennell, R. B., Saravis, C. A., and Hoagland, H.: Further

experiments with plasma proteins from schizophrenics. *In* Serological Fractions in Schizophrenia (ed. R. G. Heath). New York, Harper & Row, 1963, pp. 67-76.

10. German, G. A.: Effects of serum from schizophrenics on evoked cortical potentials in the rat. Brit. J. Psychiat. 109:616-623, 1963.
11. Ferguson, D. C., and Fisher, A. E.: Behavior disruption in Cebus monkeys as a function of injected substances. Science 139:1281-1282, 1963.
12. Frohman, C. E., Czajkowski, N. P., Luby, E. D., Gottlieb, J. S., and Senf, R.: Further evidence of a plasma factor in schizophrenia. A.M.A. Arch. Gen. Psychiat, 2:263, 1960.
13. Mangoni, A., Balazs, R., and Coppen, A. J.: The effect of plasma from schizophrenic patients on the chicken erythrocyte system. Brit. J. Psychiat. 109:231-234, 1963.
14. Buhler, D. R., and Ihler, G. S.: Effect of plasma from normal and schizophrenic subjects on the oxidation of labeled glucose by chicken erythrocytes. J. Lab. Clin. Med. 62:306-318, 1963.
15. Frohman, C. E., Latham, L. K., Beckett, P. G. S., and Gottlieb, J. S.: Evidence of a plasma factor in schizophrenia. A.M.A. Arch. Gen. Psychiat. 2:255, 1960.
16. Frohman, C. E., Latham, L. K., Warner, K. A., Brosius, C. O., Beckett, P. G. S., and Gottlieb, J. S.: Motor activity in schizophrenia; effect on plasma factor. Arch. Gen. Psychiat. 9:83, 1963.
17. Durell, J., and Ryan, J. W.: The immune lysis of chicken erythrocytes and its relationship to schizophrenia. Proc. NATO Advanced Study Institute on "Molecular Basis of Some Aspects of Mental Activity," Drammen, Norway, August, 1965.

18a. Fessel, W. J., and Grunbaum, B. W.: Electrophoretic and analytical ultracentrifuge studies in sera of psychotic patients: Elevation of gamma globulins and macroglobulins, and splitting of $alpha_2$ globulins. Ann. Intern. Med. 54:1134-1145, 1961.

18b. Kurland, H. D., and Fessel, W. J.: Distinctive protein patterns in functional psychoses. Proc. Soc. Exper. Biol. Med. 113: 249-251, 1963.

19. Sapira, J. D.: Immunoelectrophoresis of the serum of psychotic patients. Arch. Gen. Psychiat. 10:196, 1964.
20. Kopeloff, L. M., and Fischel, E.: Serum levels of bactericidin and globulin in schizophrenia. Arch. Gen. Psychiat. 9:524, 1963.
21. Dunn, W. L., and Pearce, R. H.: The clinical value of paper electrophoresis. Canad. Med. Ass. J. 84:272-280, 1961.
22. Mueller, P. S.: Plasma free fatty acid concentrations (FFA) in chronic schizophrenia before and after insulin stimulation. J. Psychiat. Res. 1:106-115, 1962.
23. Seeman, P. M., and O'Brien, E.: Sodium-potassium-activated adenosine triphosphatase in schizophrenic erythrocytes. Nature 200:263-264, 1963.
24. Fessel, W. J., and Hirata-Hibi, M.: Abnormal leukocytes in schizophrenia. Arch. Gen. Psychiat. 9:601, 1963.
25. Osmond, H., and Smythies, J.: Schizophrenia: A new approach. J. Ment. Sci. 98:309-315, 1952.

26. BLASCHKO, H.: The development of current concepts of catecholamine formation. Pharmacol. Rev. 11:307-316, 1959.
27. AXELROD, J., SENOH, S., AND WITKOP, B.: O-Methylation of catecholamines in vivo. J. Biol. Chem. 233:697-701, 1958.
28. HOFFER, A., OSMOND, H., CALLBECK, M. J., AND KAHAN, I.: Treatment of schizophrenia with nicotinic acid and nicotinamide. J. Clin. Exper. Psychopath. 18:131, 1957.
29. POLLIN, W., CARDON, P. V., AND KETY, S. S.: Effects of amino acid feedings in schizophrenic patients treated with iproniazid. Science 133:104-105, 1961.
30. CANTONI, G. L.: S-Adenosylmethionine: a new intermediate formed enzymatically from L-methionine and adenosine-triphosphate. J. Biol. Chem., 204:403-416, 1953.
31. ALEXANDER, F., CURTIS, G. C., SPRINCE, H., AND CROSLEY, A. P.: L-Methionine and L-tryptophan feedings in non-psychotic and schizophrenic patients with and without tranylcypromine. J. Nerv. Ment. Dis. 137:135-142, 1963.
32. BRUNE, G. G., AND HIMWICH, H. E.: Effects of methionine loading on the behavior of schizophrenic patients. J. Nerv. Ment. Dis. 134:447, 1962.
33. PARK, L. C., BALDESSARINI, R. J., AND KETY, S. S.: Methionine effects on chronic schizophrenics. Arch. Gen. Psychiat. 12:346-351, 1965.
34. BRUNE, G. G., AND HIMWICH, H. E.: Biogenic amines and behavior in schizophrenic patients. *In* Recent Advances in Biological Psychiatry. New York, Plenum Press, 1963, Vol. 5, pp. 144-160.
35. BALDESSARINI, R. J., AND KOPIN, I. J.: Assay of tissue levels of S-adenosylmethionine. Anal. Biochem. 6:289-292, 1963.
36. AXELROD, J.: Enzymatic formation of psychotomimetic metabolites from normally occurring compounds. Science 134:343, 1961.
37. SZARA, S.: Hallucinogenic effects and metabolism of tryptamine derivatives in man. Fed. Proc. 20:855, 1961.
38. FABING, H. D., AND HAWKINS, J. R.: Intravenous bufotenine injection in the human being. Science 123:886, 1956.
39. FRIEDHOFF, A. J., AND VAN WINKLE, E.: The characteristics of an amine found in the urine of schizophrenic patients. J. Nerv. Ment. Dis. 135:550-555, 1962.
40. ——: A neurotropic compound identified in urine of schizophrenic patients. *In* Psychopathology of Schizophrenia (eds. P. Hoch and J. Zubin). New York, Grune and Stratton, 1965.
41. TAKESADA, M., KAKIMOTO, Y., SANO, I., AND KANEKO, Z.: 3,4-Dimethoxyphenylethylamine and other amines in the urine of schizophrenic patients. Nature 199:203, 1963.
42. KUEHL, F. A., JR.: Para-O-methylation of dopamine in schizophrenic and normal individuals. *In* Amine Metabolism in Schizophrenia (eds. H. E. Himwich, J. Smythies, and S. S. Kety). Oxford, Pergamon Press, 1966.
43. BOURDILLON, R. E.: 3,4-Dimethoxyphenylethylamine in schizophrenia. *Ibid.*

12

BIOLOGIC MALADAPTATION IN SCHIZOPHRENIA*

by JACQUES S. GOTTLIEB, M.D., CHARLES E. FROHMAN, PH.D., and PETER G. S. BECKETT, M.D.†

AT A PREVIOUS MEETING of this Association in February 1961, a presentation, "Biochemistry and Schizophrenia: Implications for the Future," was made.[1] That report summarized a considerable amount of the investigative findings of the staff of the Lafayette Clinic in regard to schizophrenia, and presented the information in the form of predictions which in actuality were operational hypotheses. Since then, considerably more information has been obtained which permits elaboration and refinement of these hypotheses; this information will be presented here for your consideration.

In the previous report evidence had been presented that there is a factor in the serum of patients with schizophrenia which may have an important function in this illness. Recently a monograph, *Serological Fractions in Schizophrenia,* has been published which summarizes a great deal of the evidence of various investigators to support this finding.[2] Dr. Frohman and his associates in our biochemistry laboratories have continued to employ a biochemical assay as an indicator of the presence or the absence of this substance. This technique consists in brief of incubating plasma specimens obtained from patients with chronic schizophrenia or other illnesses, or from control subjects, with chicken erythrocytes as a tissue substrate. After the incubation, pyruvate and lactate are measured; this gives a higher lactate:pyruvate ratio for the serum of patients with schizophrenia than for control subjects. Difficult and cumbersome as this technique is, it has led to consistent findings in Dr. Frohman's hands.

---

*These studies have been supported primarily by the Department of Mental Health of the State of Michigan. Grants-in-aid have been received from the Scottish Rite Committee on Research in Schizophrenia, the National Association for Mental Health, the National Institute of Mental Health (Grant No. MH-04816), the Upjohn Company, and private citizens.

†The Lafayette Clinic and Wayne State University, Detroit, Michigan.

By employing this technique as an assay method, a great deal of information has been obtained regarding the characteristics of this serum factor. In the first place, the lactate:pyruvate ratios have been found to be at normal levels for patients suffering from other disorders, such as manic-depressive illness, diabetes, and chronic alcoholism.[3] In the second place, the mean lactate:pyruvate ratios for children with childhood schizophrenia cannot be differentiated from children as control subjects, or control adults. Patients who had childhood schizophrenia and have remained ill into adulthood are characterized by normal lactate:pyruvate ratios in spite of their gross and florid symptomatology.[3] In the third place, not all chronic schizophrenic patients are characterized by an elevated lactate:pyruvate ratio; only approximately 60 per cent of a highly selected group of chronic patients under study in our clinical research center are so characterized.[4] These two groups of schizophrenic patients — those characterized by a high lactate:pyruvate ratio and those characterized by a normal lactate:pyruvate ratio, are under intensive study, through the application of psychological, clinical, and electrophysiological techniques, with the anticipation that eventually they can be differentiated into two distinct groups of patients.

In addition to what appears to be the specificity of this substance for certain patients with chronic schizophrenia, a great deal of information has been obtained regarding the characteristics of this factor. Employing a combination of protein separation procedures and utilizing the lactate:pyruvate ratio technique as a method of following the factor, the protein in question has been isolated in what may be a pure form. The proof of its isolation has not been completed as yet. The techniques of separation of the plasma proteins consist first in the utilization of ammonium sulphate to precipitate the globulins from the other proteins, the removal of pseudoglobulins by dialysis against distilled water, the employment of curtain electrophoresis to separate the remaining euglobulins into a number of component fractions, and finally the separation of the active fraction by utilizing DEAE cellulose ion exchange chromatography.[5] The resulting fraction which retains its activity is about 1/800,000th of the proteins of the serum. In other words, from 100 cc. of blood which has about 8 Gm. of protein, 10 mcg. are obtained. This substance separates out in the range of the alpha-2 globulins and appears most probably to be a lipoprotein. Molecular weight determinations using osmotic pressure suggest that it is a large protein of about 400,000. The substance is not split by trypsin, but is split and all activity destroyed by pepsin, chymotrypsin, and papain.[6] An enzyme that will split this macroprotein and yet allow activity to be retained has not as yet been identified.

Most probably, then, this protein is large, too large to enter the cell intact. Its action on the cellular lactate:pyruvate equilibrium could be due to a small portion of the molecule acting inside the cell, or the whole molecule could be affecting the permeability of the cell from the outside. This problem has been studied in two ways: by studying its direct effect on the oxidation reduction phenomena in the cell, and by studying its effect upon cell permeability.[7] The latter studies indicate that the higher lactate:pyruvate ratios obtained by this protein are not due to an effect on passive permeability or on active transport of lactate or pyruvate. Also, it has been shown that the factor does not affect permeability toward sodium, potassium, chloride, or phosphate. Studies have been completed which suggest that cell permeability may be affected in a selective manner.[7a] On the other hand, since we are dealing with a large protein, and if we cannot definitely demonstrate any effects on permeability, it would therefore be tenable to hypothesize that this protein is a carrier of a smaller molecule which can pass through the cell membrane. This latter hypothesis is consistent with the report of the Hoagland, Bergen, Pennell group of investigators and their associates who demonstrated that activity of their isolated serum fraction, as measured by producing delay in the climbing ability of rats, passed through a membrane when dialysis was employed.[8] This hypothesis is further supported by the report of Marrazzi and his associates that electrodialysis removes a small molecule from the serum fraction which is active in depressing transcallosal synaptic transmission.[9] If this hypothesis is true, that the macroprotein is a carrier for a smaller molecule which is the active substance, then we are probably dealing with a very potent molecule of the order of a catecholamine or a hormone. Under these circumstances this substance is circulating in the blood in gamma amounts.

To make the chore of the isolation and identification of the active substance more difficult, let us consider some of the characteristics of this factor. In the first place, it has been recognized by several groups of investigators that this substance is extremely labile, and is best preserved at a pH between 6 and 9 at 4°C.; that ascorbic acid delays its disintegration, and an atmosphere of hydrogen preserves it.[10]

The processing of the serum must be initiated promptly after blood is withdrawn, for within two hours about 50 per cent of the activity it lost.[11] The chicken cells must be used immediately after their withdrawal or accurate determinations cannot be obtained.[12] Puzzling has been the loss of activity when blood or serum is transported from one hospital to another. This was first observed by Pennell and Bergen[13] and is a factor which complicates our studies, since our clinical research center is in a state hospital 30 miles from the Lafayette Clinic. This has necessitated the development of biochemistry laboratories at the state hospital for the purpose of extracting this factor.

Another phenomenon that has been intriguing has been the large variation of the lactate:pyruvate ratios from day to day in patients with schizophrenia.[14] Some of the variables responsible for this day-to-day variation are now understood. If blood is taken from patients with schizophrenia at the end of a night's sleep, the lactate:pyruvate ratio is the same as for control subjects.[14] Ten minutes of activity of the patient, however, is sufficient to produce an increase in the lactate: pyruvate ratio of patients with schizophrenia significantly different from control subjects. Exercise, then, leads to an increment which is greater for patients than for control subjects.[14] It should be mentioned, however, that control subjects under various types of stimuli show an increase in the lactate:pyruvate ratio, but of a lower order of increase than with patients. Other types of stimulating situations besides exercise, such as the administration of a cold pressor test, produce an increase in the lactate:pyruvate ratios of patients.[15] These observations, then, warrant the hypothesis that the amount of the factor in patients with schizophrenia increases when the organism is stressed, and that therefore it may be a substance which is important for adaptation through its effect upon metabolism. This further suggests that this substance may be a normal substance which in certain patients with schizophrenia cannot be adequately controlled and that therefore there may be a defect in the controlling mechanism.

Several hints that the controlling mechanism for this substance may be disturbed had already been obtained. The effects of a number of psychoactive drugs, hormones, and various neurohumoral agents had been studied in vitro on the effect of lactate:pyruvate ratios produced by incubating plasma from patients or control subjects with chicken blood cells. In these studies both epinephrine and norepinephrine in 3 to 4 times physiologic amounts reduced the lactate:pyruvate ratios significantly, and the reduction was particularly significant for the latter one.[16]

A second observation was made when Dr. Frohman was studying the lactate:pyruvate ratios on the maternally deprived monkeys in Dr. Harlow's Primate Center at Wisconsin.[17] On one of his visits to Madison the only chickens available were those that had been exposed to an outdoor temperature of 20 degrees below zero. The cells from these chickens failed to reflect any variation in the lactate: pyruvate ratios. This observation was repeated and confirmed by obtaining chickens raised in subzero weather from the upper peninsula of Michigan.

A third observation came from laboratory technicians involved in the determination of lactate:pyruvate ratios. They noted that at the time of blood withdrawal from the chicken, if the heart puncture was missed and further attempts were necessary with the chicken becoming frantic, the resulting blood from the chicken did not allow the obtaining of differential effects between control and schizophrenic plasma as determined by the lactate:pyruvate ratios. They also noted that if chickens had blood withdrawn early in the morning after which they normally flutter around for a period of time, and blood was subsequently withdrawn a second time after an hour or so, the second sample vitiated any differential findings. Under these circumstances, then, the hypothesis was entertained that if chickens were stressed, a substance developed which controlled or inactivated the schizophrenic factor. A systematic study was then initiated.

Epinephrine and norepinephrine in physiologic amounts in vitro did not reduce lactate:pyruvate ratios. However, the question was raised as to whether injection of these substances in chickens would affect their blood cells in any way and whether this would affect the lactate:pyruvate ratios of patients with schizophrenia. It was consequently determined, then, that if chickens were injected with these substances, it required five times the physiologic amount of epinephrine to result in a diminution of the effect by chicken cells on the lactate: pyruvate ratios, while a similar reduction could be obtained by a physiologic and extraordinarily small amount of norepinephrine being injected into the chickens. Further studies showed that intermediary substances such as metanephrine and normetanephrine, when injected into chickens, led to the reduction of the lactate:pyruvate ratio to about the same degrees as an injection of saline. Serotonin, injected in minute amounts, on the other hand, did not lead to a decrease in the lactate: pyruvate ratio.[18]

From these studies, then, it became apparent that when a chicken was stressed or injected with a physiological amount of norepinephrine, some substance was produced which inactivated the schizophrenic factor. Further studies have indicated that this inactivating substance was in the cell of the chicken and not in its serum. Moreover, it has been demonstrated that the intracellular substance is a protein and not a nonprotein. At the present time, then, the cellular proteins of chickens injected with the norepinephrine are being separated by curtain electrophoresis with the hope that eventually this substance that inactivates the serum factor from patients with schizophrenia can be isolated and identified. It has not been purified as yet, but it appears to be stable and probably belongs to the group of enzymes that are classified as esterases. Because of the stability of this inactivating enzyme, in contrast to the marked lability of the schizophrenic serum factor, rapid progress may be made towards its isolation and identification.

From these studies it is tempting to hypothesize that the inactivating enzyme that develops in chicken cells when stressed is similar to an enzyme in certain patients with schizophrenia which fails to be properly aroused. If such an enzyme is deficient in patients with schizophrenia, then it would be responsible for the failure of an as yet unidentified but important biologic adaptive mechanism. Intriguing as this hypothesis is, it is a long jump from a chicken cell to a human cell, but the hypothesis is extraordinarily intriguing and testable experimentally.

In the presentation two years ago,[1] it was pointed out that the factor in the serum of patients with schizophrenia interfered with intracellular metabolism necessary for the proper utilization of biologic energy in response to stress. Specifically, it had been determined that chronic schizophrenic patients were unable to increase the specific activity of adenosinetriphosphate as in control subjects following an injection of ten units of insulin, and that the specific activity of fructose 1-6 diphosphate was more disturbed in a similar way in both acute and chronic schizophrenic patients than ATP itself. Moreover, evidence had been obtained that glucose metabolism did not shift from the hexosemonophosphate shunt to the Embden-Myerhof scheme of metabolism in patients with schizophrenia who were injected with ten units of insulin in contrast to the shift in metabolism for control subjects. The above intracellular findings, coupled with the higher lactate:pyruvate ratios obtained when chicken cells were incubated with serum of patients with schizophrenia, suggests that the serum factor is inhibitory in some way to aerobic carbohydrate metabolism. A search, therefore, entailing a step-by-step analysis has been in progress, with the hope of eventually identifying the enzyme or enzyme systems which are affected by the serum factor. These studies have been most frustrating. Dr. Helen Lees, through the use of the Warburg technique, utilizing rat liver mitochondria, has demonstrated that the serum of patients with schizophrenia depresses the oxidation of succinate.[19] The effect on alphaketoglutarate dehydrogenase could not be determined because of other effects of the serum. Although the degree of suppression of succinate correlates inversely with the height of the lactate:pyruvate ratio for patients, the phenomenon does not appear to be defining the primary enzyme or enzyme system involved. Step-by-step studies therefore are in progress evaluating the effect of the factor in both the tricarboxylic acid and the hydrogen transport systems.

It is of considerable interest that Arnold and Hofmann[20] in a rather extensive investigation used succinate to overload the metabolism of their experimental subjects, both schizophrenic and controls. They too reported a highly significant difference in the metabolism of the red blood cells of schizophrenic patients in contrast to that for patients with other conditions who were used as control subjects. They confirmed our findings of an increase in the specific activities of ATP and Fl,6P for control subjects in contrast to a decrease for the schizophrenic patients when stressed with succinate. They also reported that this stressor reduced the level of ADP in control subjects in contrast to an increase for patients with schizophrenia. This also affected the ATP:ADP ratio in a differential way.

Although the serum factor has been studied only regarding its effects upon the metabolism of circulating blood cells, it is possible to conjecture that this substance passes through membranes with ease, and could affect metabolism in all the cells of the body. If this is so, then we could expect a similar metabolic effect in neural tissue. From the little that we know about the effect of this factor upon metabolism, we could only conjecture that structures of the midbrain would be more affected than those of the cortex. This is consistent with the report of Laborit[21] to the effect that midbrain structures are more dependent upon the lability of the shifts from the hexosemonophosphate shunt to the Embden-Meyerhof system of metabolism for proper function than are the cells of the cortex. With the evidence that the serum factor prevents appropriate metabolic shifts from the synthetic to the energy-releasing pathway one may hypothecate that the critical effects of this substance are, then, on cells of the midbrain. This is a tenable hypothesis also if one takes into consideration the possible neural pathways involved in the symptomatology of the patients with schizophrenia.

Although no direct metabolic studies have been done on the effect of the serum factor on neural tissue, and although neural tissue from patients with schizophrenia has not been studied, desirable as this is, one is forced to hypothesize that if the serum factor interferes with neural metabolism it should be reflected clinically, psychologically, and neurophysiologically, in ways that can be measured, thus supporting this hypothesis.

In the report that was presented two years ago[1] the relationships between the metabolic disturbances measured in the blood cells and clinical, premorbid, and early environmental factors were outlined. Significant correlations existed between the severity of the primary symptoms of the schizophrenic illness as defined by Bleuler and the degree of failure of the specific activity of fructose 1-6 diphosphate to change following ten units of insulin. Moreover, the degree of disturbance in the specific activity of ATP in its response to ten units of insulin correlated significantly with the chronicity of the process. It is difficult to understand the relationship between metabolic disturbance in blood cells and clinical characteristics unless one makes the assumption that similar metabolic disturbances are being produced in neural cells as well.

The report of Cohen and Grisell,[22] indicating a significant relationship between the degree of metabolic disturbance in red blood cells and the work output as measured by specific psychological tests for both control subjects and schizophrenic patients, is equally hard to understand unless one hypothesizes the same degree of disturbance or inefficiency of metabolic function of neural tissues, too. If the metabolism of neural cells of the midbrain is disturbed, this disturbance should be reflected in the electrical potentials of the brain. For such studies to proceed, deep electrode placement would be most desirable, as there may be but limited reflection in the electrical potentials from the cortex. It is well known, for instance, that the gross electroencephalograms of patients with schizophrenia do not reveal any qualitatively noted disturbance and appear within normal limits. However, when the electroencephalogram is studied quantitatively and the energy distribution is measured, as has been done by Goldstein and Sugerman and their associates,[23] a greater variability among a group of patients with schizophrenia characterized by a lower energy output is obtained. These findings add substance to the hypothesis that the serum factor affects neural metabolism in a selective way.

In conclusion, then, we have attempted to summarize the evidence in support of the hypothesis that there is a biologic mechanism in certain patients with schizophrenia that is not functioning properly; that this mechanism is consistently stimulated by life situations and is fundamental to driving metabolism to supply the organism with the energy needed to meet the vicissitudes of life. The hypothesis continues to the effect that a protein or a normal substance of small molecular size carried by the protein is not inactivated properly, and that the defect therefore may be in the mechanisms of inactivation rather than in the production of the factor itself. The hypothesis continues to assume that most of the cellular systems of the body are affected but that there may be some selectivity for different cellular systems of the nervous system. The metabolic disarrangements so produced is then responsible through ways poorly understood for the manifestations of the illness.

These general hypotheses are operational and subject to experimental tests. No doubt, corrections and modifications will occur as more information is obtained. The guidelines for continuing study seem clear and we shall pursue them industriously.

REFERENCES

1. Gottlieb, J. S.: Biochemistry and schizophrenia: Implications for the future. *In* The Future of Psychiatry (eds. P. Hoch and J. Zubin). New York. Grune & Stratton, 1962, pp. 103-115.
2. Heath, R. G. (ed.): Serological Fractions in Schizophrenia. New York, Hoeber Med. Div., Harper & Row, 1963.
3. Frohman, C. E., Goodman, M., Beckett, P. G. S., Latham, L. K., Senf, Rita, and Gottlieb, J. S.: The isolation of an active factor from serum of schizophrenic patients. Ann. N. Y. Acad. Sci. 96:438-447. 1962.
4. Frohman, C. E., et al.: In preparation.
5. Latham, L. K., Frohman, C. E., Beckett, P. G. S., and Gottlieb, J. S.: The isolation from plasma of schizophrenic subjects of a protein factor which has an effect on the behavior of animals. *In* Serological Fractions in Schizophrenia (ed. R. G. Heath). New York, Hoeber Med. Div., Harper & Row, 1963, pp. 33-42.

6. Frohman, C. E., Latham, L. K., Warren, K. A., Beckett, P. G. S., and Gottlieb, J. S.: Properties of a protein factor isolated from schizophrenic plasma. Fed. Proc. 22:450, 1963.
7. Latham, L. K., Loncharich, K. J., Warner, K. A., Crandall, R. G., Beckett, P. G. S., Frohman, C. E., and Gottlieb, J. S.: Effects of a protein factor isolated from schizophrenic blood on permeability. Vox Sang. 8:491-496, 1963.
7a. Latham, L. K., Warner, K., Beckett, P. G. S., Gottlieb, J. S., and Frohman, C. E.: The relationship of a plasma factor in schizophrenia to membrane permeability. Fed. Proc. 24:326, 1965.
8. Bergen, J. R., Pennell, R. B., Saravis, C. A., and Hoagland, H.: Further experiments with plasma proteins in schizophrenics. *In* Serological Fractions in Schizophrenia (ed. R. G. Heath). New York, Hoeber Med. Div., Harper & Row, 1963, pp. 67-76.
9. Redlick, T. F., Renfrew, A. G., Pieri, L., and Marrazzi, A.: Attempt to separate by electrodialysis a cerebrally active small moiety from "Taraxein-like" blood fractions. Fed. Proc. 22:569, 1963.
10. Bergen, J. R., Saravis, C. A., Pennell, R. B., and Hoagland, H.: Stabilization of a human blood factor causing behavior changes in rats. J. Neuropsychiat. 2:201, 1961.
11. Frohman, C. E.: Unpublished data.
12. ——: Unpublished data.
13. Pennell, R. B., and Bergen, J. R.: Verbal communication.
14. Frohman, C. E., Latham, L. K., Warner, K., Brosius, C. O., Beckett, P. G. S., and Gottlieb, J. S.: Motor activity in schizophrenia: effect on plasma factor. Arch. Gen. Psychiat. 9:83-88, 1963.
15. Frohman, C. E., et al.: In preparation.
16. Frohman, C. E., Latham, L. K., Beckett, P. G. S., and Gottlieb, J. S.: Effect of serum from schizophrenic subjects on cellular metabolism. *In* Serological Fractions in Schizophrenia (ed. Robert G. Heath). Hoeber Med. Div., Harper & Row, 1963 (127-35).
17. Beckett, P. G. S., Frohman, C. E., Gottlieb, J. S., Mowbray, J. B., and Wolf, R. C.: Schizophrenic-like mechanisms in monkeys. Amer. J. Psychiat. 119:835-842, 1963.
18. Frohman, C. E., Beckett, P. G. S., and Gottlieb, J. S.: Control of the plasma factor in schizophrenia. *In* Recent Advances in Biological Psychiatry (ed. S. Wortis). New York, Plenum Press, 1965, Vol. VII, pp. 45-51.
19. Lees, Helen, Greenwood, Dora J., Frohman, C. E., Beckett, P. G. S., and Gottlieb, J. S.: The effects of sera from schizophrenic subjects on the oxidation of succinate and ketoglutarate. J. Neuropsychiat. 5:534-538, 1964.
20. Arnold, O. H., and Hofmann, G.: Ergebnisse einer biochemischen Untersuchungs-methode der Schizophrenie und ihr es Erbhintergrundes. Weiner Klinische Wochenschrift 33/34:593-602, 1963.
21. Laborit, H., Leterrier, F., and Brue, F.: Tentative interpretation of phenothiazines' mechanism of action, based on action on body structures and on metabolic processes. Psychopharm. Serv. Center Bull. 2:34-42, 1962.
22. Cohen, B. D., and Grisell, J. L.: Some relations between biochemical

and psychological phenomena in normal and schizophrenic subjects. *In* Serological Fractions in Schizophrenia (ed. R. G. Heath). New York, Hoeber Med. Div., Harper & Row, 1963, pp. 203-217.

23. Goldstein, L., Murphree, H. B., Sugerman, A. A., Pfieffer, C. C., and Jenney, E. H.: Quantitative electroencephalographic analysis of naturally occurring (schizophrenic) and drug-induced psychotic states in human males. Clin. Pharmacol. Ther. 4:10-21, 1963.

13

LONG-TERM FOLLOW-UP (10-15 YEARS) OF SCHIZOPHRENIC PATIENTS WITH FUNKENSTEIN (ADRENALIN-MECHOLYL) TESTS*

by GEORGE E. VAILLANT, M.D., and
DANIEL H. FUNKENSTEIN, M.D.†

In 1950 Funkenstein, et al.[2] first published a report of a test that apparently predicted the response of schizophrenics to electric shock treatment. In brief, they noted that a majority of affective psychotics and a minority of schizophrenics either responded to a 10 mg. intramuscular injection of methacholine with a blood pressure drop that persisted for 25 minutes or longer, and to 0.05 mg. of intravenous l-epinephrine with a blood pressure rise of 50 mm. Hg or more (Group VI), or responded to the methacholine injection with a chill (Group VII). Although the percentage of schizophrenics with these responses was small, Groups VI and VII contained a very high proportion of those schizophrenics who responded to electric shock treatment to the point of leaving the hospital within a month after cessation of shock treatment. Later work, ably reviewed by Rose[9] and by Thorpe,[10] has suggested that in the hands of others the Funkenstein test does not exceed clinical judgment in reliability. Since Funkenstein's experimental conditions have rarely been precisely replicated, both confirmations and failures to confirm his work are difficult to evaluate. Nonetheless, the test in Funkenstein's hands provided significant results and has led to a number of theoretical conclusions.

One such conclusion is that schizophrenics falling in Groups VI and VII can be distinguished by their autonomic reactivity from schizophrenics who run a deteriorating course. In order to investigate if the

---

*This research was supported by the Supreme Council, 33rd Degree, Scottish Rite, Northern Masonic Jurisdiction, U.S.A.

†Department of Psychiatry, Harvard Medical School, and the Massachusetts Mental Health Center, Boston, Massachusetts.

Funkenstein test was not only correlated with short-term response to shock but also with favorable long-terms prognosis in schizophrenia, a follow-up of patients who received the Funkenstein test between 1948 and 1950 was undertaken. Many of these patients were included in the series of 72 schizophrenics reported by Funkenstein in 1952.[3]

Method

Seventy-two consecutive admissions to the Boston Psychopathic Hospital (Massachusetts Mental Health Center) were selected who had (a) been diagnosed schizophrenic upon discharge, (b) received five or more electric shock treatments, and (c) received a Funkenstein test. The Funkenstein test consists of giving to a patient, supine for 30 minutes, a saline injection and then 10 minutes later 0.05 mg. of l-epinephrine intravenously. On the following day under the same conditions 10 mg. methacholine is given intramuscularly. In each instance, the basal resting blood pressure is established and after the administration of the drug, systolic blood pressure is monitored until it returns to basal levels. The seven categories into which the patients are then placed have been adequately defined elsewhere.[3] Groups VI and VII, as defined in the introduction, were considered prognostically favorable.

Each patient's original record was reviewed, and it was recorded whether or not he was a first admission, whether he received insulin coma after electric shock, whether certain favorable prognostic factors were present, and whether or not he was eventually discharged from visit "recovered." After this information was obtained, Funkenstein's original protocols were consulted and the patient's pretreatment Funkenstein grouping was recorded. The maximum drop in systolic blood pressure after methacholine was also noted. This information was then coded and not referred to until after the completion of the follow-up. Five of the 72 cases chosen had Funkenstein tests that were incomplete or ambiguous. These cases and probably a few others were not included in Funkenstein's original series of 72 schizophrenic cases.

Six months after this information had been obtained and put aside, the 67 patients with adequate Funkenstein Tests were followed up. Follow-up consisted in first consulting the Massachusetts Department of Mental Health central files and determining whether any of the patients had required further hospitalization and, if so, for how long. The patient's subsequent charts were examined for correspondence from out-of-state hospitals and from social service agencies. The central Social Service Index of Boston and the protocols of a 3-year follow-up of patients admitted to the Boston Psychopathic in 1949[1] were also consulted. Effort was made to contact the next of kin of all those patients on whom definitive follow-up information could not be obtained from subsequent hospital admissions. Since follow-up letters proved generally ineffective, telephone contact or personal interview was used almost exclusively. The questions asked of relatives or patients were: (1) Had the patient been regularly employed? (2) Was he living independently of his parents and siblings? (3) Did he have some outside social life? Then, in a more open-ended interview, attempt was made to assess the patient's mental status, overall community adjustment, and whether further psychiatric care was needed.

The five follow-up categories that were devised were based upon the most objective available information.

0: Ten or more years in a state hospital (the follow-up period was 12-14 years.)

1: Three or more years in a hospital and inability to work regularly or to live independently of family of origin.

2: Less than three years hospitalization but inability to work for more than 50 per cent of the time the patient was in the community. (This usually meant the patient was living with parents, doing occasional menial odd jobs, and still exhibiting psychotic symptoms.)

3: Able to work more than 50 per cent of the time but unable to live apart from parents or siblings. (The patients usually had a decline in social status, limited friends, and a few psychiatric complaints.)

4: Able to work full time or to manage a household effectively, and to live independently of family of origin. (This often meant a full social life and no manifestation of prior illness.)

Results

On 89 per cent of the patients adequate follow-up was obtained for at least 8-10 years after discharge and on 63 per cent of the patients either until 1962 or until their death. Two of the patients were "lost" after discharge and six of the patients were followed only for two to seven years. Understandably, good outcome was correlated with difficulty of follow-up.

The clinical outcome of the patients can be seen in table 1. Although all of these patients received electric shock and 19 received insulin shock, the figures are comparable to other follow-up studies of schizophrenia with or without shock. The cohort probably represents a fair

TABLE 1.—Percentage of Patients Classified into each Follow-up Category

Follow-up Category	Per Cent of Patients in Each Group (n = 72)
0	29%
1	6%
2	24%
3	15%
4	26%

clinical sampling of schizophrenia and confirms the finding of many investigations that EST does not alter the long-term course of the psychosis. Although most of the patients were in the community, 59 per cent were invalids. The fact that only 23 per cent of the patients are currently hospitalized can probably be attributed to phenothiazines and to enlightened state hospital administration.

Table 2 illustrates the correlation of eventual follow-up with the original Funkenstein test results. Forty per cent of the patients with favorable (Groups VI and VII) Funkenstein tests and 43 per cent of those with unfavorable tests fell into the prognostic categories 3 and 4 and achieved what would correspond to a "social recovery." More interesting is the fact that as many of the very worst outcomes (those hospitalized for 10 years or more) as the very best outcomes (those who appeared to be leading normal independent lives) had favorable Funkenstein tests. For both the good and poor outcomes the average maximum drop in systolic blood pressure after methacholine

TABLE 2.—Correlation between Funkenstein Test Score and Clinical Outcome

	Funkenstein Group				
Follow-up Category	Unfavorable (I-V)			Favorable (VI and VII)	
0	XXXXX	XXXXX	XXX	XXXXX	XXX
1	XXX				
2	XXXXX	XXX		XXXXX	XX
3	XXXxx	x		XXXx	
4	XXXXX	XXXXx	XX	XXXXX	x

X—one patient with follow-up of 8-14 years.

x—one patient with follow-up of less than 8 years.

Since patients with ambiguous Funkenstein tests were excluded, only 67 patients are included.

was 21 mm. Hg. Age was not correlated with Funkenstein grouping. Over the long term, then, the test did not appear to differentiate the deteriorated from the remitting schizophrenic.

An incidental finding of the study was that the outcomes of the 19 patients who received insulin shock were no better than those who did not receive it. Forty-three per cent of the patients who did not receive insulin shock were in groups 3 and 4; 37 per cent of those who did receive insulin were in such groups.

The fact that seven of the 18 patients who were discharged from visit as "recovered" eventually became invalids (groups 0-2) is in keeping with the fact that the lucid period produced by electric shock treatment is often evanescent.

Discussion

One purpose of the follow-up was to test the hypothesis that schizophrenics who get well are "really" affective psychotics. It is generally accepted that the presence of symptoms suggestive of an affective psychosis mitigates the prognosis in schizophrenia, and a recent review[11] of 10 studies that examined the relationship of manic-depressive heredity to schizophrenic prognosis concluded that such heredity is correlated with schizophrenic remission. Funkenstein observed that most affective psychotics fell in Groups VI and VII and that the few schizophrenics who fell in this group *not only* responded to electric shock but also showed affective symptoms.[3] The argument can be made therefore that schizophrenics with very good prognosis should be classed with manic-depressives. The fact, however, that the remitting patients (Group 4) were not comprised principally of Funkenstein's Group VI and Group VII patients suggest that in schizophrenia neither initial response to electric shock nor similarity to affective psychosis in autonomic responsivity is correlated strongly with favorable prognosis. It would appear that remitting schizophrenics are not just misdiagnosed manic-depressives.

Secondly, although Funkenstein himself never made the assertion, many later investigators have tried to demonstrate that the Funkenstein test could be used to differentiate "process" schizophrenia (poor long-term outcome) from "reactive" schizophrenia (good long-term outcome). Geocaris and Kooiker[5] found that not one of the 25 chronic schizophrenics that they tested fell among Funkenstein's favorable groups. Hirschstein[6] hypothesized that the Funkenstein test was predicting prognosis whether or not the patient received electric shock.

He gave methacholine to 60 schizophrenic patients who did not receive shock and found that 14 of the 19 patients with a subsequent drop in blood pressure of more than 25 minutes duration (crudely equivalent to Funkenstein's favorable Group VI) got better while that group whose blood pressure returned to basal levels in less than 25 minutes showed improvement in only 12 out of 32 patients. Putting emphasis on the magnitude of the blood pressure drop after methacholine, King[7] observed that "reactive" schizophrenics experienced more severe hypotension than "process" schizophrenics. In these three studies there was the implicit assumption that fundamental differences in autonomic reactivity could be used to differentiate schizophrenics into two groups with different prognosis.

Attempting to replicate King's work, however, Zuckerman and Grosz[12] found that in response to methacholine the blood pressure fell more profoundly in "process" than in "reactive" schizophrenics. However, they deviated from Funkenstein's protocol. Laane[8] found that although none of 36 allegedly nonremitting "clear-cut schizophrenics" fell into Groups VI and VII, only one out of 12 "schizophreniform" (usually remitting) patients fell in Groups VI and VII, and this patient did not respond to electric shock. He failed to observe Funkenstein's order of drug injection.

These conflicting studies all suffer from follow-ups of just a few months. Yet schizophrenia is not an illness involving a single hospital stay, but one that encompasses decades. Thus, Funkenstein's conclusion, that autonomic response to methacholine and l-epinephrine is correlated with the short-term response to electric shock, proved reliable in his hands. But the present study would suggest that the Funkenstein test has no value in separating Bleuler's group of schizophrenias into groups with good and poor long-term outcomes.

Elsewhere Funkenstein[4] has pointed out that factors (e.g., social attitudes, perception of parents, and T.A.T. phantasies) which correlate with an individual's style of handling the acute emergency phase of stress bear no relation to ability to master stress over time. He showed that the converse was also true—factors associated with the eventual mastery of stress (e.g., integration of personality and quality of interpersonal relationships) were not correlated with the handling of stress in the acute emergency phase. In the present study it is of interest that factors that *were* correlated with long-term outcome often themselves depended upon longitudinal factors (table 3). Acute onset, premorbid adjustment, precipitating stresses, and heredity are all

TABLE 3.—Presence of Certain Factors in Poor and Good Outcome Groups

Factor	*Social Invalids (Groups 0-2) n=42*	*Social Remissions (Groups 3-4 n=30*
Onset of 6 Months or Less	45%	70%*
Symptoms of Affective Psychosis	31%	67%*
Nonschizoid Premorbid Adjustment	31%	67%*
Precipitating Event	5%	17%
Depressive Psychotic Heredity	26%	53%*

*P=0.05 (test used was the chi square).

variables that encompass a greater period of time than duration of hospital stay. In mental illness, then, "tests" may be devised to predict short-term prognosis, but unless they include a longitudinal dimension they may prove of limited value in predicting clinical course over the long term.

The writers' use of social function rather than of mental status as a criterion of recovery from schizophrenia may be criticized. The majority of psychiatric follow-up studies utilize the psychiatric interview as the instrument and the assessment of residual psychotic symptomatology as the criterion of improvement. Such methods depend upon *when* one looks at the patient. Secondly, many chronic and hospitalized schizophrenics are social invalids, but present little in the way of overt symptomatology. Thus, the use of social function over time (years hospitalized, length of effective employment post-hospitalization, and years spent independent of parental care) provides in many ways a more valid and certainly a more objective gauge of schizophrenic adjustment than presence or absence of factors like "loose associations" and "flattened" affect.

Finally, this study illustrates the benefits of keeping experimental protocols long after the original study is complete. The ultimate test of biologic parameters in mental illness must come from prospective studies with adequate follow-up.

SUMMARY

After a lapse of 14 years, 67 patients with a discharge diagnosis of schizophrenia, who received Funkenstein tests administered by Funkenstein and his associates and who were treated with electric shock, were followed up. Forty-two per cent of these patients were able to stay out of the hospital for most of the time and to work regularly. An equal percentage of patients within Funkenstein's favorable (Groups VI and VII) and unfavorable (Groups I-V) autonomic classifications showed adequate social adjustment. The tests did not distinguish between the very best and the very worst long-term outcomes. On the basis of the present data the conclusion is drawn that autonomic reactivity, as measured by the Funkenstein test, bears little relation to long-term prognosis and that the test should not be employed to defend the concept of "reactive" and "process" schizophrenia.

REFERENCES

1. Bockhoven, J. S., Pandiscio, A. R., and Solomon, H. C.: Social adjustment of patients in the community three years after commitment to the Boston Psychopathic Hospital. Ment. Hyg. 40:353-374, 1956.
2. Funkenstein, D. H., Greenblatt, M., and Solomon, H. C. A test which predicts the clinical effects of electric shock treatment on schizophrenic patients. Amer. J. Psychiat. 106:889-901, 1950.
3. ——: Prognostic tests indicating the effectiveness of treatment. Res. Publ. Ass. Nerv. Ment. Dis. 31:245-266, 1953.
4. Funkenstein, D. H., King, S. H., and Drolette, M. E.: Mastery of Stress. Cambridge, Harvard University Press, 1957.
5. Geocaris, K. H., and Kooiker, J. E.: Blood pressure response of chronic schizophrenic patients to epinephrine and mecholyl. Amer. J. Psychiat. 112:808-813, 1956.
6. Hirschstein, R.: Autonomic nervous system responses in schizophrenia. J. Nerv. Ment. Dis. 122:254-262, 1955.
7. King, G. F.: Differential autonomic responsiveness in the process-reactive classification of schizophrenia. J. Abnorm. Soc. Psychol. 56:160-164, 1958.
8. Laane, C. L.: Adrenalin and mecholyl test performed in schizophrenia and schizophreniform states. Acta. Psychiat. Neurol. Scand. 31:467-476, 1956.
9. Rose, J. T.: The Funkenstein test—a review of the literature. Acta Psychiat. Scand. 38:124-153, 1962.
10. Thorpe, J. G.: The current status of prognostic test indicators for electro-convulsive therapy. Psychosom. Med. 24:554-568, 1962.
11. Vaillant, G. E.: Manic depressive heredity and remission in schizophrenia. Brit. J. Psychiat. 109:746-749, 1963.
12. Zuckerman, M., and Grosz, H. J.: Contradictory results using the mecholyl test to differentiate process and reactive schizophrenia. J. Abnorm. Soc. Psychol. 59:145-146, 1959.

14

CURRENT REPRODUCTIVE TRENDS IN SCHIZOPHRENIA*

by L. ERLENMEYER-KIMLING, PH.D., JOHN D. RAINER, M.D., and FRANZ J. KALLMANN, M.D.

SINCE A POTENTIAL schizophrenic has to be born into this world before he can learn to pursue those disordered forms of behavior which culminate in his final break with reality, a study of reproductive trends in schizophrenia-producing family units is called for in the program of a pluridisciplinary conference concerned with the undiminished recurrence of the disease in human populations. The timeliness of such a comparative demographic analysis would seem indisputable, and perhaps the nondoctrinal character of its statistical design as well, since new cases of schizophrenia arise ceaselessly from one generation to another, and virtually all current etiologic theories assign an essential role to the family setting in which a vulnerable individual develops.

Tacitly we may even be agreed that in dealing with the old and rather sensitive problem of reproduction in schizophrenic patients, too much time has been lost by holding on to inconspicuous *pars pro toto* concepts and noncommittal procedures. The overall effect has been to perpetuate various well-entrenched remnants of the presumably outdated nature-nurture controversy in one of the most crucial clinical areas, thus keeping alive the impact of arguments and approaches used in medieval debates on the sex of angels.

VARIOUS EXPLANATIONS FOR AN INCREASED SCHIZOPHRENIA RISK IN SOME FAMILIES

In order to explain the generally observed increase in the frequency of schizophrenia in certain families, the importance of the family milieu has been stressed by some investigators, the effect of a

*This investigation is supported by Public Health Service Research Grant MH-03532 from the National Institute of Mental Health.

chromosomally transmitted specific vulnerability factor by others. Chief among the causative agents emphasized in psychogenic theories have been the ego confusion and stultification produced by an overprotective-ambivalent mother, a weak father, and faulty patterns of communication in the home. Similarly, clinical expression of a specific vulnerability factor — variously described as simple recessive, irregularly dominant, or multifactorial in its mode of inheritance—is usually assumed by geneticists to depend on complex interactions with genic and ecological modifiers.

Regardless of the etiologic working hypothesis preferred, the single family characteristic which is certain to increase a person's risk of schizophrenia is the presence of a schizophrenic parent or sibling. Clearly, therefore, it is essential to obtain, in every new generation of a nonstatic population, up-to-date information about the number and reproductive capacity of the family settings which may be expected to produce further schizophrenia cases. The need for additional prevalence data is not precluded by the consistent observation that the crucial difference between the schizophrenia risks of persons with and without the known factor of consanguinity to a schizophrenic index case (proband) has remained more or less constant everywhere,[7, 21] despite changes in mating patterns, psychiatric treatment methods, and diagnostic systems of classification. The differential schizophrenia rates, reported by many different investigators in a number of countries during the last half-century, are compared in tables 1-3. Such data serve to demonstrate, first of all, that genetic theories of schizophrenia by no means depend only on the results of twin studies.

Differential Risk Data

More specifically, a comparison of age-corrected risk figures shows that the schizophrenia rates for sensibly grouped relatives of schizophrenics have invariably been many times higher than those for contemporaries distinguished only as members of the general population.

Depending on the statistical methods and population samples used (census data with or without correction for excess mortality, sibships of the spouses of hospital patients, special demographic surveys, etc.), the general population rate may fall between 1 and 2 per cent (table 1), but has usually been found to be slightly less than 1 per cent.[10, 14, 21] Sometwhat higher figures (2 to 3 per cent) have been reported for certain isolated populations,[2] and for such special popula-

TABLE 1.—Schizophrenia Risk in the General Population and in the Sibships of Schizophrenics

Studies Compared			Relation to Index Case					
Year of Publication	*Investigators*	*Description of Population*	*General Population*	*Step-sibs*	*Half-sibs*	*Full sibs*	*DZ cotwins*	*MZ cotwins*
1932	Rüdin and Schulz	Adult hospital cases (Germany)	0.85	—	—	6.7-8.3	—	—
1935	Luxenburger	Adult twin index cases (Germany)	—	—	—	11.8	14.0	54.0
1946	Kallmann	Adult twin index cases (U.S.A.)	—	1.8	7.6	14.3	14.7	85.8
1953	Böök	Total population (North-Swedish isolate)	3.0	—	—	9.1	—	—
1953	Slater	Adult twin index cases (England)	—	—	—	5.4	14.4	76.3
1956	Kallmann and Roth	Preadolescent twin index cases (U.S.A.)	—	—	—	12.2	17.1	70.6
1962	Altshuler and Sarlin	Totally deaf schizophrenic hospital cases (U.S.A.)	2.5	—	—	11.6	—	—
1962	Garrone	Adult hospital cases (Switzerland)	1.7	—	—	14.7	—	—

tion groups as the deaf residents of New York State.[19] Although much of the variability between the findings of different investigators is due to methodological considerations, a part is probably due to differential frequencies of cousin marriages in the populations studied. Another source of variation may arise from differences in the representation of the sexes. According to Garrone,[7] the schizophrenia risk in Geneva (1901-1950) varied from 1.5 per cent for males to 1.9 per cent for females, with an overall expectancy of 1.75 per cent after some age correction* (1 per cent without any correction for age).

In contrast to the variability between studies, the diversities consistently observed between the various groups of relatives of schizophrenics have their origin in an entirely different source. This principle is most readily demonstrated in the sibships of schizophrenics (table 1), where the one factor directly related to the observed variations in the schizophrenia rate is the degree of consanguinity to the known schizophrenic subject in the family. It is clearly seen here that the closer the genetic relationship, the higher the expectancy rate. The schizophrenia risk of the half-sibs falls about midway between the rates for step-sibs (1.8 per cent) and full sibs (11.5–14.3 per cent). The significant difference which is always reported between the expectancy rates for two-egg and one-egg cotwins of schizophrenic twin index cases is no more relevant from a clinical or statistical standpoint than is the absence of a comparable difference between full sibs and two-egg cotwins,[11] or between hearing and deaf siblings of deaf schizophrenics.[1] It may also be noted here than the Geneva sibship rate reported by Garrone,[7] like his figures for the parents and children of index cases, agrees as closely with our New York State rates as do all the other European family data reviewed by Edith Zerbin-Rüdin.[21] The Swiss study was based on the families of 3810 index cases and represented all known cases of schizophrenia in Geneva between 1901 and 1950.

In evaluating the schizophrenia rates reported in the parental generation (table 2), we should bear in mind that variations in both ascertainability and mating potential are to be considered here in addition to the genetic relationship. Although it may still be true that approximately 90 per cent of new schizophrenia cases come from

*Garrone's age-corrected figure for both sexes combined was 2.51 per cent, using ages 15 through 70 as the risk period. The data recalculated by us, using ages 15 through 44 as the risk period, provide an overall expectancy of 1.75 per cent.

matings between two unaffected persons, it is definitely in the realm of possibility that present and future generations of schizophrenics may have a better chance of becoming parents than could be shown in previous studies.

To obtain data on the schizophrenia risk in descendant generations (table 3), the task of certifying schizophrenic symptoms in one parent or in both parents or in neither parent calls for particular attention, even in studies focused mainly on a search for etiologic factors in the family environment. The expectancies differ nearly as much between the children and grandchildren of schizophrenic index cases, or between the offspring of one and two schizophrenics, as they do between one-egg and two-egg cotwins. In fact, this distribution of risk data would seem to be far more consistent with the genetic theory of schizophrenia than with any other working hypothesis that has been offered.

Demographic and Evolutionary Considerations

If continuation of the search for a gene-specific vulnerability factor is regarded as plausible, or at least as not futile at our present state

Table 2.—Prevalence of Schizophrenia in the Parental Generation

Studies Compared			Relation to Index Case	
Year of Publi-cation	*Investigators*	*Description of Population*	*Parents*	*Aunts and Uncles*
1935	Luxenburger	Adult twin index cases (Germany)	11.7	—
1946	Kallmann	Adult twin index cases (U.S.A.)	9.2	—
1953	Böök	Total population (North-Swedish isolate)	12.0	—
1956	Kallmann and Roth	Preadolescent twin index cases (U.S.A.)	12.5	—
1962	Garrone	Adult hospital cases (Switzer-land)	7.0	—
1963	All family studies reviewed by Zerbin-Rüdin		5.0-10.0	0.8-2.0

TABLE 3.—Schizophrenia Risk in Descendant Generations

Studies Compared			Direct Descendants			Collateral Descendants	
				Children of			
Year of Publication	*Investigators*	*Description of Population*	*Grand-children*	*One Schizo-phrenic*	*Two Schizo-phrenics*	*Nieces and Nephews*	*Grand-nieces and Grand-nephews*
1928	Rüdin and Schulz	Adult hospital cases (Germany)	—	—	—	1.4	—
1938	Kallmann	Adult hospital cases (Germany)	4.3	16.4	68.1	1.9-3.9	—
1940	Schulz	Adult hospital cases (Bavaria)	—	—	41.0	—	—
1952	Elsässer	Adult hospital cases (Germany)	—	—	36.1	—	—
1962	Garrone	Adult hospital cases (Switzerland)	—	17.0	—	—	—
1963	All family studies reviewed by Zerbin-Rüdin		3.0-4.0	9.0-16.0	40.0-68.0	1.7-3.9	0.8-2.8

of knowledge regarding the etiology of schizophrenia, it would seem to be essential in every state concerned about the mental health of future generations to combine this search with studies of current reproductive trends and certain predictable population effects of potential evolutionary significance. Such predictions may be expressed in terms of expected changes in the forms of clinical psychopathology or mainly with respect to anticipated statistical variations in the incidence or prevalence of the disease, but they cannot be made without an understanding of some applicable principles of population genetics.

Since both our diagnostic criteria for classifying schizophrenia and efficient demographic techniques are comparatively new,[12] usable data on the frequency of schizophrenia in earlier historical periods do not exist. We do not really know, therefore, how common schizophrenia was before 1900, how it was perpetuated in certain families and societies, or which degrees of mildness or severity were favored by prevailing factors of selection relative to schizophrenic symptomatology.

The most basic theorem of modern population genetics was formulated in 1908—independently by Hardy in England and by Weinberg in Germany. Using rather simple mathematical reasoning, the Hardy-Weinberg theorem refuted the intuitive pre-Mendelian conception that a hereditary characteristic would in time spread in dilute fashion through the population as if carried by the blood.

According to the demographic principles of the Hardy-Weinberg theorem, the frequency of any given genotype in a population would remain constant from generation to generation under ideal conditions with no disrupting forces. Since such forces do operate, however, the frequency of a genotype can change over a number of generations in predictable fashions. The resultant changes may be categorized according to discrepancies from the ideal conditions required for a static ratio under the Hardy-Weinberg system.

The first condition for equilibrium is that the population be so large that no genes increase or decrease in frequency by chance variation. In a small population, with a given gene carried by only a few individuals, it would be possible for these individuals to fail to reproduce, or for none of their children to receive the gene. In such a case, the gene might disappear in one generation. This phenomenon, known as genetic drift, takes place only in small populations and can be neglected as the population increases to a very large size, as is the case for most modern populations.

The second condition for a stable Hardy-Weinberg equilibrium is the absence of new mutations which would increase the frequency of a given gene unless balanced by losses due to other mechanisms. The mutation rate for schizophrenia is not yet known. A third type of demographic force, selective migration into or out of a population group, may also lead to changes in the frequency of the gene within that group. In the case of schizophrenia, the third phenomenon may account for any increase that is found in the number of schizophrenics living under marginal socioeconomic conditions.

Selection in Schizophrenia: Assortative Mating and Differential Reproductivity

The remaining dynamic mechanisms of population change to be considered in relation to such a common pathological condition as schizophrenia, and probably the most significant ones from an evolutionary viewpoint, are the phenomena of assortative mating and selection. If matings between two carriers of the genetic vulnerability factor tend to increase the number of new schizophrenia cases, the higher incidence of the disorder in the next generation will be important for two reasons: (1) there will be clinical and social consequences for the offspring and (2) there will be an increased proportion of clinically recognizable persons who may be subjected to the force of selection.

Aside from new mutations, there is, in the final analysis, only one way for the frequency of a given gene to change in a large, random-mating and nonmigrating population: namely, through a reproductivity rate among carriers of the gene which differs on the average from that of the general population.

If carriers have more children, the given genotype will increase in frequency, thus showing a change that is referred to as positive selection, although its qualitative population effect may by no means be on the positive side. Conversely, if carriers have fewer children, the genotype will decrease, indicating a process of negative selection. In many instances, the effect of negative selection may be counterbalanced by new mutations, or by some selective advantage held by individuals in whom the character is only mildly expressed or clinically unaffected carriers. All of these mechanisms of evolutionary significance, of course, apply by extension to genes which act in constellation to produce their effects on the phenotype.

Previously Reported Mating and Fertility Patterns in Schizophrenia

Previous investigations of mating and fertility patterns in hospitalized schizophrenics were conducted in different countries and at different times, but going back only to the end of the last century. The consistent picture portrayed by these earlier studies was one of low rates of marriage and reproduction in schizophrenic populations as compared with the given general populations.[2, 4, 7, 8, 10, 11, 15-17] Obviously, prolonged hospitalization and increased mortality contributed greatly to these reduced rates.

Among the earliest fertility statistics for an urban sample of schizophrenics with virtually completed reproductive histories were the Berlin data on a consecutive series of patients hospitalized between 1893 and 1902.[10] Altogether, these 1087 patients produced a total of 2000 children, including 55 offspring of dual matings—that is, the union between two schizophrenics. The rate of nearly two children per patient was about one-half of the corresponding general population fertility. The latter rate, to be sure, was rather high by current New York standards or even compared with the general population of New York State in 1900.

Of course, such demographically significant corollaries as a gene frequency change arise only from real differences between the reproductive rates of schizophrenics and their contemporaries in the general population. This relative fertility of a given category of genotypes in a population is designated as their "adaptive value." In this sense, schizophrenics tended to have a relatively low adaptive value.

Indeed, if schizophrenics continued to produce on the average only one-half as many children as their counterparts in the general population, the proportion of schizophrenics in future generations would be certain to decrease gradually, unless fully replaced by new mutations—an improbable assumption at this time. However, recent developments in the medical and social sciences may have changed not only the life expectancies and degrees of "social atrophy" of schizophrenics, but also their opportunities for reproduction. Modern somatic and other manipulative therapies permit the schizophrenic patient to function within the community at a higher level of integration and during longer periods of remission than he ever did before. We should at least know, therefore, whether and to what extent there have also been changes in the marriage and fertility patterns of the schizophrenic population.

No one denies that the effectiveness of newly developed buffers, tending to reinforce the schizophrenic's chance of survival and to revitalize his social role, has been advantageous for the physical, and possibly for the social, stability of the affected individual. It should also be clear, however, that any consequent increase in the reproductivity of schizophrenics might lead to population changes of a less desirable nature.

Comparative New York State Data on Reproductivity

In order to appraise the extent of a progressive decrease in the selective disadvantage of schizophrenics, our New York State study of demonstrable reproductivity changes was initiated in 1960. Admissions to state hospitals during two survey periods, 1934-36 and 1954-56, were sampled. Each case drawn was reevaluated, and only conservatively diagnosed and uniformly verified cases of schizophrenia were retained as index cases to form our two samples for study. The procedure of selecting the samples, and the formulas for calculation of estimates, together constitute a probability design which ensures that the precision of any result will be calculable, and hence known.[3]

In the first phase of the study, clinical and statistical data on each index case were collected from hospital records pertaining to the admission drawn into the sample, as well as from records of earlier and subsequent admissions. The eleven hospitals* from which samples were drawn—yielding a total of 3354 verified schizophrenic index cases—consisted of Brooklyn, Central Islip, Gowanda, Hudson River, Kings Park, Manhattan, Rochester, Rockland, St. Lawrence, and Utica State Hospitals, and the New York State Psychiatric Institute. The compilation of these samples entailed the diagnostic screening of 9790 admissions.

The data extracted from these records included (1) hospitalization and treatment histories; (2) information on such personal characteristics as education, occupation, and religion; (3) data on marriage and reproduction up to the time of admission; and (4) references to the admission of other members of the family, especially of parents, siblings, spouses, or children. Diagnostic classification of the relatives from their hospital records are, of course, made by exactly the same psychiatric criteria used in compiling the samples of index cases.[3, 9]

In the second phase of the study, our research design calls for home interviews with the index case or his immediate relatives. The main objective is to obtain longitudinal data on the reproductive histories of the index cases and those of their parents and siblings, both schizophrenic and nonschizophrenic. This part of the study is not yet completed.

The age, sex, and color characteristics of the two samples at admission are compared in figure 1. The classifications by sex and age are limited in this tabulation to the 2706 white index cases for whom admission data are complete. Identical sex ratios are noted

---

*We wish to express our gratitude to the directors of these and other hospitals in New York State, as well as to their clinical and administrative staffs, for their active interest and splendid cooperation in this research project. Also, we should like to thank Mr. Robert E. Patton, director of statistical services in the New York State Department of Mental Hygiene, and various members of his staff for their untiring assistance in locating readmissions of index cases within the state.

for the two survey periods, as are similar age distributions within each sex.

Comparative Data on Marriage and Reproduction at the Time of Admission

In a previous report on 1552 schizophrenic index cases,[9] the emphasis was placed on answering the following three questions, at least tentatively:

1. Are there evidences of changes in the marital and reproductive status of schizophrenics in the later period, compared with the earlier period?

2. If changes are noted, what are the specific differences that can be discerned in the patterns of marriage and reproduction?

3. How do the marriage and reproduction rates of schizophrenics compare with those of the general population at the same period of time?

In the preliminary analysis, marital and reproductive rates were found to be substantially higher in the 1954-56 sample than in the 1934-36 cases. In accord with the findings of other investigations,[4, 10] the majority of the marriages and childbirths among these patients had taken place prior to the onset of schizophrenia. Compared with the 1934-36 group, however, the later sample not only had higher rates of marriage and reproduction before the onset of psychosis, but had also a greater number of marriages and births during the interval between onset and admission. The difference between the

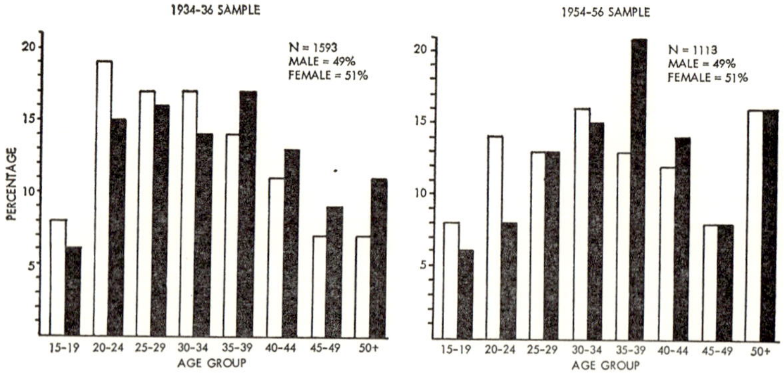

Fig. 1.—Distribution of samples of schizophrenics by age and sex.

two samples in marriage and reproduction was not accounted for by differences either in age at onset or in age at marriage. The increase in reproductivity was attributable chiefly to the increased number of marriages, rather than to changes in the fertility patterns within marriage.

Consistent with studies in other periods and other populations, the preliminary data showed marital and reproductive rates for the schizophrenics to be well below those of the general population in both survey periods, with a larger decrement for male than for female schizophrenics. Nevertheless, the outstanding feature of the findings was that marriages and total reproductivity showed a relatively greater increase for schizophrenics than for the general population over approximately the same span of time.

For the present analysis admission data are available on 2706 index cases—that is, on the majority of the white index cases in the two survey periods. Comparing the percentages of married schizophrenics in the two samples with each other as well as with the general population data (fig. 2), it is again observed that the absolute increase in the marital frequency of schizophrenics exceeds that of their counterparts in the general population. Relative increases (i.e., the absolute increase taken as a percentage of the figure for the earlier period) are even more impressive: schizophrenic women, 19 per cent; population women, 13 per cent; schizophrenic men, 55 per cent; population men, 17 per cent.

Age-specific marriage data (table 4) indicate that the differentiation

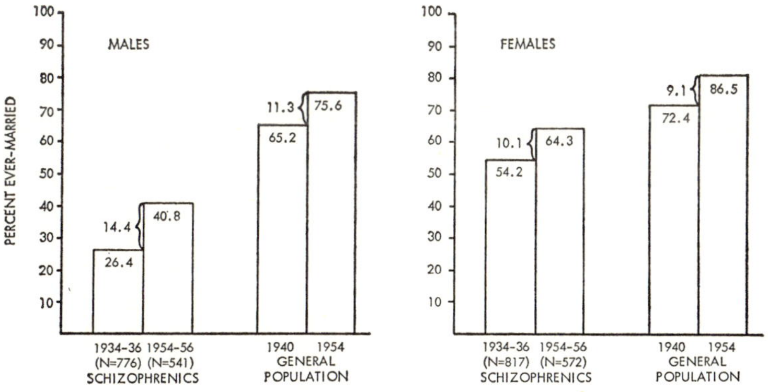

FIG. 2.—Percentages of schizophrenics ever married at admission, compared with percentages ever married in general population.

between the two samples of schizophrenics occurs at all age groups. For males, the differences are especially marked in the younger age groups (ages 15-24 and 25-34). Correspondingly greater differences in reproductivity may therefore be anticipated in the longitudinal follow-up of these cases.

TABLE 4.—Schizophrenics Ever Married, by Age at Admission at the Two Survey Periods

Age	Male				Female			
	1934-36		1954-56		1934-36		1954-56	
	Number of Cases	*Per Cent Ever Married*	*Number of Cases*	*Per Cent Ever Married*	*Number of Cases*	*Per Cent Ever Married*	*Number of Cases*	*Per Cent Ever Married*
All ages	776	26.4	541	40.8	817	54.2	572	64.3
15-24	209	1.9	117	11.1	169	19.5	80	21.2
25-34	265	20.0	160	38.1	239	54.8	158	60.8
35-44	193	46.6	136	50.7	245	70.2	198	79.8
45 or over	109	53.2	128	60.9	164	65.2	136	71.3

Another factor to be considered is the remarkably large number of marriages ending in separation or divorce. In the 1934-36 sample, 17 per cent of the female and 21 per cent of the male marriages had terminated by the time of admission; in the 1954-56 sample, 24 and 31 per cent of female and male marriages, respectively. Moreover, thc proportion of persons married more than once showed a sizable increase in the later sample. Of persons ever married by the time of admission, more than one marriage had been contracted in the 1934-36 group by 8 per cent of the women, and by 5 per cent of the men, and in the 1954-56 group by 14 per cent of the women and by 8 per cent of the men. Thus, although more contemporary schizophrenics are marrying, more of their marriages are terminated by separation or divorce. In other words, there will be more broken homes for the increasing number of children born to schizophrenics.

Data on the observed changes in reproductive patterns are given in table 5 (calculations are based on legitimate children only). These comparisons show that not only do more schizophrenic females of the 1954-56 sample marry, but also that fewer of the marriages remain childless. The increase in the number of children born per married woman reflects both the decrease in nonfertile unions and the rise in the number of children per fertile marriage. Statistics for women of the general population reveal similar but less marked changes. For male schizophrenics, on the other hand, marital fertility seems to have somewhat declined.

Measures of the total reproductivity within a group may sometimes be more meaningful than those limited to married persons. Thus, although the marital fertility of male schizophrenics has dropped, their overall reproductive rate—as measured by child per person—has actually increased slightly due to the ascending marriage rate (table 5). For female schizophrenics, the absolute increase of 0.6 children per woman (or 60 children for every 100 women) is twice as great as for the general population. In relative terms, the reproductive rate of schizophrenic women increased by 86 per cent, contrasted with a 25 per cent increase in general population reproductivity. The large fertility differential, which distinguished schizophrenics from the general population in all previous studies and still existed in our 1934-36 sample, is now in the process of disappearing.

TABLE 5.—Various Reproductive Measures for Schizophrenics and for Women in the General Population, Age 15 to End of Reproductive Period[a]

Measure	Schizophrenic				General Population[b]	
	Men		Women		Women	
	1934-36	1954-56	1934-36	1954-56	1940	1954
Total cases	723	457	653	436	***	***
Ever married (per cent)	24.8	35.9	51.4	62.2	65.0	76.3
Childless (as per cent of ever married)	27.4	26.2	28.3	19.6	26.5	18.1
Total children of persons ever married	347	279	436	556	***	***
Children per fertile marriage	2.7	2.3	1.8	2.5	2.5	2.5
Children per marriage	1.9	1.7	1.3	2.0	1.9	2.0
Children per person	0.5	0.6	0.7	1.3	1.2	1.5

[a]Ages 15 to 44 for females; 15 to 49 for males.

[b]Bureau of the Census, Current Population Reports, Series P-20, No. 108, Table 1.

Longitudinal Reproductive Data on 1677 Index Cases

In covering the reproductive histories of schizophrenics beyond the time of hospitalization during the survey years, data have thus far been collected on a total of 1677 index cases. These cases were followed through 1961, unless they had reached the end of the reproductive period (age 45 for females, age 50 for males) or died prior to that date. To provide a standard 5-7 year follow-up interval beyond admission, the marital and reproductive statuses have been evaluated as of 1941 for the 1934-36 cases and as of 1961 for the 1954-56 cases. For most of the former cases, data have also been calculated for the additional years of observation beyond 1941 (the average year of final observation being 1954).

The intersample differences in marriage and reproduction at admission (table 6) for these completed cases are similar to those found for the corresponding total groups. By the end of the 5-7 year interval following admission, both samples of completed cases had experienced small increases in marriage and reproductive rates, with intersample differences remaining fairly stable during the interval. Women in the 1954-56 group of completed cases continue to surpass their counterparts in the earlier series in all measures of reproductivity, while the male patients in 1954-56 exceeded men of the 1934-36 period in total reproductivity—that is, in the number of children per person (table 7).

Table 6.—Marriage and Reproduction of Schizophrenics (Age 15 and Over) from Admission to Last Evaluation

Sex	Period of Admission	Number of Cases	Period of Assessment: *Admission*	*5 to 7 Years Later*	*25 to 27 Years Later*
			Ever married, per cent		
Male	1934-36	461	21.5	23.9	27.1
	1954-56	295	37.3	43.4	***
Female	1934-36	535	49.0	52.5	54.0
	1954-56	386	61.9	64.0	***
			Children per person		
Male	1934-36	461	0.4	0.5	0.5
	1954-56	295	0.6	0.7	***
Female	1934-36	535	0.8	0.9	1.0
	1954-56	386	1.2	1.3	***

Another way of comparing the two groups is to consider the percentages of patients that had become parents by the time of evaluation. In the 1934-36 group, 16 per cent of the men and 35 per cent of the women had offspring by 1941; in the 1954-56 group, 32 per cent of the men and 51 per cent of the women had reproduced by 1961.

As is evident from the longitudinal trends compared in figure 3, the reproductivity of the 1954-56 sample is increasing over time at a greater rate than is true of the 1934-36 cases. For example, over 18 per cent of the children of male schizophrenics in the 1954-56 group were born during the 5-7 year follow-up interval, while less than 2 per cent of the children of the 1934-36 males were born during that interval. Even with an average of 18 to 20 years follow-

TABLE 7.—Measures of Reproduction at Time of Evaluation

Sex and Age	Period of Admission	Evaluation	Number of Cases	Children per Fertile Marriage	Children per Marriage	Children per Person	Childless Marriages (per cent)
Male							
All ages	1934-36	1941	461	2.7	1.9	0.5	30.9
	1954-56	1961	295	2.3	1.7	0.7	26.2
20-29	1934-36	1941	101	2.0	0.9	0.1	55.6
	1954-56	1961	45	1.5	1.2	0.3	20.0
30-39	1934-36	1941	167	1.9	1.2	0.2	39.4
	1954-56	1961	74	2.6	2.0	0.9	25.0
40-49	1934-36	1941	116	2.8	2.2	0.6	21.2
	1954-56	1961	79	2.3	1.8	0.9	21.0
50 or over	1934-36	1941	75	3.4	2.5	1.2	25.7
	1954-56	1961	97	2.3	1.6	0.8	30.8
Female							
All ages	1934-36	1941	535	2.5	1.7	0.9	33.8
	1954-56	1961	386	2.4	2.0	1.3	20.2
20-29	1934-36	1941	86	1.4	0.6	0.2	59.3
	1954-56	1961	42	1.5	1.3	0.5	13.3
30-39	1934-36	1941	169	2.0	1.2	0.6	37.0
	1954-56	1961	86	2.2	1.9	1.0	13.0
40-49	1934-36	1941	159	2.5	2.0	1.3	22.6
	1954-56	1961	148	2.7	1.6	1.8	15.5
50 or over	1934-36	1941	122	3.5	2.2	1.2	37.3
	1954-56	1961	110	2.3	1.5	1.0	34.3

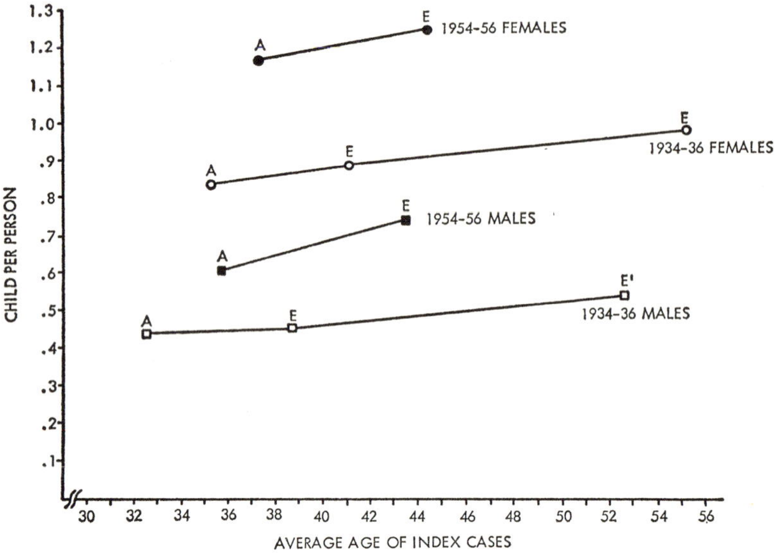

FIG. 3.—Average rate of reproduction for 1677 completed index cases over age 15. The different points of assessment for child per person are: (A) admission; (E) first evaluation, 1941 for the 1934-36 sample and 1961 for the 1954-56 sample; and (E′) final evaluation, completed only for the 1934-36 sample at the average year of 1954.

up, the 1934-36 cases failed to attain the marital or reproductive rates of the 1954-56 group at admission (table 6 and fig. 3).

The hospitalization histories of 473 completed cases reveal that a larger proportion of patients in the 1934-36 series were continuously hospitalized during the 5-7 year interval following admission than in

TABLE 8.—History of Hospitalization of Schizophrenics Subsequent to Survey Admission

Sex	Period of Admission	Number of Cases	Hospitalized Continuously (per cent)	Discharged and Readmitted (per cent)	Discharged, not Readmitted (per cent)
Male	1934-36	99	28.3	19.2	52.5
	1954-56	110	20.0	23.6	56.4
Female	1934-36	143	43.4	25.9	30.8
	1954-56	121	20.7	20.7	58.7

the 1954-56 series, and that fewer cases in the former series succeeded in remaining out of hospitals once discharged (table 8). Although final conclusions cannot yet be drawn at this stage of the study, it is expected that further analyses of hospitalization and treatment data may account for a number of the variables shaping the trend toward increased marriage and reproduction.

Reproductive Patterns in the Families of Schizophrenic Index Cases

Of 659 index cases with fully ascertained sibship data, 16.5 per cent were only children, while the remainder had a total of 2007 siblings. The average size of the sibships (including the index case) was 4.3 children per family in the 1934-36 group, and 3.8 children per family in the 1954-56 group.

A smaller difference between the two samples is found if only the net sibship size is considered—that is, the reproductive potential of the sibship. Since only 3 per cent of the siblings in the 1954-56 group failed to survive to the age of 15, as opposed to 13 per cent of the siblings in the 1934-36 group, parental matings in the two samples produced on the average 3.6 and 3.8 children who reached the reproductive years. In other words, the net reproductive potential of parents with at least one schizophrenic child in the 1954-56 sample remained relatively high despite a lower birth rate.

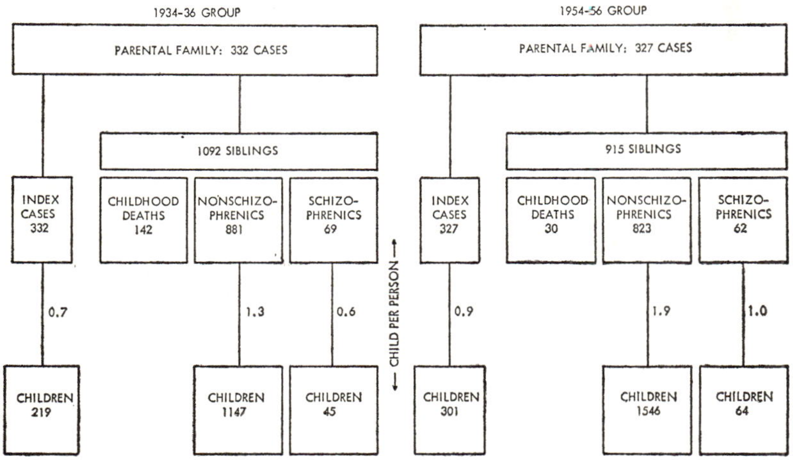

Fig. 4.—Reproductivity in the families of schizophrenic index cases.

Of prime demographic significance, and certainly requiring further exploration, is the finding (fig. 4) that while schizophrenic siblings have reproductive rates similar to those of the index cases—with a comparable trend toward increasing reproductivity in the 1954-56 group—their nonschizophrenic brothers and sisters apparently no longer follow the reproductive pattern observed in earlier studies.[4, 5, 10] Instead of having a reproductive rate between those of the schizophrenics and their contemporaries in the general population, the nonschizophrenic siblings of the index cases in the present study do at least as well in this measure as the general population. Comparison of the reproductive rates for the two survey periods indicates that for every 100 nonschizophrenic siblings, there are 60 more children born in the later sample.

In appraising the potential population effects of this finding, we should bear in mind that relatives in the present analysis have been classified as schizophrenic only if they were hospitalized and their hospital records could be diagnostically evaluated by our research staff. The classification "nonschizophrenic," therefore, may be assumed to include a certain number of unascertained cases of schizophrenia among the relatives, a methodologically relevant point that should also be considered in evaluating an even more precious byproduct of this study of reproductive patterns, the comparative schizophrenia rates for the parents and siblings of our index cases (see next section).

Apart from completing the follow-up data on those index cases who have been reintegrated into their communities in a statistical sense and on their nonhospitalized siblings and parents, the following statistical adjustments remain to be made at a later date:

1. The weighting of data pertaining to follow-up cases by a factor of 2 or 3, to correspond with the random reduction of such cases to one-half or to one-third of all cases. This step has been advisedly deferred until the work reaches its final stages, if only because any attempt to keep it current would entail considerable labor, without great profit.

2. Adjustment for overexposure, which occurs when a patient had two admissions during one of the two survey periods, and hence had double the probability of selection for patients admitted only once.

The family data still to be collected and the statistical adjustments to be made are certain to change some of the figures presented in the present set of tables. Nevertheless, it is the opinion of the investigators that the results so far obtained offer a solid basis for the conclusions drawn in this second interim report.

Dual Matings among the Index Cases and Statistically Expected Sex Differences in the Schizophrenia Rates for the Index Families Studied

The study of dual matings—i.e., marriages between two schizophrenics—has been an integral part of our research design. Thus far, 26 marriages of this kind have been identified in the present series of 2706 index cases (table 9). The dual-mating figures represent 0.9 per cent of the 1934-36 sample of index cases, 1.1 per cent of the 1954-56 cases, and approximately 2 per cent of the marriages contracted by the index cases; for obvious reasons, matings between schizophrenics outside of marriage are not included here. Under any conceptual system pertaining to the etiology of schizophrenia, it is relevant to note that the reproductive rate for dual matings (table 9) is at least as high as the marital fertility rates for the total samples. Since the marriages between an index case and another schizophrenic constitute only a small portion of the total population studied, however, statistical comparisons are to be made with caution.

The intrasample series of dual matings in schizophrenic index cases, although quite unique by itself, can be augmented by two index cases with verified schizophrenia in both parents (table 10). In these two families, one index case had nine siblings, seven of whom were schizophrenic, while the other had three siblings of whom none was schizophrenic.

As to the incidence of schizophrenia in the sibships of 546 index cases with complete family histories (table 10), it should be noted

Table 9.—Reproductive Measures for the Matings of Two Schizophrenics

Measure	Period of Admission (for index case) 1934-36	1954-56
Total dual matings (couples)	14	12
Total fertile dual matings	11	11
Total children	30	31
Children per marriage	2.1	2.6
Children per fertile marriage	2.7	2.8

TABLE 10.—Index Cases and their Siblings by Parental Mating Type

Characteristic	Total	Neither Parent Schizophrenic	One Parent Schizophrenic	Both Parents Schizophrenic
Number of index cases	546	506	38	2
Number of siblings	1823	1687	124	12
Index cases with schizophrenic siblings (per cent)	15.4	12.8	47.4	50.0
Schizophrenic siblings (per cent)	6.4	4.9	22.6	58.3

that the given schizophrenia rates have not been age-corrected according to the principles of the abridged Weinberg method[10, 14] and cannot be directly compared with the risk figures summarized in table 1. Nevertheless, it is instructive how clearly these sibship rates are apt to be differentiated by the parental mating types in regard to schizophrenia: (a) neither parent schizophrenic, (b) one parent schizophrenic, (c) both parents schizophrenic. In accordance with expectations from genetic theories, of course, the majority of the index cases come from families in which neither parent was schizophrenic. With one schizophrenic parent, the sibship rate is found to be more than four times as large as when neither parent is schizophrenic.

A question which remains to be considered in relation to the parental

TABLE 11.—Sex Differences in Schizophrenia Rates for the Parents and Siblings of Schizophrenic Index Cases

Relationship to Index Case[a]	1934-36 Number of Persons	1934-36 Schizophrenia Rate (%)	1934-36 Age Corrected Expectancy (%)	1954-56 Number of Persons	1954-56 Schizophrenia Rate (%)	1954-56 Age Corrected Expectancy (%)
Either parent	605	3.6	—	602	4.5	—
Father	306	2.9	—	297	3.0	—
Mother	299	4.4	—	305	5.9	—
Either sib	1092	6.3	10.0	915	6.8	10.9
Brother	566	6.7	10.7	460	7.0	11.5
Sister	526	5.6	9.2	455	6.6	10.3

[a]Data on schizophrenia for relatives, obtained from hospital records only.

schizophrenia rates in the two samples is the possible effect of statistically expected sex differences on comparative morbidity figures for index families (table 11). In particular, various investigators have reported that the prevalence of schizophrenia tends to be higher among the mothers than the fathers of schizophrenic index cases.[6, 13] Some studies, in fact, yielded parental schizophrenia data with approximately twice as many mothers as fathers having been classified as schizophrenic.

If there is such a sex difference in the parental schizophrenia rates observed—like the ones seen in table 11—the finding can be readily explained on the basis of the age and sex distributions of married schizophrenics. Female schizophrenics marry and reproduce more frequently than do male schizophrenics. In the present study (for both survey periods combined), only 24 per cent of the males (N = 1317), in contrast to 43 per cent of the females (N = 1389), had produced offspring by the time of admission. Moreover, it was noted in our first report[9] that the sex differential was present prior to the onset of schizophrenia.

It follows, therefore, that it is more probable for a schizophrenic ascertained as a parent of an index case to be a mother than a father. With sex differences in marriage rates as well as the degree of postmarital mobility, retroactive ascertainment of a bona fide case of schizophrenia is more likely to be effective in the mother than in the more mobile father, regardless of whether the search began with a schizophrenic son or daughter as the index case.

Finally, it may be borne in mind that, according to earlier fertility statistics for schizophrenic index families, the birth of relatively few children can be expected to postdate the onset of clinical symptoms in the schizophrenic parent. Hence, an overtly psychotic parent who is ascertainable at the time when his child becomes a schizophrenic index case will in most instances have developed the disorder during the years between the child's birth and the age of 45 (the year of life used statistically as the upper limit of the schizophrenic risk period). As women generally marry earlier and are younger when the child is born, and as they have a later age of onset in any event, they have a greater chance to develop schizophrenia during the years following the birth of the child. Male schizophrenics are less likely to marry, and if they do marry, they are often precluded from becoming fathers by the onset of overt clinical symptoms.

Sex differences of this kind are sufficient to explain a certain excess of schizophrenic mothers among the parents of schizophrenic index cases and some analogous observations.[20] At the same time, they are compatible with the reported absence of such differences among the siblings and children of comparable samples of index cases. They also agree with the finding that in studying the descendant generations of schizophrenic index families, the schizophrenia risk for the offspring is the same whether they descended from male or female subjects.

Thus, there is no evidence which either supports the hypothesis of a more damaging genetic effect exerted by an actually or potentially schizophrenic mother than by a similarly affected father, or points to a sex-linked mode of inheritance in this disorder. Instead, it would seem safe to assume that the gene-specific vulnerability factor for schizophrenia is autosomally located—that is, on chromosomes other than the pair of sex chromosomes.

Main Conclusions

1. Of the two samples of schizophrenics compared in this report with respect to their reproductive patterns, the first (with admissions in the period 1934-36) was hospitalized before, and the second (admissions in 1954-56) was hospitalized after, the introduction of the currently used active treatment methods. Among the demographic trends noted was an increased marriage rate at the time of admission in the later group. This increase was relatively greater than that reported for the general population over the same period of time.

2. There was a corresponding increase in reproductivity as measured by the average number of children per person. Contrasted with a relative increase of only 25 per cent in the reproductive rate of the general population, the comparable rate of schizophrenic women increased by 86 per cent. The absolute increase of 0.6 children per schizophrenic woman (or 60 children for every 100 women) was twice as great as the one observed in the general population.

3. According to follow-up data on both groups of index cases, the increases in marriage and reproductivity rates were found to persist during an additional observation period of 5-7 years. Moreover, a similar increase from the earlier to the later survey period was established for the reproductivity of the siblings of the index cases, both the schizophrenic and the nonschizophrenic ones.

4. The significance of these findings in terms of the mental health prospects of future generations is underscored by the fact that no representative population study on record has failed to corroborate

the genetic theory of schizophrenia. It is still justified to state categorically that the single family characteristic which is certain to increase the risk of schizophrenia in an individual is the presence of this disorder in one of his siblings or parents—provided that the classification of these other clinical cases has been in line with the principles of a conservative diagnostic system.

5. From the standpoint of population genetics, it is particularly important that the reproductive rate of schizophrenics (for males and females combined) has increased from approximately 57 to 94 children per 100 patients. The corresponding increase for female patients alone has been from 70 to 130 children per 100 women. Expressed as percentage of the general population reproductivity rate for females, the given increase has been from 58 to 87 per cent.

6. With the reproductive rate of schizophrenics tending to approach that of the general population, it seems that any selective disadvantage which schizophrenic illness may have had in terms of its evolutionary history is now in the process of disappearing.

7. With or without a genetic frame of reference, all mental health professions are now sufficiently alerted to the need of being concerned about calculable health risks in a predictably unstable home. They should be willing, therefore, to take notice of the fact that growing numbers of children are currently being born to parents, one or both of whom are known to be schizophrenic. These children are either raised in homes serving as the housing of a schizophrenic or displaced for various lengths of time to the homes of relatives, or to foster homes, or to shelters and other types of institution. The problem of preventing a vulnerable child from developing clinical symptoms of schizophrenia has not yet been solved in regard to any of these settings.

8. Until the biological disciplines exploring one or the other aspect of the complex etiology of schizophrenia come up with a reliable method for the prevention or treatment of this disorder, it is recommended that more attention be given to the attainable goals of marriage and parenthood counseling in schizophrenic families requesting such guidance.

REFERENCES

1. ALTSHULER, K. Z., AND SARLIN, M. B.: Deafness and schizophrenia: Interrelation of communication stress, maturation lag and schizophrenia risk. *In* Expanding Goals of Genetics in Psychiatry (ed. F. J. Kallmann). New York, Grune & Stratton, 1962.

2. Böök, J. A.: A genetic and neuropsychiatric investigation of a North-Swedish population with special regard to schizophrenia and mental deficiency. Acta Genet. 4:1-139, 345-414, 1953.
3. Deming, W. E.: Some statistical principles for efficient designs of surveys and experiments. *In* Expanding Goals of Genetics in Psychiatry (ed. F. J. Kallmann). New York, Grune & Stratton, 1962.
4. Essen-Möller, E.: Untersuchungen über die Fruchtbarkeit gewisser Gruppen von Geisteskranken. Acta Psychiat. Neur. Scand. (Suppl. 8), 1935.
5. ——: Mating and fertility patterns in families with schizophrenia. Eugen. Quart. 6:142-147, 1959.
6. ——: Über die Schizophreniehäufigkeit bei Müttern von Schizophrenen. Schweiz. Arch. Neurol., Neurochir. u. Psychiat. 91:260-266, 1963.
7. Garrone, G.: Étude statistique et génétique de la schizophrénie à Genève de 1901 à 1950. J. Génét. hum. 11:89-219, 1962.
8. Gibbs, C. E.: Sex development and behaviour in female patients with dementia praecox. Arch. Neurol. Psychiat 11:179-194, 1924.
9. Goldfarb, C., and Erlenmeyer-Kimling, L.: Mating and fertility trends in schizophrenia. *In* Expanding Goals of Genetics in Psychiatry (ed. F. J. Kallmann). New York, Grune & Stratton, 1962.
10. Kallmann, F. J.: The Genetics of Schizophrenia. New York, J. J. Augustin, 1938.
11. ——: The genetic theory of schizophrenia. An analysis of 691 schizophrenic twin index families. Amer. J. Psychiat. 103:309-322, 1946.
12. Kallmann, F. J., and Rainer, J. D.: Genetics and demography. *In* The Study of Population (eds. P. M. Hauser and O. D. Duncan). Chicago, University of Chicago Press, 1959.
13. Kallmann, F. J., and Roth, B.: Genetic aspects of preadolescent schizophrenia. Amer. J. Psychiat. 112:599-606, 1956.
14. Larsson, T., and Sjögren, T.: A methodological, psychiatric and statistical study of a large Swedish rural population. Acta Psychiat. Neurol. Scand. (Suppl. 89), 1954.
15. Norris, V.: A statistical study of the influence of marriage in the hospital care of the mentally sick. J. Ment. Sci. 102:467-486, 1956.
16. Ødegaard, Ø.: Marriage and mental disease: A study in social psychopathology. J. Ment. Sci. 92:35-39, 1946.
17. ——: Marriage rate and fertility in psychotic patients before hospital admission and after discharge. Internat. J. Soc. Psychiat. 6:25-33, 1960.
18. Penrose, L. S.: Research methods in human genetics. Congr. Internat. Psychiat., Paris, 6:41-54, 1950.
19. Rainer, J. D., and Kallmann, F. J.: Genetic and demographic aspects of disordered behavior patterns in a deaf population. *In* Epidemiology of Mental Disorder (ed. B. Pasamanick). Washington, D. C., Publication #60 of AAAS, 1959.
20. Rosenthal, D.: Familial concordance by sex with respect to schizophrenia Psychol. Bull. 59:401-421, 1962.
21. Zerbin-Rüdin, E.: Zur Erbpathologie der Schizophrenien. Mitt. Max-Planck Ges., H. 1-2. Munich, Max Planck Gesellschaft, 1963.

15

A NEUROTROPIC COMPOUND IDENTIFIED IN URINE OF SCHIZOPHRENIC PATIENTS*

by ARNOLD J. FRIEDHOFF, M.D., and
ELNORA VAN WINKLE, B.S.†

IN PREVIOUS STUDIES a compound was detected in urines obtained from schizophrenic patients which was not found in urines from a group of normal subjects.[1] This compound was later identified as 3,4-dimethoxyphenylethylamine. The procedures used in this identification are described in detail in prior publications.[1-3]

Since these original publications, Takesada et al, have reported that they found 3,4-dimethoxyphenylethylamine in 92 per cent of a schizophrenic population, but also in about 40 per cent of the normal subjects that they studied.[4] This is in contrast to our finding that this compound was not excreted in normals.

The structure of 3,4-dimethoxyphenylethylamine suggested that it might be a metabolite of dopamine. Normally, in man, dopamine is metabolized by monamine oxidase to 3.4-dihydroxyphenylacetic acid, which is in turn metabolized by catechol O-methyl transferase to 4-hydroxy-3-methoxyphenylacetic acid; or dopamine is metabolized by catechol O-methyl transferase initially to 4-hydroxy-3-methoxyphenylethylamine and then subsequently by monamine oxidase to 4-hydroxy-3-methoxyphenylacetic acid. All of these metabolites are excreted and can be detected in urine. Senoh et al. have shown that 4-O-mthylation can also occur in vitro,[5] but the 3-hydroxy-4-methoxy derivatives have not been identified in vivo. It has not been demonstrated previously that both the 3 and the 4 positions can be methylated simultaneously. If dopamine were methylated in the 3 and 4 positions, this would result in the formation of 3,4-dimethoxyphenylethylamine.

---

*This research was supported by U.S.P.H.S. Research Career Development Award No. MSF-14,024 to Dr. Friedhoff and U.S.P.H.S. Grant No. MH-07961 and a grant from the Schweppe Foundation

†Research Unit, Department of Psychiatry and Neurology, New York University School of Medicine, New York, N.Y.

In order to determine whether di-O-methylation of dopamine occurs, several studies were initiated.[6] In these studies five hospitalized patients with a confirmed diagnosis of schizophrenia were selected. 3.4-Dimethoxyphenylethylamine had been identified previously in the urine of each of these patients. 3-4-Dihydroxyphenylethylamine-7-H^3 was administered to each patient by intravenous infusion. Urine was collected for a period of 3 hours, and the urine from three of these patients was analyzed separately while extracts of the urine from two other patients were pooled in order to increase the concentration of radioactivity. Urine was extracted by methods that we have described previously.[1, 2] In brief, following the infusion the urine was extracted with chloroform at pH.2. The aqueous phase was adjusted to pH 9 and again extracted with chloroform. The material extracted at pH 9 was co-chromatographed in butanol:formic acid: water, 12:1-:6, with 3,4-dimethoxyphenylamine and 4-hydroxy-3-methoxyphenylethylamine. Control strips were cut and dipped in ninhydrin-pyridine reagent in order to locate the reference compounds. The chromatograms were scanned in a Tracerlab chromatogram scanner. A peak was found that corresponded in Rf to 4-hydroxy-3-methoxyphenylethylamine on each chromatogram. A second peak corresponding to 3,4-dimethoxyphenylethylamine was also identified on each chromatogram. However, this peak did not represent sufficient activity for further analysis by the isotope methods that we were employing.

The organic phase from the pH 2 extraction contained the acidic and neutral metabolites. This extract was evaporated to a small volume and applied for chromatography. The chromatograms were developed in suitable solvents and scanned for radioactivity. Control strips were cut from these chromatograms and dipped in an aniline-xylose reagent. After purification by chromatographic means, two peaks were identified: one corresponding in Rf to 4-hydroxy-3-methoxyphenylacetic acid, and another to 3,4-dimethoxyphenylacetic acid. The urine obtained from one of the subjects was extracted first at pH 9 and then at pH 2, a reversal of the procedure that we used for the other subjects, in order to eliminate neutral metabolites from the pH 2 extract. The resulting scan of the chromatogram of the extract from this patient displayed the same two peaks. The compound from the area corresponding to 3,4-dimethoxyphenylacetic acid was diluted with 3,4-dimethoxyphenylacetic acid as a carrier and was then recrystallized to constant specific activity. In all of the patients, the unlabeled compound carried the radioactivity through 3 crystallizations. These data constitute presumptive evidence that the radioactive material was in fact 3,4-dimethoxyphenylacetic acid.

In an attempt to validate these findings in vitro, liver biopsy material was obtained from two schizophrenic patients. In the first experiment tritiated dopamine was incubated with liver biopsy material, magnesium chloride, and unlabeled S-adenosyl-L-methionine iodide at pH 7.3, and peaks corresponding to both 3,4-dimethoxyphenylethylamine and 3,4-dimethoxyphenylacetic acid were identified on the chromatographic scans. However, the radioactivity recovered was insufficient for further analysis, and so in a second experiment tritiated dopamine was incubated with methyl C^{14}-labeled S-adenosyl-L-methionine, magnesium chloride, and liver biopsy material from another schizophrenic patient. Material was then eluted from the area corresponding to hydroxymethoxyphenylacetic acid. In this material the ratio $C^{14}/H^3 = 1$ after correction was made for differences in specific activity. This indicated that this material was hydroxy-methoxyphenylacetic acid. The material eluted from the area corresponding to 3,4-dimethoxyphenylacetic acid was in the ratio $C^{14}/H^3 = 2$. This was further evidence that dopamine can, in fact, be converted to 3-4-dimethoxylated derivatives in vitro.

It was possible to get further insight into the metabolism of 3,4-dimethoxyphenylethylamine from the manner in which the liver homogenate studies were carried out. In order to isolate the amines formed during the incubation, it was necessary, in some way, to prevent monamine oxidase from catalyzing the degradation of the amines to the acid derivatives. In order to do this, the liver was incubated with excess dopamine because dopamine itself is a substate for monamine oxidase. The excess dopamine would be metabolized by monamine oxidase and would, presumably, therefore block the metabolism of 4-hydroxy-3-methoxyphenylethylamine and 3,4-dimethoxyphenylethylamine to acids as they were formed. It had previously been shown by many investigators that 4-hydroxy-3-methoxyphenylethylamine is an excellent substrate for monamine oxidase, and it has been shown that 3,4-dimethoxyphenylethylamine can be metabolized by monamine oxidase, although it is not a good substrate for this enzyme.

When the liver was incubated with excess dopamine, only a small amount of 4-hydroxy-3-methoxyphenylacetic acid was formed. On the other hand, relative to the amount of 3,4-dimethoxy amine formed, a great deal of 3,4-dimethoxyphenylacetic acid was formed. This suggested that 3,4-dimethoxyphenylethylamine was being converted to 3,4-dimethoxyphenylacetic acid by an enzyme different from monamine oxidase.

It has been shown that certain phenylethylamines are metabolized by an enzyme different from monamine oxidase.[7] These include mescaline and 3,4-dimethoxyphenylethylamine. Our findings of the difference in ratio of acids and amines also suggest that the hydroxy-methoxyphenylethylamine and dimethoxyphenylethylamine are being metabolized by different enzymes.

Oates et al. demonstrated that the excretion of phenylethylamine was not very different in normals and phenylketonurics.[8] When monamine oxidase inhibitors were administered to both groups, the difference between patients and controls increased enormously. That is, the patients then excreted a great deal more amine than the controls. This finding suggests that the patients are forming more amine, but at the same time are more rapidly converting it to an acid metabolite. This possibility also exists for 3,4-dimethoxyphenylethylamine, and therefore a more accurate representation of the difference between the control groups and schizophrenic patients would be found from a study of the concentration of the acid metabolite rather than of the amine, which is an intermediate.

The relevance of our findings to the genesis of schizophrenia must be considered in the context of a number of factors. Takesada found 3,4-dimethoxyphenylethylamine in 92 per cent of a schizophrenic population, but also in about 40 per cent of a normal control group and in some patients characterized as psychoneurotics. It should be noted that the percentage of patients in whom Takesada found the dimethoxy compound is considerably higher than the percentage of patients in whom we were able to detect the 3,4-dimethoxyphenylethylamine.

Several studies have been carried out elsewhere that have delineated the phamacological activity of 3,4-dimethoxyphenylethylamine.[9, 14] The structural resemblance of 3,4-dimethoxyphenylethylamine to mescaline and the catecholamines has been of interest to other investigators. It is also of interest that 3,4-dimethoxyphenylethylamine has no sympathomimetic activity in the rabbit or the cat, and in fact produces slowing of the isolated perfused heart. It produces only a small rise in blood pressure in the cat followed by a secondary fall in blood pressure. It causes contractions of the isolated nonpregnant cat uterus and has no effect on pupillary size. It has a depressant effect on the central nervous system, and its action on smooth muscle and isolated heart is opposite to that of the closely related catecholamines. 3,4-Dimethoxyphenylethylamine has been shown to produce experimental catatonia in cats. The paramethoxy group is necessary for the production of mescaline-like effects in animals, and phenylethylamine derivatives, including mescaline and 3,4-dimethoxyphenylethylamine, that contain a paramethoxy group all have this mescaline-like action, whereas other derivatives of phenylethylamine do not have appreciable mescaline effect.

It is also of interest in the search for a relationship between 3-4-O-methylation and schizophrenia that 3,4-dimethoxyphenylethylamine is produced from dopamine as a precursor. Dopamine is found in highest concentration in the brain in the region of basal ganglia,[15,16] and all of the tranquilizers that have a profound effect in schizophrenia also produce extrapyramidal disturbances, that are presumably mediated through the basal ganglia. It has been demonstrated, in fact, that reserpine reduces the concentration of amines in the brain,[17] and chlorpromazine also produces extrapyramidal disturbances and is believed to have effects on the transport of precursors of catecholamines into brain.[18]

It should be kept in mind that 3,4-dimethoxyphenylethylamine may be found in schizophrenic patients and not in normals because all amines are being excreted in higher concentration in the urine of schizophrenic patients. Bergsman, for instance, has found that schizophrenics excrete more adrenaline than normals.[19] It is also possible that the formation of 3,4-dimethoxyphenylethylamine is related to tension and anxiety rather than to schizophrenia, and to rule out this possibility, large numbers of psychiatric patients with various diagnoses will have to be studied.

We have not yet studied dopamine metabolites formed in liver from normal subjects. Similarly, we have not shown that 3,4-dimethoxyphenylethylamine can produce any symptoms in human beings. It is a potent neurotoxic agent in animals and produces some interesting behavioral disturbances, but these behavioral disturbances occur only after the administration of high levels of this compound. In order to demonstrate a relationship between these dimethoxylated compounds and schizophrenia, a number of investigations along several lines must be carried out, some of which can best be carried out by other laboratories where patients are found under different conditions of diet, stress, and ambulation.

REFERENCES

1. Friedhoff, A. J., and Van Winkle, E.: Nature 194:897, 1962.
2. ——: J. Nerv. Ment. Dis. 135:550, 1962.
3. ——: J. Chromatogr. II:272, 1963.
4. Takesada, M., Kakimoto, Y., Sano, I., and Kaneko, Z.: Nature 199:203, 1963.
5. Senoh, S., Daly, J., Axelrod, J., and Witkop, B.: J. Amer. Chem. Soc. 81:6240, 1959.
6. Friedhoff, A. J., and Van Winkle, E.: Nature 199:1271, 1963.
7. Steensholt. G.: Acta Physiol. Scand. 14:356, 1947.
8. Oates, J. A., Nirenberg, P. Z., Jepson, J. B., Sjoerdsma, A., and Udenfriend, S.: Proc. Soc. Exp. Biol. Med. 112:1078, 1963.
9. Epstein, D., Gunn, J. A., and Virden, C. J.: J. Physiol. 76:224, 1932.
10. Geesink, A., and Den Hartog Jager, W. A.: Arch Neurol. Physiol., 24:79 1939.
11. Noteboom, L.: Proc. Acad. Sci., Amsterdam, 37:562, 1934.
12. Raymond-Hamet: Arch. Int. Pharmacodyn. 44:67, 1932.
13. Smythies, J. R., and Levy, C. K.: J. Ment. Sci. 106:531, 1960.
14. Ernst, A. M.: Nature, 193:178, 1962.
15. Carlsson, A.: Science 127:471, 1958.
16. ——: Pharmacol. Rev. 11:490, 1959.
17. Shore, P. A., Pletscher, A., Tomich, E. G., Carlsson, A., Kuntsman, R., and Brodie, B. B.: Ann. N.Y. Acad. Sci. 66:609, 1957.
18. Schwartz, D. E., Burkard, W. P., Roth, M., Gey, K. F., and Pletscher, A.: Arch. Int. Pharmacodyn. 141:135, 1963.
19. Bergsman, A.: Acta Psychiat. Neurol. Scand. 34, 1959.

16

SCHIZOPHRENIA*

by PAUL H. HOCH, M.D.†

This lecture is dedicated to the memory of Samuel W. Hamilton, whose friendship and support we valued most highly. His great understanding and compassion, blended with wisdom and practicality, gave him a unique place in psychiatry.

IN THIS LECTURE we obviously cannot cover all the facets of schizophrenia upon which volumes have been written, nor do we want to duplicate or appear to be summarizing the many excellent papers which were presented and which will be presented at this symposium. Therefore, we shall concentrate on discussing some of the aspects of schizophrenia which we have selected arbitrarily and which we feel are important from the point of view of theoretical concept, etiology, diagnosis, treatment, and social implication. In this presentation we must be excused from quoting all of those who have contributed in the past and present to the understanding of this disorder upon which opinions are so widely divergent and where the solution of a clear understanding has not appeared upon the horizon.

In schizophrenia we can delineate three historical phases. First, in the time before Kraepelin we had many partial descriptions of the clinical phenomena—the catatonic and hebephrenic pictures, for instance, which were discussed by Kahlbaum and Hecker, but with the assumption that they were separate disease entities. In the second phase, Kraepelin, Bleuler, and many others offered unifying concepts and tied together different clinical syndromes into one and separated them from other forms of mental disorder. This second historical phase contributed a great deal to our knowledge in seeing the different

*The Samuel W. Hamilton Memorial Award Lecture, Presented at the Fifty-Fourth Annual Meeting of the American Psychopathological Association, February 1964.

†Commissioner of Mental Hygiene, State of New York; Professor of Clinical Psychiatry, College of Physicians and Surgeons, Columbia University.

schizophrenic manifestations in the framework of unifying concepts, even though today some of these concepts appear to be dated and should be reformulated. In this historical phase some of the etiological ideas were already implied.

Attempts have been made to explain schizophrenia as a single disease, a reaction, a syndrome, or not one disease but different diseases with common denominators. Etiological foundations and discussions were laid to determine the extent the organic, psychogenic, or combined factors might contribute to its development. However, none of these settled the origin of the disorder, nor did they resolve many of the diagnostic, prognostic, or therapeutic problems. The chaos of the pre-Kraepelanian and Bleulerian era was mitigated by concentrating upon stressing the similarities of the different clinical pictures against the many varieties of clinical manifestations. A real or assumed security was introduced in the diagnosis of schizophrenia which probably implied more knowledge of the disorder than was actually the case. On the other hand, it permitted us to tackle many of the clinical problems empirically which formerly was not possible due to the great confusion existing because of the lack of a general conceptualization.

In the present phase, the accomplishments of the second are being more and more undone without being able to replace some of the stabilization which existed in the era of Kraepelin and Bleuler. We cannot say whether or not this is good or bad. We would only like to point out that while in one way we are continuing to introduce more refined ideas about nosology and etiology, in many instances we are also returning to phase one with all its confusion, contradictions, and subjectivities characterizing it. The present phase could be characterized by the statement which we have made in connection with Bellak's outstanding compilation in *Schizophrenia, a Review of the Syndrome*. When you read this book, you arrive at the conclusion that schizophrenia is the most important mental disease and that at the same time it does not exist.

In the beginning we would like to discuss the concepts of how schizophrenia should be described. This could be organized under the following headings:

1. A disease or a group of diseases: Bleuler spoke generally about dementia praecox or the group of schizophrenias.
2. Schizophrenia is considered a reaction.
3. A special form of maladaptation;

4. Outgrowth of a special personality structure;
5. A syndrome;
6. A special form of neurosis;
7. Special inheritance and constitutional factors.

A discussion of the different etiological theories on schizophrenia is in order in relation to the above groupings. This can be summarized under the heading as being organic in origin or due to psychological or social factors, or a combination of all theories put forth. Today the two polar positions would be to consider schizophrenia as a single disease based upon a model of a physical disease where the diversified symptomatology observed is either explained by the ramifications of the disease or due to the different compensatory mechanisms invoked in coping with it.

The other pole would assume that schizophrenia is not a disease at all, which could go as far as Szasz' statement that mental disease does not exist at all, or the position of Karl Menninger, who assumes that we have only one mental disorder with variable symptomatology, from which one variant would be that which we call schizophrenia. All the other psychiatric etiological appraisals of schizophrenia are between these extreme positions.

Many attempts have been made to treat schizophrenia as a unitary disease. The Kraepelinian concept of dementia praecox was originally based on such an assumption. Kraepelin did not commit himself exactly as to the etiology of dementia praecox, but assumed that it is due to heredity and/or a chemical deviation from the norm. Kraepelin was not alone among those who assumed a unitary disease concept for dementia praecox. The manifold symptomatology was explained, or not explained, with models such as tuberculosis, syphilis, or diabetes, where it was pointed out that they have many different and ramified symptomatologies very often appearing as though they could not be produced by one disease.

In schizophrenia practically every metabolic system, every organ, but particularly the endocrine glands, were implicated. There are numerous studies on the deviations in function of thyroid, pituitary, gonads, etc. We do not have to remind you of the many attempts made to link these pathogenetic speculations with histopathological changes in different organs of the body and epecially the brain. The discussion of the histopathology of the brain in schizophrenia could be an extensive chapter in itself. We can say here, however, that thus far whatever changes in the brain were found could not be interpreted as specific for schizophrenia; it is even possible that some of the pathological abnormalities are due to secondary changes (infection, nutritional deficiencies, etc.) which occur in schizophrenic persons but are not the cause of schizophrenia.

Of course, it is possible that newer techniques may disclose differences in cell structure and metabolism, which with newer staining techniques will disclose pathological changes we cannot see today. It is also possible that a systemic investigation of the subcortical regions of the brain may disclose pathological changes that the investigation of the cortex, on which most of the pathology of the brain was concentrated, has not disclosed. We may remind you that many considered Parkinson's disease as psychogenic until later investigations disclosed definite changes in the subcortical gray matter.

The concept of unitary disease etiology is still with us because most of the biochemical research, which we will mention later, is endeavoring to find biochemical deviations from the norm that are present in all cases of schizophrenia and to set them apart from normals and those others suffering from a different type of mental disease.

While Kraepelin considered it a disease based on a unitary etiology of unknown origin, Bleuler left the issue open. Bleuler spoke about a group of schizophrenias. Very often he treated the group of schizophrenias to be based on the same etiology, but divergent in symptomatology and outcome. At times, however, he assumed different possible etiologies as manifesting themselves in the same way (such as the concept of the acute and chronic organic psychoses). Because Bleuler assumed a hereditary background, he obviously also had to assume a single etiological factor insofar as the so-called anlage (disposition) went; but he also postulated that in addition to the anlage, other factors had to be added (namely, infections and psychogenic factors). The plural schizophrenic concept (the schizophrenias), which he used toward the different symptomatologies (hebephrenic, catatonic, paranoid, and simple) and especially in relationship to outcome, rejected the Kraepelian classifications of which the key element was deterioration. Bleuler separated the schizophrenias from other mental disorders based upon their clinical symptomatology, but not on outcome.

Even at the time of Kraepelin, schizophrenia was considered by some to be a reaction and not a disease. Hoche was the foremost advocate of this approach. Some of the strengths and weaknesses of this concept are discussed by Fish, who states that reaction is an ambiguous term. The term "reaction" can be looked upon in different ways, covering a broad range of meanings. Thus, the interaction of the illness with the environment can be called a reaction, for example, when a hebephrenic responds to an interference by others with brutal violence. Sometimes schizophrenia is provoked by severe environmental stress, and this too can be considered a reaction. Finally, schizophrenia can be regarded as an organic reaction of the brain to many different kinds of physical insults. Lastly, a general objection may be raised to the term "reaction" because most illnesses are, in fact, reactions of the organism to an interference of some kind.

In our definition, reaction would mean that the psyche responds in a certain way to environmental influences—material or psychic. Therefore, the question arises: What determines and differentiates this reaction from other mental or emotional disorders? Why do schizophrenics respond in the schizophrenic way and not with organic psychosis, a manic depressive psychosis, or a psychoneurosis? Does it differ qualitatively or quantitatively from the other disorders?

We turn now to the Meyerian hypothesis of the origin of schizophrenia, which he considered a form of maladaptation. Meyer's concept of eclectic inclusion of all factors—i.e., hereditary, constitutional, organic, and psychogenic—is, of course, a safe one, but at the same time it remains rather vague and diffuse in specificity. Up to a point it explains the matrix of schizophrenia more than the actual psychosis. The same applies to the Pavlovian concept of conditioning. There is no question that maladaptation is cumulative and conditioning is perpetuated, if not reversed; but what is the relationship between personality and schizophrenia or constitution and schizophrenia? They all contribute important background material to our present-day knowledge, but the relationship to psychosis is inconclusive. There is also no question that if you follow the biographies of schizophrenics' backgrounds into their childhood, you may find cumulative maladaptations. They cannot cope with many social, sexual, and other problems, and particularly their interpersonal relationships with others are often distorted. However, there are innumerable persons with the same organization and behavior who never become psychotic and would be considered by many as a normal part of the population, if one assumes that a certain percentage of the normal population is introverted. Some of the questions which arise may be: Are these persons variants of the "normal" or are they cases of *formes frustrées* of schizophrenia? Are they potential candidates to become schizophrenics, either spontaneously or under environmental stress? Is the personality organization of these persons just a coincidence in relationship to the schizophrenic psychosis, or are schizothymic and schizoid individuals just quantitatively different from schizophrenics? The important questions also have to be raised whether or not traits of introversion or schizoid patterns of thinking are the same in these individuals as in schizophrenics, and are they only similar but not identical to those observed in schizophrenics before the outbreak of the psychosis and after a restitution from the psychosis?

At present we have no answers to these questions. No doubt this is probably the reason research in this field slackened markedly after the very auspicious developments in the 1920's and 30's. The same applies to body types or constitutions. It is again demonstrable that some correlation (as established by Kretschmer and his school) exists, but the same arguments can be used about correlations as they are stated above. Research in this field did not progress further, because aside from descriptive and statistical correlations not much more has been worked out, and there is a question if the tools at our disposal can do more. It is necessary to demonstrate biochemically how a certain constitution functions differently from other constitutions and how this relates to psychic functioning. If asthenic habitus is seen frequently in schizophrenics, how does an asthenic constitution function differently from other constitutional types, and what is its linkage to a schizoid psyche? Of course, it must be mentioned once again there are many asthenics who have never become schizophrenic.

Both the psychobiological approach, which stresses maladaptation and behavioral disorganization, and constitutional research, linked to personality types, assume a continuum. It begins with a variant of a normal personality structure, to the abnormal but not yet psychotic, and thence to full-fledged schizophrenia. This continuum presupposes there are schizophrenic traits in normals and, of course, normal traits in schizophrenics. This is true both ways, but we believe it is a fallacy that this explains a psychosis. It explains many mechanisms in the psychosis, especially the defenses developed to cope with it, but unfortunately it does not explain the schizophrenic process itself. Schizophrenia is not simply an exaggeration of introversion or schizoid personality. These explain part of the schizophrenic process, but not the disease itself.

This brings us to the Bleulerian concept, which is still valid because it has not been disproved that the primary symptoms in schizophrenia are physiogenic or that the secondary symptoms are psychogenic. This is not new. Ferenczi and Hollos explained some of the delusions and other symptoms of general paresis in psychodynamic terms while fully recognizing the organic origin of the disease. We are able to explain the content of delusions and hallucinations in schizophrenia and in other disorders, but the delusional and hallucinatory process is not explained by its content.

The experimental psychoses brought about by the administration of LSD and other drugs clearly show that we are able to produce abnormal phenomena such as delusions, but the content of these delusions are an issue in themselves. Systemic studies in this realm have never been done because everyone is fascinated by the content, regardless of the fact that the organic psychoses and the experimental model psychoses clearly indicate that understanding the content of a delusion or hallucination does not explain the way in which a delusion or a hallucination originates. We may add here that sleeping and dreaming has a physiological basis, but it is not readily open to psychological explanation; the content of the dreams are. The difficulty, however, is where the organic symptoms stop and the so-called psychogenic symptoms begin. What is the organic basis of schizophrenia and what is psychogenic to the awareness of distorted perception, feeling of depersonalization, anxiety, and disintegration, etc.?

To overcome this difficulty and to avoid a commitment as to the disease or reaction concepts, the rather neutral designation of a syndrome was introduced. The designation of syndrome is fully justified in the clinical realm until the etiology of the disorder is known.

It is important now to discuss the four other approaches to schizophrenia—namely, the psychoanalytic theory, the newer Gestalt and existentialistic approaches, and some of the sociological theories as the causation of schizophrenia.

We will not endeavor to recapitulate here the psychoanalytic contributions to schizophrenia of Freud, Sullivan, Frieda Fromm-Reichmann,

Federn, Melanie Klein, Rado, Arieti, and many others. I would like only to touch upon the most important conceptual contributions and those analytic contributions which are of great importance from a clinical point of view. These analytic contributions have illuminated some of the motives of schizophrenic individuals about their feeling, thinking, and, in particular, their interaction with their own environment. They have also demonstrated early life experiences and parental pathology influencing the offspring. Here again many of the contributions have illuminated much of the content of psychiatric thinking replete with condensations, symbolizations, displacements, etc., without, however, enabling us to understand the basis of the loosened associations, the intracerebral ataxia (Stransky), the splitting of the psyche, the absurdities, the bizarre, and the incongruous thinking and feeling. The superstructure was again more refined and better understood without touching the basic structure itself.

Schizophrenic thinking and feeling and its linkage to the loss of reality boundaries has been explained by Jung and his school up to a point; the development of some symptoms such as paranoid delusions organized around sexual conflicts such as homosexuality has been explained by Freud. Many feel that his genetic theories are questionable. Even if we accept the libidinal fixation theories of Freud or his regression theory in relationship to schizophrenia, or the disturbances of very early object relationship and the ego boundaries by Melanie Klein, we are very often far from understanding schizophrenia as a whole. We may understand partial mechanisms as they have occurred, but we cannot understand exactly how they occurred and perhaps why they occurred. If schizophrenics regress to an earlier infantile developmental state, the question is why only schizophrenics regress so far in this manner and more deeply than the neurotic patient. Freud and others tried to resolve this question by assuming that a schizophrenic regresses further than a neurotic, and thus they established the category of narcissistic neurosis which is practically identical with a psychosis. This attitude tended to blur the boundaries between neurosis and schizophrenia and led to the assumption that a neurotic could become progressively worse and then become schizophrenic. Conversely, if a schizophrenic improved, he became a neurotic, and similar psychodynamic mechanisms could be worked out in both. Therefore, schizophrenia was considered only quantitatively different from the neuroses. It is a more deeply ramified form of a neurosis, but qualitatively there is no great difference between the two; in both, the symptoms could be understood and removed. With some modifications this, in turn, produced the optimistic attitude that schizophrenia could be treated successfully psychotherapeutically. The assumption was that if certain conflicts could be eliminated, then the schizophrenic would improve just as the neurotic. Of course, all this was supported by the prevailing idea in some circles in our time that the schizophrenias (just as the neuroses) are psychogenic in origin (even though many felt that the neuroses are a little more psychogenic than schizophrenia); to what extent these assumptions are correct can be settled only when the etiology of schizophrenia is known.

Schizophrenics have many emotional and thinking mechanisms which do not occur in neurotics. A neurotic under stress does not become schizophrenic; he becomes more neurotic. If a schizophrenic relapses, he shows a schizophrenia again and not a neurosis. Schizophrenics show many mechanisms which can be interpreted as neurotic. We pointed this out in a number of papers regarding the pseudoneurotic form of schizophrenia. It was called pseudoneurotic because we do not believe these individuals are identical with neurotics. Nevertheless, even if we should accept the point of view that the neurotic symptoms are the same as those seen in the neuroses, it must be emphasized that a schizophrenic will always show additional symptoms which do not occur in a neurotic. His emotional and thinking patterns of disorganization are specific. It is true that in incipient cases of schizophrenia this is not always easy to recognize, but more often these patients have not been properly evaluated. This has several reasons.

Some psychiatrists are preoccupied with the idea that schizophrenia is a very large entity and should be divided into several independent disorders. We have had attempts to split the paranoid form from it—some forms of the acute catatonic states such as the acute motility psychoses of Kleist, the catatonic forms described by Gjessing, the acute confusional states of oneirophrenia of Meduna, the sensitive reference psychosis of Kretschmer, the hallucinogenic delusional states of the French school, and a number of others. We also have the suggestion or inference that we should differentiate between two types of schizophrenia, one of organic origin and the other of psychogenic origin (the schizophreniform psychosis of Langfeldt).

After differentiating these different entities from schizophrenia, another group of psychiatrists stress the common features between these different groups and again call them schizophrenia. The second reason why schizophrenia is not clearly diagnosed is the preoccupation with the theoretical concepts postulated by Bleuler. We do not believe that from a clinical point of view it is important that originally Bleuler described fundamental and accessory symptoms and primary symptoms or secondary symptoms. It is quite possible, as we were one of the first to point out, that some of the primary symptoms as described by Bleuler are really secondary. It is very difficult to describe the primary symptoms of schizophrenia today. However, this does not affect clinical symptoms very much because schizophrenia today is not diagnosed, even by the most schizophrenia-minded clinician, by "primary" symptoms alone. It is more correct to say that as long as the etiology is not known, there are those who do not wish to use the diagnosis of schizophrenia because of its implications (psychiatric as to prognosis, legal as to responsibility, social, etc.). On the other hand, if we do not diagnose these patients as schizophrenic, we have no suggestions for constructive substitutes, with the exception that we may call these patients neurotic or as suffering from another undefined form of psychosis. It is then assumed that the above-mentioned negative implications will disappear, but unfortunately in most instances they overtake the patient and therapist alike. As mentioned before, we hear again and again that schizophrenia is a large entity. Seemingly, it does not really cause concern to anyone that the neuroses are an even larger entity. This is presumably because it is assumed that the neurotic is a normal variant; some even go as far as to say everyone is neurotic. Another factor in making the diagnosis of schizophrenia is the relationship of the patient's response to therapy. Some assume that if he responds to treatment, he is manic depressive or neurotic, but not schizophrenic; if he responds to psychotherapy, then there is not much difference between neurosis and schizophrenia, forgetting that psychotherapy may eliminate some symptoms, but that it does not change the matrix.

Depending upon the examiner's attitude toward schizophrenia, etiological preoccupations also influence the appraisal of the patient. All these factors enter into diagnosis, prognosis, and treatment recommendations which are full of biases, rigid positions, and confusions often based on selected case material. This in turn, leads to complete nihilism when it concerns diagnosis, prognosis, and treatment because the etiology is unknown, or to unjustified optimism in cases where it is not warranted.

In addition to the already discussed concepts of schizophrenia, we have to mention a few others but will not be able to go into many details. These are some of the newer approaches, the contributions of the phenomenological school, the Gestalt school, and, of course, the existentialistic approach to schizophrenia. Here we do not have as much perspective as we have had concerning the earlier theories of schizophrenia Nevertheless, we feel that some comments are in order. Jaspers' use of Husserl's and Dilthey's ideas contributed to a better understanding of the symptomatology of schizophrenia. There are also the contributions of Gruhle, Mayer-Gross, and Karl Schneider. Jaspers was able to show that the symptoms of schizophrenia can be divided into understandable and nonunderstandable, and that only some of the symptoms can be interpreted in psychological terms. Furthermore, phenomenological understanding does not open the door to an etiology.

The Gestalt school bases its explanation of schizophrenia on disordered perception. Even though alterations of perception were demonstrated in schizophrenia, this is not consistent and not specific. The same can be said of alterations of consciousness and awareness. They were also used to explain schizophrenic feelings and mentation. The Gestalt view in relation to delusional formation and in connection with the peculiar feelings of the schizophrenic is important. Schizophrenics feel passive and at the mercy of the environment, but at the same time they feel omnipotent or in a cosmic fusion with the world. In the light of the Gestalt theory some of these phenomena are perhaps better understood. In many instances we feel the explanations are constructs. Again partial manifestations of schizophrenics are explained, but not completely. In addition, some of the unknown constructs are used to explain other unknown phenomena. This happens in research in schizophrenia very often. The Ganzheits psychology of Petrilovitch, Pauleikoff, and others suffers from the same difficulty. Basically the same goes on here as in diagnostics. Some aspects of schizophrenic psychopathology are selected and made all-important, subordinating other pathological manifestations to the preferential lead or assumption.

We can, of course, base everything on anxiety, on existence, and ignore all else. We would like to mention here in connection with the Gestalt psychology that Conrad, the exponent of this school, introduced the concept of energy potential—namely, that "each individual has his own capability of directing his energies." Schizophrenia is looked upon by some as a disturbance of this energy potential. Somewhat similar ideas were expressed by N. Kline, Ostow, and Sarwer-Foner. Sarwer-Foner states, "Schizophrenia can be visualized as a disease of the control and channelizing of the biological energy available for contact with other people and for gratification of needs arising from such contacts. Some of this energy is expressed at a thinking level as a series of abstractions relating to a sense of the patient's self, his past, his present, and his future. In schizophrenia this disease of the control and channelizing of this biological energy is characterized by pathological deviations of this particular biological energy from gratifications or outlets permitted to other beings in that particular culture."

Unfortunately, we do not know much about the energy household in schizophrenia and not even in normals. Therefore, we will have to postpone judgment on the value of these hypotheses until we do. If we do not, it will share the same fate as the speculative libido (Freud), the elan vital (Bergson), and other attempts of a similar nature going back to Janet, who blamed the weakness of the will, "abaissement du niveau mental," in all mental conditions.

Contemporary German literature contains many articles on existentialism in relationship to psychiatry. This school originated with Heidegger and was followed later by Binswanger, Zutt, and others. In France, Sartre and his followers tried to explain schizophrenia in existentialistic terms. Discussing these interesting contributions would lead us far afield. To our way of thinking they have contributed more to philosophy. This does not mean we do not believe that philosophical theories have nothing to do with psychiatry. Everything human has bearing on it, but we do not think that philosophical exercises will illuminate schizophrenia, even though some schizophrenics may think they will. However, existentialism contributed one important theoretical fact. It focused attention on the role of anxiety, and especially that of the Daseinsangst of the schizophrenic. The relationship of many schizophrenic symptoms to this existential anxiety is important and again shows how many symptoms may occur in schizophrenia due to anxiety. Until recently, the role of anxiety was not sufficiently recognized in schizophrenia as a potent motivational force for withdrawal from reality or as a basis for acting out. Both would enable the individual to cope with overwhelming anxiety in a pathological way.

The role of anxiety can also be seen in schizophrenia if such persons are under the influence of mescaline, LSD, and some of the other psychotropic drugs, but again this existential anxiety alone does not explain schizophrenia as a whole.

We turn now to the supposedly other more tangible factors. The hereditary mechanisms in schizophrenia were studied by many, but especially by Kallmann and Slater. In our opinion the hereditary background in schizophrenia is beyond doubt. We also need more knowledge as to what is inherited: the disposition to schizophrenia which then has to be triggered by other factors to become manifest; or, as Kallmann postulates, schizophrenia as such, but its manifestation is suppressed by equally inherited defense mechanisms. There are other questions unanswered. We do not mean the specific mode of inheritance, recessive and dominant single factoral or multifactoral. We are sure this will be settled. The fundamental question is: Are all schizophrenias hereditary? If we should assume that they are not all hereditary, then how do they differ from each other and why do they look so similar? For instance, some amphetamine psychoses appear to be indistinguishable from schizophrenia; no one is able to make the differential diagnosis who does not know that the person was under the influence of amphetamine. But, based on evidence in the spontaneously occurring psychoses, we are sure schizophrenia has to be considered an hereditary disorder.

The most important issue is how the mechanism of inheritance translates itself into function. To quote Kety is to state that the biochemist must not lose sight of the possibility that the genetic factors in schizophrenia operate to determine inappropriate interconnections or reactions between chemically normal components of the brain. If that should prove to be the case, the physiological psychologist, the neurophysiologist, or the anatomist is likely to find meaningful information long before the biochemist does. We postulate, as we will discuss later, that regulative inefficiency is inherited in schizophrenia involving the functional organization of the diencephalon, mesencephalon, and reticular system which, in turn, influences the cortex.

These are all unanswered questions. It is hoped that the genetic revolution which transformed descriptive or statistical genetics into biochemical genetics wil give us a clue. What impairment is transmitted through what kind of chromosomal influence or defect? We are postulating here that an organic disorder is transmitted hereditarily. Therefore, now we should discuss in detail the work of Akerfeldt, Abood, Leach and Heath, Gottlieb and his coworkers, Hoagland and Pincus, Osmond and the Saskatchewan workers, etc. If we examine the intricacies of ceruloplasmin, taraxein, seratonin (Brody) and the research of Elkes and others, we are relieved of this task because it has been done critically and at length by Kety in *Science* in 1959 and in other publications.

After considering all this research, we are afraid to say we agree with Kety that they are inconclusive. In many instances, even though we are dealing with chemical phenomena which are supposedly more tangible than the mind, many of these findings are speculative and open to different interpretations and discussions on a clinical or on a psychodynamic level. That which is most important, however, is that the specificity of these findings for schizophrenia has not been sufficiently demonstrated. So far all these researchers have demonstrated that a single chemical metabolic factor cannot be named as the origin of schizophrenia. In has shown, however, that the regulation of metabolism in schizophrenia is not quite normal and that the homeostasis in schizophrenia is different and not as smooth as in normals.

We also would like to make some comments on social factors in schizophrenia. Lately this was especially stressed because social scientists are paying more attention to mental disease than before. Generally it has become customary to assume that schizophrenia occurs by social isolation. This is based upon studies by Faris and Dunham in Chicago and Hollingshead and Redlich in New Haven. There is no question that the lower socio-economic groups are coping with schizophrenia differently than the upper class. For instance, hospitalization is more frequent and a reluctance for assuming home care is more pronounced in the lower groups. The lack of economic means often prevents home care because no one is able to stay home with the patient and there are no means of hiring anyone to undertake such supervision. Therefore, the patient is hospitalized, and sometimes unnecessarily hospitalized for psychiatric reasons, but necessarily so for economic reasons. In addition to this, many schizophrenic patients who do not work steadily are considered to be an economic drain on the family. Nevertheless, these factors are still insufficient to claim that they are the cause of schizophrenia. It must be demonstrated that the socio-economic factors so prevalent in the lower income groups have some specific pathogenetic influence on schizophrenics or that an economic stress is able to precipitate schizophrenia in a predisposed individual. To date this has not been satisfactorily demonstrated.

Based on available statistics, a larger number of schizophrenics are found in the so-called lower socio-economic classes in larger cities because many of them move to the city motivated by vague ambitions or trying to obtain work which suits them. They also like to live within the anonymity of larger cities, surrounded by people but isolated at the same time. They often drift lower and lower on the socioeconomic scale, not being able to adapt themselves and being preoccupied with their own fantasies. In epidemiological studies only those are used who are known to social or governmental agencies, hospitals, clinics, welfare departments, etc. Many are not identified, and particularly those who remain inconspicuous.

The epidemiological studies of schizophrenia are even worse off in relationship to patients who belong in the higher socioeconomic groups. Here the obvious sources of epidemiological information are not as readily available. The diagnosis of schizophrenia is either deliberately or for rationalized reasons not made. It would be most interesting to have a good epidemiological study in the higher socio-economic groups, provided the many obstacles could be overcome in settling the important issues of incidence and prevalence. However, all such studies are difficult because (1) it is hard to specify objective diagnostic criteria, (2) competent psychiatrists vary in their diagnostic judgment, and (3) there is a gradient of severity, the severe cases being diagnosed and the others not.

Different methods are available for the treatment of schizophrenia. The treatments can be divided into the so-called organic ones such as insulin, electroshock therapy, and the different drug therapies. Then we have the psychotherapeutic procedures of which there are several variants, and then those treatments which could be classified as more indirect and based upon social manipulation, rehabilitation, and other methods. In some places these different therapeutic approaches are used independently from each other, but in many other places they are used in a combined fashion even though one or the other predominates.

The treatment of a schizophrenic is an individual affair. It should be admitted, however, based on our present knowledge, that it is not always easy to decide what kind of patient would benefit from what kind of treatment. Much of the treatment, as it is applied today, is empirical and also dependent upon the availability of psychiatric resources.

We know a considerable number of schizophrenic patients who improved sufficiently with drug treatment who did not need extensive psychotherapy, but only some support. On the other hand, there are schizophrenic patients who, even though they respond to drug treatment, do need psychotherapy. Drug treatment is capable of eliminating overt schizophrenic symptoms, but does not eradicate the matrix. We look upon drug treatment and also on insulin and electroshock therapy as treatments which are essentially quantitative in the sense that they are able to reduce symptoms often to such an extent that the patient becomes asymptomatic. Nevertheless, the high and sometimes unexpected relapse rate in schizophrenics treated by any form of therapy today indicates that the fundamentals of this disorder have not been eliminated. There are schizophrenic patients in whom the drug treatments are capable of eliminating most of the patient's gross symptoms but do not help the patient in managing some of the difficulties in his social and sexual spheres. Such patients also benefit from psychotherapy.

To what extent the different reconstructive methods of psychotherapy instead of the supportive ones are effective is an open question. At present we do not believe we have enough evidence, based upon patients who have received psychotherapy or psychoanalysis, that these attempts accomplished a great deal more than with those patients who were treated with drugs or other organic treatments. It is possible, however, that some schizophrenics will respond better to organic therapy, whereas others will respond better to psychotherapy. Essentially our position is that the treatment of schizophrenia is empirical and symptomatic regardless of what kind of treatments are used. This is, of course, axiomatic if the origin of a disorder is not known, but it must be emphasized that these different symptomatic treatments are effective with a considerable number of patients. We feel that at present the most important issue is to clarify and determine how many schizophrenic patients treated with these methods in the early phase of their sickness will become chronic. If we were able to prevent chronicity, a great deal would have been accomplished.

The treatment of schizophrenia has also important administrative and planning aspects. Where should we treat schizophrenic patients?

Formerly the tendency was to hospitalize them. Today the tendency in some quarters is the opposite and claims are made that most schizophrenics can be treated in community clinics or with short hospitalization at community centers. We believe that more schizophrenic patients can be treated in the community than before and not all have to be hospitalized, but chronicity of schizophrenia must be fully recognized in planning facilities for care and treatment. While about 80 per cent of schizophrenics will respond to modern therapies, about 30 to 40 per cent will relapse, many of them periodically for the rest of their lives. It cannot be assumed that families will be willing to accept all these patients at home. Many chronic schizophrenics can be quite trying and disruptive in the community. Five to ten per cent of the schizophrenics are antisocial to a degree that requires closely supervised hospital care. We need a great deal of research in order to have a better appraisal of schizophrenic action patterns. The present clinical or psychological test appraisals of patients is inadequate in a sense that it is unable to tell us reliably what a patient may do either spontaneously or more often under real or fancied provocation. To postulate that we have all these factors under control either with drugs, psychotherapy, or social manipulation is overstating our present capabilities.

In the foregoing we touched upon the many different problems of schizophrenia and tried, in a bird's eye view, to discuss some of the hypotheses on causation. Many speakers on the program of the Association also have expressed their views. Permit us now to bring before you in summary some of our own concepts about schizophrenia which are probably as good or as bad as some of those that we have discussed.

We consider schizophrenia basically to be an organic disorder. Much of the clinical and experimental evidence indicates that what we today call schizophrenia is a special form of integrative disorganization. This disorganization pattern is widespread and as characteristic as the so-called organic reaction types. Schizophrenia occurs in every culture and may be precipitated by different noxae in predisposed individuals. This predisposition is inherited. We could further speculate that a preeminently cortical impairment occurs in the so-called organic psychoses. On the other hand, a preeminently subcortical impairment occurs in schizophrenia or a disruption of a normal relationship between cortex and subcortex. Evidence is accumulating that if we excite the subcortical gray, psychotic manifestations occur. If we reduce the activity of the subcortical gray—for instance, with drugs such as phenothiazine and others—psychotic symptoms are reduced or eliminated. Similar observations were made if we disconnect the cortex from the subcortical gray by the means of frontal lobotomy. The regulatory disorganization in schizophrenia is a total biological affair involving the vegetative nervous system regulation, and impaired homeostasis on many physiological levels of functioning.

On a mental level, the disturbance of mental integration leads to an inability to cope in an integrative and regulative way with stimulation coming from within and without. When this regulatory inability is better understood, it would eliminate the discussion of primary symptoms. The secondary symptoms will then consist of the more subtle clinical symptoms which are present in every schizophrenic (impairment of emotional regulation, impairment of thinking processes, and impairment of action processes which were described elsewhere). The subtle symptoms become more pronounced in the grossly psychotic individual who then shows the whole gamut of symptoms such as delusions, hallucinations, and regressive phenomena which are quantitative exaggerations of the more subtle symptoms. But again we would like to call your attention to the fact that we do not know how subtle symptoms become massive symptoms.

The regulative deficiency in schizophrenia was demonstrated on many levels. We feel that this regulative inability is theoretically more important than the assumption that the disease is due to one single chemical alteration or one single metabolic disturbance. This does not mean, however, that the regulative deficiency may have no biochemical implications; it could mean that the chemical ingredients in the metabolism of schizophrenics is the same as in normals, but because of faulty regulative processes they are balanced differently, thus leading to homeostatic disruptions.

We consider schizophrenia to be far more than an "emotional disorder." It affects many facets of the person who is ill with it, and it affects the total psyche. In the older psychiatric literature the alterations in the intellectual processes of schizophrenics were stressed (impairment of associations, etc.). In the newer literature the emotional changes were stressed and probably overstressed. In our writings we have always emphasized the involvement of both the cognitive and conative aspects of the psyche. Shakow recently wrote: "If we were to try to epitomize the schizophrenic person's system in the most simple language, we might say that he has two major difficulties: First, he reacts to old situations as if they were new ones (he fails to habituate), and to new situations as if they were recently past ones (he perseverates); and second, he overresponds when the stimulus is relatively small, and he does not respond enough when the stimulus is great. With regard to reactivity, the chronic schizophrenic is certainly not a 'seething caldron.' He resembles instead the 'simmering pot' on the back of the stove which perpetually simmers at a low level. But it is a pot that does not ever provide one with a tasty pot-au-feu.

"There is a little doubt that the schizophrenic's is an inefficient, unmodulated system, full of 'noise,' and of indeterminate figure-ground relationships. What a confusing world must be the schizophrenic's when such basic modes of relating to the world are so seriously disturbed."

Arieti has also stressed cognitive functions in schizophrenia.

From a research point of view it is necessary to continue under study of other sides of the schizophrenic process, but if we do so, we should not forget that this is not a partial, but an all-pervading disorder of the psyche.

We could certainly go on discussing schizophrenia for a long, long time because schizophrenia, even though we know so much about it in many ways, is still an enigma. Nevertheless, research in this field is moving forward and making great strides.

Discussion

Recorder: JONATHAN COLE, M.D.

Comments on Dr. Kety's Presentation

Dr. Frohman: Dr. Frohman, in discussing Dr. Kety's paper, elaborated on his own data. He admitted it was true that the amount of protein fraction activity found was increased both by stress and by external stimuli. It was possible that the factor was nonspecific but that schizophrenics were exposed to unusual levels of stress. In this connection it was interesting to note that childhood schizophrenics who had grown to adulthood looked behaviorally indistinguishable from chronic schizophrenics who had become ill as adults. However, the ex-childhood schizophrenics did not show abnormal amounts of the protein factor. He admitted that his group had not proved conclusively that the abnormal levels found in adult schizophrenia were *not* due to stress or hospitalization.

Dr. Haddad: Dr. Haddad noted the exclusive preoccupation with blood and urine on the part of scientists looking for biochemical abnormalities in schizophrenia. Despite all this interest, the normal levels found in blood and urine of most chemical substances of interest in this regard were rarely available in the literature when one began to work in a new area. Why has there not been more work with cerebrospinal fluid, which would probably reflect brain abnormalities better than blood or urine? For that matter, why not study sweat and tears?

Dr. Rado: Dr. Rado stressed the response of students of psychodynamics to papers like Dr. Kety's. If they did not ignore the whole area, they would feel that the two characteristic areas of pathology in schizophrenia, the ability to experience pleasure and the normal awareness of one's own body, were totally overlooked. Dyscontrol in the autonomic area under stress also occurs early in all schizophrenic illnesses, though the phenomenon is not restricted to schizophrenics. He hoped to see biochemical studies of the awareness of pleasure and of the awareness of one's body image before too long.

Dr. Himwich: Dr. Himwich asked if Dr. Kety, in his emphasis on transmethylation of dopamine, was discounting the possible role of the transmethylation of indole substances in the biochemistry of schizophrenia.

Dr. Waelsch: Dr. Waelsch noted that the administration of large amounts of any amino acid, including methionine, could be expected to effect complex changes in the metabolism of other nitrogenous compounds. Had the general effects of large doses of methionine on such other systems been studied? Did schizophrenics show exacerbation of symptoms when they received equally large amounts of a mixture of amino acids containing a lesser amount of methionine? In short, could this be a nonspecific response to amino acid loading?

Dr. Freyhan: Dr. Freyhan underlined Dr. Kety's comment that methionine caused an exacerbation only of some symptoms in *some* schizophrenics. There was a dangerous tendency, in discussing the biology of schizophrenia, to forget the heterogeniety of these patients and the variability of their individual response to any treatment or other change.

Dr. Hoagland: Dr. Hoagland took this opportunity to report some relevant findings obtained by Dr. Bergen at the Worcester Foundation. As most of the group knew, the activity of their schizophrenic plasma fractions (which for brevity will be called taraxein) could be transferred to a normal plasma fraction by dialysis across a cellophane membrane; this implied that the molecule must be small.

Dr. Bergen now finds that normetanephrine, a metabolite of norepinephrine, has no effect, of itself, on his rat rope-climbing bioassay for taraxein. However, when normetanephrine is added to taraxein, it will double the fraction's activity in interfering with rope climbing. Also, if the rats to be used in the bioassay are pretreated for three days with isocarboxazide, the effect of a standard dose of taraxein is substantially increased. For this reason, they suspect that the taraxein effect involves a biogenic amine. In the clam heart, the effect of taraxein resembles that of a nonindole catecholamine, and differs from the effect of serotonin. He suggested that both an aberrant protein and a transmethylated catecholamine might be involved in schizophrenia. Human studies to determine the behavioral effect of taraxein in man were badly needed.

Dr. Elkes: Dr. Elkes expressed delight that the heart of *Venus mercenaria*, once found to be so exquisitely sensitive to LSD, had found its way back into psychiatric research.

DR. KETY: In summing up, Dr. Kety could only agree with Dr. Haddad's position that materials other than blood and urine should be studied in schizophrenia. However, spinal fluid, sweat, and tears were more difficult to obtain. Schizophrenic sweat had been shown to be distinguishable from nonschizophrenic sweat on the basis of smell. Some doubt had been cast on this by a study of a single schizophrenic patient at Saint Elizabeths Hospital where the foul smell had been shown to result from a treatable skin infection.

In response to Dr. Himwich's question, he was aware of psychotomimetic properties of methylated indoles such as dimethyltryptamine and dimethylserotonin. He had emphasized work on dimethoxyphenylethylamine in his informal presentation only because of its relevance to others' predictions. He thanked Dr. Waelsch for his suggestions about the possible diffuse and complex effects of a large dose of methionine on nitrogen metabolism. Personally, he had always found difficulty in becoming highly enthusiastic over this possible effect of methionine on transmethylation and, ultimately, on behavior as a basic explanation of the biochemical abnormality in schizophrenia.

He expressed interest in the findings reported by Dr. Hoagland. These reminded him of Dr. Bock's early work. Bock had found that, though metanephrine and normetanephrine had almost no effect on blood pressure, they could potentiate the actions of their parent compounds, epinephrine and norepinephrine.

In the defense of the hypotheses being studied in biochemical research in schizophrenia, he felt it desirable to note that, despite their defects and problems, they were based on much sounder data and were more accessible to exact study than was comparable work in the behavioral area.

COMMENTS ON DR. GOTTLIEB'S PRESENTATION

DR. COHEN: Dr. Frohman, many of us have followed your developing story of the isolation of a protein factor in schizophrenia with a great deal of interest. Certainly, the effort and tenacity with which you and your coworkers. Dr. Gottlieb, Dr. Beckett, and others, have pursued the search for a measureable biochemical parameter in schizophrenia must elicit from us all only the strongest admiration. And you may rest assured that we all recognize the extraordinary difficulties inherent in this elusive problem.

However, there are a number of disturbing points in the information which has been developed to date. For example, there are the reports, such as that published last year by Drs. Buhler and Ihler (J. Lab. Clin. Med. 62:306, 1963), indicating a failure to confirm the basic finding of a difference between normal and schizophrenic plasma. In the short period of time allotted here this morning, I intend to limit my remarks, however, solely to the material which you and your group have published. For it is here that some inconsistencies appear, and it is here that a set of ground rules have been developed which act as a barrier to those who consider repeating and confirming your findings.

Some of the perplexing items are of a purely biochemical nature. For example, from your estimate of 10 micrograms of active protein per 100 ml. plasma, and your estimate of a molecular weight of 400,000, the number of molecules of active protein in your test system can be calculated. In addition, from standard figures in the literature the number of chicken erythrocytes present in the test system can be calculated. Assuming a homogenous distribution of schizophrenic protein, this calculation* yields a figure of only 4

---

*Calculations are based on a test system containing 1 ml. plasma and 4 ml. of a 33 per cent suspension of chicken erythrocytes (Frohman et al., AMA Arch. Gen Psychiat. 3:263, 1960).

The number of erythrocytes in the test system is:

$$1.33 \text{ ml. packed cells} \times \frac{7.9 \times 10^{9} \text{ cells}}{\text{ml. packed cells}} = 1.0 \times 10^{10} \text{ cells.}$$

The number of chicken erythrocytes in a ml. of packed cells was estimated from average hematocrits and cell counts listed in *Blood and Other Body Fluids* (D.S. Dittmer, ed.: Fed. Amer. Soc. Exp. Biol., Washington, D.C., 1961, p. 116) as follows:

$$\frac{2.8 \times 10^{6} \text{ cells}}{\text{cu. mm. blood}} \times \frac{10^{3} \text{ cu. mm.}}{\text{ml.}} \times \frac{1.0 \text{ ml. blood}}{0.356 \text{ mls. cells}} = \frac{7.9 \times 10^{9} \text{ cells}}{\text{ml. packed cells}}$$

The number of molecules of protein factor in the test system is:

$$1 \text{ ml. plasma} \times 0.10 \frac{\mu\text{g.}}{\text{ml.}} \times \frac{1\ \mu\text{mole}}{4 \times 10^{5}\ \mu\text{g.}} \times 6 \times 10^{17} \frac{\text{molecules}}{\mu\text{mole}}$$
$$= 1.5 \times 10^{11} \text{ molecules protein.}$$

Assuming a homogeneous distribution of protein factor throughout the total volume of the system, the number of protein molecules interacting with the erythrocytes is:

$$\frac{1.3 \text{ ml. cells}}{5.0 \text{ ml. total volume}} \times 1.5 \times 10^{11} \text{ molecules} = 3.9 \times 10^{10}, \text{ molecules,}$$

or roughly 4 protein molecules per cell.

molecules of schizophrenic protein available to each erythrocyte! The available evidence points to an effect at an enzymatic level. By rough estimation for glyceraldehyde-3-phosphate dehydrogenase, one enzyme of the Embden-Meyerhof pathway, there are roughly 10,000 molecules per cell. Our current concepts of the mechanism of hormonal regulation of enzymatic activity indicate that roughly equal amounts of hormone and enzyme molecules are required for interaction. And so 4 hormone molecules affecting 10,000 enzyme molecules in an intact cell is clearly a strange result.

If we accept the concept that it is not the protein which produces the effect, but rather some protein-bound, smaller molecule, then there are other difficulties. For we are then faced with the dilemma of a small molecule which during purification involving dialysis for 3 days does not diffuse away from the protein, but subsequently in the presence of chicken erythrocytes freely diffuses to the interior of the cells to produce a measureable effect within one-half hour.

Your group has indicated the problems involved in handling and processing blood specimens, and this is a further source of difficulty and confusion. For instance, as I now understand the situation:

1. The schizophrenic protein factor is unstable and therefore "laboratories must be developed at the hospital where specimens are drawn for the primary purpose of extracting the factor," and yet the material is subsequently stable during dialysis for 72 hours.

2. The instability in whole blood has been related to an esterase within red cells which destroys the factor, and yet separation of the plasma from the cells does not stabilize the factor.

3. The drawing of chicken blood appears to present some major problems. Apparently the chicken must cooperate during the drawing of blood by heart puncture, else no effect will be noticed. Furthermore, blood drawn properly, but after a period in which the chicken "flutters around for a period of time," will prevent the differential response noted with the same chicken blood drawn earlier.

4. Further, from an initial report of the presence of an abnormal protein in schizophrenia, we have drifted slowly to a position where only some schizophrenics have it, and then only some of the time. Further, it is now found in many normals. Further, it can be increased in amount almost at will in any schizophrenic, *and indeed in any normal,* merely with some mild exercise.

All of these points and others lend so much confusion to the casual observer that it is important that we stop here before becoming too involved with new findings. For if there is indeed in schizophrenia a protein factor that can affect glucose metabolism in erythrocytes, then no one can possibly underestimate the importance of this finding, and this story should be actively pursued at many psychiatric institutions in this country. Therefore, it is contingent upon you, Dr. Frohman and Dr. Gottlieb, to make available a standard, readily accessible and reproducible test system for demonstrating the protein factor. By so doing, you can make available to yourselves a broad base of support and provide the usual broad scientific confirmation which is required for all major discoveries.

DR. WAELSCH: Dr. Waelsch stated that the remarks of the previous discussant had disturbed him. He felt the discussant had been overcritical. The problem that there might be only four molecules of abnormal protein per chick red blood cell did not bother him; after all there had been only one Mohammed and there were now millions of Moslems! The lack of solubility of the protein during dialysis and its paradoxical entry into the red cell could be effected by the action of an enzyme on the surface of the erythrocyte.

DR. HAKAREM: Dr. Hakarem expressed astonishment at the beautiful, evoked potential tracings obtained by averaging the averaged records of many schizophrenics. In his work with this technique he was sure that averaging records would be more likely to yield a flat line. How was the averaging done? What was the amount of variability observed? If the finding was real, it was very important.

DR. KETY: Dr. Kety noted, in defense of Dr. Frohman's work, that Dr. Frohman and Dr. Gottlieb had been able to correctly differentiate a significant number of chronic schizophrenic and normal controls when the material was given them at the National Institute of Mental Health under double-blind conditions. The fact that other investigators have not replicated Dr. Frohman's findings does not prove that he was wrong. On the other hand, Dr. Kety was bothered by the evanescence of Dr. Frohman's factor even in his own hands. If both no exercise and too strenuous exercise made the factor disappear, the factor might merely be measuring a predictable reduction in exercise tolerance on the part of sedentary institutionalized individuals. He would have been more impressed if the evoked potentials described deviated in the same direction as those observed by the Pittsburgh group in monkeys given schizophrenic plasma. If he was recalling their paper correctly, their results were, unfortunately, in the opposite direction. Dr. Kety wished to know more about the "progress in the characterization and purification" of the plasma fraction mentioned in Dr. Frohman's paper.

DR. FROHMAN: Dr. Frohman noted that the evoked potential work was outside his scientific area of competence. It had been done using a C.A.T. by Dr. Rodin at the Lafayette Clinic. He stressed that the clear patterns obtained by averaging the records of many subjects could be produced only by separating the schizophrenic patients into two groups beforehand on the basis of their plasma fraction activities. He noted that their finding of the fraction to begin with was influenced by its chance localization in a plasma fraction which contained very little other protein at both steps in their separation procedure. Otherwise, it might have been lost in a larger bulk of inactive protein. The molecular weight of the active protein substance was 400,000 ± 60,000. The molecule was about 65 per cent lipid in composition and also contained scialic acid. The severe lability of the active fraction stressed by Dr. Cohen was due in large part to nonspecific changes occurring over time in whole plasma. It was this that necessitated developing the laboratory at the state hospital. Once the factor was purified and stored at the correct pH and temperature, it would maintain its activity for several weeks.

COMMENTS ON DR. VAILLANT'S PRESENTATION

DR. ZUBIN: Dr. Zubin opened the discussion by asking whether the variables appearing in table 3 could all be subsumed under the single concept of acuteness of onset.

DR. VAILLANT: Dr. Vaillant replied that in this and in previous studies he had gotten much more effective separation of good and poor outcome groups by taking all five measures into account than by considering acute onset alone.

DR. ROTH: Dr. Roth then made a plea for the utilization of data of the sort presented by Dr. Vaillant in psychiatric work. Acute onset was certainly an important prognostic sign. He was personally struck by the fact that schizophrenia occurring late in life was less prone to lead to deterioration than was usually the case in younger patients. Although serious psychiatric illness occurring late in life must be considered an unhappy fate for the predominately female elderly individuals, nevertheless it would be of great importance to psychiatry to discover the mechanism by which serious illness could be postponed for so long. It was interesting also to note that in early life schizophrenia was a disease of single men and that in late life it was a disease of single women. These differences should be kept in mind.

Comments on Dr. Erlenmeyer-Kimling's Presentation

Dr. Kiser: Dr. Kiser opened the discussion by noting that data of the kind presented did not conclusively prove a genetic factor in schizophrenia. A recent methodological paper by Dr. Lilienthal in the *Journal of Public Health* had shown that having one or two parents who were alumni of the University of Buffalo, had an effect on the attendance of their children at the University of Buffalo that conformed neatly to a genetic model usually associated with recessive genetic conditions. This good fitting of nongenetic data to a genetic model should make one cautious.

The increased fertility in schizophrenics in Dr. Kallmann's later sample puzzled him. The general increase in fertility in the 1950's over the 1930's in the general population is attributable to higher socioeconomic groups who had lower fertility during the depression. If schizophrenia is, as he has been told, a disease of lower socioeconomic groups, the increase in the fertility of schizophrenics goes against the general population trend for their social class.

Dr. Freedman: Dr. Freedman noted that the children born during the thirties, when fertility was lower, are now coming to an age where they constitute the group most likely to provide new schizophrenic admissions to public hospitals. Could this decrease in the number of young adults mean the number of younger schizophrenics admitted to our mental hospitals might contain fewer severely ill schizophrenics? Does this change in the quality of the schizophrenics coming under clinical scrutiny account for their high fertility? Assuming schizophrenics are more fertile and will give birth to more potential schizophrenics, is this either bad or dangerous? One sees highly creative individuals emerging from schizophrenic parental backgrounds.

Dr. Weinstein: Dr. Weinstein suggested that if Dr. Kallmann only considered schizophrenic grandparents and the incidence of schizophrenia in their grandchildren, a better separation of genetic-hereditary from environmental factors might be obtained.

DR. HOAGLAND: Dr. Hoagland asked why schizophrenia continued to endure as a condition. What advantage could schizophrenia have for the survival of individuals affected by it?

DR. KALINOWSKY: Dr. Kalinowsky observed that the greater openness of our mental hospitals and the greater readiness with which patients were released to the community adequately accounted for the observed increase in both marriage and pregnancy rates for schizophrenics in the 1950 sample. This being true, should one not reexamine the abhorrent and generally condemned question of sterilization?

DR. KALLMANN: Dr. Kallmann responded that in compiling and presenting his data he had deliberately avoided drawing conclusions about the "dangerousness" of the observed trends. He could only guess why the schizophrenic gene might survive. His major stress was on the protection and special care needed by vulnerable children of schizophrenic parents. Schizophrenics should certainly not be encouraged to have children. He hoped that contraceptive advice would serve to avert parenthood. Psychiatrists should assist schizophrenics to question the stability of their situation and its suitability for the raising of children.

COMMENTS ON DR. FRIEDHOFF'S PRESENTATION

DR. WAELSCH: Dr. Waelsch began the discussion by asking why only the acidic metabolite of dimethoxyphenylethylamine was picked up in the urine of patients after radioactive dopamine was administered. Did this mean that the pools of the endogenous amine and the pools of the exogenous compound did not meet?

DR. FREEDMAN: Dr. Freedman asked if elevated values of this amine are found in the urine of other sick medical patients or of non-schizophrenic psychiatric patients?

DR. COHEN: Dr. Cohen suggested that differences in the metabolism of exogenous and endogenous amine could be due to metabolic contributions by intestinal flora, and that this could be evaluated if oral and parenteral routes of administration were compared.

DR. KETY: Dr. Kety presented two questions and one comment. Had

Dr. Friedhoff been able to study the metabolism of this compound by normal subjects in vivo or by normal human liver tissue in vitro? Was there any correlation between the amount of the amine excreted by schizophrenics and the amount or kind of psychopathology they manifested? He also expressed admiration of Dr. Friedhoff's careful and conservative handling of his potentially spectacular finding. The conclusions Dr. Friedhoff had drawn from his data had reflected his good judgment.

Dr. Friedhoff: Dr. Friedhoff responded to Dr. Waelsch's question by noting that the recovery of radioactive 3,4-dimethoxyphenylacetic acid in urine or from liver homogenates did not mean that the amine was not also present. Peaks were obtained on radiochromatograms corresponding to the amine. However, the amine is readily converted to the acid by monoamineoxidase. The urines of groups of the sort suggested by Dr. Freedman should eventually be done, but he had decided that work with isotopic material deserved priority since it minimized the problem of dietary variability. He conceded the possibility suggested by Dr. Cohen that gut flora might account for the production on this dimethoxy compound. However, the reduction of gut flora by an antibiotic did not alter the excretion of the compound. Normal human liver tissue had proved hard to obtain but he had just received a small amount and was beginning to study it. He wished to emphasize that it was much more difficult to prove that a chemical process did *not* occur than it was to prove that it did occur. He reported that there were no obvious correlations between the excretion of the abnormal amine and schizophrenic subtype; he was, however, hoping to study more refined measures of clinical symptoms or symptom patterns to see if these might be related to excretion of the amine.

Part IV: Clinical Research in Schizophrenia

17

EVALUATION OF OUTCOME IN SCHIZOPHRENIA

(The Long-Term Prognostic Test Index)

by ZYGMUNT A. PIOTROWSKI, PH.D., and HERMAN Y. EFRON, PH.D.*

FOLLOW-UP STATISTICS

MANY LONG-TERM EVALUATIONS of the course of schizophrenia prove that more than half of all schizophrenics remain unimproved 5 years after the onset of the manifest psychosis, and that a considerable percentage of them improve or even recover. It is reasonable to assume that there are significant psychological as well as other differences between the improved and unimproved schizophrenics at all times.

Appel, Myers, and Scheflen[1] surveyed the literature and found that 27 per cent ($\sigma = 6.3$ per cent) of 3,458 schizophrenics were "much improved" or "recovered" after 5 years. Astrup, Fossum, and Holmboe[2] recently completed their evaluation of 664 "typical schizophrenics"; thirty-seven per cent were improved or recovered after a period of 5 to 20 years, with an average follow-up of 14 years. Of 100 schizophrenics followed through life by Rennie,[20] 11 per cent were improved or recovered; of 222 schizophrenics followed for 20 years, 38 per cent were improved. Neumann and Finkenbrink[10] re-

*From the Jefferson Medical College of Philadelphia and the Veterans Administration Hospital, Lyons, N.J. The authors are indebted to Mr. Seymour V. Pollack, Associate Director, Medical Computing Center, University of Cincinnati College of Medicine, and to Dr. Elmer L. Struening, Coordinator, Program Evaluation Staff, VAH, Montrose, N.Y., for their computer analysis of the data. The study was supported, in part, by a grant from the Research Committee of the Supreme Council, 33°, Scottish Rite Freemasonry, Northern Masonic Jurisdiction.

ported a similar percentage of improvement after 20 years: 33 per cent. After 30 years, 35 per cent were evaluated as recovered by Holt and Holt.[5] Malamud and Render[9] found, after a 5- to 9-year follow-up, that of 177 schizophrenics, 10 per cent died, 58 per cent were unimproved, and 32 per cent had improved. The differences in percentages reported by various investigators would probably decrease if their follow up periods were the same and they controlled the duration of the psychosis after its manifest onset.

Another important fact is that the type of treatment does not seem to have any effect on the eventual percentage of improved schizophrenics. Available treatment methods seem to affect only the patient's subjective comfort and overt behavior, and this mainly during the first years after the onset of the psychosis. Appel et al.[1] obtained the same percentages of recovery and improvement—27 per cent ($\sigma = 6.3$ per cent) after 5 years, in 1,760 schizophrenics receiving only hospital care, and in 1,698 insulin coma-treated schizophrenics.

Long-Term vs. Short-Term Prognosis

Although in many disorders long-term prognosis appears more difficult than short-term prognosis, the opposite seems to be the case with schizophrenia. The diagnosis of incipient cases is fraught with difficulties, and a large percentage of cases are rediagnosed even after a relatively short time. The most important reason seems to be the relatively frequent variability in clinical symptoms which occurs characteristically in schizophrenics during the first three years after the onset of the illness. After three or more years, the condition of most patients quiets down; the behavior becomes much more predictable and less variable. Moreover, after a follow-up of considerable length many doubts concerning the original diagnosis disappear.[19]

Studies of schizophrenic patients treated with insulin coma reveal that the immediate result of the treatment is related to Rorschach signs of impoverishment and deficiency of thought. A large percentage of the unimproved patients produced, before and after treatment, Rorschach records resembling those of patients with confirmed brain lesions.[11, 12] The pretreatment personality of the patient who later failed to improve was much more deviant than that of the patient who later improved greatly. The emotional blunting, frequent in the unimproved, was revealed on the Rorschach test by the absence of meaningful color responses. The presence or absence of at least one meaningful color response alone identified correctly 76 per cent of the patients as either improved or unimproved.[8] However, this favorable role of meaningful color responses vanished in long-term prognosis,[16, 18] the human movement response, on the other hand, which was of minor importance in short-term prognosis,[13, 14] became of great importance in long-term prognosis.[16, 18]

Long-Term Prognostic Test Index (LTPTI): First Validations

The first long-term prognostic test index[19] was standardized largely on personality assets. Subsequent attempts at validating it were disappointing. The revised test index, LTPTI, is almost exclusively a measure of personality liabilities, or more exactly, of thinking disorders and sense-of-reality deficiencies.[16] This revised index was first validated on a group of 70 schizophrenics who, on the average, were intellectually superior and who belonged to the middle socioeconomic class, with a mean age of 28 years ($\sigma = 8.4$ years). The mean follow-up period in this 1958 group was 6 years ($\sigma = 3.7$ years); in no case was it less than 3 years.[16] The group consisted of first admissions. The 1959 group of 103 schizophrenics, 97 men and 6 women, was intellectually average, with a mean age of 34 years ($\sigma = 7.2$ years). The follow-up interval was 6.5 years ($\sigma = 2.8$ years).[17] These patients had become manifestly psychotic 2 to 10 years prior to their Rorschach test.

The patients were divided, according to the LTPTI, into those with high scores (2 or more points) and those with low scores (less than 2 points). There was a high degree of association between the follow-up status (improved or unimproved) and the low and high LTPTI scores in both the 1958 and 1959 groups, with highly significant chi-squares ($p < .01$).

Description of LTPTI Signs

The original 14 signs[16] were reduced to 12 by combining four of the signs into two.[17] The test records were scored in accordance with the system set forth in *Perceptanalysis*.[15] All signs have a weight of +2 points except: sign 12, weight of —2 points; sign 1, weight of +3 points; and signs 9 and 10, each with a weight of +1 point. The LTPTI score is the algebraic sum of the weights of the individual signs found in a test record. Each sign is scored once regardless of the frequency of its appearance in the test record. In schizophrenia, a total score of +2 points, or more, is interpreted as indicating that approximately 3 to 6 years after testing the patient will not have improved; a total score of +1 point or less is interpreted as indicating that he will most likely be improved after the same time interval. Schizophrenics who remained essentially the same with episodic exacerbations of the psychosis were grouped with the unimproved.

Sign 1. Weight: +3 points. To be credited with this sign, the patient must have produced no more than one human movement response and the sum of his weighted color responses must outnumber the sum of his human movement responses by at leat 3 ($M < 2$; $\Sigma C - M \geq 3$).

Sign 2. Weight: +2 points. Rpt or repetition. This sign, occurring frequently in organic cerebral cases, consists of applying the same visual image to at least three different blot areas; at least one of these applications must be of poor form quality.[11] The repetition may occur in the same plate or in different ones. The sign does not apply when the repetitive content are color responses, or when their verbal content is a primary sexual image (genitals).

Sign 3 (1958 signs 3 and 6). Weight +2 points. The essential feature of this sign is the vagueness and tentativeness with which the patient sees the percept (the visual image projected by him onto a specific blot area), or with which he explains the meaning of his percept. One aspect of the behavior classifiable under this sign is being troubled when asked to indicate how his image fits the blot. The patient vainly tries to add precision to his response. At times he openly professes being mystified by his own percepts. This type of test reaction resembles Plx, or perplexity, which is characteristic of cerebral organic cases.[11] Sign 3 includes also odd conceptual connections in the attempts to explain himself. It is impossible to tell what defies the patient's comprehension besides his own vagueness of thought or imagination, since the content of responses causing difficulty is not unusual or bizarre. This reaction is very different from the hypercritical attitude of the obsessive neurotic whose thoughts, imagination, and perceptions are firm and precise and who is in control of his reasoning.

Examples are: "Some sort of insect. Looks kind of poisonous. Does not look attractive to the eye. Looks like some frog. I don't know what it looks like exactly. Such things I don't know. I have no acquaintance with them" (pl. III grays); "The beginning of a bat" (pl. I), the concept "beginning" used to explain patient's vague perception of the bat. "Representing a landscape, very indefinite, very vague to me" (pl. X). "There might be two heads; it's more than that but I can't continue with this" (pl. II, tops of gray). One patient interpreted the top gray of pl. X as a "wind pipe." When questioned about it, he explained by word and gesture that he meant the anus. The differences between the wind pipe and the anus are too great and the similarities are too small to call the logical connection between the two appropriate.

A similar instance of inappropriateness is this response (pl. VII): "I believe that it is showing a division, a division of muscles and bones. If not that, a large picture of the Great Divide." The patient who gave the following response, "I know it's a bat but I don't know whether it's there; it can vary a lot" (pl. V), openly admitted the fluidity of his percept and his intellectual insecurity. A characteristic phrase is: "It's mostly a bat." Sign 3 applies when the patient is unable to clarify his idea and support it by pointing out the blot details which realistically make the shape of the blot differ from the typical form of a bat. The patient's handling of the percept as well as his verbal response must be evaluated before scoring sign 3.

Contaminations also belong in the sign 3 category. Contamination is the unwitting fusing of two or more different visual images, which pertain to the same blot area, into one unintelligible percept without the patient being able to disentangle the resulting percept.[18] Verbally, the contaminations frequently do not sound irrational or dereistic. The dereistic synthesis of fragments of images of different objects becomes apparent when one asks the patient to justify his response by indicating details of the blot which represent some of the physical features of the object apparently projected by him onto the blot. The patient who called pl. I "a female butterfly" interpreted the whole plate as a butterfly. The center of the plate made him think "of the narrow waist." These associations appeared rapidly. Before he verbalized them, he condensed them, the "butterfly" and "the waist of a woman," into "a female butterfly." The patient was not aware of what he was doing. He did not critically evaluate his associations, but contaminated them. It is not the resemblance to a woman's body that makes a butterfly female. Another patient produced "a bird's skull." Here we have a contamination of two images covering the whole of pl. I: a "bird" and a "skeletal head." An essential condition of contamination is that the patient not be clear and definite about what he is doing. The "bird's skull" is a contamination because the patient fused two different images without being aware of it, and because no real object can be simultaneously a whole bird with wings spread out and the skull of a head.

Sign 4. Weight: +2 points. Giving indeterminate form responses with self-confidence. By contrast with sign 3, sign 4 requires behavior of apparent self-confidence, or lack of concern over achievement. The patient should manifest the arbitrariness of his response. Sign 4 responses sound verbally unusual, while those under sign 3 rarely do. When the patient makes an effort to be more specific and realistic under the examiner's pressure, he fails. The corrections consist of more vague words. For a response to be classified as sign 4, it is essential that (a) the blot have some definite meaning for the patient, (b) the patient attempt to establish a correspondence between the shape of the respective blot area and the shape of the object he imagines (the visual content of his response), but fail in this endeavor. The main reason for this failure is the inability to cut out visually out of an inkblot the area corresponding to the imagined objects, without including and being disturbed by areas which should be left out, or are irrelevant; and (c) he treats the response with apparent lack of concern over his difficulties. If responses of this sort are given deliberately to create a humorous effect, they are disqualified. The verbal aspects of jokes (especially punning) resemble the verbal form of schizophrenic thinking. The difference lies in the degree of conscious self-control over the sense of reality. The normal healthy subject deliberately suspends his sense of reality and is aware of what he is doing. The patient's sense of reality is sporadically disturbed without the patient's intention and frequently without his knowledge. He does not intend to be humorous.

Examples of sign 4 are: "A bat. I don't know, not exactly but, of course, it would have to have horns" (pl. V). The top center had been interpreted as "horns" and this percept was uncritically included in the "bat" as a matter of course. The patient combined the "bat" and the "horns" into one image without giving a thought to the quality of such a percept. Another example: "I never saw a heart but it reminds me of a heart" (pl. II). The patient meant he had no idea how a heart looked and not only that he had never seen the organ, as the inquiry disclosed. "That's a city, but I don't recognize it" (pl. IX center). The patient meant that the window-like white spaces made him think of a specific city, the name of which, at the moment, escaped him and he could not "recognize" it. "Might be anything that has a shape" is perhaps the most indeterminate response. The patient behaved as if, by the use of mere words, he had communicated a definite and meaningful thought. "The picture of a divided body of most anything," "scattered pieces of paper, in half," and "I'd say, some formation of land" are other instances of meaningless responses treated by the patients who produced them as if they contained definite and meaningful information, given with ease. "If not for this (top left), it would remind me of a bay and land and island shapes" (pl. VII). However, the removal of the upper left third would contribute nothing toward making the plate look more like an island.

The employment of meaningless terms with apparent self-assurance, and with a feeling of communicating meaningfully with the examiner (solving the task meaningfully) is the essential feature of sign 4 behavior. Again, both the patient's attitude toward his own verbal response and the logical content of the verbal response must be considered before using sign 4.

Sign 5 (1938 signs 5 and 7). Weight: +2 points. Blurring of difference between imagination and sensation, confusion of description with interpretation, serious breakdown of interpretive attitude. The patient may or may not be puzzled. An extreme degree of this sign is to treat the percepts as if they were photographs of real objects. The most extreme degree is to treat the inkblot as if it were the imagined object itself. One patient who claimed that he had died was glad to find his body in pl. I; he said he had been looking for it in vain for a long time and now, at last, could give it a "decent burial." Less infrequent are milder degrees of sign 5: "Looks like little green worms. I don't think they are alive. I really don't know. It's hard to tell if they are crawling" (pl. X, top green). The patient actually looked at the blot to ascertain whether the worms were crawling. "I don't know how those musical notes got in there" (pl. I, outside dots) was the puzzled remark of another patient carefully studying the plate. "The worms have just gotten up from their chairs. I can't understand why they've gotten up" (pl. X., bottom green) was the curious response by still another patient. "That's a bat with human legs, but I'm not sure what the legs belong to, or where they go" (pl. V). This patient watched the "legs" (bottom extension) to discover the direction in which they seemed to move, back or forth. The patient is credited with the sign even if he produces no definite response, but otherwise reveals a definite breakdown of interpretive attitude. "Are these definite objects, or are they imaginary?" "Are they sometimes real?" The confusion of interpretation with description is clear in this example: "It's a butterfly and there's a line in the middle" (pl. I); "A butterfly with a line through the middle." Breakdown of interpretive attitude is also scored when the patient clearly, though indirectly, indicates that he is unaware of being the creator of a meaningful interpretation. He does so when he behaves as if there were one, and only one, correct response to the blot, because he views the blot as a picture of a real object. Even hesitation and oscillation between description and interpretation is a sign of interpretive attitude breakdown: "Looking at it sideways, it could be a blot" (pl. I). "That's a bat, but still an inkblot" (pl. V).

One variety of breakdown of interpretive attitude is "ontological mix-up"; two types of reality, concrete and abstract (empirical and conceptual), are treated as if they were homogeneous. Example: "Two men and these (top reds) are their ulterior motives" (pl. II). The patient treated both men and the motives as objects equally concrete and capable of physical separation. It is not breakdown of interpretive attitude if the subject tries deliberately to create a humorous effect, being in full control of his logical processes, or if he uses the top reds as symbolic (not literal) representation of abstract objects: motives, feelings, and other attitudes (such as is frequently done by cartoonists). Another example: "There are the men's hearts meeting together [affectionately]; their chests are frayed where the hearts got out" (pl. III). This is a breakdown in realistic interpretation because the hearts are treated as if they could act in the same manner as the men and independently of the latter. The desires of the men to join were described as if they could exist outside and independently of the men. The middle red was interpreted simultaneously both as the symbol of mutual affection and as body organs.

Sign 6. Weight: +2 points. Absurdly inconclusive explanations given in a matter-of-fact tone to at least one percept. The explanation must be inconsequential and incongruous; the form quality of the percept explained may be good or poor. The patient must not show any concern over his explanation; usually, he seems unaware of its inadequacy. The prevailing mood is one of mild hypomania. The patient gives the requested explanation readily. One patient interpreted the whole of pl. VII as "a lion taken apart" and explained, on request: "If you took this lower part here and put it in the middle, and this part (on the left) here, well, if this were moved over there and this here, etc." He got lost in the process without getting any closer to putting together one good lion. He paid no attention whether the examiner was able to follow him or not. Another patient who had given evidence of knowing that several different and equally plausible responses to the same blot area are possible, interpreted the center of pl. II as a "throat"; the reason: "because it doesn't represent anything else." The patient did not view the blots as photographs of known objects, but he could not think of an alternative interpretation of the white center. He considered the implied repetition of his interpretation as a proof of its validity. A small detail of pl. I was interpreted by another patient as "a freak human, hospitalized at birth." Asked why, he declared arbitrarily: "A freak like I've seen in the marshes at Atlantic City." Sign 6 cannot be scored without information about the patient's reasoning obtained during an inquiry.

Sign 7. Weight: +2 points. Complete absence of human content, scored either h (whole human beings) or hd (parts of human beings). All responses containing the undissected human body, whole or part, clothed or unclothed, which can be seen without dissecting the body are human content responses.[15 p.344] However, genitals are excluded from the human content category of their own (sex).

Sign 8. Weight: +2 points. F + % below 60. All the F, Fc, Fc′ responses are combined to calculate the F+%. If these three categories together total less than 10, it is advisable to include FM, and small m, for the sake of reliability of the F+%. Care should be taken to differentiate between ambiguous and poor form responses, because the ambiguous form response has only one-third the weight of the poor or "minus" form responses.[15, pp.104, 112]

Sign 9. Weight: + 1 point. Determinant scarcity; no more than 5 determinants. The frequency with which each determinant is represented in the test record does not matter. There are, altogether, 11 basic determinants: M, FM, m, c′, Fc′, F, Fc, c, FC, CF, and C.[15, p.402] Some of these determinants may appear in combination with others—for example, FMc, Mc′, CFc, Cm, etc. Such combined responses are scored for each of the separate determinants contained in them. The FMc would be scored for FM as well as for Fc; and FCMc for FC, FM, and Fc. For the purpose of counting the content categories, such FC, FM, and Fc are treated as any other FC, FM, or Fc. Only the number of separate determinant categories matters.

Sign 10. Weight: + 1 point. Content monotony; no more than 5 content categories. It is the number of different content categories represented that is essential and not the absolute frequency with which each category occurs in the test record. The most important ones are: a (whole animals); ad (parts of animals); h (whole human beings); and hd (parts of human beings); at (anatomy or part of bodies accessible to sight only after an incision, or by x-ray); sex (genitals); pl (plants and any botanical objects); obj (inanimate movable objects); arch (immovable structures built by humans, architecture); maps; la (landscapes); wtr (water or bodies of water); abs (abstract responses expressing moods); smb (symbols representing institutionalized social relations); fire; etc.[15, p.340] Each of these content categories counts as one.

Sign 11. Weight: + 2 points. No human movement responses. The patient is credited with this sign when he fails to produce even one human movement response. The patient may have signs 1, 7, 11, all three, or only one or two of them. For the scoring of human movement responses, see *Perceptanalysis*.[15, p.136]

Sign 12. Weight: — 2 points. At least 5 human movement responses regardless of form quality. This is a sign which has negative weight because it is positively correlated with improvement. When present, it reduces the long-term prognostic criterion score.

Reliability of LTPTI Scores

Scorers *A* and *B* were intimately acquainted with the LTPTI signs when they applied them to 55 cases of the 1964, or third, validation group. Their total index scores agreed in placing 89 per cent of the cases as either above or below the cut-off point; their total scores differed by less than two points in 62 per cent of the cases. Scorer *C* learned the LTPTI by reading the definitions of the signs.[16] Scorer *C* agreed in 84 per cent of the cases with scorer *A* and in 83 per cent with scorer *B*, in placing a patient in the high or low score category. Scorer *C's* total scores differed by less than two points from those of scorer *A* in 56 per cent of the cases, and from those of scorer *B* in 46 per cent of the cases. This reliability test can be considered gratifying, and its result corresponds closely with that obtained during the second validation of LTPTI.[17]

Clinical Criteria of Personality Change

The first two validation studies involved retrospective judgments of personality change during the follow-up periods. To be classified as improved, the patient had to show improvement in (a) thought processes; (b) psychosocial relations and work; and (c) attitude toward self, greater inner freedom, and less anxiety. He had to improve in all three areas to be considered improved.[16, 17] In the present (1964) validation study the goal was to evaluate the same three areas of functioning by more objective methods. Judgments of improvement in (a) thought process and (c) attitudes toward self were made by comparing ratings of the patients obtained within three days after hospital admission with ratings obtained four years (± 1 month) later. The other criterion, (b) psychosocial relations and work, was defined solely in terms of an objective evaluation of the work history. When the patient was rated entirely free of any pathological behavior on all the items of a scale on admission and he was also free of any pathology on follow-up, he was considered improved on that scale.

The patients were evaluated with the Symptom Rating Scale (SRS) developed by the Psychiatric Evaluation Project (PEP)[7] within the Veterans Administration. The SRS consists of 20 items, of which 16 are 4-point scales and four are 3-point scales. Scaling of the SRS items was based upon extensive factor analytic studies by Gurel and Cohen.[4] Although prior to the interviews that rater acquainted himself with the clinical records to be aware of areas of particular importance in each case, the ratings were based solely upon material elicited during the interviews. The work history was obtained by the PEP social worker who interviewed, separately, both the patient and a relative. In instances of unresolved contradictory information, other informants were used in order to assure accurate information. The increase in objectivity in the present study was attained at the expense of foregoing the integrative abilities that the experienced clinician utilizes in assessing behavioral and subjective changes throughout the follow-up period.

As in the previous studies, all clinical ratings were completed without knowledge of the patient's Rorschach performance. Similarly, the Rorschach records were scored without any knowledge of the patient or his history, except for his age, sex, and diagnosis.

Third Validation

The data on the present (1964) group were gathered incidental to PEP, the Psychiatric Evaluation Project.* PEP is a large-scale intra-

*As a result of a recent reorganization within the VA, PEP is now entitled the Program Evaluation Staff of the Psychiatry, Neurology and Psychology Service. However, they will be referred to as PEP since that was their title when data were collected and all relevant publications appear under that designation.

VA research group stationed at 12 psychiatric hospitals throughout the United States under the directorship of Dr. Lee Gurel at the VA in Washington, D.C.[6] The first phase of PEP, which began in 1956, included an extensive four-year follow-up study of patients admitted to the 12 hospitals with PEP units. In order to be eligible for inclusion in the study, a patient had to meet the following criteria: (a) carry a diagnosis of schizophrenic reaction; (b) never have had a lobotomy; (c) male; (d) under 60 years of age; and (e) had been in the community at least 90 of the 180 days preceding admission or readmission.

The PEP sample at the Lyons VAH consisted of 112 patients. Rorschach records were obtained from 84 of these patients by one of six psychologists (five staff members and one advanced trainee) within three weeks of admission. The remaining 28 were not tested because of a lack of time. We believe the 84 to be representative of the entire group. Of these 84 patients, 12 gave inadequate protocols—i.e., their records contained less than eight responses (answers given spontaneously during inquiry were counted)—or they produced a perseverating record with at least 50 per cent of the total number of responses being of the same content; three died before completion of the study, and one left the country and could not be evaluated. The mean age of the remaining 68 cases was 33 years ($\sigma = 8.3$). Their mean education was 9.8 grades ($\sigma = 2.4$).

As a group these patients were more chronic than those included in either of the previous studies and their test records were scantier. One of the most striking differences was the greatly reduced number of human movement and meaningful color responses. The percentage of patients with marked Rorschach deviations from the norm was much higher in the 1964 group. In the first validation group, the percentage of improved cases was 31 after 6 years; in the second, it was 23 after 6.5 years; and in the third (1964) group the percentage of cases improving on all three criteria (thinking disorders, work, and anxiety-depression) was 26 at the end of 4 years. In all three validation groups the percentages of cases with high and low LTPTI scores were practically the same: 30 per cent or 31 per cent of the patients had low scores of less than 2 points, and 69 per cent or 70 per cent had high scores of 2 or more points.

Results of Present Study

There were 47 schizophrenics who received LTPTI scores of 2

TABLE 1.—Long-Term Prognostic Test Index Scores and Improvement on All 3 Symptom Rating Scales on Follow-up (Work Output, Thinking Disorders, Anxiety-Depression)

LTPTI Score	Improved on All 3	Improved on <3 or Unimproved	Total
1 or less	11	10	21
2 or more	7	40	47
	—	—	—
Total	18	50	68

Note: $df = 1$; chi-square = 10.48; $p < .002$
$(11 + 40)/68 = .750$

points or more, and 21 who scored 1 point or less. Table 1 shows the distribution of the patients when all three criteria (work record, thought disorders, and anxiety-depression) were used simultaneously. Patients who improved on all three criteria were placed in the improved category, and the rest in the unimproved category. As was expected, patients with low LTPTI scores improved more frequently than those with high scores. The obtained chi-square is highly significant, and it is most unlikely that such a result would occur solely because of chance factors ($p < .002$). The percentage of correct predictions is 75 per cent as compared with 90 per cent in the 1958 group and 89 per cent in the 1959 group. Despite the differences in the type of patient included in the 1964 group, and despite the different method used in determining the criteria for improvement, the prognostic index was significantly related to outcome, albeit less so than previously.

BASE RATES AND LTPTI

The base rate is a statistically determined proportion of members of a class possessing a particular attribute. The base rates for improvement and, in one case (work output) for unimprovement, are very high in our sample. The base rate for the 1964 patient's unimprovement in work output was 71 per cent. In order to be rated as improved in work output, the patient had to be gainfully employed either 25 hours or more a week at the time of the four-year follow-up, or 15 hours a week, or more, for at least three months during the fourth year. The association between improved work record and low LTPTI scores, as well as unimproved work record and high LTPTI scores, was highly significant with a chi-square of 7.72 ($p < .006$).

TABLE 2. LTPTI and SRS Dichotomous Criteria of Improvement: Comparison of Efficiency of LTPTI and Base Rate Predictions

SRS Criterion	p-Value of Chi-Square	*LTPTI Predictions* Correct	False Positives	False Negatives	*Base Rate Predictions* Correct	False Positives	False Negatives
1. Work	<.006	72%	48%	19%	71%	0	29%
2. Deteriorated Thinking	<.003	53%	0	68%	78%	22%	0
3. Unmotivated	<.02	59%	14%	53%	63%	37%	0
4. Uncooperativeness	>.20	47%	19%	68%	72%	28%	0
5. Paranoid Hostility	>.90	40%	24%	77%	76%	24%	0
6. Improved on any 2 of 3 criteria (cf. Table 1)	<.05	50%	10%	68%	75%	25%	0

Had the prediction been made that none of the patients' work output would improve, the predictions would have been confirmed in 71 per cent of the cases. The LTPTI predictions were confirmed in 72 per cent of the same patients. The LTPTI put the patients in not just one class (unimproved) as the base rate would, but in both the improved and unimproved classes. While there is no significant difference between the percentages of 71 per cent and 72 per cent, this does not detract from the finding of a significant and meaningful association between LTPTI scores and changes in the work output. Moreover, base rates are not always known nor are they always reliable. A good test criterion makes the investigator independent of base rates. The p-values of the chi-squares also were unrelated to the base rates. Its improvability makes a test criterion strikingly superior to a base rate. Moreover, a dependable prognostic criterion contains clues or an explanation of what makes patients improve or fail to improve.

SRS AND LTPTI

Thinking disorders were evaluated on the basis of ratings on these SRS items: (a) Does the patient show disorganization of thought? (b) Is the patient disoriented? (c) Does the patient show bizarre postures or movements? (d) Is there a pathological memory deficit? All 21 patients with low LTPTI scores improved, and 32 of the 47 high-score patients also improved. The chi-square was 8.60 ($p < .003$).

Despite the high base rate of 78 per cent, the LTPTI proved to be significant. The base rate was 90 per cent improvement on the anxiety-depression SRS. The LTPTI failed to differentiate significantly between the few unimproved and the overwhelming majority of improved patients. Ratings of the following items provided the information for the assessment of changes in anxiety-depression: (a) Does the patient manifest evidence of depression? (b) Does the patient report feelings of depression? (c) Does the patient manifest physical symptoms of anxiety or apprehension?

When the low and the high LTPTI scorers were divided into those who improved on any two of the three SRS of table 1 and those who did not improve, the chi-square was 3.38 ($p < .05$) or still within the conventional limits of significance (cf. table 2). The association between improvement in motivation and low LTPTI scores was more significant statistically with a chi-square of 6.60 ($p < .02$). Motivation was evaluated on the SRS on the basis of these items: (a) Is the patient apathetic? (b) Compared with the average person, is he lacking in motivation toward sane goals in life? (c) How well defined are his post-hospital goals? And, if the patient was hospitalized, (d) how well defined are his goals concerning the course of his hospitalization? The SRS of "uncooperativeness" (evasiveness and lack of cooperation during interview) and of "paranoid hostility" (suspiciousness and excessive hostility) were not associated with low and high LTPTI scores ($p > .20$ and $p > .90$, respectively), as shown in table 2. The LTPTI was associated most intimately with improvement in work output, motivation, and thinking disorders. These three aspects of personality, especially thinking disorders, are more pertinent to eventual improvement and unimprovement in schizophrenia than sensitivity (paranoia) or uncooperativeness.

Analysis of variance demonstrated clearly that scoring above or below the LTPTI cutoff point is not related to age or education, at least in adult schizophrenics. A comparison of the low and the high scorers resulted in an F value for age with a probability greater than .4 and an F value for education with a probability greater than .6. The total score correlated .20 with age ($p < .10$) and —.18 with education ($p < .20$).

Low vs. High LTPTI Scores

Low LTPTI scores proved to be helpful prognosticators even in the 1964 schizophrenic group despite its high base rates on the SRS (clinical symptoms rating scales). The improvement rate of low LTPTI scorers in the following SRS categories was: Thought disorders, 100 per cent; anxiety-depression, 90 per cent; motivation, 86 per cent; cooperativeness, 81 per cent. The base rates of clinical improvement on these scales were high, above 60 per cent. If the clinical improvement base rate is high, predictions of long-term improvement based on low LTPTI scores would be correct in over 80 per cent of cases. When the LTPTI score is high (2 points or more), it is advisable to make no prediction and thus avoid the undependable predictions (cf. "False Negatives," table 2). On the other hand, when the clinical base rates of unimprovement are high, then the high LTPTI scores provide dependable predictions. The percentage of patients who failed to increase their work output was 71 per cent, and the percentage of high scorers whose work record failed to improve was 81 per cent. This relation between clinical base rates and the difference in predictive power of low and high LTPTI scores holds also for combined SRS criteria, as is illustrated by the 3-criteria scale (table 1) and the 2-criteria scale (table 2).

Most Objective Criteria

The work output as defined in the present study was an objective and reliable criterion. However, the number of days spent in the community, outside the hospital, and the number of days in the hospital until a release that lasted for a relatively long time, have a still higher reliability and are highly objective. One clinical measure of improvement was the total number of days spent in the community during the four-year follow-up period, the ICD. This is a crucial variable in evaluating treatment, particularly of chronic schizophenics (cf. Gurel, p. 527). A careful and exhaustive investigation was carried out in order to determine whether the patient spent time in any other psychiatric institution. VA records and relatives, as well as the patients, were consulted regarding hospitalization in VA installations or elsewhere. Analysis of variance revealed a highly significant finding ($p < .005$); the patients with low LTPTI scores spent more time in the community. Of the 1,460 days in the follow-up period, the low scorers remained in the community 976 days, whereas the high scorers averaged 615 days in the community, a difference of a full year.

A similar and highly related measure (cf. Gurel, p. 527) was the number of days the patient spent in the hospital prior to his "first significant release"—i.e., staying at least 90 consecutive days out of the hospital, the FSR. The low LTPTI scorers averaged exactly one year and the high scorers about two years (728 days) in the hospital before the FSR, the average difference between low and high scorers being approximately one year ($p < .01$).

In the multiple regression procedures, employed to ascertain how effectively ICD and FSR could be predicted from the LTPTI in the 1964 sample, only nine of the test signs were used. Signs 1, 4, and 12 were eliminated since they appeared very infrequently; sign 1 in one test record, and signs 4 and 12 in three records each. Table 3 contains the regression statistics. The obtained multiple R was .426 for ICD and .429 for FSR. With nine variables and 68 subjects, an R of .447 is required for significance at the 5 per cent level. In our sample the nine signs accounted for 18 per cent of the variation in ICD and FSR. When applied to other samples, weighted-composite scores derived from the original multiple correlations are almost consistently of lower predictive value. Using a double cross-validation design, we are presently studying the Rorschach signs, ICD, and FSR in a sample of 100 cases.

TABLE 3.—Multiple Regression Statistics for ICD, FSR, and LTPTI Signs

LTPTI Sign	*In-Community Days*			*First Significant Release*		
	Regression Coefficient	Normalized Regression Coefficient	% Variance Explained ($\tau \times \alpha$)	Regression Coefficient	Normalized Regression Coefficient	% Variance Explained ($\tau \times \alpha$)
2	35	.030	.002	—19	—.014	.001
3	—258	—.202*	.024	378	.270**	.078
5	—230	—.152	.016	273	.165	.024
6	239	.193*	.027	—195	—.144	.010
7	51	.037	—.005	—38	—.025	—.002
8	—146	—.114	.024	237	.170*	.043
9	92	.094	—.007	—54	—.051	—.003
10	—150	—.136	.020	68	.056	.003
11	—275	—.253**	.068	196	.165	.030

R = .426; Constant = 1474   R = .429; Constant = —367

*$p < .20$ **$p < .05$

Recognizing that the dichotomous scoring of Rorschach signs is a gross procedure and that estimates obtained from such a scoring system would give an overly pessimistic picture of the importance of the psychological characteristics underlying the signs, we were interested in obtaining an estimate of the true importance of the psychological processes involved in producing the signs. If it were possible to assess the quality of responses over a greater range, say on a 5 or 7 point continuum, then the distribution of each sign might reasonably be of the normal form. On such an assumption it would, therefore, be appropriate to compute biserial correlations between the dependent variables ICD and FSR, and the individual signs. This procedure is in contrast to our previous analyses which were based upon point-biserial (or product-moment) correlations. Regression analyses with the nine signs using biserial coefficients produced an R of .623 with ICD and .673 with FSR. Thus it appears that the psychological processes underlying the signs are of considerable importance in evaluating the course of the individual patients' schizophrenia.

Fourth Validation

This was carried out at the Medfield Foundation.* Again, the follow-up information was gathered and the calculation of the LTPTI scores were done independently. Two patients were eliminated from the study; one died and the other produced only four test responses. Three patients diagnosed "paranoid personality," "residual schizophrenia," and "psychotic reaction without clearly defined structural changes" were retained because they were psychotic and gave no sign of an organic cerebral disorder. Ten patients had LTPTI scores of less than 2 points and all improved. Eight had scores of at least 2 points; of these, three improved and five did not. Thus 15 of the 18 patients were placed correctly in their respective categories, confirming the LTPTI in 83 per cent of the cases ($p < .01$).

Factor Analysis

One method of improving the scoring of the LTPTI signs is factor analysis. The present scoring system is not based on the assumption that the signs are univocal, but that their effects are additive. Since

*Edward J. Jordan, Ph.D., Research Psychologist, and Harry Freeman, M.D., Director of Research of the Medfield Foundation at Medfield, Mass., contributed the test records and the follow-up information.

the domain of the 12 LTPTI signs is a matter of empirical observation, a factor analysis seems to be the most economical means of describing the data. The present procedure of calculating the total index score, based on the combination of different assumed factors, may obscure the unique contribution that each factor could make to a more specific prognosis.

A correlation matrix of signs was computed utilizing test records of all 259 schizophrenics of the four validation investigations. With unities as communality estimates in the diagonals, principle components were extracted to a latent root criterion of 1.00, yielding four factors. These four orthogonal factors were then rotated by means of the Varimax method.[8] Psychometrically the solution seemed quite satisfactory. Using the criterion of loadings of .30 or above, nine of the signs had unit complexity. Only signs 1, 9, and 12 had loadings greater than .30 on more than one factor; each of the remaining nine signs had such high loadings only on one factor. In future work it would appear desirable to score the signs on the four factors, assigning unit weights to each sign, and relate the factor scores with independent criteria measures. The authors are currently studying the effectiveness of factor scoring in predicting outcome for schizophrenic patients.

Factor A consists of four test signs: sign 7 with a loading of .76 (absence of human content); sign 11 loading .77 (no human movement response); sign 10 loading .76 (content monotony); and sign 9 loading .65 (determinant scarcity). This factor might be named *Constriction.* Failure to see any human beings and to produce any human movement response suggests aversion to people, lack of interest in others and in any meaningful role which one might play in interhuman relationships. The impoverished content and the limited variety of formal determinants reveal a general reduction of interest in the environment. Withdrawal and chronic depression frequently accompany such a marked reduction in perceptiveness.

Factor B consists of sign 3 with a loading of .68 (vagueness or inappropriateness of perception) and sign 5 with a loading of .51 (breakdown of interpretive attitude). This factor might be called *Doubtful Perception or Interpretation.* Sign 3 includes responses with a vague and tentative content as well as inappropriate use of abstract reasoning. Sign 5 is comprised of responses in which the mental processes of description and interpretation are confused, leading to a breakdown of interpretive attitude; sometimes there is a definite blurring of the difference between imagination and visual sensation, in extreme cases resulting in the treatment of the imagined object as if it were real. Factor B clearly points to dereistic or illogical thinking. Patients who display these signs have definite trouble in producing precise ideas or in precisely using ideas when applying them to empirical reality.

Factor C consists of four signs: sign 1 loading .55 ($M<2$; $\Sigma C - M \geq 3$); sign 2 loading .62 (repetition or intellectual perseveration; sign 6 loading .57 (inconclusive explanations); and sign 12 loading —.43 (at least five human movement responses). Perhaps the best name for Factor C is *Inappropriately Applied Energy*. Individuals scoring high on this factor possess a ready responsiveness to environmental stimulation which is poorly organized both as to goal and effectiveness of action. This factor measures essentially an ill-organized, poorly thought through and spontaneously inadequate expenditure of energy. The desire to be in active contact with the environment is indicated but it is largely ineffectual and thus unsatisfactory to others as well as to the patient.

Factor D consists of two signs: sign 4 loading .78 (indeterminate form responses); and sign 8 loading —.57 ($F+\%<60$). This factor is tentatively labeled *Sporadic Arbitrariness*. Sign 4 patients are characterized by a sporadic and ineffective arbitrariness in making statements and reaching decisions. Even when they try to be precise, they succeed only in making spurious and irrelevant changes which are meaningless in terms of sensory, empirical reality. From time to time, they are arbitrary in assigning meaning to thoughts and things. Those relatively few among them who produce very low percentages of sharply perceived forms cannot help being loose in thought and ineffectual in action, at times, and thus cannot be called arbitrary. ($F+\%<60$ is negatively correlated with Factor D.) Those with normal and superior percentages of sharply perceived forms, on the other hand, do appear arbitrary when they occasionally produce the indeterminate responses without concern for mental and factual accuracy.

Summary and Conclusions

A brief history of the development of the Long-term Prognostic Test Index (LTPTI) and scoring procedures for the index were presented. The LTPTI differs from an earlier long-term prognostic criterion[19] in that it relies almost exclusively on personality liabilities, while the earlier, less discriminating criterion relied largely on personality assets. It is noteworthy that Fisher, Gonda, and Little[3] discovered that personality liabilities are more successful in detecting organic cerebral disorders than are personality assets. A striking common feature of unimproved schizophrenics and chronic debilitated cerebral cases is the significant drop in human movement responses.

The LTPTI, based upon Rorschach responses, is intended to predict whether a schizophrenic patient will be improved in approximately three to six years after testing. In addition to the previous reports,[16, 17] indicating high interscorer agreement, further evidence confirmed the reliability of the index even for a rater who only read the scoring procedure and received no further training.

The long-term prognosis for a patient who scores 1 or below is that he will improve in all of the following clinical areas: (a) thought processes, (b) psychosocial relations and work, and (c) attitude toward self, greater inner freedom, and less anxiety. In two previous validation studies [16, 17] the percentage of correct predictions were 90 per cent and 89 per cent. Using more objective (nonretrospective) evaluation criteria in a more chronic sample of 68 schizophrenics, the percentage of correct predictions was 75 per cent ($p < .002$). In a fourth validation group of 18 patients, the LTPTI predictions were confirmed in 83 per cent of the cases ($p < .01$). The LTPTI was also significantly associated with improvement in work output, thought processes, and motivation, but was not related to improvement in cooperation and paranoid hostility.

One of the most crucial questions for prognosis in the chronic patient is how long will he remain institutionalized during the follow-up period. Of the 1460 days in the follow-up period (1964 sample), patients with an LTPTI score of 1 or less remained in the community for 976 days, whereas those with scores or 2 or more averaged 615 days in the community, a difference of a full year. Also, on the average, patients with high scores remained in the hospital one year longer than those with low scores before having a release that was followed by 90 consecutive days out of the hospital. Multiple regression analysis yielded an R of .426 between nine Rorschach signs and the number of days spent in the community.

Scores on the index were demonstrated to be independent of either age or education.

An orthogonal factor analysis was performed using data from 257 subjects. Varimax rotation of four principal component factors resulted in a meaningful and psychometrically satisfactory solution. The factors were described and tentatively identified as A, Constriction; B, Doubtful Perception or Interpretation; C, Inappropriately Applied Energy; and D, Sporadic Arbitrariness. It is suggested that in future work the signs be scored on the four factors and the factor scores be related to criterion measures. Such a study is currently being conducted by the authors.

REFERENCES

1. Appel, K. E., Myers, J. M., and Scheflen, A. E.: Prognosis in psychiatry: Results of psychiatric treatment. A.M.A. Arch. Neurol. Psychiat. 70:459-468, 1953.
2. Astrup, C., Fossum, A., and Holmboe, R.: Prognosis in Functional Psychosis. Springfield, Ill., Charles C Thomas, 1962.
3. Fisher, J., Gonda, T. A., and Little, K. B.: The Rorschach and central nervous system pathology: a cross-validation study. Amer. J. Psychiat. 111:487-492, 1955.
4. Gurel, L., and Cohen, J.: Dimensions of psychiatric symptom ratings. Unpublished manuscript. Washington, D.C.: Veterans Administration Hospital, Psychiatric Evaluation Project, 1963.
5. Holt, W. L., and Holt, W. M.: After 30 years, 35 per cent of dementia praecox recovered. Amer. J. Psychiat. 118:737-739, 1962.
6. Jenkins, R. L., and Gurel, L.: Predictive factors in early release. Ment. Hospitals 10:11-14, 1959.
7. Jenkins, R. L., Stauffacher, J., and Hester, R.: A symptom rating scale for use with psychotic patients. Arch. Gen. Psychiat. 1:197-204, 1959.
8. Kaiser, H. F.: The varimax criterion for analytic rotation in factor analysis. Psychometrika 23:187-200, 1958.
9. Malamud, W., and Render, N.: Course and prognosis in schizophrenia. Amer. J. Psychiat. 95:1039-1057, 1939.
10. Neumann, E., and Finkenbrink, F.: Statistische Untersuchungen über die Spontanremission bei Schizophrenien. Allg. Z. Psychiat. 111:17-46, 1939.
11. Piotrowski, Z. A.: The Rorschach inkblot method in organic disturbances of the central nervous system. J. Nerv. Ment. Dis. 86:525-537, 1937.
12. ——: The prognostic possibilities of the Rorschach method in insulin treatment. Psychiat. Quart. 12:679-689,. 1938.
13. ——: Positive and negative Rorschach organic reactions. Ror. Res. Exch. 4:147-151, 1940.
14. ——: A simple experimental device for the prediction of outcome of insulin treatment in schizophrenia. Psychiat. Quart. 14:267-273, 1940.
15. ——: Perceptanalysis: A Fundamentally Reworked, Expanded and Systematized Rorschach Method. New York, Macmillan, 1957. Second printing Philadelphia, Ex Libris, 1965.
16. Piotrowski, Z. A., and Bricklin, B.: A long-term prognostic criterion for schizophrenics based on Rorschach data. Psychiat. Quart. Suppl. 32:315-329, 1958.

17. ——: A second validation of a long-term Rorschach prognostic index for schizophrenic patients. J. Consult. Psychol. 25:123-128, 1961.

18. Piotrowski, Z. A., and Lewis, N. D. C.: An experimental Rorschach diagnostic aid for some forms of schizophrenia. Amer. J. Psychiat. 107:360-366, 1950.

19. ——: An experimental criterion for the prognostication of the status of schizophrenics after a three-year-interval based on Rorschach data. *In* Relation of Psychological Tests to Psychiatry. New York, Grune & Stratton, 1952.

20. Rennie, T. A. C.: Follow-up study of five-hundred patients with schizophrenia admitted to the hospital from 1913 to 1923. Arch. Neurol. Psychiat. 42:877-891, 1939.

18

THE PREDICTION OF SCHIZOPHRENIA IN INFANCY: II. A TEN-YEAR FOLLOW-UP REPORT OF PREDICTIONS MADE AT ONE MONTH OF AGE*

by BARBARA FISH, M.D., RENÉE WILE, M.S.W., THEODORE SHAPIRO, M.D., and FLORENCE HALPERN, PH.D.†

RESEARCH INTO SCHIZOPHRENIA would be advanced if it were possible to detect the disease or its antecedents early in life and to study the developing manifestations by direct observation. In adult patients, it is not yet possible to determine which biochemical and physiological dysfunctions are manifestations of the disease itself, and which are secondary to prolonged anxiety, social isolation, or other conditions secondary to hospitalization. The effects of later experiences would be minimized if it were possible to study the nascent disorder in infancy. Studies of the developing infant and child could also investigate the impact of the environment and learning on individuals with early symptoms. A rational approach to early treatment depends upon an understanding of the contribution of all these factors.

With these goals in mind, one of the authors began a pilot study in 1952 to determine whether one could detect infants who would later become schizophrenic.[6] Bender had demonstrated that characteristic deviations from normal development were present in the histories of schizophrenic children, often at birth.[1, 2] Fish hypothesized that the early deviations in development should distinguish potentially

---

*Since 1961, the work reported in this paper has been supported by a contribution of the Harriett Ames Charitable Trust, New York, N.Y.

†Respectively, Associate Professor of Psychiatry; Instructor, Psychiatric Social Work; Instructor, Psychiatry; Associate Clinical Professor, Clinical Psychology, New York University School of Medicine.

schizophrenic infants from their normal peers before the more readily recognizable psychological and social symptoms of childhood schizophrenia appeared. In this initial study, criteria for developmental abnormality were devised, based on Bender's work, and were tested on a small scale. Previous reports[6, 7] have presented the original predictions and the detailed progress of these children through the age of four years. This paper reports the outcome of these predictions, based on independent psychiatric and psychological evaluations which were performed when the children were 9 to 10 years of age.

Method

The vulnerability to schizophrenia was predicted for 16 infants selected at random from the Bellevue well-baby clinic. This was a very deprived socioeconomic population which had a high incidence of social and psychiatric pathology.[13] From the age of one month, the infants were studied for signs of deviate development. Vulnerability to schizophrenia was defined in terms of abnormally uneven neurological development, characterized by unusual combinations of retardation and precocity as compared to Gesell's norms.[6, 7, 13, 15]

Psychiatric evaluations of the parents were carried out by the original investigator, and an assessment was made of the family's socioeconomic status and their changing attitudes toward the infant. Clinical notes were also kept of the child's developing personality and problems, whether these were considered pathological or within the normal range of variation.

Results

Predictions at One Month of Age

At one month of age, three infants were judged to be "vulnerable" to schizophrenia on the basis of their abnormally uneven development.[6]

Peter's development was the most irregular. His head control was advanced for his age (he was able to lift both head and chest when prone), but his trunk was so flaccid that he could not be pulled to a sit, but had literally to be "folded up." He was abnormally underactive, showing none of the usual kicking or crawling, but only slow writhing, fish-like movements. Visual following was normal, but he showed no response to the examiner's voice. Muscle tone was doughy and he had peripheral mottling and cyanosis.

Frank showed a lesser degree of unevenness. His head control, visual following, and social responsiveness were advanced. However, he was abnormally inactive, had a more prominent tonic neck reflex than usual, and slightly doughy muscle tone and mottled skin.

Conrad showed minimal unevenness. He had increased visual alertness and normal head control, but decreased and immature motility. Tonic neck reflex was more prominent than usual. His activity tended to be slower than normal and "stretchy," rather than the usual kicking and crawling.

The remaining 13 infants were diagnosed as normal at one month of age, showing no unusual uneven development.[6, 13]

Course from One Month to Nine Years of Age

Peter, the most abnormal infant at one month of age, was the third child born to a 35-year-old schizophrenic mother. She had attended classes for retarded children in public school and was hospitalized for acute psychotic breaks at 19 years of age and after the birth of each child. P and his siblings were cared for during his first five years of life by a dull and disorganized grandmother.

After the one-month prediction, P's entire development continued to be the most aberrant of the group, with every area of functioning being affected at some time. He was apathetic and underactive until 16 months of age when he became hyperactive, impulsive, and disorganized. His postural development actually went into "reverse" in his first three months, dropping to less than 50 per cent of normal by ten months of age; after 10 months it abruptly accelerated, without any change in his environment. He showed marked scatter in developmental achievements and unusual sequences and patterns over time.

These lags and fluctuations in postural control were associated with marked anxiety in relation to gravity and an increased need for physical support and guidance in body skills in infancy and long after P had achieved independent locomotion. His body image disturbances were reflected in apractic difficulty, confusion about spatial relationships, and difficulty in learning visual motor tasks. In infancy his eye-hand coordination and fine manual skills had progressed relatively normally so that he appeared to be of average intelligence. However, development in this area became erratic after 1½ years of age, with some achievements almost at age level and others retarded, with poorly organized gestalten and figure drawings.

He began to say words at 27 months and three-word sentences at 29 months. However, he did not exploit speech normally for communication, but remained excessively fearful and inarticulate. At home and when examined, he ran around endlessly, played poorly, threw and broke toys, had severe tantrums, and did not play with his siblings or other children.

When P was 3½ years of age, a belligerent and violent stepfather entered the home and took a particular dislike to P, whom he considered the most "babyish" of all the children; he resented that P was "spoiled by his mother." The family said that P was "impossible," "naughty," and that the other children were all smarter than he.

When he was five years of age, his mother was again hospitalized for a schizophrenic psychosis and P and his two older siblings were placed in a normal child-caring institution for dependent children, where they have remained since. Both of P's siblings adapted to placement, but he continued to have difficulties.

From the beginning of placement, P stood out as a deviate child in an institution with a large number of disturbed children. He was daydreamy, aimless and confused, and unable to dress himself until he was six years of age. At nine he still had difficulty following routines and was considered to be "oversensitive, unhappy, and isolated from the group."

In school he was sullen and provocative, aggressive with teachers and his peers. He was restless and inattentive and required individual attention to do any work at all. He repeated second grade and functioned at about a year below grade level in the fourth grade when he was nine. His problems were so severe that his case worker took him into therapy, prior to our follow-up, although she was able to give such individual attention to very few.

Frank, the second most abnormal baby at one month of age, was the first child born to a 30-year-old unmarried mother. She was an intelligent, lonely, and rather timorous person who had worked as a secretary after graduating from college. On the whole, she was a good mother, sensitive and responsive to Frank, and she enjoyed him during his infancy.

Following the one-month prediction, F's development continued to be uneven, but less so than Peter's. By the third month his early inactivity gave way to hyperactivity and irritability. Thereafter, motor development showed few lags, variable precocity, and considerable scatter; at seven months he could not roll over. Visual motor development was average, except that his perceptions were sometimes fluid, and he showed unusual difficulty in establishing his own body boundaries and the boundaries of objects, especially transparent containers.

He said occasional words appropriately after ten months of age, but did not exploit new words and dropped them after one or two trials.

At 1½ years of age, without any apparent external change, he became withdrawn, irritable, clinging, and negativistic and was terrified by fears of bodily harm. He stopped talking and playing with toys and began to run around making strange noises and chattering jargon to himself. He was given mild medication (diphenhydramine) when anxiety was extreme and disrupted his functioning, and the mother was referred for casework. She was helped to tolerate F's erratic functioning and anxiety and gradually to set realistic limits for his impulsive and immature behavior. He continued to show moderately disturbed behavior until 5 years. At three years he attempted to pull his nipples to make breasts and tried to slam off his penis with the toilet seat, insisting he was a girl. Daytime urinary control was finally achieved at 3½ and bowel training at four. Placement in a nursery school at 3½ years of age seemed to accelerate the acquisition of more organized play and social patterns, but F became somewhat subdued.

By five to six years of age, F appeared much more organized, but at the expense of affective spontaneity. He showed strong attempts to conform, denying anger and other spontaneous feelings, but these were expressed in aggressive fantasy play and much anxiety in dreams. His visual gestalten and figure drawings showed combinations of both precocious and primitive features, with many rotations and confusions in direction and attempts to compensate by much heavy-handed compulsive attention to boundaries and details.

In first grade in a small private school, he showed early signs of dyslexia with reversals. The school was alerted to his dominance and perceptual difficulties, helped him promptly, and he became an excellent reader. He gained some satisfaction from being in the upper quarter of a good class. In first grade, he became a member of a local boys' club and achieved considerable status with his peers because of his athletic prowess. However, at nine he had difficulty in organizing his work, becoming so involved in obsessive details that he was often unable to complete his compositions.

Conrad, who had the least degree of uneven development at one month of age, had the most stormy and chaotic family experiences of the three infants. He was abruptly placed in an infant shelter at ten months of age when his mother had an acute paranoid break. Two months later, he was listless, apathetic, and "regressed, refused to walk."

Between fourteen months and 4½ years, C was in two foster homes.

He became more alert and soon began to walk, but he did not run until he was 3½. He continued to be underactive, slow moving, and clumsy. At 3½ he showed fear in relation to gravity and a marked lack of vigor and zest. Visual motor functioning was almost at his age level, but he was fearful in new activities and showed no initiative or spontaneous play. He began to say words and two-word sentences at two years. At 3½ his comprehension was at his age level; however, his speech was infantile, with a tendency to use his own odd vocabulary (a circle was named a "pobble," and asked what a "pobble" does, he answered, "It pimbles").

Social adaptation and relatedness continued to be fragile; he responded to each subsequent change of placement with listlessness, apathy, and regression. Conrad was always less precocious, more lethargic, and underactive than Frank, but never showed as severe developmental impairments as Peter, although Conrad suffered more disrupted placements. C's mother abruptly removed him from foster placement when he was 4½ years of age. The eight months with her was interrupted by another psychotic break and placement in a third foster home. From five to seven years of age he was in a shelter and then in two more foster placements.

In the shelter at five to seven years of age, his workers reported: "He pretended constantly that he did not understand ordinary directions and asked foolish questions that made no sense. He seemed unable to adjust to group living, was unhapy and preoccupied most of the time, put his clothes on backwards, wrong side out, and upside down. He was obstinate and had tantrums." At six, his I.Q. was 95. He spontaneously outlined his hand on paper twice; asked what hands do, he replied, "Hands shake hands; hands draw and hands put on hats."

After seven, in the foster homes he continued to be vague and daydreamy. He was so perplexed and inattentive that his hearing was tested but was found to be normal. His affect appeared bland, but sometimes he seemed desperately eager to relate and would ask, "Do you like me?" or say, "Everyone hates me," and look furious, if he was denied something. He asked persistent questions which were felt to be requests for information, such as where his elbow and shoulder were. He was a "lone wolf," rarely talking or playing with the other children in the home or in the neighborhood.

He began first grade at seven, worked poorly, and was inattentive, abstracted, and soon began to clown and disturb the class. Repeating first grade, he ran wildly about the classroom and seemed to have a "chip on his shoulder." He had no friends. He continued to be fearful and defensive in relation to learning, resented any criticism or instruction, and did not finish his work. The agency considered him to be a deviate child and referred him for psychologic and psychiatric evaluation prior to our follow-up because of his many problems .

Independent Psychiatric Evaluations at Nine Years of Age

The independent psychiatric evaluations were made by the psychiatrist (TS) who did not know the original predictions nor the subsequent course of the children. He evaluated the children at nine to 9½ years of age on the basis of a single psychiatric examination of the child. The only outside information which was made available to him was whether the child had parents or siblings at home. The pattern and pathology of the child's social relationships, affective responsiveness, reality testing, and integration were evaluated on internal evidence from the interview itself. In addition to a standard psychiatric diagnosis, the children were classified according to a behavioral typology the authors have described elsewhere.[12] The examinations were scored on a symptom severity scale developed and used by the authors for evaluating children receiving in-patient psychiatric treatment. This scale included 18 items of behavior characteristically found on the mental status examination of children.

The independent psychiatrist diagnosed Peter as a childhood schizophrenic. He diagnosed one child as having normal integration and the remainder as showing mild to moderate neurotic or personality disturbances.[13] At the request of the agency involved, the independent psychiatric examination made by their child psychiatrist consultant was used for C. This psychiatrist diagnosed C as showing predominantly a psychopathic personality organization resulting from early deprivation, with some schizophrenic features.

On the symptom rating scale, Peter's ratings were quantitatively and qualitatively more severe than the other children's. His total symptom severity score was 28 (out of a maximum possible 54 points); the remaining children ranged from 3 to 13. His score was as high and the profile of symptoms similar to those of the more seriously disturbed children examined on our in-patient service. He had moderate to severe scores on those symptoms considered to be more specific for schizophrenia: withdrawal, autistic thought disorder, and inappropriate affect. None of the other children were rated as having these malignant symptoms.

The independent psychiatrist found Peter to be a schizophrenic child (Type II[12]) with impaired, constricted, and unintegrated functioning in all areas. He was withdrawn and preoccupied, maintaining a rigid posture with eyes averted and downcast and face frozen in a frightened expression throughout the interview. He made no affective contact; despite his appearance of overwhelming tension and anxiety, he denied sadness or nervousness and admitted only to some angry feelings. Affective expression was empty and inappropriate, although overwhelming anxiety appeared to disrupt and impair his intellectual functioning. He was unable to modify this frozen affect, whether in sensitive or neutral areas. His voice had a monotonous, wooden quality with frequent and severe blocking; when he did respond, his speech was usually sparse, monosyllabic, and unelaborated.

At times, his thinking was so illogical as to seem bizarre and incomprehensible. He was confused about his own personal identity, his wishes and feelings, and was even only vaguely aware of sexual differences. He was confused in his time sense and in the identity of members of his immediate family. He admitted to hearing voices in his head in recent months and firmly believed in their reality. However, his persecutory feelings in regard to his peers were as poorly organized as the remainder of his functioning. He seemed so attuned to his inner autistic experience that external reality made little imprint.

The excessive use of denial and projection as his main defensive operations had a serious effect upon his reality orientation and gave his personality a paranoid and brittle structure. He drew back from human contact, feeling fragile and sensitive and constantly on guard against bodily as well as psychic injury. His very emptiness made chronic dependent passivity the only adaptive means possible. He was diagnosed as a childhood schizophrenic. Clinically, he appeared to be functioning on a borderline intellectual level.

In contrast, *Frank* appeared to be a moderately well-compensated neurotic child. He impressed the independent psychiatrist as being spontaneous and forthright, but under constant control. His speech was weak and squeaky with restricted movements, and his emotional tone, though generally appropriate, was always under a certain degree of constriction. Enthusiasm and overall animation were held in check, whereas anxiety was moderate to high, as evidenced by constant fidgeting, a mild hand tremor, and occasional blocking of speech, especially in relation to talk about his mother. His speech was often elaborative beyond necessity, and he occasionally became circumstantial and rambling. There was a moderate amount of easily available fantasy material which at times suggested some loosening of repression, but even here he was always logical, and if he strayed he always recaptured the goal idea. No psychotic or schizophrenic trends were detected.

F was preoccupied with loneliness and attempted to compensate for this by unrealistic fantasies of reunion with the father as an idealized hero. F's character structure seemed to be centered about an idealized masculine role with compulsive determination to win to assure his status. He channeled his hostile aggressive feelings into competitive sports and defended against them by compulsive mechanisms. His aspiration to be a "zoo catcher," was typical of his entire behavioral facade, which was one where restraint was evident in the face of the pressure of his impulses.

F became frustrated easily, but handled his disappointment by isolation and displacement. Nevertheless, there was the constant breakthrough of manifest anxiety. This did not seem to interfere significantly in his major areas of functioning. Clinically, he had good intellect and capacity for work. The pressure of his drives always demanded great counterpressures of restraint so that he often appeared tense with constriction of his emotional range. He was diagnosed as a neurotic character disorder with relatively good functional capacity and was estimated to be of average intelligence.

Conrad's independent psychiatric evaluation was the only one performed by a different psychiatrist. The agency's child psychiatrist had examined him because of his many problems; she did not know that he had been part of a study in infancy, but was aware of his mother's history, his early placements, and his maladjustments since the age of three.

At nine years of age, this psychiatrist found that C was infantile compared to other children his age. He showed an aptitude with puzzles but was generally uncommunicative and expressed himself only in response to questions. There was an uncommon poverty of expression, little contact with the examiner, or emotional modulation with a general tenor of subduedness, if not depressiveness. He was confused in his personal identity and his time-sense and showed some primitive thinking.

It was believed that he showed schizoid elements in his rather desperate efforts to relate, but that there were also poor object relations and shallowness of affect resulting from inconsistent early care. His adjustment at nine years was thought to be more psychopathic than schizophrenic and related to his early deprivation and traumatization, with possibly some early schizophrenic anlage.

Independent Psychological Evaluations at Nine Years of Age

The independent psychological evaluations were made by the psychologist (FH) who did not know the original predictions nor the subsequent course of the children, except that Peter and Conrad were in placement when tested. A complete psychological battery was administered, including the Wechsler Intelligence Scale for Children, Rorschach, the Thematic Apperception Test, Human Figure Drawings, and the Bender Gestalt Test. Norms for nine to ten years of age were used as reference points in evaluating the level of function in different areas and the presence or absence of pathology. Particular attention was paid to the integration and organization of the child's thinking and intellectual function, his perception of reality, his self-concept, and the control of affectivity and motor coordination.

The independent psychologist differentiated Peter, Frank, and Conrad from the other children because they showed pathological disorders of thinking, identification, and personality organization; their disorders were more severe than neurotic reactions and they showed serious disruption of adjustment in learning and behavior. Two additional children were diagnosed as having moderate neurotic problems. These two neurotic children were considered to have greater inner organization and less difficulty in functioning, with greater potential for change with treatment, compared to Peter, Frank, and Conrad. The remaining children were diagnosed as showing "no pathology," including neurotic problems considered to be within the "normal" range.[13]

Peter showed the most severe impairment with retarded, pathologically erratic, and deviate functioning. His total personality development seemed to have remained at a very primitive level.

Intellectually, P functioned at a defective level, his I.Q. on the Wechsler Intelligence Scale for Children being 65, with a verbal score of 75 and a performance score of 61. His subtest scores suggested that his potentialities were somewhat better than the scores indicated, going from the low defective[2] to dull normal levels.[8] He did most poorly on items involving social comprehension and judgment, where verbal facility and new learning were required. In fact, he seemed so tense, anxious, threatened, and preoccupied that it was quite difficult for him to grasp any kind of new and unfamiliar concept, even when it was carefully explained to him. On the other hand, he could function above the defective level when he was dealing with comparatively familiar tasks such as simple arithmetical problems and general information.

His functioning was not at all like what is ordinarily found in defectives: he showed a gross disparity between verbal and performance I.Q.'s, and one which went in the opposite direction than one would expect in simple deficiency. Furthermore, he showed marked variability in subtest scores, and the quality of some of his responses were far above what one might expect from a defective child and particularly one who had suffered from environmental deprivation. In the visual motor area he did not show the motor disturbances and lack of coordination that might be expected in a boy of low I.Q.; instead, he tended to split and fragment the Gestalt figures more in the manner of a schizophrenic.

In addition to limited and deviant intellectual functioning, this boy manifested impoverishment in social and emotional development. He seemed to experience himself much like a three-year-old rather than a nine-year-old. His own resources were extremely limited and his affect was shallow; he could become involved with others only on superficial levels. Unlike the typical institutionalized child, he did not go along with simple routines, nor did he share on superficial levels the more obvious, usual attitudes and reactions of the group. For example, on the Rorschach he had only two popular responses.

Most significant was the variability he manifested in his ways of perceiving and organizing his experiences. On the Rorschach there were instances when his concepts were all out of line with commonly accepted reality. The bizarreness that he revealed could not be explained solely on the basis of low intelligence, particularly since there were other times when his productions had quite a good quality. This variability, in conjunction with the regressive trends that were evident here (first giving a human interpretation to a Rorschach blot and then retreating to something inanimate), again seemed contraindicative of simple deficiency.

The disturbances that were indicated by P's test reactions appeared to be of long standing. P apparently made little effort to overcome his limitations and deviations or to compensate for them. His relatedness was shallow, social judgment was poor, and his conformity was tenuous. The best he seemed able to do was to try to avoid interaction with the environment, or failing this, to endure whatever was confronting him. He seemed to fluctuate between moments when he had a relatively good understanding of himself and his environment and moments when, unable to face the realities confronting him, all he could do was to regress and escape from himself and the world about him.

Frank was an intellectually well-endowed boy, but one who, because of his exaggerated need to conform and keep all unaccepted impulses in control, had failed to develop his own resources and find himself. He showed paranoid and schizophrenic features, with fragile defenses and reality control. His defensive operations interfered with his functioning and adjustment in practically all areas.

Intellectually F was of superior ability, his I.Q. on the Wechsler Intelligence Scale being 120 with a verbal score of 115 and a performance score of 121. Evidence of instability was seen in a wide disparity among his subtest scores, which ranged from low average[9] to very superior levels.[19] His outstanding score was on the test which requires careful discriminating observation of small details in visually presented material (picture completion). His poorest performance was on the coding test, which reflected difficulties in concentration when he had to work by himself without the guidance and support of the examiner. He seemed the kind of child whose effort and energy was directed toward carefully observing what was going on around him, on taking cues from others, and who then could go along in prescribed fashion. He had learned many isolated facts, but was overly concrete and stimulus bound and could not therefore use his knowledge or his ability when called on to apply this in new or unusual circumstances, or when he was required to use independent judgment and initiative.

This boy was seeking to present himself as a responsive, friendly, cooperative individual. Yet the disparity between his exaggerated need to comply and his actual ability to really identify with such behavior and carry it through in a consistent and constructive fashion was so great that there was constant inner tension as well as a great deal of tension between himself and his environment. At times, this tension and anxiety became such that there were breaks in reality and the emergence of disorganizing anxiety. Anxiety was reflected in the persistent excessive flight into small unessential matters, in a desperate attempt to avoid realities which he could not face (a high percentage of small details, actually twice as many as would be considered within the normal range). He also showed frequent response to the shading aspects of the blot, a response rarely encountered to any great extent at his age. Furthermore he seemed unable, in many instances, to contain this anxiety, but rather reacted to it in a diffuse, unstructured, disorganized way. On such occasions his only defense was projection of all his unacceptable impulses and flight from the threatening circumstances. His resulting paranoid attitudes were suggested by one of his Rorschach interpretations where he saw "a butterfly with two projecting guns on it, like shooting."

The end product of F's anxiety was that he departed radically from norms for his age both on the Intelligence and Projective Tests, and his efforts at coping with the tension of the testing situation left him exhausted.

Loss of objectivity was reflected in the fact that on the Rorschach a number of his responses were not in line with reality. Even when he was seeking to be purely objective, to deal with the stimulus on formal intellectual levels, he nevertheless departed from generally accepted reality 22 per cent of the time.

Despite his cooperative facade, there was indication of a great deal of oppositionalism (a number of "space" responses on the Rorschach) as well as his constant flight from more usual concepts into small, unimportant matters. While he tried to appear like a pleasant, stable, mature individual, he gave no indication of any kind of well-integrated internalized concept of himself (no M responses on the Rorschach and only one human interpretation in a very long protocol). It can only be inferred then that the facade he presented was a conscious, superimposed one, brittle in that it was not reinforced by inner strength. It is therefore very likely to be disrupted under the least pressure.

Conrad had at least average intelligence but showed deviations and impairment in all important areas. The marked emptiness, flatness, and general lack of motivation were all of an order to suggest that these limitations and resulting deviations in adjustment were of long duration. He went about relating in the only ways he knew, on superficially conforming levels, but could not even sustain this when any minor frustration arose. Diagnostically, he seemed to be a psychopathic personality, with some schizoid emptiness and detachment.

Intellectually, C functioned in the average range. His I.Q. on the Wechsler Intelligence Scale for Children being 97 with a verbal score of 100 and a performance score of 94. His performance fell to a defective level[5] where he was left entirely to himself to carry out routine assignments (coding). His next lowest score was on the test of arithmetical reasoning, where he responded impulsively. An absence of real sustained motivation and poor attention seemed to be interfering with the adequacy of his performance. When an assignment was at all difficult or required him to extend himself, he gave up with a shrug. Preoccupation also was evident, necessitating relatively frequent repetition of questions.

Lack of motivation and of any strong drive to achieve was also reflected on his responses to other tests. He approached most of his experiences in terms of the immediate and the concrete, rarely attempted to go beyond the limits of the current situation, to perceive or develop relationships between different aspects of his experiences. Instead, each circumstance was met on a rather circumscribed basis; abstract concepts, theoretical considerations, and long term planning were lacking.

Emotionally, there was a marked emptiness and withdrawal and no real capacity for positive, mutually satisfying emotional interaction. Thus on the Rorschach, C gave only one very shallow, arbitrary color response and in general seemed to be helpless in the face of emotional stimuli. He had no appreciation of what obtains between people and no ability really to feel with or for others, except on a very limited and superficial level.

It was in his stories on the Thematic Apperception Test that the inner emptiness and lack of resources became most apparent. In response to the mother-son picture he said, "A father comes home and his mother just looks worried." Questioning first produced nothing but shrugs, but finally C said, "Maybe he killed somebody." Asked to elaborate he said, "I don't know. I can't think of anything." Finally, when asked why the man might have killed somebody, he answered, "Maybe because he didn't like him." In response to the picture of a boy playing a violin he said, "He loves violins. One day he found a violin. He put it down and he kept on staring at it." Urged to make a story about the boy and the violin, C continued to look at the picture and insisted, "I don't know." In another instance all he could say was, "I don't know this. I guess he's daydreaming." Asked what happened in that case, he said, "I don't know, maybe he's sleeping, fell asleep." Lack of a rich inner life, of any real understanding of interpersonal relationships, was certainly suggested by his productions. His extreme flatness and the futility of his efforts in adjusting suggested long-standing disturbances to which he had made a kind of superficial but very limited adjustment.

Summary of Results on the Three "Vulnerable" Children

The independent evaluations made at nine years of age were in accord with the predictions of vulnerability to schizophrenia which were made at one month of age on the basis of abnormally irregular neurological development. Peter, who had the most deviate development at one month of age, continued to show the most severely disorganized development while living in a very pathological early environment. He had the longest and most profound lags and irregularities and scatter in all areas of development: motor, visual-motor, language, and social. At nine years of age he continued to show the most severe impairment and disorganization and was independently diagnosed as a childhood schizophrenic.

The two children who had less deviate development at one month of age continued to show abnormalities, but to a lesser degree than Peter. Frank showed more precocity, irritability, overreactivity, and social responsiveness in a stimulating and supportive environment; his apathy and hypoactivity gave way to a pattern of increased vigor after the first three months of life. As he grew older, he developed more outlets and mechanisms for coping with his difficulties and at nine years of age he appeared like a moderately well-compensated neurotic child to the psychiatrist.

Conrad grew up in a chaotic and stormy environment with abrupt transfer back and forth between a psychotic mother and foster and institutional placements. He showed greater apathy, lethargy, and hypoactivity than Frank, with fewer islands of precocious functioning. Although his placement experiences were more disrupted, he had less developmental impairment than Peter. At nine years of age he appeared to the independent psychiatrist to be a deprived psychopathic child with schizophrenic features.

All three children were considered by the independent psychologist to have psychiatric pathology which differentiated them from the remaining children. Peter showed the most severe impairment, with retarded, pathologically erratic and deviate functioning. Frank and Conrad had characterological problems which interfered with functioning in all areas; Frank showed paranoid and schizophrenic features with fragile defenses and reality control; Conrad showed mostly psychopathic features with some schizoid emptiness and detachment.

Discussion

Obviously one cannot generalize from this small pilot sample that abnormally irregular development in infancy will be followed by childhood schizophrenia. In order to test the hypothesis with any hope of achieving some statistical significance, several observers would have to make predictions, using these criteria on a sample large enough to compare the outcome of mild to severe deviations in development, under optimal as well as minimal nurturing environmental conditions.

Observations of older infants suggest, however, that the deviate neurological development in the schizophrenic child, Peter, was not a fortuitous finding. Fourteen schizophrenic children who had been examined before two years of age by one of the authors had shown patterns of neurological disorganization which were similar in kind to those shown by Peter.[8] In 1928, when childhood schizophrenia was relatively unknown, Gesell reported similar infants as representing "atypical growth complexes" or "pseudosymptomatic retardation," to indicate that these babies had a primary disturbance of development, which other observers at that time were inclined to attribute to environmental or emotional causes.[14, 15] Of the children described by Bergman and Escalona[3] who later developed childhood schizophrenia, one was reported to have had deviations from the age of 12 weeks which were similar to those seen in Peter.[5]

The many histories of schizophrenic children reported by Bender,[1, 2] Bradley,[4] Kanner,[17] and others indicate that disorganization of early development is a characteristic feature of childhood schizophrenia. We found that in schizophrenic children with I.Q.'s under 70, more than half had major deviations of motor development in infancy in contrast to schizophrenic children with no intellectual impairment and children with "primary" behavior disorders.[9]

To our knowledge, the current study is the first in which predictions were made at one month of age regarding the eventual development of schizophrenia based on the examination of the infants themselves. We may now compare the early development of a child who is known to be schizophrenic at 9½ with comparable data on children whose outcome is known to be less malignant.

There appears to be a spectrum of disorders in early development rather than an all or none division between schizophrenic and non-schizophrenic children. The schizophrenic child showed more severe deviations in infancy than the two children who now have borderline psychopathology. Four of the infants who were normal at one month had transient deviations later. At nine years of age these four children spanned the same range of mild to moderate neurotic disorders as did the children whose development was considered to be normal (See "Wilma," "Vera," "Carol" and "Grace"[6, 13]). A similar spectrum of varying degrees of pathological to normal developmental variations was suggested by Fish's analysis of the developmental histories of 85 disturbed children.[9]

We believe that the child's ultimate personality organization depends upon the interaction between his environment and his unique pattern of assets and impairments. The most severe early impairments are less modifiable; in children with less extreme deviations, experience plays a larger role in the outcome, as in Frank and Conrad. In a more recent study of infants born to schizophrenic mothers, a number of "vulnerable" children with moderate developmental deviations appeared to improve when placed in foster homes where optimal conditions were prescribed, depending on their particular developmental lags.[10]

The pan-disorganization of the schizophrenic child, Peter, did not appear to be a fixed neurological defect, but rather a disorder of the timing and integration of neurological maturation. In adult patients, schizophrenia is viewed as a fundamental disturbance in integrative capacity, reflected on all levels of functioning;[16] in the schizophrenic child, a comparable integrative disturbance may be reflected in measurable irregularities of development in infancy. There is a fluctuating and erratic patterning which distinguishes the course from syndromes of chronic minimal brain damage. The schizophrenic child showed acceleration and precocity as well as retardations, and a fluctuating course over the months and years of early development. The same erratic functioning occurred in the microcosm of the minutes and hours of a single examination, resulting in a profile of successes and failures not readily explained by more usual types of organic impairments. The schizophrenic child may stand erect one instant and then wobble on rubbery legs, may perceive objects, form, and space in the usual way and then suddenly appear disorganized about these relationships. A fluctuating awareness of oneself and the environment, and an erratic and unpredictable ability to function seem to be more disorganizing for the developing personality of the schizophenic child than is a stable neurological defect in functioning of comparable degree.

It is this unusual variability in functioning which leads one to characterize the schizophrenic's performance as "peculiar," and "deviate," rather than the result of any known organic impairment. We suggest that this fluctuating level of integration is itself part of a basic integrative disorder affecting central nervous system functioning in schizophrenia, and that it is related to the fluctuating states of attention and consciousness which can be observed in infancy and childhood,[8, 11] as well as in some adult patients.

ACKNOWLEDGMENT

The authors wish to thank Else Loewenthal, Research Psychologist, for her help in rendering the statistical analysis.

REFERENCES

1. Bender, L.: Childhood schizophrenia: clinical study of 100 schizophrenic children. Amer. J. Orthopsychiat. 17:40-56, 1947.
2. Bender, L., and Freedman, A.: A study of the first three years in the maturation of schizophrenic children. J. Child Behav. 1:245-272, 1952.
3. Bergman, P., and Escalona, S.: Unusual sensitivities in very young children. *In* The Psychoanalytic Study of the Child, 3/4:333-352. New York, International Universities Press, 1949.
4. Bradley, C.: Schizophrenia in Childhood. New York, The Macmillan Company, 1941.
5. Escalona, S.: Paper presented at the Meeting of the American Psychoanalytic Association of New York, 1951.
6. Fish, B.: The detection of schizophrenia in infancy. J. Nerv. Ment. Dis. 125:1-24, 1957.
7. ——: Longitudinal observations of biological deviations in a schizophrenic infant. Amer J. Psychiat. 116:25-31, 1959.
8. ——: Involvement of the central nervous system in infants with schizophrenia. A.M.A. Arch. Neurol. 2:115-121, 1960.
9. ——: The study of motor development in infancy and its relationship to psychological functioning. Amer. J. Psychiat. 117:1113-1118, 1961.
10. ——: The maturation of arousal and attention in the first months of life: a study of variations in ego development. J. Amer. Acad. Child Psychiat. 2:253-270, 1963.
11. Fish, B., and Alpert, M.: Abnormal states of consciousness and muscle tone in infants born to schizophrenic mothers. Amer J. Psychiat. 119:439-445, 1962.
12. Fish, B., and Shapiro, T.: A typology of children's psychiatric disorders:

I: Its application to a controlled evaluation of treatment. J. Amer Acad. Child Psychiat. 4:32-52, 1965.

13. Fish, B., Shapiro, T., Halpern, F., and Wile, R : The prediction of schizophrenia in infancy: III: A ten year follow-up report of neurological and psychological development. Amer. J. Psychiat. 121:768-775, 1965.
14. Gesell, A.: Infancy and Human Growth. New York, The Macmillan Company.
15. ——: Developmental Diagnosis (2nd ed.). New York, Hoeber, 1947.
16. Hoch, P., and Cattell, J.: The diagnosis of pseudoneurotic schizophrenia. Psychiat. Quart. 33:17-43, 1959.
17. Kanner, L.: Conceptions of wholes and parts in early infantile autism. Amer. J. Psychiat. 108:23-26, 1951.

19

THE CONCEPT OF PLASTICITY IN CHILDHOOD SCHIZOPHRENIA

by LAURETTA BENDER, M.D.

IN THE 1949 MEETING of the American Psychopathological Association on "Anxiety," I suggested that in childhood schizophrenia, plasticity is the specific feature of the process disorder arising in all areas of cerebral function subserving behavior.[4]

"An idea fundamental to the study of differentiation is the concept of determination—i.e., the fixation at a definite time in development of the fates of different parts of an embryo. Before the developmental fate of a part of an embryo has been fully fixed and while it is still in a pleuri-potential or plastic state, it is said to be undetermined."[37, p.135] It is this undetermined pleuripotential primitive state of plasticity which causes the maturational lag at an embryological level and characterizes all the primary symptomatology of schizophrenia in childhood.

The celebration of the Centennial of Darwin's *Origin of the Species* in the past four years emphasized the importance of the concept of evolution in our understanding of the human body, including the brain, and of human behavior. Henry W. Brosin,[24] in a paper on "Evolution and Understanding Diseases of the Mind," given at the University of Chicago Centennial *Evolution After Darwin*, delineates many of the mental and behavioral disturbances that may be related to evolution.

However, the significance of evolutionary processes in the development of the human brain, mentality, and behavior as a cause of stress in the child has not received the consideration it deserves. In all maturational lags in the child, primitive plastic phenomena appear to be the characteristic dysfunction of those brain areas most recently acquired in evolution.

The concept of plasticity is based on primitive undetermined and undifferentiated patterning in those areas of brain function most recently acquired and most actively evolving in human evolution. It is the undetermined pleuri-potential plastic state which we postulate as characteristic of those brain functions which are specifically human and the last in the evolutionary development and still evolving.

In the 1949 meeting, I said that the "concept of childhood schizophrenia includes a clinical entity which manifests pathology in all areas of behavior functioning through the central nervous system, including the autonomic or homeostatic control of the body; motor behavior or motility; perceptual patterning in each sensory field; intellectual functioning in learning process, language and thought (symbol formation and fantasy and dream creation) and the emotional social life with development of the personal and interpersonal relationships."[4, p. 132]

Arnold Gesell[31] has described the embryology of behavior as evolving through five areas of interweaving patterns:

1. Patterns in the autonomic or vaso-vegetative areas or homeostasis.
2. Patterns of sleeping and waking and states of consciousness.
3. Patterns of respiration which also anticipate speech, language, and ideation.
4. Patterns of tone in response to global perception, especially of gravity with the evolution and development of the vestibular system, from which perception of time, space, reality and object relationships evolve.
5. Patterns of motor activity arising from the tonic neck-righting responses, and from which cortical dominance patterns may also arise.

Gesell indicates that these functional patterns are the biological basis or embryology of all subsequent behavior.

In the light of Gesell's analysis of behavior of the fetal infant and our own experience with young schizophrenic children, it appears that much of the patterning of the schizophrenic child closely resembles that of the fetus. Consequently, we have concluded that the plasticity we have observed in schizophrenic children is a primitive embryological feature and accounts for lagging, regressive, and even accelerating patterns in maturation.

In childhood schizophrenia there is a marked derangement of homeostatic mechanisms. The schizophrenic infant shows a continual failure in balancing, integrating, or patterning of his primary functions under homeostatic control. As a result, stress and anxiety are experienced.

Sleep disturbances are a common complaint about schizophrenic children. As infants they often do not develop the normal pattern of sleep and waking. Later variable states of consciousness are frequently observed in the sickest children. These often find expression in their dreams.

Respiration is regarded by Gesell as the most crucial of behavior—for integrative as well as regulatory purposes. As the infant matures, respiration is incorporated into expressive behavior, and under the direction of the cerebral cortex it becomes the instrument of speech. Respiration, feeding behavior, and language are closely interwoven in the functional embryology of the individual. Respiratory difficulties are a distressing problem in many schizophrenic children during infancy. In association with homeostatic and allergic disorders, there are numerous respiratory and gastrointestinal dysfunctions. Coeliac syndrome has been reported in schizophrenic children[10, 33, 41] as an immaturity or persistence of poorly patterned tone in the intestinal tract.

Tone evolves in the fetus in response to the ever-present stimuli from gravity directly or mediated through the vestibular system. The mastering and patterning of tone is basic to all other behavior. It is by way of tonic responses that the child reacts to the outside world of reality, as well as to the internal sensations. The muscular tone of the schizophrenic child remains immature, plastic, and fetal, and it is the primary failure in responding to stimuli and relating to objects and in all future relationships.

Gesell describes the tonic neck-righting responses as the basic pattern, embryologically, for all motor and bodily activity. Normally tonic neck-righting responses dominate behavior only through the first weeks of postnatal life, and the whirling response to postural testing ceases at six or seven years. In the schizophrenic child, however, these immature responses are retained often into adulthood and are associated with excessive whirling motility and mannerisms, and preoccupations and fantasies concerning them.

Since plasticity appears to be a specific pattern of behavior in every area of function in the schizophrenic child, there is a continual interplay of opposite potentialities. As we all know, some schizophrenic children are regressed, retarded, inhibited, apathetic, mute, withdrawn, autistic, physically asthenic, puny, sickly, unsocial, unable to relate, concretistic in thinking, poverty-stricken in fantasy; others are the opposite—precocious in development, overactive, with exaggerated intellectual brilliance and creativity in fantasy, abstract in thinking, verbally or graphically productive, with invasive identifications and facile neurotic defenses, and many have various combinations of these traits.

I have frequently emphasized that lack of patterning, fluidity, maturational lags, and plasticity in all these areas of behavioral, homeostatic, motility, perceptual, ideational, and interpersonal functions characterize the primary symptomatology in the child with schizophrenia. The resulting anxiety leads to defense mechanisms which may determine the clinical picture changing under the influence of life experiences and at critical developmental epochs.[4-6, 11]

Fish[28] by examining at one month and following to 5½ years[29] a series of infants in a well baby clinic, found "that it was possible to detect an infant who later became schizophrenic by applying Bender's criteria to a random sample of infants [and that this] provides direct corroboration of her concept that the schizophrenic child is distinguished at an early age from his nonschizophrenic peers by specific biologic signs of disordered maturation. Furthermore, later development illustrated the features predicted by Bender, namely (a) overall plastic patterning of development in all areas; (b) immature homeostasis; (c) early torporous state; (d) molluscuous muscle tone; and (e) immature posture and motor activity."[29, p.22]

Fish and Alpert[30] made a study of the neurological development of infants born to schizophrenic mothers and was able to observe "deviations in the state of consciousness, vestibular function, motility and muscle tonus, as early as the first day of life and continuing into the early months of infancy."

They observed immature vestibular responses to caloric stimulation in two infants by sustained tonic deviations to the side of the slow component rather than the expected nystagmus, and this tended to persist. They called attention to Lorente de No's experimental studies[42] indicating that the rapid component depends upon the functioning of the reticular formation, and it was suggested that "the persistent tonic response in these deviate infants is related to dysfunction in the development of this system."

It is interesting in this connection that Szentagothai[43] speaks of "the inherent plasticity, or better, manifold potential specificity in the different reticular mechanisms," and refers to the work of Anokhen on the plasticity of function in reticular formation.

I have also made follow-up studies on 90 schizophrenic women, over 40 years, from 1913 when the first was admitted to the Henry Phipps Psychiatric Clinic of Johns Hopkins Hospital, through 1929-30 when individual clinical studies were made at the Springfield State Hospital where they had been transferred, to 1955-56 when, with Irene Hitchman, further clinical studies were made on those still available and a case review on the records of all others. There was a particular emphasis on the biological features. It was noted that "the picture through all these years persisted at the level we see in schizophrenic children: poor muscular tone, persistent tonic neck reflex attitudes and activities, preoccupation with body function, excreta, and body surface, and marked dependency needs."[18, p. 341] In one patient, chronic tonic disturbances in the intestines led to obstruction and final death. It was early associated with coeliac syndrome and throughout adulthood with manneristic tics of the throat and mouth.

"A continuity of the schizophrenic life pattern: a striking repetition of the clinical picture including neurophysiological and autonomic disturbances from childhood through to senility was demonstrated."[18]

Since my first publications[2] on childhood schizophrenia, the characteristic disturbance in patterned motor behavior or motility in schizophrenic children has been described. The motor development is uneven; the child is insecure and anxious in gaining new motor habits independent of the mother. Early or primitive reflex patterned activities may be retained throughout as a mode of play or expression of anxiety. Thus choreo-athetotic hand movements typical of the first months of infancy are retained and are often used compulsively or manneristically. Tonic-neck-reflex whirling, appropriate in children under seven, is retained and is almost a specific phenomenon in schizophrenic children, often continuing into adulthood. Gesell has stated that tonic-neck-reflex attitudes in the fetal infant are the beginning of all motility and motor behavior. This postural response in schizophrenics, first described by Hoff and Schilder,[38] is thus another indication of retained primitive patterning in the schizophrenic. Rotating and whirling motor play in children make up a large part of their activity. It finds expression in their dreams and fantasies and is the basis of many psychological problems such as fears of or preoccupations with losing their limbs, of expanding and contracting body boundaries, of preoccupation with flying into space, and with concern about their relationship to the outer world or the world of reality, to the nonself, and finally with their own identity in time and space.

In an attempt to quantify a test of theory and diagnostic indications of childhood schizophrenia, Helme and I[16] found that:

1. Childhood schizophrenia is characterized by a disturbance in the regulation of maturation processes at both the biological and psychological levels.

2. The dominance of tonic-neck-reflex motility is a particularly striking example of the maturational lag and unevenness in development.

3. The schizophrenic child has basic difficulties in boundaries and segregation in physiological and psychological subsystems.

4. The disorder is characterized by its pervading to some extent virtually all major areas of functioning.

5. The concept of plasticity characterizes the behavior and organization of the schizophrenic child in virtually all these areas.

The schizophrenic child also shows poor tissue and muscle tone, bodily dependence, clinging or motor compliance, and cohesiveness, tending to use the adult's body and motility in order, it would seem, to help establish his own body boundaries and center of gravity. This also points to the fluidity or plasticity in the perception of motility, boundaries, and stability. The schizophrenic child in a symbiotic relationship offers the more extreme example of these features, but they can also be demonstrated in autistic schizophrenic children.

Perceptual experiences are derived from the fetal reaction to gravity by responses in tone, at first global.[31] The vestibular system, the most ancient mechanism for perceptual motor responses,[26] evolves. In this lies the beginning of awareness of the self as separate from the non-self, of all object relationships, and of awareness of reality. In it lies also the mechanism for the patterning of tone in muscles.

In schizophrenic children, where the perceptual motor patterns remain undifferentiated, there is retained a primitive plastic pattern of tone in all muscles and tissues. This contributes also to the autonomic nervous disorders in the vascular bed, intestinal tract, etc., and to the nongratifying motility experiences leading to dependency, symbiosis, etc. Also, the infant fails to respond to changes in position when lifted or cuddled by the mother, nor does it learn to anticipate the approach of the mother by toning its muscles. Thus, object relationship is impaired, resulting in withdrawal and autism. Defects in awareness of reality and in establishing boundaries develop and contribute to body image disturbances.

A similar pattern of disturbance can be demonstrated in all perceptual areas. The Visual Motor Gestalt Test[1] is a good vehicle for demonstrating maturational disturbances and primitive plastic features in perceptual motor behavior. The schizophrenic child copying the gestalt figures shows many of the same problems which are seen in his motility. There is a tendency to use old primitive responses interlocked with the more developed capacities expected from the maturational level of the child. There is therefore an excessive use of vortical movement. Figures are also rotated to a varying degree, but often to the horizontal plane which is most primitive. Boundaries are lost so that figures influence each other in both form and position. Thus the total test makes a composition full of plastic movement. Background-foreground relationships tend to be unclear and variable.

When the visual motor gestalt function has been traced from early childhood to adulthood in schizophrenic individuals with the use of the Gestalt Test, and the body image has been similarly followed with human figure drawings, it has been found "that one sees the retention of all the infantile features in visual motor perception, gestalt formation, body image, self-perception, interpersonal relations, and reality testing and the basic characteristics—i.e., the lag in maturation and plasticity in patterning are retained throughout life and interfere with the normal development."[12]

The body image, which is the consummate perceptual experience, is distorted in many ways in the schizophrenic child: by failure in maturation, by regression, and by exaggerated preoccupations. The drawing of the human figure projects the body image and reveals the many problems of the schizophrenic from completely undifferentiated global concepts to highly articulate expressions of concern with identity, internal bodily sensations, schizophrenic whirling motility, infantile dependency needs, the unreality of the outer world, and difficulty in establishing boundaries—thus accounting for the enormously creative plastic and primitive features seen in schizophrenic art.[5]

Atypical language development, as Kanner[39] has also emphasized, is a prominent manifestation of childhood schizophrenia. One sees retardation, mutism, egocentric speech, and even precocity, as well as many aphasia-like disorders and misuse of language, based on the plastic state of the integrative function. There are especially many primitive or infantile language patterns that are retained or are readily accessible to the schizophrenic. Regression in schizophrenic language is common. Schizophrenic children are prone to left-right disorientation. Reading lags occur. It has been found, however, that the tutoring for reading lags in schizophrenic children is especially rewarding and also proves to be therapeutic for the schizophrenic symptomatology.[32]

A facile reading ability with relative high scores in verbal intelligence also occurs in schizophrenic children as another expression of plasticity.[25]

Since disturbances in learning, especially of language skills, is another type of maturational lag, this too has been interpreted[8, 12] as a plastic immaturity in those cerebral areas most recently evolved in the human, namely the cortical language areas.

There is an expanding area of knowledge concerning the evolution of the areas of the brain subserving language. It becomes increasingly evident that the nondominant, as well as the dominant, sides of the brain involve various speech functions.[40] It is argued that the "astonishing plasticity" of these rapidly evolving areas of the brain (temporoparietal cortex) account for the capacity to give rise to new functions in symbolic language.[27]

However, children with language disabilities and with schizophrenia have variable patterns of maturation in these functions. They are often not clearly patterned or patterns are not clearly determined or differentiated and are in consequence abstract, plastic, and pleuri-potential, resulting in stress for some children with developmental lags, but perhaps also allowing for potentially higher levels of maturation and creativity in others.

It is impossible in this paper to deal with all the problems of psychopathology in the development of the personality and in interpersonal relations in schizophrenia. These are the outgrowth of the primitive plastic maturation disorders in homeostasis, motility, perception, language, and intelligence with the resulting anxiety, the defense mechanisms, and the totality of life experiences. The author has from time to time dealt with them elsewhere.[2-4, 7, 12]

Through the years the therapeutic attack on childhood schizophrenia has attempted to overcome the plasticity in the autonomic nervous system and the resulting secondary symptomatology. Thus the following have been tried: metrazol, electric convulsions, subshock insulin, and psychopharmaceutical agents such as the antihistamines (Benadryl), amphetamines (Benzedrine), anticonvulsants, muscle tone stimulants (Tolserol), the meprobamates, phenothiazines, reserpines, and antidepressants.

The goal of these therapeutic efforts has been to modify the secondary symptomatology associated with retarded, regressed, and disturbed behavior of schizophrenic children. There has also been a conviction that the treatment goal was directed at some basic disorders associated with early schizophrenia. It was thought that the treatment not infrequently did succeed in nudging the lagging maturation, thus enabling the child to carry on with a more normal development. It was believed that plastic embryonic patterning, characteristically schizophrenic, in visceral vegetative functions should be overcome and that increased tone and motor patterns should be stimulated in the unstriped muscles of the vascular bed and of the respiratory and gastrointestinal systems as well as in the striped muscles of the motor systems. It was also recognized that perceptual sensitivity of the schizophrenic infant[23] and the perceptual distortions of the older child needed correction. There were, of course, other problems: anxiety and stereotyped rhythmic and manneristic motility; mutism and inadequate or inappropriate language; psychosomatic or allergic illnesses; negativistic, ambivalent, or erratic attitudes and behavior; deep-seated anxiety; and autistic, symbiotic, pseudoneurotic, pseudopsychopathic, or psychotic defenses.

Psychotherapy, which attempted to activate neurotic symptoms and strengthen body image and ego boundaries and the separation from the outer world of reality, was employed by Gurevitz[34, 35] with considerable success.[17] A 25-year follow-up on Metrazol convulsive treatment elucidated the value of this therapy in assisting in organization of defenses and remissions in some cases.[13] Several studies on the effect of electric convulsive treatment have demonstrated that a personality reorganization occurs during and after the course of treatment.[3, 14, 36]

Many of the medical treatment measures, together with new social and educational experiences for the children in the hospital, with guidance and therapy for the parents, have been sufficiently successful to justify a search for more potent and specific agents.

There is a theoretical interest in serotonin as possibly related to schizophrenia, and LSD-25 and some of its derivatives are serotonin inhibitors. Also, LSD-25 and derivatives are stimulants to the autonomic nervous system with specific effects on the tone of the vascular bed. They also have specific effects on perception, causing perceptual experiences to be more vivid. Their psychotomimetic properties might possibly break through autistic defenses. With these features in mind an effort has been made to use some of these drugs (LSD-25, UML-491 (Sansert) and psilocybin—Sandoz) in a therapeutic program.

We have made rather extensive clinical and biochemical studies in this program, on a range of clinical disturbances in 50 schizophrenic children.[19-22] Our conclusions have been that these d-lysergic acid derivates appeared to be effective as central and autonomic nervous system stimulants and as serotonin antagonists. They appeared to have some effect on the tone of the vascular system and on the organizing of perceptual experiences and the level of the mood. These changes proved to be chronic with the continuous administration of the drug and had a favorable influence on the clinical course.

Specific studies on the autonomic nervous system were made with Gloria Faretra.[21] Thirty boys (17 schizophrenic) 9 to 12 years of age received injections of saline, adrenalin, and pilocarpine before receiving medication with LSD-25, UML-491, or psilocybin and after 2 to 4 and 6 to 8 weeks of medication. Suitable clinical and psychological studies and blood pressure, pulse, and respiration were noted with each injection (Funkenstein test). The findings showed a considerable variability in the vital functions with an increasing potentiation toward normal findings. These recordings suggest evidence of plasticity in the patterning of these autonomic functions in the children, which tends to be corrected by the d-lysergic acid medication.

Conclusion

It is postulated that evolutionary processes in development of the human brain, mentality, and behavior may represent causes for stress in the child in the process of maturation.

Undetermined pleuripotential plastic states appear to be characteristic of those brain functions specifically human and last in evolutionary development, and still evolving.

Clinical experience has shown that in all maturational lags in children, primitive plastic phenomena of an embryonic nature is the characteristic dysfunction.

Childhood schizophrenia is such a maturational lag caused by an inherited factor, with a pattern of behavioral disturbance in all areas of central nervous system functions, characteristically plastic at an embryonic level.

This explains the common underlying pattern of disturbance in schizophrenia, in the visceral or autonomic functions, in perception, mentation, language, in motor activity and emotional-social behavior. It also may make understandable the great variety of clinical pictures and symptomatology which are presented by schizophrenic children.

It accounts for the response to physiological and pharmacological therapies which have aimed at reducing the plastic patterning in homeostasis, in the tone of the vascular bed of viscera and in the motor system, in perception and the affective and social behavior.

It explains the schizophrenic tendency for regressions, remissions, and even accelerated, precocious, and creative capacities and the reverberating anxiety which is at the core of the schizophrenic experience.

REFERENCES

1. BENDER, L.: The Visual Motor Gestalt Test and Its Clinical Use. New York, American Orthopsychiatric Association, 1937.
2. ——: Childhood schizophrenia: A clinical study of one hundred schizophrenic children. Amer. J. Orthopsychiat. 17:40-56, 1947.
3. ——: One hundred cases of childhood schizophrenia treated with electric shock. Trans. Amer. Neurol. Ass. 72:165-169, 1947.
4. ——: Anxiety in disturbed children. *In* Anxiety (eds. P.H. Hoch and J. Zubin). New York, Grune and Stratton, 1950, pp. 119-139.
5. ——: Child Psychiatric Techniques. Springfield, Ill. Charles C Thomas, 1952.
6. ——: Childhood schizophrenia. Psychiat. Quart. 27:663-681, 1953.
7. ——: The development of a schizophrenic child treated with electric convulsions at three years of age. *In* Emotional Problems of Early Childhood (ed. G. Caplan). New York, Basic Books, 1955, pp. 407-431.
8. ——: Problems in conceptualization and communication in children with developmental alexia. *In* Psychopathology of Communication (eds. P. H. Hoch and J. Zubin). New York, Grune and Stratton, 1958, pp. 155-176.
9. ——: The concept of pseudopsychopathic schizophrenia in adolescence. Amer. J. Orthopsychiat. 29:491-512, 1959.
10. ——: Coeliac syndrome in schizophrenia. Letter to Psychiat. Quart. 35:586, 1961.
11. ——: The brain and child behavior. Arch. Gen Psychiat. 4:531-547, 1961.
12. ——: Origin and evolution of the gestalt function, the body image and delusional thoughts in schizophrenia. Recent Advances Biol. Psychiat. 5:38-62, 1963.
13. ——: A twenty-five year view of therapeutic results. *In* Evaluation of Psychiatric Treatment (eds. P. H. Hoch and J. Zubin). New York, Grune & Stratton, 1964, pp. 129-142.
14. —— AND KEELER, R. W.: The body image of schizophrenic children following electroshock therapy. Amer. J. Orthopsychiat. 22:335-355, 1952.
15. —— AND FREEDMAN, A. M.: A study in the first three years in the maturation of schizophrenic children. Quart. J. Child Behav. 4:245-272, 1952.
16. —— AND HELME, W.: A quantitative test of theory and diagnostic indicators of childhood schizophrenia. Arch. Neurol. Psychiat. 70:413, 1953.
17. —— AND GUREVITZ, S.: The results of psychotherapy with young schizophrenic children. Amer. J. Orthopsychiat. 25:162-170, 1955.
18. —— AND HITCHMAN, I.: A longitudinal study of ninety schizophrenic women. J. Nerv. Ment. Dis. 124:337, 1956.
19. ——, COBRINIK, L. FARETRA, G., AND SANKAR, D. V. S.: Treatment of childhood schizophrenia with LSD and UML. Internat. Conf. on Biol. Psychiat. (Sakel Foundation), 1962 (in press).
20. ——, GOLDSCHMIDT, L., AND SANKAR, D. V. S.: Treatment of autistic schizophrenic children with LSD-25 and UML-491. Recent Advances Biol. Psychiat. 4:170-177, 1962 .
21. —— AND FARETRA, G.: Autonomic nervous system responses in hospitalized children treated with LSD and similar drugs. Recent Advances Biol. Psychiat. 7:1-8, 1964.

22. ——, Faretra, G., and Cobrinik, L.: LSD and UML in the treatment of hospitalized disturbed children. Recent Advances Biol. Psychiat. 5:84-92, 1963.
23. Bergman, P., and Escalona, S.: Unusual sensitivities in very young children. Psychoanal. Stud. Child 3/4: 333-352, 1948.
24. Brosin, H. W.: Evolution and understanding diseases of the mind. *In* The Evolution of Man: Mind, Culture and Society (ed. S. Tax). Chicago, University of Chicago Press, 1960, Vol. II, pp. 373-422.
25. Cobrinik, L.: Precocious reading in schizophrenic children in relation to concepts of plasticity. Read at the 1963 meeting of the American Orthopsychiatric Association, Washington, D.C., March 8, 1963 (in press).
26. Coghill, G. E.: The biologic basis of conflict. Psychoanal. Rev. 20:1-4, 1933.
27. Dobzhansky, T.: Mankind Evolving. New Haven, Conn. Yale University Press, 1962.
28. Fish, B.: The detection of schizophrenia in infancy. J. Nerv. Ment. Dis. 125:1, 1957.
29. ——: Longitudinal observations of biological deviations in a schizophrenic infant. Amer. J. Psychiat. 116:25, 1959.
30. ——: and Alpert, M.: Patterns of neurological development in infants born to schizophrenic mothers. Recent Advances Biol. Psychiat. 5, 1963.
31. Gesell, A.: The Embryology of Behavior—the Beginning of the Human Mind. New York, Harper Bros., 1945.
32. Goldberg, I.: Tutoring for reading disability as a therapeutic method in childhood schizophrenia. Quart. J. Child. Behav. 4:273-280, 1952.
33. Graff, H., and Handford, A.: Coeliac syndrome in the case histories of five schizophrenics. Psychiat. Quart. 35:306-313, 1961.
34. Gurevitz, S.: Treatment of a schizophrenic child through activation of neurotic symptoms. Quart. J. Child. Behav. 4:139-155, 1952.
35. ——: The total point of view in psychotherapy of schizophrenic children. Psychoanal. 1:62-73, 1952.
36. —— and Helme, W. H.: Effects of electroconvulsive therapy on personality and intellectual functioning of the schizophrenic child. J. Nerv. Ment. Dis. 120:213-226, 1954.
37. Hamilton, W. J., Boyd, J. D., and Mossman, H. W.: Human Embryology. Baltimore, Williams and Wilkins Co., 1962.
38. Hoff, H., and Schilder, P.: Die Lagerreflexe des Menschen. Vienna, Julius Springer, 1927.
39. Kanner, L.: Early infantile autism. Amer. J. Orthopsychiat. 19:416-426, 1949.
40. Mountcastle, V. B.: Interhemispheric Relations and Cerebral Dominance. Baltimore, Johns Hopkins Hospital Press, 1962.
41. Nichtern, S.: Immaturities in the intestinal functions in atypical development. Read at the meeting of the American Orthopsychiatric Association, Washington, D.C., Nov. 10, 1963.
42. Lorente de No, R.: Vestibular-ocular reflex arch. Arch. Neurol. Psychiat. 30:245, 1933.
43. Szentagothai, J.: Specificity and plasticity of neural structures and function. *In* Brain and Behavior (ed. M. A. Brazier). Washington, D.C.: American Institute of Biological Sciences, 1961, p. 49.

20

OFFICE TREATMENT OF THE CHRONIC SCHIZOPHRENIC PATIENT

by ALEXANDRA ADLER, M.D.*

IN RECENT YEARS, many new observations have been made about the course and outcome of schizophrenia and we have been able to follow up more cases on an ambulatory basis for a prolonged period. Although we still do not know either the cause or prevention of schizophrenia—except perhaps for some of the factors involved—we can specify procedures that might bring about improvement in the patient, as well as those that might lead to a deterioration of his condition.

The following statements relate to a group of severely affected, chronic paranoid, and paranoid-catatonic patients, under my observation from eight to eleven years. Since the management of the "borderline" and the "pseudoneurotic" schizophrenic is different and more closely related to the treatment of the neurotic patient or one with personality disorder, it will not be discussed here.

All of these cases had to be institutionalized once or twice in the past and, with one exception, initially received insulin and/or electroshock treatment. Since psychotropic drugs became available, these have been used constantly, since the patients, on account of the underlying chronic psychosis, otherwise would relapse into manifestly psychotic behavior, with recurrence or intensification of delusions and hallucinations.

There is undoubtedly not one schizophrenic patient like another, as also indicated, for instance, by the fact that the required dosage of the psychotropic drugs varies greatly from patient to patient. In this group, the daily dosage of Thorazine varies from 75 mg. to 1500 mg. All the patients came for office visits from one to three times weekly, depending on their condition and reactions.

Factors which have been found to contribute to gradual improvement of the patient's condition are:

*New York University School of Medicine, New York, N.Y.

1. Continued drug therapy, which must be adjusted and modified according to the changing symptomatology.

2. A family or, at least, a family substitute interested in and tolerant of the patient's psychotic manifestations.

3. Opportunity for continued socialization, in particular through work or, if this is not possible, participation in other group activities.

Before further discussing these three points, a few guiding principles should be pointed out upon which the interaction between psychiatrist and patient may be based. In agreement with some other investigators, it was observed that as long as the patient needs drug treatment to keep him from relapsing into delusions and hallucinations, any attempt at intensive exploration and prolonged interpretation of the symbolism exhibited through his psychotic symptoms has invariably led to a deterioration of the patient's condition. Such relapses were temporary only, probably because attempts at deeper exploration were given up as soon as undesirable effects were noted. Schizophrenic patients have an inclination toward mysticism and are likely to replace one form of mysticism by another. This is the kind of abuse they can be expected to make of an interpretation of their psychodynamics on a symbolic level. A different approach can be taken with the less seriously affected—for instance, the borderline or pseudoneurotic cases—at least as long as they remain within their diagnostic category and do not progress. The severely psychotic, when destroying objects or committing other acts of physical violence, are more inclined to understand the implications to themselves and to society when the psychiatrist, for instance, asks them, lightly, "Isn't this a crazy way to do things?" rather than when attempts are made to explain this acting-out on the ground of sexual or other symbols.

This does not imply that it is not helpful if the psychiatrist himself understands as much as possible of the patient's motivations and pattern. In particular, one has to reckon constantly with the paranoid patient's ever-present fear of anything that is stronger than himself. Therefore, even more than with other patients, giving the impression of trying to force the schizophrenic into some type of action has to be avoided as much as possible. They quickly resent and then resist force. On the other hand, sometimes most exasperating and persistent symptoms can be made to disappear by outward neglect of them, difficult as this may be for the therapist. Some schizophrenic patients, for instance, keep trying to find out how much they can get away with by giving in to their aggressive impulses in protected situations, such as by striking at parents and apologizing afterwards to the therapist. This type of acting-out, which might have been discussed at length previously, and in vain, can sometimes be stopped when the therapist suggests not to report these incidents any more, since such discussions only delay work on more important issues. In such instances the negativism of the patient is also taken into consideration. This is an approach which differs from the one that would be taken in the treatment of less severe cases. Under all conditions the patient has to feel that the psychiatrist is on his side—which is as it should be. The patient will not turn against the psychiatrist as long as he feels that he is one of the few people on whom he can count for help.

Once the paranoid patient accepts drug treatment, a most important step has been achieved. Some patients are so suspicious of anything stronger than themselves that they become terrified when they discover the power which the drugs exert upon them. In one patient, it took nine years (during which rehospitalization had been necessary because of grave paranoid-hallucinatory episodes) until the patient finally gained enough confidence to accept Thorazine and Trilafon in massive dosages and on an ambulatory basis during another relapse. He finally realized that society did not go along with his paranoid ideas and aggressive behaviour, and that cooperation with his psychiatrist served him best. Patients such as this one are the most difficult to treat on an out-patient basis. Here too, however, provided constant supervision is possible, the course may slowly lead to improvement. After a while, the patient learns to consider the psychotropic drugs as his friends, and one can achieve a great deal of cooperation from him.

Some patients learn to know, by themselves, when they need an increase or decrease of the dosage. One paranoid-catatonic patient, for instance, described how her thoughts had been "chasing" her and how she had been unable to control them; she had only "glimpses of the truth, for seconds," as she expressed it, before she was placed on drug therapy. Now, she thinks, she can work toward her "real personality." She now realizes that at times when her way of thinking again gets out of control, she needs an increase of her medication, whereas when a tired, depressed feeling overcomes her which interferes with her work in a library, a slight diminution of the dosage is indicated.

Another paranoid-schizophrenic patient had been in a hallucinatory state at the beginning of her illness and had had to be institutionalized twice. She is now working in a laboratory and takes a small maintenance dosage of Thorazine and Stelazine. Formerly, she had suffered from frequent relapses during which she had pronounced feelings of depersonalization and compulsions to utter obscene words in public. Now she feels reassured, knowing that they will yield to a temporary increase in the dosage of her drugs, whereas formerly these symptoms had prevented her from continuing her work.

In the severely psychotic, out-patient treatment hardly ever succeeds unless the psychiatrist has an opportunity to collaborate with the family or a family-substitute who provides him with objective information on the patient. It is well known how difficult it is to find a family-substitute. It would help greatly if residences were available, with trained personnel in charge, where chronic schizophrenic patients could live while under psychiatric treatment. To my knowledge, there is in the whole city of New York only one nonprofit residential set-up, accommodating about ten patients. If no appropriate living arrangement can be found, and the family declines to cooperate, the patient soon feels abandoned, a state of mind which often leads to progressive deterioration, intensification of the delusional system, and eventual acting-out.

Deterioration habitually takes place in the schizophrenic patient if he is allowed to isolate himself. Appropriate steps are therefore taken, particularly in institutions, to counteract, through group activities, the patient's tendency to seek protection through isolation. With the ambulatory patient, the same approach should be used. Particular effort has to be made to encourage activities in fields in which the patient is successful. It is well known, for instance, that some schizophrenics are quite efficient, even sometimes brilliant, in their field of work and show their psychotic trends mainly in their interpersonal relations with their families, their sexual partner, and acquaintances. The outcome of psychiatric treatment is more promising when the patient is successful in some field of human endeavor than when he has failed in all his attempts at adjustment. This also holds true of psychiatric patients in other diagnostic categories.

Whenever the schizophrenic patient is gradually guided toward a gainful occupation, a protected environment is mandatory during the first years of work. This often is difficult to find and is usually best arranged for if the patient can obtain work with a relative or a friend of the family. The patient, in constant need of protection, will often reject the efforts of organizations that provide employment for the so-called "emotionally handicapped," unless he succeeds in establishing a relationship of trust with someone in the organization. In many cases, unfortunately, such a relationship is absent, and the patient sooner or later gives up his job, indulging in a critical attitude toward the work offered him and toward his emotionally disturbed coworkers. The perspicacity of the schizophrenic in spotting other people's drawbacks is often amazing, and is evidently the result of their training in being watchful of their environment.

The severely psychotic patient also has his difficulties as a member of organized group therapy. He is inclined to be overcritical in a group in which all patients are as severely affected as he is. Consequently, he often loses interest in such a group and quits. On the other hand, with the less severely affected, he quickly notices that he is "the worst of the group," often becomes hopeless, and feels discouraged from trying to improve his ways. Of great help sometimes are rural so-called "half-way" houses, of which a few exist in this country. There patients may go voluntarily, for shorter or longer periods. Such a change of environment may help to stop a paranoid system from developing further and is particularly indicated if the patient declines to take medication.

All the efforts here referred to are becoming better organized, in particular since Cameron in Montreal and Bierer in London started opening day and night hospitals for the patient in need of a more sheltered life. The various social clubs for the emotionally disturbed, which offer organized activity for a few hours, usually on a once-a-week basis and supervised by trained personnel, have also proved to be helpful. As these increase in number, some schizophrenic patients go to a different social club every day of the week in their often desperate attempt to break through the wall which they feel separates them from human contact.

None of these organizations by themselves present a solution of the patient's problems. The chronic schizophrenic will experience failure repeatedly and success occasionally in most of them, and he will continue to need individual guidance on a long-term basis until he is able to function at the maximum of his potentialities.

As mentioned before, a lack of family, or family-substitute, makes the ambulatory treatment of the schizophrenic patient most difficult and unpromising. Sooner or later, the patient's fears usually become overwhelming, even if psychotropic drugs are administered. His unrealistic thinking tends to remain in the foreground. He often complains that drug treatment makes him more unhappy than he was before. Previously he had felt important and powerful, but now, under drug treatment, he may insist that he is just a nobody, that he had been stupid in his delusions. After a while, such patients may decline to continue to take drugs and seek for a way back to their world of phantasies, with consequent failure in all aspects of their life.

Until we have better, more specific ways of treating the severe forms of schizophrenia, our endeavors will have to remain limited, often aimed only at alleviating the patient's suffering and controlling damaging activities. The course of treatment will be wrought with exasperations and failures and may entail danger to the life and health of the patient and his family, and at times of his therapist. As in other diseases, however, a patient who has been restored to the world of the living after a hazardous siege of his illness is a rewarding experience for everyone involved.

21

SCHIZOPHRENIA AMONG ADOLESCENT STREET GANG LEADERS*

by HOWARD DAVIDMAN, M.D.,† and EDWARD PREBLE, A.B.‡

JUVENILE DELINQUENCY RESEARCH during the past 30 years has been conducted under two distinct theoretical disciplines: sociology and psychology. Sociologists investigate the social conditions that promote delinquent behavior in the individual; psychologists investigate the psychic phenomena in the individual which predispose him toward delinquency as an attempted solution of his emotional problems.

The early sociological studies of Shaw and McKay,[1] and Sutherland[2] included accounts of the individual processes involved in delinquent behavior, but argued that these processes were the same as those operating in nondelinquent individuals. The delinquent behavior of the individual was seen by them as a normal adaptation to the conditions and cultural traditions of urban slum areas. Healy and Bronner,[3] early representatives of the psychological approach to delinquency, paid attention to the social conditions related to delinquent behavior, but explained the individual's delinquent behavior as an abnormal attempt to solve the frustrations which derive from a given family and social context. The main difference between these early sociological and psychological approaches was that the sociologist viewed the individual as the constant factor, and the psychologist viewed the social context as the constant factor. In other words, the sociologist considered society to be the patient and the psychologist identified the individual as the patient—an understandable professional bias in both bases.

---

*This investigation was supported in part by Public Health Service Grant #1-R11-MH 728-A-1, from the National Institute of Mental Health.

†Associate Professor of Psychiatry, The New York School of Psychiatry, New York, N.Y.

‡Associate Professor of Anthropology, The New York School of Psychiatry, New York, N.Y.

With a few notable exceptions, the interaction between social and individual factors has received little serious attention by students of delinquency. Albert Cohen,[4] a sociology student of Sutherland, has proposed that the "delinquent subculture" provides for the delinquent a cultural solution to the psychological stresses suffered by a working-class boy who has integrated middle-class values and goals, but who is socially restricted to lower-class achievements. On the other side, Fritz Redl,[5] for example, has made a serious effort to study and treat the "genuine delinquent" within the group psychological context of his effective social environment.

The recent, influential sociological study of Cloward and Ohlin[6] reasserts the sociological determinism of the early sociological work in delinquency, invoking a revised version of Durkheim's theory of *anomie*.[7] Their conclusion is that delinquency "is not, in the final analysis, a property of individuals or even of subcultures; it is a property of the social systems in which individuals and groups are enmeshed." Cloward and Ohlin recognize "problems of adjustment" within the delinquent, but assert that these problems "are engendered by acts of social conformity performed under adverse circumstances."

Walter Miller,[8] an anthropologist, goes even further than Shaw, McKay, and Sutherland in imputing a normal, healthy psychological life to the delinquent. He states that members of street-corner gangs "are not psychopaths, nor physically or mentally defective; in fact, since the corner group supports and enforces a vigorous set of standards, it tends to recruit from the most 'able' members of the community."

The polemic between sociologists and psychologists regarding the presence or absence of pathology within the street delinquent is still a basic one today, in spite of the verbal efforts of representatives from both disciplines toward theoretical convergence. The state of this polemic has important consequences for practical measures instituted in the interest of delinquency prevention, control, and treatment. At the present time, the tide seems to be favoring the sociologists—a consequence, perhaps, of the somewhat justified disappointment with programs of action based on the psychological approach to delinquency.

It is the opinion of the authors of this paper that the reaction against the psychological approach to delinquency has gone too far and has approached the early sociological view that the street delinquent exhibits a psychologically healthy adaptation to his social environment. Our study, over a 7-year period, of the members of high status, fighting street gangs in New York City reveals a high degree of individual pathology among the members, with schizotypal[9] problems frequent, especially among those in leadership positions. Degrees of emotional problems of adaptation are evident in all gang members studied, with the seriousness of the problems being roughly correlated with the extent of delinquent behavior.

Methodology

The data on which the conclusions of this paper are based were secured by the anthropologist over a 7-year period as a "participant observer" in three lower-class urban communities in New York City.

In the initial stage of each inquiry—a period of at least one year—the anthropologist established an identity in a neighborhood both as a research worker interested in delinquency and as a professional person who could sometimes help individuals and families with social and emotional problems. After having established himself as a trusted and friendly participant in the life of the community, he secured the voluntary participation of youths from high status, adolescent street gangs who related their "life histories" in individual interview sessions of one hour in length. A minimum of 25 interviews with each of 20 subjects was recorded for the present study. The interviews were designed to obtain both developmental and environmental material. The relatively unstructured nature of the interview and the close relationship between the interviewer and the subject made it possible to elicit unconscious as well as conscious, learned responses. Dreams and other projective material were obtained.

The psychiatrist did a psychodynamic analysis of each subject based on the verbatim records of the interviews. He also studied the daily field journal records regarding the communities and the gangs which were kept during the 7-year period.

A psychologist, Dr. Murray Bilmes, interviewed the subjects and administered psychological tests (Rorschach, Thematic Apperception Test, Figure Drawings, Wechsler Adult Intelligence Scale). A summary of five typical cases are reported here.

Case #1

This 22-year-old man was, at the age of 15, the leader of the most feared street gang in the community. He achieved this position as a result of the admiration and awe which his intrepid and extravagant rageful outbursts of violence elicited. He fought often, used all types of weapons, and was known as a "sneaky" and "dirty" fighter who could attack viciously without provocation or warning. He was arrested for one homicide and probably committed one more. He began using heroin at the age of 17 and immediately became less violent. Many of his followers began using heroin, as a result of both indoctrination and emulation, and the gang changed from a fighting group to a coterie of drug addicts which soon split up into groups of two and three.

The subject has never worked, having maintained himself and his drug addiction by armed robbery, burglary, selling drugs, and "scheming" on his family, friends, and street associates. In addition to homicide, he has been arrested and served prison sentences for assault, robbery, larceny, and narcotics.

The subject fought throughout his childhood. His father became concerned about his fighting only when he was apprehended by the police. As a child he performed sadistic acts on animals and engaged in petty thefts. He did not get along well with other children. He began to have sexual intercourse at the age of thirteen and associates sexual desire with evil and dirt. In later years he suffered from ejaculatio praecox and retardata.

In recent years he has had feelings of desperation. tantrums, crying fits, and rageful, uncontrollable violent outbursts which frighten him. He expects to die young and fears for his sanity. In his last incarceration, where he was deprived of heroin, he got in so many fights that he was isolated as a security risk. Thereafter he became grandiosely delusional and planned litigious actions against the prison personnel. He regarded himself as infallible and distorted reality in a way that he had never done before. He became convinced that his wild exaggerations were true. At this time he also feared for his sanity and developed pseudohomosexual panic. After release from prison on the last occasion he went through a period of extreme agitation and quickly reverted to heroin. This time, however, the heroin did not allay his fears.

The psychodynamic report as well as the psychological report stress his chronic, pervasive fear and his explosive, unpredictable rage which endanger his life and freedom. Heroin provided a partial way out of this dilemma as well as an escape from sex, work, and normal competition, for all of which he is incapacitated and impotent. He fears for his sanity and worries lest he will kill friends or bystanders as a result of minor annoyances. There is no capacity for empathic resonance with people except in terms of violence, hero doings, vengeance for the sexual misdeeds of others, desire for huge power, and effortlessly gained money.

The family is intact. The mother and father have emotional problems, as do two older siblings, but the family has stuck together and, with the exception of the subject, avoided serious trouble. The family environment does not seem especially unfavorable.

The diagnostic impression separately arrived at by both the psychiatrist and the psychologist is of *paranoid schizophrenia.*

Case #2

This 23-year-old man has been arrested several times for felonious assaults and burglary. He is unstable in mood—at one time very dependent and jovial and at another time utterly resistive and defiant. He is prone to outbursts of rage and violence over small frustrations. The intensity and lack of control over these outbursts frighten him. He does not carry weapons, but does not hesitate to use any weapon that comes to hand in an emergency. An excellent athlete and fighter, he was well liked by the boys with whom he associated as an adolescent and became the "war counselor" for his gang.

He left school at the age of 16, worked for a short period as a mechanic's helper, and has since showed no particular ambition. He has taken money from homosexuals in exchange for their use of him. He drinks heavily and is apt to be violent, especially when drunk.

The picture is of a chronically frightened, aimless, and mistrustful youth, incapacitated for long-range, goal-directed activity. His fear of loss of inner control, which he sees as his craziness and stupidity, is matched by his desire for release of rage through combat. Drinking offers this freedom, as well as an opportunity for freer communication with other people. When sober, he is ashamed, frightened, amazed, and panic-stricken about his criminal acts—an unworthy sinner who needs to be punished.

He has been in a state of excessive fear and rage since early childhood. The mother seems to have been unavailable to him when he was a child. He ran the streets and could make contact with his mother only if he were physically hurt or in serious trouble. His memories are loaded with details of physical injury and fears of illness. He has a persistent, insatiable, dependent craving and no realistic way to obtain the money and success by which he might win his mother's attention.

He is profoundly mistrustful of the sexual aspect of girls, whom he regards as inciters of trouble who induce men into dangerous battle out of their desire for flattery. On the other hand, he is protective and warm to the desexualized and helpless image of the female. He has grave doubts about his virility and has suffered a major loss of conscious heterosexual interest. His masculinity must be proved through violence and aggressive homosexual acts. He has a pervasive feeling of helplessness and a yearning for magical success. His dreams allude to rage, violence, impotence, fears of mutilation, lack of sexual and assertive equipment, overdependence, and despair.

The diagnosis is *schizotypal organization.*

CASE #3

This 23-year-old man was a leader of boys of his street group because of his explosive violence, daring, inventiveness, and superiority at scheming and planning group raids and thefts. His history of violence, cruelty, and incorrigibility goes back to the age of five, with accounts of battle, mayhem, truancy, sexual activities, fire-setting, smoking, and drinking. There is a repeated desire to kill, dating back to the age of five; several attempts to kill animals and people were actually made. Despite opportunities, he has never been able to make a satisfactory human relationship, but could only be defiant, violent, and desperate. At the age of 16 he started using heroin and is a confirmed heroin addict today.

His parents' marriage dissolved when he was six, after the mother threw the father out of the house because of his drinking and extra-marital sex relations. Over the years, the mother has alternately rejected the subject and fostered extreme dependency on her.

The subject has served several prison sentences for assault, burglary, and narcotics. In prison he suffered from a continued feeling of tension and a need to be away from his fellow inmates for fear that they would irritate him and cause him to explode. At his own request, he was isolated in jail, where there were few troublesome stimuli. He fears contact with people because he becomes suspicious and resentful, and eventually convinced that someone has injured him. Later he realizes that the injury he resented was imaginary, and he becomes frightened about his sanity.

He has no friends now nor does he attempt to make any. He lost a girlfriend to a resented rival and feels too hurt to approach any other woman seriously. Once he dares trust someone he becomes inordinately dependent, then hostile to that person, whom he expects to force him to do the things he should despite his huge resistance. He does nothing to sustain a relationship, and people abandon him. He yearns for a normal, conventional, responsible life but can see no realistic paths open that he can follow. Whenever stress or anxiety arises, he uses magical escape routes, notably heroin.

The picture is that of a paranoid schizophrenic defended first by violent street activities, then by heroin, and eventually by self-institutionalization within prison. Psychological tests reveal pervasive mistrust, hatred, shame, and a tendency to isolate himself in situations demanding social interaction. There is no sense of strength or virility, but rather a feeling of vulnerability to attack and injury. The tests corroborate the uncertain integration and unpredictable violent outbursts. He is self-destructive, punitive and is filled with fears and guilt. The psychologist agrees that he is a disturbed person with a poor prognosis who possesses a *schizotypal organization.*

Case #4

This 23-year-old man has never worked; for the last five years he has supported himself by burglaries. He has served jail sentences for assault and burglary. He is a habitual drinker and when drunk is given to blind violence. When younger he was popular with his fellow gang members and had a few close friends. He had prestige in the gang and was a dependable fighter; however, he would assert his independence rather than exercise leadership. He would not follow anyone blindly. Violent when drunk, he is placid when sober. His blind rage is murderous when it is released: On one occasion, when sober, he "blanked out" while assaulting someone uncontrollably.

This subject trained himself to suppress and conceal his feelings, and he often acts in opposition to his emotions. This is particularly true of his pleasurable emotions and his desire for recognition, praise, and achievement. His pride depends on not being a "sucker" and precludes any revelation of his yearning for approval. As a result he keeps rigid control and maintains a flat, disinterested behavior. He expects to be robbed and frustrated if anyone perceives his tender or pleasurable feelings; he is particularly afraid of women in this connection. He ragefully defends a "good" woman's honor and is especially sensitive about any slurs on his mother. His rage is chronic, and constantly threatens to boil over, which frightens him. He welcomes incarceration and gets himself jailed by transparently ineffectual crimes when he is ready to go to jail. There he gains external control and avoids the company of females.

The childhood history shows fear of mutilating injuries, injury being expected as a punishment for his defiant anger at his mother. There is fear of new situations, repeated failures in learning and socialization, and a history of fainting and febrile hallucinosis. The life history data shows lively shame and guilt feelings about his mother and about masculine sexual desires. He sees the area of sexuality in terms of violence, exploitation, and degradation. Both parents were prone to violence in their own behavior.

He feels that he is a hopeless failure and believes that smaller, less-promising looking males will surpass and outdo him. There is a strong need to escape from those with whom he has emotional ties, despite his yearning for magical, dependent fulfillments.

He is diagnosed as a *schizotype.*

Case #5

This 23-year-old man was known as the "best fighter on the block" from the ages of ten to fifteen. During that time he was respected and feared by the other youths over whom he exercised an inconspicious leadership. He fought frequently, with minor provocation, and in a state of rage. He was aware of extreme fear of mutilation and loss of prestige, and hid this fear from others under his anger and "courageous" behavior. He dates the end of his success in life from the onset of heroin use when he was fifteen. He soon was heavily addicted, supporting his habit through daily thievery. He gradually gave up his social relations and adopted the addicted way of life with its concomitant of nonviolence. There developed an increasing feeling of loss of identity, of intellect, of personal controls, and "decent" habits, and an increasing sense of hopelessness. He felt he was slowly dying inside, losing his humanity, and losing "shape." His only dependent gratification now comes from the drug.

As a small child he was considered sickly, without any major disease. He could not sleep with the light out and suffered from nightmares of being crushed by huge animals.

His father was a dapper man and a barroom fighter who was belligerent when drunk. He beat the mother and they were divorced after four years of marriage. As a father he had a friendly interest in his son and served as a figure for identification.

The mother is described as a persistent, pseudoreasonable nagger. She remarried when he was ten. The mother seems to have provoked and encouraged her son to get into trouble so that she could then upbraid him. Their relationship became one in which they could only reach each other through anger. He developed a sullen, passive, hostile withdrawal from her anger and nagging because he knew it frustrated her. If he became openly angry, he felt that she had won the struggle.

He has no capacity for love and trust in the sexual area, having the conventional "street" attitude of the good and faithful woman being asexual. His sexual relationships have been restricted to experiences with female heroin addicts.

This man shows evidence of deficits in welfare emotions and emotional resonance. His inordinate fear and rage and awareness of failure and impotence is partly solved through heroin; nevertheless, there is gradually increasing decompensation. Feelings of depersonalization are present, and there is extreme overdependence. He shows evidence of schizotypal organization which was first masked by violent behavior and later by the effects of heroin.

Discussion

Our long-range study, based on intimate associations in the community with the subjects and their families over a 7-year period, reveals that most of the delinquent street gang members who enjoyed status and prestige on the street have emotional disorders. They are definitely not psychologically healthy members of a delinquent subculture.

Five histories were singled out for this report because they show evidence of schizophrenia. The schizophrenic disorders are of types frequently seen in adolescent offenders. They are easily misdiagnosed at hospital admission or at jail classification as psychopathic or sociopathic in etiology. Dunaif and Hoch[10] have already described these conditions in their paper, "Pseudo-psychopathic Schizophrenia." All the cases cited in their paper happen to have been sexual offenders. Their recognition of a schizophrenia masked by acting-out behavior applies to a much wider variety of offenders seen in jail and among street gang members. In current psychodiagnostic practice in the city prisons, only the most severe and obvious schizophrenias in full decompensation are diagnosed as schizophrenic. The others are termed sociopaths or passive-aggressive personalities. However, on careful examination, these individuals show signs that are consistent with Rado's criteria for schizotypal organization.[9] Rado stresses in his analysis of schizotypal organization the presence of two fundamental forms of damage of the integrative apparatus of the psychodynamic cerebral system. These are (1) an integrative pleasure deficiency, and (2) a proprioceptive disorder. Our cases show the deficiency in pleasure yield, the resultant unbalanced rage and fear, and the deficiency in pleasurably motivated behavior. At various times in their lives they show signs of decompensation under stress. There is evidence, as Dunaif and Hoch found in their cases, of overwhelming guilt.

In addition to guilt feelings, intense feelings of shame, depression, pervasive anxiety, and great uncertainty about ego-identity are observed. Perceptiveness of the emotions of other people is very poor in most cases, with a special inability to respond to the pleasurable emotions of others. There is considerable chaos and fear in sexual attitudes and behavior, a common feature of which is the experience with homosexual prostitution, always in the aggressive role.

Evidence for pathology among the street gang delinquents in this study is also found in the high percentage of converts among them to heroin addiction. Three of the five gang members whose histories are abstracted here are now confirmed heroin addicts. The ratio is approximately the same for another sixty gang members about whom we have direct knowledge.

This observation that high status fighting gang members are especially vulnerable to heroin addiction contradicts a widely held belief. Chein and his associates[11] have maintained that organized street gangs in New York City in the early 1950's were, on the whole, resistant to drug use and even provided help for those who did become addicted. They held that only a minority of addicts belonged to organized gangs and that those who did were likely to have been "anxious, inadequately functioning boys" who were peripheral or rank and file members. Cloward and Ohlin[6] adopted the same thesis in describing adolescent street addicts as "retreatists" and "double failures," who could not qualify for membership in conflict and criminal gangs.

It is our contention that large-scale heroin experimentation by street youths of New York City during the years from about 1955 to 1958 originated among high status conflict gang members and spread to other boys through indocrination and emulation. The pacific effects of heroin on aggressive behavior are well known, and we believe that the observed decrease in street gang conflict during the past five years and the increase in heroin use among street adolescents—an observation that can be verified in conversation with any candid police official, if not by statistical reports—are related phenomena.[12-15]

The evolution of behavior patterns among more than half of our subjects—street gang violence, heroin addiction, decompensation—has been a common one for street gang members of the mid-fifties in New York City, and it contradicts the "healthy street delinquent" thesis of some social scientists that is gaining popularity again today. This is not to deny that social factors may be largely responsible for the individual pathology found in street delinquents and that social conditions constitute a legitimate, even primary, target for delinquency prevention programs.

It is a mistake, however, to maintain that the street delinquent in his individual economy is an emotionally healthy person. One implication of that position is that the so-called delinquent subculture is founded upon psychodynamic imperatives independent of, or in opposition to, those that exist in society at large. Ironically, it was Durkheim, one of the great influences in modern sociology, who argued strongly against such a view. The final version of his sociology stressed the conviction that social constraints, in the form of a "conscience collective," were integrated in the psychic life of every individual in a given society.[7]

Summary

Social scientists who study the problem of street gang delinquency tend to view the individual delinquent as psychologically healthy on the presumption that his behavior represents a positive adaptation to the social conditions and cultural traditions of the urban slum community. Some go further and maintain that the street gang draws its membership from among the healthiest adolescent personalities in the community.

A 7-year psychosocial study of 20 high status street gang members in New York City refutes these contentions. Psychodynamic and sociological analyses of the life history and cultural data reveal a high degree of individual pathology, with the schizophrenic process apparent, especially among those in positions of leadership.

REFERENCES

1. Shaw, C. R., and McKay, H. D.: Juvenile Delinquency and Urban Areas. Chicago, The University of Chicago Press, 1942.
2. Sutherland, E. H.: Principles of Criminology (4th ed.). New York, J. B. Lippincott and Company, 1947.
3. Healy, W., and Bronner, A. F.: New Light on Delinquency and Its Treatment. New Haven, Yale University Press, 1936.
4. Cohen, A. K.: Delinquent Boys. Glencoe, Ill. The Free Press, 1955.
5. Redl, F.: The psychology of gang formation and the treatment of juvenile delinquents. *In* The Psychoanalytic Study of the Child. New York, The International Universities Press, 1945, Vol. I, pp. 367-377.
6. Cloward, R. A., and Ohlin, L. E.: Delinquency and Opportunity. New York, The Free Press, 1960.
7. Durkheim, E.: Suicide: A Study of Sociology (trans. J. A. Spaulding and G. Simpson; ed. G. Simpson). Glencoe, Ill. The Free Press, 1951.
8. Miller, W. B.: Lower class culture as a generating milieu of gang delinquency. J. Social Issues, Vol. 14, 3:5-19, 1958.
9. Rado, S.: Theory and therapy: The theory of schizotypal organization and its application to the treatment of decompensated schizotypal behavior. *In* Psychoanalysis of Behavior: Collected Papers (ed. S. Rado). New York, Grune & Stratton, 1962, Vol. II.
10. Dunaif, S. L., and Hoch, P. H.: Pseudopsychopathic schizophrenia. *In* Psychiatry and the Law (eds. P. H. Hoch and J. Zubin). New York, Grune & Stratton, 1955.
11. Wilner, D. M., Rosenfeld, E., Lee, R. S., Gerard, D. L., and Chein, I.: Heroin use and street gangs. J. Criminal Law, Criminology and Police Science, Vol. 48, No. 4, November-December, 1957.
12. Preble, E.: Heroin addiction among street gang adolescents in New York City. Paper read at the Sixth International Congress, World Federation for Mental Health, Paris, France, 1961. Mimeographed, The New York School of Psychiatry, Wards Island, New York City.
13. ——: Making and maintaining contact with the adolescent street addict. Paper read at the American Orthopsychiatric Association Annual Meeting, Los Angeles, California, 1962. Mimeographed, The New York School of Psychiatry, Wards Island, New York City.
14. ——: The community's role in reinforcing drug use in New York City. Internat. J. Addict. Accepted for publication.
15. ——: Narcotic use, delinquency and social policy. Bull. New York State District Branches. Amer. Psychiat. Ass., Vol. 7, No. 5, January 1965.

Discussion

Recorder: BERNARD HOLLAND, M.D.

Comments on Dr. Piotrowski's Presentation

QUESTION: What are the Rorschach signs that are pathognomonic of schizophrenia?

DR. PIOTROWSKI: Dr. Piotrowski read the following list:

The 12 clinical symptoms used to evaluate the patients' disorganization of thinking are:

1. Vagueness
2. Very poor judgment
3. Irrelevant speech
4. Rambling speech
5. Tangential speech
6. Poverty of thought
7. Confusion
8. Seems out of contact
9. Incoherent speech
10. Incongruity of thought and feeling
11. Implausible or bizarre delusions
12. Bizarre somatic ideation

Each of these 12 symptoms was rated on a five-point scale, (1) not at all, (2) slight, (3) moderate, (4) severe, (5) unratable.

QUESTION: What were the criteria which Dr. Piotrowski used for improvement?

DR. PIOTROWSKI: Patient comfortable with self; patient able to cooperate with others; patient doing useful work.

Comments on Dr. Fish's Presentation

QUESTION: In children, could you differentiate between schizophrenia and organic brain disease?

DR. FISH: Dr. Fish stated that some people consider schizophrenia is due to organic causes; others believe it is functional. The answer depends on what you consider to be the etiology of schizophrenia.

QUESTION: Does the care given by schizophrenic mothers prove to be detrimental to the children: How can you distinguish what is innate in the child and what is damage from a schizophrenic mother?

DR. FISH: Dr. Fish stated that there was always a problem in giving ideal treatment. It is obvious that a schizophrenic mother is not an ideal mother, but the pressure of society prevents removing the child from an unfavorable environment.

QUESTION: What were the criteria for determining organicity?

DR. FISH: Dr. Fish stated that evidence of organicity was failure in Bender-Gestalt tests, reading problems, and visual-motor lag.

COMMENTS ON DR. BENDER'S PRESENTATION

DR. WEINSTEIN: What evidence of organicity exists? Were there language problems, aphasia, crosshandedness?

DR. BENDER: There are language problems and aphasia in girls. Boys had more difficulty in left-right orientation. Before the age of puberty, boys had more difficulty; after puberty, more girls had difficulty.

DR. FRIEDMAN: Was there an innate biological defect that was manifest in various ages throughout life?

DR. BENDER: There were children who seemed to be normal at first, and at any time of life would manifest organicity.

DR. HOLLAND: Beginning at 1½ to 2, was the oppositional stage in these children normal? Would it fail to appear?

DR. BENDER: There are all types of variation. In some the oppositional stage appeared at a normal time. In some it could be absent altogether; it could be early or could be later.

DR. WECHSLER: Would these children have an arrested development or maturational lag?

DR. BENDER: Development of these children was highly variable. The children showed many pictures.

DR. WM. GOLDFARB: Is plasticity itself a sufficient classification? I think we need a more total view of the adaptive behavior of a child. Define organicity so research can be implemented.

DR. BENDER: I do not know how to fit plasticity into Dr. Goldfarb's adaptational viewpoint.

Comments on Dr. Adler's Presentation

Dr. Kris: Dr. Kris emphasized the importance of a steady home environment, a nonstressful environment, chemotherapy; the patient should be seen regularly; medication is important; it is important to know that many of these patients struggle with the same problems as normal people.

Dr. Kammer: Dr. Kammer stated that he had found maintenance doses of electroshock, low dose insulin useful, sometimes group therapy and/or family therapy useful.

Dr. Rümke: Can drugs be delayed, and started after psychotherapy begins?

Dr. Adler: Delaying drugs is something that must be determined by trial and error.

Dr. Rümke: How do you deal with preparation of patient for changing therapist?

Dr. Adler: Problem of changing therapist is always severe, especially for psychotic patients, and requires a great deal of preparation.

Dr. Jerome Frank: Dr. Frank commented that he found that the psychiatrist could help the patient test reality, and stressed work. He said the patient could be seen 15 minutes every two weeks and be sustained in this brief contact.

Comments on Dr. Davidman's Presentation

Dr. Bender: Dr. Bender congratulated Dr. Davidman on his paper and said it was good to know that some of the patients diagnosed in childhood as schizophrenics were able in later years, when they were adults, to confirm their early diagnosis was correct and schizophrenia remained.

Dr. Rümke: Is not some delinquency healthy? Currently and in history, many of the outstanding writers, politicians, and scientists had been rebels.

Dr. Davidman: A rebel with a cause was healthy; a rebel without a cause was unhealthy.

Question: Are aspiration tests given to these people?

Dr. Davidman: Yes. By testing they do have high aspiration.

Dr. Ogden Lindsley: What qualifies these as leaders?

DR. DAVIDMAN: Extreme violence and readiness to fight, which attracts others to them as leaders.

DR. MANDELBAUM: How can schizophrenics cooperate in a gang? Schizophrenics rarely lead; cooperation between schizophrenics is unusual; an organized escape from a mental hospital is uncommon. Is the diagnosis correct? Why is it that schizophrenics cooperate in a gang?

DR. DAVIDMAN: I am quite certain of the diagnosis from interviews and testing. Perhaps the explanation is that paranoid schizophrenics are better organized.

DR. FREYHAN: Dr. Freyhan commented that this paper dealt with an important problem—the relationship between genius, leadership, and rebellion.

DR. KRETCHNES: Dr. Kretchnes commented that genius and leadership come from all types of psychopathology.

Part V: Therapy

22

PHARMACOTHERAPY OF SCHIZOPHRENIA

by H. E. LEHMANN, M.D.*

PHARMACOTHERAPY IS TODAY the treatment of choice for schizophrenia. No other single therapeutic procedure can compete with it in terms of rapid effectiveness, sustained action, general availability, and ease of application, and it compares at least favorably with the shock therapies as far as incidence of side affects, complications, and serious risks is concerned.

HISTORY

It is one of the curious though not rare occurrences in the history of therapeutics that the first two drugs which proved to be effective in the treatment of schizophrenia were discovered almost simultaneously but quite independently and almost incidentally, neither of them as the result of a systematic search for such a treatment procedure. One of the drugs, reserpine, had been isolated as the active principle of the rauwolfia plant, which had been in use for a long time in India as a treatment for a variety of mental and emotional ills. The other drug, chlorpromazine, was the synthetic product of a pharmacologic search for a tranquilizing substance derived from an antihistaminic compound which was designed to exhibit a minimum of antihistaminic effects but maximal action on the central nervous system.

To the first observers the most characteristic action of these two drugs, reserpine and chlorpromazine, appeared to be the production of sedation or tranquilization, and the new drugs were promptly named tranquilizers. This name remained, and the whole group of drugs to which these first two belong is still commonly referred to as tranquilizers, although it is now recognized that the pharmacological

*Verdun Protestant Hospital, Verdun, Quebec, Canada.

characteristics which distinguish this group of drugs are not their tranquilizing properties (some of the drugs belonging to this pharmacologic group are actually weak stimulants) but their neuroleptic and antipsychotic action. In order to avoid confusing these new drugs with other old and new pharmaceutics which essentially and solely are tranquilizers, it is now common practice to refer to drugs as minor tranquilizers when they are only sedatives or tranquilizers but have no therapeutic effect on specifically psychotic symptoms, and as major tranquilizers when they are effective in the treatment of psychotic symptoms such as hallucinations, delusions, and thinking disorder, regardless whether a tranquilizing effect of the drugs is actually observable or not.

The special effectiveness of the major tranquilizers in schizophrenia was only discovered after the first drugs of this type had been studied for some time, as they were originally administered only for the treatment of states of general excitement and tension. There had never before been a particular pharmacologic agent for which serious claims of effectiveness in the treatment of schizophrenia had been made. All physical treatments of schizophrenia for which their proponents could show acceptable results had been of a systemic, unspecific nature—for example, fever therapy, sleep therapy, and the hypogylcemic coma and convulsive shock therapies.

Although we knew quite early that the new tranquilizers differed from the older established ones by the fact that they did not tend to produce clouding of consciousness and seemed to affect subcortical and cortical cerebral systems differentially, it required at first a certain effort to prescribe the new drugs in cases of schizophrenia to the exclusion of shock therapies. I remember distinctly the intellectual discomfort I felt when I started using chlorpromazine for the treatment of my schizophrenic patients without a very plausible rationale for such an experiment. I recall even more vividly the defensive attitude I had to adopt when a psychiatric colleague challenged me by inquiring how I could justify depriving acutely ill schizophrenic patients of insulin shock therapy and subjecting them to a new and untried procedure. During some of the recent debates on the ethics of clinical drug trials, I had several times occasion to recall these incidents of a rather recent past (i.e., 1953).

Even after it had been established clinically that the new major tranquilizers could indeed abolish such typically psychotic symptoms as hallucinations, delusions, autistic thought disorder, stupor, and withdrawal and that these drugs were therefore of considerable therapeutic value in the treatment of acute schizophrenic breakdowns, it was some time until clinicians found that these drugs were also effective in restoring to acceptable functioning a number of chronic schizophrenics who had resisted all previous attempts at treatment and had become vegetables in mental hospitals. It is likely that the "discovery" of the effectiveness of the new drugs, reserpine and chlorpromazine, in chronic schizophrenia was made by accident when it became evident that an unusually large number of chronic schizophrenic patients who had been placed on the new tranquilizing medication for the symptomatic relief of destructive or agitated behavior and who had been left on this medication for a period of several months began to show fundamental improvement of most of their psychotic symptoms.

Finally, these new drugs proved to be reliable agents for the prevention of relapses in schizophrenics in remission.[1, 2] This made it possible for the first time in the history of treatment for schizophrenia to institute an effective system of preventive maintenance therapy for large numbers of former schizophrenic patients who were now able to function in the community.

The Therapeutic Spectrum of Major Tranquilizers

Thus, the full therapeutic spectrum of most major tranquilizers comprises four functions:

1. A symptomatic tranquilizing effect in states of behavioral excitement and emotional tension.
2. A therapeutic action in acute psychotic episodes.
3. A therapeutic action in chronic psychotic conditions.
4. A preventive maintenance action in patients who are in remission from a psychosis.

Of these four therapeutic functions only the last two represent radically new developments in psychiatric therapeutics, since other reliable symptomatic tranquilizers as well as effective treatment procedures for acute psychotic conditions had already been available to the clinician before the advent of the new major tranquilizers. It may well turn out that maintenance therapy—that is, the preventive function of these drugs—constitutes their greatest value when they are viewed in the perspective of a comprehensive program for mental health.

Cure or Symptomatic Relief?

For some time clinical investigators, basic science researchers, and practicing psychiatrists belonging to different schools of thought became engaged in a heated, rather unproductive discussion of whether the new major tranquilizers could effect a "real cure" of schizophrenia or were "only symptomatic remedies." It has now been generally agreed that the answer to this question is that neither one is true. The drugs cannot bring about a "real cure" of schizophrenia since we do not know its cause, and no disease can ever be declared as cured as long as its etiology is not clear. On the other hand, the drugs do much more than provide symptomatic relief. They can produce the suppression of a whole symptom pattern—that is, of a psychiatric syndrome or a psychopathologic entity—and they can also arrest further progress of the disease process for an indefinite period of time as long as maintenance treatment with the drugs is carried out. Such therapeutic action has been referred to as compensatory treatment by Freyhan,[3] and it has been compared to insulin therapy of diabetics and digitalis therapy of cardiac patients. The fact that long, continued treatment with the new drugs in many cases seems to arrest further progress of the schizophrenic process is what distinguishes this kind of therapy from such merely symptomatic treatment as the management of acute inflammatory diseases by analgesics and steroids where the disease process under the symptomatic cover may advance disastrously.

There is no evidence that the major tranquilizers provide a specific therapy for schizophrenia. They seem to have a suppressive or inhibitory effect on functional or behavioral manifestations which are resulting from fundamental qualitative disorders of perception, conceptualization, or motivation. Because such disorders are characteristic of psychoses, and in view of the fact that no other pharmacologic agent can effectively influence these symptoms, the major tranquilizers have also been referred to as antipsychotics. Schizophrenia is the most widespread and the most typical of the functional psychoses, and antipsychotic pharmacotherapy is therefore finding its widest application in the treatment of schizophrenia.

Antipsychotic Substances

There are now at least four different chemical structures known which have antipsychotic properties. They are (1) reserpine and other rauwolfia derivatives, (2) the phenothiazines, (3) the butyrophenones,[4-6] and (4) the benzoquinolizines.[7, 8] A fifth structural formula, that of the thioxanthenes,[9, 10] is closely related to the phenothiazine nucleus. Each of these basic structures has given rise to the development of various derivatives. Reserpine and the rauwolfia derivatives are much less frequently prescribed today than the phenothiazine drugs. The first one of the latter which was used in the treatment of schizophrenia was chlorpromazine, which today still serves as a comparative standard for any new antipsychotic drug. A host of other phenothiazine derivatives has been developed by the pharmaceutical industry since then, and while the phenothiazine nucleus is common to all of them, they differ in the chemical structures of their side chains and in the nature of the halogen attached to the basic structure. Depending on these modifications, the various phenothiazine derivatives display different characteristics in regard to dose requirements and the nature of side effects they may produce. Phenothiazine derivatives with an aliphatic side chain, for instance, are less potent milligram for milligram and tend to produce somnolence and autonomic disturbances as side effects, while phenothiazine derivatives with a piperazine ring in the side chain are more likely to be mildly stimulating and to evoke extrapyramidal symptoms. The butyrophenones have been widely used as antipsychotics in Europe for some time but have only recently been given more extensive clinical trials in North America. The benzoquinolizines are still in the experimental stage. One of the thioxanthenes has been in clinical use for some time.

Neuroleptic Action

All pharmacologic agents which have proved effective in the treatment of psychotic symptoms are also characterized by their neuroleptic action. The neuroleptic action on the central nervous system is usually manifested in four different areas:

1. In the mesencephalic reticular formation where the unspecific arousal responses tend to be reduced.
2. In the hypothalamus where various symptoms originating in the autonomic nervous system may be produced.
3. In the amygdala and hippocampus where electrical activity tends to be increased, resulting possibly in the lowering of the convulsive threshold which is usually observed with the use of these drugs.

4. In the extrapyramidal system, (globus pallidus; corpus striatum), where extrapyramidal symptoms such as muscular rigidity, tremor, akathisia, and dystonia may be elicited.

Since the major tranquilizers are also frequently classified as neuroleptics, it is important to remember that any drug so classified should have the property to manifest all or at least two of these characteristics. All drugs with antipsychotic properties known today also exhibit neuroleptic effects, but some of them are apt to provoke one or two particular neuroleptic features more strongly than other neuroleptic drugs. This relative weighting of the neuroleptic action either toward the autonomic or toward the extrapyramidal side is one of the reasons for the different side effects associated with the use of different antipsychotic drugs.

Definitive Evidence of Therapeutic Effectiveness

There is now definitive evidence of the superior performance of the major tranquilizers in the treatment of acute and chronic schizophrenic patients. This has been established in several major studies organized by the Veterans' Administration[11, 12] and the National Institute of Mental Health.[13] In order to obtain a sufficiently large sample, the investigators in both studies used a pool of patients from several hospitals. The patients were newly admitted schizophrenics, well matched as to age and sex. The studies were conducted under double-blind controlled conditions. In the V.A. studies, phenobarbital was used as an "active placebo" and compared to seven different phenothiazines. In the N.I.M.H. study an inactive placebo was compared to three different phenothiazine derivatives. Kurland et al., in a a double-blind controlled experiment conducted in one hospital, compared the effects of three different phenothiazines with the effects of phenobarbital.[14]

Mass Action Principle

The three independent groups of investigators arrived at the conclusion that phenothiazines were significantly better than phenobarbital or placebo, but the three groups also found that it was almost impossible to rate the efficacy of various phenothiazine derivatives when compared with each other. Although it can be shown that reserpine and one phenothiazine derivative which is no longer in clinical use were distinctly inferior to the other phenothiazine drugs and one thioxanthene tested, it must be assumed on the basis of the evidence we have to date that whatever real differences exist between most of the currently used antipsychotic drugs are to be found only in the area of side effects and dosage levels.

In view of these findings we are today probably justified to postulate a working principle of mass action for the great majority of major tranquilizers which may be expressed by the following formula:

$$R \approx v \times f\left(D_o, \frac{I}{T_p}\right) \times T_m$$

where R is the optimal therapeutic response; the constant v which does not vary much from unity stands for the particular drug variety chosen; D_o is the optimal daily dose; T_m is the period of time during which the medication is administered; and T_p is the period of time during which the patient has manifested pathology—in other words, the duration of the psychotic process. This formula reflects the overriding importance of adequate dosage and length of administration and the relative unimportance of the particular drug chosen as long as it happens to be one of the many effective major tranquilizers.

It is possible that further clinical research might eventually bring out differences in therapeutic effectiveness between different antipsychotic drugs if such different effectiveness is correlated with specific symptom patterns. Studies which aim at the stratification of the schizophrenic patient population along the lines of symptom clusters are presenting a challenge for research in the near future and are already being conducted in some places with the help of computers.[15]

Sequence of Therapeutic Effects

At the Verdun Protestant Hospital in Montreal, Dr. T. Ban and I have been interested in the sequence of therapeutic events when a major tranquilizer goes into action. An experiment was set up in which three groups of ten acute schizophrenic patients were treated for six weeks. Each group received a different antipsychotic. The three drugs used were (1) chlorpromazine, representing the phenothiazines, (2) haloperidol, representing the butyrophenones, and (3) chlorprothixene, representing the thioxanthenes. The patients were closely followed by clinicians for the day-to-day manifestations of their psychotic condition, and at weekly intervals their behavior and mental status were recorded on a number of rating scales. The behavioral manifestations which were recorded in these conditions were brought together under three categories which designate three parameters of mental functioning. The concepts underlying this approach have been discussed in detail elsewhere.[16] The three parameters on which we oriented our observations were (1) *arousal,* which covers such manifestations as excitement, agitation, attention, and speed of movement; (2) *affect,* which refers to the expression of mood and emotional responses such as depression, anxiety, sociability; (3) *integration,* which serves as the covering concept for the higher mental functions involving perception and cognition and serves as a category in which we register hallucinations, delusions, confusion, and autistic thinking.

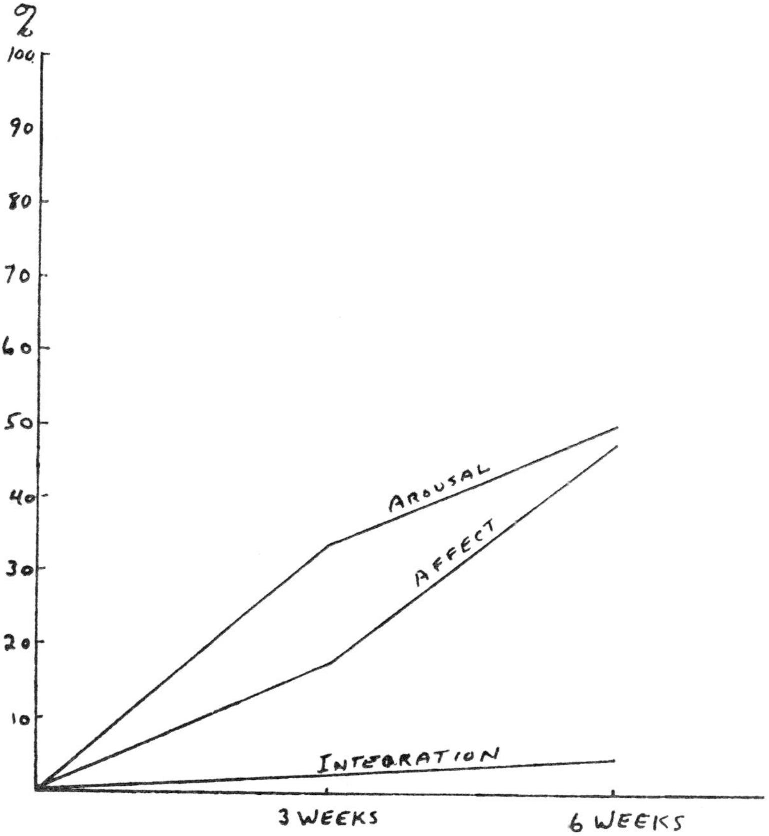

Fig. 1.—Combined cumulative significant changes in behavioral parameters during treatment with three antipsychotics: phenothiazine, thioxanthene, and butyrophenone. An upward direction of the gradient reflects improvement in the respective parameter depending on the number of the component symptoms which have shown statistically significant improvement in each behavioral category.

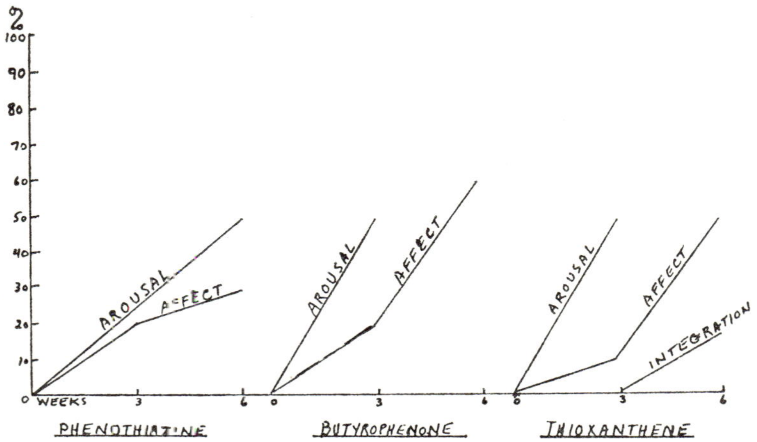

FIG. 2.—Individual cumulative significant changes in behavioral parameters during treatment with three different antipsychotics.

To our surprise, each group of patients receiving a different antipsychotic drug reacted in the same unexpected manner (figs. 1 and 2). There was a rapid improvement of symptoms on the arousal parameter as excitement and agitation subsided soon after pharmacotherapy was started. This was followed by a less rapid but still dramatic improvement in the sphere of affect, which became evident in a lessening of anxiety, tension, and depression and in greater accessibility of the patients. However, the more specific psychotic symptoms such as hallucinations, delusions, and thought disorder were hardly affected at all in the first six weeks of treatment with the three antipsychotic drugs. This was surprising to us since we had felt certain from our clinical experience that these major psychotic symptoms usually disappear within three to four weeks after an acutely ill schizophrenic patient has been placed on antipsychotic drug therapy. There were among the 30 patients of our sample some in whom such fundamental improvement did occur, but in the close follow-up studies of the whole sample on a quantitative basis the changes observed on the integration parameter were not large enough to become statistically significant.

It would appear, then, that an acutely disturbed schizophrenic patient when placed on a major tranquilizer rapidly improves in his behavior, appearance, and in his ability to make contact and to participate in the social life of his environment. However, under the surface, and well concealed by this impressive improvement which is very apparent to the nursing personnel, to the patient's family, to the patient himself, and to the psychiatrist, there is still the nucleus of the major pathology which is the essential characteristic of the patient's psychotic state—namely, the hallucinations, delusions, and thought disorder. They are weakened and much less disturbing to the patients and to their environment, but they are still there.

The pattern of improvement over time shows a very similar distribution of the therapeutic effects in each of our three groups of schizophrenic patients, suggesting a similar mode of action for each of the three chemically different major tranquilizers. A slight effect on the integration parameter—due to improvement in the symptom, delusions—appears only in the group treated with the thioxanthene, but the number of patients in each group is so small that the overall similarity of sequential symptom reduction is probably more significant than the one slight difference which might well have been due to sampling. It should also be noted that the group receiving the phenothiazine and exhibiting the least improvement had been composed of patients with higher pretreatment morbidity ratings than the other two groups, since patients were assigned to the different drugs in alternating succession as they were admitted to hospital and were not matched for degree of initial pathology.

Psychotostatic Action

On the basis of these, for us, unexpected findings—namely, that symptoms involving fundamental perceptual and cognitive functions in schizophrenic patients show little or no significant improvement after six weeks of pharmacotherapy—I am now inclined to view the action of the neuroleptics or major tranquilizers more as *psychotostatic* than as antipsychotic. Many of the patients who in the six-week period had greatly improved but had not yet become symptom-free, recovered completely in the following month or two. Unfortunately, our design of the experiment had not anticipated the need for continuing a close quantitative follow-up beyond a period of six weeks, and we have only the clinical qualitative certainty that the recovered patients a few months later no longer were hallucinated or delusional. We are now repeating the experiment, allowing a 12-week period for the follow-up evaluation of pharmacotherapeutic effects.

Vestre et al., reported similar findings in a controlled comparative study of the therapeutic effects of three phenothiazines and phenobarbital in a population of chronic schizophrenic patients.[17] At their three-week checkpoint only some symptoms, which in our framework would be assigned to the arousal and affect parameter, show improvement which is significantly greater than that obtained with phenobarbital. However, after 12 weeks there is a significant difference in the ratings of those symptoms which we would assign to the integration parameter of mental functioning (disorientation, irrelevant and bizarre speech, hallucinations) between their patients receiving phenothiazines and those on phenobarbital. It is interesting to note that the three phenothiazines rate very closely together and that the greater improvement of patients on these drugs seems to be more relative than absolute in that the significant differences in the symptom ratings are almost entirely due to the marked deterioration which took place in those of their patients who received phenobarbital.

Since other investigators have established that schizophrenic patients who received phenothiazines for long periods of time—that is, for several months or years—show in fact a gradually increasing improvement of the symptoms characterizing schizophrenic thought disorder on our integration parameter,[18, 19] one might theorize that the early and most striking effects of the major tranquilizers are those of *reversing the secondary symptoms* of a psychotic process (for example, excitement, anxiety, withdrawal, stupor, etc.) and *arresting the train of primary symptoms*, which in our conceptualization involve the integration parameter and are manifested in the form of hallucinations, delusions, and autistic thinking disorder. This suggests the further speculation that the major tranquilizers are indeed not producing any specific antipsychotic action but are characterized by their particular power of being psychotostatic—that is, by their capacity to arrest the progress of psychic disorder which, if unchecked, would lead to further impairment of the patient's contact with reality. The proposal of a psychotostatic action rather than an antipsychotic one for the major tranquilizers would also involve the supposition that the final readjustment of the disturbed basic mental functions of perception and cognition is being effected by some innate regulatory mechanisms within the central nervous system after it has been freed for this readaptive task by the action of the major tranquilizer through its reduction of the excessive influx of stimuli, both on the introceptive and extroceptive levels.

This hypothesis receives some further support from data revealed by a close analysis of the extremely well controlled N.I.M.H.–P.S.C.

Collaborative Study to which reference was made earlier.[20] Three hundred and forty-four schizophrenic patients were rated according to symptoms which were absent at the start of the clinical trial but then made their appearance after six weeks of either phenothiazine or placebo administration. It was found that of a total of 21 target symptoms the three symptoms which were most effectively inhibited or prevented from appearing by the phenothiazines and not by placebo were (1) indifference to environment, (2) hebephrenic symptoms, and (3) incoherent speech. In our classification the two last symptoms would be placed into the category of integration. It thus appears that the phenothiazines were differentiated from placebo by their power to hold specific psychotic symptoms in abeyance while they were not much more or less effective than placebo in preventing other symptoms of mental and emotional disturbance from developing over a period of six weeks. Such a prophylactic drug action seems to be related to the widely applied therapeutic effect of major tranquilizers in maintenance therapy and might well be considered to be psychotostatic in nature.

Before seriously considering such a hypothesis it would be necessary to show grounds for assuming that there really exists a basic difference between minor and major tranquilizers. Our only evidence for such an assumption is empirical and based on the observations that major tranquilizers are clinically effective in reducing or abolishing psychotic pathology, while minor tranquilizers are ineffective in this respect. Now it has been proposed that the essential early action of the major tranquilizers consists in the reduction of mental functions in the arousal and affect parameters. However, it is established that the minor tranquilizers, too, have precisely such an effect on psychological functions. Where then is the difference, if any, between these two types of psychopharmacological agents?

Differences between Minor and Major Tranquilizers

Table 1 summarizes those similarities and differences in the psychopharmacological spectra of the minor and major tranquilizers which I consider to be the most important ones in the perspective of a psychopharmacologically oriented clinician. I propose that some of the characteristics common to both types of tranquilizers constitute the *necessary* conditions but that *sufficient* factors for major tranquilizer activity are only provided when some or all of the specific factors that characterize major tranquilizers as being *different* from minor tranquilizers are also represented in a pharmacological agent under question.

TABLE 1.

Effects Common to "Minor" and "Major" Tranquilizers

a. Reduction of perceptual speed and input.
b. Reduction of psychomotor speed and output.
c. Acceleration of extinction of orienting response.

Differences in Psychopharmacological Action between "Minor" and "Major" Tranquilizers

Minor Tranquilizers	*Major Tranquilizers*
Neurophysiological Level	*Neurophysiological Level*
a. Faster frequencies in EEG during first phase of response to intravenous administration.	a. Slower frequencies in EEG during first phase of response to intravenous administration.
b. No neuroleptic action.	b. Neuroleptic action exhibited.
Animal Behavioral Level	*Animal Behavioral Level*
c. No differential inhibition of conditioned avoidance responses.	c. Differential inhibition of conditioned avoidance responses occurs.
d. Increase of "conflict behavior."	d. No increase of "conflict behavior."
Human Behavioral Level	*Human Behavioral Level*
e. Disinhibition occurs.	e. Disinhibition does not occur.
f. Tendency to employ as defense mechanisms: regression; denial; projection.	f. Tendency to employ as defense mechanisms: rationalisation; reaction formation; sublimation

Reduction of perceptional speed and input is an effect of both minor and major tranquilizers as demonstrated by the decrease of critical flicker fusion frequency. Stimulants and psychotomimetics, on the other hand, do not produce such decrease or may even cause an increase of visual perceptual input per time unit. The decreased psychomotor output of all tranquilizing drugs may be observed as reduced tapping speed or lengthened reaction time.[21-23] Accelerated extinction of the orienting response may be observed in various behavioral and autonomic manifestations as an effect of most sedative preparations and minor as well as major tranquilizers.[24, 25]

Considering now the differences between the two types of tranquilizers, on the neurophysiologic level, it is not immediately clear what connection might exist between the antipsychotic effect of major tranquilizers and the fact that they do not tend to increase the frequency of the EEG but often lead instead to a slowing of cerebral electrical activity. At least one investigator, however, has postulated that the slowing of EEG rhythms is a regular feature of all treatment methods which have proved to be effective in psychoses including not only pharmacotherapy but insulin and electroshock as well.[26]

The neuroleptic action of major tranquilizers, too, is thought by some investigators to be an essential effect which is closely related to their therapeutic effectiveness.[27, 28] There is, however, little evidence to establish a causal relation for the regular close association between the extrapyramidal or autonomic and the therapeutic effects of an antipsychotic drug.

On the level of animal behavior, the differential inhibition of conditioned avoidance response without inhibition of the escape response has served for years as a useful screening procedure for new drugs with potential antipsychotic properties.[29] A more recent observation is the differential behavior of animals in a conflict situation when they are under the influence of major or minor tranquilizers.[30] Chlorpromazine and reserpine, for instance, have no appreciable effect on the behavior of animals faced with a situation which combines a reward stimulus with an an aversive stimulus—that is food with electric shock. In contrast to this, drugs of the minor tranquilizer type (for example, barbiturates, meprobamate, and chlordiazepoxide) usually increase such conflict behavior.

On the level of human behavior, the finding that major tranquilizers do not evoke a phase of disinhibition is an important clinical fact since such a disinhibitory phase which tends to occur with most minor tranquilizers at levels of low blood-drug concentration may temporarily produce phenomena of disturbing pseudostimulation. I have previously referred to this difference in action between the two types of drugs as selective inhibition of the major tranquilizers versus global inhibition —involving cortical as well as subcortical cerebral structures—of the minor tranquilizers.[31]

To these factors, all of which are capable of experimental objective verification, I have added in the table a somewhat subjective clinical observation involving some psychodynamic concepts—namely, the tendency of a person under the influence of a major tranquilizer to employ the more constructive defence mechanisms of rationalisation, reaction formation, and sublimation, while under the influence of minor tranquilizers he is more likely to use the more malignant defenses of regression, projection and denial.

In reviewing table 1 it can be noted that the factors by which the major tranquilizers differ from the minor are all characterized by one particular feature: increased inhibition as contrasted to reduced inhibition for the minor tranquilizers. The only exception to this is possibly found in the neuroleptic action of the major tranquilizers.

Characteristics of an Ideal Drug for Treatment of Schizophrenia

In table 2 are given a number of other desirable characteristics which on theoretical grounds an ideal pharmacologic agent for the treatment of schizophrenia should possess. It is generally accepted that schizophrenics are characterized by their great variability of responses

Table 2.—Other Desirable Psychopharmacological Characteristics of Drugs to be Employed in the Treatment of Schizophrenic Conditions

a.	Decrease of variability of responses.
b.	Improvement of ability to establish and maintain a "set."
c.	Facilitation of learning (differentiation and retention).
d.	Critical restriction of ideation (fewer irrelevant and idiosyncratic responses on word association and other projective tests; no overinclusion in conceptualisation tasks).

above and below the mean when compared with a normal sample. An agent that would restrict such variability might reasonably be assumed to have a beneficial therapeutic effect in schizophrenia. Shakow and his coworkers showed long ago that one of the crucial characteristics of the schizophrenic patient is his inability to establish and maintain a "set" effectively. Shakow has now reviewed this work and confirmed his previous findings and conclusions.[32, 33] Sutton and Zubin in some carefully programmed research on crossmodal sequences of reaction time experiments have recently shown that the schizophrenic's establishment of a set or state of readiness is maladaptive in that he tends to be "overprepared" and disproportionately affected by his last trials.[34] Therefore, it would appear that a drug that could improve the establishment and maintenance of a behavioral set would also have distinct advantages in the treatment of schizophrenia. Further, since all therapeutic activity in psychoses depends on strengthening and expansion of ego resources and since such ego growth can take place only by learning, a drug ideally suited for the treatment of schizophrenia should facilitate the learning process, in particular differentiation and retention of concepts and symbols. The last item on table 2 would provide for still another desirable property of an ideal drug for the treatment of schizophrenia, by requiring that such a drug have the power of directly and critically restricting excessive and deviant ideation, since the latter is one of the primary symptoms of schizophrenia.

In a recent experiment we gave word association tests to eight schizophrenic patients who were not receiving any drugs at the time. The tests were repeated on two other occasions, each separated from the previous one by a two-day interval. On each occasion half of the stimulus words presented were identical and half of them were new words. On the second and third occasions the patients were given, prior to the experiment, either 100-150 mg. of pentobarbital or 100 mg. of chlorpromazine. The order of the drugs was alternated between patients. All word associations were evaluated on three parameters of (1) mean association time for the whole group of words in each experiment, (2) the standard deviation of the association times, and (3) the number of unusual or idiosyncratic responses.

It was found that the response characteristics for each total trial were apparently well represented in the half of the test which consisted of the identical stimulus words which were repeatedly presented on three occasions. Whatever differences were observed were apparently mainly determined by the effects of the drugs and amazingly little by practice effects. An index of improvement was set up by combining a decrease of the mean asosciation time, a decrease of the standard deviation of the association times, and decrease of unusual responses when the drug performances were compared with each other and to the performance under "no treatment" conditions. The detailed results showed clearly that the patients' associative functioning under the effects of chlorpromazine was much "better" (as defined by the three criteria given above) than under the effects of pentobarbital. There also was a tendency for patients to perform better in the association test after receiving chlorpromazine than when they received no treatment. However, this difference was not as clear-cut as that between the effects of chlorpromazine and pentobarbital. On the other hand, pentobarbital clearly produced an impairment of associational functioning when compared to "no treatment" conditions.

It seems that such a comparatively simple test model might be helpful in the screening for drugs to be used in the treatment of pyschotic conditions when efficiency and relevance of associational processes need to be evaluated. There is, furthermore, an indication from our data that the mean association times may be significantly correlated with the variability of the responses both in regard to time and content of associations, so that the mean association time of a short list of words by itself might reflect fairly reliably the action of psychotopic drugs on associational functioning.

Perceptual—Cognitive Dynamics of Schizophrenia

For some time I have held the notion that the schizophrenic individual is a person who is exposed to an excessive influx of exteroceptive stimuli. If his central processing capacity is being overloaded, he will then experience jamming of his regulatory mechanisms and react defensively by physical and psychological withdrawal from the incessant bombardment of stimuli. There is some experimental evi-

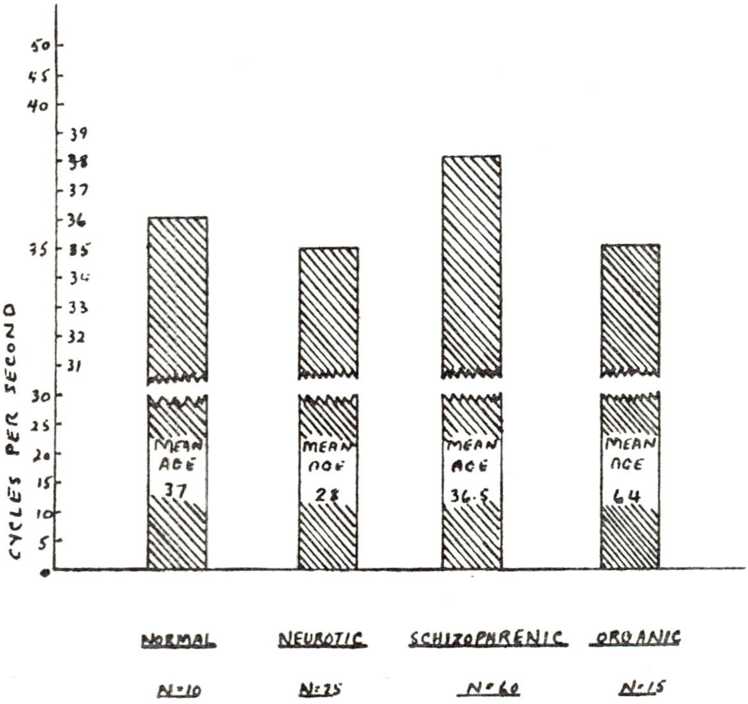

Fig. 3.—Critical flicker fusion frequency.

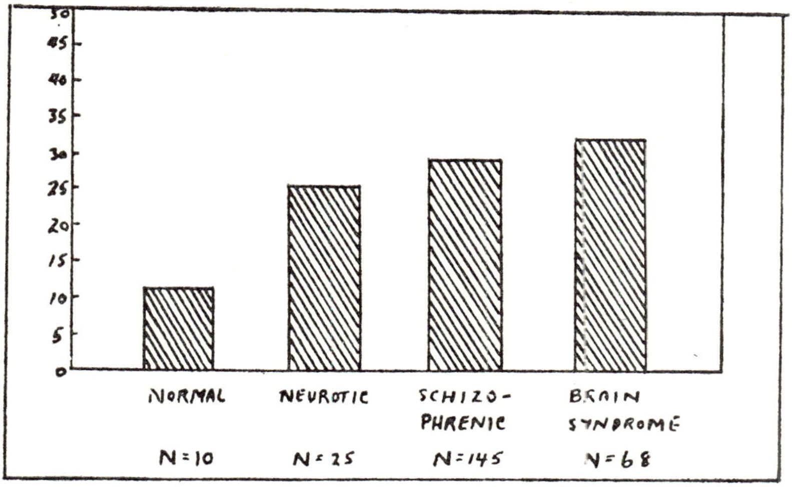

FIG. 4.—Auditory reaction time (1/100 second).

dence for this idea. In 1952 Csank and I observed that patients diagnosed as acute schizophrenics had a higher critical flicker fusion frequency than any other diagnostic group of psychiatric patients we examined. Furthermore, the schizophrenics had a higher flicker fusion frequency than our normal control group.[35] This was quite a remarkable finding, since any other known psychiatric impairment of a person's functioning would invariably result in at least temporary decrease below the normal mean of the critical flicker fusion frequency, which may be considered a measure of the central nervous system's capacity to distinguish discrete visual stimuli in the temporal field.

A group of psychiatric patients was recently examined by us and gave the same results. Figures 3 and 4 illustrate the scores of critical flicker fusion frequency and, for comparison, of simple auditory reaction time for a small group of normal controls and for larger groups of psychiatric patients divided into diagnostic subgroups of psychoneurotics, schizophrenics, and patients with organic brain syndrome. Since previous experience had indicated that chronicity of schizophrenia leads to a decrease of flicker fusion frequency (unpublished observations) and since the influence of drugs on this function is well established, the schizophrenic patients tested were in the acute stage of the disease and every effort had been made to test them before they had been placed on drugs. The trend of growing impairment from sample to sample in the psychomotor test performance (figure 2) goes in the expected direction: Reaction time is shortest in the control group and increases with increasing pathology first in the psychoneurotics, lengthens further in the schizophrenics, and finally reaches its highest value in the organic brain syndrome group. Critical flicker fusion frequency, however, is higher in the schizophrenic than in the normal or any of the other pathological groups.

These findings are certainly compatible with the hypothesis that there is a primary, possibly constitutional, susceptibility of the schizophrenic individual to be subjected to the impact of a higher number of discrete sensory stimuli per time unit of experience than most other pathological or nonpathological individuals. If he is capable of coping with this greater than average influx of discrete sensory stimuli, he might perform at a better than average level, but when the extraordinary sensitivity of his receptor apparatus is not matched by an equally extraordinary performance of his central processing apparatus, then his integration breaks down and he may become psychotic.

Integration Composed of Four Inhibition Factors

At this point it might be appropriate to outline my working conception of the integration parameter in mental functioning. Mental integration may be pictured as being composed of four structural factors:

1. The capacity to establish and to maintain an adequate *set.*
2. The capacity for adequate *differentiation* or discrimination.
3. The capacity for adequate *retention.*
4. The capacity for adequate *negative feed-back.*

The first factor, the set, depends on the subject's capacity for active inhibition of all grossly irrelevant stimuli. Only stimuli of the first order of complexity have to be filtered out in order to maintain a set —that is, only extroceptive and introceptive stimuli which are grossly incongruous to the task implied in the set. This type of inhibition may be indicated by the expression, $S_1 \overset{I}{\quad} R_1$, and it would apply to the functions involved in anticipatory sets, mental concentration, and similar behavioral phenomena.

The second factor, differentiation or discrimination, also depends on active inhibition. However, the stimuli which must be inhibited on this level are of much higher complexity than on the set-level where only the most rudimentary abstraction or filtering choice was required for the inhibition. The type of inhibition required for differentiation of stimuli of the second order of complexity may be denoted by the expression, $_{S_2}\overset{I}{\ }_{R_2}$, and it would apply to functions involved in the mental activities which comprise abstraction of concepts, intellectual focusing, reasoning by induction and deduction, and symbolic expression.

The third factor, retention, in contrast to the two previous ones depends not on active but on reactive inhibition. It is mainly nonselective and stimulus-independent. Memory functions, at least in their more biologically determined (organic) aspects, are regulated by the magnitude of this type of inhibition which, unlike the other three factors, should be at a minimum for optimal functioning and may be denoted by the expression, I_r.

The fourth factor, negative feed-back, depends on a special type of active inhibition where the response itself serves to restrict and modulate the stimulus input. Such a function is required for the establishment and maintenance of homeostasis or flexible stability of the system. This type of active inhibition may be referred to by the expression, $_{-S}\overset{I}{\ }_{R}$.

All functions involving efficient learning or adequate reality testing are dependent on intact integration of the mental apparatus. Functions involving inhibition factors 1, 2, and 4 are primarily and severely impaired in schizophrenia. Factor 3 is spared in schizophrenic patients but adversely affected in patients suffering from organic brain disease.

There are now available a number of test procedures which permit the assessment of functional models of these four factors in animals and humans. Factors 1 and 2 seem to find fairly good representation in learning and concept formation and, in more primitive form, in the full scale of conditioned behavior including studies of the orienting reflex, formation of trace reflexes, and variations of operant behavior. Factor 3 may be quantified through a variety of tests that measure retention either on the conceptual, the perceptual, or the behavioral level. Least is known about the quantitative assessment of factor 4, the negative feed-back which is responsible for homeostatic adjustments. It would appear, however, that the store of our present information on this factor will permit us to construct test models which on the behavioral level might conceivably make use of studying nociceptive responses and on the perceptual level of the operation of constancy principles. On the cognitive level our knowledge of negative feedback functioning in the handling of concepts is still rather incomplete.

Special Quality of Psychotostatic Drugs

If we accept the working hypothesis that an excessive influx of stimulus quanta leads to flooding and jamming of the integration mechanisms, it then follows that reduction of stimulus intake should be one of the basic properties of any drug that is effective in the treatment of schizophrenia. This, however, is not sufficient, for we have seen that such reduction of stimulus intake is produced by minor as well as by major tranquilizers or—to put it differently—by ordinary sedatives as well as by psychotostatic substances.

The psychopharmacologic difference between these two classes of drugs lies in their action on the inhibition factors of the integration parameter. While minor tranquilizers inhibit distracting stimuli which may interfere with the adequate maintenance of a set, they are less effective in this respect than the major tranquilizers. This is probably due to the disturbing interference of the disinhibition phase which so frequently occurs with the minor tranquilizers but not with the major. In addition, it is certain that the effect of minor tranquilizers is actually disruptive of the functioning of our second and fourth factors of inhibition which are essential for the proper functioning of differentiation and negative feedback. These drugs tend instead to produce de-differentiation and positive feedback as evidenced by their effects on behavior, cognitive functioning, and psychodynamic defence mechanisms. In producing these effects they interfere with the restitutive and reintegrating powers of the ego. These, in contrast, are left intact by the psychotostatic action of the major tranquilizers.

Elsewhere I have discussed the principles which might guide the psychopharmacologist's search for new psychoactive drugs with the use of animal models.[36] Schizophrenia, however, is such a singularly human affliction that much of the final work in research for new drugs that might be effective in the pharmacotherapy of this disease will have to be done with human subjects. In this chapter I have attempted to outline some of the general concepts, principles, and approaches that might serve as guides for systematic experiments conducted prior to and simultaneously with clinical field trials.

REFERENCES

1. U.S. Department of Health, Education and Welfare Public Health Service, National Institutes of Health: Release to Scientific and Professional Journals, February 6, 1961.
2. Blackburn, H. L., and Allen, J. L.: Behavioural effects of interruption and resuming tranquillizing medication among schizophrenics. J. Nerv. Ment. Dis. 133:303, 1961.
3. Freyhan, F. A. et al.: Mental Patients in Transition. Springfield, Ill. 1961. Charles C Thomas.
4. Delay, J., Pichot, P., Lemperiere, T., and Elissalde, B.: Presse Med. 68:1353, 1960.
5. Azima, H., Durost, H., and Arthurs, D.: The effect of R 1625 (haloperidol) in mental syndromes: a multiblind study. Amer. J. Psychiat. 117:546, 1960.
6. Enoch, M. D., and Robin, A. A.: A controlled trial of haloperidol in chronic schizophrenics. J. Ment. Sci. 106:1459, 1960.
7. Feldman, Paule E.: Clinical evaluation of Benzquinamine (P-2647) in the control of tension states and hyper-syndromes. Psychosomatics 3, No. 2, 1962.
8. Scriabine, A., et al.: Benzquinamide: a new antianxiety drug. J.A.M.A. 184, No. 4:276, 1963.
9. Gayus, Irene K., and Blanchette, J. E.: Effects of chlorprothixene in well-established schizophrenic reactions. Amer. J. Psychiat. 119:180, 1962.
10. Cohn, C. A.: Effect of chlorprothixene in patients with paranoid symptoms. Canad. Med. Ass. J., Oct. 5, 1963.
11. Casey, J. F., et al.: Treatment of schizophrenic reactions with phenothiazine derivatives. A comparative study of chlorpromazine, triflupromazine, mepazine, prochlorperazine, perphenazine and phenobarbital. Amer. J. Psychiat. 117:97, 1960.
12. Casey, J. F., et al.: Drug therapy in schizophrenia: a controlled study of the relative effectiveness of chlorpromazine, promazine, phenobarbital, and placebo. Amer. Med. Ass. Arch. Gen. Psychiat. 2:210, 1960.
13. Lasky, J. J., et al.: Drug treatment of schizophrenic patients: a comparative evaluation of chlorpromazine, chlorprothixene, fluphenazine, reserpine, thioridazine and Triflupromazine. Dis. Nerv. Sys. 23:1, 1962.
14. NIMH-PSC Collaborative Study Group: The effectiveness of phenothiazine treatment of acute schizophrenic psychoses. Arch. Gen. Psychiat. 10:246, 1964.
15. Kurland, A. A., et al.: The comparative effectiveness of six phenothiazine compounds, phenobarbital and inert placebo in the treatment of acutely ill patients: global measures of severity of illness. J. Nerv. Ment. Dis. 133:1, 1961.
16. Overall, J. E., et al.: Comparison of acetophenazine with perphenazine in schizophrenics: demonstration of differential effects based on computer-derived diagnostic models. Clin. Pharmacol. Ther. 4:200, 1963.
17. Lehmann, H. E.: Problems of evaluation and classification in psychopharmacology, psychopharmacological methods. *In* proceedings of a Symposium on

the Effects of Psychotropic Drugs on Higher Nervous Activity, Prague, October 30, 1961, to November 2, 1961. New York, Pergamon Press, 1963.
18. VESTRE, N. D., HALL, W. B., AND SCHIELE, B. C.: A comparison of fluphenazine, triflupromazine and phenobarbital in the treatment of chronic schizophrenic patients: a double-blind controlled study. J. Clin. Exp. Psychopath. 23:149, 1962.
19. PAYNE, R. W., ANCEVICH, SINGRIDA, S., AND LAVERTY, S. G.: Overinclusive thinking in symptom-free schizophrenics. Canad. Psychiat. Ass. J. 8:225, 1963.
20. ENGELHARDT, D. M., ET AL.: Long term drug-induced symptom modification in schizophrenic outpatients. Dig. Neurol. Psychiat. 31: 423, 1963.
21. GOLDBERG, S. C., KLERMAN, G. L., AND COLE, J. O.: Changes in Schizophrenic Psychopathology and Ward Behavior as a Function of Phenothiazine Treatment. Brit. J. Psychiat. 111:120, 1965.
22. LEHMANN, H. E.: Methods of evaluation of drug effects on the human central nervous system. The effect of pharmacologic agents on the nervous system. Proc. Ass. Res. Nerv. Ment. Dis. 37:126, 1959.
23. PEARL, D.: Phenothiazine effects in chronic schizophrenia. J. Clin. Psychol. 18:86, 1962.
24. VANDERBERG, S. G.: Behavioural methods for assessing neuroses and psychoses. *In* Drugs and Behaviour, eds. L. Uhr and J. G. Miller. New York, John Wiley & Sons, 1960.
25. GLIEDMAN, L. H., AND GANTT, W. H.: The effects of reserpine and chlorpromazine on orienting behavior and retention of conditional reflexes. South. Med. J. 49:880, 1956.
26. Unpublished experimental data.
27. FINK, M.: A unified theory of the action of physiodynamic therapies. J. Hillside Hosp. 6:197, 1957.
28. FLUGEL, F.: Therapeutique par medication neuroleptique obtenue en realisant systemetiquement des etats Parkinson-Formes Encephale, Num. Spec. 1956. Colloq. intern. sur les Neuroleptiques, Paris, 1955.
29. DELAY, J., AND DENIKER, P.: Caracteriatiques psycho-physiologiques des medicaments neuroleptiques. *In* Psychotropic Drugs, Proceedings, International Symposium on Psychotic Drugs, Milan, 1957. New York, Elsevier Publishing Company, 1957.
30. COOK, L., AND WEIDLEY, E.: Behavioral Effects of some psychopharmacological agents. Ann. N.Y. Acad. Sci. 66:740, 1957.
31. GELLER, I., KULAK, J. T., JR., AND SEIFTER, J.: The effects of chlordiazepoxide and chlorpromazine on a punishment discrimination. Psychopharmacologia, 3:374, 1962.
32. LEHMANN, H. E.: Neurophysiologic activity of chlorpromazine in clinical use. J. Clin. Exp. Psychopath. 17:No. 2, 1956.
33. SHAKOW, D.: Segmental set (a theory of the formal psychological deficit in schizophrenia). Arch. Gen. Psychiat. 6:1, 1962.
34. ——: Psychological deficit in schizophrenia. Behav. Sci. 8:275, 1963.
35. SUTTON, S., AND ZUBIN, J.: Effect of sequence on reaction time in schizo-

phrenia. *In* Behavior, Aging and the Nervous System (eds. A. T. Welford and J. E. Birren. Springfield, Ill., Charles C Thomas, 1964.

36. Lehmann, H. E.: Concepts, rationale and research. *In* Psychopharmacology Frontiers, Proceedings of the Second International Congress of Psychiatry, Zurich, Switzerland, 1957. ed. N. S. Kline. Boston, Little, Brown & Company, 1959.

37. ——: Selection, screening and testing of new psychiatric drugs. Proc. Third World Cong. Psychiat. 3:437, 1961.

23

THE EFFECT OF SOMATIC TREATMENTS ON CLINICAL COURSE, PSYCHOPATHOLOGICAL AND PATHOPHYSIOLOGICAL RESEARCH IN SCHIZOPHRENIA

by LOTHAR B. KALINOWSKY, M.D.*

All somatic treatment procedures in psychiatry were originally introduced for the treatment of schizophrenia. This is true for insulin coma treatment introduced by Sakel on the basis of clinical observations, but as an afterthought explained by a theory which tried to define it as a physiological treatment for schizophrenia. Although his theory could not be maintained nor the mode of action established, some of us with experience in the various somatic treatments still consider insulin, if applied adequately, an extremely valuable tool in schizophrenia.

Convulsive treatment introduced by Meduna because of a questionable antithesis between schizophrenia and epilepsy later lost its theoretical foundation by being more effective in the affective psychoses. Yet, its technical modification of electric convulsive treatment, as introduced by Cerletti and Bini, continues to be applied in large numbers of acute schizophrenics.

Psychosurgery was also meant by Moniz, as well as by his predecessor Burkhardt, for disturbed schizophrenic patients. It turned out to be the least specific method for schizophrenia but it often yields striking results in some groups of nondeteriorating schizophrenics such as pseudoneurotics and late paranoids. Already prior to the area of pharmacotherapy with neuroleptic drugs, it was obvious that psychosurgery had no specific effect on the disease. The emotional response of a schizophrenic to some psychotic experiences such as delusions and hallucinations was reduced in the same way as the emotional response of an intractable neurotic patient to his obsessions and compulsions. Today the more easily applicable neuroleptic drugs, free of

*New York Medical College, New York, N.Y.

the irreversible side effects of frontal lobe surgery, are far superior and obviously the treatment of choice in most chronic schizophrenic patients. Also, the range of target symptoms which they reach is wider than those modified by surgery. They benefit the largest number of schizophrenic patients, but they are even less specific and not better understood than the previous somatic treatments which they greatly supplement but do not replace.

Do these various treatments compete with each other—as the history of their introduction into psychiatry seems to indicate—or do they have different indications and different mode of action? In our opinion the mode of action, to be discussed later, seems to be different. Their indications certainly differ. We all agree that we do not have a truly specific treatment of schizophrenia, yet some treatments are more specific and others are less so. All of them are valuable tools in modern treatment of schizophrenia.

The first part of the topic assigned to me concerns the question whether and how somatic treatments influence the course of a schizophrenic illness. The few reliable statistics available for untreated schizophrenics prior to the introduction of shock treatments and of schizophrenic material treated by experts in the shock therapies permit the conclusion that the 20-25 per cent remission rate in untreated schizophrenics could be raised to 40-50 per cent in a mixed material of schizophrenics of all subtypes. In favorable groups of patients with acute onset and short duration of illness, figures up to 80 per cent were reliably reported. It is not surprising that the best treatment prognosis was also found in patients with the best spontaneous prognosis, such as catatonic excitement. There is some evidence that insulin is more effective than convulsive treatment, but if the latter is applied intensively with at least 15 or 20 treatments, results come close to those obtained with the more cumbersome insulin coma treatment. There is also the impression that the quality of an insulin remission is better than that of an ECT remission. The present trend among those who still use insulin, to increase the number of comas up to 100 and more, suggests that schizophrenics of several years' duration who are poor prospects for ECT can still be brought to a lasting remission with insulin coma treatment. If no lasting remission is obtained, pharmacotherapy is still a valuable symptomatic treatment, even in cases of long duration.

The main problem under debate, but unfortunately not studied by any statistical comparison of matched groups of patients, is whether an acute schizophrenic should first be treated with neuroleptic drugs or with shock treatment. Both ways of starting treatment are acceptable. Study of the psychiatric literature of the first years of pharmacotherapy suggests that neuroleptic drugs had received preference. Lately, however, the impression is that hospitals fully equipped for modern shock therapy procedures have increased the use of ECT in acute cases. This is particularly the case in psychiatric wards of general hospitals, where the time factor, because of cost and shortage of beds, favors a quick turnover. Medically ECT is often preferred because of the danger of vasomotor collapse in severely disturbed patients if treated with neuroleptic drugs, while three or four ECT's in short succession are known to be lifesaving in these cases which were formerly called "pernicious catatonia." In less acute situations an attempt with pharmacotherapy is justified and should be continued for some time after the disappearance of symptoms. It must be recommended, however, to discharge such patients only after an attempt to withdraw medication has been made. If after such withdrawal the symptoms reappear, shock treatment is indicated. If this does not lead to a remission lasting beyond the termination of treatment, it is fortunately still possible to subject the patient to a maintenance dosage of drugs.

On the negative side is the fact applicable to all available treatments that the primary symptoms of schizophrenia in the sense of E. Bleuler are least apt to respond to any kind of treatment. Defect symptoms even in fairly good treatment remissions are flattening of affect and a certain rigidity in thinking. Such scarring can be discovered in most patients after schizophrenic illness. Cases of so-called nuclear schizophrenia have a poorer treatment prognosis, yet, they do deserve treatment and often show some response. On theoretical grounds we do not consider it justified to break up the schizophrenias on the basis of treatment response into true schizophrenia and schizophreniform psychosis as has been tried by Langfeldt and by Meduna.

It cannot be questioned that the course of schizophrenia has been changed by the advent of the somatic treatments. The mere possibility to control the behavior of a patient is revolutionary since 30 years ago this could only be done with hypnotics which interfered not only with psychotic activity but with other activity as well. Since then we have many ways to modify psychotic behavior. This is evidenced by the disappearance of mechanical restraints and by the increasing number of rehabilitated schizophrenics. A question remains, however, regarding our ability to cure the disease. If we do not lose ourselves in semantics regarding specificity of treatment and actual cure of a disease, we can claim that in favorable cases we do eradicate the clinical manifestations or greatly reduce the impact of the disease. This statement seems to be permissible if we remember that there have also been observations of spontaneous cures of schizophrenia in the past, and it is not surprising that our treatments, as inadequate as they still are, increase the number of such cures. Apparently they accomplish this by supporting the natural forces of the organism to rid itself of the disease or, in other cases, make the disease latent for a long period of time.

It is undeniable that relapses are frequent with all treatments, but relapses can be treated again successfully. A clear definition of relapse is important. There are two entirely different kinds of relapse in schizophrenic patients who respond to shock therapy while under treatment. One group relapses a week or ten days after termination of treatment, representing obvious treatment failures. They differ from patients who remain in a remission for one or several years, and only then have a new outbreak of the disease. This latter group had been successfully treated but the disease obviously remains latent even in these more or less symptom-free patients, and it is apt to become reactivated by unknown causes at any time in the future. Such a new outbreak of the disease should be more clearly distinguished from the immediate return of symptoms which, by the way, find a parallel in pharmacotherapy, where successfully treated target symptoms often return within days, when the neuroleptic drug is discontinued.

It is a great progress made by pharmacotherapy that relapses can be controlled more easily and that a wider range of patients can be maintained on a better clinical level. The increasing variety of treatments enhances their social importance. It has been stressed—particularly in England, Scandinavia, and other countries—that the great strides made in social psychiatry were only possible because of the somatic treatments, and actually preceded the era of pharmacotherapy. No one procedure should be singled out in a discussion on the long-term prognosis of schizophrenia in present times. There are those who attribute much of the progress made to the older treatments; others will give credit only to pharmacotherapy. In our opinion, all the various treatments applied to the right patient at the proper stage of his illness can maintain a large percentage of schizophrenics in the community and/or enable them to benefit from various social measures. To demonstrate this statistically would be a most important research project, but it can never be successfully done with statistics on one single therapeutic approach. Those of us who were able to follow individual patients with several relapses over the last 25 years, and see them benefited by the various available methods, cannot doubt the effect that somatic treatments have on the course of schizophrenia.

The more discouraging part of this presentation will be the question of what the treatments and the many research studies connected with them contributed to our knowledge of the psychopathology and pathophysiology of schizophrenia and to our understanding of the mode of action of the various treatments. There is actually little hope that we will find a truly specific treatment for schizophrenia as long as we do not know the etiology of the disease. There was some hope that the empirical discovery of partially effective treatments might in turn contribute to a better understanding of etiologic factors. This hope did not come true. After long use of an increasing number of treatments there is still general agreement that we have no etiologic treatment for schizophrenia as we do have it, for instance, for general paresis with methods to immobilize spirochaetes or in other symptomatic psychoses by eliminating the underlying systematic disease.

How, then, do our partially effective treatments in schizophrenia work? One approach to the answer of this question was tried by von Baeyer, who studied the effect or "Eigenwirkung" of the various somatic treatments. This effect of the treatment proper can be psychopathologic or pathophysiologic, in the latter case mostly neurologic in nature. Psychopathologic changes consist of memory impairment and organic euphoria in patients under convulsive treatment, some emotional blunting or euphorization in insulin treatment, and diminished drive and reduced effective responsiveness under neuroleptic medication. These effects of the treatment itself would be equally present in normal and in schizophrenic individuals. It is usually possible during treatment to distinguish between the changes in the psychopathology of the psychosis and the effect proper of the treatment. The latter disappears after termination of treatment, and we are then able to see in what way the psychosis has changed. Such observations are necessary if we want to understand some future day the actual effect of the treatments on the psychoses. Even though it appears that the psychopathologic effect of the treatments proper, for instance, the organic reactions during convulsive therapy do not explain their therapeutic effect, this negative finding in itself is important. Further psychopathologic research into the mechanism of treatment is necessary.

An interesting chapter is the effect of drugs on the psychopathology of schizophrenia. With some neuroleptics a turbulent phase has been described, particularly with rauwolfia drugs. Of greater clinical importance is the occasional effect of antidepressants on the psychopathology of schizophrenia. Described as psychiatric complications of antidepressant drugs, they were wrongly interpreted as provocation of a schizophrenic or schizophreniform psychosis due to such drugs. They mostly concern patients in whom the predominant symptom is a depressive mood, but the shallowness of the depressive effect and the fairly young age of most such patients stand against the diagnosis of an endogenous depression. After several days or more of antidepressant medication, the patient suddenly develops an acute symptomatology with delusions and/or hallucinations and often psychomotor excitement. Thus, an acute schizophrenic symptomatology develops and is frequently interpreted either as a new complicating disease or as an aggravation of a schizophrenic psychosis which had been primarily characterized by a mere depression.

It is usually overlooked that identical occurrences had been observed in convulsive therapy. After one or two ECT's such depressed or simply withdrawn patients would suddenly develop an acute paranoid symptomatology which cannot be interpreted as organic psychotic reactions due to ECT, because the well-known organic reactions with manifold symptomatology never occur after one or two treatments and are always associated with such organic signs as confusion and disorientation. Actually such instances are explained by the disappearance of a depressive overlay in a schizophrenic patient in whom the acute symptomatology becomes manifest only after the apparent depression or catatonic withdrawal has been removed. Halpern rightly recognized such observations as an aid in the diagnosis of schizophrenia. In psychopharmacology these instances are not specific for any particular group of antidepressants and are caused by the removal of one set of symptoms rather than by toxic pharmacologic action.

There are, however, occurrences of true deliria due to antidepressant drugs. A recent paper by Lecomte and Alcalay is of particular interest for these toxic syndromes. A delirium seems to be produced by a high dosage of imipramine up to 300 or 400 mg. The patients are disoriented in time and space and have lively visual hallucinations of animals crawling all over them in their beds. The authors gave a psychopathologic analysis of these deliria which is difficult to accept and which interprets the worms these patients saw as a symbol of death and decay of the body. In any event, patients improve after this experience, but the most important fact we like to stress is that such deliria due to imipramine are quite different from the more frequent occurrence of activation of an underlying schizophrenic psychosis. There is a parallel between this pharmacologic effect and the effect of convulsive therapy, where also apart from activation of an underlying psychosis acute organic reactions with delirium-like syndromes have been described. While the activation of an underlying psychosis takes place in the beginning of treatment before any organic psychotic symptoms are present, the delirium-like syndromes occur only after a larger number of electric convulsive treatments. It may be followed by a state of temporary organic dementia without productive hallucinatory symptoms, but it may reappear once more when the patient emerges from the dementia-like organic syndrome, goes again through a delirium-like episode, and then returns to normal.

Change in symptomatology due to drugs is no more an aggravation of the illness than, for instance, the change from a catatonic stupor to a catatonic excitement. Actually, a catatonic excitement is more disturbing to the observer but it has a better prognosis than a catatonic stupor or withdrawal.

In insulin coma treatment similar changes in symptomatology have been described by Sakel himself as activation of the psychosis. Here the interpretation became somewhat complicated by the fact that hypoglycemia as such can cause an organic psychotic reaction even in nonpsychotic individuals. There are, however, patients in whom a true activation of the psychosis occurs. A parallel can be seen under intravenous sodium amytal, where an acute psychotic material can be activated, or where in patients successfully treated with insulin, ECT or lobotomy under the influence of sodium amytal or other drugs, the psychotic material can be again temporarily reproduced.

Wherever acute symptomatology occurs in the course of any treatment, discontinuation of treatment is not warranted. This had already been recognized in insulin treatment and is quite obvious in ECT. In pharmacotherapy the type of drug may have to be changed because different drugs are used for withdrawn or depressed schizophrenics and in acute paranoid syndromes. If acute manifestations occur in primarily depressed schizophrenics under antidepressants, a change to neuroleptic drugs is warranted. However, we would be inclined to use ECT as a treatment equally indicated in hypoactive depressed syndromes as well as in acute paranoid symptomatology.

This raises a question of more general importance, including the problem of the unity of schizophrenia as one disease with many different syndromes. We are referring to the fact that convulsive therapy as well as insulin coma treatment are effective in both catatonic stupor and catatonic excitement—that is, syndromes with entirely different symptomatology. We consider this as one good reason to assume that particularly convulsive therapy, in which the predictable number of usually three treatments can remove such entirely different syndromes, has a more specific effect on the basic disease than the available pharmacological agents with their effect on one set of target symptoms.

A parallel observation is that a retarded and an agitated depression require different drugs and respond differently to pharmacotherapy, while they both respond to the same number of three convulsive treatments with the same predictable disappearance of symptoms. This transgression to an observation outside of the field of schizophrenia becomes justified in view of an important observation by Helmchen and Hippius which shows that an acute schizophreniform syndrome can be precipitated by antidepressant medication, not only in unrecognized schizophrenics but also in an organic psychosis such as a general paresic. In their patient an acute paranoid symptomatology could be elicited in a depressed general paresic each time he was placed on antidepressant medication. We may add that the productive symptoms of general paresis, both depressive and paranoid, can be removed by the here undoubtedly unspecific electric convusive therapy. All these observations are listed here because one day they might help to understand how the various treatments act.

Pathophysiologic research has been applied even more widely in order to clarify the mode of action of somatic treatments. Apart from laboratory research and animal experiments, clinical observation has been used extensively and centered around the neurological manifestations common to all somatic treatment procedures in psychiatry. Differences in the neurologic concomitants of the various treatments may explain differences in the psychopathologic changes and in the clinical effects obtained. It appears that neuroleptic drugs affect a limited area of the brain as evidenced by the strio-pallidar symptoms, which may be hypokinetic in the sense of a Parkinson syndrome, or at least a certain degree of micrographia, or which may be hyperkineses such as akathisia or torticollis and dystonia. It should be realized that the neurologic concomitants of insulin and convulsive treatment suggest a much wider involvement of brain structures than the neuroleptic drugs. A patient under insulin treatment runs through the whole gamut of neurologic manifestations from subcortical areas down to the midbrain. Many studies describe these various stages which often intermingle, and observation on an insulin ward shows the great variety of neurologic manifestations in a single patient, when he goes into a coma and again when he comes out of the coma. That a convulsion affects large parts of the brain is evidenced by the observation of the brain on the operating table during a convulsion as well as by the widespread encephalographic changes and psychological alterations after convulsions.

The question arises whether such involvement of certain structures of the brain, even though reversible, is able to neutralize some unknown factor in the causation of schizophrenic illness. An important condition seems to be that treatment be given at an early stage of the disease, and that the treatment, whether hypoglycemic coma or convulsion, be applied often enough. The tendency of most experts working with insulin is to go far beyond the originally prescribed number of 40 to 60 comas, and the favorable outcome of regressive ECT, when routine ECT has failed, suggests that repeated application is necessary. Results with such intensive treatment, even in less acute cases, would indicate that the unknown damage by schizophrenic disease remains at least partly reversible for quite some time. Those symptoms which respond to neuroleptic drugs remain reversible even for many years or decades, though only while the drug is being applied. These target symptoms are usually the same which, for a short while, can also be removed with one to three convulsions by means of the so-called symptomatic ECT. Although such symptomatic treatment today is the realm of pharmacotherapy, the identical effect of maintenance ECT suggests some common denominator in the action of the two treatments.

The greatest research effort was undoubtedly made in laboratory investigations, especially by American workers. Somatic treatments immensely increased the interest of the basic sciences in psychiatry even if actual results did not live up to expectations. It was the first great disappointment that in spite of numerous studies, insulin treatment with its metabolic implications contributed nothing to the understanding of the biochemistry of schizophrenia. Some theories, such as the one by Meduna connecting certain changes of carbohydrate metabolism with various groups of schizophrenia, were not related to experiences with insulin treatment. There is essential agreement that hypoglycemia per se has no effect on the schizophrenic illness. Light hypoglycemia as obtained in subcoma or so-called ambulatory insulin treatment, even if repeated daily for many months, is considered by most workers as of little value in schizophrenia except for a symptomatic reduction of tension and for improvement of the patient's physical condition. If some investigators (such as Greaves et al.) did obtain favorable results, this is probably explained by a relatively higher percentage of deeper hypoglycemic states in such groups.

Aside from insulin other hormones were used in the treatment of schizophrenia before and after the introduction of the so-called shock treatments. Some, which had been tried on the basis of certain theories, failed to confirm these theories. This applies particularly to attempts with thyroid, where originally favorable impressions by Gjessing could not be confirmed. He combined dietary measures regarding nitrogen metabolism with administration of thyroid extract. Later, Danziger et al., saw some favorable results in periodic catatonics by raising the basal metabolism rate with thyroid alone without regard to the nitrogen balance. On the basis of the hypothesis that adrenocortical activities have some etiologic importance in schizophrenia, bilateral adrenolectomies were performed, but Apta and later others came to negative conclusions. ACTH and cortisone were recommended by Cohn et al., but Glaser and Hoch found ACTH ineffective.

The thought of bringing brain function to a temporary standstill found its reflection in various therapeutic attempts. Such thoughts were first expressed by Klaesi. However, his continuous sleep treatment did not fulfill the hope that complete rest of brain function might have a beneficial effect on schizophrenia. Some Soviet psychiatrists are inclined to base their results with both insulin and pharmacologic sleep treatment on such theoretical ideas. However, their more recent electric sleep treatment, still used by some clinicians in neurotic patients, has not found wider application in schizophrenia. It should be added that psychiatric thinking in Pavlovian terms tends to explain the effect of neuroleptic drugs with their ability to insulate the organism from stimuli. According to a summary by J. Wortis, Soviet psychiatrists see a dual therapeutic role in chlorpromazine (aminazine). It dampens overstimulation and promotes reorganization of disordered conditioned responses. Like many other explanations these are deductions from theoretical beliefs, not facts proved by clinical or laboratory findings.

The effect of chlorpromazine on the EEG pattern from stimulation of the reticular formation and studies of the antiadrenergic activity of phenothiazines led to interesting results, but neither these nor other experimental findings account for all the actions of phenothiazines in schizophrenia, nor do they contribute anything to an understanding of the disease. The difficulty in interpreting experimental findings is well illustrated by the thorough investigations by Himwich, who found that the phenothiazines and also the barbiturates suppress the midbrain reticular formation but that the rauwolfia derivatives stimulate it. It is difficult to understand in the light of such findings why phenothiazines and rauwolfia derivatives in spite of such differences have a similar effect on schizophrenic symptoms, while barbiturates have none.

The action of the newer drugs has also been explained in psychoanalytical terms. The formulation that the phenothiazines decrease what Freud called "psychic energy" available to the ego, is no more helpful in the understanding of the disease than theories following Pavlovian lines. The same can be said about psychodynamic theories developed during the first years of shock treatments. Here the particular difficulty of nonpsychological theories was presented by the fact that insulin and convulsive therapies have even less in common in psychological than in biological terms. The fact that the hypoglycemic patient becomes helpless and dependent, and that the physician becomes a mother surrogate, may explain that the patient becomes psychotherapeutically more approachable but it does not enhance our understanding of the disease. Much was made of the experience of impending death followed by the feeling of rebirth in metrazol treatment, but these experiences are missing in ECT and are rather uncommon in insulin-treated patients. A strong argument against any psychological explanation of ECT is the clinical experience that cerebral stimulation leading to a petit mal or subconvulsive response is clinically entirely ineffective, while the same psychological situation associated with a grand mal convulsive effect of which the patient is unaware, does bring about clinical changes. More valuable were attempts by Schilder to combine psychological and organic theories stating that the victory over the death threat expressed in the organic manifestations of insulin or convulsive therapy with their perceptual and aphasic difficulties enable the patient to start life and normal relations with human beings all over again. He saw equal importance in the psychological situations as in the organic process of regeneration inherent in insulin coma, but even these attempts were not very helpful in reaching new knowledge from the application of somatic treatments in schizophrenia.

Does experience with somatic treatments and their supplementation with psychotherapeutic measures support a multifactorial etiology of schizophrenia? Our answer to this question is "no." It is a false argument to claim a multifactorial theory of schizophrenia on the basis of observations that both somatic and psychological treatments can be useful. As desirable as the blending of somatic and psychological theories of schizophrenia would be, our experience with the various treatments does not help us in this direction. Attempts at an integration of different viewpoints can easily add to the confusion and obscure our lack of knowledge. Those who try to explain schizophrenia in terms of "ego psychology" would be inclined to strengthen the ego by weakening the id or reducing a strong superego. Bellak is correct in pointing out that lobotomies most effectively decrease both superego and id impulses. Seen in the context of ego psychology, a successful, modified lobotomy in certain schizophrenic patients may have the same psychological effect as successful psychoanalytical treatment, leading to strengthening of the ego by weakening the superego and the id impulses. But such a formulation, interesting as it may be, does not contribute anything to our understanding of the disease schizophrenia.

There can be no doubt that the effect of the somatic treatments, even though still unknown, lies in the organic sphere. Thinking in organic terms we might conclude that shock treatments and neuroleptic drugs in favorable cases may affect an area of the brain from which certain schizophrenic symptoms originate. Unfortunately, this area is unknown as is also the site of action of the shock treatments. But such an area, if it exists, is definitely not in the frontal lobe affected by psychosurgical methods. The neuroleptic drugs initiated new interest in such ideas of brain localization. Their site of action is often seen in parts of the brain which were also implicated in the cerebral effect of the shock treatments. Concepts expressed independently by German authors such as Ewald and Haddenbrook and by French authors such as Delay pointed in the direction of the diencephalon. Clinical observations on weight and sleep disorders by myself and electroencephalographic findings by M. Roth seem to confirm the importance of this area for the treatment effect in schizophrenia.

In this survey only few areas of research could be touched upon; others, such as the one widely accepted theory of anoxia or of the histamine effect of all somatic treatments, were not mentioned, because they did not withstand the test of subsequent clinical experience. In spite of many disappointments in research and in spite of still limited clinical results, even the most skeptical observer must admit that the somatic treatments have an enormous influence on the field of schizophrenia. Clinically the therapeutic nihilism of the past has been replaced by a pragmatic attitude which benefited not only the large number of schizophrenics, but patients with other psychiatric disorders as well. Aside from this effect on wide areas of clinical psychiatry, psychopathologic and physiologic research has been stimulated to such an extent by the somatic treatments that we can hope for a better understanding of the disease and perhaps also better understood treatments in the not too distant future.

24

EFFECT OF DIET ON SCHIZOPHRENIC BEHAVIOR

by H. H. BERLET, M.D., C. BULL, M.D., H. E. HIMWICH, M.D., H. KOHL, M.S., K. MATSUMOTO, M.D., G. R. PSCHEIDT, PH.D., J. SPAIDE, M.S., T. T. TOURLENTES, M.D., and J. M. VALVERDE, M.D.*

CONSIDERABLE ATTENTION HAS BEEN DIRECTED in recent years to the urinary excretion of indole compounds accompanying various states of mental illness, particularly because the indole nucleus is found in numerous compounds which exert effects on behavior. Serotonin, an indole compound, is a normal constituent of the brain, but with its formula slightly changed it becomes bufotenin, a psychotomimetic substance.[22] Similar compounds are psilocybin,[33] psilocin,[30, 31, 35] and dimethyltryptamine.[60] It has been suspected for a long time that such an indole may be associated with schizophrenia. One way to study this problem is to examine the urine of schizophrenic patients for breakdown products of indole metabolism, and many data have accumulated on the difference in their excretions between normal and schizophrenic subjects.[55, 56] Work from our laboratory[9-11, 13, 15] was concerned with urinary indole excretion during periods of spontaneous worsening of behavior. The average outputs of urinary indole metabolites in patients with schizophrenia varied only within normal limits when all data were considered. But a striking correlation was observed in some patients between increases in the urinary excretions of tryptophan derivatives and the exacerbations of schizophrenic activity in terms of aggravations of hallucinatory and delusional experiences as well as aggressiveness and hostility. One of the purposes of the present investigation is to reexamine the relationship between the rises of urinary indoles and the worsening of behavior.

Another attack on the biochemical aspects of this problem is that

*Thudichum Psychiatric Research Laboratory, Galesburg State Research Hospital, Galesburg, Illinois.

of loading experiments with tryptophan, an essential amino acid present in protein foods and the precursor of all the indole amine compounds in the body. Given by itself tryptophan does not evoke notable changes in the behavior of schizophrenic patients, but when administered with a monoamine oxidase inhibitor (MAOI) it produces an aggravation of the symptoms of schizophrenia of selected schizophrenic patients.[1, 43] MAOI drugs prevent the breakdown of indole amines in the body, causing them to accumulate, and the behavioral worsening is thought to be due to increases of indoles in the brain. Indeed, even in normal controls the administration of tryptophan with an MAOI drug evoked conspicuous changes resembling alcoholic intoxication and including in addition drowsiness, hyperreflexia and clonus.[38] Like tryptophan, methionine, another essential amino acid, again in combination with a monoamine oxidase inhibitor also worsened the symptomatology of schizophrenic patients.[12, 43] An important function of methionine is to make methyl groups available for the metabolic process of the body. In view of the fact that other amino acids fail to call forth behavioral changes, it seemed to Brune and Himwich[12] that tryptophan and methionine might be involved together in a common mechanism in which increases of indoles derived from tryptophan and elevated levels of methyl groups, donated by methionine, might facilitate the formation of methylated indole amines with psychotogenic properties. Indeed, Axelrod[2] has demonstrated in vitro the methylation of tryptamine and serotonin to the psychotogenic substances dimethyltryptamine and bufotenin, respectively.

There are certain bits of information in the literature on the possible presence of the methylated indole substances in the urine of schizophrenic patients. The presence of bufotenin has been reported by Bumpus and Page[16] and by Fischer et al.,[23] while Brune and Himwich[13] found a bufotenin-like substance in the urine. But Sprince et al.,[57] have made extensive chromatographic studies of urinary indoles excreted after the administration either of tryptophan or methionine, whether to schizophrenic or psychoneurotic subjects pretreated with monoamine oxidase inhibiting drugs, and they could not demonstrate methylated indoles in the urine of their subjects. We are left therefore with only suggestive evidence that methylated indoles are associated with the psychotic symptomatology of schizophrenia. In contrast to studies in this area which concentrated on the effects of increased amounts of amino acids, the present one was founded to determine whether or not reductions of the amino acids tryptophan and methionine in the diet could improve behavior and ameliorate psychotic symptoms, the reverse of the disturbances of behavior resulting from amino acid loading. If reductions of the bodily contents of indole and methyl groups to critical levels could be accomplished, it should provide the opportunity to test the theory that such methylated indole compounds are associated with the schizophrenic process.

Methods

Design

The present study was designed as the first part of a longitudinal experiment (fig. 1). All psychoactive drugs were discontinued in our patients 2-4 months prior to the initiation of the dietary experiment which was started with a control diet for 6 weeks. During this time each patient was under psychiatric observation in order to establish behavioral baselines. This period was also used for chemical determinations to establish the urinary patterns of each patient. These control observations were followed by another series of 12 weeks with a

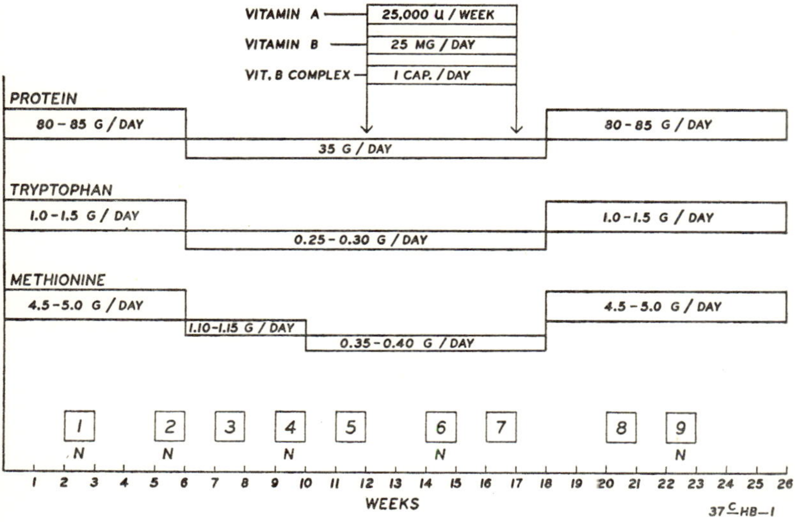

FIG. 1.—Experimental design of a longitudinal study. Part I. Low tryptophan, methionine diet, and controls. Dietary aspects of experimental design. Squares in lowest row of figure without N below indicate 5-day urine collections. Squares with N below indicate 7-day urine and feces collections, all used in the determination of nitrogen balances. The vitamin-B complex consisted of a tablet containing thiamin, 3 mg.; riboflavin, 2 mg.; and nicotinamide, 20 mg.

low tryptophan and low methionine diet representing the actual experimental part of the study. Finally, we had a second control period of 6 weeks duration with the reinstitution of the control diet, thus providing another opportunity for contrast with the experimental diet and in addition increasing the duration of the drug-free period from 2-4 months to 7-10.

Clinical

Nine chronic male schizophrenic patients with ages ranging from 39 to 59 years (mean, 53) and hospitalization periods from 6 to 28 years (mean, 19) were chosen for the study. They were picked as patients who could be managed without tranquilizing medication and yet who had active symptoms such as hallucinations or delusions which they would discuss, thereby providing indications of their mental status in addition to our other observations of their behavior. This group was maintained in a metabolic ward and was interviewed weekly by four physicians. In addition, day-to-day variations were noted by two physicians on daily ward rounds, and daily observations were noted by the trained psychiatric aides in charge of the metabolic ward. The latter recorded daily any changes in weight, eating and sleeping habits, and such behavior as socializing, alertness to surroundings, attention to appearance, and any other noteworthy changes. The psychiatric examination included such points as attention and cooperation during the interview, motor behavior, affectivity, thought content, stream of thought, sensorium and ward adjustment. For each patient a characteristic pattern of behavior was thus obtained for our initial controls. Any deviation from this individual pattern during the following experimental period was noted on a 0-4 scale according to the extent of changes and designated with a plus or minus, depending on whether there was improvement or a worsening of behavior, respectively.

Dietary

The patients were fed diets weighed before and after serving and prepared in the kitchen of the metabolic ward by a group of three workers under the supervision of one of us. (J.K.S.), a professional research dietitian, who was in charge of the dietary aspects of this investigation. Food intake records were maintained for each patient. The diets were calculated to provide 2500 calories/day, with individual caloric requirements adjusted by varying the fat and carbohydrate contents of the basic diet (calculated from Watt and Merrill.[64] The control diet as offered contained 1.0-1.5 Gm. tryptophan, 4.5-5.0 Gm. methionine, and 80-85 Gm. protein per day (calculated from Orr and Watt.[40] For the experimental diet tryptophan was reduced to 0.25-0.35 Gm./day, the minimal amount of tryptophan required for the maintenance of nitrogen balance in men.[46, 47] For the first 4 weeks methionine was decreased to 1.1-1.5 Gm./day, also the minimal daily requirement, and then was diminished further to 0.35-0.40 Gm./day for the last eight weeks.[46, 47] In order to accomplish these reductions the protein content of the diet was lowered to 35.0 Gm./day. The main protein source during the low protein phase was milk, but meat, eggs, and other dairy products were completely eliminated during this period. Nonprotein nitrogen in the form of glycine, however, was added so that the total nitrogen content of the diet offered was 4 Gm./day. All food ingredients known to contain preformed catechols and indoles were excluded from the experimental diet: bananas, avocados, plums, coffee, tea, tomatoes, pineapple, etc.[3, 8, 51, 61, 62] (see figure 1.)

Biochemical

At intervals of 2 to 3 weeks, 5-day urine collections were made; 2 during first control, 5 during low diet, and 2 during second control period. Additional 24-hour samples were collected when there were sudden behavioral changes in order to compare chemical alterations with the more dynamic transitions of behavioral disturbances. Collections of food, urine, and feces were made for 7-day periods in order to determine the nitrogen equilibrium. The actual daily tryptophan intake of each patient was calculated from the actual food consumption and protein intake. The protein intake was determined on the basis of analyses of food samples for total nitrogen. According to information published by Horwitt et al.[32] concerning the tryptophan content of diets, the average analyzed values for tryptophan in three diets was 264 mg./day. The calculated one was 25 mg. higher, indicating therefore a 9 per cent difference.

Tryptamine, total 3-indoleacetic acid, 5-hydroxyindole acetic acid, and 1-methyl nicotinamide were measured by the methods of Sjoerdsma et al.[54] Weissbach and associates,[65] Udenfriend and colleagues,[61] and Pelletier,[41] respectively. For the total nitrogen of food, feces, and urine the techniques of Scales and Harrison[49] were employed. Urinary creatinine was determined by the alkaline picrate method.[34] Urine

17-ketosteroids were measured according to Natelson,[37] and total glucocorticoids by the method of Silber and Porter,[52] and Porter and Silber.[44] Using the same samples of urine, adrenaline and noradrenaline were determined by the method of von Euler and Lishajko,[21] and dopamine according to that of Carlsson and Waldeck.[17] For 3-methoxy-4-hydroxymandelic acid a modification of the technique of Sandler and Ruthven[48] was made.

Results

Clinical

Three patients showed no significant behavioral changes during the low methionine-tryptophan period. One (A.A.) was a rather isolated, underproductive but contented individual who described simple visual and auditory hallucinations of what he called ghosts. He merely became slightly more interested and communicative and lost a mannerism which referred to his visual hallucinations. Another (R.C.) continued to be anxious, tense, and preoccupied with an elaborate bed-making ritual and similar obsessive concerns. He responded in a guarded way to auditory hallucinations and occasionally described a visual hallucination: "an ape." The third (S.P.) showed little variation in his marked underproductivity and withdrawal and continued a bizarre mannerism of pulling his disintegrating body back together again. He occasionally reported a visual hallucination of finding mice in his mouth during the low-diet period as well as the control period.

Three other patients became clearly worse during the experimental period. During the first control, one (J.V.), an intellectually oriented paranoid, became less organized in his speech to the point of being almost unintelligible at times and was less concerned about his appearance and general social adjustment. This worsening continued throughout the limited diet and second control period. Likewise, during the experimental period, another (W.C.), who had been alert although isolated and whose speech was disorganized as he described hallucinations and various peculiar ideas, became markedly less intelligible during the limited diet as well as the second control. A grandiose paranoid (J.H.), with ideas of being a general who was communicating with various high military officials and with certain persecutors, became more agitated, more actively hallucinating, and less cooperative during the limited diet and continued through the following control period.

Still another patient (O.W.), a rather grandiose intellectually oriented paranoid, fond of pseudo-philosophizing, developed a deterioration of the intelligibility of his speech during the first control period and the first half of the limited diet period. He became more coherent again during the latter half of the limited period and the second control, and at the same time became more interested in discussing fairly realistic interests instead of his bizarre somatic delusions. His overall improvements, however, were considered too little to be conclusive.

The two remaining patients fluctuated with no final improvement. J. F. fluctuated on a rather regular 6 to 16 day cycle (averaging about 8 days) between depressed, withdrawn, disinterested behavior and a boisterous, protesting, agitated state. At all times his speech was quite unintelligible except for isolated phrases. His cycles did not appear to differ conclusively in duration during the period of the limited diet, although in the equal period of 69 days there were 9 more withdrawn days and 7 fewer agitated days during the limited diet period than during the control diet. A depressed hypochondriacal patient (E.S.) with bizarre somatic delusions was observed to be

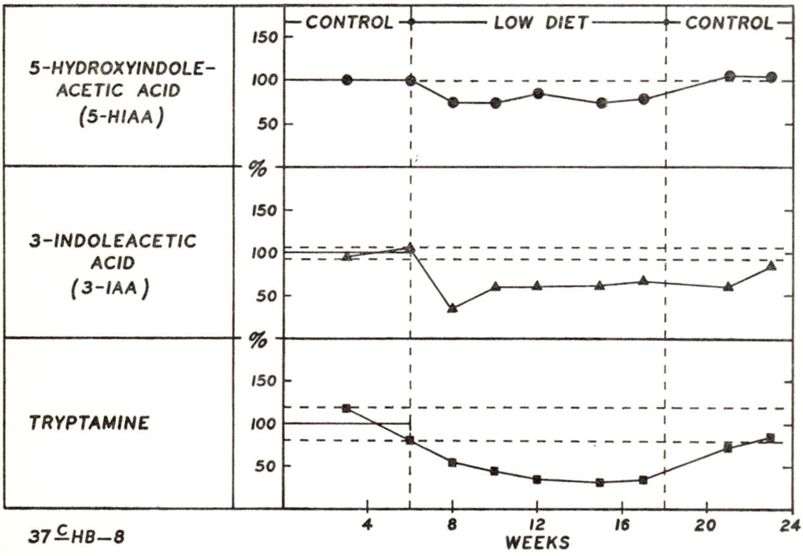

FIG. 2.—Averages of urinary excretion of 5-HIAA, 3-IAA, and tryptamine in per cent of the initial control values—100 per cent. Decreases in the three indole urinary metabolites occur during the restricted diet.

more bland during the 12 weeks limited diet and during the second control period three one-day outbursts of agitated hostile behavior. His most severe outburst occurred during the first control period.

Biochemical

One of the main goals of this study was to lower the body content of indoles and methyl groups in order to diminish the biochemical formation of psychotomimetic methylated compounds. Such a reduction was demonstrated for the indoles by the decreased urinary excretion of indole derivatives (Fig. 2). Tryptamine responded more than the other two urinary indoles to the low tryptophan intake and seemed to be the most sensitive indicator of alterations of the indole metabolism with an overall reduction of 53 per cent. Least affected was 5-hydroxyindole acetic acid (5-HIAA), which diminished by 22 per cent, and in between came 3-indole acetic acid (3-IAA) with a decrease of 32 per cent.

In contrast to our results with the indoleamines, we were not able to achieve a functional reduction of methyl groups by using the ability to methylate nicotinamide as an indicator, although our patients were on a methionine intake below that of the minimal requirement. Figure 3 shows the course of excretion of this compound which returned to almost normal levels upon the addition of 20 mg. of nicotinamide per day. The fall was therefore caused by lack of nicotinamide rather than a decreased availability of methyl groups.

Except for dopamine, the average excretion values of the catechols revealed no significant changes. Both noradrenaline and adrenaline show some variations, but the figures of the low period stay well within the limits established by the controls. The average urinary eliminations of noradrenaline were 33 μg./day during the control diet and exactly the same on the limited diet. For adrenaline the corresponding values were 12 μg./day on both diets. For VMA the values were 4.6 mg./day versus 4.7 mg./day. There was a remarkable elevation of dopamine above normal levels of eight of our nine patients during the second part of the low diet period, with average increases from 301 μg./day in the controls to 448 μg./day on the limited diet.

Both the average excretions of 17-ketosteroids and of total glucocorticoids also failed to show any significant differences between the normal and low diets, with averages for 17-ketosteroids of 14.2 mg./day and 13.1 mg./day, respectively. The corresponding daily values for total glucocorticoids were 8.0 mg. and 7.8 mg. If we omit from the aver-

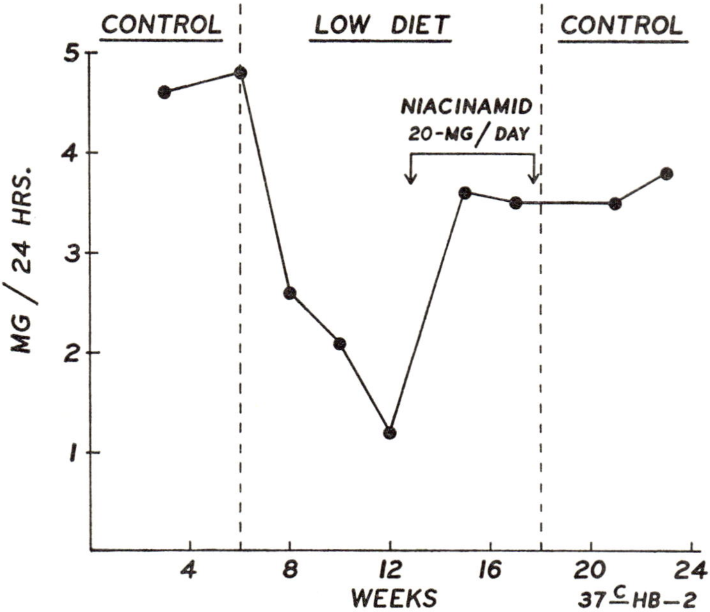

FIG. 3.—Averages of 1-methy-nicotinamide excretions during three dietary periods. The decrease in methylation was not significant after the addition of niacinamide to the diet.

ages the higher figures on two patients (J.V. and S.P.), the four values on a daily basis become 11.0, 10.5, 7.0, and 7.0, respectively.

Observations on Blood Chemistry, Weight, and Nitrogen Balance

During the initial phase of the dietary experiment, normal values were found for blood sugar, NPN, total protein, A/G ratio, cholesterol, bilirubin, alkaline phosphatase, serum glutamic pyruvic transaminase, and thymol turbidity. These evaluations were repeated in regular intervals throughout the entire study and significant alterations were not observed.

Particular attention was paid to the serum proteins as an index for protein metabolism and liver function. Total serum proteins dropped only approximately 10 per cent during the restricted diet, and the value of 6.4 mg. per cent remained within normal limits. There was no shift from the albumin fraction to the globulin fraction on the low diet. It should be noted that our low diet was specifically arranged to be compatible with physical health insofar that it supplied

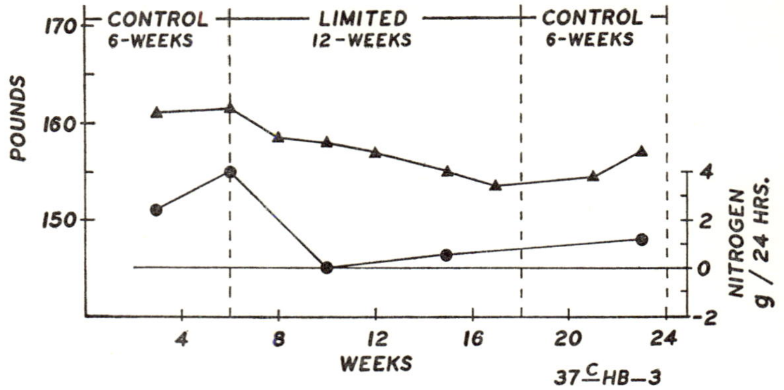

Fig. 4.—Average weights during periods of control and limited diets and average nitrogen balances. The upper curve refers to the average weight of the nine patients in pounds and the lower one to the average nitrogen balances in Gm./24 hrs. Note that all averages except one are positive.

the minimal daily requirement for tryptophan. The methylation necessary for normal liver and other body functions was not significantly reduced, while in most instances nitrogen equilibrium was maintained.

Figure 4 shows the averaged weight of nine patients during the experimental and two control periods. During the low diet only were there slight losses of weight, averaging 190 Gm./week per patient. The daily nitrogen balances were positive in 18 instances during the control diet, within the error of ± 5 per cent on 4 occasions, and negative twice. On the low diet the nitrogen balances were positive 8 times, within ± 5 per cent 5 times and negative on 5 other occasions, but the averages for all these values, presented in the lower curve of figure 4, were positive during the control diet and remained in balance during the experimental period.

Correlations between Behavior and Metabolic Changes

There were few marked changes in behavior from day to day in seven patients in our group of nine during the three observation periods, and conclusive comparisons between daily behavioral worsening and urinary excretion patterns were precluded for that reason. However, two other patients (E.S. and J.F.) exhibited episodes of pronounced exacerbations of their psychotic symptomatology or sudden changes in the character of their mental disturbances. Figures 5 and 6 reveal the average results during 5-day periods of psychotic activation as well as of increased motor activity and anxiety obtained

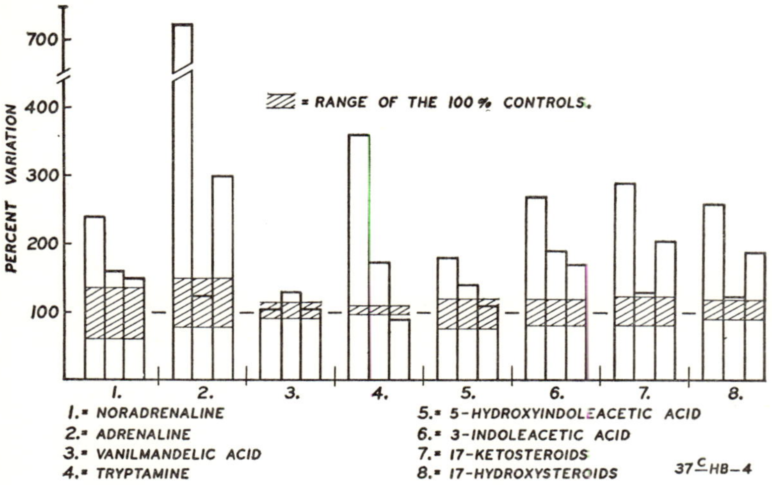

FIG. 5.—Urinary excretions of catecholamines, indoleamines, and steroid hormones during periods of aggravation of schizophrenic symptoms in patient E. S.

from two different patients in terms of indole compounds, catecholamines, and steroid hormones. The highest values for E.S. (Figure 5) were taken out of the individual daily collections of the 4- and 5-day periods of behavioral worsening and are compared with the values obtained during periods of reduced psychotic activity. On two occasions during his most severe outbursts E.S. exhibited definite increases of urinary tryptamine excretion, and rises of 3-IAA excretion occurred 3 times while 5-HIAA was only slightly elevated. Steroid

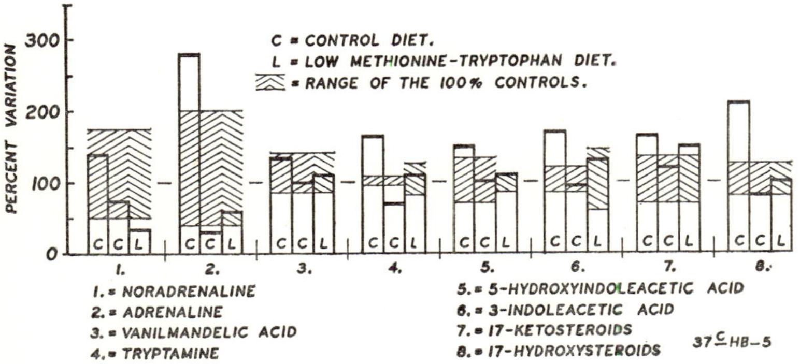

FIG. 6.—Urinary excretions of catecholamines, indoleamines, and steroid hormone during periods of aggravation of schizophrenic symptoms in patient J. F.

hormone excretions were also raised during the same period, as were the catecholamines to some extent. Similar changes are presented in Figure 6 for J. F. Increases of indole excretions were accompanied by rises of adrenaline, 17-ketosteroid hormones, and total glucocorticoids during the daily collections, but there was no such definite elevation of the average values in the 5-day collections except in one instance.

Figure 6 does not give day-to-day changes during these periods of behavioral worsening and they are presented for one such period in figure 7. This severe episode of behavioral disturbance of E.S. occurred during a control diet period and was considered extreme, with outbursts of violence and hostility accompanied by a great intensification of motor activity. This particular episode lasted for 4 days with peak excretions on the second day, though behavioral exaggerations were greatest on the third day. Marked elevations of indole excretion occurred, highest with tryptamine to 260 per cent, next with 3-IAA to 250 per cent, and the smallest rise was that of 5-

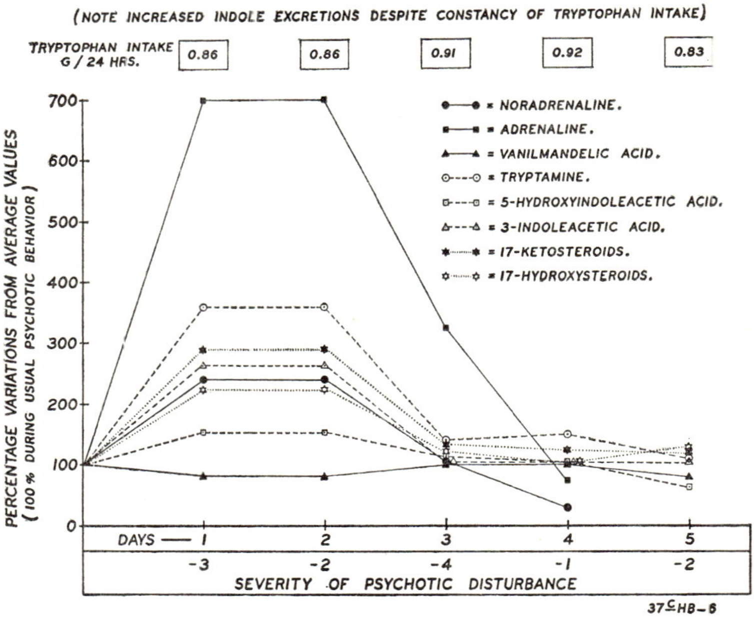

FIG. 7.—Urinary patterns during an episode of behavioral exacerbation, including aggravations of schizophrenic symptomatology as well as anxiety and hyperactivity. Except for vanilylmandelic acid, all other compounds exhibit increases. Note that the peak excretions occurred prior to the most severe behavioral disturbance, as indicated in lowest line of figure.

hydroxyindole acetic acid to 150 per cent of the controls. These three increases occurred despite a practically constant actual tryptophan intake ranging from 0.83 g./day to 0.92 g./day.

Along with these elevations, general rises were observed in almost all the other urinary compounds during these periods of behavioral worsening. Of particular interest is the increased steroid hormone excretion which correlated closely with that of the catecholamines except for vanilylmandelic acid (VMA). It appeared therefore to be of great interest to determine whether or not the excretion patterns during behavioral worsening correlated with other than psychotic symptomatology—namely, anxiety and motor activity (fig. 8). All values used were obtained on urine collected during periods without exacerbations of schizophrenic symptoms. Three patients were chosen for these comparisons, and the values of the other six were taken as

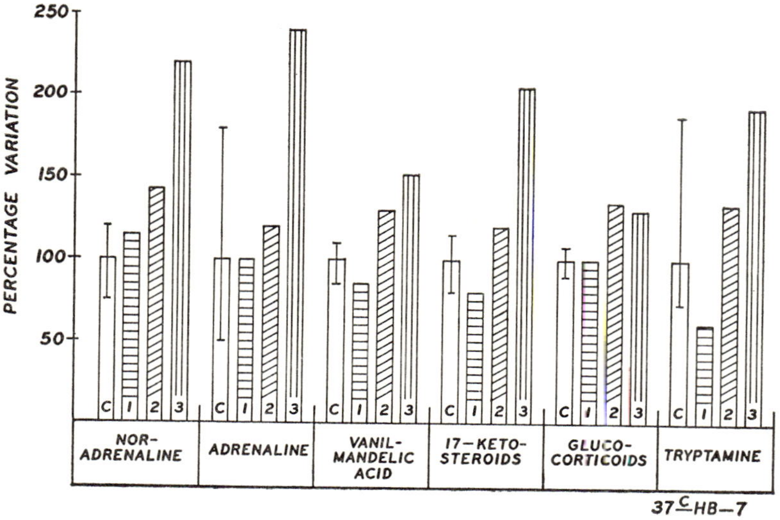

FIG. 8.—Urinary constituents, anxiety, and motor activity. Like the other six patients who revealed no great variations in motor activity and anxiety, patient I with moderate anxiety and no hyperactivity did not reveal changes in the urinary products. Patient II, however, with more anxiety and no increase of physical activity did disclose increased excretion of the catecholamines and the steroid hormones. Patient III without marked anxiety but with great hyperactivity revealed the highest results with the exception of the glucocorticoids. Note that none of these patients experienced aggravation of their schizophrenic symptoms during these periods and that tryptamine as an example of the indole urinary products failed to increase above the control values.

controls at times when they did not reveal motor restlessness. Patient I with moderate anxiety and no increase of physical activity did not show any deviations from the other six patients, but patient II, who consistently exhibited more anxiety, and patient III, without marked anxiety but with greater hyperactivity, showed increases of noradrenaline, VMA, 17-ketosteroids, and total glucocorticoids. Patient III differs from Patient II in revealing overall elevations which were much more pronounced with each of these excretory products except for the total glucocorticoids. Thus a weighing of these two variables indicated that though both were effective, motor activity would seem to be more so. These three patients did not exhibit aggravations of their schizophrenic symptoms simultaneously with their motor restlessness, and it is therefore interesting to note that they did not have an elevation of urinary indole metabolites. Tables 1a and 1b, present the ranges of actual tryptophan intake for given periods as well as the values

TABLE 1a.—Indole Excretion in Correlation to Creatinine, Tryptophan Intake, and Behavior (Patient J.F.)

	Tryptophan Intake (Gm./day)	Tryptamine (μg./day)	3-IAA (mg./day)	5-HIAA (mg./day)	Creatinine (mg./day)	Variati[illegible] of Behavio[illegible] Exacerba[illegible]
Range during Usual Behavior Control Diet	1.0-1.5	+5% to −4%	+21% to −14%	+35% to −33%	+5% to −4%	
Period I (daily) #7A	0.90-1.07	+98%	+34%	+43%	+35%	−2 to −
Period II (daily) 110/4	0.53-0.69	+192%	+43%	−2%	+40%	−4
Period III 5-day-average (#9)	0.93-1.06	−32%	−6%	−2%	−9%	−1 to −
Range during Usual Behavior Low Methionine-Tryptophan	0.25-0.35	+23% to −20%	+45% to −40%	+8% to −15%	+9% to −7%	0
Period IV 5day-average	0.24-0.34	+8%	+30%	+10%	+10%	+1 to −

for the three urinary indoles and creatinine in terms of the percentages of the levels during periods with usual behavior. The latter is designated as 0 and the steps from —1 to —4 indicate the degrees of behavioral worsening while positive numbers reveal improvement. Some of the values represent the pattern for one particular day which was selected for the highest increases of the urinary compounds in a given behavioral episode. Others were for pooled 5-day collections and thus represent the average of 5 days. Both parts of table 1 show that behavioral worsening was usually accompanied by elevations of urinary products and was greatest in periods with the most severe behavioral disturbances, as indicated by the rating of —4. On the other hand, there was little or no increase when the rating included —1 or even rose to +1. Thus there was a rough correlation between the rises of the urinary indole excretions and symptomatic activation. Similarly, the trends of creatinine changes go along with those of the indoles. Of the three tryptophan derivatives the rises in tryptamine were the greatest, except in two instances, while those with 5-HIAA were usually the least. Thus tryptamine shows the most consistent pattern when compared to behavioral variations and may therefore be the best indicator of processes which are going on during the behavioral worsening.

TABLE 1b.—Patient E.S.

	Tryptophan Intake (Gm./day)	Tryptamine (μg./day)	3-IAA (mg./day)	5-HIAA (mg./day)	Creatinine (mg./day)	Variation of Behavioral Exacerbation
ange during Usual ehavior Control Diet	1.0-1.5	+3% to −2%	+20% to −17%	+21% to −23%	+1% to −1%	0
eriod I (daily) #2	0.83-0.92	+261%	+169%	+79%	+92%	−2 to −4
eriod II (daily) #9	0.93-1.06	+73%	+95%	+37%	+4%	−2 to −3
eriod III (5 days) #10	0.80-1.03	+111%	−7%	+37%	+12%	−2 to −3
eriod IV (daily) #7A	0.90-1.07	−8%	+42%	−14%	−8%	−2 to −3

Discussion

Clinical

We were unable to demonstrate any clear relationship between the dietary restrictions of tryptophan and methionine and changes in the behavior of our schizophrenic patients. In general, four patients were unchanged (O.W., A.A., R.C., and S.P.), three became worse (W.C., J.H., and J.V.), while two (E.S. and J.F.) were disturbed to lesser degrees in regard to schizophrenic activation on the limited diet than on the control. Thus the fluctuations in behavior seen throughout the observation periods did not seem to be altered by the low methionine-tryptophan diet. The worsening in mental condition noted in three of the patients appears to have started before the low diet, although it became more clear-cut later in the study on the control diet. This impairment did not seem to be the worsening—that is, the increase in delusions, that sometimes occurs when apathetic chronic patients are stimulated by renewed close contact with a more active environment.[58] Instead, the changes involved a loosening of associations and an increase in withdrawal and apathy. It was perhaps the delayed worsening that sometimes occurs up to 6 months after discontinuing tranquilizers, according to Good et al.[26] as well as Olson and Peterson.[39] The stable behavior during the 8- to 16-week medication period, which preceded the formal 6-week control diet, was perhaps deceptive. A longer drug-free period might have eliminated the impairment in behavior observed during the experimental period. There was, moreover, no improvement afterwards during the 6 weeks in control, so it was not likely that it was a result of the restricted diet. It is at least clear that if there were any beneficial effects of restricting the tryptophan and methionine intake, they were insufficient to prevent the gradual relapsing that was seen.

The most agitated and hostile behavior of E.S. occurred in the control period, and he was more bland during the restricted period. This change may be regarded as evidence of improvement though his outbursts were brief rather than sustained, and therefore were difficult to evaluate. It is true that in the cyclical behavior of J.F. he had fewer agitated days during the period of dietary restrictions and also experiences more withdrawn days in the low diet, but these changes were not considered to indicate a clear trend towards quieter behavior since the disturbed episodes, although less frequent, were rated as more severe in intensity. In both patients, however, there were lesser degrees of psychotic activation on the limited diet, and in this connection we may point out that only in these two patients did we have the opportunity to test the effects of the low diet to ameliorate episodic behavioral worsening. But for the other seven patients the low diet could not be associated with any beneficial behavioral effects.

We should point out, however, that at no time was tryptophan entirely eliminated from the diet. Furthermore, in none of the nine patients were we able to establish a critical decrease of methyl groups, for the latter were always available in the body, as indicated by the ability to methylate nicotinamide. This availability was apparent even though the methionine intake in these experiments was reduced to one-third the daily minimal requirement and hence to a greater extent than the decreases in dietary tryptophan.

Great reductions of serotonin levels in brain and plasma of rats have been reported when tryptophan was entirely eliminated from the diet,[19] but to do so in the present study would have exposed our patients to the dangers of a negative nitrogen balance and the breakdown of body tissues. Similarly, the elimination of choline as well as of methionine could have diminished the intake of methyl groups even further, but such a drastic reduction would have resulted in fatty infiltration of the liver as well as destruction of hepatic tissues. To try to carry out the hypothesis to its logical extreme would have caused somatic effects which would be equally disastrous, if not more so, than the psychological disturbances of schizophrenia. In the present observations it is highly probable that the plasma and the tissues of the body, including those of the brain, had available metabolites of tryptophan metabolism as well as methyl groups.

Differentiation between Behavioral Changes Accompanying Indole Increases and Those of Catechols and Steroids

We wish to emphasize that under the highly controlled conditions of these observations we have been able to confirm our previous conclusions[9, 11-15] that increases of urinary indoleamine metabolites accompany worsening of psychotic behavior. Moreover, schizophrenic activation rather than withdrawal seems to be the main condition for this correlation between behavior and indole metabolism.

Increases in the severity of hallucinations and delusional thinking were always accompanied by hyperactivity and anxiety, but opportunities were available to test the separate behavioral accompaniments of schizophrenic activation in contrast to motor restlessness when the latter occurred without schizophrenic exacerbations (see fig. 8). Under these conditions urinary indoles remained low and did so even though elevations of catecholamines and steroid hormones occurred. In all instances, however, whether with or without increased severity of psychotic outbursts, marked motor activity and anxiety were associated with rises of the urinary catechols and steroids.

There is ample evidence in the literature that anxiety and motor activity can increase urinary catechols in nonpsychotic individuals during muscular work, tilting the body, and hypoglycemia as well as surgical, traumatic, and emotional stresses.[20] The steroid hormones also rise with such bodily changes as severe muscular exercise,[28] the viewing of war movies,[63] and various kinds of emotional stresses.[6, 45] These biochemical alterations are therefore characteristic of any situation in which the body reacts with stress and increased motor activity. In the present investigation, however, both constellations of symptoms occurred together as the stress and motor activity in our patients were induced by the increased severity of the psychotic symptoms.

Suggestions for an Endogenous Metabolic Factor in the Activation of Schizophrenic Symptoms

The rises of urinary tryptamine and the two other tryptophan derivatives presented in figures 5, 6, and 7 and tables 1a and 1b probably reflect similar elevations in the blood. It would seem therefore that these increases are due to a release of tryptophan in the body. Possible sources for such increases may be of endogenous or exogenous origin. In regard to the latter, it is well to point out that in comparison with the variations of the actual tryptophan intake, the rises of the indoles exceed by far the range of the daily tryptophan intake. In absolute amounts, however, the range of 0.90 to 1.07 Gm./day in Period I in table 1a could very well furnish the additional amount of precursors for the increase of tryptamine, 3-IAA, and 5-HIAA taken altogether, since tryptamine is measured in μg. and the excretion of 3-IAA and 5-HIAA did not exceed a total of approximately 40 mg./day. This explanation of an indole increase would, however, require that there was a shift of tryptophan metabolism from other pathways towards the indole pathway in our patients. The evidence for such a shift, however, is lacking except for the pathological condition of malignant carcinoid where 60 per cent of tryptophan administered is 5-hydroxylated to form serotonin instead of 1 per cent under normal circumstances.[53] We cannot estimate the importance of the exogenous factor at this time and we shall go on to evaluate the endogenous one. For an endogenous source there are various indications: a diminished food intake and especially so at a time when the caloric demand is increased by hyperactivity. Also to be considered is the practically constant intake of tryptophan during a given period of worsening. Figure 7 reveals the relatively small day-to-day variations in tryptophan intake.

In seeking the mechanism for the greater amounts of the tryptophan metabolites in the urine from an endogenous source, we note that the elimination of creatinine rose in general with that of the indole metabolites. In regard to creatinine, we may turn to the observation that the excretion of that substance is related closely to the active muscle mass of the body.[42] In fact, the urinary creatinine output is constant over long periods and under the most varied circumstances, including exercise and large variations of urinary volumes. Underweight individuals exhibit an abnormally high excretion of creatinine. In contrast, in the obese it is abnormally low. When corrective diet is successful, however, creatinine remains unchanged but becomes normal in relation to muscle mass. On the other hand, it is also true that in addition to muscle mass, other factors known and unknown influence creatinine excretion.[18] It is known, for example, that the ingestion of a diet devoid of creatine and creatinine but adequate in protein lowers creatinine as much as 30 per cent.[5] We have also observed in the present study that during the period of reduced protein intake the excretion of creatinine was diminished. The chief dietary ingredient for diminishing or increasing the creatinine output is meat, formed largely of muscle, and containing large amounts of preformed creatinine.

Our clinical observations suggest that the variations of the three tryptophan metabolites are associated with changes of appetite, for in general our patients ate less for 3 or 4 days before the exacerbations of behavior, which were accompanied by weight losses in some instances. E.S. was new to the metabolic ward, but J.F. has been on one of our two metabolic wards uninterruptedly for the last 12 years and repeatedly the psychiatric aides have successfully foretold an episode as he lost his appetite for several days before the behavioral worsening became manifest. Probably then a breakdown of muscle protein is the result of an inadequate food intake. For example, in J.F. and E.S. the calculated caloric intake per day fell from 2360 to 1330 and 2760 to 2240, respectively, during periods with activated symptoms. In accord with this possibility is the negative nitrogen balance in E.S. for the period of 7 days, including those before, during, and after the peak behavioral disturbance. This negative balance may be compared with a positive one in the previous 7-day period also on the control diet which, however, was not associated with any intensification of the psychotic symptoms. Another indication of impaired appetite and diminished food intake is the decrease in the amount of tryptophan consumed, a decrease which occurred despite the efforts of the psychiatric aides to encourage eating. For example, in patient J.F., episode 2, table 1a, the intake of tryptophan was reduced most in accordance with a behavioral rating of —4, indicating extreme symptomatic activation. Similarly with E.S., episode 1 of table 1b, the only behavorial rating of —4 for this patient was associated with his least mean tryptophan intake. It is also interesting that in both of these episodes the highest elevations of tryptamine occurred. In all instances of behavioral worsening, moreover, motor restlessness increased caloric demands at a time when food intake was reduced. In any event a possible factor for schizophrenic worsening consists in a change in muscle metabolism, as indicated by the greater elimination of creatinine, a process involving a shift of caloric supplies from exogenous to endogenous sources. The body consumed its own substance in order to obtain the calories necessary for its support, and the amino acids, including tryptophan and methionine, probably were released from muscle protein.

The first episode of E.S. in table 1b, detailed in figure 5, reveals that the peak elevation of the three tryptophan derivatives occurred before the most severe behavioral worsening and that all three derivatives receded before improvement began. In other instances, however, the rise of the urinary constituents either accompanied or immediately followed the peak behavioral disturbance. But regardless of the relationship to the peak disturbance, each period of severe symptomatic activation was preceded by an elevation of urinary indoles. Similar observations were previously made by Brune and Himwich[9] as well as Sprince et al.,[57] but in their studies, unlike the present one, the patients were on various medications. The close temporal association of behavioral disturbances with increases of urinary tryptophan derivatives suggests that tryptophan or its product, tryptamine, acts like an endogenous metabolic factor to intensify the psychotic symptoms.

Behavior of Schizophrenic Patients and Biochemical Changes in the Body

We have seen that behavioral changes in our schizophrenic patients were associated, on a temporal basis, with biochemical alterations, increases of the three tryptophan derivatives (tryptamine, 5-hydroxyindole acetic acid, and 3-indoleacetic acid) in the urine and probably in the blood. In regard to the relationship between tryptamine and behavior, we may point out that the blood-brain barrier is permeable to that amine;[27] thus the blood can supply this indoleamine directly to the brain where it may be changed chemically to a psychotogenic amine. Secondly, we have suggested that tryptophan is liberated from the body protein, especially that of muscle, and we have good evidence from animal experimentation that the brain has the ability to transform tryptophan to serotonin, an indoleamine.[25, 29] If methionine is liberated in the body during behavioral worsening, then like tryptophan it can enter the brain, and the possibility therefore exists that the two amino acids may act together to form a psychotogenic methylated indoleamine. Admittedly, there are other possibilities. For instance, we may be seeing simply effects of the increased concentrations of tryptamine, tryptophan, and methionine as individual entities rather than acting together, but all such possibilities indicate processes by which the mind of schizophrenic patients, as judged by behavioral expression, can be affected by the action of biochemical substances on the brain.

Theoretical

We have been able to confirm former observations from our laboratory which disclose a close temporal relationship between behavioral worsening and elevation of urinary tryptophan metabolites in schizophrenic patients. In addition, in the present analysis the rises of urinary creatinine are simultaneous with those of the tryptophan derivatives. Because such increases of creatinine could have originated in the breakdown of muscle substance, it is suggested that the source of the tryptophan is the breakdown of muscle protein, a conclusion which received some support from the negative nitrogen balance in the most severe of all episodes observed in the present investigation. If the loss of appetite may be regarded as a prodromal symptom of behavioral worsening, an unknown initiating cause may have precipitated the episode, with appetite impairment as an early symptom.

The increases of the tryptophan metabolites in the body seemed to act as a positive feedback to aggravate the psychotic behavior. If there was a breakdown of muscle protein, then the amino acids released into the body would include tryptophan and methionine, though admittedly we have evidence only for increased tryptophan and have none on methionine. In that regard we would like to recall the observations of Pollin, Cardon, and Kety,[43] mentioned in the introduction, revealing that only these two amino acids in the presence of a MAOI drug were able to activate psychotic symptoms in schizophrenic patients. It is also appropriate to refer again to the suggestion of Brune and Himwich[11] that tryptophan may contribute the indole nucleus and methionine, methyl groups, to form a psychotogenic methylated amine such as N,N-dimethyl tryptamine, a substance originally studied by Szara.[60] Because of the greater percentage rise of tryptamine than of 5-hydroxyindole acetic acid, a breakdown product of serotonin, our data are in accord with the production of a tryptamine-like compound rather than one resembling serotonin.

The experimental administration of tryptophan and methionine may be regarded as introducing into the body an exogenous metabolic factor which, however, does not require the presence of a monoamine oxidase inhibitor to evoke behavioral changes. The introduction of this drug may account for the fact that Brune and Himwich,[12] as well as Sprince et al.[57] reported not only similarities but also dissimilarities between the symptoms occurring spontaneously in schizophrenic patients and those provoked by the administration of a monoamine oxidase inhibitor and methionine. Increased amounts of tryptophan and methionine, whether derived exogenously or endogenously, could act as a metabolic factor by enhancing the formation of a psychotogenic indole.

The hypothetical chain (fig. 9) for behavioral worsening in schizophrenic patients would thus include: (1) an unknown initial cause with loss of appetite as an early symptom; (2) breakdown of muscle protein with release of tryptophan and perhaps methionine forming an endogenous metabolic factor; (3) the endogenous metabolic factor in turn furnishes additional materials for the formation of a psychotogenic indole; (4) and finally the action of the psychotogenic indole to enhance the severity of the psychotic symptoms.[4]

Finally, we should like to make two remarks in order to clarify the boundaries of our investigation. We have not been concerned with the nosological entity of schizophrenia per se which has, for example, been the subject of such studies as those of Friedhoff and van Winkle[24] and Sen and McGeer[50] with metabolism with catechol substances, but rather with the activation of schizophrenic symptoms and indole compounds. Secondly, we would like to know whether or not the mechanism we have suggested of symptomatic activation is specific for schizophrenic patients. Even though our subjects were schizophrenic, it is possible that a similar mechanism may be operative in other conditions. In this regard it is well to recall that Sprince et al.[57] have observed that the administration of a MAOI with methionine to psychoneurotic patients provoked rises of indole metabolites in the urine as well as hallucinations and delusions. In a personal communication, these authors informed us that one of the two psychoneurotic patients reported developed two hallucinogenic-hysteric episodes with tranylcypromine and methionine. Another psychoneurotic, not included in their paper because urinary studies were not done, experienced definite visual and auditory hallucinations on the combination of tranylcypromine and methionine. As far as these investigators could determine, neither of these two patients was subject to hallucinations or delusions prior to the administration of the combination of tranylcypromine and methionine. At present it is therefore necessary to examine the mechanism of symptomatic activation further and to determine how widespread it may be.

SUMMARY

In conclusion, we can say in the first place that dietary reduction of the bodily sources of indole and methyl groups has not been

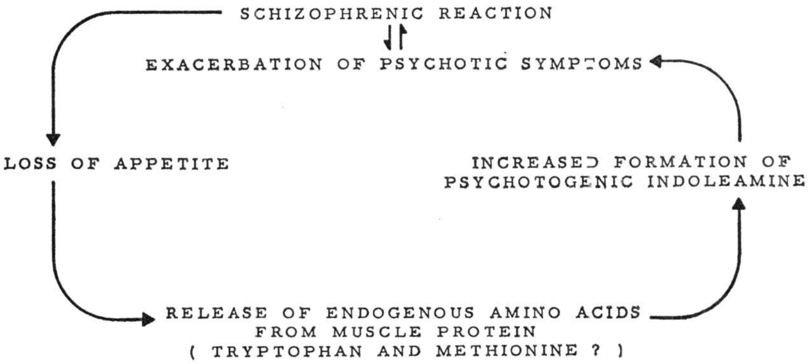

FIG. 9.—A hypothetical chain of events in behavioral exacerbation of schizophrenic patients. Figure is explained in text.

successful in affecting favorably the symptomatology of nine chronic schizophrenic patients. We feel, however, that we did not push our dietary exclusion to the limit for fear of affecting adversely the physical health of our patients.

Secondly, we have been able to confirm, under highly controlled dietary conditions, our former observations indicating that schizophrenic worsening in terms of aggravation of schizophrenic acting-out, with exacerbations of delusional thinking as well as of hallucinatory experiences, is associated with increases in urinary indoles and that these urinary changes do not accompany the kind of schizophrenic worsening characterized by withdrawal. In our patients psychotic acting-out and motor restlessness occurred simultaneously, and not only indoles but also catechols and steroids appeared in greater amounts in the urine. But when hyperactivity and affective tension were found to occur independently of increased severity of schizophrenic symptoms, only the catechols and steroids rose; the indoles remained low. Thus indoles are characteristic of schizophrenic activation, while catechols and steroids rose with increased anxiety and motor activity either with or without schizophrenic activation.

The last portion of our paper is concerned with a study of the relationships between the apparently spontaneous behavioral worsening and the urinary excretion of the three tryptophan derivatives. In our patients for whom the tryptophan and methionine contents of the diet were kept practically constant, both at control and reduced levels, the rise of the three tryptophan derivatives in the urine probably came from tryptophan produced endogenously. The simultaneous elevation of creatinine with the three tryptophan metabolites suggest muscle protein breakdown as the source of the endogenous tryptophan. This breakdown may be ascribed to the need for calories at a time when the food intake is inadequate due to a loss of appetite which occurred immediately before and during behavioral worsening. Because the exaggeration of the psychotic symptoms were always accompanied by motor restlessness, the caloric requirements were stepped up despite an insufficient intake. If the loss of appetite is a prodrome of psychotic activation, the endogenous release of tryptophan acts as a positive feedback to intensify the psychotic symptoms. Finally a theoretical formulation is suggested in which the increases of tryptophan and methionine may act together as an endogenous metabolic factor by furnishing material for the enhanced production of a methylated psychotogenic indole.

Acknowledgment

We are grateful to E. E. Haynes for hematology and blood chemistry (blood sugar, NPN, total protein, A/G ratio, cholesterol, bilirubin, alkaline phosphatase, serum glutamic pyruvic transaminase, and thymol turbidity).

REFERENCES

1. Alexander, F., Curtis, G. C., Sprince, H., and Crosley, A. P., Jr.: L-methionine and L-tryptophan feedings in non-psychotic and schizophrenic patients with and without tranylcypromine. J. Nerv. Ment. Dis. 137:135-142, 1963.
2. Axelrod, J.: Enzymatic formation of psychotomimetic metabolites from normally occurring compounds. Science 134:343, 1961.
3. Barbeau, A., and Wilkoff, L. J.: Fruits, serotonin and catecholamines. Canad. Med. Ass. J. 80:717-719, 1959.
4. Berlet, H. H., Bull, C., Himwich, H. E., Kohl, H., Matsumoto, K., Pscheidt, G. R., Spaide, J. R., Tourlentes, T. T., and Valverde, J. M.: An endogenous metabolic factor in schizophrenic behavior. Science 144: 311-313, 1964.
5. Bleiler, R. E., and Schedl, H. P.: Creatinine excretion: variability and relationships to diet and body size. J. Lab. Clin. Med. 59:945-955, 1962.
6. Bliss, E. L.: Reaction of the adrenal cortex to emotional stress. Psychosom. Med. 18:56-57, 1956.
7. Boszormenyl, Z., Der, P., and Nagy, T.: Observations on the psychotogenic effect of N,N-dimethyl-tryptamine. J. Ment. Sci. 105:171-181, 1959.
8. Bruce, D. W.: Serotonin in pineapple. Nature 188: 147, 1960.
9. Brune, G., and Himwich, H. E.: Effects of reserpine on urinary tryptamine and indole-3-acetic acid excretion in mental deficiency, schizophrenia and phenylpyruvic oligophrenia. Acta of the International Meeting on the Techniques for the Study of Psychotropic Drugs, Bologna, June 26-27, 1960.
10. Brune, G. G., and Himwich, H. E.: Biphasic action of reserpine and isocarboxazid on behavior and serotonin metabolism. Science 133:190-192, 1961.
11. Brune, G. G., and Himwich, H. E.: Indole metabolites in schizophrenic patients. Arch. Gen Psychiat. 6:324-328, 1962.
12. Brune, G. G., and Himwich, H. E.: Effects of methionine loading on the behavior of schizophrenic patients. J. Nerv. Ment. Dis. 134:447-450, 1962.
13. Brune, G. G., and Himwich, H. E.: Biogenic amines and behavior in schizophrenic patients. *In* Recent Advances in Biological Psychiatry, ed., J. Wortis. New York, Plenum Press, Inc., 1963, pp. 144-160.
14. Brune, G. G., and Pscheidt, G. R.: Correlations between behavior and urinary excretion of indole amines and catecholomines in schizophrenic patients as affected by drugs. Fed. Proc. 20:889-893, 1961.
15. Brune, G. G., Pscheidt, G. R., and Himwich, H. E.: Correlations between the behavior of patients with mental disturbances and effects of psychoactive drugs on some urinary products. The Third World Congress of Psychiatry, June 4-10, 1961. Toronto, University of Toronto Press, 1961, 111-117.
16. Bumpus, F. M., and Page, I. H.: Serotonin and its methylated derivatives in human urine. J. Biol. Chem. 212:111, 1955.

17. Carlsson, A., and Waldeck, B.: A fluorometric method for the determination of dopamine. Acta Physiol. Scand. 44:293-298, 1958.

18. Consolazio, C. F., Johnson, R. E., and Pecora, L. J.: Physiological Measurements of Metabolic Function in Man. New York, McGraw-Hill, 1963, p. 262.

19. Culley, W. J., Saunders, R. N., Mertz, E. T., and Jolly, D. H.: Effect of tryptophan deficient diet on brain serotonin and plasma tryptophan levels. Proc. Soc. Exp. Biol. Med. 113:645, 1963.

20. von Euler, U. S.: Noradrenaline. Springfield, Ill., Charles C Thomas, 1956.

21. von Euler, U. S., and Lishajko, F.: The estimation of catecholamines in urine. Acta Physiol. Scand. 45:122-132, 1959.

22. Fabing, H. D., and Hawkins, J. R.: Intravenous bufotenine injection in the human body. Science 123:886-887, 1956.

23. Fischer, E., Lagravere, T. A. F., Vasquez, A. J., and DiStefano, A. O.: A bufotenin-like substance in the urine of schizophrenics. J. Nerv. Ment. Dis. 153:441, 1961.

24. Friedhoff, A., and van Winkle, E.: The characteristic of an amine found in the urine of schizophrenic patients. J. Nerv. Ment. Dis. 135:550, 1962.

25. Gal, E. M., and Marshall, F. D., Jr.: The hydroxylation of tryptophan by pigeon brain in vivo. *In* Biogenic Amines, Vol. 8: Progress in Brain Research, eds. H. E. Himwich and W. A. Himwich. Amsterdam, Netherlands, Elsevier Publ. Co., 1964, pp. 56-60.

26. Good, W. W., Sterling, M., and Holtzman, W. A.: Termination of chlorpromazine with schizophrenic patients. Amer. J. Psychiat. 115:443-448, 1958.

27. Green, H., and Sawyer, J. L.: Correlation of tryptamine-induced convulsions in rats with brain tryptamine concentration. Proc. Soc. Exper. Biol. Med. 104:153-155, 1960.

28. Hill, S. R.: Studies on adrenocortical and psychological response to stress in man. AMA Arch. Int. Med. 97:269-298, 1956.

29. Himwich, W. A., Claman, M. A., Pscheidt, G. R., Kohl, H. H., and Knapp, F. M.: The role of the liver in the production of behavioral responses to indole compounds. Recent Advances Biol. Psychiat., Chapt. 6, Vol. 6 (ed. J. Wortis). New York, Plenum Press, 1964, pp. 183-189.

30. Hofmann, A., and Troxler, F.: Identifizierung von Psilocin. Experientia 15:101, 1959.

31. Horita, A., and Weber, L. J.: The enzymic dephosphorylation and oxidation of psilocybin and psilocin by mammalian tissue homogenates. Biochem. Pharmacol. 7:47, 1961.

32. Horwitt, M. K., Harvey, C. C., Rothwel, W. S., Cutler, J. L., and Haffron, D.: Tryptophan-niacin relationships in man. J. Nutr. 60: (Suppl. 1): 1-43, 1956.

33. Isbell, H., Wolbach, A. B., Wikler, A., and Miner, E. J.: Cross tolerance between LSD and psilocybin. Psychopharmacologia 2:147, 1961.

34. Jaffé (method of): In Practical Physiological Chemistry, eds. P. B. Hawk, B. L. Oser, and W. H. Summerson. Philadelphia, Blakiston Co., 1949, p. 840.

35. Kalberer, F., Kreis, W., and Rutschmann, J.: The fate of psilocin in the rat. Biochem. Pharm. 11:261, 1962.

36. Knox, W. E.: Phenylketonuria. *In* The Metabolic Basis of Inherited Disease, eds. J. B. Stanbury, J. B. Wyngaarden, and D. S. Frederickson. New York, McGraw-Hill, 1960, p. 394.

37. Natelson, S. (ed.): Microtechniques of Clinical Chemistry of the Routine Laboratory. Springfield, Ill.: Charles C Thomas, 1957, pp. 238-241.

38. Oates, J. A., and Sjoerdsma, A.: Neurologic effects of tryptophan in patients receiving a monoamine oxidase inhibitor. Neurology 10:1076-1078, 1960.

39. Olson, G. W., and Peterson, D. B.: Sudden removal of tranquilizing drugs from chronic psychiatric patients. J. Nerv. Ment. Dis. 131:252-255, 1960.

40. Orr, M. L., and Watt, B. K.: Amino acid content of foods. Home Economics Research Report No. 4, U.S.D.A., Washington, D.C., 1957.

41. Pelletier, O., and Campbell, J. A.: A rapid method for the determination of N^1-methylnicotinamide in urine. Anal. Biochem. 3:60-67, 1962.

42. Peters, J. P., and Van Slyke, D. D.: Quantitative Clinical Chemistry Interpretations, Vol. 1, 2nd ed. Baltimore, Williams and Wilkins, 1946, p. 908.

43. Pollin, W., Cardon, P. V., and Kety, S. S.: Effects of amino acid feeding in schizophrenic patients treated with iproniazid. Science 133:104-105, 1961.

44. Porter, C. C., and Silber, R. H.: A quantitative color reaction for cortisone and related 17,21-dihydroxy-20-ketosteroids. J. Biol. Chem. 185:201, 1950.

45. Price, D. B., Thaler, M., and Mason, J. W.: Preoperative emotional states and adrenal cortical activity. AMA Arch. Neurol. Psychiat. 77:646-656, 1957.

46. Rose, W. C.: Amino acid requirements of man. Fed. Proc. 8:546, 1949.

47. Rose, W. C., Lambert, G. F., and Coon, M. J.: The amino acid requirements of man. VII. General procedures; the tryptophan requirement. J. Biol. Chem. 211:815, 1954.

48. Sandler, M., and Ruthven, C. R. J.: The estimation of 4-hydroxy-3-methoxymandelic acid in urine. Biochem. J. 80:78, 1961.

49. Scales, F. M., and Harrison, A. P.: Boric acid modifications of the Kjeldahl method for crop and soil analysis. J. Ind. Engr. Chem. 12:350, 1920.

50. Sen, N. P., and McGeer, P. L.: 4-Methoxyphenylethylamine and 3,4-dimethoxyphenyl-ethylamine in human urine. Biochem. Biophys. Res. Communications 14:227-232, 1964.

51. Shaw, K. N. F., and Trevarthen, J.: Exogenous sources of urinary phenol and indole acids. Nature 182:797-798, 1958.

52. Silber, R. H., and Porter, C. C.: The determination of 17,21-hydroxy-20-ketosteroids in urine and plasma. J. Biol. Chem. 110:923, 1954.

53. Sjoerdsma, A., Weissbach, H., and Udenfriend, S.: A clinical, physiologic and biochemical study of patients with malignant carcinoid (argentaffinoma). Amer. J. Med. 20:520-532, 1956.

54. Sjoerdsma, A., Oates, J. A., Zaltzman, P., and Udenfriend, S.: Identification and assay of urinary tryptamine: Application as an index of monoamine oxidase inhibition in man. J. Pharmacol. Exp. Therap. 126:217-222, 1959.

55. Sprince, H.: Biochemical aspects of indole metabolism in normal and schizophrenic subjects. Ann. N.Y. Acad. Sci. 96:399-418, 1962.

56. Sprince, H.: Indole metabolism in mental illness. Clin. Chem. 7:203-230, 1961.

57. Sprince, H., Parker, C., Jameson, D., and Alexander, F.: Urinary indoles in schizophrenic and psychoneurotic patients after administration of tranylcypromine (Parnate) and methionine or tryptophan. J. Nerv. Ment. Dis. 137:246, 1963.

58. Stone, A. A., and Eldred, S. H.: Delusion formation during the activation of chronic schizophrenic patients. AMA Arch. Gen. Psychiat. 1:177-179, 1959.

59. Sutton, H. E., and Road, J. H.: Abnormal amino acid metabolism in a case suggesting autism. AMA J. Dis. Child. 96:23, 1958.

60. Szara, S.: Dimethyltryptamine: Its metabolism in man; the relation of its psychotic effect to the serotonin metabolism. Experimetia 12:441-442, 1956.

61. Udenfriend, S., Lovenberg, W., and Sjoerdsma, A.: Physiologically active amines in common fruits and vegetables. Arch. Biochem. Biophys. 85:487-490, 1959.

62. Waalkes, T. P.: Sjoerdsma, A., Creveling, C. R., Weissbach, H., and Udenfriend, S.: Serotonin, norepinephrine and related compounds in bananas. Science 127:648-650, 1958.

63. Wadeson, R. W., Mason, J. W., Hamburg, D. A., and Handlon, J. H.: Plasma and urinary 17-OHCS responses to motion pictures. Arch. Gen. Psychiat. 9:146-156, 1963.

64. Watt, B. K., and Merrill, A. L.: Composition of foods—raw, processed, prepared. U.S.D.A. Handbook No. 8, Washington, D.C., 1950.

65. Weissbach, H., King, W., Sjoerdsma, A., and Udenfriend, S.: Formation of indole-3-acetic acid and tryptamine in animals: A method for estimation of indole-3-acetic acid in tissues. J. Biol. Chem. 234:81-86, 1959.

25

INHIBITORY CONDITIONAL RESPONSES IN SCHIZOPHRENIC PATIENTS

by JOSEPH H. STEPHENS, M.D., SOON MO CHOI, M.D., and JOHN E. PETERS, M.D.*

LITTLE IS KNOWN IN THIS COUNTRY about Soviet psychology and psychiatry in spite of an increase in recent years in the number of translations of the Russian literature. Pavlov's theory of higher nervous activity and elaborations of this theory provide the basis for most Russian experimental work in this field. Unfortunately, this theory is usually confusing to American readers both in its terminology and in its basic assumptions. Nevertheless, the actual results of experimental work may be useful empirically even if the theories that led to the experiments are imperfectly understood, rejected, or theoretically unsound.

Aside from the work of Gantt, Astrup, Alexander, Reese, Sutherland, and a few others, human conditioning along traditional Pavolvian lines has received little attention in our psychiatric literature.[1-4] In Astrup's recent book, *Schizophrenia: Conditional Reflex Studies,* 1105 references are given, of which only 164 are in English. Of these only 53 are directly concerned with human conditioning of any type.

The work reported in this paper is an outgrowth of our limited study of the Russian literature. It concerns human conditioning experiments in psychiatric patients, although some will doubtlessly not consider our experimental procedure conditioning in the Pavlovian sense. The experiments most similar to those we are here reporting are those studies of children made by Wortis and Choi.[5] The present work, in contrast to Gantt's, is not based on classical Pavlovian methods but bears some resemblance to a method elaborated by Ivanov-Smolensky.[6]

---

*The Pavlovian Laboratory, Department of Psychiatry, Johns Hopkins University School of Medicine, Baltimore, Maryland.

Experimental Method

The patient is seated in the experimental room in a comfortable chair with armrests. Attached to the right armrest is a rubber bulb which the subject squeezes as described later. On the left arm rest is a device which photoelectrically measures plethysmographic changes in the middle finger of the left hand. On the wall which the patient faces are colored lights which serve as stimuli. There are eight lights, one green, one white, three red of graded intensity, and three yellow of graded intensity. The tester sits to the left of the patient and operates a control box which can turn on the lights or produce a high- or low-pitched tone. Stimuli are presented for one second at a time. An Ofner polygraph records the intensity with which the patient squeezes the bulb and the plethysmographic changes. It also records the time at which the signals, auditory and visual, are given. A tape recorder is used for giving verbal directions to the patient. The test is comprised of the following steps.

1. Orienting responses are measured by presenting each stimulus at 15- to 30-second intervals without comment.

2. A tape recording with the following instructions is played twice: "Here is a bulb which you are supposed to squeeze. You have seen a series of lights and heard two sounds. Whenever a red light or the high-pitched sound comes on, I will tell you to squeeze. Whenever a yellow light or low-pitched sound comes on, I will tell you not to squeeze." Even though the tape says, "I will tell you to squeeze," this is not actually said in the early part of the experiment. The connection, or so-called verbal conditional reflex, is accomplished by nearly all patients merely in the course of the above instructions.

3. All of the signals are now again given at 10- to 15-second intervals without comment. If the patient does not squeeze to the red light and the high tone or does squeeze to the yellow light or low tone, the tape is played again. If the patient still does not squeeze at the appropriate time, he is directly instructed to do so until a stable response is established. It is the modification by procedural maneuvers of this established response that we are chiefly concerned in studying in the test.

Let us digress for a moment to point out that although squeezing a bulb to a sound or a light after verbal instruction may not appear to be a conditional reflex, many Soviet experimenters think otherwise. Milerian states the following: "Studying the physiological mechanism of voluntary actions Pavlov concluded that 'every mechanism of movement of the will is a conditioned associated process subordinated to all the laws of higher nervous activity described.' Voluntary actions are causally conditioned; their apparent 'spontaneity' is the outcome of complex determining influences both from the immediate and the more remote aims of life. In his analysis of man's voluntary actions Pavlov showed that this complex conditioning was the essence of willed activity, and that there is no absolute difference between voluntary and involuntary behavior."[7] The present authors are not ready to assume that verbal associations obey the same laws developed by Pavlov with salivary conditioning in dogs.

Luria has written extensively on the role of language in the formation of temporary connections such as those formed in our experimental procedure where a light or tone becomes a signal to squeeze or not to squeeze a bulb.[8] To discuss in detail why Soviet writers call such temporary verbal connections conditional reflexes would, however, be beyond the scope of this paper.

4. The neutral green and white signals are now each given twice at 15-second intervals to test for generalization in the Pavlovian sense.

5. The three red lights of varying intensity and the high-pitched tone are now given, first preceded by the white light with a half-second overlap in order to test for external inhibition in the Pavlovian sense.

6. A conflicting signal, red and yellow light simultaneously, is now given at 15-second intervals. If the patient asks for clarification, he is told simply to do his best.

7. All of the signals are again given one at a time to measure whether the above conflict has brought about a change in responses.

8. A red signal is now given three times at 7-second intervals. One half-second after the third presentation of the red light the high pitched tone is given. The high-pitched tone is then given three times at 7-second intervals, followed the third time in one half-second by the red light. Both of these procedures may be repeated several times if the response is abnormal. Failure to respond when a second positive immediately follows a positive signal of different quality is termed "negative induction" by Pavlov.

9. A second tape recording is now played twice with these instructions: "Now I am going to say the words, 'right' or 'wrong.' That is, if you give the right response, I will say 'right.' If you make a

mistake, I will say 'wrong.' Later I will ask you to say right or wrong yourself, but you will keep squeezing just as before."

10. At 15-second intervals a red light, a yellow light, the high tone, and the low tone are now given. If the patient's response is correct, the tester says "right." If the patient is wrong, the tester says nothing. The neutral green and white lights are also presented without comment.

11. All signals are now given again, including last of all the combination of red and yellow, and the patient is asked to say "right" or "wrong" to his response. This is to measure mutual interference of verbal and motor systems, or (to use the Pavlovian terminology) mutual interference of the first and second signaling systems.

12. Step 11 is repeated with the additional instructions, "Continue to say "right' or 'wrong' and squeeze the bulb, but also tell me why you do as you do." This gives a further test of verbal interference.

Case Material

The patients tested were all inpatients at the Henry Phipps Psychiatric Clinic. They ranged in age from 14 to 52. There were 25 schizophrenics, 25 neurotics, and 10 patients in a mixed group of character disorders and adjustment reactions of adolescence. This group consisted of six adjustment reactions of adolescence and four character disorders. This is, of course, too small a number for statistical comparison with the other groups, but we will present the results with this fact in mind. Twenty-five normal volunteers served as controls. The schizophrenics were subdivided into two clinical subgroups: 10 "process" patients, expected to have a poor outcome, and 15 "nonprocess" patients, expected to have a good outcome. This was done on the basis of carefully defined subgroups of schizophrenia as previously discussed by Stephens and Astrup.[9]

Results

We found no outstandingly consistent differences in plethysmographic responses in the different patient groups and the controls. Some of the controls and some of the patients gave an appreciable vasoconstriction to the presentation of the conflicting stimuli, but further experimentation is needed in the search for meaningful correlations of autonomic data and the clinical picture. Orienting responses and

and responses to neutral stimuli before the conflict signals had been given were not significantly different in the different groups. Those parts of the test showing any significant differences in the different clinical groups are those with which figures 1-5 are concerned.

In figure 1 we see that the schizophrenic patients exhibit significantly greater external inhibition than the other groups.

Figure 2 shows that twice as many patients in the schizophrenic group as in the neurotic group showed disturbed responses after the conflicting signals were given. Two of the patients diagnosed as adolescent maladjustment also gave disturbed responses after the conflicting signals, although these responses were not qualitatively as severe as those seen in the schizophrenics. The types of disturbance seen in this part of the test were increased latency of response, paradoxical responses (strong signals giving weakest responses), ultraparadoxical responses (reversal of responses), and complete disappearance of all responses for short periods. Four schizophrenic patients showed increased latency periods of from 2.5 to 8 seconds. Six also showed periods of disappearance of all responses lasting up to 80 seconds. Ultraparadoxical and paradoxical responses were seen in five of the schizophrenics and in none of the neurotics.

In figure 3 we see that negative induction was noted four times

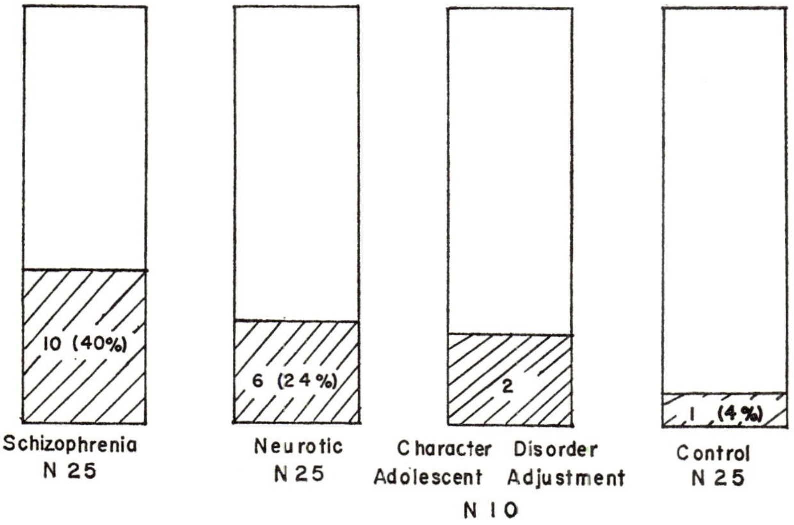

FIG. 1.—External inhibition.

as often in schizophrenics as in neurotics. No negative induction was noted in the other patients or controls.

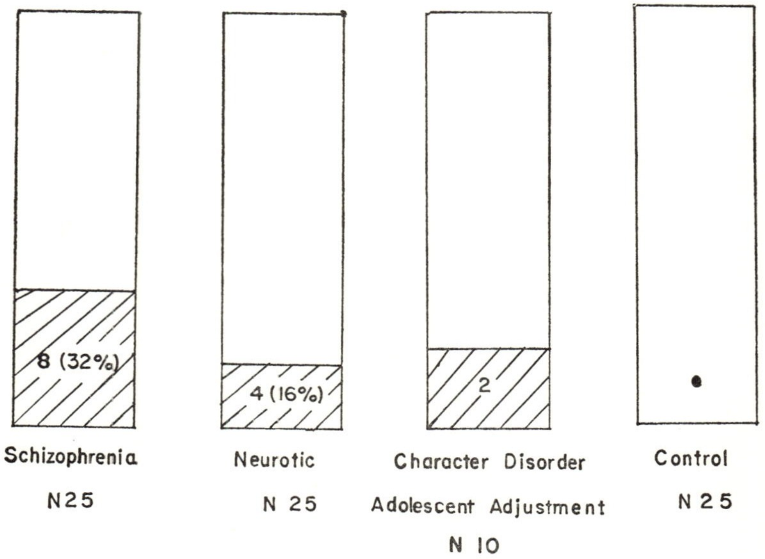

FIG. 2.—Disturbed responses after presentation of conflicting signals.

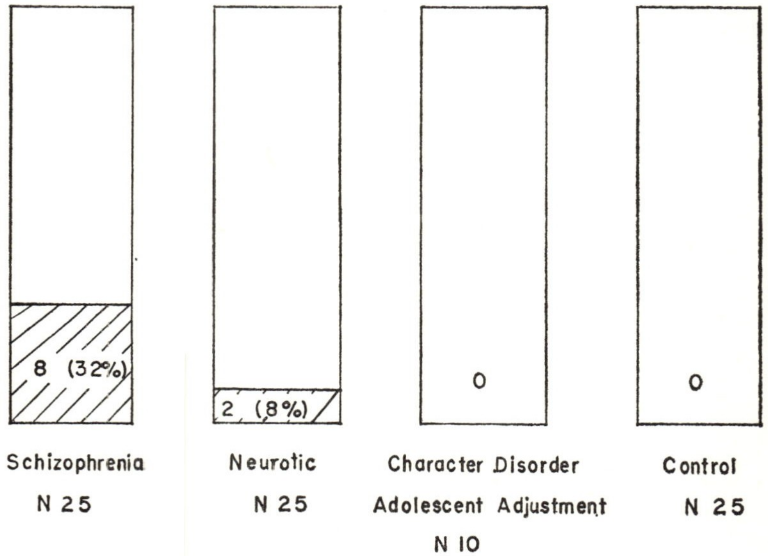

FIG. 3.—Negative induction.

In figure 4 we see a disturbed verbal response noted mainly in the schizophrenics. It is when the patient, in step 11 outlined above,

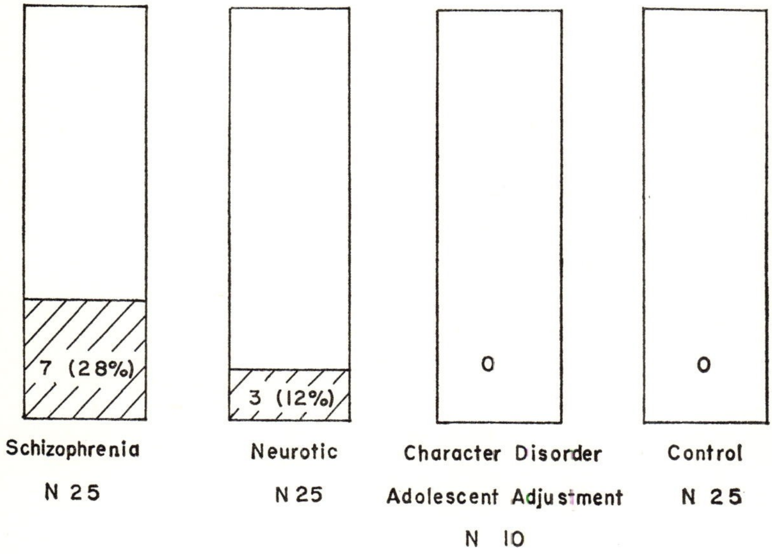

FIG. 4.—Disturbed verbal response.

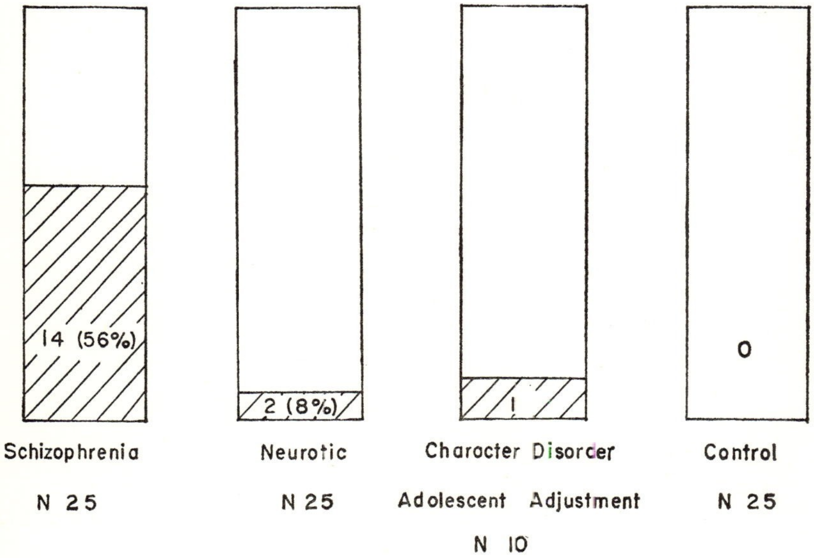

FIG. 5.—Disturbed response with verbal interference.

says "wrong," not when he makes a mistake, but when the negative signal (yellow light or low tone) is presented and he quite correctly does not squeeze the bulb.

Figure 5 shows disturbed motor responses when the patient is asked to say "right" or "wrong" and to give a reason for his response. The different types of disturbed responses noted here include the evoking of responses by neutral signals, reversal of responses, delayed responses, marked diminution in the size of responses, and inhibition of all motor responses in spite of continued verbal responses.

Figure 6 shows significant differences in "process" and "nonprocess" schizophrenics. The "process" patients are considered to be clinically much sicker.[9]

Ten of the 25 schizophrenics were given Thorazine in doses of from 200 to 800 mg. daily. One other schizophrenic was on 100 mg. Mellaril daily. None of the other patients were obtaining high doses of Thorazine, although one neurotic patient was on 75 mg. daily. One neurotic was on Tofranil, 75 mg. daily, and two were on 2 and 4 mg. of Stelazine daily.

Figure 7 compares schizophrenics receiving or not receiving drugs. It is apparent that the pathological test results are not due to a drug effect. Actually the patients receiving drugs have in general

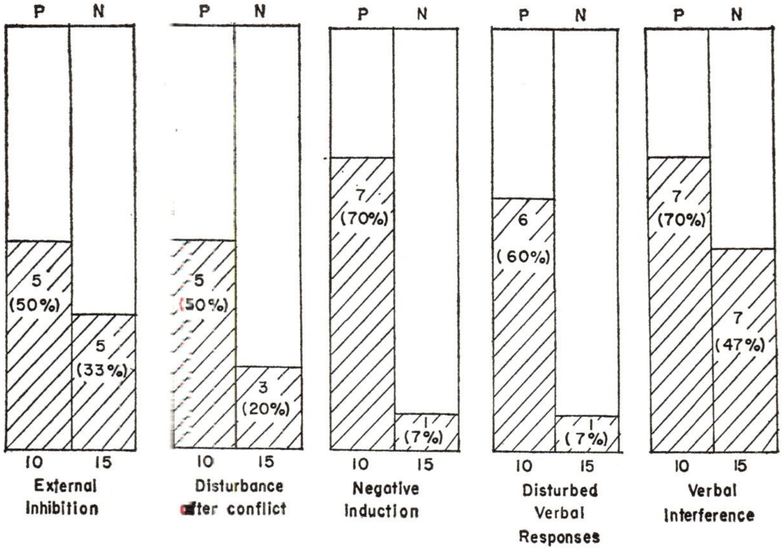

FIG. 6.—Differences in "process" (P) and "nonprocess" (N) schizophrenics.

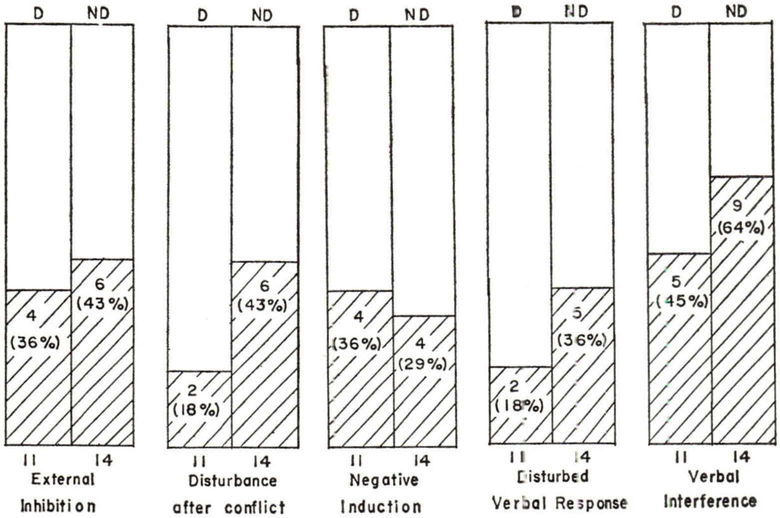

FIG. 7.—Differences in schizophrenics receiving drugs (D) and not receiving drugs (ND).

somewhat less pathological responses. Vinar has noted in his experiments that improvement in the cooperative working of the two signalling systems during the treatment with neuroleptics was a prognostically favorably finding. [10]

DISCUSSION

We have shown marked inhibitory responses in schizophrenic patients as compared with neurotics and normals. Character disorders and adolescent adjustment reactions also showed less inhibitory responses than schizophrenics, but our sample here was small. These inhibitory responses have been characterized by increased latency period, paradoxical and ultraparadoxical responses (phasic phenomena), negative induction, external inhibition, and complete inhibition of all responses for short periods of time. The normal responses of the controls is in keeping with Vinar's observation that he has never found phasic phenomena or disturbances in the cooperative functioning of the two signalling systems in healthy individuals.

Recent Pavlovian theorists would no doubt relate our findings to Pavlov's concept of schizophrenia as a state of heightened inhibitability of the cerebral cortex. Speaking in another conceptual framework, we consider our findings quite possibly the result of a disturbance of perception or attention. Vinar has pointed out the need for being cautious in interpreting the results in physiological terms when using the verbal-motor conditioning method. He also notes that one should especially here take into account the factor of social interaction between the experimenter and the experimental subject.[10] The disturbed responses we have seen in the schizophrenics may have been merely a measurement of negativism and distrust on the part of the patients. Jus has pointed out the dangers of too facile a replacement of psychopathological terminology by physiological terminology.[11] We do not, however, have sufficient evidence to give either a purely physiological or psychological explanation for our findings.

It is of particular interest to us to find that "process" schizophrenics show a greater disturbance than "nonprocess" schizophrenics. This is further evidence against the concept of schizophrenia as a homogenous entity.[9]

It is too soon for meaningful follow-up studies on our patients, but it is possible that the test we have described may have some prognostic value. We plan to test this possibility in the future. It will be of special interest to follow the progress of those patients who were not considered to be schizophrenic but who gave disturbed responses similar to some of the schizophrenics.

REFERENCES

1. Gantt, W. H.: The conditional reflex function as an aid in the study of the psychiatric patient. *In* Relation of Psychological Tests to Psychiatry (eds. P. H. Hoch and J. Zubin). New York, Grune & Stratton, 1952.
2. Astrup, C.: Schizophrenia, Conditional Reflex Studies. Springfield, Ill., Charles C Thomas, 1962.
3. Alexander, L.: Apparatus and method for the study of conditional reflexes in man. Arch. Neurol. Psychiat. 80:629-649, 1958.
4. Reese, W. G., Doss, R., and Gantt, W. H.: Autonomic responses in differential diagnosis of organic and psychogenic psychoses. Arch. Neurol. Psychiat. 70:778-793, 1953.
5. Wortis, J., and Choi, S.: Psychophysiological factor analysis in retarded, neurotic, and psychotic children. *In* Recent Advances in Biological Psychiatry, Vol. V (ed. J. Wortis). New York, Plenum Press, 1963.
6. Ivanov-Smolensky, A. G.: Essays on the Pathophysiology of the Higher Nervous Activity. Moscow, Foreign Languages Publishing House, 1954.
7. Milerian, E. A.: Involuntary and voluntary attention. *In* Recent Soviet Psychology (ed. N. O'Connor). New York, Liverright, 1961.

8. Luria, A. R.: Genesis of voluntary movements. *In* Psychology in the Soviet Union (ed. B. Simon). Stanford, Calif., Stanford University Press, 1957.

9. Stephens, J. H., and Astrup, C.: Prognosis in "process" and "non-process" schizophrenia. Amer. J. Psychiat. 119:945-953, 1963.

10. Vinar, O.: The possibilities of the use of conditional reflex methods in clinical psychiatry. *In* Psychopharmacological Methods, (ed. Z Votava).

11. Jus, A.: The theory and practice of psychiatry in Poland. Amer. J. Psychother. 16:676-692, 1962.

Discussion

Recorder: WILLIAM GOLDFARB, M.D.

Comments on Dr. Lehmann's Presentation

Discussion focused on the two aspects of this report—namely, the clinical application and effects of drugs, and Dr. Lehmann's theoretic speculation regarding the nature of schizophrenia and the presumed role of neuroleptic drugs in this latter regard. Dr. Glueck pointed to the necessity for assisting the chronic patient to select beneficial adaptive patterns after positive response to drugs. Dr. Lehmann responded that when the chronic schizophrenic was ready for reintegration, he would himself be impelled to seek the proper life choices for him. Dr. Hoch concerned himself with the problem of preventing the high number of relapses after good response to drugs. Factors influencing such relapses include the improper application of drugs, and the sudden loss of drug reactivity and the need for switching to a new drug. All discussants were fascinated by Dr. Lehmann's notion that schizophrenia results from excessive stimulus inflow ("jamming"). Dr. Hoch, for example, felt the problem was in the processing of stimuli rather than the inflow. Dr. Zubin also cautioned that the flicker fusion data distinguishing pathological and normal groups are open to question and may be revised when more refined measures of response are achieved. Further, he again emphasized that more than stimulus input was involved in the total experience embodied by the flicker fusion experiment—e.g., transmission, central coordination, and output. The patient's level and stability of activation or arousal at the moment of stimulation particularly need appraisal.

Discussion of Dr. Lehmann's Presentation

by Sidney Malitz, M.D.

It is most unfortunate that Dr. Lehmann was unable to read his entire paper this morning, because then we would have had an opportunity to see the total scope of his integrative faculties operating at full capacity. I have never ceased to admire the orderly manner in which he sorts out data and utilizes set, differentiation, retention, and negative feedback in a most harmonious fashion and in the finest tradition of clinical psychiatry. While it is certainly true that most of the pioneer discoveries in psychiatry have not emerged through systematic search, and this applies also to psychopharmaceuticals as Dr. Lehmann has mentioned in his paper, it is also true that the most valuable contributions have been made by men like Dr. Lehmann who have had the sustained curiosity, the cognitive awareness, and the integrative capacity to draw inferences and come up with educated hunches, later corroborated by experiment, which advance the parameters of our psychiatric knowledge. In these areas the schizophrenic is usually sadly lacking.

Dr. Lehmann points out several interesting observations in his paper which bear reemphasis. One of these is the value of neuroleptic agents in improving, or at least diminishing, psychotic and disruptive symptomatology in some chronic schizophrenic patients. I say some, because we all have seen chronic schizophrenics who have not responded to drugs after 6 weeks, 12 weeks, or much longer periods. We still do not know why. Perhaps the cluster analyses of the new computer science will eventually help us in this area.

Dr. Lehmann describes clearly the difference between major and minor tranquilizers both on a behavioral and neurophysiological level. He charts most dramatically, in quantitative fashion, a belief that many of us have long held: that while there is a rapid action on arousal and affect in schizophrenics receiving neuroleptics, the integrative capacity is little affected, and very late at that. The term psychotostatic implies a slowing down of disruptive inflow rather than a reversal or qualitative alteration. An analogy can be made to the overloaded switchboard operator who becomes confused and unable to handle her calls properly because of the tremendous flow in incoming and outgoing traffic. She makes errors, keeps people waiting, connects the wrong parties, and may show sharp bursts of inappropriate affect. This occurs every day at noon at our hospital, when in addition to the regular load, people are calling each other to make luncheon dates. If we had the authority to regulate the rate of calls or to rip out a considerable percentage of the telephone cables, our switchboard operator would soon get back her integrative capacity, the remaining calls would be promptly and accurately put through, and her affect would once more become appropriately and properly modulated.

On one small point, I must take issue with Dr. Lehmann. It is his belief that minor tranquilizers are associated with more "malignant mental mechanisms" such as regression, projection, and denial, while the major tranquilizers evoke a tendency to employ the more constructive defense mechanisms of rationalization, reaction formation, and sublimation. It has been my observation that the type of mental mechanism employed by an individual will relate much more to his particular personality, past experience, and severity of psychopathology than to the category of medication he receives. When the complex barrage of stimuli impinging on the patient is reduced or slowed down by drugs, he will usually select that adaptive pattern of defense best suited to his individual resources.

I do have one question. It is not clear to me how minor tranquilizers are disruptive. Perhaps Dr. Lehmann could elaborate.

I should like to congratulate Dr. Lehmann for his clear, concise exposition of the current drug treatment of schizophrenia and his helpful suggestions for research to clarify further some of the many problems still remaining.

Comments on Dr. Kalinowsky's Presentation

Discussion of this paper ranged over many issues. Dr. Freyhan began by stressing the importance of directing treatment to specific target symptoms. Drugs could not feasibly be used to treat the schizophrenic or "schizophrenia," and it was more pertinent to use drugs for the specific treatment of accessible symptoms. The questions, "How long has the patient had his illness?" or "Which patients benefit from treatment?" are less significant than a selective treatment of specific symptoms. Dr. Roth referred to problems of classification. He doubted the value of classifying on the basis of treatment response. He recommended an operational approach in which primary symptoms would be those which show a high degree of covariation with all other symptoms. He also emphasized the importance of early identification and treatment. Dr. Zubin raised a question regarding the long-term effects of drug treatment and wondered whether the drugs were really for maintaining the patient out of the hospital, or was the illness being cured? Referring to the efficacy of maintenance treatment, Dr. Kohl indicated that drugs kept patients out of hospitals for longer periods, although not permanently. Similarly, Dr. Friedman suggested that drugs improved the social functioning of patients, even if statistical readmissions were common. In his final summation, Dr. Kalinowsky again stressed the need for an inclusive program of somatic therapy, including insulin and ECT as well as drugs. Like some other speakers, he stressed the continuing value of clinical and subjective approaches and also agreed to the importance of psychotherapy in maintaining patients after somatic treatments had induced improvement.

Comments on Dr. Himwich's Presentation

In discussing the Galesburg results, Dr. Hoch questioned whether the clinical findings might not be specific for excitement rather than schizophrenia alone. Dr. Himwich agreed that increased motor activity and anxiety led to the urinary changes and could be interpreted whether such excitement was found in a schizophrenic or not.

SUMMARY COMMENTS

by Leslie B. Hohman, M.D.

There has been a tendency in American psychiatry to enlarge the symptomatology to be included under the diagnostic category of schizophrenia. This tendency has reached a point where to many psychiatrists the diagnosis has no other meaning than that the patient is disturbed.

In spite of the fact that Adolf Meyer frightened American psychiatrists into avoiding diagnostic categories by calling them poor diagnosis labeling, the fact remains that there can be no scientific approach to evaluation of cases without adequate diagnosis. How is it possible to judge the efficacy of treatment without knowing the natural history of any clinical syndrome? Any scientific approach in medicine requires accurate diagnostic criteria for prognostication, to say nothing of the practical aspects of prognostication.

Recently, several published studies on prognosis (mainly from continental but also American clinics) have shown clearly that what has been included under the heading of schizophrenia is clearly affective disorders symptomatology. This type of case has a high recovery rate and will obviously distort any accurate study of outcome of mental disease. The situation is even worsened by including delirium states under the rubric of schizophrenia.

We still stand at that stage in psychiatry where we can only study symptom complexes since we do not know the causes of mental disease. All variations of speculation as to causes still remain in the realm of speculation; even if some beliefs as to causality have assumed the realm of conviction and like religious belief have to be based on faith.

Meyer's approach studied symptom complexes as malignant or benign and summed up each case as entirely malignant, or a mixture of malignant and benign, or benign and malignant, or entirely benign.

It is possible to equate benign with reversibility, and malignant with nonreversible.

It is obvious that any "either-or" classification into schizophrenia or manic-depressive must require jamming of facts to fit these limited categories. Repeated European studies have tried to solve the problem by making many subdivisive categories under the heading of schizophrenia, or have attempted a whole new grouping for cases which are neither manic-depressive nor schizophrenic but a new middle group. These attempts have always failed to meet any general acceptance. In my opinion, one of the chief difficulties in more accurate evaluation of symptom complexes has been the failure to recognize the various variety of affects wtih their appropriate biologic concomitants and their "consistent with" delusional and hallucinatory content disorders. A recognition of additional affective states (fear, anger, bewilderment, anxiety, suspicion, amorousness, awe, awfulness, jealousy, absence of any feeling, and confusion) can save many cases from being dumped into the group of schizophrenics and can avoid the false recovery rates for schizophrenia.

It should be urged in making a diagnosis of a malignant symptom complex that the symptoms should be clearly defined. They should not be in diagnostic statements such as flat affect or bizarre delusions. Too often these diagnostic statements represent, not factual observation, but conviction about the diagnosis in the mind of the observer.

Although Bleuler formulated his concepts of schizophrenia over 50 years ago, no essential important change of symptomatology has been brought forward: insidious onset, chronic course, intermittent attacks, at times some remission of symptoms, but never restitutio ad integrum. His primary symptoms of (1) disturbances of association and affectivity, (2) the predilection for fantasy as against reality, and (3) the inclination to divorce one's self from reality (autism) with hallucinatory and delusional material constitute his secondary group of symptoms and have importance today. His definition of particular distortion of association and affectivity is particularly valid.

To avoid the difficulty of a grouping of symptoms into primary and secondary ones, I would propose to continue Adolf Meyer's stressing of the importance of passivity feelings or behavior that appears to be the dramatization of passivity; that is, the patient acts as if he were being governed or controlled by outside influence.

I would include the following description of schizophrenic thinking and talk, negative aspects in talk, affectivity, and passivity attitude and its dramatization.

Characteristics of Schizophrenic Thinking and Utterances

1. Tends to be vague (to the point of meaninglessness).
2. Stilted, affected, high-flown, and elaborate talk (may involve cadence).
3. Fragmented (to word salad).
4. Beside the point (Beireden).
5. Blocking.
6. Not infrequently interrupted by listening to or answering voices.
7. Often circumstantial.
8. Neologistic (made-up words) or neosemes (old words with odd meanings).
9. Mystical, fantastic, "symbolic," pseudo-religious, pseudo-scientific concepts.
10. Mumbling and very low voice (not understandable).
11. Mutism.
12. Mimetic movements accompanying talk show rapidly shifting expression (wiping off) and mixed expressions at same time.
13. Distorted thinking may not appear in spoken language but only in written material.
14. May show ambivalence (positive and negative at same time or in rapid succession).
15. Illogical talk, loosening of logical bonds. May be impossible to see connections between ideas, words, phrases, or sentences.
16. Negativistic utterances (not uncooperative).
17. Rut-like repetitions (stereotypies). Talk may be reduced to a single word, phrase, or sentence.
18. Proper grammatic construction disappears but often only in the discussion of delusional material.
19. Echolalic speech (repeats only what is said to the patient).
20. Episodic explosive affect.

Negative (Nonschizophrenic) Aspects (Speech)

1. Normal talking on neutral topics, shifting to abnormality when sensitive areas are approached.
2. Cadence and form may be good.
3. May be able to sustain normal speech and thinking for long periods.

Other Important Negative Aspects

1. Absence of pervasive affect.
2. Clear sensorium (dream states and delirious states are often like schizophrenia).
3. Memory good.
4. No consistency of delusional or hallucinatory material with any pervasive affect.

Passivity Attitude and Its Dramatization

1. Change in personality with increasing inactivity.
   a. Slump in personal appearance and personal care (bathing).
   b. Slump in energy and drive and ambition.
   c. Slump in ability to concentrate on work.
   d. Gradual loss in interest in work, reading, activity, exercise.
   e. Gradual loss of ability to make contacts with people (staying by themselves—avoiding contacts with people, eye avoidance).
   f. Loss of affection for people (often close relatives).
   g. Prolonged lying in bed.
   h. Avoidance even of excretory functions (severe constipation or holding of urine).
2. Maintenance in early stages of the syndrome or reaction of large portions of normal affectivity and normal drives, which results in conflict and struggle with the inactivity or passivity feelings. This results in:
3. a. Irritability in attempting to avoid contacts.
   b. Refusal to accept willingly the passivity feelings and projecting the cause of the abnormal feelings onto the outside world. Rejection of guilt.
   c. Dramatization or acting out to protect or justify the passivity attitude.
      (1). Autistic creations or delusional systems. Wishfulfilling systems.
      (2). Paranoid systems (grandiose or persecutory).
      (3). Total rejection of outside world (catatonic stupor).
4. a. Partial suicide.
      (1). Emasculation attempts, gouging out an eye.
   b. Hallucinations of odor, especially of a sexual nature, or body odor perceived as ideas of reference.

These two sets of symptoms are practically always symptoms of an irreversible schizophrenic process.

Part VI: Diagnosis, Classification, and Prognosis

26

SOCIAL COMPETENCE, THE PROCESS-REACTIVE DISTINCTION, AND THE NATURE OF MENTAL DISORDER*

by LESLIE PHILLIPS, PH.D.†

THE PSYCHIATRIC CATEGORY OF SCHIZOPHRENIA has usually not been considered a single diagnostic entity. A wide range of biological, psychological, and social characteristics have been found to be associated with the disorder, yet no consistent relationship between all these observations and its traditional subtypes has been discovered. Consequently, some division of the schizophrenic syndrome has been sought which better articulates available data with the heterogeneous manifestations of the disorder.

Most widely accepted is a distinction between what have been called the process and the reactive forms of schizophrenia. A certain homogeneity has been remarked within each of these categories. The process form of the disorder is the more classical schizophrenic syndrome—that is, one characterized by a life history of ineffectuality, emotional dulling and severe disturbances in thought, and an unfavorable outcome. Reactive schizophrenia has been described in more optimistic terms: as subsuming a history of greater social adequacy, greater emotional reactivity in the psychosis, a lesser degree of thought disturbance, and a more favorable prognosis. Earlier investigators believed that the process form of schizophrenia is constitutional or genetic in origin, while the reactive or less typical pattern of the disorder was

---

*This study was supported by the Dementia Praecox Research Project, Worcester State Hospital, and a research grant (M-896) from the National Institute of Mental Health, United States Public Health Service.

†Worcester State Hospital and Clark University, Worcester, Massachusetts.
The writer is greatly indebted to Dr. William Vogel who has made many constructive suggestions at various stages in the writing of this paper.

considered to be the consequence of more psychogenic determinants, and as mimicking the more ominous pathology of process schizophrenia.

Today, opinion is divided on whether any sharp distinction between the process and reactive forms should be maintained. While some writers emphasize the value of this differentiation, others propose that the two types of psychosis should be thought of as endpoints on some continuum of lesser to greater pathology.

Developmental theory suggests that all types of schizophrenia and, indeed, all of psychopathology may be seen as an interlude in the total life pattern. On the basis of developmental theory, the whole life history, including the premorbid and postmorbid phases, can be viewed as a reflection of the way in which the person copes with the increasingly complex tasks which society poses for the maturing individual. This theory leads us to evaluate the way in which the person meets his societal tasks in the premorbid and postmorbid periods, and to view the period of psychosis as a consequence of failure to cope with the developmental tasks which confront every person.

Zigler and the present investigator[23] have made use of an index of "social competence" to assess the ability to meet the expectations set by our society for the person growing into adulthood. Our measure of social competence includes items which reflect socieconomic potential and the likelihood that age and sex role expectations will be fulfilled. Social competence, then, corresponds to the individual's level of psychosocial development.

Zigler and the present writer have noted that the level of social competence achieved in the premorbid period is associated with the types of symptoms manifested in psychopathology. Specifically, it has been observed that a patient's symptoms tend to reflect a consistent picture of the degree of personal responsibility which he accepts for his present difficult situation. Thus, one cluster of symptoms is indicative of a self-critical "turning against the self." Two other sets of symptoms imply a rejection of personal responsibility, either by blaming or attacking others, or by withdrawal from traumatic circumstances. We have labeled these latter symptom clusters respectively as "turning against others" and as "avoidance of others."[17]

Zigler and I hypothesized that symptomatology in a psychotic phase is consistent with, and an integral element of, a total life pattern and that this totality differs between patients who can be labeled as process or reactive schizophrenics. We therefore tested the assumption that, within a schizophrenic population, symptom manifestation would shift according to the achieved level of premorbid social competence. Consistent with developmental formulations, which emphasize that increasing maturity implies increasing responsibility for the self, we proposed that schizophrenics scoring at higher levels of competence would exhibit a greater tendency to symptoms indicative of a "turning against the self." In contrast, the pathology of those of lower competence should more likely reflect either a "turning against others" or an "avoidance of others." Because we believe that the developmental position is of general validity in psychopathology, we also proposed that these same relations between premorbid social competence and the symptom picture should be maintained among a nonschizophrenic psychiatric population as well. Our hypotheses were confirmed in samples of 298 schizophrenic and 508 nonschizophrenic patients. In addition, the data supported the feasibility of treating the process-reactive distinction in any mental disorder as a continuum, measurable in terms of three levels of premorbid social competence, rather than as a sharp dichotomy.[24] Thus, a process-reactive dichotomy unique to schizophrenia appears to be an unnecessary and untenable construct. In its stead, a consistent and continuous relation appears between premorbid history and the symptoms of psychiatric disorder quite independent of traditional classifications.

The writer believes that these findings have certain more general implications for the nature of mental disorder. First, though, I want to summarize the argument to this point: each individual is confronted with meeting the developmental tasks posed by our society. In psychopathology, the person's premorbid competence in mastering these tasks is reflected in his symptomatology. Those of higher competence tend to manifest symptoms indicative of a self-critical attitude and of taking responsibility for one's difficulties. Those of lower competence show symptomatology which reflects an avoidance of personal responsibility expressed either in turning against others or a withdrawal from threatening relationships.

These relations hold independent of diagnostic category—that is, both within and external to the schizophrenic syndrome. We have also observed that patients of higher premorbid competence tend to manifest a more favorable prognosis than those of lower competence. Thus, our data suggest that the form taken by psychopathology is part of a total life pattern which flowers out of the person's premorbid social effectiveness. The process-reactive distinction in schizophrenia then is generalizable to all of psychopathology and reflects life patterns established in the premorbid period.

As noted above, the process and reactive forms of disorder have been considered to be determined by organic and psychosocial factors, respectively. Because of the reformulation of the process and reactive dichotomy which has just been outlined, I now want to address myself to the insights into the nature of psychopathology which are contributed by the organic and psychosocial positions. The major theoretical positions are in fact more legitimately considered a threesome, represented by the biological, psychological, and social orientations. Here, however, I shall consider the contributions of only two of these —the biological and the social. These represent, respectively, a commitment to the dominance of heredity, or constitutional or biochemical factors versus environmental influences on the manifestation of disorder. Psychological thinking on causation in mental disorder, which means primarily psychoanalytic theory, is unclear about its organic or environmentalistic commitment, particularly in the severe disorders.[5] For this reason, and also because I plan to review psychological theory in mental disorder in a future paper, this will not be considered further here.

Before going on to a very brief evaluation of the relative significance of biological and social factors for psychopathology, one other comment seems necessary. The contrasting positions of heredity versus environment, or organic versus psychosocial origins of mental disorder, arouse strong feelings and touch off biases which influence their acceptance or rejection, quite independent of their factual strength or weakness. They seem to arouse strongly held values as to whether man is governed by his origins or is actually a free agent in control of his own destiny. Thus, it is a striking fact that the genetic base for mental disorder is generally accepted as axiomatic among European psychiatrists, while virtually all American psychiatrists are committed to the thesis that early childhood experience is the dominant determinant of later adjustment. The parallel contrast between the more fixed, tradition-oriented society of Europe and the more fluid open society of the United States is obvious. In an analogous contrast, Pastore[16] has compared the attitudes of 24 biologists, psychologists, and sociologists on the heredity-environmentalist issue with their political opinions. Of the 12 scientists classified as "liberal" or "radical," 11 were environmentalists, while of the 12 conservatives, 11 were hereditarians. It is clear that a good deal more emotional heat than scientific coolness enters into these convictions. The writer's commitment to the prepotence of social factors in the onset of mental disorder will quickly become apparent, and the reader is warned to make his own corrections for this bias.

THE BIOLOGICAL BASES OF PSYCHIATRIC DISORDER

Despite decades of investigation, the yield in established facts on the biochemical and constitutional bases of psychiatric disorder is dishearteningly small. A recent review by Hoagland[6] on the work in the biochemistry of schizophrenia gave voice to this disappointing state of affairs. He expressed serious doubt that biochemical solution for schizophrenia is to be found in such substances or functions as taraxin, pineal extracts, serotonin in the brain, mescaline, lysergic acid, or peculiarities of the adrenal cortical system. What we have learned to date convinces him that "we are still groping pretty much in the dark." A recent review by Kety[9-11] came to a similar conclusion. Observed relationships between "constitutional" or innate somatic factors and psychiatric disorder are also generally weak or contradictory.[18] Only genetic factors have found consistent support as associated with the manifestations of mental disorder. Any evaluation of genetic studies, however, must first consider that only schizophrenia and manic-depression have been reported as based on some inherited predisposition, while the neuroses and personality and character disorders are more ambiguous in origin.

Genetic investigations largely have made use of twins because identical twins carry a larger component of common inherited potential than do fraternal twins, while it is assumed that both types of same-sexed twin pairs share on equally similar environment. Hence, to the extent that psychopathology is the consequence of purely genetic factors, it should more frequently occur together in identical than in fraternal twins. The shared inheritance of fraternal twins is no greater than that of ordinary siblings.

Systematic studies on the cooccurrence of schizophrenia, or "probable" schizophrenia in twins, have been carried out by Essen-Möller,[4] Kallmann,[7] Luxenburger,[12] Rosanoff et. al.,[19] and Slater.[21] Quite similar figures were reported by all these investigators. The coincidence of schizophrenia in identical twins ranged from 67 per cent to a high figure of 91 per cent. In contrast, the reported cooccurrence of this psychosis in fraternal twins ranged for the most part between 10 and

17 per cent. These figures are quite comparable to the 14.2 per cent given by Kallmann for siblings.

However, these observations cannot be taken as support for the older, genetic position that "heredity is everything, environment nothing," since inherent in modern genetic theory itself is the recognition that environment factors interact with the genes in the production of all the characteristics of an organism. The term "heredity," as used nowadays, implies that organisms possess different potentials for development under the influence of the same environmental factors.

Thus, a gene is not presumed to produce directly any specific personality or behavior trait, nor is it the sole or absolute determiner of a trait. Rather, a gene merely sets into motion a sequence of processes, including the action of other genes, metabolic processes (both pre- and postnatal), psychological processes, and ultimately, interpersonal relationships. In this vein, Kallmann[8] has proposed that genes exert their influence through the body chemistry. Further, he has said, "No psychodynamic concept is inconsistent with the general biological premise that 'heredity acts, in part, by influencing the selection, and in fact the creation, of the environment of the given individual.' "

Essen-Möller likewise believed that what was inherited was a "characterological defect," rather than the predisposition to any particular form of mental disorder. This assumption is in contradiction to the distinction (mentioned earlier as hypothesized by a number of investigators) between the etiologies of the process and reactive forms of schizophrenia. They presumed that process schizophrenia was "organic" in origin—that is, either genetically, constitutionally, or biochemically determined while the reactive form of the psychosis was thought to be psychogenically determined. In the light of our discussion it seems more appropriate to consider any possible genetic factors to be associated with the total life pattern rather than with direct initiation of specific psychotic states.

It is possible that further findings will strengthen the case for the physical basis of mental disorder. It may be, for example, that genetic factors will be discovered to be unequivocally involved in all forms of psychopathology and not only in schizophrena and manic depression. Perhaps the penetrance of the genes which may be associated with the manifestation of psychosis will be found, after all, to be so highly determining of pathology that predisposition can be considered virtually identical with the likelihood of disorder. And perhaps we will find answers to what Kallmann[7] has told us we do not yet have answers for in genetics—namely (1) why the joint occurrence of schizophrenia in families is so much more common in same-sexed individuals, particularly females, and (2) why the ratio of male to female cases of schizophrenia changes with different age levels. In general, males are overrepresented in childhood behavior disorders while underrepresented in adult psychoses. Finally, it may be that some genetic explanation will be discovered and substantiated for the observed differences in the incidence of psychosis and of the various forms of disorder in single versus married persons, and in lower versus middle and upper classes. For the present, however, the limits of our knowledge make it difficult to foresee how answers to these questions can ever be devised within a purely genetic framework.

Social Bases of Psychiatric Disorder

It is evident that in the light of modern genetic theory it is necessary to consider social and environmental factors in order to achieve a rounded picture of the nature of psychopathology. In fact, the available literature indicates that social and cultural factors may contribute substantially to the incidence and form of mental disorder. It is not possible within the confines of the present paper to review all the available data, but I have chosen three sets of findings which are relevant. They are presented in the following sequence: (1) Ethnic differences and symptom diversity within a diagnostic category, (2) coping potential and symptomatology, and (3) cultural change and symptomatology.

Ethnic Diversity and Symptom Differences within a Diagnostic Category

Biologically oriented investigators tend to minimize the profound divergences in disorder directly traceable to ethnic and societal differences. The fact is that even disorders which carry the same diagnosis, and which have been considered by psychiatrists of a genetic bent to be a unitary disorder, vary in symptomatology according to the society in which they are observed. The writer has already reported, for example, on the different characteristics of schizophrenia which can be seen in more or less socially competent persons.

Similary, schizophrenics drawn from different ethnic groups often manifest widely divergent symptom pictures. For example, Opler and Singer[15] have described a group of schizophrenic patients of Irish ancestry as latent homosexuals and as being dominated by fixed delusions revolving about sin and guilt. In contrast, they characterized a group of schizophrenics of Italian ancestry as often overtly homosexual, as frequently hypochondriacal, and as being marked by violent acting-out behavior with only slight, scattered, and changeable delusions.

This ethnic diversity in symptomatology might be hypothesized as corresponding solely to genetic differences, but this assumption is not easily maintained for other observations of symptom differences. For example, Japanese schizophrenics in Japan are described as physically assaultive[20] while Japanese schizophrenics in Hawaii are described as suspicious, having ideas of being controlled or influenced[3] Thus persons of the same racial stock, carrying the same diagnosis, develop different kinds of symptoms depending upon the society in which they live.

We are told also that paranoid schizophrenia appears to be relatively rare in backward societies, and where present, shows little tendency toward abstract and complex systematization of delusional thought. And, finally, it has been suggested that amok, latah, and Arctic hysteria, all states of confused excitement and maniacal attack, are primitive forms of schizophrenia.[2]

Coping Potential and Symptomatology

It is not enough, however, to show that the form of a disorder differs from one culture group to another. The next consideration is whether any regularities can be established between the characteristics of a society and its dominant psychopathologies.

The available literature suggests that the relationships reported above between individual social competence and symptom formation are also true both for social classes and societies and their dominant forms of psychopathology. Social classes and societies which are deficient in coping with the environment are marked by psychopathologies which differ from those appearing in more effective classes and societies. Lower class patients tend to act destructively against others or to become seclusive, while middle class patients are likely to manifest ideational symptomatology and to express themselves as feeling guilty and depressed.[14]

In technologically backward societies, pathology is also likely to correspond to an immature level of individual psychological development with an emphasis on action disturbance, a profound disorganization in thought, and a self-centered tendency to blame others for one's difficulties. In contrast, pathology in technologically more advanced societies more often parallels a higher level of individual development. Action symptoms are more inclined to be restricted and pathology to be expressed in thought, which in terms of its formal organization remains intact. The content of the patient's preoccupations more frequently center on a feeling of personal guilt, indicative of a pathologically exaggerated sense of moral responsibility for the welfare of others.

Benedict and Jacks[2] have proposed that the type of pathology common in nonliterate societies suggests that there hostility is directed outward, whereas in Western society this hostility is more often directed inward. That is, in advanced cultures "the external function of society in preventing crime is partly handed over to the inner processes of guilt and atonement." Benedict[1] likewise says that "Western culture presents a significant contrast to many nonliterate cultures in the mechanisms of conscience. In backward societies all responsibility is shifted to supernatural powers, to the virtual exclusion of ideas of free will and personal responsibility with consequent minimal self-reproach and feelings of guilt."

Cultural Change and Symptomatology

Level of technological development, or coping potential, is obviously not the sole determinant of society's predominant forms of mental disorder. Another factor which appears to influence the types of pathology manifested is the speed with which a society is changing. Rapid changes in American social values over the last half century is a prime case in point.

In this period we find in the United States a much increased awareness and tolerance of personal motives, including violence and sexuality, which previously would have been severely disapproved. These changes in values and tolerance in our own society have had inevitable consequences for the nature of its psychopathology. Extension in the range of experience which is permissible corresponds in time to a decrease in those disorders which are manifestations of repression, and of conflict and feelings of guilt over impulse expression. For example, conversion hysteria, once so common in repressive Victorian society, has virtually disappeared in the United States,[22] while the incidence of manic-depressive disorders has been reduced by 60 per cent within the last 50 years and is now far less common than schizophrenia.[13] Correspondingly, this century has witnessed general increase in violence, theft, and the addictions. Both these trends may reflect a lessened tendency to blame oneself for wrongdoing and a decreased harshness in the moral tone of society.

Present-day tolerance for the previously tabooed has not eliminated psychopathology or deviant behavior from our midst. Wheelis[22] has commented that the psychoanalyst is being increasingly faced with disorders which do not conform to the traditional syndromes. Most common today in the practice of psychoanalysis, he believes, are patients who suffer from vague states of discomfort, from a sense of isolation, and a lack of goals and direction. They come to the therapist complaining of loneliness, doubts, insecurity, unhappiness, lack of fulfillment, boredom, and restlessness. Perhaps the reported increase in the incidence of schizophrenic disorders is associated with a generalized increase in a sense of isolation and alientation pervasive in American society.

The writer's concept of the relation between social factors and pathological forms can be condensed into one brief statement. Rather than judge psychiatric symptoms as expressions of disease, we can see them simply as the person's behavior as he tries ineffectually to cope with the problems which are unique to his life. His symptoms *are* the person caught in difficulties beyond his capabilities for mastery. Their nature expresses that particular person's circumstances, his values and place in society, as well as reflecting the values of his time and culture. Regularities in symptomatology which we recognize as diagnostic syndromes can then be seen to express the common elements of human experience which mark a particular historical period and society.

REFERENCES

1. Benedict, P. K.: Socio-cultural factors in schizophrenia. *In* Schizophrenia (ed. L. Bellak). New York, Logos Press, 1958, pp. 694-729.
2. Benedict, P. K., and Jacks, L.: Mental illness in primitive societies. Psychiatry 17:377, 1954.
3. Enright, J. B., and Jaeckle, W. R.: Ethnic differences in psychopathology. Paper read at the Pacific Science Congress, Honolulu, Hawaii, August 1961.
4. Essen-Möller, E.: Psychiatrische Untersuchungen an einer Serie von Zwillingen. Acta Psychiat., Kbh., Suppl. 23, 1941.
5. Fenichel, O.: The Psychoanalytic Theory of Neurosis. New York, W. W. Norton & Co., Inc., 1945.
6. Hoagland, H.: Biochemical aspects of schizophrenia. J. Nerv. Ment. Dis. 126:211-220, 1958.
7. Kallmann, F. J.: Heredity and Mental Disorder. New York, W. W. Norton &Co., Inc., 1953.

8. ——: The genetics of mental illness. *In* American Handbook of Psychiatry (ed. S. Ariet:). New York, Basic Books, Inc., 1959 pp. 175-196.
9. Kety, S.: Biochemical theories of schizophrenia. Part I. Science 129:1528-1532, 1959.
10. ——: Biochemical theories of schizophrenia. Part II. Science 129:1590-1596, 1959.
11. ——: Biochemical theories of schizophrenia. Part III. Science 129:3362-3363, 1959.
12. Luxenburger, H.: Die Manifestationswahrscheinlichkeit der Schizophrenie im Lichte der Zwillingsforschung. Allg. Z. Psychiat. 103:174, 1934.
13. Malzberg, B.: Important statistical data about mental illness. *In* Arieti, S. (Ed.) American Handbook of Psychiatry (ed. S. Arieti). New York, Basic Books, 1959, pp. 161-174.
14. Myers, J. K., and Roberts, B. H.: Family and Class Dynamics in Mental Illness. New York, John Wiley & Sons, Inc., 1959.
15. Opler, M. K., and Singer, J. L.: Ethnic differences in behavior and psychopathology: Italian and Irish. Internat. J. Soc. Psychiat. 2:11, 1956.
16. Pastore, N.: The Nature-Nurture Controversy. New York, King's Crown, 1949.
17. Phillips, L., and Rabinovitch, M. S.: Social role and patterns of symptomatic behaviors. J. Abnorm. Soc. Psychol. 57(2):181-186, 1958.
18. Rees, L.: Constitutional factors and abnormal behaviors. *In* Eysenck, H. J. (Ed.) Handbook of Abnormal Psychology (ed. H. J. Eysenck). New York, Basic Books, 1961, pp. 344-392.
19. Rosanoff, A. J., Handy, L. M., Plesset, I. R., and Brush, S. The etiology of so-called schizophrenic psychoses with special reference to their occurrence in twins. Amer J. Psychiat. 91:247-286, 1934.
20. Schooler, C., and Caudill, W.: Symptomatology in Japanese and American schizophrenics. Personal communication, Oct. 1963.
21. Slater, E.: Psychotic and neurotic illnesses in twins. M.R.C. Spec. Rep. Ser. No. 278 (London, H.M.S.O., 1953).
22. Wheelis, A.: The Quest for Identity. New York, W. W. Norton & Co., Inc., 1958.
23. Zigler, E., and Phillips, L.: Social competence and outcome in psychiatric disorder. J. Abnorm. Soc. Psychol. 63(2):264-271, 1961.
24. Zigler, E., and Phillips, L.: Social competence and the process-reactive distinction in psychopathology. J. Abnorm. Soc. Psychol. 65(4):215-222, 1962.

27

A CROSS-CULTURAL APPROACH TO CLASSIFICATION IN SCHIZOPHRENIA AND OTHER MENTAL DISORDERS*

by JOSEPH ZUBIN, PH.D., and MITCHELL L. KIETZMAN, PH.D.†

THE PURPOSE OF THIS PAPER is to analyze the problems presented by cross-cultural studies in the diagnosis of mental disorders and to delineate an approach which may permit fairer cross-cultural comparisons. Beginning with the basic assumption that mental disorders are the joint product of deviations from the norm in the patient's biological equipment as well as in his environmental experience, an attempt will be made to obtain indices of mental disorder based on deviations in both of these components. Hopefully, they will not be occluded or exaggerated by differences in the social-cultural-environmental milieu of different groups nor by the potentially different diatheses of people in varying geographical locations. In the course of such an undertaking, the relative contributions of biology and environment to the etiology of mental disorders can perhaps be more clearly highlighted.

Two assumptions underlie this approach. The first is that at the present time incipient mental disorders are detected and diagnosed largely on the basis of observed deviation from social-cultural expectations. Since such expectation is highly dependent on social-cultural norms, cross-cultural comparisons of mental disorders are fraught with much difficulty. To the extent that cultural expectations differ from country to country, deviations from such frameworks cannot be compared directly. The techniques most useful for detecting these deviations are largely the inventorying of overt behavior either through

---

*The preparation of this paper was aided in part by Grants MH 09191, MH 07466-01, MH 07776-01, MH 03546-04, MH 07478-01, CD 00029-05, and by post-doctoral fellowship grants to Dr. Kietzman (MPD-16,094 and NSF 42197).

†Biometrics Research, N.Y. State Department of Mental Hygiene, and Columbia University, New York, N.Y.

observational and/or interviewing methods. How to minimize the differential influence of sociocultural factors in the application of these techniques is our first problem.

The second assumption is that in addition to the culture-bound indicators of mental disorders there may exist culture-free or culture-fair indicators of vulnerability on which comparisons can be based regardless of the social-cultural milieu. The culture-fair are to be sought first in the cross-culturally invariant deviations from expectation (if any exist) which characterize mental disorders. The culture-free indicators must be relatively independent of previous experience and may be either (1) biochemical (2) neurophysiological, or (3) behavioral. The search for the biochemical indicators is a major undertaking now in full swing, but thus far has not yet yielded results which are diagnostically useful. The neurophysiological approach is less well known and its results too are still very tentative. Such techniques as evoked potentials and EEG patterns fall into this category. The behavioral approach is to be distinguished from the uncontrolled observational or clinical approach discussed previously by the fact that while the observational approach is largely naturalistic and uncontrolled (although it can be made systematic), the behavioral approach is based on the laboratory technique of controlled stimulation. (It should be further noted that continued success of the biochemical and neurophysiological approaches is highly dependent upon the further development of behavioral techniques). One promising approach is to focus on the initial component of the response of the patient to stimulation in the various sense modalities. The first 1,000 milliseconds following stimulation can become the testing ground for the culture-free or culture-fair indicators, on the presumption that the learned behaviors from the social-cultural environment may not be able to express themselves quickly enough to influence the response until after the brief initial phase has passed.

Although the culture-dependent techniques are better developed and better known (interviewing, projective tests, conceptual tests, etc.), there are already quite a number of techniques in the culture-free area which can be exploited. Both areas, however, suffer from a common shortcoming—the absence of accepted systematic standard techniques for their investigation. If we could systematize and objectify the techniques already in use, we could improve diagnostic methods considerably by reducing the irrelevant "noise" introduced into the diagnostic procedures. This is the immediate purpose of this paper in contrast with the long-range purpose of discovering better techniques for discriminating the mentally ill from the mentally well.

Culture-dependent techniques can be improved in the following manner: The mental status part of the mental examination can be made more objective by the use of a systematic interviewing schedule and accompanying inventory for recording both the verbal and the motor behavior of patients. Similar techniques can be developed for evaluating the other parts of the mental examination—the social adaptation of the patient, the anamnesis, and ward behavior. Specific methods for developing each of these will be discussed.

Culture-free indicators have to be sought in laboratory experiments in which the speed, accuracy, and temporal or spatial integration of responses to specified types of stimuli can be measured and contrasted in patients and controls.

Finally, methods have to be developed for integrating the data emanating from such studies, so that the natural lines of cleavage in the patterned data (if such are found) can be discovered. On the basis of these cleavages, the population of mental patients can be fractionated into homogeneous subgroups which will either parallel the old diagnostic categories in part or in whole, or establish new categories for further evaluation.

The need for cross-cultural investigations arises from the fact that the data on hospitalized mental patients show tremendous differences among countries and even within regions of the same country. The variability in incidence and prevalence rates has many sources. Some of these sources of variation are inevitable today, resulting from our lack of knowledge of etiology. Others inhere in the diagnostic task itself, since in the last analysis diagnosis is based on human decisions that are never flawless. But there are some sources of variation which are avoidable under properly controlled (e.g., culture-fair) conditions.

A catalog of the sources of these variations would include (1) cultural differences in the initial detection of mental illness, (2) theoretical assumptions regarding the nature of mental illness, and (3) the specific methods of arriving at the diagnosis.

Cultural Factors in the Initial Detection of Mental Illness

The detection, rather than diagnosis, of mental disorders is made largely by laymen—the patient himself, his family, friends, neighbors, the community and its public officials (policemen, sheriffs, etc.). In the U.S. and especially in the U.K., because of the National Health Service, the general practitioner plays the role of a secondary screen, before the psychiatrist is brought in. Thus, at least the initial detection of mental illness is based largely on those aspects of the patient's behavior which deviate from expected social-cultural norms. As a result, social-cultural forces tend to bias the apparent prevalence of mental illness. While estimation of the true prevalence of all illnesses suffers from this difficulty[6] there are certain criteria by which the presence or absence of most nonpsychiatric illness can usually be established independently of the patient's behavior (action, feelings, attitudes, emotions and thoughts). In most mental disorders, however, the patient's behavior is the sole basis for making diagnoses. To the degree that such deviant behavior constitutes the basis for suspected mental illness, environmental factors (cultural, social, and physical) may inhibit or facilitate bringing certain types of patients to the psychiatrist for diagnosis. This is one reason why different cultural groups may show different rates of diagnosed mental illness, and this source of variability is definitely attributable to environmental influences. Furthermore, environmental factors may play a large role in determining what label to place on the patient when he comes to the attention of the diagnostician.

An example of the cultural differences in initial detection or in diagnosis or in both is afforded by data recently provided by a cross-cultural study at McGill University.[42] They sent questionnaires to the network of psychiatrists and social scientists with whom they had established contact through their semiannual review publication. This questionnaire contained a list of 26 symptoms or signs, inquired about the main locale in which the respondent worked and made his observations, the cultural group which predominated in his practice or field work, and included a variety of other questions. The results indicated that the following items were never reported as *infrequent* in schizophrenics: (1) social and emotional withdrawal, (2) auditory hallucinations, (3) delusions (in general), and (4) flatness of affect. These four symptoms reportedly occur transculturally but in the remaining 22 items out of the 26, definite associations were found between frequency of reported appearance of a symptom and some broad sociocultural grouping. Thus, delusions of destruction and religious delusions are quite infrequently reported except in Christians and Muslims. Visual hallucinations apparently appear most often in African and near Eastern groups and delusional jealousy is most common in Asians, irrespective of religion. Depersonalization seems to be most frequent in urban populations while delusions of grandeur are most frequent in rural populations.

Since this study was based on a questionnaire, it is not clear whether the traits under examination differ in frequency among the different sociocultural groupings or whether social-cultural factors biased the answers to the questionnaire.

The role of the general practitioner in referring patients in the U.K. was studied by Rawnsley and Loudon.[48] Substantial variation in rate of referral among practitioners was found which could not be accounted for by specific social and demographic factors, selective recruitment of psychiatric patients, clinical severity, diagnosis, age, civil state, or occupation. General social and attitudinal factors on the part of the general practitioner and the community were largely responsible for the variation in referral rate.

Theoretical Assumptions Regarding the Nature of Mental Illness

The theoretical models for the mental disorders that now vie for acceptance are so many that this is hardly the place to review them. We shall limit ourselves to a few and illustrate their implication for diagnosis. One school of psychiatry denies any specificity to mental disorders, maintaining that there is only one kind—the failure to adapt or adjust to the environment. Diagnosis is either impossible or of no value in this system.

At the opposite end of the spectrum is the school that maintains that psychiatric diagnoses are based on pathognomonic factors or syndromes of such factors which are universally characteristic of each category of disease in all environments. While there is substantial agreement in this school regarding the universality of symptoms of psychosis, especially the frank psychoses, the agreement regarding neurosis, character, and personality disorders is far from unanimous.

Between these two extremes there are various compromises. In the middle of the range may be found the point of view which assumes that until indexes that are independent of culturally determined behavior become available (as was the case for general paresis, mongolism, PKU, etc.), we shall have to depend on behavioral deviations from social-cultural norms for our diagnoses. Since these deviations are so highly dependent on the environmental context which provides their frame of reference, different environments may well elicit different types of deviation, and cross-environmental comparisons may be impossible.

If we exclude the first school of thought, which denies the usefulness of diagnosis entirely, the two other points of view both agree that there is more to mental illness than the deviations from the expected norms. There must be in addition some vulnerability, perhaps in the neurophysiological substrate, which characterizes those who develop mental illness. If this neurophysiological substrate is relatively free of differential social-cultural effects it may be useful as an independent criterion in the diagnosis of the mental disorders.

Specific Methods of Arriving at Detection and Diagnosis

Even if the environmental forces elicited the same or similar types of deviation from a patient regardless of his country of residence or socioeconomic level, we could not achieve diagnostic comparability. The individual factors in the patient's behavior are weighted so differently by the family, the community, and the diagnosing psychiatrist that a consequent increase in the variability of detection and diagnosis must result. Insofar as the social-cultural norms differ from country to country and even within different regions of the same country, it is to be expected that deviations from such shifting standards cannot be directly comparable. Even the self-reports (or absence of reports) of inner feelings that are elicited by the psychiatrist are culturally influenced and interpreted by both the patient as well as the examiner, which again may lead to increased variability across cultures.

One of the sources of variability in diagnosis reflects the differences in diagnostic procedures and labels attached to the same patients by different examiners even within the same culture and sometimes even within the same hospital.

The unreliability of psychiatric diagnoses has been documented in a multitude of studies. As an example of such studies one can point to the recent investigations of Beck et al.[4,5] They found that agreement on diagnosis was reached in only 54 per cent of the cases, but that there was almost perfect agreement for a specific symptom (depth of depression), an indication that for *observations* of behavior good agreement exists. Two-thirds of the disagreements seemed to be chargeable to the nosological system itself, which in addition to its lack of clear criteria requires impractically fine distinctions (e.g., between psychophysiological reaction and conversion reaction) and which force decisions between neurotic symptoms and personality disorder when both are present. The remaining third of the discrepancy was attributable to variability in procedure on the part of the examiners.

Kreitman[31] has reviewed the studies in which different observers examined the same patients or comparable groups of patients. He found only 5 studies of this type in the literature, a testimony to the fact that careful studies of reliability of diagnosis are rare. In all but one of these studies, the examinations that were compared were *repeated* examinations. In only one study were the patients observed simultaneously by the same group of observers. The percentage of agreement varied with the different diagnostic groupings. When broad groupings were used, agreement ranged from 89 per cent to 59 per cent for the psychoses as against 46 per cent to 24 per cent for the neuroses. For the more specific diagnoses, the agreement was lower. Pasamanick[44] examined the diagnoses allotted after ward assignment to groups of female patients quite homogeneous in age, residence, educational status, type of admission, and marital status, who had been admitted to the same hospital and had been randomly assigned to the different wards. The greatest discrepancy in diagnosis between the wards was for neurosis and character disorders. The organic disorders seemed to have drawn the highest agreement in all the studies.

The basic rationale for investigation is that the detection and diagnosis of mental disorders today depend to a significant extent on aspects of behavior of the individual which deviate from social-cultural norms. These deviations constitute the symptoms on the basis of which the diagnosis is made. Some of these symptoms may be found to be universally characteristic of patients across all cultures, others may be more culture-dependent. In the case of those categories of illness whose characteristics seem to be independent of culture, there should be no difficulty in identifying similar disorders in different cultures. For those disorders which are manifested in behaviors that are culture-bound, it will be very difficult to identify similar disorders in different cultures since their characteristic behaviors will, of course, be different. The first step in the direction of preparing tools for improving diagnosis is to develop objective measures for detecting deviations from expected behavior in the particular cultural milieu in which the patient finds himself. For this purpose systematic interviewing with objective recording of behavior during the interview and with objective evaluation of the content of the interview is necessary if comparable results are to be obtained for different interviewers.

However, there may be more to mental disorder than this externally observable deviation in behavior. Unless we find the additional factors which underlie the external behavior, we will never be able to make comparisons across cultures except for those illnesses which have behavioral characteristics that are universal. What can these additional factors be? Apparently, if one made the assumption that underlying the externally observable behavior there is a graded vulnerability which differentiates those who develop the illness from those who do not, it might perhaps be possible to obtain indicators of this vulnerability which are culture-free or culture-fair. By culture-free measures we mean those which characterize a vulnerable individual but which remain immune to environmental influences. If such techniques are not discovered, we could settle for culture-fair measures, by which we mean measures that, though subject to the influence of cultural forces, nevertheless still permit the detection of vulnerability across cultures.

What is the nature of this vulnerability? It may have a hereditary basis, or it may develop as a result of trauma-producing experiences very early in life or perhaps even in intrauterine existence. This is no place to argue the question as to the origin of the vulnerability, but it is necessary to recognize that some assumption regarding vulnerability is important for analyzing the development of deviant behavior of the type we call mental disorder.

We have two choices before us. If we assume that this vulnerability is produced by environmental stresses and strains, then it might be possible to subject individuals to a variety of stimuli of a mildly noxious sort to determine their response to such stimulation. It would be ideal, of course, to perform such studies on neonates so as to determine which individuals seem to be more sensitive to stress-producing loads. This, however, is a hazardous procedure, and furthermore we do not know whether the immediate response to the stress-producing load will be indicative of future responses, since it is the repeated presentation of such stimuli which may be basic to the development of vulnerability. On the other hand, to try to determine a genetic basis for this susceptibility is again a problem which is beyond us at the present time. For this reason, we might avoid the problem of the etiology of these conditions and simply test in the early adult schizophrenic for signs of deviation in some culture-free or culture-fair response that would indicate his vulnerability. Whether this deviation is the cause or the result of the illness cannot be determined now. However, if longitudinal studies reveal the presence of these deviations in individuals long before their clinical symptoms appear, we may have more faith in the possibility that they are not produced by the illness.

One area for the investigation of such indexes is the biochemical analysis of the body fluids. This is now rather widely investigated and is hopefully yielding results that will be of interest. A second approach is to try to examine the neurophysiological response system which may yield indicators of vulnerability. In this study we propose to make a thorough sampling of those techniques that might differentiate the vulnerable from the nonvulnerable. Hopefully this technique would not be as subject to the influences of cultural forces as are the behaviors which are now used for diagnostic purposes. A third approach is behavioral and focuses attention on the initial components of the response to specific stimulation in the various sense modalities. The first 1000 milliseconds following stimulation offer an opportunity for obtaining culture-free indicators of mental illness since the cultural influences may not be able to make themselves felt until after the initial component of the response is finished.[70]

The model we have in mind consists of four elements: (1) the input of the stimulus, (2) encoding of the information and its propagation to the higher centers, (3) interaction with stored memories of previous experience, and (4) emission of response. Mental disorder may interfere with one or more of these four components or with all of them. Elkes[18] has suggested that the encoding of the input and the interaction between the propagated information and stored memories may be at fault in schizophrenia. In an attempt to relate the model to culture-free indicators, it is clear that culture-free deficiencies can occur at any one of the interfaces between the processes or in the processes themselves, but the content component—stored memories—since these are so very much the product of past experience, is perforce culture-bound.

One may raise a question regarding the stability and regularity of each of these four components in normals. It is well known that considerable individual differences exist with respect to the reception, encoding, and retrieval of information in the nervous system and that the intraindividual variability in this respect is also considerable. Furthermore, it is a well-established observation that for both interindividual and intraindividual variability patients exceed normals. We might extend our model to include the postulate that each portion of the central nervous system, since it is never static even in the idling state (when no external stimulus impinges), has its own rhythmic cycle of activity. Therefore, successively impinging stimuli, even though they be identical, must produce different responses depending on the duration of the particular cycles which they hit and on the particular phase of the rhythmic cycle which is impinged upon. This may explain the basic variability in the usual responsiveness of an organism. If all cyclical activity had the same duration and stimuli impinged in phase, perhaps the variability would be reduced considerably. If we now postulate further that one of the characteristics of the mentally ill (especially schizophrenics) is greater fluctuation in their rhythmic cycles (less similarity from cycle to cycle in duration and intensity of discharge), we may attribute the differences between patients and normals not to any of the four basic components discussed earlier, but to the inordinate variability of the rhythm of their cyclic activity in the idling state. This may also be at the bottom of the oft-reported variability in schizophrenic reponses. This is a rather loosely structured model requiring considerably more specification before it can be subjected to test, but it does not present any apparent impossibilities.

One essential step in applying the proposed model based upon rhythmic cycles is the provision of methods for assessing the *idling* state—the initial state of the organism before any stimulus is applied. The measures that generally have been used to study the idling state are of three different types: (1) autonomic, such as the heart rate, galvanic skin response, and pupillary response; (2) skeletal somatic, as, for example, electromyographic recordings; and (3) cortical, as reflected in the electroencephalogram.

The nonspecific system probably exerts an influence on all of these, but in the intact organism it cannot be measured directly and must be inferred from its influence on the other three. We need not be concerned as some are about the lack of correlation between the measures of these three types of systems, since their cycles may be out of phase and the ordinary loads which each system carries (e.g., the heart) even in the idling state differ considerably from system to system. All we need to require of our measures is not correlation across individuals but systematic patterning of the measures in the three systems across successive occasions in the same individual.

It would be well, however, to obtain a single measure which would represent the organism's idling state. One may speculate, for example, whether the variety of rhythmic cycles which characterize the firing of the different sets of cells in the three systems may not, with the help of the other bodily cycles (metabolic rates, etc.), give rise to an organismic time-clock which characterizes the organism and which may constitute the basis for the difference in time judgments which have been observed between patients and normals. Organismic time may turn out to be some type of average of the individual cycles characterizing the various systems of the body. If organismic time can be used as a measure, the individual differences in this measure may well be related to the first 1000 milliseconds of an individual's response, and in this way serve to bolster the possibility that it is in this brief time period that the differential between patients and normals is likely to be found.

The concept of organismic time may be regarded as an intermediary between sidereal time and subjective time experience. Thus, there are three time clocks to be taken into consideration in the analysis of behavior: (1) sidereal clock, independent of the organism (measured in seconds); (2) organismic clock, dependent on the rate of cycling of the internal milieu (measurable in orgs); and (3) a subjective clock related somehow to the organismic clock (measurable in chrons).

What support can be provided for the hypothesis that the subjective time sense (in chrons) may be based on some aspect of physiological functioning in the various parts of the organism (organismic time measured in orgs)? Over 40 years ago Piéron[46] suggested the possibility that if the speed of organic processes (measured in orgs) is modified by variations in temperature, mental time (subjective time measured in chrons) will increase or decrease proportionately.* Following Piéron's suggestion, François[22] and Hoagland[25] demonstrated that by elevating an individual's body temperature it is possible to modify his behavior so that he counts or taps at a faster rate. Carrel[13] and Lecomte du Noüy[33] postulated that the reason why wounds take longer to heal in the aged is attributable to the slowing down of organismic processes in their *milieu intérieur,* and this in turn leads to

*It must be noted, however, that the variations in temperature referred to here are the variations in the internal milieu. Simply varying external temperature is not enough, since the initial effect of an external change may introduce compensatory homeostatic changes in the internal milieu, and it is the temperature of the internal milieu that we are concerned with.

the impression in the aged that sidereal time is speeded up, since fewer orgs and corresponding chrons occur per second of sidereal time. Fischer, Griffin and Liss[21] found that organismic time (their term is neuronal time) is accelerated in nervous tissue characterized by the higher metabolic rates, as evidenced by the greater dye-sorption in such areas. LSD-25, according to them, raises the body temperature and leads to more rapid counting and tapping per second. Lhamon Goldstone and Goldfarb[34] at last year's symposium reported that the less chronic schizophrenic patients, presumably the more agitated, demonstrated the greatest overestimation of clock time, and therefore the fastest organismic time (as did subjects who received stimulants). The chronic schizophrenic patients and the schizophrenic patients in remission showed less overestimation of time than normals, and therefore their organismic times presumably would be slower than that of the normals and than that of the less chronic schizophrenic patients.

The important point here is not to analyze in detail the results of time judgment studies, but to use them as an example of how to relate behavioral measures (time estimation, in this case) to organismic time, especially in psychopathology. There seems to be no general statement possible about the relationship between changes in organismic time and changes in behavior. To clarify the relationship, however, it is necessary to distinguish between two types of response involving time duration that are inversely related to each other and thus are related in opposite ways to changes in organismic time. Responses of the first type consist of the perception of environmental change, per se, and these are postulated to be inversely related to changes in organismic time. For example, perceived environmental changes would appear slower as organismic time becomes faster. Responses of the second type are not perceptual, since they are not responses to specifiable environmental changes. Instead, they are conceptual responses that are dependent upon memory storage of previous environmental changes. Tapping behavior following the instructions to "tap once every second," when the subject has no clock as a referent, would be an example. Responses of this type are believed to bear a direct relationship to organismic time and would therefore speed up as organismic time became faster.

The importance of distinguishing between these two types of response can be illustrated by analyzing some recent studies of velocity perception done by Held and White[24] and by Carlson and Feinberg,[12] using very similar measurement techniques. These investigations are of particular interest because Held and White studied sensory deprivation effects (which have been related to psychotic behavior) and Carlson and Feinberg compared schizophrenics and normals. In these studies Held and White interpreted prolonged response time results as indicating that their subjects underestimated the velocity of a moving object which, in terms of our formulation, would be related to a speeding up of organismic time. However, Carlson and Feinberg found that upon repeated testing over 13 weeks, their subjects also gave longer response times, which they suggest might be due to the likelihood that repeated testing would be less demanding and eventually the task would become routine, and perhaps even boring. Under these conditions organismic time presumably would slow down, not speed up, as would be demanded by the interpretation of the longer response times proposed by Held and White. When we analyze the technique used by these investigators, we find that subjects had opportunity to utilize both classes of response we suggested earlier—the perceptual and the nonperceptual. They made perceptual judgments of the velocity of the moving object while it was in sight, as suggested by Held and White. They also had to estimate its velocity when it was out of sight. This nonperceptual (conceptual) time judgment came at the end of the trial, and we suggest that it was relatively more important in producing the longer response time than the perceptual component. In other words, rather than interpreting these results in terms of underestimation of the velocity of a perceived moving object, which would suggest a faster organismic time, we interpret them in terms of a prolonged response (an overproduction) by the subjects of the period of time required for the hidden moving object to arrive at the goal. (A similar suggestion was made by Carlson and Feinberg.) This interpretation then leads to the conclusion that in both studies a slower motor response time suggests a slower organismic time.

Ponomarev, a Russian investigator,[47] supports our interpretation in a report concerning the effect of drugs on the response to a continuously visible moving object. Under these conditions Ponomarev found that caffeine, presumably a stimulant, produced longer or delayed response, while a bromide, presumably a sedative, produced shorter or premature responses. These apparently paradoxical results become more understandable if we remember that the response under consideration here is based upon a perceived rather than inferred change in the environment and that it bears an inverse relationship to changes in organismic time. Thus, if the caffeine makes organismic time go faster, the moving object should appear slower, and there should be an increase in the number of longer or delayed responses.

We have presented only a brief sketch of the concept of organismic time as it relates to behavioral changes and psychopathology. The organismic time construct, as presented here, is more or less similar to such general terms as excitation, activation, or arousal. It is expected that future development of the construct, however, will include not only the notion of change in organismic times, but also investigation of the magnitude of change, and the problem of the rate of organismic times, per se. There is considerable discussion in the literature about significant physiological and/or psychological time constants. The neuronic shutter theory, originally proposed by Meister,[40] and subsequently mentioned by Lindsley[35] and Ellingson,[19] suggests that the 8-12 cps alpha frequencies of brain waves might serve as a shutter device that give a person periodic views (averaging 100 msec) of his environment. Subsequent investigations by Lansing,[32] Callaway,[11] and Dustman[17] support the general idea of this theory by showing that the reaction time to light pulses can be significantly reduced if the pulses are presented at a particular phase of the alpha brain waves. Venables[61] reported finding a periodicity in reaction times for nonpatients and schizophrenic subjects, and he also showed that although the two groups had the same absolute periodicities, they were out of phase of about 10 milliseconds.

We do not, however, have to wait for pure culture-free indicators. Even if they do bear a cultural impress, they occur so rapidly that the cultural-experiential impact cannot loom very high. For example, the startle pattern seems to be a transcultural response to a sudden noise, parts of which (e.g., the eye blink) occur within the first 40 milliseconds after stimulation on the average and seem to be relatively free of habituation. The entire startle response seems to be finished by about 1500 milliseconds after stimulation. While the psychopathological correlates of startle are not very striking, other types of responses that occur in the first 1000 millisecond range do seem to be promising and will be presented in this paper.

There is a hypothesis which finds favor with many American psychiatrists and psychologists that certain illness resulting from continued exposure to noxious stimulation may not exhibit initially any neurophysiological or biochemical signs. In such cases, a thorough survey of the historical development of the individual would have to be undertaken in order to identify the experiences which lay behind the development of the disorder. The decision whether to adopt the assumption of initial vulnerability or to reject it must be made on the basis of strategy rather than possibility. The assumption that traumatic experiences per se produce the illness without the help of any original hypersensitivity or vulnerability is not as susceptible to experimental testing as is the assumption that the patient possesses certain vulnerabilities which have led to the illness.

The latter requires direct experimental exploration of some leads which already exist. The former requires a retrospective analysis of past experience or a longitudinal prospective study of potentially mentally ill individuals—a much more difficult if not impossible task. However, adopting the assumption that there is some vulnerability in each patient to begin with, we may discover some patients in whom no vulnerability seems to be present. These might be the individuals who upon closer examination would reveal a life history which was quite deviant and reflected many more traumatic experiences than those who do not develop the illness.

Let us assume that in a given environment there are a certain number of vulnerable types and a certain number of nonvulnerable types. It should be pointed out that by "vulnerable" we mean an individual possessing certain characteristics which, if he were exposed to specific pressures would lead to an illness. In other words, "vulnerability" and "nonvulnerability" are ad hoc concepts dependent for their status on demonstrable evidence that in some situations such people have proved vulnerable. This does not preclude the possibility of finding vulnerability in some of our current "nonvulnerables" if new situations such as radiation effects, etc., are discovered that transfer the previously "nonvulnerable" to the "vulnerable" class. Nevertheless, these types are distinguished from each other, in the ideal case, by comparing profiles of characteristics exhibited for a variety of culture-free measures. Since the measures we use have as their aim the establishment of a typology of susceptibility to various kinds of psychopathology, we must further assume that in *another* environment the distribution of types into two categories—vulnerable and nonvulnerable—may be reversed. Thus if type A has the inborn error of metabolism producing PKU (phenylketonuria), if environment I provides a diet containing phenylalanine, then A will develop mental deficiency. On the other hand, if the individual of type A lives in environment II, which is free of phenylalanine, a normal pattern of behavior will ensue.

Any one of the vulnerability types (A, B, C . . .) could possibly be associated with any one of the psychopathological or normal behavior patterns, depending on the social-cultural-physical pressures. Conversely, anyone characterized by one of the possible psychopathological patterns could possess one or another of either the vulnerable or nonvulnerable substrates. An individual can fall into one of four categories: (1) vulnerable in environment I and exhibiting psychopathology—the mentally ill; (2) not vulnerable but temporarily exhibiting psychopathology—the pseudomentally ill; (3) vulnerable but not exhibiting psychopathology—the latent case; and (4) not vulnerable and not exhibiting psychopathology—the mentally well.

The visibility or detection of the individuals who are vulnerable as well as of the overtly psychopathological depends to a large extent on the environment in which they live. Since the tolerance of communities for eccentricity varies considerably from environment to environment, the number of detected individuals belonging to the vulnerable and psychopathological class will also vary. Thus, the alleged greater tolerance for eccentricity in the U.K. and the lesser tolerance for drug addiction and alcoholism in the U.S. may explain in part some of the discrepancies in incidence rates. If objective indicators of vulnerability and deviant behavior become available as a result of the proposed study, future population studies can be made more comparable across social-cultural environments.

One may ask why we have chosen the United Kingdom and the United States for our first comparative study. The reasons are as follows: first, the common language; second, the basic disparity in the social-cultural-environmental factors; and third, the available cooperative efforts already in existence. These two countries are sufficiently far apart in social-cultural environments to produce discernible differences in incidence of two major psychoses (manic-depressive psychosis and schizophrenia) and yet not so far apart that we would be likely to run into patently noncomparable diagnoses such as running amok, *delire passionel*, etc. Let us now turn to the available culture-dependent and culture-free techniques.

The Culture-Dependent Techniques

A. Observational and Interview Techniques

If we accept the assumption that mental disorders are now detected and diagnosed on the basis of social-cultural deviations, it becomes necessary to develop techniques and instruments for objectively measuring such deviations. The clinical interview which now constitutes the basis for diagnosis is an unstructured free-floating interview which varies from clinician to clinician and which is unsuited to the purposes of scientific investigation.

Unless a systematic procedure is introduced for collecting information, diagnoses will vary from observer to observer even for the same patient. In order to increase agreement among observers four controlled procedures are being developed: (1) the Mental Status Schedule, (2) the Social Adaptation Schedule, (3) the Structured Clinical Interview, and (4) the Ward Behavior Inventory.

The application of rating scales to the classification of mental patients has a long history despite its relatively recent development.

Father Moore[41] was one of the first to rate the behavior notes in case history material. He factor-analyzed the results, arriving at dimensions not unlike those which Kraepelin had developed earlier through clinical observation. The Malamud-Sands scale[36a] was the next one to be developed. Since then, Lorr[36] and Wittenborn[67] have provided scales for psychiatrists for rating the behavior of mental patients.

1. Mental Status Schedule.[58] This technique consists of an interview schedule for the mental status examination and a matching inventory of 248 dichotomous items descriptive of small units of pathological behavior. The schedule contains questions arranged in a definite sequence designed to provide for follow-up of incomplete responses. Most of the questions are open-ended so as to encourage the patient to reveal his own mentation. Properly administered, the interview has the "feel" of the clinical evaluation. However, unlike the usual clinical interview the provision of a specific schedule of questions, a fixed order of presentation, and a uniform coverage of the same areas of psychopathology with each patient make it more likely that the differences observed will be due to actual differences among patients rather than to different interviewing procedures. This technique yielded reliabilities of the order of .90 or more when several groups of patients were evaluated independently by three psychiatrists. Moreover, it has distinguished significantly between the amount of psychopathology shown by inpatients, clinic outpatients, and former inpatients on follow-up.

2. Social Adaptation Schedule (in preparation). This technique follows the form of the Mental Status Schedule in that the patient is examined by means of a structured interview and observations are recorded on an inventory of dichotomous items descriptive of small units of pathological behavior. However, it differs from the examination of the mental status in that the focus is not on symptomatology but on the presence of disturbed functioning as seen mainly in disturbances in social adaptation. The patient is examined for evidence of disturbed functioning in any of the following areas of adaptation: (1) use of leisure time, (2) friendship patterns and involvement in social activities, (3) work adjustment, (4) sexual and marital adjustment, (5) school or vocational training and (6) level of aspiration. The technique has been designed so that it can be used to supplement the examination of the mental status or can be used on a separate occasion as an independent instrument.

With regard to the anamnesis, we have not yet developed an instrument for this area. It is important, however, to realize that obtaining information on the entire spectrum of a person's developmental history is a research task of the first magnitude. In the experimental approach to this problem it is necessary to develop techniques which will focus on particular critical periods in the history of the individual. It is proposed to begin with a focused interview dealing with the question of the status of the patient a year before he came for help and, by focusing on this particular period, arrive at more objective information. A second focus might be the adolescent friendship patterns of the patient, since in some current research we have found this phase of development important in prognosis, especially with regard to type of onset. A third focus might bear on early childhood, especially based on history obtained from the family. In all of these aspects of the anamnesis, at least two members of the family ought to be interviewed for cross-checking purposes. While this may sound impractical for everyday use, it should not be beyond the range of a research project. In fact, the Katz Adjustment Scales[28] are based upon questioning relatives of patients. Hopefully, the more intensive methods used in this research can form the basis for more practical approaches in the future.

3. *Structured Clinical Inventory.*[9] This instrument is similar in form to the Mental Status Schedule but differs from it in purpose. Instead of focusing on mental status evaluation, it focuses on the general social and psychological adjustment of the patient and is intended primarily for use by the social scientist. Emphasis is placed on *evoking* immediate and salient pathology rather than on probing for a wide range of specific information as with the Mental Status Schedule.

4. Ward Behavior Inventory.[8] This instrument capitalizes on the observational opportunities afforded nurses and ward attendants in everyday contact with the patients. The WBI consists of 150 items rated true or not true. All the items describe observable behaviors as seen during a 48-hour span of observation. Neither retrospective material nor dynamic inferences are included. Total scores reflect global pathology and provide evidence of change in response to treatment. The Ward Behavior Inventory has proved itself reliable when raters are properly trained and motivated.[8] Reliability coefficients ranged from .40 for untrained raters to .84 for well-trained and well-motivated observers. Follow-up studies indcate that the global pathology score correlates at a low but significant level with outcome in terms of length of time out of hospital. WBI scores of 107 patients followed for 1 year had a correlation of .23 with an Outcome Index (1961). Several drug studies have proved the instrument sensitive to change. Among these are the NIMH 9-hospital collaborative study of phenothiazine therapy conducted by the Psychopharmacology Service Center[16] and an unpublished study of the efficacy of a psychic energizer for seniles. Future work with the WBI will focus on analysis of patterns of items and identification of cluster of patients possessing similar symptomatology.

B. Conceptual Techniques

1. Verbal Behavior. Another conceptual or experience-bound area involves verbal behavior experiments in which the output of the interviewer is manipulated through reinforcement techniques to yield measures of self-referred affect. Apparently schizophrenics differ from normals only in one aspect of verbal behavior in these experiments—in their tendency to extinguish more quickly after reinforcement is discontinued.

A measure of comprehensibility of schizophrenic speech has become available through the use of the "cloze" procedure. This technique demonstrated that the speech of schizophrenic patients is less predictable than that of matched normal subjects. This was shown to hold for early as well as chronic schizophrenics.[50]

Interviews with patients and informants close to the patient have been used to obtain information on performance and interaction within the household and in other primary social groups, for the classification of patients in terms of social role.

Standardized interview procedures have been used to obtain samples of speech behavior to be analyzed in terms of certain measures of vocabulary and grammatical structure for comparison with normal individuals of the same sublinguistic (dialect) background.

2. *Thinking Disorder.* A series of conceptual tests has been developed to detect deviation in the thinking processes of the schizophrenic. The Metalog Test,[10] which measures ability to shift from one to another meaning of a given word, and a variety of sorting tasks have been utilized in the investigation of schizophrenia with special reference to overinclusiveness, anomalous grammatical structure, etc.

The use of psychological tests as adjuncts to diagnosis dates back to Kraepelin's clinic. For the most part, the tests in use today, e.g., intelligence tests, vocabulary, sorting tests, projective tests, etc.—depend heavily on social-cultural influences. A review of these tests would constitute a review of the armamentarium which clinical psychology has developed. As an example of one of the techniques which has proved useful in the diagnosis of psychotics, one can point to the work of Payne.[45] By utilizing a variety of conceptual tests Payne was able to differentiate three main aspects of thought disorder in psychotic patients: abnormal slowness or "retardation," "over-inclusion," and "concreteness." The schizophrenic group stood highest in overinclusion, but did not differ from a depressed group in "retardation," while "concreteness" did not show up as a characteristic of any psychotic illness.

C. *Sociological Variables*

In connection with an ongoing study of the residents of an old age home, techniques have been developed for the investigation of the degree of isolation experienced by an individual and its significance for subsequent adjustment to a home for the aged.[65] Similarly, techniques for the measurement of persuasibility, conformity, and integration into the home have been developed. These techniques are perhaps the most significant for discovering the types of social-cultural deviations which relate to mental disorders. In the aged it was found, for example, that the senile dementia cases proved to be quite conforming while the functionally ill were very low in conformity.

In the same vein, patients with senile dementia made a favorable evaluation of a home for the aged while patients with functional psychiatric disorders evaluated the home negatively. On a measure of integration into the activities of the home and on a scale of *anomie* both types of mental patients rated lower than the normal residents. Neither group differed from the normals in persuasibility. With the techniques such as these we can discover the specific dimensions in which various types of the mentally ill deviate from social-cultural norms.

D. Anthropological Variables

While a comparison of American culture with such a closely similar culture as the British will probably not reveal differences as dramatic as comparison with an exotic culture, it is nevertheless important to identify differences that may contribute to the discrepancies in the rates of the mental disorders. At all events, since at least the *detection* of mental illness is highly influenced by cultural forces, care must be taken to determine the equivalence between the two countries with regard to such general customs as greeting, bereavement, courtship, and other characteristics of social interaction.

In order to develop a measuring instrument which will be useful cross-culturally it will be necessary to find the concrete behavioral equivalents in the two cultures which characterize the categories found useful in detecting psychopathology. It will be necessary also to evaluate the relative importance within the different cultural systems of the corresponding concrete behaviors. To these ends careful anthropological investigation will be required. In attempting to establish normative baselines it would also be useful to assess the particular social-cultural milieu of the patient and the nature of the social groupings in which the patient has been a member. Questions should be formulated on the patient's household—its members, their activities, their child-rearing practices, their contact with the patient, with each other, and with others outside the household; on the patient's employment in terms of social structural considerations—coworkers he was in contact with, the nature of his and their contact, etc.; and similarly with respect to other major involvements of the patient. With all of this, there should also be obtained a description of overall behavior—not merely of the symptomatic behavior, but of the ordinary behavior of the patient. Such information should be obtained from several informants.

The patient's entry into the hospital should be systematically observed, perhaps in terms of a simple interaction framework. which can be used also by observers of his initial interview and of his behavior on the ward. Another approach, which should be seen as complementary rather than alternative, is the direct intensive study of several selected subcultural groups for the careful establishment of behavioral, structural, and evaluative norms relevant to the mental patient's behavior and to his incorporation in a community. As a supplement to these approaches, it might be useful to explore the possible value of such techniques as the semantic differential[43] in comparing mental patients with culturally similar normal subjects. Such comparisons would yield information regarding attitudes, personal value systems and conceptual frameworks in which the patients deviate from the normals.

The degree of rapport or interaction between patient and diagnostician can be gauged objectively by utilizing the cloze technique discussed previously. If a sample of speech obtained from the psychiatrist were given to the patient with every fifth word deleted and the patient required to supply the missing words, and similarly if the patient's speech production were treated in the same way and given the psychiatrist to fill in, some measure of the degree of rapport between the two could be obtained. If more than one psychiatrist were involved, different degrees of understanding between patient and diagnostician could be related to the evaluation.

Culture-Free or Culture-Fair Techniques

In order to simplify the presentation of the variety of techniques available for evaluating pathology in ways that are culture-free or culture-fair, a table has been devised (table 1) which presents the variety of responses the subject is capable of, and the types of stimulation which may be used to elicit these kinds of behavior.[68]

It can be readily seen that as one ascends the columns of the table one begins to get involved more and more with culturally determined responses, but even the lowest rung on the ladder—the physiological—is not always entirely free of social-cultural influences. However, it seems plausible that the effect of hyperventilation on the EEG, for example, is less dependent upon culture than is speed of reading on the Stroop Cards. Some of the behavioral techniques which we have developed and which fall in this category of being less dependent on social-cultural norms are (1) pupillography, (2) cross-modality reaction time, and (3) some measures of temporal resolution in vision and audition.

Most clinically oriented workers wonder how functions so far removed from overt behavioral deviations can help in diagnosis. This

TABLE 1.—Examples of Measurable Activities as Functions of Stimulus Variables

LEVEL OF OBSERVED BEHAVIOR	STIMULUS VARIABLES											
	IDLING STATE		ENERGY VARIABLES				SIGNAL VARIABLES					
	NONE		APPROPRIATE ENERGY		INAPPROPRIATE ENERGY		CONFIGURATIONS		SIGNS		SYMBOLS	
	VARIABLE	FUNCTION	VARIABLE	FUNCTION	VARIABLE	FUNCTION	VARIABLE	FUNCTION	VARIABLE	FUNCTION	VARIABLE	FUNCTION
Conceptual	—	Reverie and fantasy	Uniformly diffused light	Fantasy	Inversion of gravitational attraction	Subjective account of experience	Aircraft forms or silhouettes	Recognition of identity of forms	Practical trouble-shooting test	Diagnosis of trouble	Stimulus word in association test	Association to stimulus word
Psychomotor	—	Spontaneous movement	Painful stimulus	Arm withdrawn	Electroshock	Movements of limbs	Star-shaped maze	Mirror tracing	Classical delayed response stimuli in animal experimentation	Successful response by animal subject	Reinforcement of affect in focused interview	Electromyographic response
Perceptual	—	Spatial and temporal orientation	White noise	Orientation to direction of sound	Pressure stimulation above retina	Phosphene	Rotating Benham Disc	Subjective color experience	Usual visual alternatives in animal discrimination experiment	Selective response of animal subject	Musical chords	Pitch discrimination
Sensory	—	Background noises; cortical gray	Light of graded intensity	Threshold response	Electrical stimulation of thermal receptors	Warmth or cold sensation	Patterned light stimuli	Visual threshold	Infant's faint cry	Mother's auditory threshold	Words or sentences presented tachistoscopically	Visual threshold
Physiological	—	BMR; basal EEG; basal PGR	Increase in carbon dioxide concentration	Change in rate of respiration	Pressure on carotid sinus	Change in heart rate	Photic driving	Change in EEG pattern	Bell ringing in Pavlovian conditioning	Salivation	Verbal instructions to prevaricate	Effect on PGR

has been trenchantly pointed out by Cartwright, Kirtner, and Fiske in a recent report.[14] They say, "The business of neurosis and recovery exists and is exhibited only in the contexts of the self, family, friends, employers, and clinical practitioners. . . . A desirable conceptual variable in the domain of neurosis and recovery through psychotherapy would likely have at least one principal quality: observers in different roles can systematically agree or disagree about it. *A second prerequisite would be that of inherent meaningfulness.* All observers might easily agree that, following a sudden loud noise, a patient's galvanic skin response has changed in a certain direction and amount. But what such a change might signify would be unclear. In particular, its relevance to daily functioning in ordinary interaction with others is in doubt. Yet it is precisely for such daily functioning that the appropriate conceptual variables must have inherent meaningfulness."

It is apparent that an insatiable curiosity motivates these writers. We still don't know why the Wasserman test works, nor how aspirin brings about its effects. Why we should *demand* more from neurophysiological techniques before they are accepted as diagnostic aids in the mental disorders is beyond our comprehension.

The culture-free measures can serve two functions. First, though no measures can be said to be completely culture-free, the way in which culture might affect such measures as pupillary response to light sitmuli is indirect, unlike the direct way in which culture influences primarily conceptual measures such as vocabulary. The major way in which culture will tend to influence the culture-fair tests is likely to lie not in the function under measurement, but in the subject's approach to the testing situation—e.g., in the subject's understanding of the purpose of the test, in the degree of fear experienced, in his motivation, attention, cooperation, etc.—in other words, specifically in those variables which also tend to contaminate comparisons of schizophrenics and normals even when they come from the same cultural background. But it is these very contaminations that the experimental culture-fair techniques have been constructed to minimize.*

Secondly, to the extent that it is possible to minimize cultural influences on such measures, the findings may reflect the presence of

*Such designs include obtaining complete functions rather than isolated points of measurement for each individual, comparisons of slopes of functions rather than level, the measurement of functions under idling state conditions and under load conditions, and finally, the use of the range of variation within a population as a basis for assessing observed deviation.

"organic" factors (vulnerability) relatively independent of social-cultural etiology in at least some part of the mentally ill population. One may then use similarity in response on the psychophysiological measures as part of the pattern of behavioral characteristics which may prove to be invariant across sociocultural boundaries.

This culture-fair substrate underlying the behavior of groups of mentally ill patients may also be used to investigate the possible differential effects of culture on behavior. If the underlying organic factors are identified, the individuals who are characterized by these factors and who exhibit behavior pathology can be compared with those who do not, to determine the types of differential interaction between physiological and cultural factors which led to pathology in one group but not in the other group.

This interaction between physiological and cultural factors is only one aspect of the interaction possible in our heuristic table in which the physiological, sensory, perceptual, psychomotor, and conceptual responses are elicited by energy or symbol stimuli.

In actual experience, these heuristic elements do not occur in isolation any more than chemical elements occur in the pure state in nature. For example, the experience of fear involves the entire spectrum of responses from physiological to conceptual. Following the usual analysis, the sight (sensory and perceptual) of a fear-inducing object usually leads to an immediate appraisal of its dangerous character (conceptual based on stored memories) and is accompanied by visceral (physiological) excitation and may lead to flight (psychomotor). It has been possible to demonstrate experimentally that in order to obtain a "true" emotional experience, all of these levels of response are essential. Thus, merely inducing the physiological component through the injection of adrenaline will not evoke a true emotion[37] nor will the induction of an emotional mood by means of moving picture episodes lead to a true emotion when the physiological component is blocked.[55] The required interaction between sensory and conceptual responses is attested to by the recently developed detection theory of Tanner and Swets[60] in which a manipulation of expectancy (a conceptual component) can vary the threshold. The placebo effect, especially in pain studies, has been shown to be a reflection of conceptual expectancy. Even in animal experiments, such as Harlow's[23] monkeys or Birch's[7] rats, the role of stored memories in determining the response to stimulation is well known. The role of the interaction between physiological and conceptual components in therapy, especialy in behavior therapy, is now the focus of attention.[69]

While the conceptual component, representing the stored memories of previous experience, seems to enter into most responses so that there is always the chance that cultural effects will contaminate our search for culture-free or culture-fair techniques, it may be possible to reduce the conceptual component to a minimum, if not to exclude it entirely. Examples of such responses are the higher activation levels of early schizophrenics, which Mednick[39] and others postulate. The linking of body fluids to psychoses may present another culture-free or culture-fair differential.

Our theoretical and methodological interests in the short-time domain of 1000 milliseconds or less leads us to compare schizophrenic and normal subjects by considering experimental studies which employ brief periods of time for their independent and/or dependent variables. Probably one of the best-documented experimental differences between schizophrenic and normal subjects is that patients display longer and more variable reaction times. In addition, there are a number of reaction time studies which, while demonstrating the longer reaction times of patients, also provide some interesting additional data.[59] We already have mentioned Venables' report[61] of periodicity of reaction times in which normals and schizophrenics demonstrated 100 millisecond periodicities which were out of phase with each other by 10 milliseconds. Venables and Tizard[64] reported a "paradoxical" reaction time effect in which for some patients reaction time decreased as the stimulus intensity increased, up to a certain stimulus intensity, but beyond this intensity reaction times increased. Unfortunately, this effect did not persist beyond the first day of experimentation and as far as we know a replication has not been reported.

Using another, more complex, type of psychomotor task, King[29] demonstrated that schizophrenic and normal subjects differ in their ability to tap in synchrony with a repetitive click presented 1-3 seconds apart. These results show that normal subjects in such a task tend to anticipate or respond before the synchronizing stimulus is given,* while schizophrenic subjects respond after the stimulus presentation. Similar differences between normal and schizophrenic subjects in a synchronization task was reported by Abell.[1] In an even more complex, but somewhat related task, Carlson and Feinberg[12] reported that

*Also reported in Bartlett and Bartlett.[2]

schizophrenics demonstrate a greater inability than normals to synchronize a circularly moving clock hand with a predetermined spot on a clock face. The patients tended to respond later than the nonpatients, so that for them the clock hand went further beyond the target than for the normal subjects. In a study of motion perception, Johansson, Dureman and Sälde[26] described a technique that successfully differentiated a group of normal subjects from a group of psychiatric patients characterized as autistic and socially isolated. Their technique was based upon the observation that two objects moving in opposite directions are perceived as moving much faster than their actual speeds. Under these conditions the autistic subjects seemed to be less influenced by the illusion of the two moving objects since they judged their objective velocity more accurately than the normal subjects.

If patients differ from nonpatients in some physiological, time-processing characteristics, then one might expect differences between patients and normals in their capacity to receive and integrate temporal events in their environments. This would logically be true, especially if the environmental temporal components happen to be of the same time duration as the impaired or modified physiological temporal processes or mechanisms. Since our emphasis is upon intervals one second or less, it is necessary to consider environmental time constants of the same magnitude. Considerable data are available concerning such temporal parameters as pulse frequency, pulse duration, and the time between pulses. Behavioral phenomena such as critical flicker frequency, apparent movement, two pulse thresholds, auditory localization, and masking can all be characterized as temporal, environmental manipulations in the 1000 millisecond domain. If patients are found to differ from nonpatients in psychophysical investigations of these effects, and if adequate methodological precautions have been taken to minimize the nonsensory contributions to these psychophysical determinations, then such patient-nonpatient differences may provide us with a culture-fair or culture-free technique for detecting pathology.

An important "if" in the above formulation is in regard to the minimization of nonsensory components in the threshold determinations. For example, Clark, Rutschman, Link, and Brown[15] recently argued that numerous previous studies of critical flicker frequency in which patients were found to have lower CFF thresholds than normal subjects simply reflected a criterion difference—a difference between normal and patient subjects in their willingness to say they saw the flickering light as fused. A recent CFF study by McDonough[38] is noteworthy in that it reports that reactive schizophrenics demonstrated *higher* CFF thresholds than normals. It is more difficult to explain a higher CFF threshold for the patient group as being due to a criterion difference, and thus these results, if replicated, are suggestive of actual perceptual differences between patients and normals.

A number of studies of apparent motion have shown that schizophrenics require longer periods of time between light pulses than normals to produce a motion effect.[51-54] It has been shown also that schizophrenics require longer exposures of a stimulus display for recognition[20] and for the correct differentiation of groups of dots which are spatially ordered.[27]

King[30] failed to find differences between schizophrenics and normals in the time between two pulses of light that produced for the subjects the appearance of a single flash. Venables,[63] however, used the same two-pulse technique with an added noise background and found that while the noise did not influence the normal subjects two-flash performance, it changed the thresholds of the schizophrenic subjects. Venables[62] also related the two-flash thresholds to changes in skin potentials. He reported a negative correlation between skin potentials and two-flash threshold for schizophrenic subjects and a positive correlation of the same variables for normal subjects. Venables suggests these findings for the patients as being related to a parallel arousal of autonomic and cortical activity attendant with a lack of control of cortical activity by the regulatory activity of the reticular formation.

In support of the idea of patient-normal differences in cortical excitability and responsiveness are investigations by Shagass and Schwartz.[56, 57] These workers recorded evoked potentials to two discrete, electrical stimuli presented to the wrist and separated by brief periods of time. From these electrophysiological data they plotted the resulting "recovery" functions for the effects of the first stimulus upon the amplitude of the evoked potential to the second stimulus. Schizophrenic subjects were found to require a longer temporal separation between pulses than normal subjects for the amplitude of the second evoked potential to return to its baseline, suggesting that they display less cortical excitability and responsiveness than normals.

With the aid of objective measures of both varieties—the culture-bound as well as the culture-free—a new approach can be made to the development of more homogeneous diagnostic groupings. At the present time, much of the research in psychopathology suffers from the great heterogeneity which characterizes today's diagnostic classifications. Even when there is full agreement on the part of a diagnostic team regarding such diagnoses as schizophrenia or neurosis, the individual patients in each category are far from a homogeneous group, even with respect to the variables which presumably characterize each category. Bleuler has pointed to this fact by substituting for Kraepelin's "dementia praecox," the term "groups of schizophrenias." The heterogeneity in the category of neurosis is too well known to require documentation.

Heretofore, the technique applied to the statistical classification of patients has been factor analysis, either direct or inverse, of the correlations obtained from a sample including rotation to simple structure. Such techniques are elegant and quite suitable if the underlying population from which the sample is drawn has a multivariate normal distribution. Were this the case, there would be no need to search for better classifications, because our population is already homogeneous. However, if we start with an assumption of homogeneity and wind up with a conclusion of heterogeneity, the only justifiable procedure is to reject factor analysis as inapplicable. For this reason, once heterogeneity is established, we discard factor analysis and base our new analysis on the test profile of each patient expressed in standard scores. The usual method of correlating profiles (inverse factor analysis) takes into consideration only the shape of the profiles and neglects entirely the distance between profiles. For this reason, we deal with two measures of distance—discrepancy in shape and discrepancy in level—and group together all patients who show the greatest similarity with respect to these two measures. In this way, under certain assumptions (normality of multivariate distributions as well as zero correlation within each subgroup) a fractionation of the sample into homogeneous subgroups becomes possible.

Summary

The behavioral changes which accompany the development of mental disorder have been classified into two major divisions: culture-bound and culture-free or culture-fair. Present day methods of detecting and diagnosing mental disorder are largely based on culturally deviant types of behavior so that there is a need for developing culture-free or culture-fair techniques. Even the culture-bound techniques, however, suffer unduly from variations in their application which produce diagnostic variability that could be reduced by proper controls. Methods for introducing such controls are provided through such techniques as standard interviews and inventories of behavior that can be objectively scored and evaluated. Experimental methods have been developed for studying verbal behavior itself, the carrier-wave of our culture. These can be applied to differentiating diagnostic groups. Advances in the development of culture-free techniques are not as great. Yet, certain derivatives of reaction time studies, pupillography, evoked potentials to ulnar stimulation, etc., promise well to provide us with serviceable tools. When these objective methods are applied to populations of mentally ill, the new techniques for fractionating populations into homogeneous subgroups may yield new classifications of the mentally ill which will be more homogeneous and more suitable for future investigations.

REFERENCES

1. Abell, A. T.: Sensory-motor synchrony and schizophrenia: a study of temporal performance. Dissertation Abstr. 23:1776-1777, 1962.
2. Bartlett, N., and Bartlett, C.: Synchronization of a motor response with an anticipatory sensory event. Psychol. Rev. 66:203-218, 1959.
3. Reference 3 does not appear in the text.
4. Beck, A. T.: Reliability of psychiatric diagnosis: 1. critique of systematic studies. Amer J. Psychiat. 119:210-216, 1962.
5. ——: Reliability of psychiatric diagnoses: 2. A study of consistency of clinical judgments and ratings. Amer. J. Psychiat. 119:351-357, 1962.
6. Berkson, J.: Limitations of the application of fourfold table analysis to hospital data. Biom. Bull. 2:47-53, 1946.
7. Birch, H. G.: Sources of order in the maternal behavior of animals. Amer. J. Orthopsychiat. 26:279-284, 1956.
8. Burdock, E. I., Hakerem, G., Hardesty, A. S., and Zubin, J.: A ward behavior rating scale for mental hospital patients. J. Clin. Psychol. 16:246-247, 1960.
9. Burdock, E. I., and Hardesty, A. S.: Structured clinical interview and inventory. Paper read at E.P.A., Atlantic City, May, 1962.
10. Burdock, E. I., Sutton, S., and Zubin, J.: Personality and psychopathology. J. Abnorm. Soc. Psychol. 56:18-30, 1958.
11. Callaway, E., III: Factors influencing the relationship between alpha activity and visual reaction time. EEG Clin Neurophysiol. 14:674-682, 1962.
12. Carlson, V. R., and Feinberg, I.: Response-time of schizophrenics in a perceived velocity task. J. Psychiat. Res. 1:247-255, 1963.
13. Carrel, A.: Physiological time. Science 74:618-621, 1931.
14. Cartwright, D. S., Kirtner, W. L., and Fiske, D. W.: Method factors in changes associated with psychotherapy. J. Abnorm. Scc. Psychol. 66:164-175, 1963.
15. Clark, W. C., Rutschmann, J., Link, R., and Brown, J. C.: Comparison of

flicker-fusion thresholds obtained by the methods of forced-choice and limits on psychiatric patients. Percep. Mot Skills 76:18-30, 1963.

16. COLE, J.: Evaluation of drug treatments in psychiatry. *In* Evaluation of Psychiatric Treatment (eds. P. H. Hoch and J. Zubin). New York: Grune & Stratton, 1964.

17. DUSTMAN, R. E.: Phase of alpha brain waves reaction time, and visually evoked potentials. Unpublished doctoral dissertation, University of Utah, 1963.

18. ELKES, J.: Schizophrenic disorder in relation to levels of neural organization. *In* Chemical Pathology of the Nervous System (ed. J. Folch-Pi). New York, Pergamon Press, 1961, pp. 648-665.

19. ELLINGSON, R. J.: Brain waves and problems of psychology. Psychol. Bull. 53:1-34, 1956.

20. FESANARO, G.: Studi sulla rapidita della percezione visiva. Nota II. Rapidita di percezione visiva di immaginin in movemento in alcune offezione neuro-psichiatriche. Acta. Neurol. Napoli 7:323-331, 1952. (*Ophthal. Lit.* 6 (7): 887, abstr. 4763, 1954).

21. FISCHER, R., GRIFFIN, F., AND LISS, L.: Biological aspects of time in relation to (model) psychoses. Ann. N.Y. Acad. Sci. 96:44-64, 1962.

22. FRANÇOIS, M.: Contribution à l'étude du sens du temps. La température interne comme facteur de variation de l'appréciation subjective des durées. Année Psychol. 28:188-204, 1927.

23. HARLOW, H. F.: The heterosexual affectional system in monkeys. Amer. Psychol. 17:1-9, 1962.

24. HELD, R., AND WHITE, B.: Sensory deprivation and visual speed: an analysis. Science 130:860-861, 1959.

25. HOAGLAND, H.: The physiological control of judgments of duration: evidence for a chemical clock. J. Gen. Psychol. 9:267-287, 1933.

26. JOHANSSON, G., DUREMAN, I., AND SÄLDE, H.: Motion perception and personality. I. Nord. Psykologi 3:113-120, 1955.

27. KASWAN, J. W.: Tachistoscopic exposure time and spatial proximity in the organization of visual perception. Brit. J. Psychol. 49:131-138, 1958.

28. KATZ, M., AND LYERLY, S. B.: Methods for measuring adjustment and social behavior in the community. Psychol. Rep. Monogr. Suppl. 4, 13:503,535, 1963

29. KING, H. E.: Anticipatory behavior: temporal matching by normal and psychotic subjects. J. Psychol. 53:425-440, 1962.

30. KING, H. E.: Two pulse and flicker-fusion thresholds for normal and schizophrenic subjects. Percept. Mot Skills 14:517-518, 1962.

31. KREITMAN, N.: The reliability of psychiatric diagnoses. J. Ment. Sci. 107: 876-886, 1961.

32. LANSING, R.: Relation of brain and tremor rhythms to visual reaction time. EEG Clin. Neurophysiol. 9:497-504, 1957.

33. LECOMTE DU NOÜY, P.: Biological Time. New York, MacMillan, 1937.

34. LHAMON, W. T., GOLDSTONE, S., AND GOLDFARB, J. L.: The psychopathology of time judgment. *In* Psychopathology of Perception (eds. P. H. Hoch and J. Zubin). New York, Grune & Stratton, 1964.

35. LINDSLEY, D. B.: Psychological phenomena and the electroencephalogram. EEG Clin. Neurophysiol. 4:443-456, 1952.
36. LORR, M.: Multidimensional scale for rating psychiatric patients: Hospital Form. Vet. Adm. Tech. Bull 1:10-507, 1953.
36a. MALAMUD, W., AND SANDS, S. L.: A revision of the psychiatric rating scale. Amer. J. Psychiat. 104:231-237, 1947.
37. MARANON, G.: Contribution à l'étude de l'action émotive de l'adrenaline. Rev. Franç d'Endocunol. 2:301-325, 1924.
38. McDONOUGH, J. M.: Critical flicker frequency and the spiral aftereffect with process and reactive schizophrenics. J. Consult. Psychol. 20:150-155, 1960.
39. MEDNICK, S. A.: A learning theory approach to research in schizophrenia. Psychol. Bull., 55:316-327, 1958.
40. MEISTER, R. R.: A hypothesis concerning the function of the occiptal alpha rhythm in vision. Unpublished doctoral dissertation, University of Chicago, 1951.
41. MOORE, T. V.: The Essential Psychoses and Their Fundamental Syndromes. Studies in Psychology and Psychiatry, III. Baltimore, Williams and Wilkins, 1933.
42. MURPHY, H. B. M., WITTKOWER, E. D., FRIED, J., AND ELLENBERGER, H.: A crosscultural survey of schizophrenic symptomatology. *In* Proceedings of the Third World Congress of Psychiatry. Montreal, Canada, McGill University Press, 1961, Vol. 2, 1309-1315.
43. OSGOOD, C. E., SUCI, G. J., AND TANNENBAUM, P. H.: The Measurement of Meaning. Urbana, Ill., University of Illinois Press, 1957.
44. PASAMANICK, B., DINITZ, S., AND LEFTON, M.: Psychiatric orientation in relation to diagnosis and treatment. Amer. J. Psychiat. 116:127, 1959.
45. PAYNE, R. W., AND HEWLETT, J. H. G.: Thought disorder in psychotic patients. *In* Experiments in Personality (ed. H. J. Eysenck). London, Routledge and Kegan Paul, 1960, Vol. 2.
46. PIÉRON, H.: Les problèmes psychophysiologiques de la perception du temps. Année Psychol. 24:1-24, 1923.
47. PONOMAREV, M. F.: An experimental investigation of certain motor reactions in connection with time perception. Problems Psychol. (Vopr. psikhol). 3:79-88, 1960.
48. RAWNSLEY, K., AND LOUDON, J. B.: Factors influencing the referral of patients to psychiatrists by general practitioners. Brit. J. Prev. Soc. Med. 16:174-182, 1962.
49. SALZINGER, K., AND PISONI, S.: Reinforcement of verbal affect responses of normal subjects during the interview. J. Abnorm. Soc. Psychol. 60:127-130, 1960.
50. SALZINGER, K., PORTNOY, S., AND FELDMAN, R. S.: Verbal behavior of schizophrenic and normal subjects. Ann. N.Y. Acad. Sci. 105: 845-860, 1964.
51. SAUCER, R. T.: A further study of the perception of apparent motion by schizophrenics. J. Consult. Psychol. 22:256-258, 1958.
52. SAUCER, R. T.: Chlorpromazine and apparent motion perception by schizophrenics. J. Consult. Psychol. 23:134-136, 1959.
53. SAUCER, R. T., AND DEABLER, H. L.: Perception of apparent motion in organics and schizophrenics. J. Consult. Psychol. 20:385-389, 1956.

54. SAUCER, R. T., AND SWEETBAUM, H.: Perception of the shortest noticeable dark time by schizophrenics. Science 127:698-699, 1958.
55. SCHACHTER, S., AND WHEELER, L.: Epinephrine, chlorpromazine and amusement. J. Abnorm. Soc. Psychol. 65:121-128, 1962.
56. SHAGASS, C., AND SCHWARTZ, M.: Reactivity cycle of somatosensory cortex in humans with and without psychiatric disorder. Science 134:1757-1759, 1961.
57. SHAGASS, C., AND SCHWARTZ, M.: Excitability of the cerebral cortex in psychiatric disorders. *In* Physiological Correlates of Psychological Disorder (eds. R. Roessler and N. S. Greenfield). Madison, Wisc. University of Wisc. Press, 1962, pp. 45-60.
58. SPITZER, R., BURDOCK, E. I., AND FLEISS, J.: The mental status schedule: a preliminary report. Paper read at Amer. Psychiat. Assoc., St. Louis, May 1963.
59. SUTTON, S., AND ZUBIN, J.: Effect of sequence on reaction time in schizophrenia. *In* Behavior, Aging and the Nervous System (eds. J. E. Birren and A. T. Welford). Springfield, Ill., Charles C Thomas, 1964.
60. TANNER, W. P., AND SWETS, J. A.: A decision making theory of visual detection. Psychol. Rev. 61:401-409, 1954.
61. VENABLES, P. H.: Periodicity in reaction time. Brit. J. Psychol 51:37-48, 1960
62. VENABLES, P. H.: The relationship between the level of skin potential and fusion of paired light flashes in schizophrenic and normal subjects. J. Psychiat. Res. 1:279-287, 1963.
63. ——: Changes due to noise in the threshold of fusion of paired light flashes in schizophrenics and normals. Brit. J. Soc. Clin. Psychol 2:94-99, 1963.
64. VENABLES, P. H., AND TIZARD, J.: Paradoxical effects in the reaction time of schizophrenics. J. Abnorm. Soc. Psychol. 53:220-224, 1956.
65. WALTON, H. J., GRANICK, R., AND NAHEMOW, L.: Psychiatric illness and adjustment in a home for the aged. Ann. N.Y. Acad. Sci. 105:897-918, 1964.
66. WARD, C. H., BECA, A. T., MENDELSON, M., MOCK, J. E., AND ERBAUGH, J. K.: The psychiatric nomenclature. Arch. Gen. Psychiat. 7:198-205, 1962.
67. WITTENBORN, J. R.: Psychiatric Rating Scales. New York, The Psychological Corp., 1955.
68. ZUBIN, J.: A biometric approach to diagnosis and prognosis. *In* Psychosomatic Medicine, the First Hahnemann Symposium (eds. J. H. Nodine and J. H. Moyer). Philadelphia, Lea and Febiger, 1962, (table 3, p. 78).
69. ZUBIN, J., AND KATZ, M.: Psychopharmacology and personality. *In* Personality Change (eds. D. Byrne and P. Worchel). New York, John Wiley & Sons, 1964.
70. ZUBIN, J.: Introduction, Symposium on the first 1,000 milliseconds. Paper read at the Amer. Psych. Ass., Philadelphia, 1963.

28

TWO YEARS OF A HOME CARE STUDY FOR SCHIZOPHRENICS*

by BENJAMIN PASAMANICK, M.D., JOSEPH L. ALBINI, PH.D., FRANK R. SCARPITTI, PH.D., MARK LEFTON, PH.D., and SIMON DINITZ, PH.D.†

OVER THE YEARS, it has been alleged that the state mental hospital has failed to live up to its expectations as a therapeutic institution for the mentally ill. The victim of general social neglect—resulting in inadequate facilities, personnel, and funds—the mental hospital, it is held, has proved largely incapable of treating effectively the one million patients who annually are admitted to its care.

The historic inadequacies of the mental hospital and the increasing magnitude of the problem made it inevitable that new approaches to the care and treatment of the mentally ill would be sought. In addition to attempts to upgrade the status of the mental hospital and gear it more directly to therapy rather than long-term custody, recent proposals have called for the development of home and community care programs as substitutes for hospitalization. These proposals have resulted in the passage of legislation establishing community mental health centers.

These centers, once operative, will represent a radical departure from previous approaches, since the emphasis will be directed toward providing patients with adequate care in the community setting. In view of this new emphasis, the results obtained during two years of a controlled study of the relative efficacy of maintaining schizophrenic patients at home under nursing care with and without drug therapy as opposed to hospitalization, may be suggestive of what might reasonably be expected from the community mental health center approach.

---

*This study was supported by Public Health Service Research Grant MH 07874 from the National Institute of Mental Health. Sandoz, Inc., and Smith, Kline and French Laboratories supplied the drugs.

†Research Division, Department of Psychiatry, Ohio State University, Columbus, Ohio.

Method

The design of this controlled study and the problems encountered in its implementation have been described in detail in a previous paper.[1] Only a brief summary statement of the methods will therefore be included.[2]

In the latter part of 1961 a clinic, the Institute Treatment Center, was established in downtown Louisville, Kentucky. Staffed by a study director, a part-time psychiatrist, a psychologist, a social worker, and five nurses with public health nursing experience, this center was given responsibility for the conduct of the study. The establishment of this clinic at some distance from Central State Hospital, located outside of Louisville, necessitated the employment of a hospital psychiatrist, working on a part-time basis, to screen all newly admitted patients to determine their eligibility for inclusion in the study. When a newly admitted state hospital patient meets the criteria—a diagnosis of schizophrenia, nonsuicidal or homicidal, between 18 and 60 years of age, from Louisville or the nine surrounding counties, and having a family or someone else willing to accept and provide supervision for the patient in the home—the patient and relatives are brought to and interviewed at the Treatment Center. If the clinic staff psychiatrist confirms the diagnosis and deems the patient suitable for the program, and if the family expresses willingness to cooperate, the patient is accepted for the study. The study director, using a deck of random cards, assigns the patient to one of three groups: home on drugs (40 per cent), home on placebo (30 per cent), or hospital control (30 per cent).

The randomly assigned hospital control patients are returned to Central State Hospital. The home care patients are returned to their families. Shortly after the return home, the public health nurse assigned to the case visits the patient and family. The same nurse makes weekly calls for the first 3 months, bimonthly visits for the second 3 months, and monthly visits thereafter. On each visit the nurse leaves the prescribed medication for the patient. She also completes a written report on the status of the patient which is then reviewed by the staff psychiatrist.

In addition to the initial psychiatric evaluation and psychological test battery and the social history at intake, nurses' progress reports, interviews with "significant others," and a variety of other formal measures are routinely administered to all patients, including those appropriate for the home care, failure patients, and the hospital control patients.

Within a few months after the start of this home care study, it became evident that Central State Hospital would not be able to supply a sufficient number of patients to fulfill the requirements of the study design. As a result, Louisville General Hospital was asked to refer schizophrenic patients to the Treatment Center and consented to do so. This source has yielded only a very small number of new patients. Similarly, all outpatient clinics, social agencies, and physicians in the area were asked to refer suspected schizophrenics to the Treatment Center. The increasing number of these referrals have compelled the Center to act as a community screening agency. Nevertheless, some ambulatory schizophrenics have been uncovered. If the illness in these cases is severe enough to warrant hospitalization, and the other criteria are also met, these community, referred patients are accepted into the program. A separate deck of randomized cards is used to place these community patients into two groups: home on drug or home on placebo. The data gathered on these community patients are analyzed separately from the Central State Hospital subjects.

The Patient Population

In the two years of this controlled study, 226 patients had been admitted to the program. Of these, 161 were Central State Hospital patients and 65 were community agency or physician referrals. Of the Central State Hospital patients, 64 were placed in the drug home care group, 45 in the placebo home care group, and 52 were assigned to the hospital control or "natural" group. Of the 63 community referrals, 36 were placed on drug home care, 27 on placebo home care, and two were hospitalized. For the purposes of the analysis which follows, 15 patients have been eliminated from consideration. These include the 13 patients who refused to cooperate or who left the community (administrative failures) and the two community referred hospital controls.

Social Background Data

The data in table 1 indicate that the patients in the five groups in the study—Central State referred drug or placebo home care, hospital controls, and community referred drug or placebo home care—do not significantly differ in age, sex, race, or marital status. Patients in all five groups were, at the time of admission to the study, approximately 35 years of age; most were female, some two-thirds were white, and nearly three-fifths were married. Although not significantly different, due largely to the small sample sizes, the community referral cases tended to be over a year younger and to consist of a higher percentage of married subjects than the Central State Hospital patients in the program.

TABLE 1.—Demographic Characteristics of Patients

Category	*N*	*Mean Age*	*Per Cent Male*	*Per Cent White*	*Per Cent Married*
Central State Patients					
Drug	64	35.1	41	69	53
Placebo	45	35.8	31	67	55
Hospital Control	52	37.6	27	63	60
Community Referred Patients					
Drug	36	33.8	36	69	69
Placebo	27	33.9	30	67	63

Psychiatric Status—Psychiatrist's Ratings

At admission to the program, all patients were evaluated by the staff psychiatrist, using the revised Inpatient Multidimensional Psychiatric Scale (Lorr IMPS scale). This scale contains 10 subscales or syndromes, four of which combine to provide a schizophrenic disorganization morbidity score. The four subscales are: motor disturbance, disorientation, conceptual disorganization, and retardation and apathy.

Table 2 contains the mean morbidity scores for schizophrenic disorganization of the five categories of patients. The mean score of the Central State Hospital patients at admission was 39.2 for the drug home care, 48.0 for the placebo home care, and 43.8 for the hospital controls. These scores were not significantly different from each other and all were higher than the one-rater or two-rater mean morbidity score obtained by Lorr on his norm sample of 476 hospitalized patients. This would indicate that the Central State Hospital patients in the study do not constitute the more favorable risks or the less severely impaired.

The community referral patients, however, were rated at intake as less severely ill than the Central State Hospital patients in the drug and placebo home care groups. The mean schizophrenic disorganization scores of the community referral patients were 30.0 in the drug home care group and 35.7 in the placebo home care group (see table 2).

TABLE 2.—Schizophrenic Disorganization (IMPS) Morbidity Ratings by Psychiatrist and Nurses of Patients at Admission

Category	Psychiatrist's Ratings			Nurses' Ratings		
	N	*M*	σ	*N*	*M*	σ
Central State Patients*						
Drug	60	39.2	19.3	59	16.0	14.8
Placebo	42	48.0	28.5	42	23.9	18.4
Hospital Control	52	43.8	21.3	—	—	—
Community Referred Patients*						
Drug	31	30.0	14.8	31	10.6	10.7
Placebo	26	35.7	17.2	26	14.8	15.2

*Excludes ratings of "administrative failure" patients.

Psychiatric Status—Nurses' Ratings

The Lorr IMPS scale was also used by the nurses to rate the home care patients. These ratings were made on the first visit to the home and at specified periods thereafter. The results of the initial nurses' ratings, as shown in table 2, are similar in direction to those obtained by the staff psychiatrist. These findings on schizophrenic disorganization are as follows:

1. As has also been found in other studies, the nurses consistently rated the same patients as being significantly less impaired than the staff psychiatrist rated them as being.
2. The initial ratings of the nurses indicated that the Central State Hospital patients, drug and placebo, were significantly more impaired than the community referral patients.
3. Nurses and psychiatrist ratings of the same home care patients resulted in a Pearsonian correlation coefficient of $= +.525$ and a Spearman-Brown rank order correlation coefficient of .444.

Psychological Test Scores

The psychological battery administered to the subjects at admission to the study and at specified subsequent intervals consisted of a sequential reaction time test, the WAIS, the Bender Gestalt and the Porteus Mazes. The results obtained in the initial administration are displayed in table 3. These findings suggest (1) that the drug, placebo, and hospital control groups did not significantly differ from each other on most of these measures, and (2) that the Central State

Hospital subjects were significantly different from the community referral patients on most of these tests.

TABLE 3.—Psychological Test Scores at Admission

	Reaction Time		WAIS		Bender Z		Porteus Mazes QE		Porteus Mazes IQ	
Category	*Total*	*σ*	*Mean*	*σ*	*Mean*	*σ*	*Mean*	*σ*	*Mean*	*σ*
Central States Patients										
Drug	1824.9	550.7	81.9	16.5	103.8	35.7	40.3	20.4	81.6	32.6
Placebo	2221.8	1326.8	80.2	19.2	107.7	28.0	35.7	15.7	80.1	32.3
Hospital Control	1971.9	638.0	71.4	13.6	116.9	35.7	32.9	14.5	66.2	31.0
Community Referred Patients										
Drug	1655.1	501.3	88.0	17.0	99.3	32.6	38.0	14.7	98.7	35.5
Placebo	1650.0	399.5	91.0	17.4	91.5	27.2	42.1	26.6	96.8	31.0

In more specific terms, using the total of the medians of 20 blocs of five trials each, the three Central State groups did not statistically differ from each other in reaction time but were significantly slower in reaction time than the community referral cases. Similar results were obtained on the WAIS IG scores as prorated from six subtests.[3] On this intelligence test, however, the hospital control patients scored significantly lower in IQ than the home care patients. On the Bender Gestalt, using Z scores derived by Pascal and Suttell, the hospital control patients showed significantly more pathology than the home care patients.[4] Finally, using the QE (error quotient) score on the Porteus Mazes, the controls showed significantly less pathology than the home care subjects. On the IQ score derived from the Porteus Mazes, the hospital controls were found to be significantly lower in IQ than the home care patients, as would have been predicted from the WAIS.

RESULTS

Home Care versus Hospital Control Patients

In order to determine the effect of home care treatment as opposed to hospitalization, it is of interest to contrast the experiences of the drug and placebo patients with those of the hospitalized patients in the "natural" group. After 2 years, the findings indicate the superiority of home care treatment in terms of the amount and percentage of time spent at home by home care and hospital control patients.

Table 4 and figure 1 show that the 60 Central State Hospital referred drug home care patients spent 20,314 days at home, or 91.1 per cent of their time in the program. The 42 Central State Hospital referred

TABLE 4.—Total Amount of Patient Time Spent at Home and in Hospital

Category	*N*	*Days at Home*	*Days in Hospital*	*Total*
Central State Patients*				
Drug	60	20314	1968	22282
Placebo	42	12492	3634	16126
Hospital Control	52	14004	6264	20268
Community Referred Patients*				
Drug	31	8207	633	8840
Placebo	26	5607	823	6430

*Excludes data on "administrative failures."

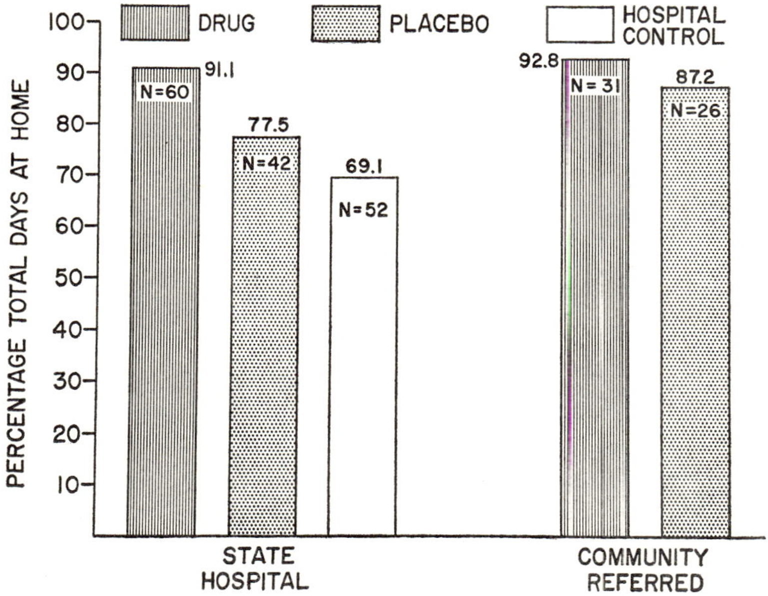

FIG. 1.—Percentage of total days spent at home by drug, placebo, and hospital control patients and by referred patients.

placebo home care patients spent 12,492 days at home or 77.5 per cent of their days in the study. The 52 hospital control patients spent 14,004 days at home or 69.1 per cent of their project days. The gap in the length of time spent at home has been steadily narrowing between the placebo home care patients and the hospital controls. It seems likely that in the next reporting period, 6 months hence, the placebo home care patients and the hospital controls will be even closer to one another in their home and hospitalization records.

Table 4 and figure 1 also indicate that the community referred patients in the drug and placebo home care groups have spent even more time at home than the comparable Central State Hospital referred patients. There are two major explanations for this finding. First, community referred cases, as indicated earlier, were rated by both the psychiatrist and nurses as showing less glaring psychiatric symptoms at admission to the study. Second, these community referred patients have not yet been at risk on the project for as long a period of time. Major intake of community referred subjects began 6 months after the intake of Central State Hospital subjects.

Drug versus Placebo Home Care Successful Patients

During the 2-year period under study, 50 of the 60 (83.3 per cent) Central State Hospital referred drug home care patients have remained continuously in the community. These 50 successful patients have spent an average of 350.8 consecutive days at home. In contrast, significantly fewer of the Central State Hospital referred placebo home care subjects, 15 of 42 (35.7 per cent), have remained continuously at home during this period. These 15 successful patients have spent an average of 336.2 consecutive days at home. This success-failure comparison is shown in figure 2.

Of the community referred patients, 24 of the 31 on drug home care (77.4 per cent), in comparison to 16 of the 26 on placebo home care (61.5 per cent), have remained continuously at home. This difference in the success rates of the drug and placebo community referred home care groups is not statistically significant. The average successful drug patient in the community referred group has spent 285.1 consecutive days at home, and the average successful placebo patient has spent 231.2 days. In time, and with greater exposure, the rates of success of the community referred patients, particularly in the placebo group, should approximate those of the Central State Hospital referred subjects.

Drug and Placebo Home Care Failures

Operationally defining failure as a hospital admission, the 10 Central State Hospital referred drug home care failure patients have experienced 19 hospital admissions and a mean of 196.8 inpatient hospital days. The 27 Central State Hospital referred placebo home care failures have been hospitalized 36 times and have spent an average of 134.6 days of inpatient hospital time. The 52 hospital control patients spent a mean of 80.1 days in initial hospitalization, and in 24 subsequent hospitalizations they spent an additional 40.4 days. That is, the drug home care patients were saved all of the time spent by the hospital controls in initial hospitalization, and even the placebo patients were saved much of this time (see fig. 3).

In regard to the community referred subjects, the 7 drug failures had 8 hospital admissions and a mean of 90.4 days hospitalization, while the 10 placebo failures had 14 hospital admissions and spent an average of 82.3 days in the hospital.

Initial Psychiatric Evaluation and Success and Failure

Using the initial Lorr IMPS ratings by the staff psychiatrist and the nurses of Central State Hospital referred home care patients, there is a pronounced trend for the future successful patients to have

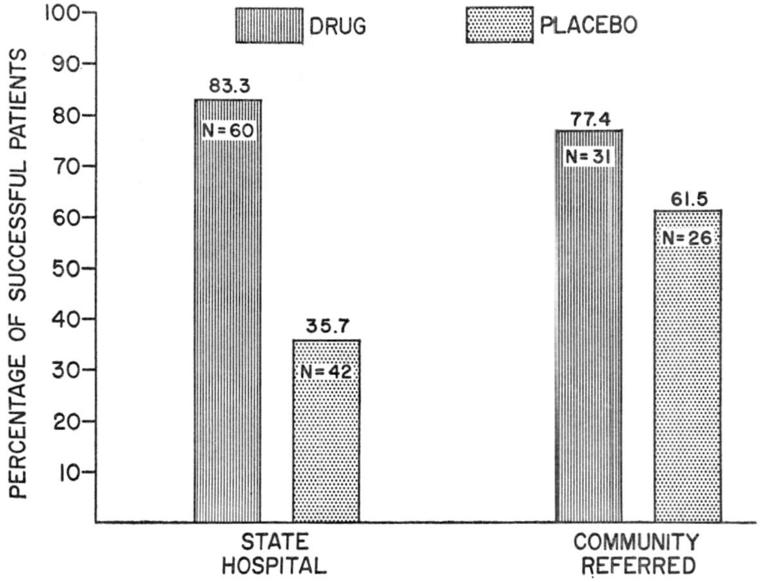

FIG. 2.—Percentage of successful patients in drug and placebo groups by state hospital and community referral.

been rated as less impaired than the future failures. This trend is primarily observable in the drug group (table 5). Unfortunately, the relatively small number of failure cases and the large intragroup variance precluded this trend from attaining statistical significance.

Psychological Evaluation and Success and Failure

Except for the results on the Porteus Mazes error quotient, all of the other initial psychological test scores pointed in the direction of differentiating future successful from future failure patients. On the sequential reaction time test and the Bender Gestalt, the future failures in both the drug and placebo groups were either slower in reaction time or showed greater pathology. On both the WAIS and the Porteus Mazes IQ, the future failures were lower, but not significantly so.

Despite the small number of failure cases, these psychological test scores frequently differentiated, at a significant level, success from failures. This was particularly consistent for the Central State placebo group.

Thus the initial Lorr scale psychiatric evaluations were more likely to distinguish to some degree success and failure in the drug

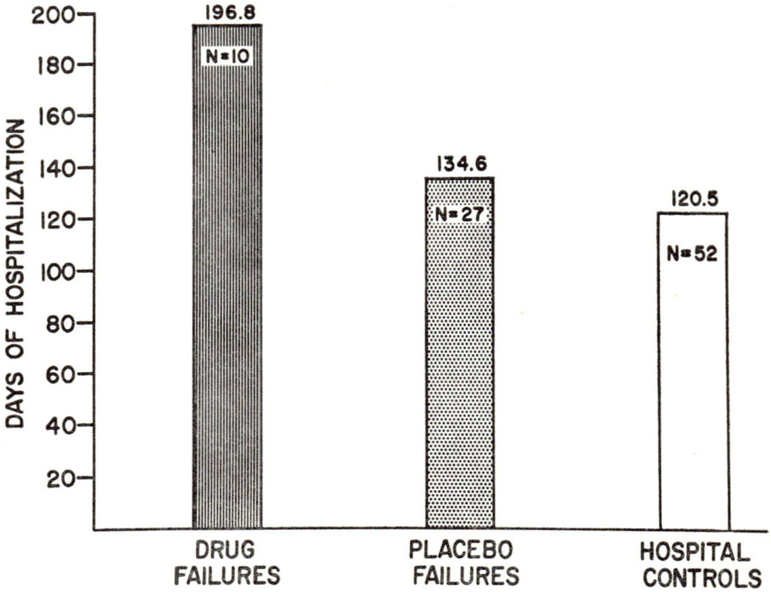

FIG. 3.—Average number of days of hospitalization of drug and placebo group failures and of all hospital controls.

TABLE 5.—Psychological and Psychiatric Test Scores of Success and Failure Patients at Admission

	Reaction Time Block Total	*WAIS Mean*	*Bender Gestalt Z Mean*	*Porteus Mazes*		*IMPS Psychiatrist Rating Mean*	*IMPS Nurses Rating Mean*
				QE Mean	*IQ Mean*		
Central State Drug							
Success	1790.0	82.8	103.3	40.3	83.6	37.0	14.3
Failure	1990.8	77.5*	106.0	39.8	71.4	49.9	23.9
Central State Placebo							
Success	1664.4	86.8	96.1	36.1	96.1	47.8	18.4
Failure	2522.0*	76.6*	113.8*	35.5	71.8*	48.1	27.0

*Statistically significant difference.

home care group, and the initial psychological evaluations to discriminate the successes or failures in the placebo home care group. Drug intervention by preventing the hospitalization of many patients of moderately severe initial psychiatric impairment probably introduces a much greater degree of variability into the psychological test scores of the successes and thereby reduces predictability. In the placebo group, successes are more homogeneous in test scores measuring pathology, and therefore predictability is likely to be greater. Psychiatric ratings, being more directly focused on classical pathological symptoms, are more likely to screen out the very severely impaired for whom even drug intervention is inadequate to prevent hospitalization.

DISCUSSION

The results at the end of two years of this controlled study indicate that an intervention program utilizing public health nursing practices and psychoactive drugs can prevent the hospitalization of 80 per cent or more of seriously ill schizophrenics randomly assigned to home care. Experience also indicates that once the drug home care patients have successfully remained at home for 6 months, their success rate does not greatly decline wtih additional exposure ranging up to 2 years. There are several reasons for this, but perhaps the two most important are the changes in medication available to the psychiatrist and the great effort made by the field staff in conserving home care patients—both drug and placebo. Comparison of the drug home care with the placebo home care patients, as well as with the hospital controls, leaves little doubt that many of the drug patients have indeed been saved hospitalization.

With time, the experience of the placebo home care patients approaches that of the hospital controls. The "public health nurse—placebo effect" combination becomes increasingly attenuated, and the support provided by the nurse on home visits is insufficient to prevent hospitalization. Thus, 21 of the 27 placebo failures were hospitalized within 6 months. Despite equally heroic efforts by the field staff and the usual medication changes, most of the placebo patients are hospitalized in due course.

The hospital controls, the "natural group," do fairly well after their initial hospitalization of approximately 80 days on the average. Sixteen of the 52 controls required subsequent hospitalization.

On the other hand, the experience of the community referred ambulatory schizophrenics is different from that of the state hospital referred patients. In the ambulatory schizophrenic sample, the experience of the drug and placebo groups did not differ significantly. In integrating this result it should first be noted that the community referral cases have had, thus far, considerably less exposure on the project than the Central State Hospital patients. In time, it is likely that placebo failures will increase sharply while drug failures will increase very little. This prediction is based on the experiences of the state hospital patients at a comparable period of exposure. In addition, the initial psychological and psychiatric evaluations indicate that the ambulatory patients were indeed less severely impaired than their state hospital counterparts. Since they were already maintaining themselves in the community without intervention, drug medication and the support of the nurses were less necessary and effective.

REFERENCES

1. Scarpitti, F., et al.: Problems in a home care study for schizophrenics. AMA Arch. Gen. Psychiat. 10:143, 1964.
2. See also Pasamanick, B., et al.: Home versus hospital care for schizophrenics: a controlled study of the use of drugs and public health nursing care. J.A.M.A. 87:177, 1964.
3. Karras, A.: Predicting full scale WAIS IQ's from WAIS subtests for a psychiatric population. J. Clin. Psychol. 19(1):100, 1963.
4. Pascal, G., and Suttell, B. J.: The Bender Gestalt Test: Quantification and Validity for Adults. New York, Grune & Stratton, 1951.

29

RELEASE AND COMMUNITY STAY CRITERIA IN EVALUATING PSYCHIATRIC TREATMENT

by LEE GUREL, PH.D.

A CENTRAL PROBLEM in any evaluation of psychiatric treatment is the selection and operational definition of appropriate criteria. Typically, the more comprehensive the treatment, the more likely is the researcher to use actuarial criteria of a public, albeit global, nature. This is particularly true in studying both specific therapies and overall hospital effectiveness with inpatient functional psychotics. It has become axiomatic that the primary criterion measure here be some variant of hospital release/community stay; inhospital change without release is largely academic, and more sophisticated measures of community adjustment and readmission are logically dependent on release and community stay.

There are, however, many possible ways in which release/community stay can be defined, and conclusions may vary from study to study in accord with the specific methodology used. One researcher may use a cross-sectional criterion involving whether the patient is in an institution 90 days, or 1 year, or 10 years after admission. Another uses a longitudinal index which relates time in hospital to time in community over a given total period—some for a 1-year period, others for a 5-year period.[1] One researcher may define release when the patient physically exits the hospital. Another acknowledges release in accord with the administrative action of final discharge, even though this may occur at exit in one case and as much as a year later in a second case.

Definitional differences have obvious importance for the reader who seeks to reconcile discrepant findings. However, prior knowledge of the effects of procedural variation has even greater importance in initiating research, since choice of a given procedure will have far-reaching impact on data collection methods. One purpose of the present study was to identify for future use valid criterion measures which could be collected with minimum cost and effort. There is a vast practical difference in the resources needed to identify the fact of hospital release vs. establishing patient whereabouts 5 years after admission vs. determining whereabouts over a period of years. The first measure requires only clerical notation; the last requires frequent follow-up contacts. The general issue for both reader and researcher, then, is how different criteria relate to one another, and to what extent they yield comparable results. Specifically, this methodological inquiry reports data which (1) clarify relationships between certain alternative and part-whole methods of computing release and community stay, and (2) reflect the extent to which procedural variations affect conclusions about treatment effectiveness.

PROCEDURE

Subjects

Subjects were of two kinds, hospitals and patients. When dealing with outcome criteria, per se, the sample was composed of patients; when release and community stay were of interest as steps in the operational definition of hospital effectiveness, we dealt with an N of hospitals. This distinction is reflected below in the organization of the "Results" section into two parts. Part II deals with the general issue of release and community stay as criterion measures and is based on a sample of patients; Part I is specifically oriented around how the same data relate to issues of hospital effectiveness.

The hospital sample was the 12 VA psychiatric hospitals participating in the Psychiatric Evaluation Project (PEP).[2] The patients were male functional psychotics who were predominantly schizophrenics, being admitted or readmitted to the 12 hospitals; who were less than 60 years of age; who were without tuberculosis, organic brain disease, or psychosurgery; and who had been out of a psychiatric facility for at least 3 of the 6 months preceding admission. Intake of subjects began in the fall of 1956 and continued until 120 subjects per hospital were obtained or until a cutoff date in September 1957. Practically all qualified admissions during the intake period were selected, and the sample of 1319 patients was essentially the total population of eligibles.

Follow-Up

Patients were followed over a period of 4 years from admission. Those who left the hospital were seen by a psychiatric social worker at regularly scheduled intervals, as were persons who knew of the ex-patient's activities. Subjects who moved beyond the areas served by PEP social workers were referred to other VA facilities. If readmitted, the patient was interviewed by the PEP psychologist. These procedures made possible a determination of all periods of institutionalization, and this single body of information was used to describe release and community stay in different ways and over different time periods.

Criteria Studied

Of the measures discussed here, an a priori position was taken that the single most meaningful measure of treatment success for nongeriatric, inpatient functional psychotics is how much of a total follow-up period they spend in the community. Such a measure, unmodified incommunity days (ICD-U), served as a standard to which other measures were usually compared. ICD-U was determined by summing all days during which a subject was not in any psychiatric or penal facility. A pass, which in the VA cannot exceed 72 hours and which does not remove a patient from bed occupancy status, was treated as inhospital time. ICD-U was computed for the first 6 months, second 6 months, second year, third year, and fourth year following admission, and these were summed to yield appropriate totals for cumulative time periods.

When used as an index of treatment success, ICD-U is open to several legitimate criticisms. Included in ICD-U were days on elopement (AWOL) and leave of absence (LOA) status. It may be argued that most AWOL's constitute short, self-granted passes, that an LOA is merely a "vacation," and that neither ought to be credited as treatment success. Since LOA's and AWOL's were known to be common, a modified measure of incommunity days, ICD-M, was computed for each of the time periods for which ICD-U had been determined. ICD-M does not credit any LOA or an AWOL of less than 30 consecutive nights as time out of the hospital.

One might also argue that a count of individual days is too fine a measure and that hospital and community stay ought to be defined in larger and more clinically meaningful units. Such a measure is reflected here by incommunity months (ICM). A total ICM was computed for the 4-year period by rounding to the closest whole month all periods out of an institution of 30 or more consecutive nights and disregarding any institutionalization not involving at least 15 consecutive nights.

A fourth and final variation in computing community stay was suggested by Ullmann's work on the effectiveness of foster home care.[3] ICD and ICM are subject to the disadvantage of assigning to the admitting hospital responsibility for patient outcome over the total follow-up period. It can be argued that, once the patient enters another treatment institution, the original hospital should not be held accountable for subsequent outcome. In meeting this objection, PEP-responsible time (PRT) was determined by summing the number of days in all periods from admission to the original PEP hospital to admission to some other psychiatric or penal facility. Treatment success was expressed as the ratio of ICD-U during PRT periods to total PRT, and is called the per cent success/PRT (success relative to PEP-responsible time). It defines the percentage of days on which the patient was not institutionalized out of the total number of days for which the original PEP hospital was held "responsible." Success/PRT index was computed for the first year, second year, and combined third and fourth years following admission and for their cumulative combinations.

It is sometimes desirable or necessary that a cross-sectional determination be utilized as an index of treatment outcome. This is the case, for example, when state-wide records are available[4] or when resources permit only a one-time follow-up. Patient whereabouts on a given date following admission were determined by using the same definitions of modified and unmodified status as were used with ICD. Unmodified whereabouts (W-U) records as a treatment failure a patient in any psychiatric or penal facility on the exact date in question. Modified whereabouts (W-M) differs from W-U by counting as in the hospital LOA status and an AWOL of less than 30 consecutive nights. W-U and W-M were determined at the 45th, 90th, 135th, 180th, 365th, 730th, 1095th, and 1460th day after admission. These points were selected as most likely to yield important comparisons between hospitals.

Finally, three measures of length of hospitalization were determined. These reflect the number of inhospital days from study admission to a first significant release (FSR). In contrast to the longitudinal and cross-sectional criteria discussed above, FSR indicates how long a patient was hospitalized. In further contrast to community stay criteria, FSR data have the important advantage of relative ease of data collection. A release criterion, once defined, can be established with high reliability, usually on the basis of routine hospital records.

The three variants of first release discussed here are FSR-30, FSR-90, and FSR-90-D. FSR-30 defines a first significant release as a hospitalization followed by 30 or more consecutive nights out of that hospital; FSR-90 treats as a first significant release a hospitalization followed by 90 or more consecutive nights out of that hospital. By comparison, FSR-90 depends on a more rigorous definition of what constitutes release. The third FSR measure, FSR-90-D, is simply the expression of FSR-90 as an early vs. late dichotomy. The cutting point between 274 and 275 days was determined on the basis of preliminary analyses and indicates whether or not the patient was released within 9 months.

In summary, then, this study dealt with three measures of treatment success and with alternative ways of defining them. (1) FSR-30 and FSR-90 reflect length of hospitalization prior to release. (2) Whereabouts, W-U and W-M, reflects institutionalization or noninstitutionalization on specific dates after admission. (3) ICD and ICM reflect time in community over specified follow-up periods. These three major categories are summarized in table 1.

Depending on whether variables were dichotomous or continuous, phi, point biserial, or Pearson r's between all measures were computed on an IBM 7090 computer. Most of the intercorrelations in Part I of the "Results" section were based on an N of 1274 subjects. Forty-five subjects of the original 1319 died during the follow-up period, and their data were discarded. An additional 24 patients were directly transferred to other hospitals. Since no meaningful measure

TABLE 1.—Summary of Release and Community Stay Criteria

A. Release Criteria

1. *FSR-30:* Length of hospital stay followed by 30 nights out.
2. *FSR-90:* Length of hospital stay followed by 90 nights out.
3. *FSR-90-D:* Early FSR-90 = 274 or less; late FSR-90 = 275 or more/none.

B. Longitudinal Criteria

1. *ICD-U:* Unmodified incommunity days.
2. *ICD-M:* Modified incommunity days.
3. *ICM:* Incommunity months.
4. *Per cent success/PRT:* ICD-U during PEP-responsible periods.

C. Cross-Sectional Criteria

1. *W-U:* Unmodified whereabouts.
2. *W-M:* Modified whereabouts.

of first release was possible in these 24 cases, the N in computations involving FSR was reduced to 1250. Findings presented in Part II were based on the N of 12 hospitals. Because parametric statistics with so small an N are suspect, parametric measures of relationship were supplemented with parallel sets of rank-order correlations.

Results: Part I

Modified vs. Unmodified

Whether LOA status and short AWOLS are credited toward time out of the hospital can be seen in tables 2 and 3 to have very limited significance. Correlations of corresponding modified and unmodified criteria ranged from .889 for the 45-day whereabouts to .997 for ICD in 3 years. Not only were relative effects due to LOA and AWOL quite small, inspection of the means indicates that absolute influence was also minimal. The difference in the two methods of computing incommunity days amounted to an average of 21.3 days per patient, a difference of less than 2 per cent relative to the total 1460 days of follow-up. Nevertheless, that over 60 per cent of patients accumulated LOA or AWOL time makes it easy to see how this issue could have appeared important. Nor can this 60 per cent average be attributed to the influence of any single group of hospitals; no hospital had less than 43 per cent of its patients with some AWOL/LOA time.

ICM and Responsibility

Table 2 indicates further that whether incommunity time was counted in daily units or in monthly units was unimportant. ICM correlated .990 with ICD-U and .975 with ICD-M.

The utility of introducing the concept of responsibility to correct for readmission to other hospitals can be evaluated from the correlations in table 2 of the ICD and ICM variables with per cent success during PEP-responsible time. Again, it would appear that such a correction can have only minimal effect, particularly during those periods least removed from admission. As before, however, it is understandable that, on an a priori basis, this might be an issue of concern to the critical reader. Twenty-nine per cent of patients released via an FSR-90 were subsequently admitted to other institutions. The effect of this 29 per cent, if distributed over every patient in the sample, would result in an average of 159.2 days for which we would

TABLE 2.—Means, Standard Deviations, and Intercorrelations of Longitudinal Criteria (N = 1274)

Variable	Mean	S.D.	Intercorrelations													
			1	2	3	4	5	6	7	8	9	10	11	12	13	14
1. ICD-U in 6 months	48.0	54.5	—	981	864	863	704	702	621	620	566	563	560	862	709	581
2. ICD-M in 6 months	43.1	53.1			837	854	684	692	604	610	549	553	545	835	689	563
3. ICD-U in 1 year	152.6	121.2				993	876	873	782	779	715	707	708	978	867	722
4. ICD-M in 1 year	143.9	121.4					867	872	772	777	705	703	701	970	858	712
5. ICD-U in 2 years	384.7	234.3						996	949	948	893	881	886	854	960	864
6. ICD-M in 2 years	370.6	238.3							943	948	886	879	882	851	956	857
7. ICD-U in 3 years	626.4	343.6								997	975	959	966	762	906	924
8. ICD-M in 3 years	607.3	350.6									970	959	964	759	905	920
9. ICD-U in 4 years	876.3	456.2										982	990	696	848	936
10. ICD-M in 4 years	855.0	476.2											975	688	837	919
11. ICM in 4 years	28.2	15.3												689	841	928
12. % success/PRT in 1 yr.	41.9	33.4													883	735
13. % success/PRT in 2 yrs.	52.5	32.5														894
14. % success/PRT in 4 yrs.	59.8	31.6														—

TABLE 3.—Means, Standard Deviations, and Intercorrelations of Cross-Sectional Criteria (N = 1274)

Variable	Mean (% out)	S.D.	Intercorrelations															
			1	2	3	4	5	6	7	8	9	10	11	12	13	14	15	16
1. W-U on 45th day	13.5	34.2	—	889	495	542	359	380	274	285	198	213	173	179	155	153	131	136
2. W-M on 45th day	11.0	31.3			487	544	331	363	258	264	180	193	163	166	145	141	115	120
3. W-U on 90th day	28.7	45.2				901	645	696	477	506	307	323	244	244	213	212	183	179
4. W-M on 90th day	24.6	43.1					607	660	452	476	302	319	238	234	211	207	159	158
5. W-U on 135th day	40.8	49.1						927	699	735	374	391	253	248	246	254	209	209
6. W-M on 135th day	37.2	48.3							687	722	390	412	276	277	260	269	221	223
7. W-U on 180th day	49.1	50.0								942	470	493	291	290	281	278	250	259
8. W-M on 180th day	46.1	49.8									466	490	282	288	270	278	254	262
9. W-U on 365th day	59.0	49.2										957	401	404	363	357	266	270
10. W-M on 365th day	57.1	49.5											400	411	370	369	274	278
11. W-U on 730th day	65.9	47.4												949	482	484	421	427
12. W-M on 730th day	63.7	48.1													489	498	419	424
13. W-U on 1095th day	67.0	47.0														960	548	554
14. W-M on 1095th day	65.2	47.6															558	566
15. W-U on 1460th day	68.3	46.5																986
16. W-M on 1460th day	67.7	46.8																—

not assign responsibility to the original hospitals. This, of course, is more than 10 per cent of the total follow-up period and is of absolute, even if not of relative, significance. This finding should serve to caution both clinician and researcher against the too ready assumption that nonreturn to a specific hospital means community stay; in a large proportion of present cases, it did not.

First Significant Release

Table 4 presents means, standard deviations, and intercorrelations of the three FSR criteria and their correlations with selected community stay criteria. The means for FSR-30 and FSR-90 were computed by assuming that patients not released during the 4-year follow-up were then released on the 1461st day. It will be noted that FSR-30 and FSR-90 were so highly related as to be considered almost identical ($r = .950$). In fact, all but 23 of the 1142 patients who achieved an FSR-30 also achieved an FSR-90, and in only 87 additional cases were the values of FSR-30 and FSR-90 other than identical.

Although mean length of hospitalization preceding release was approximately 1 year, over 60 per cent of the sample started an FSR-90 during the first 9 months (early FSR-90-D of 61.5 per cent). This seeming discrepancy is a function of the skewing which resulted from assigning FSR over so long a period as 4 years. By way of contrast the median for FSR-90 was at 6 months; 49.4 per cent of the patients initiated an FSR-90 before the 181st postadmission day.

FSR-90-D, the dichotomization of FSR-90, is seen in table 4 to be a fair approximation of the continuous parent variable ($r_{pb} = .756$). Interestingly, FSR-90-D was somewhat superior to the continuous distribution of FSR-90 as a predictor of community stay during earlier postadmission periods. As is evident from the last group of correlations in table 4, those with the noncumulative ICD periods, this occurrence in part reflects the high specificity of FSR-90-D as a predictor of community stay during the period of which it is the midpoint. In brief, the computation of FSR-90 over a 4-year period made it a better predictor of overall community stay, whereas its expression as the FSR-90-D dichotomy was a better predictor of community stay during earlier postadmission periods.

Cross-Sectional (Whereabouts) Criteria

Relationships of the cross-sectional criteria to one another and to the FSR criteria have been presented in tables 3 and 4. Table 5 presents correlations between incommunity days and unmodified whereabouts on given follow-up dates. In order to be minimally redundant, parallel tables giving the relationship of W-U to ICD-M, of W-M to ICD-U, and of W-M to ICD-M have been omitted; in no instance did a correlation in any of these three omitted tables differ more than .031 from the corresponding coefficient in table 5.

Several facts about the whereabouts criteria are evident from an inspection of tables 3, 4, and 5. It is apparent from table 3 that, except for certain adjacent checkpoints, one in/out status was only minimally predictive of another. The highest values (about .7) occurred

TABLE 4.—Relationship of Release Criteria to Community Stay Criteria (N = 1250)

			Correlation Coefficients		
	Mean	S.D.	FSR-30	FSR-90	FSR-90-D
FSR-30	349.9	427.5	—	950	710
FSR-90	380.9	447.1		—	756
FSR-90-D (% early)	.6152	.4865			—
ICD-U in 6 months			—569	—570	—632
ICD-U in 1 year			—721	—741	—856
ICD-U in 2 years			—790	—820	—747
ICD-U in 3 years			—784	—814	—664
ICD-U in 4 years			—755	—785	—612
ICM in 4 years			—749	—780	—610
% success/PRT in 1 yr.			—723	—742	—852
% success/PRT in 2 yrs.			—789	—819	—746
% success/PRT in 4 yrs.			—748	—780	—618
W-U on 45th day			—283	—278	—273
W-U on 90th day			—422	—421	—449
W-U on 135th day			—530	—525	—590
W-U on 180th day			—574	—583	—710
W-U on 365th day			—581	—616	—582
W-U on 730th day			—514	—538	—314
W-U on 1095th day			—483	—500	—326
W-U on 1460th day			—377	—394	—266
ICD-U in 2nd 6 months			—713	—742	—875
ICD-U in 2nd year			—691	—725	—505
ICD-U in 3rd year			—593	—616	—372
ICD-U in 4th year			—521	—544	—355

Note: Correlations of FSR criteria with ICD-M and W-M have been omitted in order to save space. In no instance did these values differ more than .021 from the corresponding ICD-U and W-U values presented above.

in the block of correlations between the 135th and 180th day. On the other hand, whereabouts on the 135th day was only minimally predictive of whether or not the patient was institutionalized at checkpoints beyond the 180th day. It is clear, therefore, that fairly large numbers of patients in at one time were out at a later time (as would be expected) and/or that many of those out of an institution at one point were reinstitutionalized at a later date.

In spite of this pattern of shifting patient whereabouts, the cross-sectional criteria were, within very narrow limits, surprisingly good predictors of the longitudinal incommunity day criterion. The values in table 5 indicate that a checkpoint date slightly beyond the midpoint of a time interval was a reasonably good predictor of incommunity days during the interval. For example, whereabouts on either the 90th or 135th day predicted fairly well ICD-U in the first 6 months, as did whereabouts on the 180th day for ICD-U in the total first year. These values, of course, were somewhat inflated by patients who never left the hospital and by patients released late in the follow-up period. Nevertheless, the vast difference in effort required to determine whereabouts as compared to determining total incommunity days is such that a cross-sectional criterion would seem a useful measure in situations of limited resources.

In a practical situation, one could, of course, combine a dichotomous FSR criterion with knowledge of cross-sectional whereabouts in order to project ICD over a period for which a detailed ICD follow-up was impossible. For example, the .714 correlation of whereabouts on the 730th day with ICD-U over the total 4 years can be raised to .823 in a multiple correlation adding early vs. late FSR-90-D. As a further

TABLE 5.—Relationship of Unmodified Longitudinal and Cross-Sectional Criteria (N=1274)

	6-month ICD-U	1-year ICD-U	2-year ICD-U	3-year ICD-U	4-year ICD-U	ICM
W-U on 45th day	614	451	368	325	295	295
W-U on 90th day	842	664	546	439	444	436
W-U on 135th day	854	769	622	543	490	488
W-U on 180th day	737	825	688	604	554	550
W-U on 365th day	419	687	764	705	650	643
W-U on 730th day	300	383	636	720	714	705
W-U on 1095th day	288	372	510	667	746	739
W-U on 1460th day	250	314	431	533	650	641

example, one could assume that it was impossible to complete more than 1 year of a contemplated 3-year ICD follow-up. A multiple correlation based on FSR-90-D and W-U on the 365th day would predict ICD-U over 3 years at the level of R = .771. These illustrative values compare not unfavorably, in view of the greater effort required to predict later ICD-U from knowledge of ICD-U during an earlier follow-up period.

Readmission

The relatively low correlations between whereabouts at nonadjacent checkpoints, and between whereabouts and ICD, suggest that readmission was a not infrequent occurrence. The design of this study was not ideally suited to providing information about readmission, per se, a major reason being that the sample to begin with was composed largely of readmissions. Nevertheless, several of the present findings are of interest. To preserve clinical meaningfulness, readmission was defined as involving an institutional stay of 15 or more consecutive nights.

Of the 1250 patients who did not die or who were not directly transferred, 1142 (91.4 per cent) achieved an FSR-30. Of these, 65.3 per cent (N = 746) were later readmitted to a psychiatric or penal facility sometime during the 4-year study period. Because FSR-90 involves a more stringent criterion of release, readmission rates with FSR-90 were somewhat lower than for FSR-30. Of the 1119 patients with an FSR-90, 710 (63.4 per cent) were later readmitted. To provide a uniform exposure period, it was determined that 1108 of the patients who achieved an FSR-30 did so within the first 3 years; 42.1 per cent (N = 467) were readmitted within one year of the FSR-30 exit. Of the 1089 whose FSR-90 began in the first three years, 37.7 per cent (N = 411) were readmitted within 1 year of the FSR-90 exit.

Results: Part II

To this point, release and community stay criteria have been dealt with in the abstract, in the sense of being of general research interest. The data have shown that different criteria and different definitions of the same criteria were less—in some cases, considerably less—than perfectly related. This raised the possibility that most of the departure from unit relationship was contributed by particular groups of patients. If so, and if such patients came from a particular hospital, that hospital's criterion scores, since they were averages of patient criterion scores, could show considerable fluctuation. This issue was of particular concern in the larger PEP research, a study with hospitals as units and only indirectly concerned with patient outcomes, per se. The data which follow deal with the same criteria and definitional differences discussed above; however, in contrast to what has gone before, criterion scores at this point are for hospitals as subjects. In brief, having examined orderings of patients on the criteria under study, we now examine relationships between orderings of hospitals.

Reliability

Averaging patient scores to yield a hospital's criterion score is analogous to a summing of the test items which make up a person's score on a psychological test. Just as test reliability can be assessed by correlating scores on equivalent halves, it is possible to assess in the same way the use of patient criterion scores to arrive at a hospital's criterion score. It is recognized that, while useful in exposition, identifying test items with patients, personality inventories with the present criterion measures, and a test subject with a hospital is by no means a perfect analogy. Limitations notwithstanding, both the analogy and the use of methods like the Spearman-Brown formula appear instructive in furthering understanding of the data.

Patients in the 12 hospitals were randomly split into halves, and mean scores on 33 criteria were computed for each of the $(2 \times 12 =)$ 24 halves. Product-moment and rank order correlations between the half-test scores are presented in the first two columns of table 6. The third column gives estimated whole-test reliabilities computed by using the product-moment coefficients in the Spearman-Brown formula. Since these data are believed to be unique in dealing specifically with the reliability of effectiveness measures for service institutions, their significance is difficult to assess. However, compared with the reliability of instruments commonly used in social science research, it appears that, with the exception of certain cross-sectional criteria, the estimated whole-test reliabilities are quite satisfactory.

In connection with the lower split-half reliability of the whereabouts measures, it should be noted that utility and reliability seem to be inversely related. An early checkpoint like 45 days would not be very useful for hospital comparisons, because so few patients were out of the hospital. Yet the fact that the bulk of patients were scored as institutionalized made for a highly reliable measure. The point is that

TABLE 6.—Split-Half Product-Moment and Rank Order Reliability Coefficients (N=12)

	rho	r	Estimated Reliability
1. ICD-U in 6 months	769	789	882
2. ICD-M in 6 months	783	839	912
3. ICD-U in 1 year	699	665	799
4. ICD-M in 1 year	699	735	847
5. ICD-U in 2 years	671	701	824
6. ICD-M in 2 years	671	748	856
7. ICD-U in 3 years	832	813	897
8. ICD-M in 3 years	839	826	905
9. ICD-U in 4 years	867	865	928
10. ICD-M in 4 years	839	856	922
11. W-U on 45th day	754	882	937
12. W-M on 45th day	811	847	917
13. W-U on 90th day	860	829	906
14. W-M on 90th day	923	924	960
15. W-U on 135th day	705	639	780
16. W-M on 135th day	698	689	816
17. W-U on 180th day	282	414	585
18. W-M on 180th day	455	525	689
19. W-U on 365th day	568	513	678
20. W-M on 365th day	435	458	628
21. W-U on 730th day	460	618	764
22. W-M on 730th day	434	582	736
23. W-U on 1095th day	552	682	811
24. W-M on 1095th day	629	784	879
25. W-U on 1460th day	456	614	928
26. W-M on 1460th day	425	604	922
27. ICM in 4 years	811	881	937
28. % success/PRT in 1 year	587	612	759
29. % success/PRT in 2 years	532	626	770
30. % success/PRT in 4 years	783	844	916
31. FSR-30	853	789	882
32. FSR-90	734	807	893
33. FSR-90-D	491	650	788

split-half reliability can be only one of the indexes on which to assess the value of a criterion measure.

Although most of the reliabilities in table 6 were satisfactory for practical use, that their size left something to be desired has implications for the matter of sample size. Just as adding equivalent items will raise the reliability of a psychological test, the reliability of these criteria would have been increased by having more subjects per hospital. With the exception of one hospital which had 77 subjects, N in the study hospitals ranged between 95 and 116. The point to be noted is that, while not small, the patient samples in the present study were none too large and that similarly designed studies in the future should ideally be based on larger patient samples.

Stability of Hospital Standings

Tables 7, 8, and 9 parallel tables 2, 3, and 4. The product-moment correlations* in these tables indicate to what extent the standing of hospitals on one criterion measure were similar to their standings on another measure, and it is from them that conclusions can be derived about use of these criteria to assess hospital performance.

Values in tables 7, 8, and 9 are in general higher than those in tables 2, 3, and 4. However, aside from their generally higher levels, interpretation of the correlations based on hospital scores coincides with the major findings of the earlier analyses. The essential equivalence of the modified and unmodified methods of criterion definition, for example, was amply confirmed. It is also evident that longitudinal and release criteria yielded a considerably more stable ordering of hospitals than did the cross-sectional criteria.

Although hospital scores at adjacent checkpoints or during adjacent cumulative ICD periods were generally highly correlated, there was an interesting exception to this pattern. The intercorrelations of whereabouts at the 45th, 90th, 135th, and 180th day fell into a fairly orderly progression until seemingly disrupted between 6 months and a year. There was a relatively greater drop in the correlations of whereabouts on the 365th day with whereabouts at other checkpoints. Like the checkpoints preceding the 365th day, correlations for the 730th, 1095th, and 1460th days seemed to fall into regular patterns, except when correlated with the 365th day. This is simply noted here and will be discussed below in connection with the intercorrelations of cumulative FSR-90 acquisition rates.

---

*Parallel rank order correlations were computed throughout because of the small N. In no case were differences between the two sets of values large enough to alter interpretation of the data, and only the product-moment values are reported here. The rank-order correlations are reported in a more detailed presentation of these data in PEP Intramural Report 63-3, available upon request to the Director, Program Evaluation Staff, VA Hospital, Washington, D.C. 20422.

TABLE 7.—Product-Moment Intercorrelations of Hospital Means on Longitudinal Criteria (N = 12)

Variable	1	2	3	4	5	6	7	8	9	10	11	12	13	14
1. ICD-U in 6 months	—	992	927	930	795	812	748	758	727	735	742	934	789	701
2. ICD-M in 6 months			919	932	779	803	728	743	702	715	721	925	770	674
3. ICD-U in 1 year				996	956	964	929	933	907	911	915	999	955	893
4. ICD-M in 1 year					941	957	914	924	890	900	902	995	941	877
5. ICD-U in 2 years						996	990	986	973	967	975	948	995	960
6. ICD-M in 2 years							985	988	967	968	974	957	993	956
7. ICD-U in 3 years								997	994	989	992	923	988	983
8. ICD-M in 3 years									991	993	992	928	988	983
9. ICD-U in 4 years										993	997	903	975	993
10. ICD-M in 4 years											989	908	974	985
11. ICM in 4 years												912	977	992
12. % success/PRT in 1 year													948	889
13. % success/PRT in 2 years														971
14. % success/PRT in 4 years														—

TABLE 8.—Product-Moment Intercorrelations of Hospital Means on Cross-Sectional Criteria (N=12)

Variable	1	2	3	4	5	6	7	8	9	10	11	12	13	14	15	16
1. W-U on 45th day	—	981	964	942	771	764	647	613	423	478	417	339	382	383	365	419
2. W-M on 45th day			959	938	727	732	606	574	418	483	371	296	306	306	304	364
3. W-U on 90th day				990	866	873	775	764	488	555	547	475	501	503	480	534
4. W-M on 90th day					880	891	796	783	527	595	558	499	493	497	475	525
5. W-U on 135th day						988	887	908	495	567	615	578	655	673	648	693
6. W-M on 135th day							922	936	549	624	634	597	672	691	664	709
7. W-U on 180th day								983	709	754	836	816	758	760	697	715
8. W-M on 180th day									592	657	809	797	733	732	665	692
9. W-U on 365th day										981	684	640	647	649	650	625
10. W-M on 365th day											689	659	638	630	628	621
11. W-U on 730th day												979	804	766	685	678
12. W-M on 730th day													726	678	592	583
13. W-U on 1095th day														992	972	966
14. W-M on 1095th day															985	978
15. W-U on 1460th day																993
16. W-M on 1460th day																—

TABLE 9.—Rank Order and Product-Moment Correlations of Release Criteria with Community Stay Criteria (N = 12)

	FSR-30		FSR-90		FSR-90-D	
	r	*rho*	*r*	*rho*	*r*	*rho*
FSR-30	—	—	987	937	924	899
FSR-90			—	—	935	965
FSR-90-D					—	—
ICD-U in 6 months	—723	—636	—686	—643	—780	—642
ICD-U in 1 year	—888	—853	—862	—888	—942	—900
ICD-U in 2 years	—941	—916	—913	—930	—941	—942
ICD-U in 3 years	—969	—909	—954	—951	—944	—949
ICD-U in 4 years	—969	—888	—966	—916	—934	—897
ICM in 4 years	—967	—881	—960	—909	—931	—906
% success/PRT in 1 yr.	—893	—853	—869	—888	—941	—900
% success/PRT in 2 yrs.	—937	—909	—922	—916	—956	—942
% success/PRT in 4 yrs.	—952	—860	—959	—881	—932	—890
W-U on 45th day	—532	—629	—462	—622	—554	—603
W-U on 90th day	—631	—622	—578	—615	—675	—582
W-U on 135th day	—776	—755	—766	—783	—857	—789
W-U on 180th day	—885	—874	—857	—832	—905	—841
W-U on 365th day	—787	—652	—744	—610	—799	—694
W-U on 730th day	—877	—839	—852	—804	—740	—750
W-U on 1095th day	—866	—818	—918	—895	—858	—823
W-U on 1460th day	—827	—636	—889	—797	—867	—809

Another interesting fact emerges with respect to the generally accepted need for a lengthy follow-up period. It will be noted in table 7 that a 2-year follow-up would have resulted in a not dissimilar ordering of hospitals from that at the end of 4 years. Product-moment correlations between the 2-year and 4-year ICD scores were about .97, as was the correlation of per cent success during PEP-responsible time in 2 years with success over 4 years. It would appear that a 2-year follow-up so closely approximates the criterion value of a 4-year follow-up as to be considered completely adequate for the kinds of situations in which these data were collected.

It will be recalled that release criteria were of special interest here because of their relative ease of collection. It is evident from table 9 that release criteria correlated highly with the more laboriously collected and seemingly more meaningful community stay data. In spite of many possible arguments against release figures as measures of

TABLE 10.—Product-Moment Intercorrelations of Cumulative FSR-90 Acquisition Rates (N = 12)

Variable	1	2	3	4	5	6	7	8	9	10	11	12	13
FSR-90 within:													
1. 1 to 15 days	—	875	788	760	756	747	682	504	377	236	—010	—011	005
2. 1 to 30 days			944	914	874	872	780	579	390	304	—018	004	—005
3. 1 to 45 days				976	952	941	812	652	500	470	204	214	209
4. 1 to 60 days					974	974	896	759	656	625	352	352	336
5. 1 to 75 days						988	922	812	685	637	437	450	447
6. 1 to 90 days							946	855	729	678	443	444	431
7. 1 to 135 days								938	836	752	543	559	540
8. 1 to 180 days									925	858	712	722	696
9. 1 to 274 days										971	851	821	781
10. 1 to 361 days											893	854	810
11. 1 to 729 days												978	965
12. 1 to 1094 days													990
13. 1 to 1459 days													—

hospital effectiveness, the empirical data indicate that they hold considerable promise as practical equivalents of the long-range criteria with greatest face validity.

Patterns of Patient Release

It was noted earlier that a shift in the relative standings of hospitals seemed to occur around 6 months and/or 1 year. In order to clarify release pattern differences between hospitals, cumulative FSR-90 rates were computed for each hospital for the 13 overlapping periods listed in table 10. The period shortly after admission was deliberately overrepresented; eight of the 13 categories are concerned only with the 6 months following admission. This emphasis on early release was thought to be consistent with both the findings discussed so far and, more generally, with contemporary emphases on brief hospitalization.

Before examining the release patterns described by FSR-90 rates, it should be noted that a second set of FSR-90 rates was computed by dropping from consideration all patients whose FSR-90 had been achieved through an AWOL or AMA exit. Correlation of these "approved" FSR-90 rates with total FSR-90 yielded values that were never less than $r = .939$ and $rho = .899$; this finding demonstrates the very minimal effect on hospital standings of differences in FSR-90 which resulted from exits without staff approval. This finding was not without some element of surprise, however, since AMA and AWOL exits accounted for fully 13.6 per cent of all FSR-90 exits.

Intercorrelations of the 13 sets of cumulative FSR-90 rates in table 10 indicate that, over a period of time, sizable shifts occurred in the relative standings of hospitals. Their orderings on early release bore only the faintest resemblance to orderings on total releases within 2 years, 3 years, or 4 years. Obviously, some hospitals achieved relatively high rates of early release but then showed little or no increment from the release of additional patients. A patient entering such a hospital would have a high probability of quick release, but, should he remain too long, his chances of release would rapidly diminish. Conversely, it would seem that there were hospitals which were slow to release patients, but, once started, they caught up and exceeded the release rates of hospitals which had shown a short-lived burst of quick releases.

Further inspection of table 10 complements earlier impressions of change in the relative positions of hospitals around 6 months and/or

1 year postadmission. Regularities in the progression of correlation size seemed to be disrupted between 1 and 2 years and, to a lesser extent, between 180 and 274 days. It was in large part from preliminary versions of the data in table 10 that 274 days was selected as the most satisfactory point at which to dichotomize FSR-90. In retrospect, this would seem to have been at least as good a choice as any other, since FSR-90 within 274 days correlated highly with the three long-term rates but still reflected some of the hospital differences in early release. As such, dichotomizing at 274 days compromises between over-emphasis on either too short or too long a view of the release process.

In a further examination of release rate patterns, table 11 presents data for four selected hospitals on cumulative FSR-90 acquisition within each of the 13 periods previously noted. Deviations of each hospital's FSR-90 rates from the total sample values are indicated on the lines labeled "Difference." Upper and lower limits of the full range of deviations for all 12 hospitals are indicated at the bottom of table 11. Deviations for the four example hospitals are also represented in figure 1 where a hospital's release curve indicates that its FSR-90 rate was better or worse than the all-patient rate.*

Several things are apparent from table 11 and figure 1. Relative to other hospitals, Hospital D illustrates a situation of unswerving uniformity; it had the dubious distinction of defining the 12-hospital lower limit for every one of the 13 time intervals. Hospital B illustrates a situation of moderate change in relative standing. Hospitals A and C, on the other hand, demonstrate a more dramatic shift in relative position. Hospital C got off to a much slower start than did Hospital A, but, by the end of 6 months, C's release rate had picked up momentum and continued at a favorable rate. By the end of the 4-year follow-up, Hospital C had released about 10 per cent more of its admissions than had Hospital A.

Change in relative standing is important here only secondarily because of what it tells about individual hospitals. Its major importance lies in a demonstration that evaluation of mental hospital effectiveness through use of cohort release rates will be considerably influenced by length of the study period. It is apparent from figure 1, for example,

*A slightly more accurate method would have been to compare a hospital's release pattern against the other 11 hospitals. However, such a refinement involves much computation and, except for accentuating highest and lowest deviations, would not materially further illustration of release pattern differences.

TABLE 11.—Hospital Differences in Rate of Cumulative FSR-90 Acquisition

	Cumulative Per Cent FSR-90 Acquisition by Day												
	15	30	45	60	75	90	135	180	274	364	729	1094	1459
All patients	3.5	7.1	11.8	17.5	21.8	26.4	40.4	49.4	61.5	69.1	83.2	87.2	89.5
Hospital A:													
% FSR-90	15.1	20.8	24.5	31.1	34.9	41.5	53.8	56.6	65.1	67.9	75.5	79.2	83.0
Difference	11.6	13.7	12.7	13.6	13.1	15.1	13.4	7.2	3.6	—1.2	—7.7	—8.0	—6.5
Hospital B:													
% FSR-90	6.3	10.5	16.8	26.3	32.6	37.9	56.8	63.2	77.9	82.1	93.7	94.7	95.8
Difference	2.8	3.4	5.0	8.8	10.8	11.5	16.4	13.8	16.4	13.0	10.5	7.5	6.3
Hospital C:													
% FSR-90	0	1.7	4.3	12.9	15.5	24.1	45.7	57.8	72.4	79.3	88.8	92.2	93.1
Difference	—3.5	—5.4	—7.5	—4.6	—6.3	—2.3	5.3	8.4	10.9	10.2	5.6	5.0	3.6
Hospital D:													
% FSR-90	0	0	0	1.0	1.9	5.8	16.3	26.9	41.3	50.0	69.2	73.1	76.0
Difference	—3.5	—7.1	—11.8	—16.5	—19.9	—20.6	—24.1	—22.5	—20.2	—19.1	—14.0	—14.1	—13.5
All-hospital range of differences:													
Upper limit	11.6	13.7	12.7	13.6	16.0	16.8	16.4	13.8	16.4	13.0	10.5	7.5	6.3
Lower limit	—3.5	—7.1	—11.8	—16.5	—19.9	—20.6	—24.1	—22.5	—20.2	—19.1	—14.0	—14.1	—13.5

that a criterion of release within 60 days or 90 days would lead to a considerably different evaluation of hospitals than would a criterion of release within 2 years. While choice of criteria is tailored to a particular problem, it is clear that for many research problems a criterion of release within too brief a period following admission would be of questionable validity.

The undesirability of too brief a follow-up will not surprise even the novice researcher. What is of considerably more interest is the implication that use of cumulative release over too long a follow-up period can be equally undesirable. There apparently comes a point when more effective hospitals (effective in terms of release rates) have so few cohort members remaining to be discharged that they are left to mark time while less effective hospitals catch up. As a result, the range of interhospital differences is attenuated. After such a "point of diminishing variance," a single set of cumulative release rates would fail to discriminate hospitals as sharply. The data in table 11 suggest that, in the present study, such a point came at about 2 years.

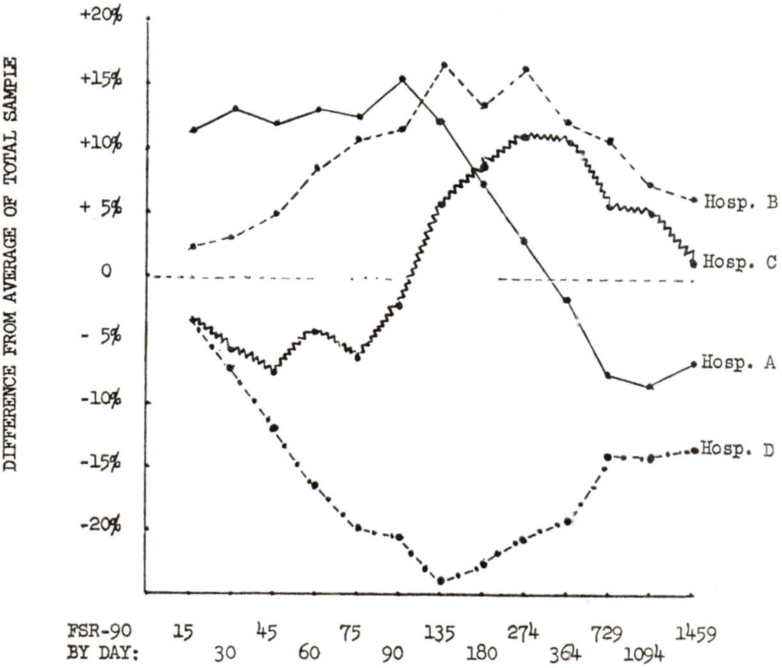

FIG. 1.—Hospital differences in rate of cumulative FSR-90 acquisition.

Discussion

Researchers would perhaps differ among themselves on the major problems involved in evaluation of psychiatric treatment. However, high on any list of major methodological issues would be the question of appropriate criteria. The present paper has been concerned with identification and clarification of operational definitions of patient release and community stay and with their application as criteria of mental hospital effectiveness. Several of the reported findings only serve to emphasize and support research practices already in common use. For example, the data on split-half reliability underline the importance of basing measures of hospital performance on a large enough N of patients to insure adequate reliability of the criterion. Findings such as this require no elaboration here, and the present discussion is limited to findings which uniquely clarify methodological issues or raise questions about the validity of generally accepted practices.

One general finding appearing in several forms throughout this study was that differences in operational definition of a particular criterion construct can only minimally influence derivative conclusions about hospital effectiveness. This generalization seemed to hold even when the absolute influence of variations in definition was large. Such was the case, for example, in introducing the concept of responsibility into the measurement of incommunity stay; per cent success/PRT showed uniformly high correlations with incommunity days. Measurement of incommunity stay in monthly rather than daily units seemed to have been of little consequence, either absolutely or relatively. Similarly, whether or not debatable community stay in the form of LOA's and short AWOL's was counted was seen as unimportant in the measurement of hospital effectiveness. Neither did the difference between 30 days and 90 days as a requisite nonreturn time nor the difference between medically approved and total release rates affect the use of first significant release as a measure of hospital performance. In brief, it appears that considerable variation would have to be introduced into the operational definitions of release and community stay before such changes materially affected hospital comparisons.

Also of interest was the extent to which different—although obviously related—criterion measures were roughly equivalent to one another. An extreme instance of this was evident in the fairly high correlations of as crude an index as whether institutionalized on a single day near the middle of a time period with as refined a measure as a daily determination of institutionalization. Even more impressive was the extent to which length of hospitalization, expressed here in the FSR indexes, could be used to approximate daily measurement of incommunity stay. The finding of r's in the 80's and 90's suggests that, because such data are routinely available, we could make greater use of them in treatment evaluation and that we would need be less apologetic about their use. Even when its variance was restricted by dichotomization, release rate yielded almost as much criterion information for purposes of comparing hospitals as did detailed measures of community stay.

One place where our results suggest extreme caution is with the use of a whereabouts criterion—that is, with status as simply in or out of an institution on a specific date. The fact of not infrequent readmission imposes very definite limits on the usefulness for interhospital comparisons of a single whereabouts criterion. As judged from the correlations of whereabouts and ICD criteria, the validity of the single cross-sectional criterion for assessing hospital performance is restricted to very specific time periods.

The data reported make it clear that hospitals differed considerably in the speed with which they returned patients to the community. One hospital released only 2 per cent of its sample within the first 75 days after admission; two other hospitals had each released about a third of their patients within the same period. Yet the two hospitals which were roughly equivalent on release within 75 days of admission differed considerably in the percentage of their admission samples released within 9 months, or 2 years, or 4 years. Quite obviously, hospitals do differ in the total number of releases within a given time period. What is more important to the researcher is that, varying with the exposure period, the pattern of interhospital differences can vary considerably.

This finding illustrates the importance of selecting a release criterion far enough removed from admission to reflect as much of the shifting pattern of hospital standings as is appropriate to a specific problem. On the other hand, a release rate computed over too lengthy a period can minimize and obscure differences between hospitals. It would seem that the researcher must be prepared to avoid both the Charybdis of premature evaluation and the Scylla of an overly long and less meaningful follow-up. In this study release rate within 2 years was seen as more than just as good; it was actually to be preferred to release within 4 years.

Summary

This study reported the reliability of, the effects of definitional variations in, and the relationships between three major classes of release and community stay data often used as criteria in the evaluation of psychiatric treatment. These were (1) length of institutionalization, (2) postadmission cross-sectional whereabouts, and (3) postrelease longitudinal whereabouts. The data were based on a 4-year follow-up of 1274 male functional psychotics admitted or readmitted to 12 VA NP hospitals.

Results indicated that definitional differences were of little consequence either in relative or in absolute terms. However, the time period defining a criterion measure can be of considerable significance. It was suggested that several different, albeit related, criterion measures are useful in complementing each other to yield varying perspectives on treatment outcome. Implications were discussed and illustrated for selection in situations of limited resources of criterion measures which would require minimum time and effort and which would approximate more laboriously collected criteria.

Acknowledgment

The author wishes to acknowledge that he is but one of a large group involved in the work of which this study is a small part. He is particularly indebted to the PEP psychologists and social workers who collected the data and to Dr. R. L. Jenkins under whose direction the PEP study was initiated.

REFERENCES

1. Burdock, E. I., and Hardesty, A. S.: An outcome index for mental hospital patients. J. Abnorm. Soc. Psychol. 63:666-670, 1961.
2. Jenkins, R. L., and Gurel, L.: Predictive factors in early release. Ment. Hosp. 10:11-14, 1959.
3. Ullmann, L. P.: Home Care Placement of Neuropsychiatric Patients. Washington, Psychiatric Evaluation Project, 1961.
4. Lehrman, N. S.: A state hospital population five years after admission: a yardstick for evaluative comparison of follow-up studies. Psychiat. Quart. 34:365-373, 1960.

Discussion

Recorder: MORTON KRAMER, Sc.D.

COMMENTS ON DR. PHILLIPS' PRESENTATION

DR. ROTH: Dr. Roth stated that the latah and amok are forms of hysteria. The Shaman is a gifted, hysterical leader and not psychotic. Dr. Roth added that he is unaware of any society that has given a known psychotic a position of leadership.

Dr. Roth emphasized that it is important to separate the biological and sociological variables and factors in etiological considerations. He illustrated this by some phenomena he has observed in the schizophrenia of old age. This group consists primarily of single women living in isolation. He carried out investigations to determine whether the isolation was primarily a cause or effect of the schizophrenia. Evidence suggestive of the isolation as being an effect of the schizophrenic process was that these women had always been self-isolated; they were arrogant, cold, difficult persons. When compared with a control group of women with affective disorders, the schizophrenic women were quite different. For example, among the schizophrenic women there was a high proportion with illegitimate children. Not one of 20 cases investigated had married the father of the illegitimate child. This is quite different from the experience of a comparison group of women with affective disorders who had had a similar experience. (It was not clear as to how many of the mothers of the illegitimate children in the comparison group married the fathers.)

There were some other observations that suggested the isolation of these schizophrenic females was related to such social factors as (1) some were the youngest members of sibship and were most likely to be left alone in childhood and adolescence since fewer parents and sibs were alive; (2) 30 to 40 per cent suffered from deafness. Thus, biological and social factors reinforced each other.

DR. VON MENDELSSOHN: Dr. Mendelssohn stated that Dr. Phillips spoke of form and content, but not in the same sense as Dr. Hoch had in the address of the preceding day. Dr. von Mendelssohn reiterated the importance of separating content from form.

DR. POLLACK: Dr. Pollack emphasized the importance of developmental patterns in explaining types of psychopathology. For example, in relation to the marked preponderance of males among adolescents with psychopathology, there may be some relationship to early brain damage and complications of pregnancy in the mother.

DR. KRAMER: Dr. Kramer emphasized the need to be more critical in the assessment of changing patterns of first admission rates for specific disorders. For example, the rapidly decreasing rate of first admission to state hospitals for manic depressives does not mean a decreasing incidence of the disorder per se. With the increasing number of community facilities, such as psychiatric services in general hospitals, outpatient psychiatric facilities, increasing numbers of private psychiatrists, etc., one must have knowledge of the effect of such facilities on producing the changes in admission rates to mental hospitals for specific disorders. It is quite possible, for example, that the incidence of manic depressive psychosis has remained the same over the years, but that the pathways to treatment of persons affected with such disorders has changed so that a higher proportion go to the general hospitals, the private psychiatrist, etc., thus accounting for the smaller proportion coming to the large state mental hospital.

DR. PHILLIPS: Dr. Roth has noted that 30 to 40 per cent of a group of schizophrenic women whom he observed suffered from deafness and thus were socially isolated. This is an extremely high prevalence of deafness, and I don't know whether Dr. Roth is implying that social isolation in schizophrenia is usually associated with deafness or whether he considers this rate as unique to the group under observation. No one can quarrel with the notion that deafness is organic in nature and that it can reinforce a person's tendency toward isolating himself socially. But this is not to imply that it is the biological aspect of deafness which is the determinant of social isolation. It is the deaf person's psychological *response* to his deafness which isolates him, not deafness per se. Many people overcome this handicap as others overcome the barriers of language, values, and ethnic differences.

I am not clear what Dr. von Mendelssohn means by the distinction between form and content. Of course, we know that the content of hallucinations will differ from one person to another and from one society to another. However, I had something very different in mind when I suggested that the dominant formal characteristics of disorder differ from one social class or society to another and change over time as the dominant values of a society change. Recently, for example, we have found that a person's dominant role orientation, combined with his dominant modality (i.e., action, thought, or affect dominance), as these are both expressed in his symptomatology, determine the psychiatric diagnosis assigned to him at the upper limits of diagnostic reliability. Role orientation and symptom modality are, to my way of thinking, formal characteristics of mental disorder. Many investigators, however, have found that these formal characteristics of disorder, dominant modes of role and symptom modality, vary from one social class or culture to another.

I have some difficulty in following Dr. Pollack's argument. I am not quite sure if he means that the complications of pregnancy presumed to be associated with adolescent disorders in males affect primarily male fetuses.

I can only agree with Dr. Kramer that we cannot accept psychiatric hospital admission rates as reflective of either true incidence or prevalence rates for the various disorders. We need far better statistics than we now possess on the appearance of different forms of disorder in the general population. However, we must distinguish between the problem of absolute versus relative rates for the various disorders. My position was that the relative rates of disorders had appeared to change over time. Undoubtedly, community psychiatric facilities are now seeing patients who previously would have entered the mental hospital. But we must remember that hospitalization rates for manic-depressive disorder have continuously decreased as far back as we have available data—that is, since 1910. The very recent increase in community facilities cannot account for the gradual decline in hospital admissions for manic-depressive psychosis over a period of more than a half-century. Further, it is difficult to believe that the most severe forms of psychiatric disorder—such as hebephrenic and catatonic schizophrenia, which are now almost never seen in hospitals—are now treated in community facilities. This is all the more difficult to accept when we note that an increasing proportion of patients entering hospitals are exhibiting milder and nonpsychotic forms of disorder.

Comments of Dr. Zubin's Presentation

Dr. Hoch: Dr. Hoch stated that Dr. Zubin's approach is a praiseworthy attempt to make data on diagnosis more objective and then more comparable. Dr. Hoch indicated that he agreed with Professor Rümke's approach, which stresses subjective appraisal of schizophrenics and emphasizes the importance of the clinical approach, the "feel" of the clinician. He hopes that Dr. Zubin's approach will clarify what can be objectified and what cannot be. Dr. Hoch added that he fully agrees with Jaspers that some symptomatology displayed by schizophrenics is understandable only to schizophrenics and not to normal observers. He encourages research of the type advocated, but he also raised doubts that the problems of diagnosis will be clarified before the etiology of schizophrenia is known.

DR. WECHSLER: Dr. Wechsler emphasized the need to define culture as well as the disorder being studied. He illustrated this by problems he has encountered in defining culture in relation to IQ testing. Children place on symbols different meanings which are derived from the significance of the symbolic object in the cultural group in which the child lives. For example, to children living in a kibbutz the concept of buying (sugar, for example) is quite meaningless, since no one buys items in the kibbutz. Similarly, the response of Iraeli children to a pig with a missing tail in a projective test yielded a "phooey." Culture is a method of communicating an environmental experience.

DR. RÜMKE: Dr. Rümke emphasized the importance of distinguishing form and content. For example, the schizophrenic has delusions (form), but the content of the delusion differs as a result of environmental factors and experiences undergone by the patient. For example, in the south of a small country, the persons are much more romantic, and in the north much more frigid. Such differences reveal themselves in content of the delusions of sick persons from these areas. He also emphasized the importance of style, mode, and tempo of communication that characterizes persons in different countries and within different areas of the same country. Schizophrenics may speak quite rapidly in one country, slower in another.

DR. RADO: Dr. Rado emphasized the basic importance of psychodynamics and cautioned against its elimination in the diagnostic process and in research dealing with unraveling the diagnostic process.

DR. LEHMANN: Dr. Lehmann raised the problem as to whether schizophrenia is a concept or a symbol. He wondered how one can weight the relative importance of physical characteristics, biological variables, significant social patterns, "the praecox feeling" that Dr. Rümke indicated was important, and the psychodynamic variables. Dr. Lehmann raised the question as to whether schizophrenia is a diagnostic term that should be eliminated from the psychiatric nomenclature.

DR. ZUBIN: We agree with Dr. Hoch that only when the etiology of schizophrenia is known on an objective basis will it become possible to diagnose schizophrenia properly. While waiting for this millennium to arrive, whatever help objective approaches can yield in reducing the unnecessary noise in the diagnostic system would be of great value, not only in current classification but eventually in the establishing of the existence of an etiological agent itself.

Dr. Wechsler's request for a definition of culture is well taken and should be given proper attention. The very fact that the symbols in the various cultures have different significance make it necessary to search for culture-free or culture-fair indicators. These cannot be found in culturally transmitted symbols but must be sought elsewhere, perhaps in the neurophysiological realm. Dr. Rümke's reference to the "praecox feeling" and Dr. Rado's insistence on psychodynamic considerations are also well taken. However, as long as these remain private events in the mind of the psychiatrist and are not made public, it becomes very difficult to make comparisons not only across cultures but even within cultures. Only by providing indicators that are public and readily recognizable can we hope to make progress in detecting schizophrenia.

Regarding Dr. Lehmann's final suggestion that perhaps schizophrenia has outlived its usefulness, we agree that this may be the case, but only with the help of objective indicators can we ever verify such a hunch. If we get a multivariate distribution of behaviors which can be subjected to methods of fractionation for finding the natural lines of cleavage among the variables, we may be able to demonstrate that what is now called schizophrenia can be regarded as a composite of five or six different types of illnesses.

COMMENTS OF DR. PASAMANICK'S PRESENTATION

DR. WORTIS: Dr. J. Wortis raised two questions: (1) What does Dr. Pasamanick think of the quality of state hospital care in Kentucky? (2) What improvements could he envisage in that system?

DR. VON MENDELSSOHN: Dr. von Mendelssohn stated that the opening of the day hospital center at St. Elizabeths has attracted a type of patient not too evident prior to the establishment of this facility. He asked Dr. Pasamanick whether the program that he described had any tendency to attract a different type of patient than was usually admitted to the Kentucky State Hospital.

DR. COLE: Dr. Cole asked Dr. Pasamanick to comment on the effectiveness of Public Health Nurses without psychiatric training in the follow-up of patients at home as compared to Public Health Nurses with such training. He was particularly interested in the relative success of the two types of nurses in keeping patients out of the hospital.

DR. ZUBIN: Dr. Zubin asked Dr. Pasamanick to comment on measures other than days in and out of hospital that he may have considered in his research—such as employment history, various facets of social adjustment, etc.

DR. HOCH: Dr. Hoch commented on the quality of patients who are kept out of the hospital and those who are rehospitalized. He stated that it is not always possible to maintain very sick patients in the community. The issue is whether it is possible to maintain sick schizophrenics in the community in a manner so that they function in a satisfactory manner and stay out of trouble.

DR. PASAMANICK: I am very grateful to the discussants for their kind and thoughtful remarks and questions. First, in reply to Dr. Wortis, I would say that the quality of state hospital care in Kentucky is no better and no worse than it is in the average state hospital system in this country—that is, on the whole, quite poor. The improvements that could be suggested would take up at least the content of another paper. If I had to summarize them briefly, the outlines in the guide being promulgated by NIMH for community mental health care are those I would follow as the beginnings of adequate care.

As to Dr. von Mendelssohn's comments, it probably would be sufficient to indicate that our patients were not attracted to our program but, on the contrary, were largely already committed patients who were randomly assigned to the three different types of care, and that (as I further indicated) these were seriously and acutely ill schizophrenics rather than the neurotically ill individuals frequently attracted to new programs.

I am afraid that I am unable to give Dr. Cole any definitive information on the point he raises, since only one of our five nurses had had psychiatric training, and this would really be insufficient to make any worthwhile comparisons. I think a lot would depend upon the type of psychiatric training the nurse had received. I could conceive of some of it as being seriously handicapping, particularly when highly questionable psychodynamics and psychotherapy are involved. I think the brief training we gave our nurses stood them in good stead.

In reply to Dr. Zubin, we secured data on items of social adjustment on the patients as well as a few on other family members. These will be analyzed when the study is completed and reported on at that time. They have as yet not been looked at.

Finally, I must agree wholeheartedly with the comment made by Dr. Hoch. Our impression at this time is that, on the whole, our patients in the community functioned at least as well as those in the hospital, and that while there were many dissatisfactions with the quality of their functioning, they did not create an undue amount of trouble, since three-quarters or more of them on drugs managed to remain unhospitalized—in contrast to those on placebo, where getting into trouble generally led to hospitalization. I do not think that the threshold to determination of "trouble" was raised in this care program to any major degree. If it had, I think we would have retained even more in the community.

Comments on Dr. Gurel's Presentation

Dr. Zubin: Dr. Zubin commented that he found Dr. Gurel's paper difficult to comprehend because it seemed to lack a scientific model as the basis for its formulation. Dr. Zubin reviewed the various indexes that he had developed in his research on effectiveness of hospitalization—an index of stagnation, the occlusive index, and various other outcome indexes. Basically, he was trying to obtain measures that quantified outcome for three basic groups of patients: first, a group that after a period of hospitalization returned to the community and was never rehospitalized; a second group that moved back and forth between hospital and community; and a third that, once admitted, never returned to the community.

Dr. Cole: Dr. Cole commented also that Dr. Gurel's paper was interesting but difficult. He felt that Dr. Gurel's research represented the phenomena of a large project with an extensive amount of data which can now be extensively analyzed as the result of a research worker having access to a computer. At one time analyses were much more limited and selective because of the limitations imposed by computational difficulties and time limitations for obtaining various permutations and combinations of indexes computed from the same data. The computer now performs these operations quite rapidly and yields large volumes of tabulations and computations for the investigator to consider. Dr. Cole asked Dr. Gurel to comment on the interhospital differences and rates at which patients were released.

Dr. Kramer: Dr. Kramer commented on the findings that the FSR 30 and 90 at the end of 2 years yielded essentially the same scoring of hospitals as resulted at the end of 4 years. He pointed out that the significance of the finding related to the problem that was being investigated. If the delineation of factors associated with the development of a chronic hospital population was the focus of the investigation, then it was important to determine why the FSR rates remained the same between the second and fourth years of hospitalization.

Dr. Gurel: Dr. Gurel responded by noting that data as to the why of interhospital differences in release rates and in building a chronic population, as reflected in Dr. Cole's and Dr. Kramer's questions, were still being developed and would be presented in PEP Intramural Report 64-5. (Ed. note: This paper has since been published.) He also agreed with Dr. Cole's point about computers, citing one of the PEP papers in which it was said that "the electronic computer has the vices of its virtues: it curses us while it blesses us." One of the blessings is the opportunity to lay to rest, as was attempted in this paper, the debate about some minor methodological issues and thereby curtail much of the haggling and criticism which characterizes the implementation of treatment criteria.

APPENDIX

Membership of American Psychopathological Association*

Officers:

Jerome D. Frank, M.D., Pres.
Department of Psychiatry
Johns Hopkins University
Baltimore, Maryland

Franz J. Kallmann, M.D., Pres.-Elect
722 West 168th Street
New York 32, New York

Seymour S. Kety, M.D., Vice-Pres.
National Institute of Mental Health
Bethesda 14, Maryland

Fritz A. Freyhan, M.D., Secretary
William A. White Building
Saint Elizabeths Hospital
Washington 20, D.C.

Bernard C. Glueck, Jr., M.D., Treasurer
Box 2070
Hartford, Connecticut

D. Ewen Cameron, M.D., Councillor
Psychiatry and Aging Research
Veterans Administration Hospital
Albany, New York

Benjamin Malzberg, Ph.D., Councillor (L)
Research Foundation for Mental Hygiene, Inc.
119 Washington Avenue
Albany, New York

Committee on Program

Paul H. Hoch, M.D., Chairman
722 West 168th Street
New York 32, New York

Joseph Zubin, Ph.D.
722 West 168th Street
New York 32, New York

Members:

Theodora M. Abel, Ph.D.
Palisades
Rockland County, New York

David Abrahamsen, M.D.
1035 Fifth Avenue
New York, New York

Nathan Ackerman, M.D.
43 East 78th Street
New York, New York

Alexandra Adler, M.D.
30 Park Avenue
New York, New York

Leo Alexander, M.D. (L)
433 Marlboro Street
Boston, Massachusetts

George S. Amsden, M.D. (L)
Acworth, New Hampshire

Leslie R. Angus, M.D.
1120 East Market Street
Danville, Pennsylvania

Silvano Arieti, M.D.
22 East 72nd Street
New York, New York

Irma Bache, M.D. (L)
1 East 356
Pentagon Building
Washington, D.C.

---

*(L) = Life Member
(H) = Honorary Member

Walter W. Baker, Ph.D.
Eastern Pennsylvania Psychiatric Institute
Henry Avenue & Abbottsford Road
Philadelphia, Pennsylvania

Lauretta Bender, M.D.
44 Malone Avenue
Long Beach, New York

Herbert Birch, Ph.D.
Department of Pediatrics
Albert Einstein College of Medicine
New York, New York

H. Waldo Bird, M.D.
325 Barton Shore Drive
Ann Arbor, Michigan

Paul Bergman, M.D.
Clinical Center, Rm. 2N-238
National Institute of Mental Health
Bethesda, Maryland

James Birren, Ph.D.
Section on Aging
National Institute of Mental Health
Bethesda, Maryland

Henry Brill, M.D.
Pilgrim State Hospital
West Brentwood, L.I., New York

Eugene Brody, M.D.
University of Maryland
School of Medicine
Baltimore, Maryland

Albert Browne-Mayers, M.D.
55 East 86th Street
New York, New York

Hilde Bruch, M.D.
4 East 89th Street
New York, New York

A. Louise Brush, M.D. (L)
55 East 86th Street
New York, New York

Dexter M. Bullard, Sr., M.D. (L)
M.H.A.
500 W. Montgomery Avenue
Rockville, Maryland

Ernest W. Burgess, Ph.D.
University of Chicago
1225 East 60th Street
Chicago, Illinois

Dale C. Cameron, M.D.
Saint Elizabeths Hospital
Washington, D.C.

Douglas G. Campbell, M.D.
490 Post Street
San Francisco, California

Eric T. Carlson, M.D.
60 Sutton Place South
New York, New York

Edward J. Carroll, M.D. (L)
121 University Place
Pittsburgh, Pennsylvania

James P. Cattell, M.D.
880 Fifth Avenue
New York, New York

G. Brock Chrisholm, M.D. (H)
Seawood, West Coast Road
R.R. 2, Victoria
British Columbia, Canada

John A. Clausen, Ph.D.
1963 Yosemite Road
Berkeley, California

Hollis E. Clow, M.D. (L)
121 Westchester Avenue
White Plains, New York

Robert A. Cohen, M.D.
4514 Dorset Avenue
Chevy Chase, Maryland

Jonathan O. Cole, M.D.
7111 Edgevale Street
Chevy Chase, Maryland

Oskar Diethelm, M.D. (L)
New York Hospital
525 East 68th Street
New York, New York

Roy M. Dorcus, Ph.D.
University of California
Los Angeles, California

John M. Dorsey, M.D. (L)
Wayne State University
Detroit, Michigan

Leon Eisenberg, M.D.
2610 Whitney Avenue
Baltimore, Maryland

William W. Elgin, M.D. (L)
Sheppard & Enoch Pratt Hospital
Towson, Maryland

Joel Elkes, M.D.
Johns Hopkins Medical School
Baltimore, Maryland

Milton H. Erickson, M.D. (L)
32 West Cypress Street
Phoenix, Arizona

Jack R. Ewalt, M.D.
72-76 Fenwood Road
Boston, Massachusetts

Raymond Feldman, M.D.
9900 Old Spring Road
Kensington, Maryland

Max Fink, M.D.
Missouri Institute
5400 Arsenal Street
St. Louis, Missouri

Barbara Fish, M.D.
550 First Avenue
New York University
New York, New York

Arthur N. Foxe, M.D. (L)
9 East 67th Street
New York, New York

Richard L. Frank, M.D. (L)
15 East 91st Street
New York, New York

Alfred M. Freedman, M.D.
161 West 86th Street
New York, New York

Arnold J. Friedhoff, M.D.
32-25 168th Street
Flushing, New York

John Frosch, M.D.
1 Gracie Terrace
New York, New York

Daniel H. Funkenstein, M.D.
74 Fenwood Road
Boston, Massachusetts

W. Horsley Gantt, M.D.
Johns Hopkins Hospital
Baltimore, Maryland

Bernard Glueck, Sr., M.D. (L)
University of North Carolina
Box 1020
Chapel Hill, North Carolina

Murray Glusman, M.D.
50 East 72nd Street
New York, New York

William Goldfarb, M.D.
530 West End Avenue
New York, New York

Jacques Gottlieb, M.D.
Lafayette Clinic
951 East Lafayette
Detroit, Michigan

Milton Greenblatt, M.D.
11 Burnside Road
Newton Highlands, Massachusetts

Roy R. Grinker, Sr., M.D.
Michael Reese Hospital
29th Street & Ellis Avenue
Chicago, Illinois

Ernest M. Gruenberg, M.D.
722 West 168th Street
New York, New York

A. Irving Hallowell, Ph.D.
Box 14, Bennet Hall
University of Pennsylvania
Philadelphia, Pennsylvania

Ward C. Halstead, Ph.D.
5537 University Avenue
Chicago, Illinois

David Hamburg, M.D.
Department of Psychiatry
Stanford University Medical School
Palo Alto, California

Donald M. Hamilton, M.D. (L)
21 Bloomingdale Road
White Plains, New York

Irving B. Harrison, M.D.
159 Soundview Avenue
White Plains, New York

Lynwood Heaver, M.D.
2651 E. 21st Street
Tulsa, Oklahoma

Morris Herman, M.D.
30 East 40th Street
New York, New York

Harold E. Himwich, M.D.
State Research Hospital
Galesburg, Illinois

Hudson Hoagland, Ph.D.
Deerfoot Road
Southboro, Massachusetts

Leslie B. Hohman, M.D. (L)
Duke Medical School
Durham, North Carolina

Bernard Holland, M.D.
Emory University
Woodruff Building
Atlanta, Georgia

William A. Horwitz, M.D. (L)
722 West 168th Street
New York, New York

Joseph Hughes, M.D.
111 North 49th Street
Philadelphia, Pennsylvania

Howard F. Hunt, Ph.D.
722 West 168th Street
New York, New York

William A. Hunt, Ph.D. (L)
Northwestern University
Evanston, Illinois

Paul E. Huston, M.D.
500 Newton Road
Iowa City, Iowa

Lissy Jarvik, Ph.D., M.D.
722 West 168th Street
New York, New York

George A. Jervis, Ph.D., M.D.
Letchworth Village
Research Department
Thiells, Rockland County, New York

Lothar B. Kalinowsky, M.D. (L)
115 East 82nd Street
New York, New York

Abram Kardiner, M.D. (L)
1100 Park Avenue
New York, New York

Solomon Katzenelbogen, M.D. (L)
9305 Parkhill Terrace
Bethesda, Maryland

William Raymond Keeler, M.D.
484 Avenue Road
Toronto, Ontario, Canada

Edward J. Kempf, M.D. (L)
Wading River
Long Island, New York

Isabelle V. Kendig, Ph.D. (L)
Sandy Springs, Maryland

Richard D. Kepner, M.D. (L)
P. O. Box 3119
Honolulu 2, Hawaii

H. E. King, Ph.D.
University of Pittsburgh Medical School
3811 O'Hara Street
Pittsburgh, Pennsylvania

Lawrence Kolb, Sr., M.D. (L)
6645 32nd Street N.W.
Washington, D.C.

Vojtech Adalbert Kral, M.D.
4145 Blueridge Crescent
Montreal, Canada

Morton Kramer, Sc.D.
9612 Sutherland Road
Silver Spring, Maryland

Emma Layman, Ph.D.
104 West 2nd Street
Mt. Pleasant, Iowa

Zigmond M. Lebensohn, M.D.
2431 K. St. N.W.
Suite 215
Washington, D.C.

Heinz E. Lehmann, M.D.
6603 LaSalle Boulevard
Montreal, Quebec, Canada

Alexander H. Leighton, M.D.
319 Rand
Cornell University
Ithaca, New York

Paul V. Lemkau, M.D.
615 N. Wolfe Street
Baltimore, Maryland

David M. Levy, M.D.
47 East 77th Street
New York, New York

Sir Aubrey J. Lewis (H)
The Maudsley Hospital
Denmark Hill, S.E. 5
London, England

William T. Lhamon, M.D.
Cornell University Medical School
525 East 68th Street
New York, New York

W. T. Liberson, Ph.D., M.D.
Chief, Physical Education and Rehabilitation Service
Veterans Administration Hospital
P.O. Box 28
Hines, Illinois

Ogden R. Lindsley, Ph.D.
Behavior Research Laboratory
Harvard Medical School
Metropolitan State Hospital
Waltham, Massachusetts

Maurice Lorr, Ph.D.
1521 Erskine Street
Washington, D.C.

Reginald S. Lourie, M.D. (L)
Children's Hospital
Washington, D.C.

John W. Lovett-Doust, M.D.
University of Toronto
2 Surrey Place
Toronto, Ontario, Canada

Hans Lowenbach, M.D.
Duke University Medical Center
Durham, North Carolina

Donald J. MacPherson, M.D. (L)
1101 Beacon Street
Brookline, Massachusetts

Sidney Malitz, M.D.
722 West 168th Street
New York, New York

Robert Malmo, Ph.D.
1025 Pine Avenue, West
Montreal, Canada

Edwin E. McNiel, M.D. (L)
3875 Wilshire Boulevard
Los Angeles, California

William C. Menninger, M.D. (L)
Menninger Foundation
Topeka, Kansas

James G. Miller, M.D.
Mental Health Research Institute
University of Michigan
Ann Arbor, Michigan

Neal E. Miller, Ph.D.
Department of Psychology
Yale University, 333 Cedar Street
New Haven, Connecticut

John Money, Ph.D.
Phipps 400, The Johns Hopkins Hospital
Baltimore, Maryland

Thomas Verner Moore, Ph.D., M.D. (H)
Ven. P.D. Pablo Maria Moore
O. Cart.
Cartuja de Miraflores
Apartado 43
Burgos, Spain

Robert S. Morrow, Ph.D.
16 Pietro Place
Dobbs Ferry, New York

Leon Moses, M.D.
19 East 74th Street
New York, New York

Hobart Mowrer, Ph.D.
445 Gregory Hall
University of Illinois
Urbana, Illinois

Harry M. Murdock, M.D.
Sheppard and Enoch Pratt Hospital
Towson, Maryland

Henry A. Murray, M.D. (L)
48 Mount Auburn Street
Cambridge, Massachusetts

J. Martin Myers, Jr., M.D.
Institute of Pennsylvania Hospital
111 North 49th Street
Philadelphia, Pennsylvania

Leo P. O'Donnell, M.D. (L)
36 Elm Street
Pawling, New York

Raymond L. Osborne, M.D. (L)
140 East 54th Street
New York, New York

Joseph B. Parker, Jr., M.D.
University of Kentucky
Medical Center
Lexington, Kentucky

Benjamin Pasamanick, M.D.
Columbus Psychiatric Institute
Ohio State University
Columbus, Ohio

Grosvenor B. Pearson, M.D. (L)
3101 W. DeBazan Avenue
St. Petersburg, Beach 6, Florida

Harris P. Peck, M.D.
120 Woodridge Place
Leonia, New Jersey

Zygmunt A. Piotrowski, Ph.D. (L)
1025 Walnut Street
Philadelphia, Pennsylvania

Phillip Polatin, M.D. (L)
5281 Independence Avenue
New York, New York

Max Pollack, Ph.D.
Hillside Hospital
Glen Oaks
Long Island, New York

Hyman L. Rachlin, M.D. (L)
35 Park Avenue
New York, New York

Sandor Rado, M.D. (L)
235 East 73rd Street
New York, New York

John Rainer, M.D.
9 Innisfree Place
Eastchester, New York

F. C. Redlich, M.D.
333 Cedar Street
New Haven, Connecticut

David McK. Rioch, M.D. (L)
4607 Dorset Avenue
Chevy Chase, Maryland

Janet MacKenzie Rioch, M.D.
719 Monroe Street
Apt. 203
Rockville, Maryland

Margaret Rioch, Ph.D.
4607 Dorset Avenue
Chevy Chase, Maryland

Eli Robins, M.D.
Department of Psychiatry
Washington University School of Medicine
St. Louis, Missouri

Fred V. Rockwell, M.D. (L)
Grasslands Hospital
Valhalla, New York

Howard P. Rome, M.D.
Mayo Clinic
Rochester, Minnesota

David Rosenthal, Ph.D.
National Institute of Mental Health
Bethesda, Maryland

Saul Rosenzweig, Ph.D.
Department of Psychology
Washington University, Box 150
St. Louis, Missouri

Mathew Ross, M.D.
333 Commonwealth Avenue
Chestnut Hill, Massachusetts

Theodore Rothman, M.D.
415 North Camden Drive
Beverly Hills, California

William S. Sadler, M.D. (L)
533 Diversey Parkway
Chicago, Illinois

George S. Saslow, M.D.
University of Oregon
Medical School
Portland, Oregon

Isidor W. Scherer, Ph.D.
8934 Bradmoor Drive
Bethesda, Maryland

G. Wilson Shaffer, Ph.D. (L)
Johns Hopkins University
Baltimore, Maryland

Charles Shagass, M.D.
The Psychopathic Hospital
State University of Iowa
500 Newton Road
Iowa City, Iowa

David Shakow, Ph.D. (L)
National Institute of Mental Health
Clinical Center
Bethesda, Maryland

Alexander Simon, M.D. (L)
Langley Porter Clinic
San Francisco, California

John L. Smalldon, M.D. (L)
Denver Hospital & State School
Taunton, Massachusetts

George W. Smeltz, M.D. (L)
Marlborough-Blenheim Hotel
Atlantic City, New Jersey

Lauren H. Smith, M.D. (L)
111 North 49th Street
Philadelphia, Pennsylvania

Harry C. Solomon, M.D. (L)
74 Fenwood Road
Boston, Massachusetts

Rene A. Spitz, M.D.
12 Rue Robert de Traz
Geneva, Switzerland

Edward J. Stainbrook, M.D.
1200 N. State Street
Los Angeles, California

Gregory Stragnell, M.D.
388 Homewood Road
Los Angeles, California

Joseph G. Sutton, M.D.
5 Roosevelt Place
Montclair, New Jersey

Hans C. Syz, M.D. (L)
The Lifwynn Foundation
52 South Morningside Drive
Westport, Connecticut

William S. Taylor, Ph.D. (L)
27 Langworthy Road
Northampton, Massachusetts

Harry A. Teitelbaum, M.D.
5605 Greenspring Avenue
Baltimore, Maryland

William B. Terhune, M.D. (L)
Silver Hill Foundation
Box 1114
New Canaan, Connecticut

Charles B. Thompson, M.D.
The Lifwynn Foundation
52 South Morningside Drive
Westport, Connecticut

Kenneth J. Tillotson, M.D. (L)
1265 Beacon Street
Brookline, Massachusetts

Harvey J. Tompkins, M.D.
Department of Psychiatry
St. Vincent's Hospital
New York, New York

James S. Tyhurst, M.D.
University of British Columbia
Vancouver 9, British Columbia
Canada

Vladimir G. Urse, M.D. (L)
Cook County Hospital
Polk and Wood Streets
Chicago, Illinois

Roy McL. Van Wart, M.D. (L)
10431 Bellogio Road
Los Angeles, California

Heinrich B. Waelsch, M.D., Sc.D.
722 West 168th Street
New York, New York

James Hardin Wall, M.D. (L)
121 Westchester Avenue
White Plains, New York

Raymond W. Waggoner, M.D.
University Hospital
1313 East Ann Street
Ann Arbor, Michigan

David Wechsler, Ph.D.
Bellevue Hospital
New York, New York

Edith Weigert, M.D.
12 Oxford Street
Chevy Chase, Maryland

Edwin A. Weinstein, M.D.
7101 Pyle Road
Bethesda, Maryland

Livingston Welch, Ph.D.
Hunter College
695 Park Avenue
New York, New York

Louis Wender, M.D. (L)
59 East 79th Street
New York, New York

Frederick L. Weniger, M.D.
108 Franklin Road
Pittsburgh, Pennsylvania

Louis J. West, M.D.
University of Oklahoma
Medical Center
800 N.E. 13th Street
Oklahoma City, Oklahoma

Robert W. White, Ph.D.
Department of Social Relations
Harvard University
Cambridge, Massachusetts

John C. Whitehorn, M.D.
210 Northfield Place
Baltimore, Maryland

George B. Wilbur, M.D. (L)
Cove Road
South Dennis, Massachusetts

William Preston Wilson, M.D.
Duke University
Medical Center
Durham, North Carolina

Cecil L. Wittson, M.D.
9651 North 29th Street
Omaha, Nebraska

Joseph Wolpe, M.D.
University of Virginia
School of Medicine
Charlottesville, Virginia

S. Bernard Wortis, M.D. (L)
410 East 57th Street
New York, New York

Past and Present Officers of the American Psychopathological Association

Presidents

1912	Adolf Meyer
1913	James T. Putnam
1914	Alfred R. Allen
1915	Alfred R. Allen
1916	Adolf Meyer
1917	Adolf Meyer
1918	Smith Ely Jelliffe
1921	William A. White
1922	John T. MacCurdy
1923	L. Pierce Clark
1924	L. Pierce Clark
1925	Albert M. Barrett
1927	Sanger Brown II
1928	Ross McC. Chapman
1929	Ross McC. Chapman
1930	William Healy
1931	William Healy
1932	J. Ramsay Hunt
1933	Edward J. Kempf
1934	Edward J. Kempf
1935	Nolan D. C. Lewis
1936	Nolan D. C. Lewis
1937	Nolan D. C. Lewis
1938	Samuel W. Hamilton
1939	Abraham Myerson
1940	Douglas A. Thom
1941	Roscoe W. Hall
1942	Roscoe W. Hall
1943	Frederick L. Wells
1944	Frederick L. Wells
1945	Bernard Glueck
1946	Robert P. Knight
1947	Frederick L. Wells
1948	Donald J. MacPherson
1949	Paul Hoch
1950	William B. Terhune
1951	Lauren H. Smith
1952	Joseph Zubin
1953	Clarence P. Oberndorf
1954	David McK. Rioch
1955	Merrill Moore
1956	Oskar Diethelm
1957	Howard S. Liddell
1958	Leslie B. Hohman
1959	Harry C. Solomon
1960	David Wechsler
1961	William Horsley Gantt
1962	Lauretta Bender
1963	D. Ewen Cameron
1964	Jerome D. Frank

Vice-Presidents

1924	William Healy
	George H. Kirby
1925	J. Ramsay Hunt
	Sidney L. Schwab
1927	Ross McC. Chapman
	Edward J. Kempf
1928	Edward J. Kempf
	E. Stanley Abbott
1929	Edward J. Kempf
	E. Stanley Abbott
1930	J. Ramsay Hunt
	Herman N. Adler
1931	J. Ramsay Hunt
	Herman N. Adler
1933	Albert M. Barrett
	Trigant Burrow
1934	Albert M. Barrett
	Trigant Burrow
1935	J. Ramsay Hunt
	Smith Ely Jelliffe
1936	J. Ramsay Hunt
	Smith Ely Jelliffe
1937	Samuel W. Hamilton
	Ray G. Hoskins

Vice-Presidents

1938 Lydiard H. Horton
Hans Syz
1939 Roscoe W. Hall
Douglas A. Thom
1940 George S. Sprague
Bernard Glueck
1941 Frederick L. Wells
Lowell S. Selling
1943 Frederick L. Wells
Lowell S. Selling
1944 Lowell S. Selling
Flanders Dunbar
1945 Thomas V. Moore
Robert P. Knight
1946 Paul H. Hoch
Thos. A. C. Rennie
1947 William C. Menninger
Ruth Benedict
1948 Ruth Benedict
Lauren H. Smith
1949 Arthur N. Foxe
Norman Cameron

1950 Harry M. Murdock
William S. Taylor
1951 Harry M. Murdock
Lauretta Bender
1952 William Horowitz
S. Bernard Wortis
1953 David McK. Rioch
Merrill Moore
Howard S. Liddell
1955 Oskar Diethelm
Howard S. Liddell
1956 Leslie B. Hohman
1957 David Wechsler
1958 David Wechsler
1959 Clara Thompson
1960 Theodora M. Abel
1961 Donald M. Hamilton
1962 D. Ewen Cameron
1963 Jerome D. Frank
1964 Franz J. Kallmann

Secretaries

1921 H. W. Frink
1922-1926 Sanger Brown, II
1927-1929 Martin W. Peck
1930-1939 L. Eugene Emerson
1940-1948 Merrill Moore
1944-1951 Samuel W. Hamilton
1952-1960 Donald M. Hamilton
1961-1964 Fritz A. Freyhan

Treasurers

1924-1942 William C. Garvin
1943-1951 Joseph Zubin
1952-1964 Bernard C. Glueck, Jr.

INDEX

Abstract ideas, concepts of, 40-41, 72, 80-81
Abstraction, impairment of, 135
Acute schizophrenia, compared with chronic cases, 223-224
Adaptation
  biologic maladaptation, 233-241
  social, 498-499
Adaptive struggles of patients, 63-70
Addiction to drugs, by street gang delinquents, 381-382
Adenosine triphosphatase, sodium-potassium-activated, 228
Adenosine triphosphate activity, 238, 239, 240
Adenosylmethionine, tissue levels of, 228, 229
Admission rates in hospitals, 554, 555
  readmission rates, 538
Adolescence
  deterioration in, 3, 7, 9
  street gang leaders, 372-373, 386-387
Adrenaline. *See* Epinephrine
Adrenocortical activity, in schizophrenia, 421
Adualism, 41-43
Affect, in chronic schizophrenia, 132
Affective stimuli, and avoidance behavior, 149
Affective psychotics, prognosis of, 248
Age
  and behavior patterns of chronic patients, 194, 196
  of married schizophrenics, 273
  of schizophrenics, 255, 261, 262
Aged, studies of, 501, 553
Alcoholic patients, LSD affecting, 221
Amine excretion, in schizophrenia, 281, 311
Amino acids
  and behavioral changes, 426
  effects of feedings of, 228, 303
Amnesia, in schizophrenia, 46
Amphetamine psychoses, 295
Anger, assessment of, in chronic patients, 186, 190-202
Anhedonia, 66, 76, 167
Anthropological variables in illness, 502-503
Antidepressants, effects of, 417-418, 419
Antigenic abnormalities, studies of, 226
Anxiety
  affecting learning, 133
  role in schizophrenia, 294-295
  and symptom formation, 19
Aphasia, speech in, 102, 103, 220
Aretaeus, 2
Arousal, withdrawal correlated with, 133
Asch phenomenon, 213
Asclepiades, 2
Association, looseness of, 100
Association tests, chlorpromazine affecting, 403
Assortative mating and selection, 258-259
Ataractic drugs, and emotional responses to stimuli, 154-158
Autism, infantile, awholism in, 46
Autonomic nervous system, in childhood schizophrenia, 362-363
Autonomic processes
  Funkenstein test for reactivity, 244
  in schizophrenia, 132-133
Aversive reactions, drugs affecting, 154-158
Aversive stimuli, response to, 130-131, 147, 221
Avoidance behavior
  gradients of, 162, 163-164
  origins of, 166-175
  and reaction times, 144
  stimuli affecting, 133
  and symbolic stimuli, 147-152
Awholism, 46-47

Barbiturates, action of, 422
Behavior patterns
  age factors in, 194, 196
  in catatonics, 194, 198
  of chronic schizophrenics, 182-203, 222-224
  in female patients, 190-197
  in hebephrenics, 200, 202
  in male patients, 190-197
  and metabolic changes from diet, 434-439
  in paranoid schizophrenics, 194, 198
  in pseudoneurotics, 200, 202
  in psychoneurotics, 200, 202
  punishment and reward affecting, 129-175, 221-222
  and time judgment, 493
Behavioral scientists, contributions of, 205-217, 483, 490
Benzoquinolizines, 392
Bentaine, effects of, 228, 229
Biochemical studies, 14, 225-231, 295-296, 302-304, 475, 483, 490
  antigenic abnormalities, 226
  dietary studies, 432-434
  lactate:pyruvate ratio, 226, 233-238

protein abnormalities, 225, 227, 234-235, 302, 304-308
taraxein, 225, 303
Biological factors in psychopathology, 474, 475-477, 553
Biological maladaptation, 233-241
Biological motivation in schizophrenia, 134-135, 222
Bleuler, Eugen, 11-12, 284, 286, 289, 292, 468, 510
Blood pressure, in Funkenstein test, 244
Body image, in schizophrenic children, 360
Brain
convulsive therapy affecting, 420, 423
pathology in childhood, 384
in schizophrenia, 285-286, 299
Brengelmann picture-recognition test, 92
Bufotenin, 425
in urine, 426
Butyrophenones, 392, 394-397

Caffeine, affecting responses, 494
Carbohydrate metabolism studies, 238-239
Catalepsy, early description of, 3
Catatonia
from dimethoxyphenylethylamine, 281
early concepts of, 5, 6
test scores of behavior patterns in, 194, 198
treatment of, 419
Catecholamines
diet affecting excretion of, 435
formation of, 228, 303
levels in stress, 442
Celiac syndrome, in schizophrenic children, 356, 358
Celsus, 2
Censure, effects of, 130, 136-138, 152-175
Childhood schizophrenia
body image in, 360
celiac syndrome with, 356, 358
language disorders in, 360-361
perceptual behavior in, 359
plasticity in, 354-363, 385
postural control in, 336, 358
prediction of, in infancy, 335-353, 357, 384
reading ability in, 360
respiration in, 356
sleep disorders in, 355
tonic neck reflexes in, 336-337, 356
treatment of, 361-363
verbal behavior in, 360
visual motor Gestalt test in, 359-360
Children
adolescent street gang leaders, 372-383, 386-387
awholism in infantile autism, 46
development of, family milieu affecting, 167-171, 222
preschizophrenic, 171
of schizophrenic parents, 260, 262-265, 267, 269
Chlorpromazine, 392
affecting EEG, 421
affecting speech, 119, 125
association tests after, 403
discovery of, 388
and emotional responses to stimuli, 155-158
extrapyramidal disorders from, 281
therapeutic effects of, 394-397
Chlorprothixene, therapeutic effects of, 394-397
Chronic schizophrenia
behavior patterns in, 182-203, 222-224
compared with acute cases, 223-224
office treatment of, 366-371, 386
responsiveness in, 132
thought disorder in, 85-87
Classification of disease, cross-cultural approach to, 482-511, 555
Clinical aspects of schizophrenia, 1-76
adative struggles, 63-70, 75-76
cognition, 37-48, 71-72
evolution of concepts, 1-18
hallucinations, 49-61, 72-75
pseudoneurotic schizophrenia, 9-36, 71
Clinical Inventory, Structured, 182-202, 499
Cloze procedure, use of, 102-104, 107, 118, 119, 221, 500, 503
Cognition, schizophrenic, 37-47, 219, 300
adualism, 41-43
awholism, 46-47
characteristics of, 469
in chronic schizophrenia, 85-87
and concretization process, 38, 40-41, 72, 80-81
drugs affecting, 404-406
overinclusive thinking, 77-96, 219
paleologic thought, 43-46
and perception, 92-93
and progressive teleologic regression, 38-40
and reaction time, 88-91
remission of symptoms affecting, 83
tests of, 501
Color responses in schizophrenia, 313-314
Communication. *See* Verbalization
Community stay data, after treatment, 527-552, 559
Compensatory adaptation, 67
Computers, use of, 560

Concept formation, punishment affecting, 138
Concept-learning experiment, 93-94
Conceptual dysfunctioning, assessment of, in chronic patients, 186, 189, 190-202
Conceptual expectancy, 506
Conceptual techniques in diagnosis, 500
Concreteness, abnormal, 135-136
Concretization process, 38, 40-41, 72, 80-81
Conditional responses, inhibitory, 453-462
Conflicts, in discrimination, 169
Confusion, early concepts of, 4
Constitution, concept of, 13
Contamination of images, in Rorschach test, 316
Convulsive therapy
  brain changes from, 420-423
  in catatonia, 419
  in childhood, 362
  delirium from, 418
  effectiveness of, 412, 413-414
  effects of, 416
  and Funkenstein test, 244-249
  psychodynamic theories of, 422
  reactions to, 417
Coping potential, and symptomatology, 478-479
Creatinine
  excretion of, 443
  intake of, and indole excretion, 438, 439
Cultural factors in psychiatric disorders, 477-480
  See also Social factors

Deafness, and schizophrenia, 255, 554
Decompensated schizotypal behavior, 67
Degeneracy, concept of, 5
Dejection, assessment of, in chronic patients, 187, 189, 190-202
Delinquency, juvenile, 372-383, 386-387
Delirium, from antidepressants, 417
Delusions
  early concepts of, 4
  form and content of, 289, 556
  and overinclusive thinking, 83-85
Dementia, 4
  praecox, 3, 5, 7, 9-10, 285
  senile, 501
Demographic and evolutionary considerations, 256-258
Depreciation of self, assessment of, 187, 190-202
Depression
  concreteness in, 81
  overinclusive thinking in, 81
  treatment of, 417-418, 419
Detection of illness
  cultural factors in, 484-486
  specific methods for, 487-497
Deterioration in schizophrenia, 3, 7-9, 68, 286, 369
Deterrents of war, studies of, 208-209
Development in infancy, and prediction of schizophrenia, 350, 357, 385
Developmental theory of schizophrenia, 472-473, 554
Diagnostic categories, 467-470
  anthropological variables, 502-503
  conceptual techniques, 500-501
  cross cultural studies, 482-511, 555
  cultural factors in initial detection of illness, 484-486
  culture-dependent techniques, 484, 497-503
  culture-free techniques, 484, 489, 503-510
  interview techniques, 182-203, 497-500
  mental status schedule, 498
  nature of mental disorder, 471-480, 486-487, 553
  social adaptation schedule, 498-499
  sociological variables, 501
  specific methods for, 487-497
  structured clinical inventory, 182-202, 499
  thought disorder studies, 501
  variability in, sources of, 486, 557
  verbal behavior studies, 45, 220-221, 500
  ward behavior inventory, 188, 500
Diencephalon, role of, 423
Diet, 425-449, 467
  and behavior changes, 434-439
  biochemical studies, 432-434, 445
  changes from, compared with changes in stress, 441-442
  clinical results of, 430-432
  endogenous factors in behavioral worsening, 442-444
  theoretical implications, 445-447
Dimethoxyphenylethylamine in urine, 229, 230, 277-282, 304, 310-311
Dimethyltryptamine, 425
Disarmament agreement, mechanisms of, 209-210
Discrimination learning, 92
  capacity for, 406
  conflicts in, 169
Disintegrated schizotypal behavior, 67
Disorganization pattern in schizophrenia, 299
Dissociation, 77-78
Divorce, frequency of, 264

Dopamine
derivatives of, 229, 277, 310
diet affecting excretion of, 432
Double-bind situations, reactions to, 123, 168, 170, 171
Drive reduction, 123, 131
Drug addiction, of street gang delinquents, 381-382
Drug-induced hallucinations, 60, 73-74
Drug therapy. *See* Pharmacotherapy
Dualism, lack of, 41-43

Economic conditions of schizophrenics, 258, 296-297
Einstellung rigidity, 80
Electric convulsive therapy
in childhood, 362
effectiveness of, 412, 413-414
and Funkenstein test, 244-249
psychodynamic theories of, 422
Electroencephalography, 240-241
chlorpromazine affecting, 421
Electrophysiological studies, 509
Energizing aspects of schizophrenic behavior, 131, 133-134
Energy potential, concept of, 294
Environmental factors in mental disorders, 474, 477-480, 489
See also Social factors
Epidemiological studies, 297
Epinephrine
diet affecting excretion of, 432
excretion in schizophrenia, 281
formation of, 228
and lactate:pyruvate ratio, 237
tests with mecholyl, 244-251
Errors, fear of, 141
Erythrocyte studies, 226, 227, 233, 240
Escape from double-bind situations, 123
Escape training, instrumental, 131
Esquirol, J. E. D., 4
Ethnic diversity in symptomatology, 477-478
See also Social factors
Etiological theories of schizophrenia, 285-297
Evaluation of outcome of schizophrenia, 312-334, 384
See also Rorschach tests
Evaluation of treatment, and community stay data, 527-552, 559
Evolutionary and demographic considerations, 256-258
Exchange programs, international, 211-212
Existentialism, 294
Expectancy, conceptual, 506
Extinction, speed of, in schizophrenia, 99, 123-124
Eysenck's factor of psychoticism, 82, 96

Factor analysis, 510
in long-term prognostic test, 329-331
Failure threats, effects of, 137
Fallout shelter builders, attitudes of, 209
Families
deviant relationships in, 136, 149, 222
parent-child relationships, 136, 149, 222
reproductive trends in schizophrenia, 252-275
role in therapy, 369, 386
schizophrenogenic mothers, 157, 167
Fatigue process, in retardation, 91, 96
Fatty acids, free, in plasma, 228
Fear, assessment of, 186, 190-202
Feed-back, negative, 407
Fertility patterns in schizophrenia, 259-260, 273, 309
Fixation studies, in animals, 172
Flicker fusion studies, 464, 508
drugs affecting, 404-406
Follow-up studies
long-term, 312-334, 384
of predictions in infancy, 335-353
of release and community stay data, 527-552, 559
Foreign aid programs, effectiveness of, 212, 214
Fragmentation of wholes, 46-47
Free fatty acids in plasma, 228
Freedom rides, psychological studies of, 216
Freud, S., 12-13, 290
Fructose 1-6 diphosphate activity, 239, 240
Frustration, response to, 137, 172
Functioning, purposive, in schizophrenia, 132
Funkenstein tests, 244-251

Galen, 2
Galvanic testing, results of, 132
General practitioners, referrals by, 486
Generalization in learning, and over-inclusive thinking, 93-94
Genetic factors in schizophrenia, 14, 222, 295-296, 474, 475-477, 489
manic depressive heredity, 248
reproductive trends, 252-275, 309-310
Gestalt explanation of schizophrenia, 293-294
Gestalt test, in schizophrenic children, 359-360
Glucocorticoid excretion, diet affecting, 432
Glucose metabolism studies, 226, 238
Greek description of mental illness, 2
Griesinger, W., 12

Group therapy, 370
Guilt feelings, of street gang delinquents, 381

Habit, and national behavior, 216
Habit strengths of responses, 134, 135, 145, 147, 171
Hallucinations, 49-61, 73
  complexity of, 53-55
  drugs causing, 60, 73-74, 417
  form and content of, 289, 554, 556
  general characteristics of patients, 52
  methods of study, 50-52
  perceptual qualities of, 57-58
  projection of, 56
  reactions to, 55-56
  reality of, 55
  temporal aspects of, 53
Haloperidol, therapeutic effects of, 394-397
Hamilton Memorial Award Lecture, 283-301
Hardy-Weinberg theorem of population genetics, 258
Hebephrenia, 6, 200, 202
Heboidophrenia, 6
Hemolysis of erythrocytes, 227
Heredity
  manic depressive, 248
  and schizophrenia. *See* Genetic factors
Heroin addiction, of street gang delinquents, 381-382
Hindu description of mental illness, 1
Hippocrates, 2
Historical aspects
  of pharmacotherapy, 388-390
  of schizophrenia, 1-17, 283-284
Home care study, 515-526, 557
  and hospital control patients, 520-522
  method of study, 516-517
  patient population, 517-520
  placebo home care, 522-523
  psychiatric evaluation, 518-519, 523
  psychological evaluation, 519-520, 524
  social background data, 517-518
Homes for out-patients, 369, 370
Homosexuality, and paranoia, 84
Hormone therapy, 421
  See also Insulin
Hospitalization, reasons for, 296, 299
Hospitals
  admission rates, 554, 555
  and home care study, 515-526, 557
  interhospital differences, 547, 551, 560
  readmission rates, 538
  release and community stay data, 527-552, 559
Hostility, assessment of, 186, 190-202
Hypoglycemia, effect of, 421, 422

Ideation, incongruous, assessment of, 186, 190-202
Idiotism, 4
Idling state, assessment of, 491
Imipramine, delirium from, 417
Immune lysis of erythrocytes, 227
Inappropriate responses to Rorschach test, 316
Incongruous behavior, assessment of, 186, 190-202
Indian description of mental illness, 1
Indole compounds, excretion of, 425
Infancy, prediction of schizophrenia in, 335-353, 357, 384
  See also Children
Inhibitory conditional responses, 453-462
Inspection methods, international, 209-210
Inspectional science, 63-65
Instrumental escape training, 131
Insulin
  and ATP activity, 238, 240
  and plasma free fatty acid levels, 228
Insulin therapy
  brain changes from, 420
  in catatonia, 419
  effectiveness of, 248, 412, 413
  effects of, 416
  psychodynamic theories of, 422
  reactions to, 418
Integrative apparatus, psychodynamic, 66
International relations
  cooperative projects, 215
  exchange programs, 211-212
  inspection methods, 209-210
  negotiations, 211-213
  psychological factors in, 205-217
Interview techniques, 497-500
  with chronic schizophrenics, 182-203
Introspectional science, 63-65
Inventory
  clinical, structured, 182-202, 499
  ward behavior, 188, 500
Isolation
  effects of, 501, 553
  in schizophrenia, 296, 297, 369

Jung, C. G., 11, 290
Juvenile delinquency research, 372-383, 386-387

Kahlbaum, K., 5-6
Kendall's coefficient of concordance, in speech studies, 108
Ketoglutarate oxidation, 239
17-Ketosteroid excretion, diet affecting, 432
Klein, Melanie, 290

Kraepelin, Emil, 6-8, 12, 13, 284, 285, 286
Kretschmer, E., 13

Lactate:pyruvate ratio, studies of, 226, 233-238
Language. *See* Verbalization
Leadership, in adolescent street gangs, 372-383, 386-387
Leaders, national, behavior of, 206
Learning
 anxiety affecting, 133
 discrimination, 92
 generalization in, and overinclusive thinking, 93-94
 punishment affecting, 146
 reinforcement affecting, 158-166
 social, 170, 222
Lethargy, assessment of, 187, 189, 190-202
Leukocytes, abnormal, 228
Lobotomy, effects of, 412-413, 423
Long-term prognostic test index, 312-334, 384
 See also Rorschach tests
Looseness of association, assessment of, 100
Lymphocytes, abnormal, 228
Lysergic acid diethylamide
 affecting language, 220
 affecting perceptual tests, 93
 in alcoholism, 221
 in childhood schizophrenia, 362-363
 delusions from, 289
 and overinclusive thinking, 220
Lysis of erythrocytes, 227

Magic, infantile craving for, 67
Maladaptation, biologic, 304-308
Mania, early concepts of, 3, 4
Manic depressive psychosis
 heredity and schizophrenic remission, 248
 incidence of, 554, 555
Marriages between two schizophrenics, 260, 271-274
Mecholyl test, results of, 244-251
Melancholia, early concepts of, 3, 4
Memories, storage of, 490, 493, 506, 507
Memory functions, 407
Mental illness
 of national leaders, 206
 nature of, 471-480, 486-487, 553
Mental Status Schedule, 498
Mescaline
 resemblance to dimethoxyphenylethylamine, 280, 281
 similarity to adrenaline, 228
Metabolic changes, affecting behavior, 434-439
Metalog test, 501
Metanephrine, effects of, 304
Methacholine test, results of, 244-251
Methionine, effects of, 228, 229, 303, 426, 427-448
Methylated indole substances, in urine, 426
Methylation of catecholamines, 228, 303
Metrazol therapy, 422
 in childhood, 362
Meyer, Adolf, 9, 10, 287, 467
Michelson Project, 208-209
Monoamine oxidase
 action of inhibitor, 426
 and dopamine metabolism, 277
 effects of, 311
Monologue procedure, in speech studies, 104
Morel, B. A., 4-6
Motion, perception of, 493-494, 508
Motivational state, in schizophrenia, 131-135
Motor development in infancy, and prediction of schizophrenia, 350, 358
Movement response to Rorschach test, 315, 321
Mysticism of patients, 367

National conflicts, psychological factors in, 207
 See also International relations
Neck reflexes, tonic, in infancy, 336-337, 356
Negative feed-back, 407
Negative reinforcers, effects of, 169-170
Negotiations, international, 211-213
Neuroleptic action of tranquilizers, 392-393, 401
Neurological deviations in infancy, and prediction of schizophrenia, 350
Neuronic shutter theory, 495
Neurophysiological studies, 483, 487, 490, 505
 biochemical research, 225-231, 302-304
 biologic maladaptation, 233-241, 304-308
 dimethoxyphenylethylamine in urine, 229, 230, 277-282, 304, 310-311
 long-term follow-up of Funkenstein tests, 244-251, 308
Neuroses
 concreteness in, 81
 and dimethoxyphenylethylamine in urine, 280
 interview profiles of patients, 200, 202
 and schizophrenia, 290
Niacin, as therapy, 228
Nicotinamide, methylation of, 432, 441

Nicotinic acid, as therapy, 228
Nitrogen balance, diet affecting, 434
Norepinephrine, diet affecting excretion of, 432
Normetanephrine, effects of, 303
Noxious stimuli, effects of, 131, 495
Nuclear schizophrenia, prognosis of, 414
Nuclear test ban, 215
Nurses, Public Health, 516, 558

Object classification test, 79
  in chronic schizophrenia, 85-86
Object sorting test, 79, 219
  in chronic schizophrenia, 86
  schizophrenic failure in, 100
Office treatment of chronic patient, 366-371, 386
Organic disease
  in childhood, 384
  in schizophrenia, 285-286, 299
Organismic time, 492
Overinclusive thinking, 77-96, 219
  in chronic schizophrenia, 85-87
  and delusions, 83-85
  and generalization in learning, 93-94
  phenothiazine affecting, 86, 87-88
  and reaction times, 88-91

Pain, responses to, 131
Paleologic thought, 43-46, 99
Paralogical thinking, 99
Paranoia
  delusions in, 83-85
  drug therapy in, 368-369
  early concept of, 4, 6, 7
  fears in, 367, 368
  test scores of behavior patterns in, 194, 198
Paraphasia, 220
Paraphrenia, 5
Parents. *See* Families; Genetic factors
Parergasia, 10
Paresis, general, treatment of symptoms in, 419
Passivity attitude, 470
Peace Corps, principles of, 214
Perception
  assessment of dysfunction, 187, 188, 190-202
  and delusion formation, 85
  disorders in schizophrenia, 293
  drug behavior, 93, 158, 404-406
  in schizophrenic children, 359
  of speech, studies of, 102, 103
  studies of, 45
  and thought disorder, 92-93
  of velocity, 493-494, 508
Perceptual qualities of hallucinations, 57-58
Performance in schizophrenia, prediction of, 129-175, 221-222
Personality of patient
  clinical criteria of changes in, 321-322
  and long-term prognosis, 313, 314
Pharmacotherapy, 298, 388-408, 464-466
  antidepressants, 417-418, 419
  antipsychotic substances, 391-392
  in childhood, 362-363
  as cure or symptomatic relief, 391
  effectiveness of, 393
  effects of, 412-424
  and emotional responses to stimuli, 154-158
  extrapyramidal disorders from, 281
  history of, 388-390
  ideal drug, 402-404
  and inhibitory responses, 460
  major and minor tranquilizers, 399-402, 465
  mass action principle, 393-394
  neuroleptic action, 392-393, 401
  and office treatment, 368-369, 386
  in paranoia, 368-369
  and perceptual-cognitive dynamics, 404-406
  and placebo home care, 522-523
  psychostatic action, 397-399
  qualities of psychostatic drugs, 408
  sequence of therapeutic effects, 394-397
  therapeutic spectrum of agents, 390
Phenobarbital, compared with phenothiazines, 398
Phenomenology, 1-76
Phenothiazines, 392
  action of, 422
  affecting overinclusive thinking, 86, 87-88
  therapeutic affects of, 394-397
Phenylketonuria, and phenylethylamine excretion, 280
Phobias
  counter-phobic cats, 172
  and regression, 40
Picture-recognition test, 92
Pinel, Philippe, 3
Placebo home care, 522-523
Plasticity in childhood schizophrenia, 354-363, 385
Pleasure capacity, defect in, 66, 76, 167
Population studies of reproductive trends, 252-275
Postural control, in infancy, 336, 358
Prediction of performance in schizophrenia, 129-175, 221-222
  factors influencing, 152-175
  and origins of avoidance behavior, 166-175

and premorbid adjustment, 140-141, 152-153
and reward reinforcement, 158-166
role of punishment, 130-147
symbolic stimuli and avoidance behavior, 147-152
and tranquilizing medications, 154-158
Prediction of schizophrenia in infancy, 335-353, 357, 384
Pregnancy, complications of, 554, 555
Premorbid adjustment, and behavior under censure, 140-141, 152-153
Premorbid social competence, 472-473
Preschizophrenia child, 171
Presidential address, 205-207
Process form of schizophrenia, 248, 471, 474
inhibitory responses in, 456, 460
Prognosis
follow-up statistics, 312-313
Funkenstein test for, 244-251
long-term vs. short-term, 313-314
studies on, 467
test index, long-term, 312-334, 384
See also Rorschach tests
Proprioceptive disturbances, 66, 76
Protein
factor in schizophrenia, 225, 227, 234-235, 302, 304-308
serum, diet affecting, 433
Proverbs test, 79-80, 85
Pseudomutuality concept, 168
Pseudoneurotic schizophrenia, 19-36, 67, 71, 291
developments during treatment, 28-35
diagnosis of, 20
interview profiles of patients, 200, 202
past history, 25-28
presenting complaints, 22-25
primary clinical symptoms of, 20-21
Pseudopsychopathic schizophrenia, 380
Psilocin, 425
Psilicybin, 425
in childhood schizophrenia, 362-363
Psychiatric Evaluation Project, 322-323
Psychoanalytic contributions to schizophrenia, 289-293
Psychology, 77-224
behavior patterns, 182-204, 222-224
overinclusive thinking and retardation, 77-97, 219
prediction of performance, 129-179, 221-222
verbal behavior, 98-127, 220-221
See also Behavior
Psychoneurotics. *See* Neuroses
Psychosurgery, effect of, 412-413, 423
Psychotherapy, in childhood, 362
Psychoticism, tests of, 82, 96
Psychotomimetic drugs, 60, 73-74, 228, 280, 281
See also Lysergic acid diethylamide
Public Health nurses, role of, 516, 558
Punishment
affecting behavior, 129-175, 221-222
role of, 130-147
stimuli symbolizing, 147-152
Purposive functioning, in schizophrenia, 132
Push-pull responses, analysis of, 150, 161
Pyruvate:lactate ratio, studies of, 226, 233-238

Rauwolfia derivatives, 281, 388, 391, 392, 422
Reaction times
and overinclusive thinking, 88-91
punishment affecting, 144, 222
studies of, 507
Reactive schizophrenia, 248, 471, 474
Readability, measure of, 103
Reading ability, in schizophrenic children, 360
Readmission rates in hospitals, 538
Reconstruction of sentences, 103, 105, 106, 108-117, 120-122, 220
Referral rate among practitioners, 486
Regression, progressive teleologic, 38-40
Regulative deficiency in schizophrenia, 300
Reinforcers, primary and secondary, 131, 133
Reinforcement
effects of, 124, 125, 130
and learned rewards, 158-166
negative, effects of, 169-170
rewards and punishment affecting, 145-146, 221
verbal procedures, 145-146, 164-165
Relapses, treatment of, 415
Release and community stay data, 527-552, 559
patterns of release, 546-549
readmission rates, 538
Remission of symptoms
affecting thought disorder, 83
and manic depressive heredity, 248
Repetition
response to Rorschach test, 315
in speech, rate of, 102, 124-125
Reproductive trends in schizophrenia, 252-275, 309-310
comparative data on marriage and reproduction, 262-265
demographic and evolutionary considerations, 256-258
differential risk data, 253-256
dual mating studies, 271-274

longitudinal reproductive data, 266-269
mating and fertility patterns, 259-260
New York State data, 260-262
reproductive patterns in families, 269-270
risk of schizophrenia in some families, 252-253
Research in schizophrenia, 312-383
adolescent street gang leaders, 372-383, 386-387
evaluation of outcome of schizophrenia, 312-334, 384
office treatment of chronic patient, 366-371, 386
plasticity in childhood schizophrenia, 354-363, 385
prediction of schizophrenia in infancy, 335-353, 384
Reserpine, 391, 392
discovery of, 388
extrapyramidal disorders from, 281
Residences for out-patients, 369, 370
Respiration, in schizophrenic children, 356
Responsiveness, in schizophrenia, 131
Retardation
fatigue process in, 91, 96
and overinclusive thinking, 77-96, 219
Retention, capacity for, 407
Rewards
affecting behavior, 129-175, 221-222
ineffectiveness of, 151, 159
reinforcing effects of, 158-166
social, effectiveness of, 161, 164
Rigidity, Einstellung, 80
Roman description of mental illness, 2
Rorschach prognostic test, 313-334, 384
absence of human content, 320
and base rate predictions, 324-325
and breakdown of interpretive attitude, 318-319
and clinical criteria of personality change, 321-322
color responses, 313-314
and contamination of images, 316
content monotony, 320-321
description of signs, 314-321
determinant scarcity, 320
factor analysis of, 329-331
first validations of, 314
fourth validation of, 329
inappropriate responses, 316
incongruous explanations for percepts, 319-320
low vs. high scores, 326-327
movement response, 315, 321
objective criteria in evaluation, 327-329
and personality of patient, 313, 314
and Psychiatric Evaluation Project, 322-323
reliability of scores, 321
repetition response, 315
results of study, 323-324
self-confidence with meaningless responses, 317-318
and Symptom Rating Scale, 322, 325-326
third validation of, 322-323
vagueness of response, 315
Russian-American negotiations, 212

Schizophrenia, Hoch lecture on, 283-301
Schizophrenogenic mothers, 157, 167
Schizotypal organization, 381
Schizotype, working theory of, 66-70
Selection and assortative mating, 258-259
Self-depreciation, assessment of, 187, 190-202
Senile dementia, 501
Serotonin, 425
antagonists of, in childhood schizophrenia, 362
diet affecting levels of, 441
and lactate:pyruvate ratio, 237
Set, establishment of, 406
Sex distribution
in parental schizophrenia rates, 272-273
of schizophrenics, 261, 262
Sexual attitudes
assessment of deviance, 187, 190-202
maladjustment, and effects of punishment, 140-141, 152
of street gang delinquents, 380, 381
Shelter builders, attitudes of, 209
Shock therapy. *See* Convulsive therapy
Siblings, schizophrenic, reproductivity of, 270
Sit-in campaigns, psychological studies of, 216
Sleep disorders, in schizophrenic children, 355
Sleep treatment, 421
Slowness, in schizophrenia, 80
Social Adaptation Schedule, 498-499
Social clubs for out-patients, 370
Social competence, 472-480, 553
Social factors
censure, effects of, 130, 136-138
cross-cultural approach, 482-511, 555
culture-dependent techniques to detect illness, 484, 497-503
culture-fair indicators of vulnerability, 484, 489, 503-510
culture-free indicators of vulnerability, 484, 489, 503-510
in initial detection of illness, 484-486

in juvenile delinquency, 372-374, 382
maladjustment, and effects of punishment, 140-141, 152
in psychiatric disorders, 474, 477-480, 489
rewards, effectiveness of, 161, 164
in schizophrenia, 296
Social learning, 170, 222
Socioeconomic conditions of schizophrenics, 258, 296-297
Sociological variables in illness, 501
Sodium-potassium-activated adenosine triphosphatase, 228
Somatic treatments, effect of, 412-424, 466
Sorting tests, 79, 219
in chronic schizophrenia, 86
schizophrenic failure in, 100
Spatial conflict, responses to, 150
Spearman's rank order correlation coefficient, 108
Speech. *See* Verbalization
Speed of functioning, measures of, 82
Startle response, 495
Steroid hormone levels in stress, 442
Stimulants, affecting responses, 494
Stimuli
affecting schizophrenics, 124, 125
aversive, response to, 130-131, 147, 221
noxious, effects of, 131, 495
responses to, 464
screened out, 91, 92
symbolic, and avoidance behavior, 147-152
Stress, hormone levels in, 442
Structural Clinical Interview, 182-202, 499
Student exchange programs, 211-212
Succinate oxidation, 239
Surgery, effect of, 412-413, 423
Sweat, studies of, 304
Sydenham, describing mental illness, 3
Symbolic stimuli, and avoidance behavior, 147-152
Symbols, cultural aspects of, 556
Symptom complexes, description of, 467-470
Symptom Rating Scale, 322, 325-326

Tachistoscopic, test, 92
Taraxein, 225, 303
Teleologic regression, progressive, 38-40
Temperature changes, effects of, 492, 493
Thinking. *See* Cognition
Thioxanthenes, 392, 394-397
Thought processes. *See* Cognition
Thyroid extract therapy, 421
Time judgment studies, 492-493
Tonic neck reflexes, in infancy, 336-337, 356
Toxins, early concept of, 8, 10, 11
Tranquilizers. *See* Pharmacotherapy
Transmethylation process, 225, 228, 230, 303
Treatment of schizophrenia, 297-299, 388-462
in childhood, 361-363
diet, 425-449, 467
effect of somatic treatments, 412-424, 466
home care study, 515-526, 557
hormone therapy, 421
office treatment of chronic patients, 366-371, 386
pharmacotherapy, 388-408, 464-466
relapses with, 415
release and community stay data, 527-552, 559
sleep therapy, 421
Tryptamine derivatives, metabolism of, 229
Tryptophan
dietary, effects of, 427-448
excretion of derivatives of, 425
monoamine oxidase inhibitor with, 426
Twins, studies of, 475

UML-491, in childhood schizophrenia, 362-363
Unitization method, in speech studies, 104, 105, 107-108, 116, 117
Urine
dimethoxyphenylethylamine in, 229, 230, 277-282, 304, 310-311
indole excretion, 425

Vague responses to Rorschach test, 315
Vanilylmandelic acid excretion, diet affecting, 437
Variability in diagnosis, sources of, 486, 557
Velocity perception studies, 493-494, 508
Verbalization, 45, 220-221, 500
in aphasia, 102, 103, 220
characteristics of, 469
chlorpromazine affecting, 118, 125
cloze procedure, 102-104, 105, 107, 118, 119
and conditional reflexes, 455
evaluation of communicability, 106-108
extinction studies, 99, 123-124
factors affecting, 45
and outcome of illness, 119-122
perception of speech, 102, 103
rate of speech 117-119

reconstruction method, 103, 105, 106, 108-117, 120-122
repetition of words, 124-125
in schizophrenia, 98-126
in schizophrenic children, 360-361
speech samples and subjects, 104-106
unitization method, 104, 105, 107-108, 116, 117
Vesania, 5
Vigotsky test, 219
Violence, national impetus for, 216
Visual hallucinations, 49-61, 73
Visual Motor Gestalt Test, in children, 359-360
Voluntary actions, analysis of, 455
Von Domarus principle, 43-44, 71, 99
Vulnerability, 496-497, 506
and development of schizophrenia, 222
indicators of, 484, 489

War prevention, and role of behavioral scientists, 205-217
Ward Behavior Inventories, 188, 500
Weight, diet affecting, 434
Wholes, fragmentation of, 46-47
Willis, T., 3
Withdrawal
arousal correlated with, 133
mechanisms in, 135-136
symbolic cues for, 150
Word association tests, chlorpromazine affecting, 403
Worry, assessment of, in chronic patients, 186, 190-202